Fighter Squadron
441 Squadron from Hurricanes to Hornets

Fighter Squadron
441 Squadron from Hurricanes to Hornets

Larry Milberry

CANAV Books

Copyright © Larry Milberry 2003
All rights reserved. No part of this book may be reproduced in any form or by any means without prior written permission of the publisher.

Library and Archives Canada Cataloguing in Publication

Milberry, Larry, 1943-
   Fighter squadron : 441 Squadron from Hurricanes to Hornets / Larry Milberry.
Includes bibliographical references and index.

ISBN 0-921022-16-6

   1. Canada. Canadian Armed Forces. Tactical Fighter Squadron, 441--History.
   2. Fighter planes--Canada--History. I. Title.

UG635.C2M548 2004   358.4'33'0971   C2004-903622-X

Design: David O'Malley & Ryan Thompson
   Aerographics Creative Services, Ottawa

Proofreading: Dave Burton, Pickering, Ontario; Ralph Clint, Toronto; William A. Flynn, League City, Texas; Hugh A. Halliday, Orleans, Ontario; Lambert Huneault, Windsor, Ontario; Ron Pickler, Burlington, Ontario; Robert J. Thorneycroft, Calgary

Printed and bound in Canada by Friesen Printers Ltd., Altona, Manitoba

Published by
CANAV Books
Larry Milberry, publisher
51 Balsam Avenue
Toronto, Ontario M4E 3B6
Canada

Mustang 3s served 441 from May to August 1945, when the squadron disbanded. (Sid Bregman)

Front Endpaper
A 441 Spitfire taxies in Normandy, and (below) Mustang 9G-E in a rare in-flight photo taken during the squadron's dying days in 1945. (Sid Bregman)

Silver Foxes at war's end atop one of their Mustangs at Digby: F/O D.C. "Don" Gildner, F/L D.H. "Don" Kimball, DFC, F/L A.A. Smith, DFC, F/O G.D. Morrison, F/L H.E. Derraugh, S/L R.H. Walker, F/O George E. Heasman and P/O J.A. McIntosh. Kimball was 441's leading ace with six kills and one damaged. (CF PL45116)

The Sabre that brought 441 its greatest fame in the 1950s. Here is a Sabre fresh from the production line at Cartierville. Then, Sabres at Decimomannu, Sardinia, where 441 did gunnery training. (CANAV Col., Lou J. Hill)

441's officers at North Luffenham in 1953. On the wing are Jean Gaudry, Don Williamson, Bob Simmons, Gord McDonald, Norm Ronaason, Les Benson, Ray Jolley, Murray Neilson, Bob Haverstock and adjutant Bill Felhaber. Standing are Fern Villeneuve, Neil Burns, Steve Atherton, Don Hanson, Ralph Annis, Jack Turner, Len Fine and engineering officer Doug Cooke. In front are Pete Cranston, Rocky Paquette, Don McIlraith, Gar Brine, Dean Kelly, Bill Gill, Slim Walker, Jack Ecker and Ken Branch. (441 Sqn)

Half Title Page
F/L Sid Bregman of 441 took some of the few air-to-air photos of RCAF Spitfires overseas. Here, is 441's 9G-Y during a flight from Hawkinge, Kent in the fall of 1944. Sid had set this up as a special photo mission.

Title Page
CF-18s on the line at Tyndall AFB during "William Tell 88". (Larry Milberry)

Back Endpaper
Starfighter days at 441. First, 104785 between missions at Baden-Soellingen. Then, a CF-104 with a heavy load of cluster bomb canisters. (CF PCN79-119, via G. Wenham)

Canada's high time Starfighter pilot was 441's John David with some 3200 hours on type. (CF BS78-1293)

In 2002, Todd Lemieux of Calgary provided 441 with this 1975 Corvette. Seen around it on a May morning in 2003 are pilots Miles "Milhouse" Selby, Rob "Crack" Carter, Des "Deuce" Brophy, Chris "Bypass" Bijdevaate (Dutch exchange), Mike "Migs" French, Reagh "Rage" Sherwood, Mike "Woody" Woodhouse, Brehn "Noodle" Eichel, Shawn "Loaf" Hartzell, Chris "Hammy" Hamilton and Rob "Thorney" Thorneycroft. (Larry Milberry)

In 2003 Canada's CF-104 pilots spent a week on an Alaska cruise aboard SS Veendam. Across the front in this souvenir photo from the left are Herb Sievert (441), Bert Davis (441), Jim Cratchley (441) and Paul Manson (441). Over Paul's left shoulder is Ken Mowbray (441). The next four across are Charlie Paul (441), Ted Lewis (441), Ron Chercoe (441) and Sky King (441), then are Bill Turnbull (441, flying suit), Bob Edwards (441, cardigan), Jim Jones (441) and Phil Engstad (441, flying suit). In the black vest is Red Willet (441) then (behind him and to his left) Doug Fenton, Ken McLeod (441), Harv Roddick and Jack Frazer (flight suit). The next quartet shows Bob Nicholson, Dan Graham, Rae Simpson and Gorm Jensen (441). The bunch in the back from the left are Bob Christie, Ron Ellis (441), Gerry King, Dave Koski, Ray Learmond, Chris Tuck, Romeo Lalonde, Jack Watson, Ron Coleman (partially or totally hidden), Reg White, Pete Caws (441), George Kirbyson, Guy Fabi, Ray Sawchuk (flight suit). (via D.S. "Doug" Fenton)

LCol Billie Flynn leads the change-of-command flypast at Cold Lake on September 1, 1999. (Larry Milberry)

Contents

Foreword 7

Preface 9

CHAPTER 1
Defending Canada: 1942-1943 13

CHAPTER 2
Invading Great Britain 23

CHAPTER 3
Invading France.. 30

CHAPTER 4
Air Defence of Great Britain................................ 42

CHAPTER 5
Pilot Profiles 47

CHAPTER 6
Decorations and Heraldry 64

CHAPTER 7
Rebirth of the Squadron 69

CHAPTER 8
The NATO Commitment 78

CHAPTER 9
On to Marville 97

CHAPTER 10
Gunnery 105

CHAPTER 11
Training, Exchanges and Prangs 121

CHAPTER 12
Sabre Days Waning 131

CHAPTER 13
The Starfighter Years 137

CHAPTER 14
Supersonic at 1 Wing 143

CHAPTER 15
Pulling Up Stakes 169

CHAPTER 16
Flight Safety 175

CHAPTER 17
Profiles and Events 187

CHAPTER 18
Starfighters Fading 204

CHAPTER 19
A New Start 225

CHAPTER 20
William Tell 239

CHAPTER 21
A Changing World 250

CHAPTER 22
Squadron Losses 254

CHAPTER 23
More of the Nineties 257

CHAPTER 24
Exchanges 269

CHAPTER 25
441 in Task Force Aviano 274

CHAPTER 26
Recent Times 298

Glossary... 315

Bibliography 316

Index 317

The Silver Foxes flew the magnificent Lockheed CF-104 Starfighter from 1963 to 1986. Here is a famous 1983 pose of "Checkerbird" 104880. (CF)

Foreword

Fighter Squadron: 441 Squadron from Hurricanes to Hornets is one of the best such histories ever published. The project began in 1991 with some basic research, but progress was slow. In 2002, however, Larry Milberry became interested in publishing the finished product. Using the talents and tenacity of an aviation history sleuth, he organized material already gathered, sought out members and former members of the 441 Squadron family, collected their stories, then skillfully wove it into a thorough history.

The book begins with the exciting wartime years when, as 125 Squadron, we were flying Hurricanes on the East Coast. In 1943 we went overseas to serve with distinction as 441 "Silver Fox" Squadron in Great Britain and Normandy. Next came the exciting postwar years flying the Vampire, F-86 Sabre and CF-104 Starfighter. Larry ends this magical ride with a look at present day 441 Squadron flying the CF-18 Hornet.

Fighter Squadron is dedicated to all the men and women who have served, and who will in the future be a part of this great organization. After all, they are the ones who have made 441 Tactical Fighter Squadron such an incomparable success.

CHECKER, CHECKER!!

R.J. Thorneycroft
Lieutenant-Colonel (Retired)
Commanding Officer
441 Tactical Fighter Squadron
July 2001 -- August 2003

Silver Foxes gathered on July 30, 1979 for the CO's 1000-hour Starfighter flight. Aircraft '785 was especially painted for the occasion. Standing are Doug Barton, Dave Trask, Terry Cosgrove, John David, Larry Crabb (the CO), Dave Richards, Phil Murphy, Mike Jephcott, Luc Trepenier and BJ Ryan. In front are Rick Gelinas, Dave Owen, Mex Tremblay, Gary Lacroix, Gord Loney, Rob Porter and Ted Delange. (Crabb Col.)

Preface

Fighter Squadron: 441 Squadron from Hurricanes to Hornets is the story of a legendary Canadian flying unit. Although there are more than 40 books covering Royal Canadian Air Force and Canadian Forces squadrons, none compares to this one in scope and production quality. *Fighter Squadron*, however, did not get easily into print, for books are daunting things. No sooner can such a project begin, than people realize how deeply they are in over their heads. It's easy to find more immediate and rewarding things to do, so onto the back burner goes the book. In 441's case this is how things went for several years.

My connection with 441 dates to the early 1980s, when I was researching for such book as *Sixty Years* and *The Canadair Sabre*. This interest grew when, about 1990, I was introduced to a stash of historic files collecting dust in a closet at 441. It was here that I learned of wartime pilot R.J. "Bob" Lacerte's good efforts in the 1970s to compile the squadron's WWII history.

In the mid-1990s, 441 alumnus Sky King got behind an effort to produce a squadron book, but things again languished. Then, while at Cold Lake in 1999, I heard from LCol Billie Flynn that 441 was not yet ready to give up on its project. In 2001 I talked things over with his successor, LCol Rob Thorneycroft, suggesting that he start by contacting researcher Hugh A. Halliday. This was done and Hugh soon was at work in the National Archives and in the DND Directorate of History, scouring 441 Operational Record Books, relevant personnel documents, etc. He also began interviewing Silver Foxes from various eras. I did the same, picking up where I had left off years earlier. Meanwhile, Hugh kept me busy distilling floppy discs packed with raw 441 history. Through various networks, such as the Canadian Fighter Pilots Association, SPAADS and the CF-104 alumni, Silver Foxes were invited to chip in, which some did.

All this was the research phase of the book — the "grunt work" and, gradually, a story began unfolding. Along the way a few surviving wartime Silver Foxes became enthusiastic supporters: Sid Bregman, Norm Brunton, Jake Copeland, Alex Graham, Bob Hayes, Arthur Jewett, Guy Mott, Bruce MacKenzie and Harry Pattinson. Even though Jake was beset by Alzheimer's, his wife, June, arranged for an interview. During my afternoon with them in Ottawa, Jake was amazingly lucid, once the topic of Spitfires arose. Harry Pattinson was in rehab by this time so, when I visited his place in Renfrew, it was his wife, Lynne, who opened the doors. Besides the interviewing, log books, albums, scrapbooks, and old correspondence helped to round out each man's story. Pilots Bob Lacerte, Lamont M. "Lal" Parsons, and Hugh Ritchie, though passed on, also helped by way of their memorabilia.

Sabre era people who supported our efforts included Ralph Annis, Bill Bain, Don Bergie, Carl Bertrand, Norm Bigg, Bruce Burgess, Bob Carew, Garth Cinnamon, Ronald Clayton, Elizabeth Constantine, Gary Corbett, D.A. "Dave"

F/L W.W. "Bill" Brown, an outstanding 441 Spitfire pilot. Here he chats in Normandy with the Marshal of the RAF, A/C/M Tedder. Brown was killed by flak on August 13, 1944. In 2003 the Silver Foxes had a Northern Alberta lake named in Brown's honour. (CF PL31062)

Cummings, Bernie Curran, Calvin Drake, Bob Durnan, Jean Ecker, R.J. "Jack" Folkins, Tom Gigliotti, Don Gilkinson, R.G. "Ron" Hayman, Carole Heard, L.J. "Lou" Hill, J.W. "Bill" Hind, D.W. "Doug" Howlett, John "Ray" Jolley, Tom Koch, Claude LaFrance, Leo Lalonde, Alan Lockhart, Bill Lynn, J.L. "Jack" MacArthur, Ron MacGarva, Andy and Alison MacKenzie, Arnold G. Matthews, Ian R. McDonald, R.G. "Bob" Middlemiss, D.H. "Don" Myles, Murray "Buzz" Neilson, Dennis Paproski, Remi Paquette, Les Price, Rogers E. Smith, K.R. "Ken" Stacey, Larry Sutton, Don Syms, Harry Tate, Fern Villeneuve, Douglas "Duke" Warren, Charles Winegarden and Bill Worthy. Nan Baggs and Tes O'Mara provided a glance at the lives of young RCAF wives and mothers of the 1950s. Nan, the widow of 441's Larry Spurr, and Tes, the widow of 441's Hank O'Mara, loaned some memorable photos.

Old time Silver Foxes recall the Sabre era as a glorious time when 441 was ready to take on Soviet might in Europe. Here a shiny new Sabre 5 taxies at Cartierville in the spring of 1954. Shortly afterwards it flew to North Luffenham to join 441. (CF PL52197)

Going out of their way with CF-104 history were such Silver Foxes as C.D. "Doug" Barton (USAF), Gerry Bayles, Ross Betts, D.C. "Dave" Burt, Brian and Sandy Castledine, R.G. "Bob" Christie, Larry Crabb, Ted Delanghe, D.V. "Dan" Dempsey, R.J. "Bob" Endicott, D.L. "Doug" Erlandson, D.S. "Doug" Fenton, John E. Greatrix, Mike Hoch, David Huddleston, John Hutt, Gorm Jensen, Garry "Sky" King, Klaus Kropf, Romeo Lalonde, L.E. "Ted" Lee, Ken Mowbray, Mike Major (USAF), Paul D. Manson, Robin "Red" Morris, M.C. "Mike" Nicholas (USAF), Larry O'Brien, Peter Riley, R.J. "Ray" Saulnier, Wally Sloan, W. "Bill" Turnbull, Bill Van Oene, Nigel Walpole, Judge Wenham, Morley White, and Gordon P. Zans.

When it came to the CF-18 Hornet, I was assisted by the likes of Jeff Beckett, Travis Brassington, Richard Brosseau, D.C. Burt, Dave Burton, Rob Chapman, W.A. "Billie" Flynn, Chris Hadfield, Terry Hunt, Marc Ouellet, Rob Parker, Glenn Phillips, Craig Richmond, Pierre Rochefort, Kurt Saladana, Graham Sinclair, Kirk Soroka, Pierre St-Amand, Tim Strocel, Ian Struthers, Rob Thorneycroft, Paul Umrysh, Bob Wade and Mike Woodfield. Their offerings frequently concerned ordinary life on squadron - the kind of history rarely found in official publications.

Over the years I made many trips to Cold Lake, Ex. Maple Flag always being a good excuse to travel west. Once again the object was to get to the "hands-on" level, where things happen. After all, if you want the real history, there's nothing better than getting out on the flightline, walking the hangar floor, visiting the shops, talking to the folks, and logging as many nights in the mess as possible. I also got to strap into a Hornet several times, to blast off for some yanking, banking and barfing. Through the auspices of NDHQ I visited Aviano, but before the Balkan Rats were in the shooting war. During the air offensive, LCol Billie Flynn invited me to see the real action. Sad to say, however, I was in a state of panic, putting the finishing touches on the first two volumes of *Canada's Air Force at War and Peace*. I couldn't go, so talk about an opportunity missed! Meanwhile, Mike Valenti and I had been covering "Willy Tell" at Tyndall AFB, Florida, including in 1988, '92 and '94 when 441 was present. In May 2003 a final visit to 441 was in order. Mike accompanied me to copy hundreds of photos from 441's albums, and what a gold mine these proved to be.

Photos can set an aviation book apart from the ordinary effort, and no publisher is more renowned for its photo treatment than CANAV Books. This standard was set back in the 1970s by McGraw-Hill Ryerson editor Robin Brass. In my first book, *Aviation in Canada*, Robin placed the photos "front and centre", and pressed me for informative captions. The book became a best seller, survived five printings and set a standard that has been emulated by numerous other publishers.

As usual, with the 441 project many photos originated with the RCAF/CF (unfortunately, photographers rarely are identified). Many other photos used were loaned by past or serving members, or aviation photo buffs like Tony Cassanova and Andrew Cline, both of Aviation World fame, and by Mike Valenti. Occasionally, you may turn the page and be startled by what the candid camera delivers, but you'll enjoy the overall results. While this book has lots of airplane photos, I strove to make *Fighter Squadron* a "people book", for people are what aviation, at any level, is really about.

Many others assisted in getting *Fighter Squadron* into the air. Dave Burton, Ralph Clint, Billie Flynn, Bert Huneault, Ron Pickler and Rob Thorneycroft were dogged proof readers, so not many faux pas are likely to pop up (not that some haven't evaded our eagle eyes). Cpl Short of 441 provided historic documents, photos and memorabilia that he had gathered and

Original postwar Silver Foxes celebrating at North Luffenham a few days before the CO, S/L Andy MacKenzie, left for his Korean tour. Behind are Don Hanson, the CO, Slim Walker and Dean Kelly. In front are Jack Ecker, Pete Cranston, Bob Simmons, Ralph Annis, Gord McDonald and Les Benson. (441 Sqn)

Recce "One-O-Fours" from Marville in a mid-1960s echelon left set-up shot. (Huddleston Col.)

Hornet '754 taxies at Aviano for a July 1998 "Allied Force" patrol. The warload is light – wingtip AIM-9s, two 500-lb bombs, a FLIR pod and one external fuel tank. For an all-up mission, a Hornet could carry three tanks, a FLIR pod, two 1000-lb bombs, and several AAMs. Note the 441 markings and the name by the canopy of 441's renowned Maj Jeff "Beck" Beckett. (Larry Milberry)

catalogued in his spare time. When I needed people identified, Cpl Bill Chisholm of 441 was a key resource. Matthew and Simon Milberry helped with data management, relaying e-mails, etc. Sky King remained supportive throughout the project.

Others assisted as *Fighter Squadron* took shape. Providing information, checking facts, lending photos, publications, etc. were: G.R. "Bob" Ayres, Bill Baggs, A.E. "Barney" Barnard, Fabiana Bohemier, Capt Ben Bond, Robert Bracken, S.E. "Syd" Burrows, Lloyd C. Campbell, David Clark, Les Corness, John L. Den Ouden, Ken Duff, Ron Eldridge, Stephen Fochuk, Monique Halliday, Shirley Hiebert, Hrant Keskek, Janet Lacroix, G. Lang, Roger Lindsay, Jim Lyzun, John Melson, John Meuse, Carl Mills, Ken Orr, Garnet "Red" Ovans, Jules Plamondon, Todd Pomerleau, Geoff Rankin-Lowe, Lisa Simkins, Turbo Tarling, David Thompson, Siegfried Wache, Wilf White and Gordon S. Williams.

Besides these individuals, several institutions and companies helped with photographs and other material and services: Bombardier Aerospace, Canada Post, Canadian Forces Joint Imaging Centre, Department of National Defence (4 Wing Cold Lake, Directorate of History and Heritage, NDHQ), Imperial War Museum, Library and Archives Canada, Public Record Office (London, UK). Apologies to any whose names have been missed.

As to getting *Fighter Squadron* finally into print, that's another story. In the last year of work, much new 441 history surfaced. I decided to make room for this, reminding myself that there is nothing more pitiful than the cheapskate's approach of setting artificial boundaries. Naturally, *Fighter Squadron* ballooned, setting back production by months and sending costs through the roof. In this way the book gives new meaning to the term "labour of love". But what true supporter of Canada's aviation heritage would prefer a half-baked book, let alone complain about the price (about the same as a couple of good ol' Canadian 2-4s)?

With *Fighter Squadron*, CANAV's enviable record in financing books remains in tact. It has never so much as applied for a publishing grant, my position always being that, if a book is worth the publishing, get on with it, but don't oblige your neighbours to foot the bill. A note about weights and measures, before you begin reading. Assuming that we all are able to convert easily from one system to another, CANAV uses Imperial units, since these remain common in global aviation.

Larry Milberry

The Hawker Hurricane, 125 Squadron's first fighter, flew in England in 1935. A revolutionary monoplane, the first version had a 1030-hp Rolls-Royce Merlin, a top speed of 315 mph, and impressive firepower - eight .303 machine guns. The RCAF accepted the first of 50 Hurricane Mk.Is from the UK in 1939. From June 1942 it added 450 Mk.XIIs (1300 hp, 340 mph) built in Fort William by Canadian Car and Foundry. Shown is a flight of 125 Squadron Mk.XIIs. A handful of Canadian-built Hurricanes survives, including (in 2004) 5667 with the Fighter Factory in Sussex, Virginia. (Sid Bregman Col.)

CHAPTER

Defending Canada
1942 - 1943

125 Squadron Days

In the early 2000s, 441 "Silver Fox" Squadron was flying CF-18 Hornets from 4 Wing in Cold Lake, Alberta. A renowned Canadian fighting unit, 441 traces its beginnings to a predecessor - 125 Squadron. The formation of 125 was linked to Canada's reaction to the war situation early in 1942. Japan's attack on Pearl Harbour, followed by offensives against Hong Kong, Malaya, the Philippines and the Dutch East Indies, fed rumours and fears that the enemy was about to attack the west coast of North America. The feeling was heightened when Japan launched a major offensive in the islands off Alaska - this was no imaginary threat. These fears resonated on Canada's east coast, already panicky over U-boat incursions into the Gulf of St. Lawrence and the waters off Halifax.

Thus did the RCAF expand its air defence and anti-submarine forces. In the spring of 1942 eight new Home War Establishment fighter squadrons formed on the coasts. The second of these, 125 Squadron, would begin operations at Sydney, Nova Scotia. It came into being under an Organization Order of April 17, 1942, to take effect on the 20th. It was not until the 27th, however, that 125 Squadron graduated from being a paper unit. The "Org Order" stated that squadron and flight commanders should be pilots with recent fighter experience, preferably with overseas service. The first commanding officer, F/L Charles W. Trevena, qualified, having flown with No.1 (RCAF) Squadron during the Battle of Britain. His successor, F/L Robert William Norris, who took over on June 3, 1942, was credited with one enemy aircraft probably destroyed and one damaged in the Battle of Britain. Several other pilots were from 118 Squadron at Dartmouth, where they recently had traded their obsolete Grumman Goblins for Curtiss P-40 Kittyhawks.

On April 27 WO Lamont M. "Lal" Parsons flew 125's first

S/L R.W. "Bob" Norris commanded 125 Squadron at Sydney and Torbay. He flew in the Battle of Britain with No.1 Squadron (RCAF) in 1940. Norris, who finished the war in Bomber Command, passed away in Belleville, Ontario on November 7, 2002. (CF PL36585)

Pilots reached 125 Squadron from various backgrounds. "Lal" Parsons and "Pat" Pattinson, for example, came from 118 Squadron at Dartmouth. There they flew the Grumman Goblin, a flight of which is shown over Nova Scotia. In the case of P/O Guy Mott, he had been flying Kittyhawks on the West Coast with 14 Squadron. Others were "sprogs" - new pilots who arrived at 125 directly from training. (CF PL5954)

aircraft, delivering Harvard 3337 from Dartmouth to Sydney. For its first few weeks, 125 was busy assembling crated Hurricane Is. In this period, Parsons was commissioned and became 125's first flight commander. On June 7, seven Hurricanes and two Harvards flew from Sydney to Stephenville, Newfoundland, escorted by a

Officers of 125 Squadron in late 1942. Seated are P/O McDonald (Adjutant), S/L Norris (CO), F/L Harry Pattinson (OC "A" Flight) and F/O Lamont Parsons (OC "B" Flight). Behind are P/O's Rhodes, Guy Mott, John Gilmartin, Jack Boyle, WO "Bud" Young and P/O Trujillo. (441 Sqn Col.)

While at Dartmouth, some RCAF pilots, F/L Pattinson included, occasionally flew "Merchant Ship Fighter Unit" Hurricanes ashore for maintenance. While at sea, these "Hurricats" stood ready to be catapulted aloft, should German bombers attack. Shown at Dartmouth is MSFU "Hurricat" NJ-P. (Pattinson Col.)

The Hurricane was noted for its ruggedness, something that F/O Harry Hindmarsh of 125 Squadron learned the hard way. Here is the aftermath of his close encounter with an RCN Fairmile. (Pattinson Col.)

Bolingbroke and a Canso. From there, shepherded by the Bolingbroke, they reached Torbay via Gander on 9th. At Torbay the job was to help defend the nearby port of St. John's. Meanwhile, most of 125's groundcrew had sailed aboard the SS *Caribou* from Sydney to Port aux Basques. From there they travelled by rail to St. John's (the Caribou would be sunk by a U-boat in the Cabot Strait in October 1942 with the loss of 118 lives.)

Popular aviation magazines in 1942 were speculating about possible aerial threats to North America, including raids by Fw.200 Kondor bombers, and strikes from aircraft carriers. On nothing more than a reconnaissance mission, however, an Fw.200 lacked the range to penetrate much further west than Iceland, while construction of Germany's only aircraft carrier, the *Graf Zeppelin*, already had been halted in favour of increased U-boat construction. Thus, from its start, 125 Squadron was looking for a role, something that caused its pilots some frustration. Something useful for 125 Squadron, however, was the chance to take part in the war games with the Newfoundland garrisons. In an exercise of September 27, 1942, an "invading army" was attempting to capture Torbay airport. FSgt Guy E. Mott had just taken off on patrol when his aircraft developed a coolant leak and his cockpit filled with smoke. Mott climbed to 1000 feet and bailed out, landing in

Conception Bay. Thus did he become the first 125 pilot to join the "Caterpillar Club" (members were airmen who had parachuted to safety).

Mott's wingman, Sgt John William Gilmartin, was unable to contact base by radio, so returned immediately to Torbay to report the crash. He then took off in a Harvard and guided a small fishing boat from the outport of Bauline. Aboard were Charles H. Butler, Ambrose King, Chesley King, James S. Legrow and Reginald Legrow. They didn't reach Mott a moment too soon. By the time they hauled him aboard, he had been in the frigid water for 35 minutes.

Two days after Guy Mott's dunking, two pilots were doing a sector reconnaissance. As part of the exercise they attacked an "invading force" of five Fairmile anti-submarine vessels in Conception Bay. P/O Harry A. Hindmarsh took his role most enthusiastically, clipping the mast guy wires of a Fairmile and losing part of his starboard wing and aileron. Happily, he got home. A few weeks later Sgt. Gilmartin became the second 125 pilot to qualify for the Caterpillar Club, after a faltering engine obliged him to "hit the silk".

The extent of 125 Squadron operations was evident by the resources expended. Total manpower varied between 36 and 46, of whom 15 to 20 were pilots. The average aircraft establishment was 10 Hurricanes and two Harvards. Assuming that fog was not blanketing the area, each day the squadron would fly two dawn and two dusk patrols. The rest of the time was dedicated to lectures and air exercises – formation flying, aerobatics, dogfighting, night flying, etc. In July 1942 gasoline was so scarce that the squadron had to borrow from United States Army Air Corps units at Torbay. Meanwhile, the aging Hurricane Is grew

Sten Lundberg of 125 Squadron sketched "Heading Out to Sea", showing Hurricanes armed with depth charges. Then, a snapshot of Lundberg at Torbay in 1942. Later, he flew with 416 Squadron, but was shot down and became a POW. Postwar, he was one of Canada's early commercial helicopter pilots, flying for his father's aerial survey company. (441 Sqn)

A typical Hurricane Mk.XIIA. Then, an impressive 125 Squadron line abreast formation with St. John's and the Newfoundland coast below. (Bregman, Pattinson Cols.)

The RCAF supplied home defence squadrons with Harvards for on-going training. (Sid Bregman Col.)

difficult to maintain, and spares were scarce. On September 18 (at the height of a U-boat campaign in the Gulf of St. Lawrence) 125 had only one serviceable aircraft. Next day the figure was zero. Through October, serviceability never exceeded five Hurricanes, and on 24 days the number varied between one and three.

Hurricane XIIs replaced the Mk.Is in November 1942. Not only did serviceability soar, but so did the pilots. That July they had competed with each other to see who could reach the highest altitude. A record had been set at 28,200 feet by Sgt Sten Lundberg. With the newer machines and improved oxygen masks, they soon surpassed 30,000 feet and, on May 3, 1943, P/O Mott reached 35,400.

The Canadian-built Mark XII was essentially the British Mark II with wings strengthened to carry 250-pound bombs. For anti-submarine patrols 125 fitted either two 100- or 250-pound armour-piercing bombs, or two 250-pound depth charges, then went patrolling for U-boats. S/L Norris seems to have promoted anti-submarine scrambles as a means of encouraging his men. He explained their mission: "It is our duty to show that a fighter squadron can be used for more than one thing and thus make our own position much more interesting, while we are waiting to protect our shores from enemy aerial activity. It is our duty to show the BR [Bomber-Reconnaissance] Squadrons that we are needed as much as they are, and that our skill and knowledge are as good as theirs."

Besides U-boat hunting, 125 trained for other tasks. On December 11, 1942 it proudly reported achieving its first night interception, FSgt Charles Kusiar (Hurricane 5502) catching a 145 (BR) Squadron Hudson over Signal Hill. That day's record of flying (in many ways typical) shows a bit of a Home Defence squadron's routine. The squadron reported having eight Hurricanes and one Harvard serviceable, six and one unserviceable. With these resources they conducted 2 dawn patrols, 4 formation flights, 2 night formation practices, 1 test on a glide path indicator, 1 night scramble, 2 instrument practice trips, 2 astern deflection attacks, 2 practice scrambles and 2 sector recces.

The most formidable enemy at Torbay was the weather. More than one sortie concluded with a pilot groping to find the field after meeting unexpected fog or snow squalls. Pilots were trained in woodcraft (building shelters, snaring game, ice fishing, and building fires), lest they crash-land or bail out in bush country. Such hazards were underlined on February 17, 1943. A Hudson was missing and 125 sent five aircraft to search. Suddenly, unexpected winds and blinding snow struck the area. Two aircraft reached base, but three Harvards force-landed. F/O "Lal" Parsons with his passenger, Cpl Allan J. White (rigger), landed wheels up near Kelligrews with only slight damage to propeller and flaps. The aircraft later was towed home. P/O Ernest B. Rhodes with Cpl Gordon H. Sinnott (electrician) landed on a lake near Heart's Desire. They returned to Torbay by horse-drawn sleigh, while the aircraft was flown home on March 5. P/O John J. Boyle with LAC Arnold B. Jensen (engine fitter) alighted on a frozen lake near Carbonear. Although the flaps were damaged, S/L Norris later was able to fly this Harvard home. As to Parsons, referring years later, Bruce MacKenzie of 125 Squadron would describe him as having "taught us to fly in all kinds of weather."

From June to December 1943 the squadron again was in Sydney, where the weather improved and flying increased. The pattern of "non-combat" operations continued, while pilots watched enviously as one or two comrades periodically would be posted overseas. Due to engine failures, two more pilots joined the Caterpillar Club - P/O Rhodes (August 7) and P/O Norman Brunton (November 30). On October 13 A/V/M A.E. Godfrey, Deputy Inspector-General of

I got my first chance to fly a Hurricane on June 18 at Torbay, taking up Mk.I No.1353 - quite a decrepit old kite. After familiarizing myself with the Hurricane's basic characteristics, I returned to land. I selected flaps and gear down but, on final, I must have re-selected "flaps up" (that was not impossible to do, since both functions were controlled by the same lever). The aircraft landed beautifully and I rolled ... and rolled. I applied left brake, I applied right brake, learning that air brakes are not the greatest. Finally, I was off the end of the runway. I swung around with hard left rudder and ... smack, right into a great rock! It was either that or go off a steep bank. In the aftermath, I got away with the incident, since F/O Pattinson, our "A" Flight commander, took the blame, explaining to the CO that he had been remiss in not warning me of the tricky gear/flap lever.

Prime Minister Churchill inspecting airmen at Uplands on the occasion referred to by Bruce MacKenzie. (CF PL6510)

the RCAF, visited 125 and ordered a scramble at short notice, deliberately doing this at noon-hour, when flights were most likely to be under-staffed. The scramble was followed by a formation fly-past by 12 Hurricanes. Godfrey complimented pilots and groundcrew for their high state of efficiency, then informed them that they were to proceed overseas in January 1944.

Torbay Tales

Bruce M. MacKenzie was honoured to have served on 125 and 441 squadrons from beginning to end. A prairie boy, he had graduated from high school in 1940, then worked as a store clerk at a paltry wage. Tired of this, in the summer of 1941 he joined the RCAF. Starting there at $2.80 a day seemed like a financial bonanza to a young man hoping to attend university. After the usual RCAF preliminaries at Manning Depot in Brandon, then at Initial Training School in Regina, MacKenzie was off to 19 Elementary Flying Training School at Virden, Manitoba. There he soloed on a Tiger Moth after a mere eight hours of training.

MacKenzie next was posted to 2 Service Flying Training School at Uplands to face the challenge of the Harvard. One day Winston Churchill paid a visit to watch a British Commonwealth Air Training Plan station in action. And action he got. The station commander ordered all serviceable Harvards into the air, to give the great man a top show. Included in the flying was Bruce MacKenzie, but he botched his takeoff, nearly pranged into a snow bank, then into the control tower, from where "Winnie" was observing. In spite of this, in April 1942 MacKenzie won his Wings. Soon he was posted to Sydney in the initial 125 Squadron pilot cadre. He describes what followed:

We sailed for Newfoundland aboard the ferry "Caribou", disembarked at Port aux Basques, then travelled by train across Newfoundland. The train swished and swayed as it rolled along on its narrow gauge rails. We heard all kinds of stories about how it sometimes was marooned by gale force winds - I later experienced such a marooning. This trip was the first time that I ever encountered white porters on a train.

Work hard, play hard. Life on any RCAF station included lots of sports and other fun. Parties such as this in Torbay's mess were greatly enjoyed by everyone. (Sid Bregman Col.)

125 Squadron alumni in Ottawa for the 1998 Canadian Fighter Pilots Association convention: Norman Brunton (St. Petersburg, Florida), Guy Mott (Sarnia, Ontario), Clem Gerwing (Calgary), Lal Parsons (St. John's) and Bob Hayes (Irondale, Ontario). In May 2003 Brunton and Gerwing related a few memories from 125 days. Brunton, who grew up in New Jersey, fell in love with the Spitfire when he saw one at the 1939 New York World's Fair. He joined the RCAF in August 1941, training on Finches and Ansons. He joined 126 Squadron at Dartmouth, then transferred in August 1942 to 125. Once overseas, he and some others soon left 441 at Digby, Brunton going to 403. Gerwing, who grew up in Lake Lenore, Saskatchewan, joined the RCAF in July 1941. He learned to fly at Virden, Manitoba on Tiger Moths, then got his Wings in Ottawa on Harvards. While waiting in Halifax to get overseas, he was posted to 125. Commenting in 2003 about the coastal patrols flown by 125, he chuckled: "Before long it became quite evident that the Germans weren't coming." Posted overseas, Gerwing soon experienced real war - there were devastating raids on Bournemouth while he was there. From here, he joined 17 Squadron (Spitfires) in the Far East. With him there was Herb Ivens (ex-125), who later was a Japanese POW. Postwar, Gerwing found his calling in leather goods. In 2003 he finally retired from his long-time business, Alberta Boot. (Larry Milberry)

Sgt Brunton (right) with F/O Parsons, then Sgt Gerwing, Sgt Hayes and P/O Mott as young pilots in Torbay some 60 years earlier. (Guy Mott Col.)

When F/O Guy Mott got his posting overseas, he decided on a small celebration. Meanwhile, late in the afternoon, two of us servicing bods were the only inhabitants of the hangar (the weather was a washout, but two groundcrew mechs were required on readiness alert). The ensuing boredom was suddenly broken by F/O Mott showing up. In one hand he had an almost full bottle of hooch, in the other he had some glasses. "Would you fellows care for a drink of this rot gut?" he asked.

Now, I didn't think that we should be drinking in the hangar, but ... how often does an ordinary erk get offered such an enticing treat from a friendly officer? I guess the other erk must have wondered the same but, after giving it a quick thought, we dove right in.

The previous week someone had swiped my coveralls. That meant that I had to sign an E-26 and pay for a new pair. I was pretty cheesed at that, so printed "ELDRIDGE" in big, ugly letters across the back of my new pair. Well, after we all had a few snorts from F/O Mott's bottle, I found him staring bleary-eyed at my back. "ELD ... RIDGE", he stammered. "I can smell your name wherever I go." I

Guy Mott with Mr. and Mrs. Ambrose King in Bauline, Newfoundland on June 26, 1987. (Parsons Col.)

While we didn't do much flying at Torbay, we gained a lot of confidence in bad weather operations (once we were so completely snowed in that G/C Grandy, our station commander, had no way of getting from St. John's to the 'drome other than on snow shoes). F/O Lal Parsons was especially valuable in teaching us the ropes. On typical patrols we could go far out to sea, then return to find the airport fogged in. Our radios were poor, so we weren't always in contact with the control tower. On other occasions, while doing night flying, we used to go over St. John's where, on our radios, we might pick up the latest episode of the "The Green Hornet" radio drama.

On one unforgettable night exercise I taxied out in a Hurricane that had a duff radio. After Guy Mott landed in a Harvard, the tower flashed me the green light to take off. Assuming that the tower would hold Guy at the end of the runway, I lined up, poured on the throttle and headed down the runway. Then, as my tail came up, there was Guy taxiing back towards me! Well, all I could do was kick on hard right rudder, then I felt our wingtips brush. I got airborne, climbed out and flew for an hour. Upon returning, my radio still was u/s, so the tower flashed me the green light and I landed. Guy explained how he also had taken evasive action to the right. As the saying goes, I guess our numbers were not up at the time. As to responsibility for this near disaster, apparently the controller was relieved of his duties for wrongly giving me the green light.

One of 125 Squadron's ground crew ("erks" as they often called themselves) was Ron Eldridge. Years after the war he wrote to 441 pilot Bob Lacerte about some fun that three squadron members had one day:

Some of those at the February 19, 1989 ceremony: Harold Butler (son of the late Charles H. Butler, boat crew), Rev. Silas G. Rogers (United Church), Ambrose King (boat crew), Mrs. Miriam King (widow of Chesley King, boat crew), Phyllis Swyer (daughter of Reginald Legrow, boat crew), James Legrow (boat crew) and Lal Parsons. (Parsons Col.)

didn't know if he meant to say "smell" or "spell", but we all chuckled. As F/O Mott left us, I wished him the best of luck in his new posting. "Thanks," he answered. "I'll probably need it where I'm going." Happily, "Lady Luck" was with him and he came home in one piece.

In 1987 there was a 125 Squadron reunion in St. John's. On February 20, 1988 Lal Parsons wrote to 441 Squadron telling of this, and of a special service that followed:

Last September I wrote and brought you up to date on the tidying up of things after the '87 reunion. At that time I told you about our oversight in not having acknowledged the fine work of the people of the fishing village of Bauline in rescuing Guy Mott, after he had parachuted into the cold waters of Conception Bay on September 27, 1942. Well, it has now all been done. There were offers to finance the plaque, but Guy decided this was something he would like to look after himself. So he decided on the wording, and sent in a fine bronze plaque.

Bauline is a small community and, like a lot of our smaller places, is a one-denominational place. There is a little United Church there. The minister and the Board of Stewards were approached for permission to place this plaque in their sanctuary. The request really got a good reception and yesterday, Sunday, the plaque was presented and dedicated.

It was a lovely service, all built around the presentation. The anthem "I was wrecked on a lonely and desolate shore", from an old Redemption song book, was followed by the sermon by the Rev. Silas Rogers about the paradox of the Gospel "strength is weakness", referring to the challenges that bring out the best in people. Then came a solo entitled "Precious Memories", by the son of the people whose house Guy had been taken to. A scripture lesson was read by the daughter of one of the men in the boat. Two other men who were part of the boat's crew were present.

The plaque was dedicated by the minister, and the unveiling done by the oldest lady in the community, Mrs. Meriam King, a lady of 86 years and widow of the man who owned the boat. During the service, the congregation was told of the incident, then there was a reception in the church hall. It was really a very touching and tasteful service, put on by a very sincere and down to earth people used to the hazards of the North Atlantic.

It was unfortunate that more of the squadron could not have been there, and certainly too bad that Guy could not attend. But road conditions are so uncertain and conditions have to be about one hundred percent to navigate the hilly road down into Bauline. For Guy to come this time in the year and have the function postponed did not seem practical. I phoned him right after the service and sent him the bulletin and other material this morning, and will maybe have a tape for him when I see him in a week or two in Sarnia.

Losses

On August 27, 1942 Sgt D.B. Ruggles of Kenora, Ontario was practicing low level formation flying in Hurricane 1360. Suddenly he pulled up in a steep turn, stalled, and dove into the ground near Hopeall. Another 125 loss came from a larger tragedy. On December 12, 1942, LAC Gomer Couture Bellerive, an electrician, was one of more than 140 killed (16 being RCAF) in a fire that destroyed the Knights of Columbus Hostel in St. John's. Bellerive had joined 125 only a week earlier. FSgt Charles W. Kusiar of 125, who arrived quickly at the fire, assisted rescuers with floodlights and crowd control. Squadron adjutant P/O W. McDonald spent several days helping to identify the dead. Ruggles and Bellerive were 125's only fatalities in Torbay days.

Sad times came inevitably to 125 Squadron. This was the send-off from St. John's for Sgt Ruggles. As his casket was entrained for Gander (where he was buried), an honour guard fired a volley and the station band played. (Mott Col.)

Wings over Seas

September 15, 1943

- Introducing our "Skipper", **Squadron Leader Norris**, who has seen action in England, and the enemy is hoping his posting here remains permanent.
- **Flying Officer Pattinson**, the senior Flight Commander and "Chief of the Rumble Club", is an old timer in the Service, and the Squadron benefits from his experience.
- **Pilot Officer Parsons** is at home here in his native land. If he is not tearing the skies apart with an aircraft, he is ripping roads apart with "Tangerine" [the squadron "staff car"].
- **Pilot Officer Stevenson** is a new addition to the Squadron and, from all accounts, is a good Yankee.
- **Flight Sergeant Mott** has seen service in many squadrons and, at present, is taking pills to increase his stature.
- **Sergeant Lundberg**, the Swedish Ace, has an American goose confirmed.
- **Sergeant MacDonald**, or "Crash" to his pals, is at present basking in sunny Toronto, but will be back in action soon.
- **Sergeant Kusiar**, the "Mad Russian", is also on leave and promises to return with a harem.
- **Sergeant Gilmartin** is as yet almost hairless, but anyone wishing to see this interesting individual in that state had better hurry, as a salesman selling hair tonic has made a sale.
- **Sergeant Hayes**, the sleeping beauty, alias "Horizontal", is still alive and well.
- **Sergeant Gerwing**, Casanova of the West, is lucky in cards and lucky in love.
- **Sergeant MacKenzie** is the beauty of the Squadron and can exist for days on a diet of peaches and cream.
- **Sergeant Dean**, "The Professor", is a native of the west, and is the only married "Non-Com" in the outfit — and is he married!
- **Sergeant Brunton**, a newcomer to the Squadron, hails from New Jersey, and has passed the initiation with flying colours.

We hope that this proves a satisfactory introduction to the pilots. More news next issue.

Squadron pilots at Torbay in 1943. Standing are Sgt R.C. "Bob" Hayes, FSgt Guy E. Mott and Sgts Norm Brunton, J.W. "Bill" Gilmartin, WO MacIntosh, H.L. "Professor" Dean, Bruce M. MacKenzie, C.F. "Clem" Gerwing, Sten T. Lundberg, C.W. "Bill" Kusiar and A.J. "Alex" McDonald. In front are P/O Harry Hindmarsh, P/O Harry Pattinson, S/L Bob Norris, P/O Lamont Parsons and P/O McDonald (the adjutant). Of these, Alex McDonald would be lost overseas, while Lundberg would do a stretch as a POW. (All, Norman Brunton Col.)

"The Boys" in a less formal scene at Torbay.

In the September 15, 1943 edition of "Wings over Seas", Torbay's station newspaper, FSgt Johnny West, under the banner "Slip Stream", wrote a light-hearted column introducing 125's pilots.

Armed with 250-lb depth charges, 125 Hurricanes patrol for U-boats off Newfoundland. Nobody on squadron ever spotted a U-boat, although large whales sometimes were mistaken for the enemy.

Norm Brunton in Torbay days.

Great fun at Torbay. First, the program describing an evening of formal entertainment, then an informal get together in 125's readiness shack.

FSgt Johnny West during an outing in St. John's where he has picked up a couple of bottles of hooch. West was another of the 125 alumni lost overseas.

A typical crew on readiness at Torbay in May 1943. Behind are AC Fellows, LAC Chick, AC Craigmyle, P/O Lundberg, LAC Goodin and LAC McGonigle. In front are LAC Head, Sgt Flynn, LAC Nadler and Cpl Mitch Hill.

Pilots Wally Hill and Bud Young amuse the squadron mascots at Sydney in 1943.

Torbay old timers at Cold Lake for 441's 50th anniversary: Clem Gerwing, Sten Lundberg, Bob Hayes, Guy Mott, Don Kimball and Bruce MacKenzie. (Bob Hayes Col.)

LCol Ian Struthers, then 441 CO, with 125 CO Bob Norris. They were attending 125's reunion in St. John's in 1987. (Bob Hayes Col.)

Supermarine Spitfire Mk.IX "9G-Y" of 441 Squadron in an aerial photo by Sid Bregman. When such code letters as "9G-Y" appear, they are easily interpreted. The first two letters are the squadron identifier ("9G" signifies 441); the next letter indicates the particular aircraft, i.e. aircraft "Y" of 441.

CHAPTER
Invading Great Britain

The Squadron Goes Overseas

The decision to post 125 Squadron overseas was part of a larger plan. The withdrawal of Japanese forces from the Aleutians in August 1943 had removed the most conspicuous enemy threat on the Pacific coast. Thus, by that autumn the excessive scope of the Home War Establishment was accepted. Even the number of home-based anti-submarine squadrons was reduced, the introduction of four-engined Liberators having greatly enhanced RCAF capabilities.

In this period a new RAF formation (83 Group) was taking shape. One of its purposes was to support First Canadian Army, once the Allies had returned to western Europe. With 83 Group in view, six RCAF home fighter squadrons transferred to the UK. To avoid confusion with existing RAF squadrons, they were renumbered in the 400-series:

HWE Unit	Command	Overseas Sqn Number	Aircraft
123 (AC) Sqn	EAC	439	Typhoon
125 (F) Sqn	EAC	441	Spitfire
127 (F) Sqn	EAC	443	Spitfire
14 (F) Sqn	WAC	442	Spitfire
111 (F) Sqn	WAC	440	Typhoon
118 (F) Sqn	WAC	438	Typhoon

With this reorganization the HWE was not entirely without fighters. Nos.126 and 129 squadrons of Eastern Air Command had their establishments rise from 15 to 18 Hurricanes, while No.1 OTU at Bagotville was to have 12 ready for action at 30 minutes notice. No.125 flew its last operational sorties on November 2, 1943. Thereafter, it concentrated on training and preparing for overseas. F/L Henry Wallace McLeod, DFC, arrived from No.1 OTU to spend 10 days lecturing 125 about fighter doctrine, and instructing in air-to-air firing and formation tactics. A Malta fighter ace, McLeod was an inspiring example, as much for his hawkish enthusiasm as for his record (he later took 127/443 Squadron overseas, leading it until killed in action in September 1944).

The initial movement order envisaged 125 sailing in the last week of January 1944, but personnel did not start reporting to No.1 "Y" Depot in Lachine (a Montreal suburb) until the 13th. That meant a last-minute rush to complete paperwork (including personnel documentation) and to arrange for Christmas leave. Flying training ceased on December 19. Three days later, all personnel left Sydney for three weeks of home leave, before meeting again at Lachine. At that time unit strength was 120 all ranks (19 officer pilots, 4 NCO pilots, 2 other officers and 95 airmen in all trades). Five of the pilots had been with 125 since its formation.

When 125 reassembled at Lachine, it was organized pandemonium. Nos.14 and 127 squadrons were also part of the move, and all were busy with the pre-embarkation routine of documentation, photographing, blood typing, accounting, etc. On January 19 the three squadrons marched to the railway station, slipping along the icy roads under the weight of personal baggage. Two trains moved them to Halifax, where they embarked aboard the troopship SS *Louis Pasteur*. On the 21st they put to sea unescorted. Six days later they were at anchor in Liverpool's Mersey estuary.

"Hurry up and wait" is a service maxim, and those aboard the *Louis Pasteur* had to do just that. Their vessel remained at anchor and rumours spread to explain the delay. The reason was simple – overcrowded docks. Finally, on January 31, *Louis Pasteur* moved into the harbour and the squadrons disembarked. Trains whisked the Canadians to Bournemouth, a British peacetime resort, now home to No.3 Personnel Reception Centre, the main point where Canadian and Australian air force personnel were accommodated, pending deployment elsewhere. Here

W/C J.E. "Johnnie" Johnson, DSO and 2 Bars, DFC and Bar, commanded 144 (F) Wing from March to July 1944. As such he often led 441. After the war, he remained close to his RCAF compatriots, rarely missing a Commonwealth Aircrew Reunion in Winnipeg, or a CFPA convention. (CF PL43239)

the men drew flying clothing, took night vision tests, and went through more paperwork, while becoming accustomed to British conditions, from blackouts to afternoon tea.

On February 8, 1944 the newly-arrived squadrons were formally renumbered 441, 442 and 443 squadrons. A week later they entrained for RCAF Station Digby in Lincolnshire, where they constituted 144 (RCAF) Wing. W/C James E. Walker, DFC, of Edmonton commanded the wing, while RAF W/C J. E. "Johnnie" Johnson, DSO, DFC, was Wing Commander (Flying) responsible for day-to-day operations. A member of the RCAF with 11 enemy aircraft to his credit, Walker was a veteran of North Russia and North Africa, while Johnson, associated with the RCAF for more than a year, was to many an "Honorary Canadian". (Walker would die in the crash of an Auster on April 25, 1944.) S/L Bob Norris accompanied 441 to Digby, but his posting as CO of 125 Squadron ended in February and he transferred to Bomber Command.

Mobility within 144 Wing would be vital in forthcoming operations, and 2 Tactical Air Force, to which 144 Wing belonged, had a standard pattern intended to achieve that end. Thus did 441 become a unit of pilots only, plus a handful of clerks. The mechanics and armourers now became 6441 Servicing Echelon, part of a larger pool of 144 Wing servicing resources. While the new system ultimately permitted speedy transfers of men and machines during mobile warfare, its use when operating for long periods from fixed bases was arguable. Some felt that this system created artificial distinctions between aircrew and those who cared for their machines, so was detrimental to groundcrew morale. Nevertheless, Canadian pilots strove to maintain links with those who serviced and armed their Spitfires. At a time when food was rationed, aircrew were allowed a generous issue of six eggs per week. In his unpublished memoir, Bruce MacKenzie recalled: "One of our favourite tricks, to make sure that aircraft maintenance were looking after our airplanes, was to hide an egg behind the tail wheel or some other inconspicuous spot around the aircraft, and then see if our maintenance people found them. It was a humorous check up and a way of sharing what was provided for the pilots with the fellows who made sure we stayed airborne."

Now known as the "Silver Fox" squadron, 441 began a program of

S/L George U. Hill, DFC and 2 Bars, commanded 441 from March 11, 1944, until shot down on April 25. (CF PL21694)

intense ground training (lectures, films, skeet shooting, etc.), until its Spitfire Vs arrived on February 22. As soon as they had drawn parachutes and completed cockpit drills, the pilots tried out their new machines, with which they soon were at home. Meanwhile, 441 was adding pilots with operational experience and, on March 12, Spitfire IXs began arriving. On the 18th the squadron moved to Holmsley South, a few miles northeast of Bournemouth. All this was overseen by veteran RCAF fighter pilots S/L George U. Hill, DFC, and S/L James D. Hall. The fiesty Hill became CO on March 11. A former steeplejack, Dieppe veteran, and ace from the Mediterranean theatre with a dozen kills, he had three DFCs (his story is recounted in detail in *The Tumbling Sky*). As to Hall, he later commanded 443 Squadron, but was killed in action in June 1944.

Accommodations at Holmsley South initially were in Nissen huts but, once the groundcrew arrived by train, all ranks moved into tents. The first few days involved digging slit trenches – as much to practice for the future, as to meet an existing threat. Meanwhile, cannons and machine guns were tested and harmonized, while Spitfire IXs were modified to carry jettisonable fuel tanks. The first operational sorties came on March 27, when F/Os William R. Chowen and Leslie C. Saunders scrambled after an unidentified aircraft. Since a cap had been left off his oil tank, Saunders returned early, but Chowen intercepted the "bogey" (a lone USAAF Mustang) half way across the English Channel.

Next day was much better. American 8th Air Force B-17s were attacking airfields in France. Two 144 Wing squadrons were to fly a supporting sweep. S/L Hill was ill, so W/C Edward P. Wells, DSO, DFC (RNZAF), led the twelve 441 Spitfires. W/C Johnson assumed double duty, leading 442 Squadron and the Wing (443 was on an air firing course). They first proceeded to Tangmere to refuel, then took off at 1400 hours. To avoid radar detection, the formation crossed the Channel on the deck, climbing to 10,000 feet as they neared France. At this point Johnson developed R/T trouble. He remained with the formation, but had Wells lead.

Don Kimball rose in 441 to be OC "A" Flight. In 2003 Bruce MacKenzie remembered him as "super, delightful and calm", and as a serious chess player. Kimball also was a good shot, becoming 441's leading ace with 6 e/a destroyed and one damaged. (CF PL45117)

Pilots of 441 at Funtington in May 1944. Standing are Jake Fleming, Alex McDonald, Bill Dunning, Don Kimball, Alex Graham, Tom Gamey, Leo Cashman, Wally Hill, Freddie Wilson, Sandy Saunders, Lou Plummer, Bruce MacKenzie and Johnnie Johnstone. In front are Johnnie West, Guy Mott, Tom Brannagan, Danny Browne, Les Moore and Bill Draper. (Guy Mott Col.)

The Spitfires crossed the coast at St. Valery, before heading south towards Chartres. The Luftwaffe airfield at Dreux, west of Paris, presented a tempting target - 20 to 30 aircraft parked in the dispersals. As 442 flew top cover, Wells led 441 into the sun, echeloned them to starboard, then dove to strafe Dreux from south to north. He fired on a control tower, then blasted a twin-engined Me.410. W/C Johnson, joining the fray with F/O Percy A. McLachlan as wingman, shot up what he thought to be a Ju.88. F/O Thomas A. Brannagan strafed a vehicle, a machine gun position and a flak tower, before shooting up an unidentified single-engine machine and an Me.410, all the while manoeuvring to avoid obstructions. Johnson reported both of Brannagan's targets "destroyed".

"White Section" of 441 pulled up to 7000 feet, drawing intense light flak, while "Black Section" dove for its crack at the field. F/L Leslie A. Moore damaged an He.111 and an Me.410 (the latter shared with F/O Ronald G. Lake and F/L Guy Mott). Lake damaged another aircraft, while P/O Donald Hugh Kimball scored strikes on a Ju.88. The final tally was 4 enemy aircraft destroyed, 4 damaged. Reporting the action later, W/C Johnson credited their success to surprise (the enemy probably had not expected an attack so far inland), inattentive flak gunners, and good tactics (attacking out of the sun). Of 11 pilots from 441, ten had participated in the strafing (FSgt Ross A. MacMillan had flown as a spare with 442). Of the ten, four had previous combat experience, while six were on their first operation. A few days later, cine footage shot during the action was the highlight of a training session.

On April 1, 1944, 144 Wing moved to Westhampnett, Sussex (a satellite of Tangmere). This was to give it experience in the frequent transfers that were expected, once France was invaded. Later, 144 Wing moved to Funtington, Sussex, where 441 rejoined it on April 23. The road convoy with the servicing echelon arrived three days later. The organization of these convoys was a problem troubling 83 Group. Traffic jams, lost drivers and general confusion were common (on the continent most such difficulties would be resolved, in part through practice, but also by breaking convoys into easier-to-manage units).

In the early morning of April 25 W/C Johnson led 441 and 443 on a sweep in support of B-17s and B-24s bound for German and French targets. Southeast of Laon the Spitfires spotted six Fw.190s climbing to intercept. In a few minutes all

Toronto school chums Jake Fleming and Lou Plummer seem to have arrived by coincidence on 441 Squadron. (CF PL29400)

In the air over Europe the Silver Foxes were wary of two dangerous opponents – the Me.109 and the Fw.190. (David Thompson Col.)

six were destroyed - two each by Johnson, 443, and 441. F/O John Wallis "Jake" Fleming and F/L Lloyd "Lou" Plummer of 441 (by coincidence, boyhood chums from Northern Vocational school in Toronto) chased one that was escaping, took turns shooting bits from it, then watched the German pilot bail out at 1000 feet (his Focke-Wulf crashed into a house). On returning to base, however, S/L Hill and P/O Sparling of 441 were missing.

After an intense huddle, with several pilots reporting what they had seen, and W/C Johnson mapping everything out on a blackboard, their fate was surmised. Johnson had seen two Spitfires shoot down an Fw.190 in the main battle. As Fleming and Plummer had bagged their victim some 15 miles away, it was assumed that Hill and Sparling had shot down the sixth e/a, then fallen prey to some unknown hazard. In reality, Hill and his wingman had indeed sprayed an Fw.190, which blew up so violently that both Spitfires were damaged. Sparling's radio was knocked out. Although he managed to get within 10 miles of England, he was never seen again. Debris had lodged in Hill's engine, which promptly packed up. He crash landed, evaded capture for more than a month, but finally was betrayed and arrested by the Gestapo. He would endure almost a year of captivity, partly in solitary confinement. In this way were the Silver Foxes blooded – and bloodied. S/L Hill was succeeded by S/L John Danforth "Danny" Browne, formerly of 403 Squadron. A native of Florham Park, New Jersey, he had enlisted in the RCAF in March 1941. Browne would remain with 441 until his tour expired in July. Aside from the new CO, other veteran pilots were posted to the squadron, providing more than a dash of experience.

Sub-Form 540, Operations Record Book, 441 (RCAF) Squadron

"Sub-form 540, Operational Record Book" is the record of day-to-day operations for any RCAF wartime squadron. Although often a drab document, the "540" is where researchers turn for the general picture of what was going on at any time. To this data they may add details from combat reports, personal diaries, interviews with veterans, etc. In this way does a more informative and lively historical narrative emerge. Here are some excerpts from 441's Sub-Form 540 for April 1944, when it mainly was training for the coming invasion.

April 1, 1944 *The squadron moved to RAF Station Westhampnett, Sussex along with 144 Airfield. Fifteen pilots flew, one stayed behind to bring an aircraft which was then unserviceable, and the remainder proceeded by road convoy. All personnel, upon arrival, were accommodated in tents. Pilots practiced circuits and landings on the new aerodrome.*

April 5. *Two new Spitfire IX aircraft were flown in from 83 Group Support Unit, bringing the number of Spitfire aircraft up to establishment strength of 18.*

April 8. *The squadron, led by C.1075 S/L G.U. Hill, DFC and 2 Bars, went on a sweep to Rennes. J.17857 F/L L.A. Moore was forced to return by jettison tank trouble.*

April 12. *J.20224 F/O E.L. Prizer was posted to 83 Group Support Unit. The squadron flew to Hutton Cranswick, Yorks. to take the air firing and bombing course. Fifteen Spitfires and the Auster III were flown up. Three pilots were left behind to bring aircraft which were unserviceable. Two pilots were in charge of a road convoy bringing the Servicing Flight and the remainder travelled by rail.*

April 15. *Weather prevented use of the ranges, so pilots took part in skeet and revolver shooting. Cine films were shown during the afternoon.*

April 19. *Practice bombing and air/ground firing occupied the whole day. The scores on the latter showed a marked improvement with J.11283 F/O R.G. Lake turning in a score of 120 hits out of 300, or 40%.*

April 21. *Weather permitted only limited use of the gunnery range. No bombing was done. However, the top score for air/ground firing was turned in by J.16591 F/O P.A. McLachlan – 123 hits out of 300, or 41%.*

April 23. *The squadron returned to 144 Airfield, now at Funtington, Sussex, all aircraft being flown in during the morning.*

April 24. *During a sweep, this squadron, using 90-gallon jettisonable tanks, made the deepest penetration into enemy occupied territory yet made by Spitfire IX aircraft.*

April 25. *On an early morning sweep led by the Wing Commander Flying, 441 and 443 squadrons attacked and destroyed six Fw.190s. The score was evenly divided, 2 destroyed by the Wing Commander Flying, 2 by 443 Squadron and 2 by this squadron. J.25138 F/O J.W. Fleming and J.26508 L.A. Plummer shared one destroyed, and C.1075 S/L G.U. Hill, DFC & 2 Bars, and J.29535 F/O R.H. Sparling shared the second. The latter two pilots failed to return to base. C.1075 S/L G.U. Hill, DFC & 2 Bars was seen to land in a large field. While two of his pilots circuited, he left the aircraft and ran towards a large woods nearby. His loss is assumed due to technical failure. J.29535 F/O R.H. Sparling, his No.2, flew back with the squadron. He, by a pre-arranged sign, notified a fellow pilot that his R/T was unserviceable, but continued on the course until about ten miles off Portland Bill, England. There he was seen to turn east on a possible course to Bournemouth, but has not been seen or heard of since. The Acting Commanding Officer, J.17857 F/L L.A. Moore, flew with three other pilots on extensive searches for F/O Sparling, but no trace was found of him or his aircraft. The squadron was on readiness and during the evening was scrambled three times, but all proved uneventful.*

April 26. *J.9068 A/S/L J.D. Browne (Pilot) was posted in from 403 Squadron to take command of the squadron. C.12368 F/O F.A. Ruggles (A.&S.D. Admin.) report in from RCAF Station Middleton St. George, Durham, for adjutant duties. The road convoy finally arrived from Hutton Cranswick, Yorks. with the servicing personnel. Since the 23rd April their work had been done by members of the Aircraft Maintenance Section and a squadron of servicing commandos. Six aircraft went on this squadron's first dive bombing mission, each dropping a 500 lb. bomb on enemy gun emplacements. Fourteen practice bombing sorties were also flown.*

April 27. *The squadron took part in two escort sweeps. Both were uneventful. Three pilots acted as pall bearers to the late Wing Commander J.E. Walker, Commanding Officer, 144 Airfield Headquarters. A wreath was placed on the grave by members of the squadron.*

April 29. *J.9036 S/L J.D. Browne led the squadron for the first time. This was a six aircraft dive bombing show and the mission was abandoned due to clouds.*

Starting on April 26, the Silver Foxes had begun dive bombing in France. Tactics involved peeling off from about 10,000 feet, lining up on target, then releasing bombs at roughly 4500 feet. Transportation targets were priority for, once the invasion commenced and Allied troops got ashore, it would be a race to see which side could put more forces into the battle area. Thus did the Allies pummel roads, bridges, railway lines, yards and junctions, truck convoys ("MT" or motor transport) horse-drawn wagons and airfields. There also were "special targets", including V-1 flying bomb launch sites, and radar sites.

W/C James E. Walker, DFC and 2 Bars, while still a flying officer. Early on he had flown Hurricanes in north Russia, where he made his first kill. Later, he led 243 Squadron in North Africa. He rose to command 144 Wing, then died meaninglessly in an Auster accident. His tally of enemy aircraft is noted as 9 - 4 -12 (plus shared victories). (CF PL7189)

A 441 pilot and his "steed". The Spitfire Mk.IX's main offensive armament was its prominent 20-mm cannons. (Sid Bregman Col.)

Destroying the latter would make detection of Allied ships and aircraft more difficult, and hinder Luftwaffe air control at its most basic level.

All this was part of the grand air plan in preparation for a Normandy invasion. For May alone 13 of 28 Silver Fox operations involved dive bombing. Results could be dismal or excellent, as with seven hits on a V-1 site at midday on May 25, followed by eight hits on a similar target that evening. Fighter pilots on such sorties had one great fear - anti-aircraft fire, or flak. There might be none, or the flak might come up in streams, first as accurate, high-level 88-mm bursts, then (below 10,000 feet) 40-mm cannon fire, finally (below 1000 feet) small calibre fire. Three 441 Spitfires were damaged by flak on May 19.

The hazard of flying through debris thrown up by explosions also concerned pilots, but there was little worry of German fighters. These were seldom seen, since the Luftwaffe was concentrating on defending its homeland, with a plan to deploy quickly to France once the invasion began. Thus, it was a red-letter day should Spitfires meet enemy fighters. However, there was the occasional kill, as when a French Caudron transport, impressed into German service, was spotted on April 28. Spitfires from 441 left it a blazing wreck, F/Ls Tommy Brannagan and Les Moore sharing the credit. (Born in Hamilton, Ontario, Moore had been educated in the US and was a US citizen. He later earned a DFC with 441, and an AFC with 53 OTU. Later he joined 402 Squadron, where he died in March 1945, while strafing a train.)

Another rare brush came on May 5, when 144 Wing was sweeping the Lille-Mons-Douai area. Several 441 pilots were flying with 443, so the ensuing events were a joint affair. Outward bound, W/C Johnson spotted an Fw.190 and shot it down. About 30 minutes later several Fw.190s appeared and S/L H.W. McLeod of 443 attempted a bounce. The Germans broke to port and the fight was on. McLeod bagged an Fw.190, while P/O Frederick A.W.J. Wilson scored hits on another, following it down low, before having to evade an attacker. He did not see his target crash, but McLeod confirmed the kill.

Meanwhile, P/O Thomas C. Gamey and F/O Percy A. McLachlan had gone after another Fw.190, following it to tree-top level, before Gamey delivered a telling burst. His quarry crashed and exploded. McLachlan was seen to attack another Fw.190, but he did not return to base. From New Westminster, British Columbia he was the second 441 pilot killed. Unlike many who simply vanished, we now know exactly what happened to him. As reported in The *JG.26 War Diary*, a JG.26 pilot, Warrant Officer Peter Crump, had come to the aid of a comrade, but too late – McLachlan had done his work. McLachlan then headed home, periodically rocking his wings to check for pursuers. Despite the low altitude, Crump found McLachlan's blind spot and stayed in it, matching every Spitfire manoeuvre from behind. Approaching the coast, the Canadian apparently relaxed his vigil. Crump zoomed up beneath and fired. The Spitfire flicked onto its back and crashed into a line of trees. McLachlan was Crump's 28th victim. His name later was inscribed on the Runnymede Memorial, dedicated to aircrew with no known grave. Subsequent to that, his body must have been recovered, as *They Shall Grow Not Old* states that he is buried in Belgium. The Commonwealth War Graves Commission records only the Runnymede commemoration. As to Gamey, he later served with 443 Squadron, where he died in action in January 1945.

The Allies and the enemy knew that D-Day was coming, but few guessed where the invasion would begin. The same maps and geographic surveys were available to both sides. Areas with narrow beaches and steep cliffs could be ruled out – the lessons of Gallipoli in 1915 and Dieppe in 1942 had been learned. Two places seemed apparent – the Pas de Calais (a shorter route by sea) and Normandy. The Germans put more faith in the former. After all, that was the route they had examined most carefully in 1940, when planning Operation Sea Lion, their unfulfilled invasion of the UK. Allied bombing and reconnaissance had reinforced this evaluation (although wrecking railways in the Pas de Calais was almost equally useful in isolating Normandy). In an effort to be strong everywhere, the Germans had fortified both areas with beach obstacles, mines, and concrete bunkers. RAF defences had effectively blocked every attempt by the Luftwaffe to reconnoitre the Allied staging areas. Meanwhile, the enemy was bombarded with information and disinformation – a "bodyguard of lies", as Winston Churchill put it.

In preparation for D-Day, 144 Wing took part in Ex. Fabius (May 3-4), a rehearsal for the big day. On May 14 the wing moved to Ford, from whence it continued its sweeps, escorts and dive-bombing. Throughout the month there had been a steady reinforcement of pilots so that, by the end of May, 441 had 27 on strength. There was a pep-talk on May 24 from Air Marshal Sir Arthur Coningham, Air Officer Commanding 2 TAF. Then, more ominous things began to happen. Leave was cancelled, movement outside the airfield was restricted, and, on June 4-5, the groundcrew all over England began painting black and white "invasion stripes" on their aircraft.

F/O Percy McLachlan while on 403 Squadron. Note his casual dress and stance. RAF officers might object to such swagger, but RCAF pilots rarely got worked up about appearances. (CF PL19233)

Occasionally, some VIP would drop in on 441. Here, S/L Brannagan watches over his boys as A/C/M Sir Arthur W. Tedder, Marshal of the Royal Air Force, and A/V/M Broadhurst, AOC 83 Group, visit. Then, Tedder chats with F/L Guy Mott as F/L Bill Brown looks on. (CF PL31059, PL31061)

P/O Gil Brochu (below) of 441 visits his brother F/O Leopold Brochu, then on Halifax bombers with 425 Squadron. (CF PL30737)

Early on the evening of June 5, 441 sent a dozen Spitfires to patrol the English Channel between Selsey Bill and St. Catherine's Point. The scene below was awesome. From Southampton and Portsmouth, spilling out of the Solent and Spithead, the sea was filling with ships bound for France. About 2200 hours S/L Browne led another patrol over the armada. This time, FSgt Victor Armand Gilbert "Gil" Brochu suffered engine failure and bailed out at 800 feet over the Channel. His dinghy inflated and he scrambled aboard. As Browne and the others landed, they were summoned for a wing briefing. W/C Johnson told them officially what they already knew – D-Day was tomorrow. Then he gave them their orders for first light. His address was recorded and later broadcast on the BBC. Meanwhile, 42 hours would pass before Brochu finally was picked up off the coast of France and taken to hospital in Southampton.

CHAPTER 3
Invading France

Normandy

At 0625 hours on D-Day 441 was airborne, flying four patrols from then until final touchdown at 2150. There was flak on two missions, and P/O Wilson had to force-land at base after being hit. The scenes below of ships and smoke were exciting, yet they conveyed little of the fierce fighting in progress. German aircraft were absent, and almost as scarce on June 7 (443 Squadron shot down an Me.109 and damaged another). Due to weather, air operations were scrubbed on the 9th, resumed on the 10th, and scarcely were interrupted thereafter. Movement between squadrons was fluid, with pilots traded back and forth between units as required. About midday of the 10th, six 441 aircraft (with an RAF pilot tagging along) took off to sweep around Evreux, S/L Browne leading. That done, they landed on an airstrip that army engineers had bulldozed inside the beachhead. Refuelled and rearmed, they took off to patrol around Argentan before returning to Ford. The rest of 144 Wing also patrolled, dropped in briefly at the strip, then flew home. Thus, the three Canadian squadrons

Part of the D-Day fleet lies off Normandy in June 1944. Then, 441 Spitfire "9G-Y" is readied for a sortie. Fuel, oxygen and ordnance would be replenished, and even the windscreen would be cleaned. (Hugh Ritchie Col., IWM CL1698)

may have been the first Allied aircraft to operate in France since June 1940.

Where was the Luftwaffe through this tumultuous period? Its interventions were few and unsystematic, for it was in chaos. It had few ground attack aircraft (the Russian Front had devoured them). Between January and April 1944 the enemy had waged a futile night bombing campaign directed chiefly at London (and intended as retaliation for attacks on German cities). Thanks to radar-guided night fighters, radar-ranged anti-aircraft guns, and proximity fuses, this "Little Blitz" had left the Luftwaffe with a shell of a bomber force.

Luftwaffe plans for forward deployment, once the invasion began, immediately went off the rails. Allied air attacks had driven enemy aircraft from the fields closest to the invasion beaches so that, on the morning of D-Day, only two German fighters strafed Allied troops. Nevertheless, by pulling aircraft from Italy, and bringing up other reserves, they did add 998 fighters, plus a few other aircraft to their Normandy assets. But these numbers proved meaningless, for the German air control system had been crippled by bombing even before D-Day, and attempts to move up any unit were harried at every turn. German signals systems broke down, and aircraft serviceability, which had been as low as 50% - 60% before the invasion, fell lower. At the outset, the enemy underestimated the odds. A squadron of Fw.190 fighter-bombers, moved from St. Quentin to Laval for use against the beachhead, was instructed to proceed with a mechanic crouching behind the armoured seat of each aircraft. American fighters intercepted them and shot down five. Fighter-bombers themselves could not hope to reach their targets without escort, and Allied air attacks on Laval were relentless. This particular squadron was wiped out in six days.

German confusion appeared in many other ways. New pilots arriving in France sometimes could not find their bases - the camouflage that hid the fields from Allied aircraft also frustrated Luftwaffe crews. Personnel long accustomed to lavish permanent bases now were thrust into field conditions for which the Allies had been training for months. With almost no air reconnaissance, and unsure as to what was being deployed against them, German intelligence had serious gaps, e.g. some "ships" attacked and damaged by the Luftwaffe were actually derelicts sunk offshore to create artificial harbours. Squadrons such as the Silver Foxes now looked for other kinds of action, targets of opportunity being commonly sought. This was dangerous work. On June 12 P/O John E. West had to bail out over the Channel. But his 'chute snagged in the tailwheel and he was carried to his death - 441's third combat loss. The 14th concluded with a late evening escort of bombers raiding Le Havre. When 443 spotted some German aircraft, it chased them, but 441 stuck with its charges.

The next day 11 Dakotas carried ground personnel from Ford to B.3 Ste. Croix-sur-Mer on the Normandy coast, joining a party that had gone there by sea on the 13th. The Spitfires followed, and that evening flew their first patrol from what was intended to be a fixed base in France. Things did not go smoothly. The field had no lights and, as the Spitfires returned from their mission, they had problems finding it. Three pilots landed at another field (one overshot the runway without

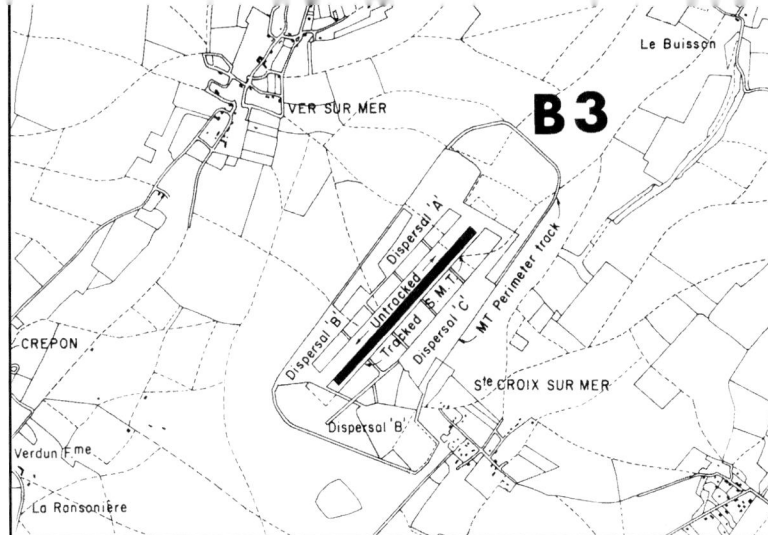

The layout of B.3 Ste-Croix-sur-Mer, 441's first ALG. Built by the 24th Airfield Construction Group, B.3 was ready for operations on June 9, 1944. The sole runway was 4200 x 540 feet of which 3900 x 120 were "tracked", i.e. covered in perforated steel plate (shown in black). Taxi, dispersal and marshalling areas were turf. (via David Clark)

injuries). Nine others returned to Ford, rather than chance a night landing.

Once settled in at B.3, 441 lived in an unmistakable world of war. Artillery rumbled by day, enemy bombers and Allied flak barrages filled the night. Everyone dug slit trenches. Landing strips were heavy with dust churned up by aircraft. Water truck crews vainly tried to suppress the dust, which got into everything. On June 30 a Spitfire had to make a one-wheel landing because dust had fouled the undercarriage.

Finding German aircraft was like winning a lottery, but 441 cashed in on June 22, when scrambled after enemy fighters reported near Domfront. From 10,000 feet two Fw.190s were spotted. F/O William Wood Lindsay ("Bill") Brown, F/O Bill Chowen and FSgt Ross MacMillan took turns firing at one, which crashed and exploded. The other was shot down by F/O Jake Fleming, whose combat report notes: "I was flying on the port side of Black Leader as Black Five. I sighted two aircraft on the deck and immediately went down on them. I took the leading aircraft and opened fire at approximately 400 yards. He broke immediately and pulled straight up in the air. I held my fire and, when within 50 yards of him, I saw strikes and then he blew up. I flew through the debris and upon returning to base

Spitfires often were called in with Typhoons or medium bombers to hammer bridges, rail junctions, etc., but German armour and MET also were good prey. (NAC PA137361, CF PL42344)

found that a piece had been knocked off the tip of my propeller. Also, only one cannon fired. I claim one Fw.190 destroyed." One of these victories, whether Fleming's or his comrades', was notable, the victim apparently being Major Josef Wurmheller of JG.2, a veteran of battles dating to September 1939. With 100 Allied aircraft to his credit, he wore the Knight's Cross.

With few German aircraft about, 144 Wing reverted to bombing and strafing. An "armed reconnaissance", as such a sortie was called, was basically spent looking for trouble. The term "MET" (Motorized Enemy Transport) figured largely in 144 Wing records, and successes were classified as "flamers" (seen to be on fire), "smokers" (left smoking) and "damaged". This system was roughly parallel to grading aerial victories ("destroyed", "probably destroyed" and "damaged"). F/L Mott was particularly busy at this dangerous, low-level work. After all, enemy fire, whether from flak gunners or infantrymen with automatic weapons, could bring a hot reception. It is difficult to assess the impact of any particular attack although Operational Research officers subsequently concluded that claims of enemy vehicles destroyed often were exaggerated. More equipment was simply abandoned by the enemy than destroyed. On the other hand, the policy of drenching the theatre with Allied air power was effective. At the very least, it forced the enemy to make his significant deployments by night.

June 30, 1944 was another jackpot day, 441 dispatching two sections of six aircraft each. The first was led by S/L Browne at 1214 hours), the second by W/C Johnson (airborne at 1230). Browne was the first to engage enemy aircraft. His combat report provides a first-hand account:

Having joined the RCAF in September 1940, Alan Johnstone was one of the many "Yanks" in the RCAF who, once the US had entered the war, remained in the RCAF, rather than transfer to the US forces. (CF PL31037)

I was flying as White One leading five aircraft on an armed recce south of Caen. We had gone above cloud (6500) to cross the bomb line and turned south-east. Passing over a gap in the cloud, I saw a Fw.190 sliding underneath at 4000 feet in the Gace area, and half rolled the section behind him. There were ten '190s in a loose formation heading towards Caen. Upon sighting us they broke into cloud, so I climbed to 9000 feet, where I perched over the hole waiting for one to come out ... I selected one in the cloud gap and from line astern set him on fire with a two-second burst of cannon and M/G. The rest of the section were engaged at this time. I claim one Fw.190 destroyed. Cine film used.

"The rest of the section were engaged" ... yes, indeed! Jake Fleming was shot down by an JG.26 Fw.190, and taken prisoner. Bill Chowen came back with bullet holes in his hood. Meanwhile, controllers were directing W/C Johnson and the rest of 441 to the scene. By now a dozen Me.109s were in the fray. Johnson noted how they also were using cloud cover, but he managed to shoot down one. His 33rd kill, this made him the RAF's top fighter pilot. F/O Mott dived on a '109, sending it down in flames. F/L Alan Johnstone, separated from his companions in cloud, emerged into the clear just as a Messerschmitt sought cover. He snapped off a one-second burst, sending the enemy down. Imprudently, Johnstone descended to photograph his victim and was attacked. He escaped into cloud, chased and damaged another '109, then flew home a wiser man.

A Pilot's Log Book

Typical of 441 pilots in this period was F/O Bruce MacKenzie. Excerpts from his log book (from D-Day June 6, 1944 to month's end - 26 sorties flown) describe an exciting time, one that any young man would have been thrilled to experience - and survive.

Date	Sortie/Time	Notes
June 6	**Patrol over beach head** 2:00 hours	Patrolled beaches. Saw second British Army land. Light A/A fired at us from ships off shore. Terrific barrage by naval guns.
June 6	**Patrol over beach head** 2:10	Saw big tank battle north Caen. Lots burning. Saw glider troops land. One went in river. F/S Brochu missing (picked up).
June 7	**Patrol over beach head** 2:15	Over Sword, Juno & Gold. A few Huns about. 1 Me.109 dest., 443 1 prob. dam.
June 8	**Patrol over beach head** 2:10	Over Sword, Juno & Gold. Nothing much around. F/O Dowdy crash landed on beach, caused by flak.
June 12	**Patrol over beach head** 2:15	Penetrated deep into Laval. Didn't catch anything. Flak from Caen. Alex Graham flipped over on takeoff.
June 12	**Patrol over beach head** 2:05	Penetrated deep into east, south behind Le Havre. Johnny West tried to bail out. Chute caught on aircraft.
June 15	**Ford to B.3 in France** 1:00.	Uneventful. Was 40 min. over drome waiting to get in. Very dusty, 4 crack-ups.
June 16	**Inland patrol.** 1:00	Me.109s over Caen. 1 dest 443, 1 dest. W/C JEJ., 4 Spits missing 443. Lost #2, returned to base early.
June 25	**Dive bombing** 0:40	Bomb troop and gun emplacements at "Cheux" SW Caen. Heavy flak.
June 25	**Dive bombing** 0:30	Bomb tanks and artillery observation SE Caen. No flak, fair results.
June 27	**Recce for Huns** 1:00	Sighted 7, chased them far inland towards Rouen. Didn't catch any.
June 29	**Armoured recce** 1:20	After transport, 5 trucks dest., 4 dam.
June 29	**Armoured recce** 1:10	A few Huns reported, none seen. Penetrated deep south west. Shot up motorcycle & truck.
June 30	**Patrol over beach head** 1:30	Nothing sighted. Lots of Marauders & Bostons going in. 10 a/c dest, 4 to 441. Jake Fleming missing.

Brannagan Takes Over

On July 1, 1944 S/L Browne left the squadron, his tour finished. "B" Flight Commander T.A. "Tommy" Brannagan was promoted to squadron leader to take over 441. Bill Brown now led "B" Flight. By the standards of recent events, that day was fairly routine - one dive-bombing attack on a bridge, one Spit holed by flak (shrapnel lodged in a pocket flashlight of the pilot's Mae West), and the rest of the day washed out by weather. June 1944 had proved momentous - the busiest in 441's brief history - 866 operational hours, 76 non-operational. July was the second most intense - 852 operational hours, 65 non-operational. However, in air-to-air combat it would be 441's most successful month with 31 confirmed kills. All this was amassed in just six days of savage fighting, and all for the loss of two RCAF pilots.

The first of these scraps began on July 2 with a series of noon-hour patrols. Three sections, each of four Spitfires, were airborne. Blue Section, led by F/L Moore, was the first to score. They spotted several e/a on the deck near Lisieux, heading west towards Caen. Moore quickly downed two Me.109s. F/L Ron Lake almost collided with an Fw.190 before shooting it down, fired at a '109 and missed, fired again, watched it crash, then expended his remaining ammunition on another '109, which Moore finished off. Five kills (and an immediate DFC for Moore). But there was a price - F/O Alex McDonald was missing - but not lost. He had chased an Fw.190, scored strikes, and seen the pilot bail out. Then flak nailed McDonald at the moment of his triumph. His engine quit and he was too low to bail out. He crash landed, but his Spitfire turned over, trapping him in his harness. In a subsequent evasion report, McDonald described what followed:

Bruce MacKenzie as a sprog LAC training on Tiger Moths, then overseas on Spitfires. (MacKenzie Col.)

Tom Brannagan while with 403 Squadron in March 1944. In 2004, Windsor, Ontario re-named its airport terminal building in hometown boy Brannagan's honour. (CF PL28560)

A young Frenchman came running across the field and pulled me out. We ran along the hedgerow into a very thick wood about half a mile away. Another Frenchman came along behind and, while the first one was away fetching me some clothes, he kept watch. The first one then returned with civilian clothes, a French-English dictionary and a small map of the local vicinity.

I hid my equipment in the bush and went with the Frenchman, who kept watch for me, and lunched at his farm. After the meal I went to another farm close by where, in the evening, a girl who could speak some English, came along with the Frenchman who had pulled me out of my plane. From here, my journey was arranged.

Many such reports ended this way, vaguely hinting at adventures to come. Happily, McDonald filed another report which picked up the story:

The Frenchman who had pulled me out of my aircraft was named Roland Piel. The other, who gave me lunch, was called René... The girl who came along to the farm, and who spoke English, was Gaby Delauney. I stayed at this farm for one week, during which time she brought me an identity card. The farm was owned by Lucien Dupais ... Every day the girl brought me the latest war news.

Nothing particular happened until the following Sunday night, when I was taken by Lucien Dupais to Roland Piel's farm who, I learned, had destroyed my aircraft during the week. The Germans only discovered the plane three days afterwards and, when they asked him if he knew anything about the pilot, he told them that [he] had run away into the woods.

After being at Piel's farm for two days, I asked Gaby Delauney what the chances were of getting through the lines. She explained that she had been to see the Resistance people at Blangy [Blangy-le-Chateau], but that I could not get through until the end of the month.

I stayed on at the farm until 2 August, during which time the Germans called on three occasions, looking for butter. The Piels treated me very well, giving me plenty of food and a change of clothes every week.

On 3 August I left together with André Piel (the farmer's brother) and Gaby Delauney for Blangy, where I met the local Chef de Résistance, whose name was Brébert and number was 2052. He had been over to the Piels' farm the day before to make arrangements for my journey. The same day I left Blangy by bicycle with Brébert's son for Le Mesnil Eudes.

On the way there we were stopped by a German officer and about ten soldiers and had our passes checked, but managed to fool the Germans by Brébert explaining that I was dumb and we reached our destination safely. At Le Mesnil Eudes we met another Resistance man who took me by bicycle to St. Jacques. I don't know his name, but he was referred to as and looked like Tarzan. He took me to a farm owned by Dufray.

The next morning, together with Dufray, I left for a farm just northwest of St. Paul de Courtonne. This was the local Resistance Headquarters and I stayed there for four days, meeting Flight Lieutenant Logan, RCAF, Flight Sergeant Gilleade, RAF, Flight Officer Izzard, USAAF, Staff Sergeant McGeary, USAAF, and a Dutch refugee.

On 8 August we all left with the local Chef de Résistance, Francine ... for a farm at Preaux. While we were here we saw any amount of military transport with Red Cross markings, used for carrying all types of equipment.

On 10 August we were joined by various Resistance people and a Major MacLeod, USAAF, and from here until the morning of 17 August, my story is identical to his [MacLeod's report is not available]. On the morning of 17 August I left Cheffreville with Sergeant McGeary at about 0930 hours to get through the lines. McGeary was stopped by German guards at St. Martin du Mesnil Oury. I did not see him again.

I eventually contacted British troops (51 Division) at Vieux Pont, in which vicinity I saw two Spitfires hit by flak at 1900 hours. One plane spun into the ground and blew up. The pilot of the other baled out and was captured. I think they were both from 403 Squadron. [On this day F/O H.V. Boyle of 403 Squadron was killed in action.]

The next big scrap came in the evening of July 5. W/C Johnson was leading. Armed recce was the mission, but a low ceiling precluded ground attacks. Controllers gave permission to sweep the Alençon area. There, a break in the clouds revealed 12 or more Fw.190s. The Spitfires were at 8000 feet, the enemy at about 5000. Within minutes Johnson had shot down his 34th and 35th enemy aircraft, while other pilots claimed the following:

F/O William Chowen	2 Fw.190s destroyed (1 shared with Mott*)
F/L G.E. Mott	2 Fw.190s destroyed (1 shared with Chowen)
S/L T.A. Brannagan	1 Fw.190 destroyed; 1 Fw.190 damaged
P/O Wallace D. Hill	1 Fw.190 damaged
F/O Donald H. Kimball	1 Fw.190 destroyed
F/O Bruce M. MacKenzie	1 Fw.190 damaged
F/O John W. Neil	1 Fw.190 destroyed

* The enemy unit was probably JG.11, which took a beating that day (see Jean-Bernard Frappé, *La Luftwaffe face au débarquement allié*). Brannagan's "damaged" seems to be unconfirmed by 2 TAF. The 441 ORB mentions a "damaged" by FSgt E.G. McClinton, but this is not substantiated.

The Mott/Chowen victory shows the degree to which reports were assessed. Bill Chowen had been seen to collide with an enemy aircraft and was dead, so that German fighter was credited to him. Mott originally claimed one kill, plus a damaged. His combat report notes:

I took my section down by half rolling and coming up on one FW with great excess speed. I closed in giving a short burst and had to pull up in case of collision. I saw strikes and flashes on Fw.190's fuselage from my burst and, as I was on top of a zoom, I saw a Spit give him a quick burst. The Fw.190 blew up in the air. This aircraft was not claimed by any pilot in our Wing and this could have been F/O Chowen who did not return, as I saw the parachute from the other aircraft he destroyed before me shortly after.

Immediately after my first combat I closed in on another Fw.190 and followed him into a small cloud firing. He had entered cloud before I fired and, as we came out the other side, I saw him spiralling down and crash in a field. I also saw another enemy aircraft crash about the same place and about the same time.

The Intelligence Officer collected reports from at least three pilots. In the end he concluded that Mott had hit an Fw.190 (which he claimed as damaged), but that Chowen had finished it off (turning the "damaged" claim into a shared "destroyed"). Mott then added an Fw.190 on his own. Chowen attacked another, scored hits, then collided with it, the Spitfire's wing slicing into the Fw.190's tail. The German bailed out, Chowen did not. For the next several days 441 had no claims, other than for MET.

New pilots joined 441, including Gil Brochu, safe following his dip in the Channel. The squadron rested on July 7, while rain gave everybody a break on the 10th and 11th. Even the 12th was low-key with only 22 sorties. Then came July 13, and another bonanza. Brannagan had led the Silver Foxes off at 2010 on an armed recce around L'Aigle. At 2035, flying at 8000 feet, he spotted a dozen Fw.190s on the deck, apparently headed for the battle area and carrying what were reported as long range tanks (more likely they were bombs). The squadron dived and the result was a massacre. Only one Spitfire was hit (in the confusion a Spitfire damaged MacKenzie's aircraft), while 441 registered 10 kills:

F/O William J. Myers	3 FW.190s destroyed
S/L Tommy Brannagan	2 FW.190s destroyed
F/L Jack C. Copeland	1 FW.190 destroyed
F/O Don H. Kimball	1 FW.190 destroyed
F/O Bruce M. MacKenzie	1 FW.190 destroyed
F/L Guy Mott	1 FW.190 destroyed
F/O Lloyd Plummer	1 FW.190 destroyed

Bill Myers' report details his "hat trick":

Squadron Leader Brannagan spotted 12 Fw.190s on the tree tops from about 8000 feet. I flew abreast of him, pulling up about 180-75 yards behind the 190s. I fired a two-second burst at one of the enemy aircraft, which blew up and disintegrated in the air. The rest did a hard break port which I did also. I got onto the tail of

F/O Lou Plummer, S/L Brannagan and F/O Bill Myers in a typical Normandy setting. (CF PL30730)

another 190 and opened fire at 200-250 yards range, 15 degrees deflection. After a short burst he went on fire and slithered into the ground bursting into flames. This was also confirmed by Squadron Leader Brannagan. At this time I saw three Fw.190s on my tail firing. One burst hit my port wing. Pulling hard, I found myself 75-degrees - 90 degrees from the Fw.190, giving him a ring and quarter. I gave him a burst and then I pulled up two rings at 300 yards. Dropping my nose I noticed he was hot and began to slowly turn towards the ground. Before he hit, he was in a flat spin and I gave him another two second burst blowing him up. I saw numerous fires burning on the ground and two parachutes. I claim three Fw.190s destroyed. Cine gun used.

A newspaper report dated July 15 in London, England (source unknown), described the action of the 13th. This was the type of item that filled newspapers at this stage of the war. Details were sufficient enough to suggest that there was little worry as to censorship:

Meanwhile, more details were made available of the shooting down of 10 Focke-Wulfs on Thursday by the RCAF Spitfire squadron led by Sqn. Ldr. Tommy Brannagan of Windsor, Ont. It was the squadron's second spectacular victory in little more than a week, giving them a score of 15 confirmed kills in two sorties, a record unequalled by any fighter squadron in Normandy.

Three of the German aircraft destroyed Thursday fell before the guns of F/O Bill Myers of Windsor, Ont., a veteran of between 80 and 90 operational flights, whose only previous score was a half-share in the destruction of an enemy dive bomber. Brannagan himself got two and Flt. Lieuts. G.E. Mott of Sarnia, and J.C. Copeland of Toronto, and F/Os Lloyd (Lou) Plummer of Toronto, B.M. MacKenzie of Stettler, Alta. and D.H. Kimball of Onatucket, N.B., each got one.

Three of Thursday evening's victors also shared in the previous five-plane triumph, when Brannagan shot down two, and Kimball and Mott each got one. Brannagan has been in command of the squadron for only a fortnight. The youthful airman, who started his second tour without any rest period, said that Germans "didn't have a chance because, apparently, they didn't see us until we were right down on them." He said the FWs were carrying bombs.

The story of Thursday's encounter was told by Myers and Plummer as they sat in a Normandy apple orchard. The squadron was on armed reconnaissance over the enemy lines, "looking for trouble". Just south of Argentan they sighted 12 German planes in formation about 10,000 feet below them.

The German formation might have gone unmolested if the sun's reflected light had not bounced off their tops, said Myers. Brannagan spotted the reflection and led the squadron in a plunge at about 400 miles an hour, which brought the Spitfires down about three miles behind the unsuspecting enemy.

"We flew behind them at tree-top level, and the CO told us to hold our fire until we were able to close in on them," Myers continued. "Three of them were shot down before they even knew they were bounced."

"And the rest it," interjected Plummer, "was just a slaughter." Some of the FWs blew up in the air; others hit the ground and then blew up, and Plummer said, "It was a great sight to see fires breaking out all over the place on the ground."

In another press report, datelined "Courtenay Edwards, A Normandy Airfield", Brannagan gave even more details of the fight:

Before attacking I wanted to make absolutely sure they weren't American Thunderbolts, which the FWs resemble. We dived beneath them and held our fire until we were only 50 yards away. When I saw the black crosses, I gave the order to shoot.

It was all over inside three minutes. Seven went down in 60 seconds. Not until I and my No.1 had each knocked down a Hun simultaneously in a two-seconds burst did Jerry know we were after him. Even then the formation did not break up immediately. They didn't know what to do. I am not surprised, in the circumstances, that they didn't show more fight. They just didn't have the chance.

Only three pilots baled out of the ten aircraft we saw crash. After the first seven went down, we split up a bit and had to chase some of the Huns. Only two got away. They were all carrying drop tanks, which some hastily jettisoned, when they saw what was happening.

They were heading towards the Brest Peninsula. Only one of the FWs returned our fire. One of my pilots, Flt. Lieut. Ray Sim, a Canadian, was on his first operation. He would have got a Hun had he been better placed.

The big victory of July 13 was the last hurrah for 144 Wing, which was disbanded the next day, as 2 TAF wings were expanded to four squadrons each. Under this arrangement 442 Squadron joined 126 Wing, 443 joined 127 Wing, and 441 moved to B.11 Longues to join 125 Wing (RAF) that included 132, 453 and 602 squadrons with Australians, Poles, Norwegians and Free French. This entailed no changes in operations, although the new airfield (near Bayeux) seemed more vulnerable to Channel fogs than had St. Croix. Of this period, in his memoir Bruce MacKenzie was unhappy about 441 joining a RAF wing:

I do believe that, if we had had a senior Squadron Leader still with us (such as S/L George Hill) we would never have been sent to join this 125 RAF Wing. It was really a letdown. The morale of the squadron was not nearly so good thereafter, and the only thing that really kept spirits up was the fact that we had Brannagan looking after us. There wasn't the same spirit as in the days when we flew with 442 and 443 with all that intense competition. 441 had ended up with the highest score of the three squadrons and we had wanted to keep it that way.

Six pilots were airborne for a late afternoon patrol on July 17, F/L Bill Brown leading. Ground control reported e/a at 25,000 feet. The Spitfires followed instructions for an intercept. They were at 22,000 when they sighted six Fw.190s about 1000 feet higher over Brann. Brown put the sun behind him and gave chase for several minutes, ending close to Verneuil. The Germans were inattentive, for Brown was able to close within 50 yards before firing. His target caught fire and exploded. The enemy, now alerted, accepted the challenge. Two of them chased Brown, but he escaped into cloud, re-emerged and found an Fw.190 positioned like a sitting duck. He latched onto its tail but, before he could fire, the '190 banked, its hood dropped away, and the pilot bailed out.

From the summer of 1944 the Luftwaffe still had many skilled veterans, but more than its share of tyros rushed through the flying schools. These reached combat units with perhaps 160 hours of flying time – less than half that of their Allied opponents. Jean-Bernard Frappé, listing enemy losses day by day, offers proof of this. German casualties fell heavily upon the junior ranks. Of 20 German fighter pilots reported shot down in the Normandy area on July 17, only four held commissions. The poor watch kept by Fw.190 pilots on this occasion was symptomatic of the Luftwaffe's decline, as was the willingness of the occasional pilot to abandon his aircraft prematurely.

F/O Don Kimball witnessed Brown's first victory, then bore in on the fellow's wingman, who tried to escape by diving. Kimball stuck with it to 4000 feet, firing short bursts at extreme range. Bursts at 800 and 700 yards produced no results, but another at 500 yards delivered strikes around the wing roots and fuselage. Both machines continued through cloud to 3500 feet, when Kimball fired a final burst from 500 yards. The '190 streamed black smoke and kept right on going into the ground. Of all this action, F/O Bruce MacKenzie commented, "Not enough to go around."

Next day F/O Mott led the squadron on a morning patrol. From 26,000 feet he spotted two Me.109s at 10,000 feet. The Spits dove steeply, so much so that pilots found their windscreens frosting over, making it hard to aim. The Germans scattered, but Mott followed one, snapping off short bursts that finally did the trick. The enemy pilot jettisoned his hood, climbed to about 700 feet, and hit the silk. Meanwhile, F/Ls Jack Copeland and A. Johnstone, also having frosting problems, harried a '109 from 4000 feet down to 100, before it crashed.

One could almost view this as a game, but not quite. When 441 scored again, even the combat reports gave more than a hint of horror. During an early morning, low-level armed recce of July 27, ground control advised Mott that there was "trade" nearby. He spotted two Fw.190s, shot down one, while Don Kimball bagged the other. The grim realities were expressed in their reports. "The pilot tried to get out of the cockpit, but was evidently hit and crashed with the plane", wrote Mott. Kimball's statement was equally morbid: "The pilot baled out at 100 feet, but he seemed to hit the ground before his parachute opened."

With strength still 25 to 27 pilots there were now opportunities for 441 to take leave in Britain. Events out of the ordinary included escorting Bomber Command "heavies" during a daylight raid on German positions (July 30). The intervals between air battles were marked by the routine of uneventful defensive patrols, inconclusive dive bombing, and strafing in the face of flak that worsened by the day. The tally of flamers and smokers mounted, but few were as spectacular as an ammunition truck that S/L Brannagan torched on August 3. German gunners, in their turn, hit two 441 Spitfires on August 4 and 5. Each time the pilots got down, one reaching base, the other crash-landing at a neighbouring strip.

On August 6 the redoubtable Guy Mott went missing. He had been leading an armed recce, when his engine quit (whether for flak or mechanical reasons he could not say). Unable to glide to American lines, he bailed out at 2000 feet. Having concealed his parachute, harness, helmet and Mae West, he began walking northwards towards Vire. That night he hid in a hedge, while German soldiers and vehicles passed nearby. Approaching some farm houses, Mott discovered they still were held by the enemy, so headed in another direction, only to find himself passing between two light guns, heavily camouflaged and guarded by two soldiers, talking loudly. Mott strode by, ignoring them. They, in turn, made no attempt to stop him. Dressed in blue, with his tunic over his arm, he may have confused them as to his identity. Now he found a farm house with civilians, who responded when he gave a "V" sign. Six families, forced from their homes in Vire by the ground battle, were sheltering here. They shared what food they had with the fugitive. Mott hid in a barn, while scavenging German troops dropped by. About noon of the 8th three vehicles pulled into the farm yard. Drawing Allied artillery fire, two left immediately. The third caught fire and set the house ablaze as well. The civilians joined Mott in the barn that night but, on the 9th, he was able to greet advancing American troops. Soon he was back at Longues and given leave in Britain.

Meanwhile, the Silver Foxes were adding to their MET record, with variety added by an air/sea rescue patrol and attacks on barges in the Seine (August 9). The Germans now were retreating from Normandy, providing many targets as they left. Following two months of seeming stalemate, things were changing fast. On August 12, 125 Wing began moving forward, shifting from B.11 Longues to B.19 Lingèvres, a longer strip (5000 feet), which allowed wider dispersal of aircraft and vehicles. By August 13 the Spitfires were at their new base, and strafing continued.

While Bill Brown's aircraft was mauled by flak on August 9, the 13th was deadly. Attacking a road convoy, Brown took hits and tried to make base. Suddenly, his Spitfire went out of control and disappeared into heavy ground haze east of Vire. Brown was buried in the Ranville Cemetery, Calvados. On January 1, 1946 the London Gazette announced him as Mentioned in Dispatches. Tommy Brannagan was luckier than Brown. Hit by flak on August 15, he crash-landed behind German lines and was captured.

Pilots undoubtedly found low-level attacks exciting, but some targets were petty. The Spitfires were chasing individual motorcycle riders as well as trucks. On the other hand, some days were rewarding beyond imagination. From August 18 the Germans desperately were trying to extricate themselves from Falaise, and Allied air power was marshalled to make sure that they did not. Pilots of many squadrons savaged men, horses,

The starboard wing of Bruce MacKenzie's "9G-M" after being clobbered on August 20, 1944. A pilot was fortunate to survive such severe damage. (MacKenzie Col.)

guns and vehicles on the roads. Between 1500 and 2030 hours 441 was constantly in the fight, with Spitfires landing, refuelling and rearming in record time, then setting off again. In those 5 ½ hours they logged 40 sorties, dropped nearly seven tons of 250- and 500-lb bombs, fired 4126 20-mm rounds and 19,529 .303 rounds. They claimed 15 flamers, 16 smokers and 26 damaged. There was no doubt of one target – two trucks that blew up as only ammunition carriers could. Weather and diminishing targets gave the pilots some respite, but danger lurked even on quiet days. Hit by flak, F/O Bruce MacKenzie belly-landed at base on August 20. The squadron Operational Record Book reported this in a matter-of-fact manner, but MacKenzie (in his memoir) described it more vividly:

> We had been given strict instructions not to attack any motor transport draped with a red cross and also to make sure, doubly sure, that the motor transport we were attacking were not of the Allied forces... It was my duty ... to identify what was below us, then report to the remainder of the flight to attack or not to attack. We were down at about 400 feet, George Heasman was my number two. It was quickly apparent that we were dealing with German motor transport, augmented by the fact that they were shooting 40-mm cannons at us ... There was a loud bang on my starboard wing and, looking out, I could see a huge hole just inside the wing tip, about the middle of the wing. This almost flipped the plane over and it took full aileron just to keep the aircraft in flying position.
>
> I'd lost a lot more height ... and was just barely above the tree tops and holding the joy stick as hard over to the left as I could... I could hear the others calling for instructions, but my transmitter was not functioning. I heard George Heasman telling them, "Yes, get down, those are definitely German transports, you should be attacking them. MacKenzie's got a hole blown in his wing, so we'll have to head back." Head back we did, and my thought was, this aircraft is not very stable ... I'd better get up high enough, so that I can bail out, but I'd better get back over my own lines first ... After we got suitable height, about 8000 feet, I made many attempts to escape the aircraft. Each time that I would let go of the joy stick, the aircraft would do a roll and the centrifugal action of this would just make it impossible for me to get out safely.
>
> The next thing was to check the stalling speed. I didn't know whether the aileron was damaged, I didn't know if the flaps would function properly, I didn't know if the starboard gas tank had been punctured. On checking the stalling speed, I found it was about 160 miles per hour. We then returned to our base and I called in that I was going to have to attempt a wheels up landing ... I came around and did a very wide, swinging approach, didn't dare put the flaps down. I didn't want to have any wheels down because I would have to be going too slow for the required landing speed with such a high stalling speed... I came screaming in and the fellows on the ground afterwards told me that they were saying to themselves, "Put your flaps down, put your flaps down". Of course, I knew that I shouldn't attempt that or I would be in real difficulty. I came in, cleared the fence and kept the aircraft flying just above stalling speed... I kept it as level as possible. It hit the ground and very shortly skidded to a stop.

By August 22 the focus of action had shifted to the Seine River, where the enemy was crossing under constant air attack. There still were chances to register flamers and smokers, but enemy aircraft were just rumours, so far as 441 was concerned. Flak and small arms fire remained the greatest hazard. P/O Heasman took a burst in the engine and rifle fire punctured his wings on August 23. On the evening of August 28 the squadron was relieved of operational duties. The Battle of Normandy was over, the war was entering a new phase.

Normandy to Nijmegen

From August 26 S/L R.H. Walker was in charge of 441 Squadron. By now the war was moving towards Germany, so squadrons were perpetually on the move, catching up to the fighting. With operations temporarily suspended, 125 Wing's road convoys headed for Thomer, eight miles south of Evreux, but that was still too far from the fast-receding front. The next base was B.40 Beauvais, 130 miles on, 441 arriving there on September 2, a day after the Luftwaffe had vacated the place. Supporting road convoys came up that evening. Operations resumed on September 3, with patrols flown as far as Brussels, but the only opposition was flak. Even B.40 was not near enough to the battlefield so, on September 4-5, 125 Wing leap-frogged another 75 miles to B.52 Douai. Flak claimed F/L Raymond G. Sim's aircraft on the 14th, although he evaded capture. Still, the Spitfires were operating at extreme range from the front, so a move was made to B.70 Antwerp, 90 miles distant. These moves gave some personnel an opportunity to

S/L R.H. "Kelly" Walker, the longest-serving 441 CO, was in charge from August 1944 to August 1945, when 441 disbanded. (CF PL15852)

visit battlefields of the First World War (they were pleased to find the Vimy Ridge Memorial intact). Some squadron members, on leave from one base, had problems finding their units a week later.

The Silver Foxes moved into B.70 on September 17, 1944, Day 1 of Operation Market Garden. This was otherwise known as the Battle of Arnhem, Field Marshal Montgomery's attempt to seize bridges over the Lower Rhine and open a way into the heart of Germany. Of three bridges to be taken, Nijmegen and Grave were captured. A third, at Arnhem, could not be held. Fighting raged until the night of September 25/26, when remnants of the Allies' beleaguered airborne forces were evacuated.

The Luftwaffe did not play a major role at Arnhem. It was enemy ground defences that did the job of harassing the Allied aircraft dropping supplies and attacking German troops. Rather, the Luftwaffe appeared in greater numbers further south, attacking bridges in Allied hands. For 125 Wing this presented magnificent opportunities. The results were spectacular. As 441 patrolled the area on the first day, it spotted many fires, but no German aircraft. It was very different on September 18, when two patrols (1145-1300 hours and 1450-1555 hours) produced the following results:

S/L R.H. Walker	1 Bf.109 destroyed (shared with F/L Johnstone)
F/L A. Johnstone	1 Bf.109 destroyed (shared with S/L Walker)
F/O George E. Heasman	1 Bf.109 destroyed
F/L R.G. Lake	1 Bf.109 destroyed

F/O George Heasman and friend astride a 441 "Spit". (CF)

Walker's combat report illustrates many elements of the air war, and shows what the enemy was up against. Even in a forward battle area, with units just arrived, the Spitfires enjoyed the benefits of radar direction and controllers. The Germans often seemed to be hunting without direction. They could be aggressive when alerted, but their air discipline betrayed inexperience. Walker describes his first patrol:

I was leading 441 Squadron on a patrol over the Nijmegen area, flying north, when we heard Kenway report Huns flying west of Eindhoven at 20,000 feet. The squadron orbitted to port and, after a few minutes flying, we saw 20 plus Me.109s flying north at 14,000 feet. They turned and flew down the Rhine. We climbed to approximately 15,000 feet and, observing a straggler on the starboard side of the formation. I attacked this aircraft from dead line astern. It took no evasive action whatsoever when, at a range of 400 yards, I gave a 5-second burst, bringing myself to 50 yards range. I observed a strike on the starboard side of the engine, and a piece of metal flew off the aircraft from in front of the cockpit. White smoke immediately came from the damaged part of the fuselage and the aircraft went down at a 45 degree angle towards the earth. I broke off the attack at this point, as aircraft came in at us at six o'clock and I saw no more of the plane. But F/O MacKenzie, who saw the E/A which F/O Heasman claims as destroyed, also saw a few minutes previously an aircraft burning on the ground and, as we were the only aircraft in the vicinity at the time, this must have been the Me.109 which F/O Johnstone and I claim as destroyed (shared).

While Walker had not witnessed the end of his '109, his wingman, F/O Johnstone, had fired on it after the CO broke away. This may have been unwise - Walker turned to avoid enemy aircraft and presumably Johnstone was exposing himself as a target. But he got away with it, scoring hits that changed the white smoke to black while the e/a's undercarriage came half-way down. At 6000 feet he broke away to follow Walker. Johnstone was also unable to see the final results of his fire. Confirmation came from F/O MacKenzie. Meanwhile, F/O Heasman had become separated. On his own he spotted several '109s in line-abreast formation, dived on one, and scored strikes. He saw the hood fly off, but had to avoid other aircraft, so did not observe its fate. Cine gun film confirmed he had hit the '109. F/O Kimball witnessed the pilot bailing out.

The second patrol that day produced one kill, but showed how far the Luftwaffe had fallen. F/L Lake chased four '109s in a shallow dive from 14,000 feet down. He could get no closer than 1000 yards and finally snapped off a burst. One German pilot began weaving. As he did, Lake closed to 300 yards. By now they were down to about 1000 feet. The '109 started into a turn as Lake followed. They had swung through three-quarters of a circle, when Lake fired a 3-second burst, getting strikes on the wings and cockpit. "The aircraft half rolled and went straight in," wrote Lake, adding, "F/O [Harry] Plewes, who was flying Black 4 and was with me all the time, also saw the strikes and the aircraft burst into flame and crash to earth."

On the second patrol, pilots reported vapour trails rising vertically from 15,000 to 25,000 feet, then fading. Ten miles southwest of Munchen-Gladbach they reported cranes and other heavy equipment in quarries. The vapour trails and mysterious rolling stock seemed to be connected. They were - the Germans were just beginning their V-2 rocket attacks on Britain. Allied airmen would see many more such trails. These early ballistic missiles heralded a new and frightening type of warfare.

For several days 441 was more on the fringes of the battle than in it. They flew their patrols, watched 4-engined Stirlings dropping supplies to the Nijmegen bridgehead, and sat out one rainy day (September 23). Having moved rapidly forward to catch up to the land battle, they were now uncomfortably close to it. German artillery found the airfield, destroying two

Typhoons, and damaging six 441 Spitfires. Slit trenches and steel helmets, not used since Normandy, reappeared. During an escort mission on the 24th, a 441 section observed Dakotas dropping supplies to pockets of British paratroops still holding out around Arnhem. It was a futile operation, most of the supplies falling into German hands.

The first patrol of September 25 was uneventful, the second featured a savage fight - ten 441 Spitfires against 30+ Fw.190s and Bf.109s, apparently a mixed force of fighters and fighter-bombers aiming for the Nijmegen bridge. Control gave no warning. S/L Walker was at 5000 feet when he spotted the enemy. There was no time for strategy as he led his aircraft down for a 15-minute brawl. The most dramatic combat report was that filed by F/O Don Kimball:

> *I was flying White 1 in 441 Squadron led by S/L Walker and saw approximately 30 Me.109s at 1000 feet about 4000 feet below our formation. Time 1435. I went in to attack, firing a three-second burst cannon and machine gun and saw strikes on an Me.109 on wing roots, fuselage and cockpit... I saw enemy aircraft crash and flame.*
>
> *By this time the enemy formations had broken around and I broke round on the tail of another Me.109. I saw strikes on the fuselage and wing roots. The enemy aircraft caught fire and crashed after a 3-second burst. I had to break around as other enemy aircraft were firing at me. From then on I was alone with about 12 enemy aircraft milling around me. After three or four minutes of this, a cannon shell hit my bottom petrol tank. I managed to break away from the enemy aircraft and landed at Eindhoven short of petrol.*

Success is commonly measured by enemy aircraft destroyed, but the most important aspect of this fight was that the Germans had been compelled to drop their bombs short of target. The Nijmegen bridge was never knocked out. That triumph aside, 441 had acquitted itself well. The final tally for September 25 was:

F/O Don H. Kimball	✪ ✪	2 Bf.109s destroyed
F/O Harold E. Derraugh	✪	1 Bf.109 destroyed plus one damaged
S/L R.H. Walker		2 Bf.109s damaged
F/O J.A. McIntosh		1 Bf.109 damaged *

*The squadron ORB also mentioned a Bf.109 damaged by F/O Les Saunders. No combat report of this seems to survive, and his claim was not logged by 2 TAF HQ.

Unhappily, this operation produced some of 441's heaviest casualties, apparently at the hands of JG.26. F/O Bernard Boe of North Vancouver was shot down and killed. FSgt Osman McMillan of Windsor, Ontario was trying to force-land his damaged Spitfire, when he crashed fatally into a gully. McMillan died wearing the rank of a flight sergeant but, when his commission was confirmed, he would be recorded in Commonwealth War Graves Commission documents as an officer.

September 25 concluded with another escort of Dakotas still trying to supply the paratroopers at Arnhem. Next day some of the fiercest air battles around Nijmegen occurred, but 441 seemed to be up at almost all the wrong times, so could claim no kills exclusively for itself. The Wing Commander (Flying), W/C Alan G. Page, RAF, shot down a Bf.109 while leading 441 but, on this occasion, the enemy gave as much as he got. F/O McIntosh had to force-land at Eindhoven with battle damage. Luftwaffe efforts to destroy the bridges continued. On September 27 it flew some 300 sorties, keeping up the pressure from dawn to late afternoon. No.83 Group flew 398 sorties, shooting down 46 enemy aircraft for the loss of nine pilots. Ultimately, the only damage done to the Nijmegen bridge was caused by German frogmen, and even that was superficial (the Germans also had tried floating mines downsteam to destroy the bridge, an effort frustrated by log booms constructed by the Canadian Forestry Corps).

The first 441 patrol of the 27th paid off richly. F/L Mott, leading one section near Arnhem, spotted 20 Bf.109s with either bombs or long range tanks, and closed to engage. The dogfight went from 5000 down to 1500 feet and ended with three Messerschmitts destroyed - two in flames and one as the pilot jumped. The successful pilots were F/Ls Jack Copeland and Ron Lake, and F/O Sidney Bregman.

The Silver Foxes flew their last patrols with 2 TAF on September 30, fighting their last air-to-air action of the war. Six Spitfires patrolling around Nijmegen observed two Me.262 bombers (likely of KG.51) swoop in towards the bridge. Ron Lake attacked, but both jets escaped using their speed, plus cloud. Lake knocked pieces from one for a "damaged".

In six months on operations 441 had flown 2730 sorties, destroyed 56 enemy aircraft, and inflicted varying degrees of mayhem on MET - 158 flamers, 137 smokers and 195 damaged. They had destroyed one locomotive (plus one damaged), sunk a barge, and shot up various other targets. Along the way they reported 14 pilots missing (one rescued from the Channel, three evaders, three POW, and seven killed). The war had seven months to run, and 441 would continue to serve honourably, but nothing would ever match those hectic, glorious months from March to September 1944.

Spitfires "9G-A" and "9G-H" in their dispersal somewhere in Normandy. Note how natural camouflage was used.
(Hugh Ritchie Col.)

In the Field with 441

AN ALBUM

Groundcrew of No.6441 Servicing Echelon service a Spitfire in Normandy. (Guy Mott Col.)

F/O Lou Plummer lines himself up with one of the local Belgian beauties. (CF PL30048)

Living quarters were well-camouflaged at this 441 ALG. Then, beneath the meshing. The man on the left is F/O Alexander James McDonald, killed in action September 25, 1944. (Mott and Bregman Cols.)

Pilot Hugh Ritchie of 441 does his laundry. Ritchie was a seasoned fighter pilot by 1944. Born in 1913, he joined the RCAF in June 1940 as "an old man" of 27. He served overseas from January 1942, but did not join 441 until December 1944. (Hugh Ritchie Col.)

Every airman had a collapsible canvas tub for laundry, shaving or bathing. Here, F/O Myers washes down. (CF PL31070)

441's famous staff car, an oversized Plymouth. (Mott Col.)

Hugh Ritchie of 441 takes a break but is ready to scramble. (441 Sqn.)

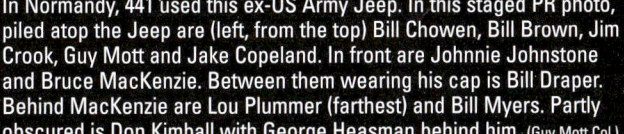

441 had a Spitfire "run about" like this one for beer delivery. This is how it was done - a 90-gallon "jet tank" made an ideal keg. (NAC RE20423)

In Normandy, 441 used this ex-US Army Jeep. In this staged PR photo, piled atop the Jeep are (left, from the top) Bill Chowen, Bill Brown, Jim Crook, Guy Mott and Jake Copeland. In front are Johnnie Johnstone and Bruce MacKenzie. Between them wearing his cap is Bill Draper. Behind MacKenzie are Lou Plummer (farthest) and Bill Myers. Partly obscured is Don Kimball with George Heasman behind him. (Guy Mott Col.)

CHAPTER 4

Air Defence of Great Britain

441 Spitfires ready for operations. (Sid Bregman Col.)

Hawkinge - Escort Days

"Once again this squadron realized that nobody loves an 'orphan'. Just when we had finally caught up with the Army and enough German aircraft were being seen to give the pilots a chance to fatten their score, without explanation or warning the squadron was relegated from 2 TAF to 11 Group, Air Defence Great Britain and turfed back to England." Such was the bewildered complaint of 441 Squadron which, on September 30, 1944, was transferred from Antwerp to Hawkinge near Dover on the south coast of Kent (F/O Bruce MacKenzie noted of this day in his log book, "From 2nd TAF to ADGB, worse luck!"). Several elements were involved in the switch. With the Luftwaffe on the ropes, Bomber Command was increasingly conducting daylight raids, but these needed escorts. While most RCAF fighter squadrons had been deployed in No.83 Group, 2 TAF, 402 Squadron had remained in England, available for tasks ranging from chasing V-1s, to shepherding medium and heavy bombers on daytime operations. It was undoubtedly an arbitrary decision but, when "higher ups" decided to rotate 402 to the continent, somebody had to replace them in ADGB. That "somebody" was 441. The fact that it was the only RCAF squadron in 125 Wing was probably a factor.

While 402 and 441 traded places, their servicing echelons did not - 6402 SE remained at Hawkinge, 6441 at B.70. While the Silver Foxes undoubtedly regretted being pulled from Europe, Hawkinge offered permanent quarters and more comfortable leave prospects. Thus, 441 would be spared the coming winter (to be one of the most miserable on record) and the dreadful accommodations in Holland and Belgium. The squadron flew its first escort on October 5, covering 24 Bostons to a target near Nijmegen. The trips were longer than before (this one lasted 2:15 hours), but there was no mistaking that the tempo had slowed. From 412 sorties (593 operational and 101 non-operational hours) in September 1944, flying fell to 123 sorties (200/67 hours) in October, and 113 (200:45/113:10 hours) in November.

The modus operandi for escorting differed greatly from what the Silver Foxes had known. It even differed from the tactical escort missions flown the previous spring. For one thing, weather was more crucial as to an operation being a "go" or "no go". It had to be favourable both in England and over the target. Thus, there were spells when little or nothing was happening (e.g. October 16 - 24 and October 30 - November 4). Twice (December 3 and 8) the Spitfires landed at Brussels when weather turned foul. On the continent the Spitfires sometimes carried 45-gallon drop tanks, but now they routinely used 90-gallon tanks. These caused problems, often failing to jettison properly. There were 18 early returns in October, 14 in November and 19 in December, usually meaning two Spitfires coming home - the one with the problem, plus its escort. On several operations one or two extra aircraft took off to cover for these cases of DNCO - duty not carried out. In the absence of the Luftwaffe, the Spitfire pilots were now spectators to the wider dramas of raids played out below. They paid their first visit to Germany on October 6, watching as 120 Halifaxes attacked oil targets in the Ruhr. Oil was the target again on October 12, most of the bombers being RCAF from 6 Group.

On October 14 Bomber Command mounted a huge daylight raid on Duisburg, followed by another that night. Apart from strategic considerations (the city was a major inland port), the raid was a demonstration of Allied power, Bomber Command pouring almost 10,000 tons of bombs into the target in 24 hours. The Silver Foxes saw seven bombers shot down by flak. They next accompanied Bostons on October 15, heavy bombers on the 25th, and again on the 28th. The 28th involved 700 Lancasters and Halifaxes raiding Cologne. Flak was intense, but only five bombers were lost.

Weather over the target on October 28 had been clear but, as the Spitfires turned for home, they met cloud and icing. South of Brussels, F/O Alexander James McDonald and P/O Gil Brochu were seen letting down with Bruce MacKenzie and Guy Mott and others of 441. It was a radar letdown through cloud and severe icing. On regaining base, all pilots reported instruments frozen and hoods frosted over. They waited patiently for McDonald and Brochu, who had gone missing before. This time they did not make it. Brochu, a member of the squadron since June 1943, crashed and died in Belgium. McDonald, who had joined 125 Squadron in April 1943, simply vanished - another name on the Runnymede Memorial for those with no known graves. These would be 441's last operational casualties.

On October 29, 441 was escorting heavy bombers attacking fortifications, coastal guns and dikes on Walcheren Island as the 2nd Canadian Division stormed the place during the Battle of the Scheldt. F/O Bruce MacKenzie flew on this operation, later noting in his log, "Gun positions Walcheren. Good bombing. Island pretty well sunk." Subsequent escort missions were uneventful (save for watching flak shoot down the occasional bombers and observing V-2 trails). A major operation supported American troops on November 16. This marked the end of Guy Mott's tour - he was replaced as "A" Flight commander by Don Kimball. The number of pilots who had served in both 125 and 441 was dwindling. Indeed, the unit was fast losing much of its "corporate memory" as veteran pilots finished their tours, to be replaced by rookies.

The last 441 escort mission was on Christmas Eve, covering 170 bombers attacking Lohausen airfield, Dusseldorf. The Battle of the Bulge was at its height, and the attack was one of several intended to minimize Luftwaffe support of the German offensive. Photographs showed the target well cratered. The balance of 1944 ebbed away in seasonal festivities. The squadron diarist had taken pains to describe a party on December 23 at which 90 children from schools near Folkestone were entertained with movies, games, Father Christmas, and treats unheard of in rationed Britain. The same scribe was more circumspect about the next few days. His entry for the 25th read only "Christmas Day". There was probably little else to report, for 441 was preparing to move again.

A gang of the Silver Foxes in a candid shot. (Sid Bregman Col.)

Dining in the UK

In the 1980s Spitfire pilot R.J. "Bob" Lacerte of 441 compiled a rough history of his time on squadron. Although based on the official records, his manuscript also contained some human interest material. Included is Lacerte's description of a 125 Wing officer's diet - 441's days of English cuisine:

Welsh Rabbit – *a coarse toast covered with cheesy powdered egg spread.*

English Hare – *roasted hare legs made to pass as chicken drumsticks (the rest of the carcass went into soups and stews).*

Australian Mutton – *prepared using various camouflaging recipes, the only actual choice being with or without the wool.*

Horse Meat – *passed off as ham steaks, yet surprisingly tasty if you didn't know the difference, or were too hungry to care.*

Bangers – *imitation breakfast sausage made from ground soybean cereal soaked in suet, and fried.*

Brussel Sprouts – *the staple dinner vegetable guaranteed to fill you with so much gas that you felt full when only part way through a meal.*

Chicory – *reportedly a coffee substitute, but really not a decent substitute for anything.*

Yorkshire Pudding – *supposedly made fresh daily in the Mess kitchen, but rumours claim that it came from the same place that made our inflatable rubber dinghies.*

Kippers – *the smelliest herring-like fish. Took ages to get the bones out!*

The Silver Foxes divided their resources. Headquarters and "A" Flight were at Skaebrae, "B" Flight was further north at Sumburgh in the Shetland Islands (the flights changed places at the end of February). On those first few days, as gales whipped the area, personnel may well have asked what sin had brought them to this place. Operations were more akin to those in Torbay, than to their recent adventures in France, Belgium, even Kent. Between bouts of foul weather they managed to fly 205 hours in January, 257 in February, 397 in March. This, however, was really operational training - ASR duties, the odd, uneventful scramble, but mostly routine patrols, formation practice, air-to-sea firing, dive bombing, dog fighting, GCI exercises and fighter affiliation with RAF Coastal Command. The only thing approaching combat was on January 13. On that day four pilots flew within 30 miles of the Norwegian coast, while Mosquitos attacked shipping. The Spitfires were to help with ASR, but were not required.

A brutal reminder of the price of war. Hugh Ritchie of 441 took this photo of fresh graves in France. In time such casualties were disinterred for reburial in national war cemeteries.

Banished to the Orkneys

On December 27, 1944, 441 Squadron left Hawkinge, ground crews following by rail next day. Their destination was Skaebrae, a storm-tossed outpost in the Orkney Islands. One could not get much further away from the war than this. Why Skaebrae? There is no clear answer. Sooner or later, every squadron had to serve in such a place, it seems. Even a remote area merited fighter protection, and the naval base at Scapa Flow obviously qualified. What better way to offer it than to use the place for "rest tours". 611 Squadron had drawn the short straw October to December 1944. Now it was 441's turn. Strategically, the base was insurance against prowling German reconnaissance aircraft and a forward location for Allied units doing recce, shipping sweeps and anti-submarine patrols. By any description, however, Skaebrae was a backwater, reached by air or rolling ferry boat. Pierre Clostermann, a pilot and author, wrote, "Skaebrae in winter might just as well be the North Pole." A poem widely known in RAF circles described it thus:

This bloody town's a bloody cuss -
No bloody trains, no bloody bus,
And no one cares for bloody us -
In bloody Orkney.

The bloody roads are bloody bad,
The bloody folks are bloody mad,
They'd make the brightest bloody sad,
In bloody Orkney.

All bloody clouds and bloody rains,
No bloody kerbs, no bloody drains,
The Council's got no bloody brains,
In bloody Orkney.

Everything's so bloody dear,
A bloody bob for a bloody beer
And is it good ? - no bloody fear,
In bloody Orkney.

The bloody flicks are bloody old,
The bloody seats are bloody cold,
You can't get in for bloody gold
In bloody Orkney.

The bloody dances make you smile,
The bloody band is bloody vile,
It only cramps your bloody style,
In bloody Orkney.

No bloody sport, no bloody games,
No bloody fun, the bloody dames
Won't even give their bloody names
In bloody Orkney.

Best bloody place is bloody bed
With bloody ice on bloody head
You might as well be bloody dead
In bloody Orkney.

A 6402 Servicing Echelon fitter runs up a Spitfire, then another scene as a 441 pilot taxies for takeoff. (Sid Bregman Col.)

To lose a man in battle was tragic, but that, at least, had some meaning. A loss on an exercise, however, was maddening. On January 23, 1945 two Spitfires went out on formation and homing practice, but separated. One came home, the other did not. WO Joseph Eloi "Boe" Bohemier of Ste. Anne, Manitoba was plotted north of Lerwick when he asked for a homing. He acknowledged, then vanished. Aircraft and launches scoured the area, but it was as if the mists had swallowed Bohemier. On March 10, 1945 F/L Ernest W. Martin of Toronto and F/O Reg Perkin left Skaebrae on a GCI exercise. History repeated itself - they lost touch. Like Bohemier, Martin vanished without trace.

On February 13, 1945, 441 celebrated its first anniversary overseas. F/O Reginald W. Perkin composed a squadron song, set to the music of "MacNamara's Band", that summarized a varied year:

We are the boys of 441
As everyone must know.
We've been in France, and Belgium too,
And where the north winds blow.
We must admit of flak a bit
We really are adverse
But flying over water boys,
Is what we hate the worst.

Chorus:
We like our beer and whisky clear
We also take to rum.
And ladies sigh with open eyes
For more of 441.

Return to Hawkinge

The squadron's tour in purgatory ended on April 3, 1945 as it left Skaebrae, replaced by 329 Squadron. All of 441 flew out in Dakotas, returning to Hawkinge and the bomber escort role, with hand-me-down Spitfires. There were a few new twists, as on April 10 - 11, when they flew to B.90, Petit Brogel in Belgium, then escorted bombers to marshalling yards in southern Bavaria. A similar operation was tried on April 12-13, again staging from Petit Brogel for a raid on Swinemunde. This time they missed the bombers (which were eight minutes late). It hardly mattered, for the Luftwaffe was beyond being a threat. On April 16, 441 flew from Hawkinge to B.86 Helmond in the Netherlands. Two days later S/L Walker led a dozen Spitfires as 900 Lancasters and Halifaxes blasted the German island fortress of Heligoland. The fireworks were spectacular with plenty of secondary explosions. Yet another escort on the 25th (from Petit Brogel) involved 480 bombers (192 from 6 Group) taking apart another island fortification at Wangerooge. It was Bomber Command's last raid of the war, and 441's final operation. Their work was linked to that of the heavy bombers but, with the Eastern and Western fronts now fusing in Germany, Bomber Command had run out of targets.

The Silver Foxes moved to Hunsdon, Herfortshire on April 29, but the switch was meaningless. VE Day arrived on May 7 and two days of celebrations eclipsed all other events. On May 12 ten pilots formed part of an escort to ships removing the German garrison from Guernsey. They swept over the island in victorious formation - 441's war was finally over. Or was it? On May 17 it moved again, with 442 Squadron, back to Digby. Now it began converting to Mustang IIIs. It took no imagination to guess what was coming - the Pacific theatre with long-range escort missions against Japan. Nevertheless, the most significant event here was another fatality - F/O Eddie McCabe crashed near Hull during a cross-country flight, 441's last wartime casualty. Hopes for a Pacific role faded even before Japan's surrender. As July closed, orders came that 441 was to disband effective August 7. The last few days were spent ferrying Mustangs into storage. Now it was time to go home.

After D-Day, 441/6402 held various formal and informal celebrations, from fly-bys to dances.
(441 Sqn Col.)

CHAPTER 5

Pilot Profiles

F/O John Edward West

Life and death are cloaked with ritual, whether of individuals or institutions, and the events surrounding these are important to all participants. Before leaving 441 Squadron's wartime experiences, we might look back on some practices as a reminder that, beyond strategy and tactics, fighting and waiting, there were other stories, distinct but related. The training of a fighter pilot is one such.

In almost all respects, F/O John Edward West was typical of the men who served in 441. His background and training may illustrate what many of his comrades experienced. West was born in Halifax of native Haligonians on October 11, 1917. West had three brothers and five sisters, younger brothers Frank R. West and Richard P. West also being in the RCAF. He was educated in Nova Scotia, first at Hopewell (1924-1935, up to Grade XI), then in New Glasgow (1935-1937, completing to Grade XII). Thereafter he worked in a steel foundry on clerical jobs, before becoming an office clerk with a Halifax construction company.

West presented himself at the RCAF recruiting centre in Halifax on July 7, 1941. The interviewing officer noted him as being 5 feet 6 3/4 inches and 167 pounds. He was described under various headings - Approach ("confident"), Carriage ("upright"), Dress ("neat, conservative, clean"), Physique ("medium"), Speech ("clear"), Response ("quick") and Manner ("alert, confident, sincere"). He listed his sports as swimming, football and softball, although his hobby was unusual - "psychology"! He had one hour of flying dual and 15 minutes experience as a passenger, yet the interviewer also noted, "Has built own plane and tried to fly it. Result - crash. Good experience." The officer concluded, "Very good pilot material."

West was formally sworn in as an Aircraftman, 2nd Class (AC2) on July 7, but was not posted to No.1 Manning Depot in Toronto until July 21. Having been kitted, tested and given his first experience at drill, he was posted to 1 SFTS at Camp Borden. This was not a training assignment, for he was in a "holding pattern", waiting for a vacancy in the BCATP pipeline. West most likely did guard duty at Camp Borden. Then, on October 10, 1941, he was posted to 5 ITS in Belleville. This was where aircrew training really began. He was on course from October 13 to December 5, 1941, taking mathematics, armament, signals, drill, hygiene, law, discipline, etc.

Described as "a bright determined type, a hard and conscientious worker", West graduated 23rd in a class of 107, and was promoted to Leading Aircraftman. He was taken on strength of 17 EFTS in Stanley, Nova Scotia, on December 6, 1941. Here he logged 29:50 hours of dual daylight time, 3:10 of dual night time, 28:15 solo (day) and 6:30 instrument flying "under the hood" - all in the Fleet Finch. He also completed 11 hours in the Link Trainer. His flying instructor wrote of him as having "No outstanding weakness - good all around student." Ground school consisted of courses in airmanship, airframe, aero engines, signals, theory of flight, air navigation, aircraft recognition and armament. Again, West impressed his instructors, who wrote, "Good student. Of average intelligence only, makes up for this by good solid work. Quiet, well-mannered and disciplined, is mature, well-liked and a natural leader". West graduated 9th in a class of 28 (in the absence of a logbook it is difficult to identify his instructors, but at EFTS he was regularly tested by F/O Kenneth S. Molyneux, an outstanding officer who would be Commended for Valuable Services in the Air in 1943).

West now advanced to 8 SFTS in Moncton. There he would log (on Harvards) 51:25 hours dual by day, 8:10 dual by night, 57:35 daytime solo, 8:10 night solo, 28:05 on instruments, and 22:15 in the Link. He seemed to falter here, being considered weak at instrument flying. His ground school marks also dropped - he scored 119 out of a possible 200 in airmanship and maintenance, 88 out 150 in navigation, and 35 out of 100 in signals. West held up better in armament and meteorology. His progress had been slow, his ability assessed as "low average", yet the CFI seemed loath to be harsh, concluding, "He is keen and diligent and with more experience should prove satisfactory in all service requirements."

West graduated on June 19, 1942 with the rank of sergeant, but was not recommended for a commission. He was posted to 126 Squadron at Dartmouth, where he "put up a black", pranging Hurricane BW845 following an air-to-ground firing exercise of September 7, 1942. Having undershot the runway, he opened the throttle, went round, and finally touched down. The undercarriage collapsed, but he was not hurt. On October 28, 1942 West joined 125 Squadron at Torbay.

47

Moving from posting to posting, or coming or going on leave, RCAF students such as Johnny West and Jake Copeland got to know train schedules all over Canada. (NAC PA136261)

If one's posting was overseas, a sea voyage was in the cards. Most Allied troopships were converted ocean liners. Here S.S. *Louis Pasteur* nears Quebec City in August 1945, bringing thousands of Canadians home from the UK. (CF PL36920)

Promotion came at regular intervals, consistent with RCAF policies. Six months after winning his wings, West became a flight sergeant, six months later, a WO2. On July 21, 1943, he was commissioned as a pilot officer (he routinely had been described by S/L Norris as a "good NCO type", but Norris finally recommended a commission). Promotion to flying officer followed in another six months.

A record of West's flying in Canada shows that he had logged an impressive 570:50 hours, mostly on the Hurricane at 126, then 125 squadrons. Before going overseas, he told his mother that, in the event of his death, his estate should go to the education of his two youngest sisters. However, unlike many others, he did not write a formal will. Throughout his career he would have a clean conduct sheet.

On June 12, 1944, returning in Spitfire MH447 from an operational patrol over the Normandy beaches, he began to fall behind and lose height. He tried to bail out at about 1000 feet, but his parachute snagged in the tailwheel, and he went down with the aircraft. West seems to have lived modestly - at his death he left an unpaid mess bill of one pound.

Jake Copeland

Jack Cameron Copeland, often called "Jake" by his RCAF compatriots, was born in Brantford, Ontario on October 25, 1918. Before the war he studied mining engineering at the University of Toronto. Graduating in 1940 at the top of his class, he went to work in Northern Ontario for Hollinger Mines. Soon, however, he was drawn into the war, first as a volunteer in the Algonquin Regiment, which he joined in North Bay in March 1941. Soon, however, he transferred to the RCAF and was selected for pilot training. On July 16, 1941 he had his first training flight, going up in Fleet Finch 4582 with instructor Len Fitton at 12 EFTS in Goderich. He soloed on the 29th and finished the course with 54:35 hours. Copeland now moved to 1 SFTS at Camp Borden, flying first with Sgt Aistrop in Harvard 2649 on September 19, 1941. He finished here with 148 hours and an "Above Average" assessment, something rare at any level in the BCATP.

Soon, Copeland was aboard ship for the UK, first stop being Bournemouth. There he received his posting - to 5 FIS (Tiger Moths) at Perth, Scotland for the instructor's course. After 222:55 hours here, he earned his instructor's category and joined the staff at 4 EFTS at RAF Brough in Yorkshire. Before anyone was posted from the UK to the BCATP in Canada, the RAF wanted some assurance that he showed some promise. The task at 4 EFTS was to screen such pilot candidates, who fairly poured through Brough.

Jake Copeland as a youthful RCAF pilot. (Copeland Col.)

At Brough FSgt Copeland would learn about hard work and long hours - RAF style. In June 1942, for example, he logged 91:15 hours. So it would go for the months ahead. A typical day for him meant 6 to 9 flights. On July 22, 1943 he passed his 1000th flying hour, then ended his tour on October 22. He now had 1309:25 flying hours - quite a phenomenal figure, and nearly all on Tiger Moths. Copeland's CO, S/L H.A. Howes, sent him on his way to RAF College at Cranwell with an "Above Average".

From Tiger Moths, Copeland was destined to fighters, but he needed to "brush up" on something heavier. Beginning on November 5, therefore, he flew the Miles Master through to February 25, 1944. This would have been an excellent lead-in for what came next - Spitfire conversion at 57 OTU at Eschott. This was Copeland's aviation dream finally come true. On March 4 he first flew a "Spit", taking up "PW-C" for 15 minutes. Now came all the typical exercises, whether low-level or formation flying, practice air fighting, or gunnery.

The course took to May 10, then came a brief wait for a posting. Thus, from May 26 - 30 Copeland was at 1 Tactical Exercise Unit at RAF Tealing near Dundee, Scotland. This was a pilot holding unit, where a fellow could get in a few extra hours. Then came word that Copeland was to report to 441 Squadron, stationed since June 15 at B.3 Ste. Croix-sur-Mer.

With the invasion in full swing and the enemy still threatening to push the Allies back into the Channel, life on any fighter squadron was wild. F/L Copeland, anxious to start doing his part, first flew with 441 on June 23, taking up Spitfire IXc"J". There was little time for orientation, Copeland getting straight into the fray. Fortunately, he made careful log book entries. These give a snap shot of exciting, dangerous and uncertain times. Most sorties were armed recces, but Me.109s and Fw.190s were reported on the prowl, so these also were sought. Sorties usually took an hour, but longer if a 45-gallon belly tank was used. Copeland's log is packed with entries describing vehicles and road convoys shot up. In these excerpts one can almost hear the roar of the Merlin engine, smell the exhaust and cordite, and feel the "G", as 441 roared across Normandy:

July 5 *"Engage 12+ Fw.190s. Starboard aileron shot off. Crash landed at B.2 OK. Attacker shot down by W/C Johnson."*

July 13 *"Destroyed one Fw.190. Squadron, led by S/Ldr, destroyed 10."*

July 18 *"Sighted two Me.109s at 10,000 feet, from 26,000. Destroyed one, shared with F/L Johnstone."*

August 4 *"Had to make a flapless, brakeless landing. Ran off runway and broke prop."*

August 6 *"F/L Guy Mott hit by flak. Baled out OK near Vire. Mott safe, returned August 9."*

W/C A.G. Page, the RAF "Winco Flying" at B.3, was not happy about Copeland bringing home a damaged Spitfire on July 5. Page endorsed his log book accordingly. One wonders what got into the winco's head to penalize one of his pilots for what surely was a good show. For August, Copeland logged 32:05 operational hours, 4:30 non-operational, on most days flying at least two sorties. On July 15, 441 moved from B.3 to B.11 Longues, on August 13 to B.19 Lingèvres, on September 2 to B.40 Beauvais and on September 5 B.52 Douai. Pilots like Copeland had to get used to this constant packing, moving and unpacking, sometimes under enemy fire.

In mid-September 441 was embroiled in the airborne assault around Arnhem. On the 17th, it moved to B.70 Antwerp. For the 18th Copeland, flying sorties around Nijmegen, noted: "Encountered about 18 109s. S/L Walker and F/L Johnstone - 1 destroyed, F/O Heasman - 1 destroyed, F/L Lake - 1 destroyed." On July 26 he reported a German jet near the Nijmegen bridge, but it was too fast for him to engage. Next day he flew three Nijmegen sorties, bagging one Me.109. On the 30th in the same area he chased an Me.109, then two Me.262s, but had to admit "no joy" for his efforts.

On September 30, 441 was recalled to the UK, F/L Copeland noting in his log, "402 Spit 14s took over." Now at Hawkinge, 441 was on bomber escort duty. Copeland's first operation in this new period was escorting Bostons on October 5. The next day he was covering a Halifax daylight raid against synthetic oil plants in the Ruhr. For October 7 he noted, "300 Lancs bombing Emmerich. Weather unfit, returned." (The Spitfires may have been recalled, but not the bombers. This raid by 340 Lancasters

A spread from Jake Copeland's log book specifying action in September - October 1944. (Larry Milberry)

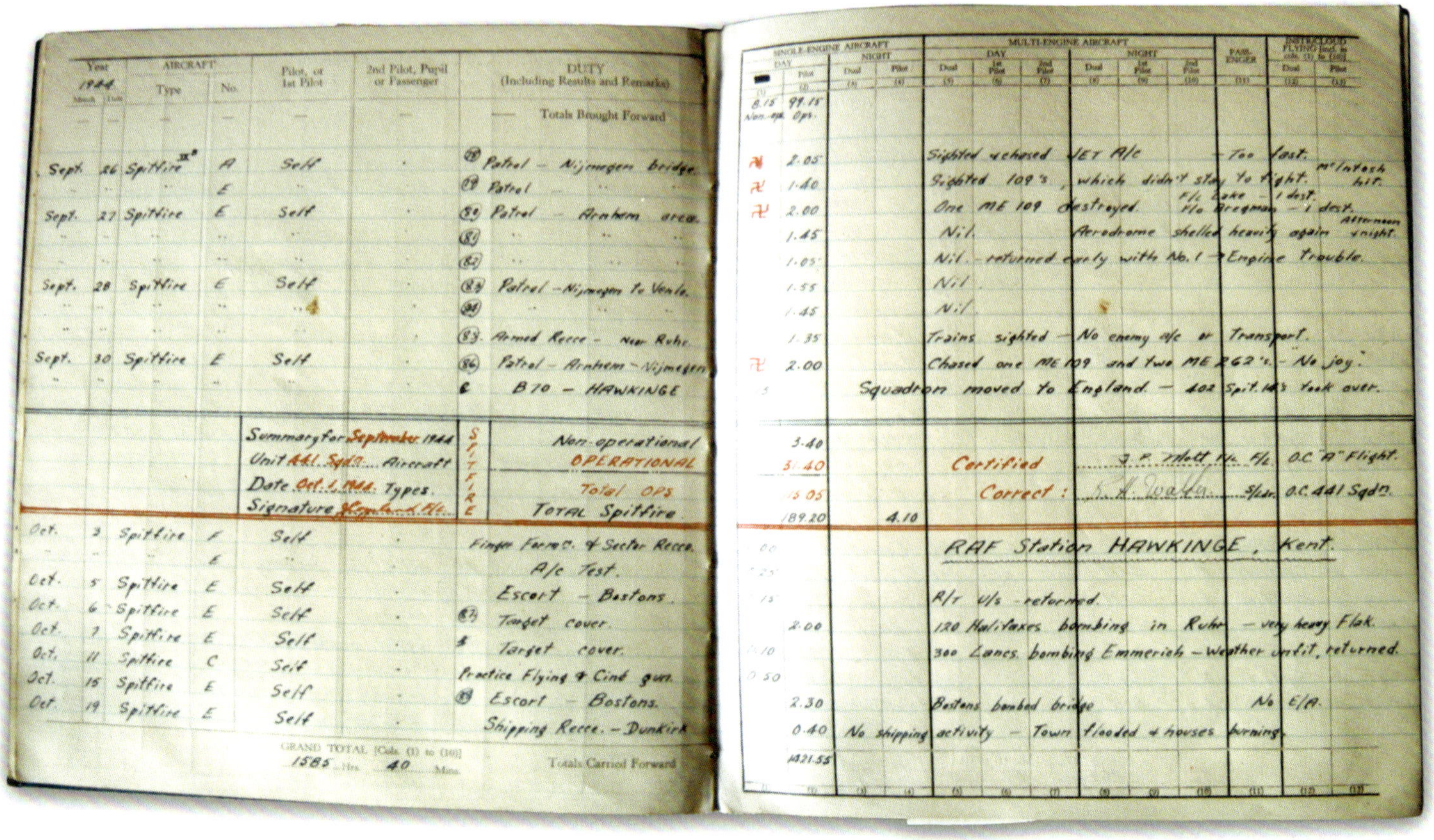

and 8 Mosquitoes was a devastating blow to Emmerich, some 3000 buildings being destroyed or damaged.) On October 19 Copeland noted, "Shipping recce, Dunkirk. No shipping activity. Town flooded and houses burning." November 10 was something special: "Escort Dakotas. VIPs to Paris - PM Churchill and Eden. Engine rough, returned." For November 16 the task was to cover 418 Lancasters to Duren: "Very cold. Art Jewett baled out OK". Copeland logged his final 441 operation on December 18, 1944, flying on this occasion 132 Squadron Spitfire "FF-W".

Now came the squadron's sojourn in the Orkneys and its conversion to Mustangs. After this F/L Copeland received 30 days of "special leave". Sailing on February 1, he disembarked in New York eight days later, then hurried home to Brantford, where his fiancée, June Jackson, awaited. Within a few days June and he were married. The pair had met at a dance in 1942, June then being a student at McMaster University. By this time she was at Oxford University Press in Toronto on the editorial team working on *The RCAF Overseas*.

F/L Copeland now returned to England, disembarking on April 21. He was posted to 58 OTU at Hawarden in Wales for a Spitfire refresher course (May 12 to 17), but soon was ordered home, sailing aboard SS *Stratheden* on July 22, reaching Canada on the 31st. On September 4 he appeared at No.4 Release Centre in Toronto and was discharged a week later. He had flown 147:40 operation hours on the Spitfire IXc and recorded 2.5 kills. He received a Mention in Dispatches on June 14, 1945. Total time in his log was 1630:45 hours. While Copeland received an MiD, he originally had been recommended for the DFC. In such cases, the usual result was no gong or, perhaps, a lesser one. S/L R.H. Walker had put up Copeland for a DFC on January 7, 1945:

> Flight Lieutenant Copeland has just left for one month's leave in Canada, having served actively overseas for three years. He instructed for 18 months on Tiger Moths and is credited with one tour of operations with this squadron.
>
> During his first few engagements, this officer was twice hit by enemy fighters, but in both cases, brought his badly shot-up Spitfire back to crash land on the aerodrome. Demoralizing as this was, he continued to carry the attack to the enemy and, in his next two engagements, destroyed a Fw.190 on the 13th July 1944, and shared a Me.109 destroyed with his No.2 on 18th July 1944. Both of these successes were obtained in the Argentan area. While providing cover for the paratroop attack at Arnhem on 27th September, he attacked and destroyed an additional Me.109. These successes have been achieved while flying protective patrols over the front line from D-Day until after the Arnhem show. He has destroyed 22 enemy road transport and damaged two barges by shooting up the Huns ahead of our army from Normandy to Holland. On one occasion he was hit by flak in the Falaise Gap area, but again brought his aircraft back safely to base.
>
> Flight Lieutenant Copeland has displayed great courage and determination to seek out and destroy the Hun wherever he could be found and has contributed largely to the fine record of his squadron. I therefore recommend the immediate award of the Distinguished Flying Cross.

Jack Copeland now left aviation, returning to the University of Toronto to study mechanical engineering. Instead going back into mining, he now opted for a 27-year career with Canadian International Paper in Gatineau, Quebec. There he worked his way through the masonite, fibreboard and plywood mills, ending as head of all three, then moving to corporate HQ in Montreal. Thereafter, he spent several years in Ottawa with the Department of Industry, Trade and Commerce, retiring in 1983 and settling in west end Ottawa.

One may wonder what the wives and girlfriends of those overseas did during the war. One way or another most worked in the war effort - in factories, schools, hospitals, offices, etc. In September 2002, June Copeland recalled a few of her wartime memories:

> I worked at Oxford University Press from the fall of 1943 to the fall of 1946. The office was in Toronto on University Avenue just north of Dundas, in a charming old building called "Amen House". Built of stone, it was four or five stories high with mullioned windows. William and Irene Clarke headed "OUP" and also Clarke-Irwin, along with Mrs. Clarke's brother, Arthur Irwin. The editor with whom I worked was W.W. Robertson. I started at $18.00 a week, working up to about $25.00.
>
> Those days in publishing were very exciting. I met A.Y. Jackson, who did a jacket art for British High Commissioner Malcolm Macdonald's book "Down North". One day, while working in the library, I had a spirited conversation with David Lewis, who later was such a big name in politics with the NDP. I did some editing on "The RCAF Overseas: The Fifth Year", published in 1945. When it came to "The Sixth Year", I was eagerly awaiting mention of Jack's name.

Jake Copeland peruses his log during an August 2002 interview session. Then, Jake with his wife June, and 441 compatriot Arthur Jewett at the 1998 CFPA convention. (Larry Milberry)

A New Brunswick Son

Arthur Jewett was born at Aroostook Junction, New Brunswick on July 24, 1923, the son of a CPR worker and subsistence farmer. Young Arthur helped with the chores and delivered milk at 8 cents a quart. When he was eight years old, he saw his first airplane. In 1942 he joined the RCAF, starting at Manning Depot in Lachine, a Montreal suburb. Next, he was at Camp Borden on tarmac duty- washing and helping to fuel aircraft. ITS at Toronto followed, then came EFTS at Goderich. Jewett's first flight was in Tiger Moth 1224 on March 31, 1943 with Sgt Ribble. He soloed on April 23, finishing the course on May 15 with a flight in Tiger Moth 255. His time at this stage totalled 56:50 hours.

Jewett now was posted to SFTS in Ottawa, starting his flying on the Harvard on May 19. His "50-hour" test came on June 21. Training was intense, as shown by Jewett's log for the week of July 19 - 23 - 7:20 hours of dual instruction, 4:55 day solo and 3:00 night solo. There were 15 flights, including five on the 22nd. This was no game for anyone lacking self confidence. Jewett finished his course on August 3 with 77:15 hours dual (day) on the Harvard, 66:00 solo (day), 7:20 dual (night) and 15:35 solo (night).

By now Jewett was pegged for the fighter world and posted to Course 18 at No.1 (F) OTU in Bagotville. There he started with a flight in Harvard FE385 with F/O Miron on September 21, 1943. On the 25th he flew the Hurricane for the first time and was immediately engrossed in the intensive OTU world - day and night, formation and low level flying, dog fighting, cross-country trips, etc. For October 1943 he flew the Hurricane for 21:30 hours, the Harvard for 11:55.

Even in training, young fellows like Jewett could meet death head on. He noted, for example, how Sgt Bailey had been killed in a Hurricane. "Probably blacked out", he entered in his log (this was Raymond W. Bailey, RAF, killed on November 15). OTU sped by, Jewett finishing with 49:25 hours in the Hurricane, 20:25 in the Harvard. Posted overseas, he sailed from New York aboard the RMS *Queen Mary*. In his draft were several others from Course 18 - Neil Burns, Jake Copeland, Jimmy Flood and Alex McIntosh. As Jewett recalled, "We enjoyed the trip and drank all the way across to Greenock, then took the train down to Bournemouth." There he was surprised to meet a friend from Aroostook - Charles Gaines, then on 519 Squadron doing weather flights. Gaines would die in August 1944 in a Ventura, crashing minutes after takeoff, apparently because some control locks had not been removed. Death would touch Arthur Jewett many more times before war's end.

From Bournemouth P/O Jewett was posted to 57 OTU at Eshott, near Newcastle, flying there first on March 3, 1944 in a Miles Master. The next day he took up Spitfire "PW-K", a 15-minute flight about which he noted in his log, "I'm glad there weren't any pictures" (Jake Copeland soloed at Eshott in "PW-C" on the same day). On the 14th there was tragedy at Eshott as F/O Flood collided with another Spitfire. The other pilot spun in and died, while Flood force-landed (he would die in action in August 1944 near Dieppe while with 421 Squadron.) OTU was busy - in March Jewett logged 24:40 hours on Spitfires, 1:50 on Masters.

Sid Bregman had these photos of Arthur Jewett in his wartime photo album.

April brought more misery. For some reason a USAAF P-47 one day flew through the Eshott circuit, colliding with a Spitfire flown by a Norwegian student, identified by Jewett as Sgt Knaghjneum. Both planes crashed fatally, Jewett commenting in his log, "Ruined my dinner." Another student on OTU, FSgt Cyril Jewell (RAF), was killed, colliding with power lines. When he returned from a flight that day, Jewett found that his belongings had been removed from his room, and that his bed was ready for a new occupant. It seems that someone in the orderly room had confused him with the unfortunate Jewell and wasn't wasting any time getting the paper work and formalities completed.

Arthur Jewett finished at Eshott on May 11 with a flight in Spitfire VB "JZ-H". He left with 69:50 on Spitfires, then travelled to No.1 TEU for some advanced training on the Spitfire I, II and V, including on the gyro gun sight. He left after 18:25 additional hours, the CO noting in his log, "This pilot is gyro trained." Jewett now was posted to 441 Squadron at B.3, where he arrived from England by Dakota. He learned that he was the replacement for a pilot who had made a wheels-up landing and been turfed off squadron by W/C Johnson. The winco called in Jewett for a quick introduction. Jewett recalled in 1998 that Johnson was "very brief and very sharp." He simply warned Jewett to do just what he was told, then dismissed him. Jewett made his first 441 flight in Spitfire "9G-Y" on July 9, 1944. Three days later he was on a patrol with F/O Bill Draper as lead and got home with only two gallons of fuel remaining. Johnson disciplined Draper for this, also dismissing him from 441.

All the daily action came hot and heavy for the sprog pilot. Jewett noted for July 17: "6 Fw.190s sighted. F/L Brown 2 destroyed, F/O Kimball 1 destroyed." On August 13 he was on patrol as No.2 to F/L W.W. "Bill" Brown. He went down after some German trucks. Brown, a seasoned member of 441, followed. Seconds later Brown was shot down and killed - they had been lured into a flak trap. For September 14 Jewett noted that F/L R.G. Sim had not come home from a strafing mission. Soon it was learned that he had been hit and bailed out. Local civilians assisted him and he returned safely on October 29 (Sim later joined 443 Squadron and assisted in

51

Art Jewett's buddy "Mac" McIntosh in 441 Mustang (and motorcycling) days. (Sid Bregman Col.)

shooting down a Ju.88 on May 3, 1945). For September, Jewett logged 23:00 hours, 19:30 on ops.

In the fall of 1944 the Silver Foxes were based near Antwerp. One evening Art Jewett and J.A. "Mac" McIntosh went on the town, since they didn't have to fly the next morning. Eventually, they got a taxi back to their quarters, a large house commandeered as billets. Their driver was uneasy about his two well-oiled passengers and let them off short of destination. The boys started strolling along a street then, inexplicably, began shooting out windows with their .38 sidearms. They finally reached home, making a lot of noise as they stumbled about. The pilots, who had to be up at sunrise to fly, did not like this and words were exchanged. Jewett then put some bullets into the ceiling. He and McIntosh at last were subdued and a kangaroo court was convened. F/L Copeland, Jewett's old buddy from Bagotville days, was infuriated, suggesting that the offending duo be taken outside and shot, then the CO sent everyone to bed. The incident blew over, but Jewett and McIntosh did suffer one punishment - they could only carry sidearms when flying. Upon landing, they had to turn them over.

On November 16, 1944 Jewett was on a bomber escort to Duren, which was being softened up ahead of a US Army push. Poor Duren suffered 3127 civilians killed. Neither was this a great day for Arthur Jewett, who was on his 52nd operational sortie. Over Duren at 20,000 feet his engine died. He glided as far as possible towards Allied positions, then bailed out, coming down at Frelenberg, Germany. Luckily, the Americans had taken this area and Jewett was back with 441 on November 20, having gotten to know a little about the ground war by going on a few patrols with the Americans. He was back in the air on the 25th, doing an air test.

Cameras were "verboten" on RCAF operations but, thank goodness, some airmen pooh-poohed the rules. Here is another outstanding Sid Bregman view of a 441 Spitfire. Not even the RCAF got such good photos in Normandy.

The Mustang, well-liked by most fighter pilots, came too late to see action with 441. (Sid Bregman Col.)

On January 1, 1945 Jewett again had engine failure. He was over the North Sea, but glided to safety. For this good show W/C R.A. Barton, OC of RAF Skaebrae in the Shetlands, inscribed a green endorsement in Jewett's log: "When flying Spitfire MK926 at RAF Sumburgh on 1 January 1945, F/O Jewett force-landed without further damage after an engine failure, thereby displaying sound judgment and good airmanship."

On April 11, 1945 F/L Jewett completed his 55th and final op, flying Spitfire "9G-N" on a 2:50-hour trip: "Escort Lancs to Bayreuth. Uneventful. Nice bombing." In April 1945 the Silver Foxes moved to Hawkinge from where, on May 12, they took part in a 2½-hour Victory Sweep to the Channel Islands. After returning to base, the pilots were reprimanded for being too enthusiastic with their beat-up. Jewett made his last Spitfire flight on May 31. Now 441 began converting to the Mustang III. Jewett flew this type initially at Digby on June 1. He didn't fall in love with it, recalling in 1998, "I didn't care for the Mustang. It seemed heavy and awkward compared to the Spitfire. It did, however, have plenty of range."

Although the war in Europe was over, there still were casualties. On June 18 Jewett was on a flight from Bognor to Portsmouth, Southampton and Bournemouth when he spotted a parachute in the sea. Later he heard that it was from F/O Vernon F. "Junior" McClung, a 25-year-old 442 Squadron pilot from Stoney Creek, Ontario. McClung had been flying Mustang KH694 from Digby, when he suddenly dove into the sea. A logbook entry on July 24, 1945 reads, "Cross-country. My birthday. McCabe killed. Spun into a junk yard. convenient." F/O Edward J. McCabe, age 21 from Toronto, had gone straight into an auto wrecker's yard near Hull.

By this time many young RCAF aircrew had become hard and cynical beyond imagination. They had been on so many ops, killed so many of the enemy, been shot down, bailed out, crash landed, evaded, been wounded, recovered, gone back on ops, became hardened drinkers, and generally seemed inured to the misery in which they dwelt. It was a whirlwind existence and one that these young men neither deserved nor enjoyed. They pined to be home with their mothers and fathers, brothers and sisters, wives and children. Thus was it a happy day for Jewett when he made his last flight, taking a Mustang from Digby to Molesworth, and recording in his log, "441 Squadron officially disbanded today. C'est la guerre." He had flown 682:45 hours, including 254:45 on Spitfires and 37:15 on Mustangs.

Back home, Arthur Jewett returned to university in Sackville. There he met a secretary, Joyce, whom he married in 1948. Life was not smooth sailing, however, for Jewett suffered psychologically and drank heavily. He quit school,

Arthur Jewett with RCAF Spitfire historian Robert Bracken at the 1998 CFPA. Arthur has a copy of Robert's book, *Spitfire: The Canadians*. Then, Arthur at home in Fredericton in 1999. (Larry and Stephanie Milberry)

but got involved with Alcoholics Anonymous and off the bottle. He worked in construction and eventually got on with New Brunswick Power, remained there to 1987. By 2003 he was a widower in Fredericton, busy with family life and in community affairs, especially fund-raising for charities. He still enjoyed his great pastime of fly fishing, only using one fly in his whole life - the Royal Coachman dry fly. Besides fishing, he still played the piano and skied (he always specified "downhill ... never cross country"). As to the booze, in August 2003 he reported, "On September 30 it will be 49 years since I have had one ounce of C2H5OH."

Arthur Jewett following his CF-18 flight with 441 Squadron CO, LCol Dave Burt. (441 Sqn)

In May 1997 Arthur Jewett was visiting his daughter in Cold Lake, where she was teaching. Word got around that there was an old Spitfire pilot on base. This reached the ear of LCol Dave Burt, CO of 441. Jewett was invited to visit his wartime squadron. LCol Burt had a sense of history. He appreciated the sacrifice that young men had made for Canada nearly 60 years earlier. It only seemed right to the CO that the old timer should see what the Silver Foxes were doing now. The best way to do that was to strap Arthur Jewett into a CF-18 Hornet and take him flying. That is what happened on June 3, 1997. Jewett spent 1:10 hours aloft that day in Hornet 188916 with LCol Burt as his personal tour guide.

Toronto Boy - Sidney Bregman

Born in Warsaw, Poland on April 9, 1922, Sidney Bregman came to Canada as an infant, then spent his boyhood in Toronto. Following his elementary education, he attended Central Technical School, taking the aeronautics option. Like many other "Central Tech" graduates, his first job was on the shop floor at de Havilland Canada, earning about 40 cents an hour. Meanwhile, he was taking flying lessons with Patterson and Hall Aircraft at Barker Field on Dufferin Street. In November 2002 his instructor, Vi Milstead (later an Air Transport Auxiliary pilot), checked her log. There she found that she had flown with Bregman several times between August 28 and October 13, 1941, mainly in Cub CF-BIT.

With war in the headlines and the grind at de Havilland less enticing by the day, Bregman decided to join the RCAF. Following ITS at Belleville, he was posted to 13 EFTS at St. Eugene in eastern Ontario. There he flew initially on September 1, 1942, going up in Fleet Finch 4543 with his instructor, Mr. Lewis. The course ended on October 23 with Bregman having logged 73:50 hours. Following some leave, he reported in at 2 SFTS at Uplands, where flying commenced on October 31 - a sortie with F/O Anderson in Harvard 3099. The typical course ensued, Bregman succeeding and earning his Wings after a final flight of February 15, 1943. By this time his log showed 229:00 hours on the Finch and Harvard.

Bregman now began fighter OTU at Bagotville. There he began with a series of Harvard "famil" flights, his first with F/L Merritt in FE504 on March 16, 1943. On the 28th his flight commander was happy enough with Bregman to send him on his first fighter sortie - 55 minutes in Hurricane 5647. There followed a flurry of sorties, whether low level, formation or instrument flying, practicing RT, aerobatics, air-to-air/air-to-ground gunnery, cine camera practice, climb-to-height sorties (as high as 25,000 feet), etc. On May 10, 1943 Bregman was finished at Bagotville. His OTU experience totalled 75:05 hours, 47:10 noted as on an "operational" type, i.e. the Hurricane. The Chief Flying Instructor, S/L L.G. Schwab, and Chief Instructor, W/C E.M. Reyno, were pleased with the results.

Wasting no time, the RCAF posted Bregman to 127 Squadron, an Eastern Air Command fighter unit at Gander under S/L P.A. "Pappy" Gilbertson. For Bregman, things began on June 5 with P/O Taylor showing him around the area in Harvard 2897. Three days later he flew the Hurricane, taking up 5496, then he easily slipped into the daily routines. For June

Sid Bregman as a 19-year old in the RCAF. He was on guard duty at Camp Borden, some months before beginning flight training. (Sid Bregman Col.)

Hurricanes beat up the Bagotville flightline at 1 (F) OTU. Converting to the Hurricane was a huge thrill for any young pilot. (CANAV Books Col.)

Sid Bregman with his favourite Spitfire "9G-Q", then views of "Queenie" at rest, and aimed towards the butts, having its cannons harmonized. (Sid Bregman Col.)

alone Bregman would log 50 sorties, 31 in the Hurricane for 27:25 hours, 29 in the Harvard for 23:00 hours. This was just great - a fellow got bags of flying in a challenging environment (weather-wise), and nobody was shooting at him!

On July 18, 1943 the squadron moved to Dartmouth, where all the usual sorties continued - dawn and dusk patrols, gunnery, army co-operation, GCI training, etc. Dartmouth for Bregman included one dicey event. Upon landing one day, he found that his brakes had failed. These worked by air pressure, of which Bregman had none. Rather than go off the end of the runway into a ditch, he turned onto a taxi way. Straight ahead, however, was a guard house. Just as the guard scampered to safety, the Hurricane demolished the little shack. Happily, all turned out well, with no one hurt and little damage to the Hurricane. Bregman's log shows his last flight with 127 as November 29, 1943. About this time the paperwork was underway that would close down the squadron, then revive it in the UK as 443 Squadron. The last 127 sortie was on December 14 - a dawn patrol by two Hurricanes.

January 13-20, 1944 Bregman was at "Y" Depot at RCAF Station Lachine (Montreal) awaiting entrainment for Halifax and embarkation overseas. The crossing was made, then all former 127 personnel on the draft reported to Bournemouth. In Bregman's case, he was there from February 1-12 awaiting orders. Next, he spent two months with 443 at Digby (later at Holmsley South). On February 24 at Digby he enjoyed his first Spitfire flight, taking up Mk.VB "BL319". P/O Bregman now was posted on some useless duties somewhere in the north but, when the train stopped in London, he and his travelling mate got off and visited RCAF HQ. There they pleaded their case - they wanted a decent posting. Some strings were pulled and they were diverted to 61 OTU at Rednal for the Spitfire OTU.

OTU ran from April 13, 1944 to June 11, by when Bregman had 65:00 hours on the "Spit", 2:05 on the Master. A few days then were spent at 1 TEU, then two days at 83 Group Support Unit at Bognor Regis. While a new pilot might spend some weeks in this TEU/GSU "holding pattern" awaiting a squadron, the invasion was underway, so Spitfire pilots were needed. Thus did P/O Bregman quickly join 441 Squadron at B.3. There he made a local flight on July 9 in Spitfire Mk.IXb "9C-S". On the 12th he flew his first operational sortie - 1:15 hours noted as "Patrol. Base - Courseulles. Uneventful." The sortie wasn't exactly "uneventful". Lead had taken Bregman down to strafe a rail target. As he clung tightly to Lead's wing, ack-ack came up. Then there was an explosion ahead, with rubble

thrown up. On returning to base, Bregman found a ding in his propeller spinner, slight damage from their strafing pass. Bregman flew three more sorties by day's end on the 12th.

What followed was usual for a young fighter pilot chalking up his sorties over Normandy. On July 18 Bregman made a log book notation: "2 Me.109s destroyed by F/Lt Mott and F/Lts Copeland and Johnstone". On an escort sortie of July 30 he noted, "700 bombers bomb area around Caumont". Next day Bregman noted, "Crossroad bombed. One staff car hit." In this way did the Allied tactical air war in Normandy proceed - launching hundreds of fighter sorties daily to pick off enemy targets one by one. For August 9 Bregman was on an air-sea rescue sortie, likely spotting for aircrew down in the Channel. Later that day he was on another do, strafing Seine barges. August 18 was busy - three sorties against tanks and roads jammed with MET. This would seem to have been the "shooting gallery" connected with the German break-out from the Falaise Gap. By day's end 144 Wing had accounted for some 200 MET destroyed. For August, F/L Bregman flew 31 times for 34:10 hours, 30:50 being on ops.

While on a sortie on September 27 around Nijmegen, F/L Bregman's engine quit. Realizing that his drop tank somehow had fallen away, he switched to his main tanks and the engine restarted. The CO then sent Bregman and his wingman back to base. Suddenly an Me.109 passed across Bregman's nose. Its pilot was not paying attention, so this was a gift - Bregman downed the enemy fighter, expending only 11 rounds in doing the job. On the 30th he had a squirt at an Me.262, but that was a typical engagement with the speedy jet - not much of a chance for a Spitfire.

On October 1 the squadron moved to Hawkinge, where the pace slowed. Most operations now were bomber escorts. On October 5, for example, Bregman was escorting Bostons to a target near Nijmegen. On the 14th he went to Duisberg in the Ruhr on Op. Hurricane, where 957 Lancasters, Halifaxes and Mosquitos bombed with devastating effect. On October 28 Bregman flew cover for the 733-bomber raid on Cologne. Such sorties were lengthy for a Spitfire - 2:15 hours for Nijmegen, 2:20 for Duisberg, 2:20 for Cologne. At one point during the October 28 sortie, 441 was in solid cloud. Each pilot was concentrating, keeping visual contact with another Spitfire left, right or ahead. Suddenly, Lead called that his flight instruments were inoperative - his pitot tube had frozen. Lead poured on power and left the formation, which then split every which way. Bregman, for his part, dove quickly under the cloud. At first he was disoriented, then was relieved when he spotted the Canadian war memorial at Vimy Ridge. Next, he spotted a squadron of Spitfires heading home. He cautiously formed up with them, and returned to base.

Bad weather obliged 441 to recover at Brussels on December 8, after escorting Lancasters. After refuelling, they flew to B.67 Ursel near the Belgian coast. Arriving back from town in the morning, the pilots found their aircraft covered in snow. It was up to the pilots to do their own snow clearing, then they fired up. No one had informed them, however, about cold-weather starts. Thus, no sooner were the fellows airborne, than all were complaining of oil splashing back to obscure windscreens. Back everyone went to clean up the mess and try again. It all panned out, the flight reaching Hawkinge the next day.

On December 24 Bregman escorted bombers striking airfields at Düsseldorf and Essen. Four days later 441 began their "rest" in the Shetlands. For January, Bregman flew only seven trips (5:20 hours); for February, seven (4:30). March, however, when his flight moved to Skaebrae, saw flying increase, Bregman logging 35 sorties for 27 hours. On March 15 he flew four times, e.g. "Flight formation, land at Wick". Practice dive-bombing with 250-pound bombs was included in this period.

On April 3 the squadron was back at Hawkinge, Bregman flying his first operation that month on the 7th - a 1:55-hour trip escorting 15 Lancasters from 617 Squadron and two Mosquitos from 5 Group bombing shipping at Ijmuiden, Holland. On some of these ops Bregman was astounded by the sight of heavy flak bursting nearby. For a moment the sky would seem full of black smoke, with shrapnel flying every which way. On April 10, 441 positioned to B.90 Petit Brogel from where, next day, it covered 100 Halifaxes, 14 Lancasters and 8 Mosquitos bombing railway yards at Bayreuth, a city to the northeast of Nürnberg. At 2:50 hours, this was Bregman's longest Spitfire sortie. A similar operation was flown on April 16, when 441 positioned to B.86 Helmond, in order to escort bombers on the 18th. The target that day was the port, town and airfield on Heligoland, an island off the southwest Danish coast. This was one of Bomber Command's last big raids (969 bombers). Heligoland was plastered, but only three Halifaxes were lost - a sure sign that Germany was on its knees. This op turned out to be the last of the war for F/L Sid Bregman.

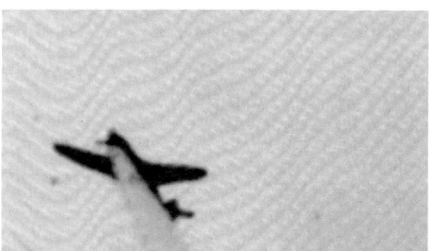

The moment of truth - gun camera film of the Me.109 falling to Sid Bregman and "9G-Q" on September 27, 1944. (Sid Bregman Col.)

By now people on 441 were wondering how soon they could get home. On May 12, the squadron joined in a mass "Victory Sweep" over the Channel Isles, and on the 23rd made its last move, returning to Digby. May was quiet for Bregman, with only 12 flights for 10:05 hours. Of special note, his flight of May 30 in "9G-Q" was his last of the war in a Spitfire. He had logged 264:40 Spitfire hours, 110:15 on ops. Next day he flew Mustang III "9G-Y", his first experience on type.

The Mustang now took over at 441. The squadron put up a good show of flying through June and July, including Victory flypasts. On July 6 Bregman had a pleasant flight in the squadron Auster. He flew the Mustang III 28 times in July for 23:20 hours then, on July 30, flew Mustang IV "Y2-T" of 442 Squadron for 50 minutes. With that his wartime flying was over. His log book showed 817:15 hours on all types. Bregman now left England for home, sailing from Southampton aboard the *Empress of Britain*. The ship came up the St. Lawrence to disembark its passengers at Quebec City, from where they entrained for Montreal and Toronto. At one of these points Bregman almost got run over while crossing the street - he wasn't re-acclimatized to traffic moving in the left lane!

Bregman soon enrolled in the School of Architecture at the University of Toronto. Graduated in 1951, he went into partnership, the firm becoming Bregman and Hamann. It grew to have nearly 200 employees and counted among its projects such Toronto skyline features as the Toronto Dominion Centre, Eaton Centre, and First Canadian Place. Sid Bregman retired in 1985, although he never lost his interest in aviation and occasionally flew a light plane. Otherwise, he was an avid sailor and lover of art. His interest in architecture also remained strong. In November 2002 he addressed the graduating class in architecture at the University of Toronto.

In the early 1990s Sid Bregman heard that Spitfire MJ627 ("9G-Q") was being restored in England by Maurice Bayliss. He arranged for a visit to see his favourite old 441 mount, the one in which he had shot down his Me.109. Then, on March 5, 1997 he and his friend Anthony Jurak were visiting Bartow Airport near Tampa, Florida in Jurak's T-28. While there they met Harry Stenger, whose company had restored a two-seat Spitfire. Bregman happened to show Stenger his log book. Stenger, astounded at seeing such an authentic bit of Spitfire history, invited Bregman to fly in Spitfire PT462. Thus, half a century after his 441 Squadron tour, Sid Bregman again enjoyed that thrill of flying the magnificent Spitfire.

Sid Bregman, Service Record

Unit	From	To
13 EFTS, St. Eugene, Ontario	1-9-42	3-10-42
2 SFTS, Uplands	25-10-42	19-2-43
1 (F) OTU, Bagotville	14-3-43	14-4-43
127 Sqn, Gander	4-6-43	17-7-43
127 Sqn, Dartmouth	17-7-43	23-12-43
"Y" Depot, Lachine, Quebec	13-1-44	20-1-44
3 PRC, Bournemouth, UK	1-2-44	12-2-44
443 Sqn, Digby, UK	12-2-44	12-3-44
443 Sqn, Holmsley South, UK	12-3-44	12-4-44
61 OTU, Rednal, UK	12-4-44	15-6-44
1 TEU, Tealing, UK	16-6-44	3-7-44
83 GSU, Bognar Regis, UK	4-7-44	7-7-44
441 Sqn, B.3 Ste-Croix-sur-Mer, France	8-7-44	19-7-44
B.11 Longues, France	19-7-44	13-8-44
B.19 Lingèvres, France	13-8-44	2-9-44
B.40 Beauvais/Nivillers, France	2-9-44	5-9-44
B.52 Douai, France	5-9-44	17-9-44
B.70 Antwerp, Belgium	17-9-44	30-9-44
Hawkinge, UK	30-9-44	31-12-44
Sumburgh, Shetland Islands	31-12-44	4-3-45
Skeabrae, Orkney Islands	4-3-45	2-4-45
Hawkinge, UK	3-4-45	30-4-45
Hunsdon, UK	30-4-45	17-5-45
Digby, UK	17-5-45	14-7-45
Molesworth, UK	14-7-45	8-8-45

Sid Bregman in the cockpit of PT462 in May 1997. (Sid Bregman Col.)

Sid Bregman's Album

In the spring of 1945, 441 traded its beloved Spitfires for Mustangs, some of which were camouflaged, others in natural finish. (Sid Bregman Col.)

From "square one" it was the erks who made operations possible - not a prop could turn without them. In RCAF fashion, they could look like a rough-and-ready bunch. (Sid Bregman Col.)

F/L H.E. Derraugh, S/L R.H. Walker (CO) and F/O J.A. McIntosh with one of their new Mustangs. (CF PL45121)

Sid Bregman enjoying a beer with two local lassies, while 441 was at Hawkinge. Then Moira Thompson, a girlfriend, who was a Royal Navy WREN. (Sid Bregman Col.)

Spitfire squadrons often had a little Auster to buzz around on business or pleasure. Here, F/L Bregman poses with 441's Auster LB327. Built in 1942, it survived the war, being struck off RAF strength in May 1946. (Sid Bregman Col.)

Taken during leave in London - an airman's souvenir snapshots. (Sid Bregman Col.)

Some 441 fellows (Dewar left, Bregman right) show off a manly-looking motorcycle. (Sid Bregman Col.)

Sid Bregman sailed home aboard the *Empress of Britain*. Here is the great liner on a postcard of the day. Then, the deck with a mob of Canadian "vets" anxious to get back on home soil. Finally, the view of Quebec from the ship. (Sid Bregman Col.)

P/O Alex Graham with his 441 Spitfire "Pam" - Pam was the young RAF WAF code and cipher officer, whom he met and later married at Digby (inset). A Regina boy, Graham joined the RCAF in 1941. Following EFTS at Regina and SFTS at Yorkton, he earned his Wings and was posted overseas. He began on Spitfires with 91 Squadron at Hawkinge then, in October 1942, joined 411 at Digby. On a training sortie from there on January 28, 1943 he collided with another Spitfire, which took off his tail. The second machine, piloted by P/O G.F. Brown of Toronto, crashed fatally, but Graham was able to bail out with injuries. In March 1943 he joined 402 Squadron, where he completed 59 operational sorties, before being posted to 441 in March 1944. Here he completed 35 "ops" until injured on June 12. On this occasion he was taking off on the wire mesh runway surface at Ford, when a tire blew and his Spitfire somersaulted. Graham was rushed to hospital, where X-rays showed grave spinal fractures. The remedy was a vertebrae fusion, followed by six months in a body cast - Graham's flying days were done. Back home, he studied medicine at the University of Western Ontario, from where he graduated in 1950. Henceforth, he practiced in St. Thomas, Ontario until 1993. (Graham Col.)

Legacy

A squadron's heritage hangs on the quality of its people. In the case of the Silver Foxes, some members served from 125's inception to its disbandment as 441. These individuals provided a solid foundation to the squadron, and were role models for any new people joining it. Others contributed only for a tour, then left to bolster another squadron, to instruct at OTU, etc. Others, through no choice of their own, served only briefly. In the case of C.A. "Alex" Graham, after many operations on 402 and 411 squadrons, he reached 441 just before D-Day. He would not complete a 441 normal tour. Instead, he suffered grave injuries on crash-landing a few days after D-Day. Then there were the irrevocable losses - the eleven 125 and 441 pilots who died fighting and in accidents. The sum of all such stories constitutes the 125/441 wartime legacy.

Harry Pattinson

Focusing upon individual members helps illustrate how 441's rich heritage came about. F/L Harry Pattinson's story is that of a young man emerging from the Great Depression, getting into flying, cutting his teeth at 125 Squadron, carrying his experience overseas, then continuing to serve Canada in the postwar era. Born in Hamilton on March 25, 1917, as a boy Pattinson was fascinated by aviation. No doubt he visited Jack Elliot's old airfield along the Hamilton beach, bicycling or hiking there. While still in his teens, he was hanging out at the new municipal airport where, in 1938, he joined the Hamilton Aero Club. On September 18 he took his first flying lesson, going up with chief club instructor Ernie Taylor in J-2 Cub CF-BHR. He soloed in the same Cub on February 5, 1939 and, on April 21, earned Canadian private pilot licence #2986.

With the war, most recreational flying ceased, so pilots like Harry Pattinson had to busy themselves with school or at their jobs. In most cases, however, they soon got into the war effort. That usually began with a visit to the RCAF recruiting office. In Pattinson's case he beat most fellows into uniform - he had joined Hamilton-based 119 (Aux) Squadron before war broke out. At that time 119 became a coastal squadron, and Pattinson entered the BCATP training stream. Following RCAF indoctrination, he was posted to 1 EFTS at Malton, near Toronto. There, on December 18, 1940, Mr. T. Evans took him aloft in Fleet Finch 4413 on his first instructional trip.

Being experienced on light aircraft, it is no surprise that Pattinson soloed the next day. He finished his course on January 28, 1941, having logged 54:45 hours on the Finch. Now he was posted to 1 SFTS at Camp Borden where, on February 20, Sgt Wesley H. McIntosh took him flying in Yale 3371. He soloed on the 24th, then carried on to April 16, by when he had logged 139:35 hours on Yales and Harvards.

Pattinson left 1 SFTS on April 27 with an "Average" rating, and was posted to Rockcliffe to fly Grumman Goblins at 118 (F)

Harry Pattinson as a sprog LAC learning to fly in Hamilton. Then, his membership card, signed by club treasurer E.B. Hale (later G/C Hale, Station Commander at North Luffenham in 441 days). (Pattinson Col.)

Squadron. (By this time, however, it was clear that the biplane Goblin was useless as a fighter. Oddly, in a scam of a decision that only could have been made in Ottawa, 15 of these 200-mph clunkers had been purchased in 1940. Meanwhile, no combatant in the "real war" was flying anything less than a 300+mph Hurricane or Me.109!) At Rockcliffe, Pattinson first flew a Goblin on May 13, 1941. His squadron now moved to Dartmouth, Pattinson ferrying Goblin 345 there via Mont Joli on July 21. Happily, 118 quickly converted to the Curtiss Kittyhawk. Pattison first flew this type (aircraft 815) on November 11, 1941. Life at 118 centred mainly around coastal patrols, seeing off and greeting convoys, troopships and warships; exercising with coastal artillery units; and doing weather checks and fighter affiliation (a typical sortie of January 25, 1942 was logged as "Harbour entrance recce").

For his entry of March 10, 1942 Pattinson wrote: "No.2 F/S Isralson crashed into Bedford Basin in heavy snow storm and was killed". The death of the 21-year old from Hanley, Saskatchewan would have smitten everyone at 118 Squadron, but such a loss was a brutal fact of life in 1942. Pattinson's Kittyhawk flight of April 24 would be his last at 118. The squadron was preparing to deploy to Alaska, and some of its veteran pilots were being posted to help establish new Home War Establishment fighter squadrons from Tofino to St. John's. Pattinson soon got word that he would join 125 Squadron. He flew first there in Harvard 3337 on April 29. Soon, ex-RAF Hurricane Is were being test flown and 125 was in business. For this period, Pattinson's log shows Hurricane Is 1352 - '55, '57 - '60, '62, '63, '75 and '77.

Anticipating 125's role in the U-boat war, Pattinson flew Lysander 451 on May 21: "Practice with full load, 2 x 250 lb depth charges, 2 sea markers and a rear gunner [Sgt MacDonald]". Pattinson led the way to Torbay on June 14, arriving in Harvard 3337. The pilots were elated to hear that they soon would re-equip with Hurricane Mk.XIIs. Pattinson took up his first (No.5484) on November 8, 1942, a 55-minute test flight. His log thereafter shows Mk.XIIs 5482, '84, '85, '90, '93, '95, 5501 and '02. A sortie of March 11, 1943 in 5490 was his first carrying 2 x 250-lb depth charges. On March 27 he was flying 5495 on a search for Harvard FE525 (it isn't known to where FE525 had wandered, but records show that it survived the war).

After 72:15 hours in the Goblin and 115:00 in the Kittyhawk, F/L Pattinson was deemed to be "tour expired" at 125 and was posted overseas. At this time S/L Norris endorsed his log, "Above the average". No doubt there was a great thrash in the mess to honour Pattinson's leaving. Hangovers having subsided, 125 soon returned to work while, on April 2, 1943, F/L Pattinson boarded a USAAF B-24 Liberator (No.124326, aircraft commander 1Lt Buckingham) at Torbay. They flew to Gander, then stopped at Goose Bay and Presque Isle (Maine), before letting off Pattinson on the 4th in New York. From there he embarked for the UK. His next log book entry is for a June 15, 1943 flight with 403 Squadron in Miles Master DL782. This was at RAF Kenley with F/O Bob Middlemiss.

Four days later Pattinson flew 403's "KH-X" for an hour - his first Spitfire flight. On July 8 he noted: "Rodeo 242. St. Valery - LeHavre - Etretat. 1:25, first operational flight. No Huns sighted." Pattinson was in the "real" war at last. At 403 he came to know some of the RCAF's finest airmen, typical being his CO, S/L F.E. Grant, and Malta veterans F/L Bob Middlemiss and F/L Noel Ogilvie. Frequent "Rodeos" were conducted (sweeps over enemy territory looking for any sort of action), but there also were "Ramrods", raids usually by medium bombers on cross-Channel targets. The Spitfires were along to fend off enemy fighters. On a Ramrod of September 6, 1943 Pattinson had to land at Friston when he ran low on fuel - he had

Goblins at Mont Joli, Quebec, while 118 was moving from Rockcliffe to the East Coast on July 15, 1941. Then, "Pattinson's Folly" - the Goblin that he belly landed at Dartmouth. (Pattinson Col.)

four gallons after shutting down. He also notes this day: "110 Fort crews pulled out of Channel in about 2 hours. Short of gas and ditched. Stuttgart raid."

F/L Pattinson flew his last 403 sortie on September 27. It had been a brief tour - 27 ops for 39:25 hours. Next, he was posted to India, sailing on the SS *Strathmore* on October 25. Off France their convoy was attacked by the Luftwaffe, but Pattinson's ship escaped. He later noted in his diary, "We landed OK in Bombay on 26/11/43." What went on in those two months likely could fill a chapter. Pattinson now joined 10 Squadron, Indian Air Force. Beginning on December 22, he was flying Hurricanes and Harvards, mostly training and often moving base. In November 1944 he joined 67 Squadron at Comilla, near Dacca. Here he first flew the Spitfire on December 11, 1944. From now on he was busy with daily combat along the Burma coast. Typical of his log book entries is that of December 24: "Took off from Cox's [Cox's Bazaar]. Shot up a launch and a couple of bashas [huts] on the way home. Destroyed or damaged a couple of M-boats. Landed with 3 gals. gas." For January 9, 1945 he notes an air-sea rescue Walrus shot down, and six Japanese Oscar fighters over his base. On January 17 his task was to escort Lord Louis Mountbatten and his party, who were flying around Burma in tiny L-5 utility planes. They landed late: "Erks held lights for us and jeeps on runway. 1:40". Of 18 Spitfire sorties flown by Pattinson in March, 15 were operational.

On April 14, 1945 Pattinson was forced down in a rice paddy, when his "jet tank" stopped feeding. He flew his last of 80 India-Burma operations on April 27. On July 26 he sailed from Calcutta aboard the SS *Carthage*, docking in Southampton on August 13. F/L Pattinson came home in September aboard the SS *Nieu Amsterdam*. The ship, carrying 7900 returning Canadians, docked in Halifax on September 9, 1945. Pattinson now was posted to Centralia as a test pilot. There he met Lynne McLeod, a young RCAF WD. They soon married. Other postings came to Aylmer and Rockcliffe, where Pattinson flew with the Experimental and Proving Establishment. There his tasks included acceptance flying on North Stars and experimental aerial survey work with a modified Canso. By 1953 Pattinson was at St. Hubert, where he first flew the Vampire on June 8. Later, he served with the Toronto reserve squadrons on Sabres and T-33s. Beginning in 1958 he had a ground tour at the radar site in Foymount, Ontario. A NORAD tour at Syracuse, NY came next. During this time he kept up his flying on the T-29 and T-33. In 1964 he retired from the RCAF, his last flight being with F/L Marr in T-33 21373 on February 17, 1964. By this time S/L Pattinson's log book showed experience in a wide range of aircraft including: Finch - 89:05 hours, Canso - 91:30, T-33 - 194:45, Expeditor - 239:05, Spitfire - 267:05, Hurricane - 331:50, Harvard - 660:35. Upon retirement, Harry and Lynne Pattinson took up farming in the Ottawa Valley. One of Harry's joys now was attending 125/441 Squadron, or Canadian Fighter Pilots Association, reunions. There he was revered by all as the flight commander from Torbay who had led by example, and taught his pilots to survive in the worst of weather.

Spitfire LV675 "R-RD" of 67 Squadron was flown in combat in India-Burma by F/L Pattinson. Here it is ready for action, then somewhat bent, with the pilot wondering what's next! (Pattinson Col.)

Lynne McLeod and Pat Pattinson enjoying an evening out at Toronto's Royal York Hotel in 1945. As a WD, Lynne was a member of the RCAF Women's Precision Drill Team, renowned at events around North America. (Pattinson Col.)

Death of a Fighter Pilot

As soon as a pilot went missing, a telegram would be dispatched to his next-of-kin. Next, his personal effects would be gathered. These would be sent with an inventory to an RAF Central Depository for safe-keeping. Meanwhile, the missing man's CO would compose a letter to concerned family members, striving for truth without brutality, and sympathy without banality. On July 8, 1944, for example, S/L Brannagan wrote to Mrs. W.R. Chowen, then living in Agincourt, Ontario.

Before you receive this letter you will have been informed by RCAF Overseas Headquarters that your husband, J.26678 F/O W.R. Chowen has been reported missing in action.

Bill took off with the rest of the squadron on an armed reconnaissance over enemy territory on July 5, 1944 but, unfortunately, did not return to base. The squadron encountered a considerable number of enemy aircraft of which at least seven were destroyed. Bill was seen diving after an enemy aircraft and, during the engagement which followed, he was seen to collide with his opponent. Part of the wing was torn off and his aircraft was seen to fall earthwards. However, in view of the fact that the engagement continued, it was impossible to see whether he baled out or not.

Your husband was a particularly popular member of 441 Squadron. as well as of the entire Airfield. His readiness to join in the various activities of the Officers' Mess made him many friends and his loss will be greatly felt here.

His personal effects have been carefully collected and forwarded to R.A.F. Central Depository where they will be held until better news is obtained or, in any case, for a minimum of six months before being forwarded to you.

May I now express the great sympathy which all of us feel with you at this anxious time, and you can rest assured that, if any news of your husband is obtained, we shall get in touch with you immediately.

The inventory of Chowen's belongings was numbing in its detail. Apart from uniform items, it included the contents of his toilet case - tweezers, a cigarette case, razor kit, commando razor kit, two combs, a shaving brush, spool of thread, message note book, Waterman's pen and pencil, breviary, scissors, a nail file, diary, two packs of playing cards. Also itemized were his silk scarves (2), handkerchiefs (3), and towels (5). Other items were "one photo of Mrs. Chowen" and "one photo album with snaps", a clock and a pipe.

Although not intended to describe operations, the letters of condolences could sometimes relate inspiring events to comfort the next of kin. S/L Walker had two similar notes to compose on September 28 - to a widow and to a mother. That to Barney Boe's wife was typical:

In the afternoon of September 25, 1944, nine of our aircraft took off on an operational patrol over enemy territory. During the patrol a large number of enemy aircraft, on their way to attack a very important target, were intercepted. In the dog fight that followed the enemy aircraft were forced to jettison their bombs and, through the heroism of these pilots, a major victory was won. Our aircraft became separated during the conflict, and so it was impossible to see what happened to all our men. However, a number of enemy aircraft were destroyed. Unfortunately your husband did not return to this base and up to the time of writing no word has been received from him.

Some families were contacted more than once. Sgt Gilbert Brochu went missing on June 6, 1944. The customary letter went out the next day, but he was safe, soon returned to the squadron and was commissioned. When he went missing again on October 28, S/L Walker suggested that he might simply have lost his way, leaving room for hope, but this time it was final. Brochu's brother, Leopold, had been visiting the squadron at the time, and personally handled Gilbert's effects.

Sometimes a letter was more encouraging. W/C J.E. Johnson, writing on April 27, 1944 to Mrs. G.U. Hill, could report that her husband had been seen to land in a large field and walk away from the aircraft "without apparent injury". On August 17 W/C Page could assure Mrs. Brannagan that her son had landed behind enemy lines and probably was a POW. When the news was bad, however, there was no doubting the grief at home. Some of it came back to the officers who wrote those sympathetic letters. Families tried to put on brave faces. Alex McDonald had gone missing once during the summer, then turned up. When he went missing again on October 28, the family and the squadron hoped for another happy ending. McDonald's mother, Ellen, wrote, "Alex was so happy with you all and so keen on flying that we shall always feel he had his wish in getting overseas at last granted."

Yet some would suffer anguish almost unimaginable to those who have never had to deal with such tragedies. Mrs. Ina McMillan of Windsor, Ontario, mother of Osman, may have lacked eloquence, but her heartfelt letter to S/L Walker in November 1944 was a *cri de coeur* for a generation of families scarred by a war fought thousands of miles away:

I have just received your letter of September 28th and I have been expecting a letter from some members of the squadron ever since I received the telegram from Ottawa September 30th notifying me about Oz's death, which came as an awful blow to his sisters and myself. It's terrible, makes one wonder if there's any justice when a clean living and decent boy like Oz is cut down like that. I've tried to make myself believe it just couldn't be true. Ottawa makes so many mistakes; they said Oz was buried in Molenbrock, Holland. When my other son was killed, they gave us a different place of his burial, but his Wing Commander had written us and gave us all the particulars and the correct place of his burial and my relations visited his grave. I am sure you have given me Oz's correct resting place, for I really want to bring his body home and, if I can't, I'll have his body taken to England and buried beside his brother. That's what Oz and I agreed on before he went overseas. If anything should happen to him, and they found his body, he was to be brought home or else buried beside his brother. So please write and tell me if you saw my boy after he was killed and tell me just what he was like, and don't hide anything from me. I can take it and I won't tell his sisters if it's too bad, but we do want to bring him home. You see, Oz was the youngest in the family and we loved him very deeply. I can hardly believe I'll never see my happy Oz again. His father just died shortly before Oz went overseas, so he left home with a heavy heart. We had so much sorrow the past three years. I've had four deaths in the family. Oz was my last hope and I was so built up on his return. I'm heart broken, he meant so much to his sisters and I. My other son was on his return trip from Bremen, Germany when he was brought down over the English coast, a mistake in the heavy fog, his 19th trip. Please answer and tell me all you can about how Oz was after he was killed. God bless you and keep you safe.

Osman's brother, FSgt Alexander T. McMillan, had died with 408 Squadron on October 21, 1941. He is buried in Nottinghamshire. Walker could not give Mrs. McMillan the assurances she sought about repatriating her son's body. McMillan still lies in Holland, separated from his brother by narrow seas, and from his family by an ocean and half a continent.

CHAPTER 6
Decorations and Heraldry

From time to time Canadian military personnel were singled out for honours and awards. Everyone, of course, qualified for certain medals - the Canadian Volunteer Service Medal was accorded to every man and woman who voluntarily joined Canada's forces, with a Maple Leaf clasp added if they served overseas. The more visible honours, however, were limited, regulated and the subject of considerable paperwork.

Canadians received British decorations in accordance with policies and procedures stated by the British Air Ministry and related organizations. Other than the Victoria Cross and George Cross, which could be awarded posthumously, for most other decorations a recipient had to be alive when recommended. To this general rule there were two exceptions - Mentions in Dispatches (an honour signified not by a medal but by an Oak Leaf on the 1939-45 Star), and some foreign awards.

The distribution of honours worked on a quota system. Most gallantry awards involved Bomber Command, which also had the heaviest losses. By 1944 a Distinguished Flying Cross or Distinguished Flying Medal was awarded for every 100 operational hours flown by Bomber Command. That meant that if a Lancaster squadron flew 1000 hours in a month, ten men could be recommended for "gongs" such as the DFC. In other commands the criterion was different. For Fighter Command and 2 TAF it was one decoration for every 300 operational hours.

A decoration began with a recommendation drafted by a flight commander or squadron CO. Sometimes the task was delegated to the squadron adjutant. The recommendation went up through the chain of command, where it might be re-written, edited, sometimes sent back, and finally passed to an Air Ministry Committee in London that made the final cut. The King usually rubber-stamped the results, which were then formally announced in the *London Gazette*. In the case of RCAF personnel, parallel publication in the Canada Gazette was routine. Once a man had been awarded a DFC, he was entitled to wear the ribbon. The medal came later, sometimes at a Royal investiture with King George VI pinning on the gong. Many received their awards from less lofty people - senior officers, Governors-General, etc. Hundreds chose simply to receive their medals by mail.

Between the deed and the final reward lay considerable paper - "staff work" at its most personal. A case in point is F/O Boyd W. Dunning of 441 Squadron. S/L Walker first recommended him for a DFC on October 31, 1944, then followed through with another submission on November 9. Walker went into much detail describing Dunning's work which, to that date, had run to

This officer, as 2 i/c of his Flight, has just completed his second tour of operations against the enemy. In spite of being persistently aggressive in the air, he has no credited score, but by pure guts and determination has attacked the enemy whenever he could be found. His first tour was completed from Malta as an NCO in 1942 and from where he did sweeps, rhubarbs and dive bombing into Sicily. He did patrol and protected the Malta convoys. On one occasion was attacked and hit by four Me.109s, but through superior airmanship did shake them off and land safely at Malta. He returned to England and joined this squadron just before "D" Day and did 25 hours protective cover over the beach head in the first few days. He then dive bombed and strafed the enemy from Normandy to Holland, destroying or damaging 25 enemy transport. During his two tours he had participated in 193 sorties against the enemy and has always shown great courage and determination in pressing home his attacks, in spite of heavy opposition.

B.W. "Curly" Dunning, MiD, taps a potable water tanker. Above is his CO's rejected DFC recommendation. (UK13328)

243 operational hours on 193 sorties (92 patrols, 36 sweeps, 29 armed recces, 17 scrambles, 8 escorts, 6 dive bombing missions, and 5 "Rhubarbs"). He also had 15 enemy vehicles destroyed and 10 damaged.

The recommendation seems to have been turned back, but on November 23, only two weeks after the previous submission, Walker was sending off yet another, repeating much of the above, but adding comments that Dunning's leadership and experience had been "an inspiration to the junior pilots." After more than a month, with no sign of an award, another submission went forward (January 7, 1945). The Station Commander at Skaebrae may have undermined Walker when he wrote on the document, "I am unable to confirm the operational record of this pilot, as his first tour was completed in Malta." In the end, Dunning received recognition in more modest form - the *London Gazette* of June 14, 1945 reported that he was MiD.

Walker was equally persistent in getting a DFC for F/O Donald H. Kimball. The first submission (unsuccessful) was dated August 30, 1944, at which time Kimball had flown 94 sorties (122:30 hours), had four enemy aircraft destroyed in the air, one damaged on the ground, plus numerous ground targets damaged. Walker wrote: "This officer has displayed on his brief tour of operations from April 1944 exceptional keenness in leading his section into and destroying the Bosh whenever he could be found. His achievements are exceptional and his future bright. I strongly recommend the immediate award of the Distinguished Flying Cross."

Walker tried again, putting recommendations forward on October 31 and November 25. The latter document now credited Kimball with 148 operational hours and 115 sorties (51 patrols, 31 armed recces, 16 sweeps, 7 dive bombing missions, 4 escorts, 3 scrambles, 2 Roadsteads, and 1 Ramrod). His score was even more impressive than when first described - 6 enemy aircraft destroyed in the air, 1 damaged on the ground, 1 locomotive damaged, 9 vehicles destroyed and 24 damaged. The CO wrote:

As a section leader in "A" Flight, F/O Kimball has shown on all occasions exceptional keenness to seek out and destroy the enemy. On March 28, 1944 he attacked Dreux aerodrome in the face of heavy flak and damaged a Ju.88. In July, whilst covering the invasion operations, he destroyed four enemy aircraft over the beach head. On September 25, 1944, while on patrol over Nijmegen Bridge, with orders to protect the same at all cost, the squadron intercepted 50 plus enemy aircraft proceeding to attack the bridge. In the fight that ensued, this officer, though alone and having been hit in the petrol tank by cannon fire, continued to engage the enemy and destroyed two Me.109s. He retired only when, having fired all his ammunition, shortage of petrol forced him down at a forward base.

This officer, in a short period of operations, has proved a fine leader and is definitely Flight Commander material. F/O Kimball now has six enemy aircraft destroyed in the air, one damaged on the ground, and 33 enemy road transport destroyed. In view of the above achievements, I strongly recommend the immediate award of the Distinguished Flying Cross.

On December 29, 1944 the London Gazette announced that F/O Kimball had been awarded the DFC:

During his tour of operations this officer has displayed exceptional keenness and determination. As a section leader he has taken part in numerous patrols, armed reconnaissances and fighter sorties. He has destroyed four enemy aircraft in the air and one on the ground in addition to much enemy road and rail transport. Flying Officer Kimball has shown himself to be an outstanding fighter whose achievements against the enemy have been brilliant.

Scrutiny of the documents leaves one wondering about just when the award was approved, and which submission brought it about. The published citation mentioned destruction of "four enemy aircraft in the air and one on the ground". Yet, Walker's final submission had updated Kimball's score to six and one. It appears that, somewhere along the way, a clerk had forwarded the original recommendation of August 30 (converting the Ju.88 damaged on the ground on March 28, 1944 into a "destroyed") and had overlooked Walker's submissions of October 31 and November 25! Kimball ultimately chose to receive his DFC by mail in March 1949.

Squadron Emblem

Sooner or later squadrons were informed that they should get themselves a proper badge and motto, to be duly approved by the Royal College of Heralds (i.e. the Chester Herald). Most squadrons took this seriously. Others did not - until rudely advised otherwise. No.441 Squadron appears to have treated the subject seriously enough, but did not address it until after the intensive summer and autumn of 1944.

The squadron badge approved in December 1945 by the King and Chester Herald. (441 Sqn)

There was time enough for such matters once they returned to England. Surviving correspondence between the squadron and the College of Heralds in October and November 1944 show some of the problems in choosing a suitable symbol. An Indian's head was in contention, but 421 Squadron had already been offered that. A husky dog was considered, but 437 Squadron already had pre-empted that one. On December 9, 1944, 441 wrote to the Chester Herald, "This squadron has tentatively chosen the 'Silver Fox' for its name", and forwarded two sketches for a proposed badge. Subsequent correspondence demonstrates the problems of communications between specialists in different fields. On December 13 the Royal College of Heralds wrote:

> Thank you for your letter of the 9th of December telling us that you would like a silver fox's mask as a Badge.
>
> We could show the head couped or erased at the shoulder and I shall have a rough sketch made showing the Badge in a rather more heraldic treatment than that adopted in your sketch.
>
> Will you please let me know your reasons for selecting a silver fox, as I always give these when putting Badges for approval. Are you nicknamed the Silver Fox Squadron?

The 441 adjutant, F/L Frank A. Ruggle, writing on behalf of the CO, replied on the 19th:

> Your suggestion as to whether the badge should be couped or erased at the shoulders is not completely understood and it would be appreciated if you could do a rough sketch of each for approval.
>
> The Silver Fox is a national wild animal of Canada and the squadron would use the nick-name of the Silver Fox Squadron.

The heraldic terms "couped" and "erased" were puzzling, but matters began to jell on February 2, 1945 when the Chester Herald returned two sketches for a proposed badge, one showing the fox in profile and one "affrontee" (facing outwards). S/L Walker replied, favouring the latter design, but suggesting that the hair on the throat be shortened, the animal appearing too shaggy for a proper fox. He also advised the Chester Herald that the motto "Stalk and Kill" had been chosen. The latter acknowledged this information, and, with the agreement of diverse parties, including RCAF Overseas HQ and the King himself, approval was a matter of course.

Eloi Bohemier was born in St. Norbert, Manitoba on December 1, 1923. His parents Jean-Marie and Florida later moved to Ste-Anne, where the 12 Bohemier children were raised. Eloi proved to be a sharp-minded boy, playing guitar, clarinet and accordion, painting in watercolours, and excelling in sports. With the war, he and brothers Celestin, Eulace and Lionel all joined the RCAF. In 1973 Manitoba named some 4200 provincial geographical points for its war dead. One of these is Lake Bohemier, named in Eloi's honour, and found in the Cormorant Lake region. (via Fabiana Bohemier)

Winding Down

Years after the war, Bruce MacKenzie expressed some final thoughts about his time with 125/441 Squadron:

> My 131st and final operational flight, led by a Belgian wing commander, was over the Heinbach Dam area on December 8, 1944. On returning, we refuelled at Brussels. From there we took off for Hawkinge, but had to land at Brugge on account of bad weather. We counted our blessings, for who knows what awaited us had we tried pushing through. Next morning we were able to leave, but not before cleaning 12 inches of heavy snow off our wings.
>
> After Christmas 441 was posted to the Orkneys, but I was left to watch as the boys departed - I had completed my tour. No Orkneys for me and I was grateful. Instead, I went on leave up to Edinburgh, but did not stay where I had indicated on my travel orders. Thus, when I returned to Hawkinge, I was reamed out to no end. Instead of embarking for Canada early in January, I was banished to an operational training station. There I bumped into F/L Prizer, an American who had been with us on 125.
>
> On this sojourn I got re-acquainted with the Hurricane, then I heard that all experienced fighter pilots were being held in the UK on account of the Battle of the Bulge. Next I spent six weeks at Catfoss flying Spitfires on a pilot gunnery instructors course. Once graduated, we all would become instructors training pilots being sent to the Far East to finish off Japan.
>
> Finally, my leave home came through and I sailed aboard the SS Ranchi, a converted merchant ship with its hold crammed with East Indians. On May 8, while we were in mid-Atlantic, word came of the fall of Germany. We all hoped that this news also had reached the German U-boats still lurking about. We received a tumultuous welcome upon sailing into Halifax harbour. From here we boarded trains for the trip across Canada.

Pilots of 125 Squadron fame meet in Ottawa in 1980: Bob Hayes, Guy Mott, Jack Boyle, Pat Pattinson and Sten Lundberg. (Pattinson Col.)

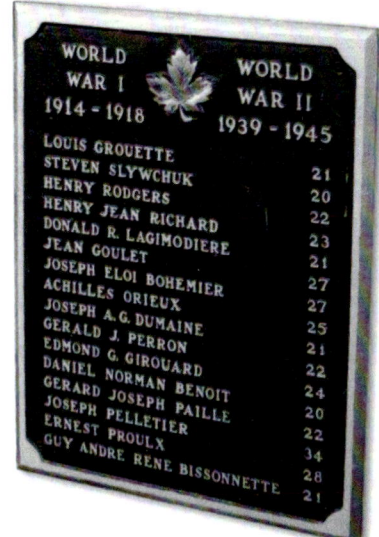

The plaque commemorating the young men of Ste-Anne, Manitoba, who were lost in WWI and WWII. Listed is Joseph Eloi Bohemier, killed in 1945 while on 441 Squadron. (Larry Milberry)

Arthur Jewett discusses the old days with squadron mates Ron Lake (centre) and Guy Mott at the 1998 CFPA convention. Then, a contingent of old timers at Cold Lake in 1992 for 441's 50th anniversary: Jake Fleming, Bob Lacerte, Danny Brown, Bruce MacKenzie, Guy Mott, Johnnie Johnson, Kelly Walker and Jake Copeland. (Larry Milberry, Bruce MacKenzie Col.)

Now I had the choice of getting "demobbed" in Winnipeg, going to a gunnery school, or going out to the Far East. My choice was the former - I was anxious to get on with my university studies. Once demobbed, I took a high school refresher course in Calgary and was ready for university that September.

Looking back at it all, I felt that I had been very lucky to survive. I think in terms of the leadership of Lal Parsons, our flight commander in Newfoundland. He taught us about flying in the worst of weather, and led in establishing squadron camaraderie. F/L Mott also was a key leader. Many of us would always regret that he had not succeeded S/L Brannagan. On the other hand, we also were disappointed with the RAF winco who commanded 125 Wing, when we were shuffled into that organization. It also was a disappointment that so few Spitfire pilots - those doing dangerous dive bombing and strafing - were recognized for their efforts with a decoration.

"Remember When"

While researching his squadron's history, Spitfire pilot Bob Lacerte compiled a list of "remember when" anecdotes:

Remember when ... the pilots bought a beat-up 1934, 2-door Ford from a used car lot in Harbour Grace. It came to grief when Harry Pattinson, "Adj" McDonald, and the Station dental officer ditched her on the way home from a party in St. John's.

Lal Parson, instead of joining up on Harry Pattinson during a dawn patrol, tried his best (in the darkness) to formate on a light house.

Harry Hindmarsh beat up a Fairmile in Conception Bay, losing eight feet off one wing.

Ross MacMillan belly-landed W/C Johnnie Johnson's personal Spitfire, while delivering tomatoes for the winco's wife.

A Spitfire V crash-landed near us and our maintenance boys recovered it and made it serviceable. As no one claimed the "Spit", we used it to ferry in beer from England. Woe betide the pilot who made a rough landing back at base when the belly tank was full of "joy juice"!

Don Kimball won the DFC. Not bad, since, originally, he had tried joining the Army!

Bruce MacKenzie won the Croix-de-Guerre with Silver Star after he had destroyed two enemy aircraft and damaged four others.

The CO decreed that no farm stock was to be liberated to supplement our meager rations. Who returned with a heifer draped over the hood of a jeep? Of course, the story was that it had been "killed in action". Another day scroungers Lacerte and Lake came up with a bushel of ripe tomatoes. We were all quite "loose" for the next few days.

French-speaking pilots Brochu, Lacerte, Monnette and others bartered with farmers for some local produce. Who came back with two cocks and organized a cock fight?

Guy Mott organized a "raiding party" to Paris, three days after its liberation. There we drank much champagne and "acquired" a US Army jeep for the squadron.

We used to dump a bag of hard tack into a hole, soak it in gasoline, then get a good campfire going to boil up our tea.

When 441 banged up some mess furniture and a few bodies at our Christmas '44 squadron party. Is that why we got our sudden posting to the Orkneys?

When Gil Brochu commandeered a big Plymouth sedan from a village priest. Now 441 had a staff car! The priest, by the way, did it "for the glory of France"!

The beautiful Canadair F-86 Sabre prototype at Cartierville, near Montreal, in August 1950. Test pilot Al Lilly flew it first on August 8.
(North American Aviation, Canadair D6560,)

CHAPTER 7
Rebirth of the Squadron

A Changing World

By the end of December 1946, the RCAF, which had more than 215,000 members in 1944, had shrunk to 12,735. What remained of the Regular Force centred mainly upon aerial photography, transport, and search and rescue. It was expected that the Auxiliary would play the greater role in air defence. In 1947 Air Marshal W.A. Curtis, himself a former Auxiliary member, became Chief of the Air Staff.

For a time the RCAF operated with wartime veterans, and it was not until November 1947 that the first postwar aircrew trainee intake began training. The graduates received their Wings in June 1948. Meanwhile, the world was not turning out to be the peaceful place that everyone had expected in 1945. The Soviet Union was increasingly suspicious of America and Western Europe which, in turn, resolved to prevent any spread of Soviet influence. Thus began the Cold War.

For a time public attention was riveted on events elsewhere. There was the bloody partition of India, and the deteriorating situation in Palestine, but a coup d'état in Czechoslovakia and the beginning of the Berlin Airlift in 1948 really caught the West's attention. In reply, on April 4, 1949 the North Atlantic Treaty Organization was born, with Canada as a founding member. Meanwhile, Canada's armed forces already were being bolstered and modernized. The RCAF acquiring its first jet aircraft in January 1948 (the de Havilland Vampire, most of which equipped Auxiliary squadrons) was unrelated to international events, but subsequent growth was driven by the Cold War. When Korea exploded in June 1950, such growth accelerated.

RCAF Strength, All Ranks

Date	Regular Force	Auxiliary	Total
January 1, 1944	215,200		215,200
April 1, 1945	164,846		164,846
March 31, 1948	13,832	1121	14,953
March 31, 1949	14,552	1427	15,979
March 31, 1950	17,274	2369	19,643
March 31, 1951	22,359	3147	25,506
March 31, 1952	31,511	4810	36,321

Canada, having abandoned its traditional indifference to international events outside the Commonwealth, fully expected to shoulder its portion in collective security. The question (home defence aside) was what its role should be. Correspondence circulating in RCAF HQ in 1950 estimated an immense Soviet bombing capability. Suggestions were that the USSR soon would have 1000 Tu-4 bombers (copies of the B-29), plus Il-28 and Tu-16 twin-engined jet bombers. North America could be reached only by Tu-4s carrying 10,000-pound bomb loads on one-way missions. Britain, being closer to Soviet bases, would be more vulnerable. The Soviets, it was felt, might fly missions at night and in bad weather using pathfinder and blind bombing techniques, although Western intelligence doubted that they had the necessary radar.

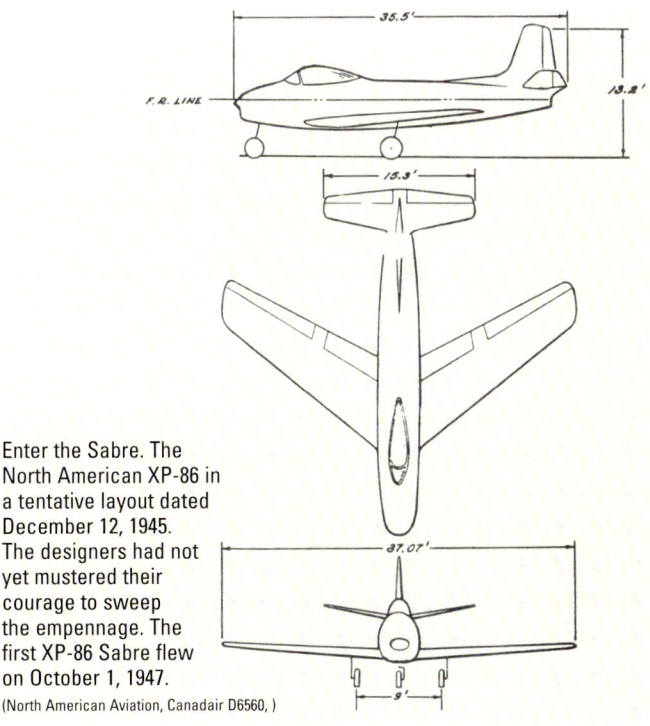

Enter the Sabre. The North American XP-86 in a tentative layout dated December 12, 1945. The designers had not yet mustered their courage to sweep the empennage. The first XP-86 Sabre flew on October 1, 1947.
(North American Aviation, Canadair D6560,)

Planners working with these assumptions concluded that Canada needed a defence force of nine squadrons equipped with Avro CF-100 all-weather fighters. Britain's defences needed bolstering with nine further RCAF squadrons, of which at least four would fly CF-100s, the rest having licence-built North American F-86 Sabres. Writing to his counterpart, Air Marshal Curtis, in December 1950, RAF Chief of the Air Staff, Sir John Slessor, declared, "From the point of view of the Air Defence of the United Kingdom, our most difficult and dangerous period is from now until 1953." Contemplating a forthcoming 421 Squadron deployment to the UK (where it would fly RAF Vampires and Meteors), Slessor described RCAF units as being "a most valuable addition to our air defences during a most awkward period."

Enter the Sabre

The North American F-86 Sabre is one of the most revered of postwar fighters. Ordered for the RCAF in 1949, it came along at just the right time, a "golden age" in aviation history when exciting technology was being introduced and when military budgets were generous. The Sabre was a beautiful, modern machine, yet one around which the aura of classic aerial combat lingered. Its successor, the CF-104 Starfighter, would be dubbed by the press "The Missile With a Man in It", but the classic lineage from Sopwith Camel through Spitfire to Sabre seemed to represent a smooth evolution. The Sabre had no fancy computers. Its gunsight might have had radar ranging, but entering a target's wingspan still was done by twiddling a knob.

Early Sabre production at Cartierville. Canadair was "a natural" to build the Sabre for the RCAF. It had strong leadership, a modern plant and a trained labour force anxious for work in Canada's vibrant postwar economy. For more about Sabre production refer to *The Canadair Sabre* and *Canadair: The First 50 Years*. (Canadair D6952)

The RCAF needed Sabres for the NATO role. Ottawa's decision to station them overseas was accompanied by a commitment to train NATO aircrew. This was further proof that, as a NATO ally, Canada was solid. There were doubts, however, that Sabres would serve long in Britain, since specifications for new RAF fighters exceeded the Sabre's. Britain's new Supermarine Swift, however, proved disappointing, so the RAF had to equip several squadrons with Canadian-built Sabre 4s, pending delivery of the Hawker Hunter.

By early 1951 Canada's NATO commitment had been modified. The RCAF now would form part of an

AC1s R.L.S. King and J.R. Charnley of 441 with belts of .50 cal. machine gun ammunition for Sabre 19195. Then, a display of a Sabre's six "Fifties". In this era the UK, Western Europe and USSR favoured cannons as fighter armament, while the Americans liked .50 calibre. While cannons used more destructive explosive ammunition, they fired slowly. Machine guns used non-explosive bullets, but had a higher rate of fire. (CF PL53042, CANAV Col.)

"Integrated Force". Its contribution would be organized (tentatively) along tactical lines, being self-supporting, and consisting of 11 squadrons - 10 on the Continent with a back-up in Britain. All this would be supported by rear headquarters, an air materiel base, repair and salvage facilities, and communications systems. With Canada now so committed to the air defence of Western Europe, the RAF was disappointed - it had hoped to keep RCAF squadrons defending Britain for as long as possible.

The RCAF commitment began to take shape in October 1951, when 410 Squadron ferried 48 Sabres to NAS Norfolk, Virginia. The Sabres were craned aboard the aircraft carrier HMCS *Magnificent*, which then sailed to Halifax, boarded the rest of the squadron, and crossed the Atlantic to Glasgow. There the Sabres were offloaded and towed to nearby Renfrew airport. From there they flew on to North Luffenham. On November 1, RAF Station North Luffenham officially was transferred to No.1 (Fighter) Wing, RCAF, 410 taking possession of its facilities on November 15. In February 1952, 441 Squadron, which also crossed aboard HMCS *Magnificent*, joined 410. These were the last such seaborne deliveries. Between May 30 and June 15, 1952, 439 Squadron completed Operation Leapfrog I, ferrying 21 Sabres across the Atlantic via Goose Bay, Greenland and Iceland. With their arrival, No.1 (F) Wing was complete. Once in place, the three squadrons operated under 12 Group, RAF Fighter Command.

An advanced echelon of No.1 Air Division HQ was established in Paris in August 1952. Between September 28 and October 11, Op. Leapfrog II brought 416, 421 and 430 squadrons across the Atlantic to RCAF Station Grostenquin, France. These constituted No.2 (F) Wing - the first RCAF organization based in Europe since March 1946. No.1 Air Division HQ formed in Paris on October 1 as part of 4th Allied Tactical Air Force. The location was temporary - in April 1953 "Air Div" HQ moved to Metz, France. On March 7, 1953 Nos.413, 427 and 434 squadrons left Canada for Zweibrucken, West Germany, where they formed No.3 (F) Wing. Nos.414, 422 and 444 Squadrons, which made the trip between August 27 and September 4, comprised No.4 (F) Wing at Baden-Soellingen, West Germany. Finally, early in 1955, No.1 (F) Wing moved to Marville, France. No.1 Air Division with its 12 Sabre squadrons was complete.

As NATO grew (most notably after West Germany gained membership), the role of No.1 Air Division began to change. With day fighter strength expanding, Canada was asked to reduce Sabre strength in favour of CF-100s. There followed another series of trans-Atlantic delivery flights (Op. Nimble Bat from November 1956 to August 1957) in which 419, 423, 440 and 445 CF-100 squadrons flew to Europe. The Sabre squadrons disbanded (410, 413, 414 and 416) soon re-formed in Canada with CF-100s.

The Sabre years would be the of happiest times for those serving in No.1 Air Division. Their aircraft were superb, and morale and operational efficiency were high. In August 1958, June 1959 and September 1960 RCAF Sabre teams would win the Guynemer Trophy, emblematic of gunnery supremacy among NATO's air forces. Through the Sabre years, Canadian NATO schools taught two generations of "service brats" - the children of military personnel serving overseas. A military radio network served Canada's NATO bases and linked them to Canada. A European Grey Cup game was played each November. At a more personal level, many who had not brought out families, found wives abroad. To marry a foreign national required Air Division Headquarters permission, which was not always granted. A statistic for the period December 1, 1958 to November 30, 1959, dealing with approved foreign marriage applications, showed how geography (and the location of an RCAF base) shaped the selection process. Of 117 submissions allowed 55 involved a German mate, 38 French, and only 14 British. Other nationalities were Dutch (3), Danish (2), Italian (2), Belgian (1), Luxembourg (1) and Indian (1).

RCAF Sabres scramble from Volkel, Holland, while on exercise in July 1953. By this time the RCAF had 12 day fighter squadrons in NATO. (CF PL80349)

The officers of 441 Squadron at St. Hubert in Vampire days. Standing are Doug Cooke (EO), Jack Ecker, Bob Middlemiss, Larry Spurr, Slim Walker, Andy Mackenzie, "Willie" Weeks, Les Benson, Gord McDonald, Murray "Buzz" Neilson and Steve Atherton. In front are Bob Simmons, Don Hanson, Ray Himmelman, Bruce Sheasby (instructing from the OTU), Garnet "Gar" Brine and his pooch "Checkers", Ray Jolley and Ian McDonald. (via Andy MacKenzie)

441 Back in Business - St. Hubert Days

When 441 Squadron was reborn, the instrument of that act was Organization Order 1/51 of February 1, 1951, stating: "Plans for the development of Air Defence Group call for the formation of additional fighter squadrons. It has been decided that 441 Squadron will form at RCAF Station Chatham, New Brunswick." This was to occur March 1 with squadron functions defined as: "(a) To carry out training in air interception. (b) To carry out air interceptions as directed by the Group Commander, Air Defence Group." An amendment was published on February 15 - St. Hubert replaced Chatham.

The new squadron began taking shape on schedule, initially under experienced veterans. S/L A.R. "Andy" MacKenzie, DFC, was the first CO. Momentarily, he commanded little more than his own staff, some groundcrew, and a pool of aircraft, but others began arriving on March 19. A/F/L Larry Spurr and F/L Robert G. Middlemiss, DFC, became 441's "A" and "B" Flight Commanders. Spurr, who had flown Spitfires during the war, arrived from 410 Squadron. There he had been on 410's Vampire aerobatic team, the Blue Devils. Middlemiss, a Malta Spitfire pilot, had attended RAF Central Fighter Establishment, where he first flew jets. Besides such wartime "retreads", 441 also had

Vampire BT-H taxis at St. Hubert ("BT" was 441's postwar code, "H" identifies the particular aircraft). Then, 441 mechanics service a Vampire. This natty type served 441 from March to June of 1951, when the Sabre took over. A few years earlier a bitter controversy had raged in the newspapers headlines. Going at each other were those favouring the modern Sabre and those boosting the popular postwar "Buy British" trend. The latter argued that the RCAF could have several Vampires for the price of a Sabre. Happily, good sense prevailed. (Ray Jolley)

F/L Larry Spurr, one of 441's original flight commanders. He later would down a MiG-15 in Korea. Then, flight commander F/L Bob Middlemiss with F/O's Don Hanson and Bob Simmons. Spurr and Middlemiss had been Spitfire pilots during the war. (Ray Jolley)

F/Os D.H. "Steve" Atherton and G.R. "Gar" Brine back from a 441 Vampire sortie. The Cold War would cost the lives of hundreds of RCAF aircrew, whether in training or on operations. Brine was killed during a May 3, 1954 sortie, when Sabre 19400 plunged into Miramichi Bay near Chatham. On May 15, 1956 Atherton lost his life in Sabre 23261, when his engine failed soon after takeoff from Chatham. (Ray Jolley)

several "sprog" pilots - recent graduates of the postwar training system.

On March 20, 441 Squadron flew its first sector recce with 3 Vampires and 2 Harvards. Next day, 416 Squadron Mustangs appeared over St.Hubert from Uplands to taunt 410 and 441. The Silver Foxes retaliated next day, the ORB noting, "Bounced 416 at OW [Ottawa] twice with three-Vampire formation." Later in the day 416 shot up St. Hubert, but F/O W.R. "Willie" Weeks, P.C. "Slim" Walker and D.H. "Steve" Atherton "caught them cold over river". Weeks, Walker and Atherton illustrate the talent in 441's initial pilot cadre. Weeks, recipient of the DFC, gained his experience flying Spitfires with 442 Squadron. Like most at war's end he left the RCAF, then took out a short service commission 1950 - 54. Walker had shot down a Japanese fighter on the Burma front in 1944. Atherton represented the new generation. Born on September 22, 1928, he joined the RCAF in September 1949, flew with 441 from February 1952 to March 1954, then with 410 to December 1955. Next he instructed on Sabres at Chatham. On May 15, 1956 he died near there while attempting to crash land in Sabre 21261.

On March 29, 1951 the day's activities were simply recorded: "Squadron picture taken but negative pack broke on camera... Ping pong table set up in pilots' room. Flew 14 hours 50 minutes."

Otherwise, these early days were full of activity, whether with flying, ground school, sports, partying or family life. New personnel kept arriving - tradesmen, admin staff, pilots, etc.

On April 2, Harvards from 441 helped search for two missing 438 Vampires, but the day ended fruitlessly. On April 4, the squadron began training with drop tanks on the Vampires. Next day three aircraft carried out a mock attack on 416. On the 9th the weather spoiled plans for flying, so "A" and "B" flights went after each other in volley ball. Also on the 9th F/Os Les Benson and Don Hanson were in a VIP guard of honour at Dorval regarding a state visit by French President Auriol. The diary entry for April 12 was a prelude to many complex air defence exercises:

"Big Photo" operation commenced and first section on hand at 0520 hours. "Firefly Control" called first "Scramble" at 0837 hours, the section getting off in four minutes. The "enemy", which consisted of American B-29s, B-50s and B-36s, dropped some window [aluminum chaff] in the Dorval area and there was no interception. During the day various forms of sabotage were encountered and one chap tried to run off with one of our Vampires. S/L MacKenzie caught him just as he was starting the engine. Another man with a camera was picked up by the Security Guard which we had stationed

F/O Jack Ecker doing ops officer duty at St. Hubert. (Ray Jolley)

around the hangar. At 1830 hours we finished the day with no interceptions. Flew 25 hours and 5 minutes.

Weather curtailed Ex. Big Photo the next day, and the squadron reverted to flight-sized exercises. On April 16 F/O Hanson flew to Quebec City with a part for a helicopter involved in the Vampire search. A key event occurred on April 18, when A/F/L Larry Spurr and F/O D.B. "Don" Simmons began converting to Sabres, beginning with ground school at the Sabre Mobile Technical Unit. When F/L R.E. Kent of 416 disappeared between Chatham and Ottawa on April 20, 441 also joined in that search. The wreck and Kent's body soon were found in northern New Brunswick.

For April 23 the diarist noted: "F/O M.B. Neilson went missing at 1630 and the whole squadron waited anxiously for some word. At 1750 F/O Neilson phoned from Rimouski saying that he had made a forced landing out of fuel at this town. A 104 (K) Flight Dakota is to leave in the morning with a crew." This "gen" was followed up by the entry of the 24th:

> *S/L MacKenzie left at 0715 with the 104 (K) Flight Dakota en route to Rimouski via Mont Joli. After a delay the plane arrived in Rimouski around 1100 hours. F/O Neilson had guarded the plane all night as it was impossible to get a guard flown in last night. Neilson explained that his radio failed on the last leg of his navigation trip and he looked for the St. Lawrence River. On finding the river he headed for Mont Joli but ran out of fuel at Rimouski, forcing him to land wheels-up on a turf field. On completing the inspection the group left for Mont Joli and took off at approximately 1600 hours, arriving here around 1800 hours.*

In May 2003, Murray Neilson recalled his prang. Neilson had joined the RCAF in 1949 at age 18. For the April 23 sortie, he had been on air fighting from Chatham with two other pilots, when his electrics failed. Flying in cloud, he searched for a way down, finally descending, then breaking cloud to spot Rimouski's grass runway. He put Vampire 17063 down smoothly on its belly. His sortie had lasted an amazing 2:05 hours without underwing tanks - for the final 25 minutes he had been gliding. (After leaving 441 at North Luffenham, Neilson worked in RCAF

G/C W.R. MacBrien was a leading figure in postwar RCAF fighter plans and organization. (CF PL30265)

intelligence, then instructed at Moose Jaw, where he flew with the Goldilocks aerobatic team. He left the RCAF in 1965 to fly for QANTAS in Australia, then joined CPA, from where he retired in 1980.)

Initially, 441 had been reporting to Air Defence Group. Formed in December 1948, ADG was commanded by G/C W.R. "Iron Bill" MacBrien, OBE. As of June 1, 1951, however, this organization was elevated to command status under A/V/M C.R. Dunlap, CBE. In spite of such changes, life at 441 was routine. On May 18, for example, F/Os Don Atherton and Bob Simmons flew to Centralia for the graduation of some NATO pilots. About this time some construction was due for St. Hubert, so 441 prepared to go on detachment to Dorval. Ten more 441 pilots were assigned to the MTU on May 21. On May 31 the squadron diarist noted: "Perfect weather and our last day for squadron exercises in the Vampire. GCI, homings and air tests comprised the day's work... We flew 11 hours, 50 minutes. Our next move is to Dorval Airport, where we are to fly F-86E Sabres." On June 2 A/F/L Spurr and F/Os Simmons and Weeks flew a Vampire airshow at Quebec City. The squadron moved to Dorval on June 6.

On June 13, 1951 F/Os John E. "Jack" Ecker and Don Simmons were named to check out on the Sabre, in order to begin ferrying some from Canadair. Three days later there was an escape and evasion exercise. Pilots were dropped off 18 miles from base and had to make their way back without capture. This was to simulate wartime conditions, and was something that the retreads knew all about. On June 19 the first 441 Sabre (19124, BT-B) reached Dorval. Next day the diary reported: "We witnessed the first Sabre crash today, when F/O Found of 410 Squadron went off the end of Runway 10, smashing the ILS hut and ruining the aircraft."

On June 22 F/Os Simmons and Weeks were notified that they would attend a 10-week USAF gunnery course in Nevada. Soon, A/F/L Spurr was off to fly Sabres with the 93rd Fighter Squadron at Kirtland AFB, New Mexico. On June 26 he got news of his promotion to flight lieutenant, the diarist noting gleefully: "Spurr was tossed into the swimming pool before buying the drinks." On July 5 all 441 pilots wrote a final exam on the F-86. The results made them shine - the average mark was 94.5%. For July 12 the diary reported that F/Os Bob Simmons and Steve Atherton were busy painting the first checkerboards on 441 Sabres. Meanwhile, the squadron's numbers were growing, the diarist reporting on July 19, "More Sabres have been delivered this week and we have a total of nine. F/O Hanson is the proud father of a baby girl". On July 26-27 they did the high altitude indoctrination program at the Institute of Aviation Medicine in Toronto.

On August 9 the diarist noted with pride, "We put up our first four-plane formation on Sabres and it seemed to be a good show." A squadron briefing on August 20 by G/C Stevenson of AFHQ dealt with the topic of 441 going overseas. Other events suggested a quickening pace. For example, the Hon. Brooke Claxton, Minister of National Defence, and Sir Arthur Henderson, UK Minister for Air, inspected 410 and 441 at Dorval, even as the squadrons re-packed for St. Hubert, where flying commenced the next day (in spite of on-going construction).

The Battle of Britain flypast took place over Ottawa on September 16, participants being four Sabres (441), three Vampires (413) and 12 Mustangs (416). On this detachment

441 did its first firing with Sabres, using the Winchester range south of Ottawa. On September 7 S/L MacKenzie left to join a USAF squadron destined for overseas - he was to discuss the concept of flying Sabres across the North Atlantic. MacKenzie accompanied a typical USAF operation, but aboard a USAF C-54. His later report would go a long way towards the RCAF adopting the overseas ferry concept and lead to Operation Leapfrog.

On October 9 five 441 Sabres ferried to Norfolk, Virginia, followed by 11 more on the 15th, 22nd and 25th. From there 441 would embark for England. However, disaster struck on October 23, when Expeditor KE-118 crashed into Mount Bruno: "We lost our armament officer, F/O Harry Driscoll... Two civilians from our hangar also were killed, Mr. Ralph Nichols, a GE rep, and Mr. Roy Pelletier, a Sperry man." Their funerals would be the first for postwar 441. On October 30 the squadron paraded in Montreal in honour of the 1951 Royal Visit. New personnel steadily joined 441, one being F/L Eric Dean Kelly, who arrived on December 7 to take over "B" Flight. On December 27 F/O Cranston had a scary experience - a jammed elevator on landing. The diarist noted: "Through use of power, he landed safely and later heard that a bolt had come loose and jammed his actuating mechanism."

Commanding 441 in its postwar beginnings was S/L A.R. "Andy" MacKenzie, DFC. (CF PL53038)

Early 441 Sabre pilots (except Raynor who was 410 Squadron). Standing are Jack Ecker, Murray Neilson, Ken Jorgenson (USAF), Gar Brine, G.A. "Gord" McDonald and Ray Jolley. In front are Don Hanson, Steve Atherton, Ray Himmelman, Len "Speed" Bentham and Art Raynor. Jorgenson spent about a year at 441, then was posted to Korea. Raynor died in a flying accident in the UK in April 1952. (Jean Ecker Col.)

NCOs and airmen of 441 Squadron in the same 1951 period at St. Hubert. (Jean Ecker Col.)

Checking out some 441 graffiti - Steve Atherton and Don Simmons. (Ray Jolley)

F/Os Remi Paquette and Gord McDonald at Dorval with 441's first Sabre. (CF PL53043)

Norm Ronaasen took this candid shot of some of his zany squadron mates in the mess at St. Hubert. Behind are Fern Villeneuve (pouring beer into Jack Ecker's ear), Rocky Paquette, Bob Haverstock with Buzz Neilson in front of him, Jean Gaudry with Jack Turner in front of him, Bob Simmons and Frank Wise. In front are Ecker, Ralph Annis, Slim Walker, Andy "Haggis McBagpipe" MacKenzie, Don Simmons and Bob Middlemiss. (A.R. MacKenzie Col.) ** 1 name missing

441's three types in 1952 - Sabre, T-33 and Harvard. Then, a 4-plane section scrambles from St. Hubert. (Ray Jolley)

A wintery 441 flightline scene at St. Hubert. Soon the squadron would be aboard ship for the UK. (CF PC-67)

CHAPTER 8

The NATO Commitment

HMCS *Magnificent* docked in the Clyde River near Glasgow, its deck crowded with Sabres. "Maggie" made two voyages transporting Sabre 2s to the UK. Later it returned some Sabre 5s to Canada. (CF)

North Luffenham Days

While 441 worked up at St. Hubert, No.1 Air Division was taking shape. Organization Order 135/51 of November 23, 1951 laid out the objectives:

Organization Order 100/51 dated 17 July 1951 advised that during 1951-52 three RCAF fighter squadrons (F-86s) would be located in the UK to operate under the command and control of an RCAF Fighter Wing Headquarters. It was further stated that, notwithstanding the fact that, while in the UK, the primary mission of these squadrons would be to carry out operational training with the RAF. The Wing was also to be considered as the initial component of the Air Division of 11 squadrons which Canada is contributing to the integrated forces of NATO. In accordance with the plan, 441 (F) Squadron, presently located at St. Hubert, will be the second squadron to proceed to the UK to form part of 1 Fighter Wing, RCAF, North Luffenham.

Relocation to North Luffenham was to be effective February 1, 1952. The function of the unit was: "To train and co-operate with RAF squadrons, units and formations as directed by the Air Officer Commanding-in-Chief, RAF Fighter Command through the Commanding Officer, 1 Fighter Wing Headquarters." A memo of December 20, 1951 outlined how the move was to be effected. Personnel, dependents included, were to assemble at the St. Hubert Drill Hall at 0900 on February 12 with baggage for customs inspection, and to receive their steamer tickets and rail berthing cards. At 1900 hours on February 13, 441 would leave Montreal by rail for Saint John. Baggage was limited to 150 pounds (train) and 200 pounds (ship).

Although dependents might accompany RCAF personnel (at their own expense), official policy was clear: "This offer of assistance is not to be interpreted as encouragement for personnel to have their dependents accompany them to the UK, as living conditions in the UK, and particularly in the North Luffenham area, are such that it is undesirable for dependents to accompany personnel." In a sign of the times, the squadron diary added: "You may make arrangements with MacDonald Inc., PO Box 1929, Place d'Armes, Montreal, Quebec, to ship 1000 cigarettes per month at a cost of $ 4.00 per 1000, postage paid."

A diary note on January 11, 1952 was historic: "Today is the last day of flying for 441 (F) Squadron until we reach

England." Apart from preparing for the move, personnel had embarkation leave from January 21 to February 4. This was followed by numerous social events, including a "Fighter Stag" on February 8 attended by pilots from all squadrons in the area, plus some OTU instructors from Chatham. On February 13 the Silver Foxes sailed for the UK aboard the Canadian Pacific liner *Empress of France*. In an age of speedy but cramped air travel, one may look back fondly on the days when people crossed oceans on such vessels, but nostalgia overlooks things such as sea sickness - and there were two very rough days during 441's passage.

The squadron disembarked at Liverpool on February 20. Since 410 Squadron already was in England, many of its pilots were in the welcoming party. Personnel immediately entrained for North Luffenham. No.1 Wing's historical report states that the newcomers arrived at 2330 hours and that 410 staged an informal reception, the late hour notwithstanding. One may wonder just how "informal" - next day two 410 Sabres were damaged in crash-landings (without injuries). On February 26 S/L MacKenzie made the first 441 flight at "North Luff" in poor weather.

Authorities had been right about dependents sailing to Britain at this time. The first members of 1 Wing at North Luffenham had found the place run down, barracks even missing sheets. The first drafts were accommodated in local hotels, and every trailer that could be scrounged was used until service quarters improved. Crowded though they were, trailers proved easier to heat than drafty, half-insulated British houses. Such early problems would be resolved by the time 441 arrived, but Britain remained a dreary

The *Empress of France* at Liverpool to disembark 441 Squadron. (A.R. MacKenzie Col.)

The main gate at North Luffenham, as Sabres streak by for the station photographer. (CF PL62073)

S/L MacKenzie climbs aboard his Sabre for a sortie from North Luffenham. After a 10-year RCAF career Sabre 19150 ended its days with the Greek Air Force. (CF PC2619)

One of the great "North Luff" flightline scenes. As the CO's Sabre is serviced, Dean Kelly does one of his well-known "scorch-pasts". (CF PC2619)

place, far from the cheery tourist trap that evolved years later. In the short run, however, this all meant that pilots and mechanics often arrived without the stabilizing influences of families. It is hardly surprising that, on February 27, S/L MacKenzie gathered his men for a briefing about deportment in the UK (he previously had congratulated them for their conduct aboard the Empress of France).

For those wives accompanying their husbands, culture shock was severe. Unless they had been "war brides", they had much to learn. One year after 1 Wing formed, it published a retrospective (1 Fighter Wing: The First Year, 1951-52), noting:

> There are quite a few Canadian Home Fires burning in and around North Luffenham. The wives are doing a splendid job to make their husbands and families comfortable and happy. But it isn't easy to get started.
>
> What with the shortage of housing, many have to stay in rooming houses, small inns, trailers and ancient dwellings, some without modern conveniences. However, the usual Canadian adaptability and versatility have overcome many of the difficulties.
>
> After securing a dwelling, the second big step seems to be cooking. There are many types of stoves and several systems of fuelling. Fuel is not too plentiful, central heating is rare. Then comes purchasing with ration coupons and, with that, getting to know the new terms for various commodities that are known in Canada by another name. Of course one gets on to the monetary system after six weeks or so. That is not too difficult, because the merchants in the area are very courteous and helpful. Though occasionally, they have difficulty understanding the Canadian housewife.
>
> After finding a place to live, mastering the stove and learning the grocer's language, there is a transportation problem to face. It takes about a month before you decipher rail and bus schedules.

Squadrons arriving in Britain hit the ground running, and 441 soon was ready for operations. Predictably, however, it

When his Sabre had a compressor stall and caught fire, F/O Ronaasen was quick in getting back onto the runway at North Luffenham. 19183 was repaired, only to end years later in a crash with the Turks. (via Bill Bain)

wasn't long before there was trouble. On March 6 F/O Norm Ronaasen made an emergency landing. Of this the wing reported: "Six aircraft up after MET briefing with S/L MacKenzie leading the first formation. On return to base and during the landing, No.4 had engine trouble when trying to overshoot. F/O E.N. Ronaasen, the pilot, was forced to land due to lack of power and, following touch down, his engine burst into flames, burning completely through aft fuselage section. He did an excellent job of controlling his Sabre past

Dean Kelly with friends E.G. "Irish" Ireland and Cec Brown at the 1998 Canadian Fighter Pilots Association convention in Ottawa. (Larry Milberry)

F/L Kelly hangs in for photos alongside an RAF Dakota. The Sabres have automatically popped their leading edge slats to improve slow-speed control. (CF PL62501)

the others ahead of him ..." March 19, 1952 was another 441 highlight: "This date marks the first year of operations for our squadron... The weather was down all day ... We ran and hiked for approximately 5 miles, which gave everyone ample exercise." The 22nd brought a wing scramble, 22 Sabres launching in under six minutes to intercept B-50s and Lincolns.

Almost every week in this period 1 Wing had RAF visitors looking over the Sabre. There also was basic RCAF public relations to be done. In March 1952 this included a flypast for Air Ministry cameras and a one-man airshow for Air Cadets, F/L Dean Kelly performing for the youngsters. Airshows increased - no fewer than ten 441 Sabres appeared at airshows throughout the British Isles on September 20. The next step was to form an aerobatic team, the pilots being F/Os Garnet Brine, Fern Villeneuve, Ralph Annis and Jean Gaudry. Winter soon ended the airshow circuit, but through 1953 the team would be busy. Its achievements are covered in Dan Dempsey's book, *A Tradition of Excellence: Canada's Airshow Team Heritage*. A *Flight* magazine article of September 19, 1952 describes a display put on for the press at North Luffenham:

> *From flying control we saw the ranks of Sabres, resplendent in their squadron markings. Those of 439 (Tiger) Squadron have a yellow stripe, edged in red, on the fin, and red diamonds on a yellow band round the nose. Proclaiming 441 (Silver Fox) Squadron*

The first 441 aerobatic team was in steady demand for UK airshows. Here, Gar Brine leads in BT-146, No.2 is Fern Villeneuve in '162, No.3 is Ralph Annis in '152 and No.4 is Jean Gaudry in '165. (Remi Paquette Col.)

(S/L A.R. MacKenzie, DFC) is a black-and-white checkered nose and a similarly checkered band round the tail, and for 410 (Cougar) Squadron (S/L D. Warren, DFC) there are red and white chevrons on the tail and white diamonds on a red ring round the nose.

In obviously bumpy conditions the standard of formation flying was as near perfect as we could hope to see, and equally admirable was the individual aerobatic performance of F/O Ronaasen. Of all his manoeuvres the most spectacular was one in which, to the best of our knowledge, the Sabre has not yet been equalled – the multi-turn vertical roll. This, we were assured, is a matter of delightful simplicity. After 550 knots or so have been built up on the clock, the control column is eased back until the Sabre is climbing absolutely vertically. Then the stick is moved over, perhaps three or four inches and, with a mere 10-lb pressure, kept there; and round goes the Sabre, six, eight, ten - even twelve times, over a height band of 10,000 - 13,000 feet.

Another most impressive performance, again demonstrated by F/O Ronaasen, is the fly-over at 115-120 kt, with the Sabre apparently disintegrating, so large are the projecting areas of leading-edge slats and fuselage air brakes. Landings are somewhat "hotter", due to the necessity for keeping the tail end of the fuselage off the runway.

collision." There would be many more such sombre entries in the coming years.

On April 24 F/O Don McIlraith had rudder trouble, spinning from 30,000 to 10,000 feet before recovering. On May 8 there were dogfights with Meteors over East Anglia. In one scrap F/O Villeneuve lost an underwing tank. On June 5 F/L Walker and F/O Brine visited Pferdsfeld, Germany, the 441 diary noting it as "a field that the Canadian government contemplated buying for operations". Also in June, field reps from Bristol visited 441 to get familiar with the Sabre, which they soon would be overhauling. The wing grew with the arrival of 439 Squadron. It was escorted on June 15 on its final leg from Canada by five 441 Sabres. On June 23 there was a big exercise with "enemy" F-84s, Meteors, Canberras and B-50s. G/C E.B. "Ed" Hale, North Luffenham station commander, led some of this flying, and also offered lectures about Korea, where he recently had finished a short tour.

On July 1, 1952 three 441 Sabres attended the airshow at RAF West Raynham. It was an exciting occasion, 441's diarist

On April 1, 1952 F/O Ronaasen had another "dicey do", landing at RAF Ansty with low fuel. Ansty, a Chipmunk EFTS, had only 3300 feet of runway, but Ronaasen got off OK after the drop tanks on his Sabre had been removed. On the 18th the diarist wrote: "Our squadron learned with regret of the loss of F/Os Kerr and Rayner of 410 Squadron in a mid-air

Officers of 441 Squadron at North Luffenham in 1952. Behind are Les Benson, Bill Felhaber (Adj), Don McIlraith, Slim Walker, Doug Cooke (EO), Ian McDonald, Dean Kelly, Norm Ronaasen, Andy MacKenzie, Pete Cranston, Jean Gaudry, Bob Haverstock, Jack Ecker, Murray Neilson, Jack Turner, Ray Jolley, Fern Villeneuve and Ralph Annis (in front of Fern). In front are Gord McDonald, Don Hanson, Don Williamson, Ray Himmelman, Gar Brine, Steve Atherton, brothers Don and Bob Simmons, and Rocky Paquette. (Ray Jolley Col.)

noting many of the types present, most of which flew that day: Avro 707B, Boeing B-29, D.H.110, Vampire and Venom, Hawker 1067, North American B-45, Republic F-84, Supermarine Attacker, Seafire and Swift, and Vickers Valiant. There also was a live demonstration of a seat ejection from a Meteor. The diarist boasted that day of how "F/L Kelly demonstrated a Sabre to its full extent." Kelly already was famous for his air displays. In January 2003, Remi Paquette of 441 recalled how pilots looked to Kelly as their role model. That is not to say that they would follow in his footsteps every time. They would not, for example, try his loop off the runway following touchdown. Having pulled this off, all Kelly had to say was, "In a Sabre 2 that is not a good idea!" However, with him as lead, the boys would practice GCAs into North Luffenham with the weather "at limits" (200 foot ceiling, visibility half a mile). In later years Dean Kelly would amaze crowds with the Voodoo, putting on such a tight show that he rarely left the confines of the airfield. While being so skillful at aerobatics, Kelly also was regarded as one of the RCAF's most safety-minded pilots.

On July 11, 1952 the squadron visited Belgium where, two days later at Melsbroek, F/L Kelly wrung out his Sabre and went supersonic. On the 15th King Beaudoin sent a Dakota to North Luffenham with his aide, Maj Van Lirde, who was to interview Kelly "on behalf of the King on the reasons for the sonic shock wave". This topic really seemed to fascinate everyone in the early years of supersonic flight, with countless telephone calls and other enquiries being made by curious citizens. A typical letter-to-the-editor appeared in a British magazine *circa* 1952, M.H. Hengeveld writing: "While staying in the country, near Nottingham, I saw a Sabre flying at considerable speed and certainly under 6000 feet. The aircraft went into a shallow dive and almost immediately the whole house was shaken by a really tremendous boom. At this point the aeroplane was travelling across my line of vision at two to three miles distance."

Hengeveld wanted to know more about the science of the supersonic boom, while others wanted to know why their windows were being broken any time a jet fighter "boomed" their neighbourhood. One such case was reported in Flight (with their love for "dropping booms", RCAF pilots may have been the culprits involved).

> Damage to a 200-year old cottage at Woodhorn, Oving, near Chichester, Sussex, as the result of a supersonic bang, has been claimed by the tenants, Mr. and Mrs. F. Potter. Besides a number of cracks in various parts of the walls, the front door frame and one of the bedroom floors had also moved. The occurrence was reported to the Air Ministry. This claim seems to have brought to a head the various stories of supersonic bangs breaking windows, blowing people off their bicycles and a variety of other effects. The Ministry of Supply has promised an investigation into any claims for damage due to this cause."

In this period 441 began surpassing 500 flying hours per month, a squadron minimum set by 1 Wing COpsO, W/C R.T.P. Davidson. On July 29 F/L Kelly flew to Vickers Armstrong at Chilbolton for a fly-off against the RAF's new fighter, the Swift. His impressions were noted by the squadron diarist: "It appears at this time that the Sabre is superior to the Swift in all respects except thrust of engine." The RAF soon accepted the Swift to be a dud, the few production aircraft being sent to photo recce units. To save the day, the RAF adopted the Canadair Sabre 4. In another comparison, in July 1952 a Sabre from 441 flew against an RAF Venom. The Venom's excellent climb rate was noted, but so was its slowness.

The Supermarine Swift was one of several RAF fighters evaluated by Dean Kelly. Although sleek-looking, its performance disappointed RAF hopes. (RAF)

The diary entry for August 19, 1952 is worth citing as an example of general training under way:

> The only flying today, other than a test flight, was in conjunction with two wing scrambles against Meteor aircraft from the Day Fighter Leaders School. The first scramble was at 1040 hours and our squadron flew eight aircraft along with eight of 439 (F) Squadron. F/L Kelly was the wing leader. The interception was made under the control of "Gaper" and "Comment" GCI. Contact was made with 16-plus Meteors between 35,000 and 40,000 feet over East Anglia. The show was quite successful, our pilots keeping a high mach number during the engagement. The second scramble was at 1445 hours. F/L Kelly again led the wing, our squadron and 439 (F) Squadron, both supplying eight aircraft. One section of four aircraft from our squadron, not having drop tanks, climbed separately and failed to make contact. The remainder of the wing engaged the Meteors over the East coast. The show was quite successful. On the return trip F/O Ronaasen ran short of fuel with an unserviceable radio and returned to base.

Since there were runway repairs on August 21, 441 spent the day in lectures about atomic weapons. Next day it was at the Holbeach range for air firing. This ended in a bit of excitement: "F/O [Don] Williamson chalked up one wing tip and aileron confirmed, as he landed his Sabre. An aileron change is underway and the aircraft should be serviceable within 24 hours." A few days later 441 went by bus to Nottingham for dinghy drill at the Victoria Baths. The week also involved familiarization with small arms issued for base defence. Everyone was required to take part in such training. In early September the Chief of the Air Staff, Air Marshall W.A. Curtis, visited North Luffenham. On his departure on the 3rd, four 441 Sabres tried escorting him, but had to quit, since his Dakota was only making 115 knots.

On September 12, 1952 F/O Williamson had another surprise. After landing, the rear fuselage of his Sabre (19152) came away and was left on the runway! Consequently, all RCAF Sabres were subject to a special inspection. On the 15th

Life at North Luffenham was never dull, whether flying or not. At this Officers Mess affair, the CAS, Air Marshal Curtis W.A., is being honoured by 441. From the left the crowd includes: Jack Ecker, Les Benson, Gar Brine, Ian McDonald, Ray Himmelman, Murray Neilson, Steve Atherton, Slim Walker, Jean Gaudy, Doug Cooke, A/M Curtis, Rocky Paquette, Bob Simmons, Andy MacKenzie, Gord McDonald, Don Simmons, Bill Felhaber, Don Williamson and Pete Cranston. The black armbands were a sign of respect - King George VI recently had died. Then, the CAS on the flightline with Andy MacKenzie and his boys - Jack Ecker, Buzz Neilson, Rocky Paquette, Dean Kelly, Slim Walker, Gord McDonald, Ralph Annis, Don Simmons and Ray Jolley. (441 Sqn Col.)

A/V/M R.L.R. Atcherley (RAF), North Luffenham station commander G/C Ed Hale, and 441's S/L MacKenzie. Atcherley asked MacKenzie about flying the Sabre. This was arranged, MacKenzie taking up the A/V/M's Meteor, Atcherley a 441 jet. MacKenzie was ready for the docile Meteor, but Atcherley learned a thing or two in a hurry about handling the swept-wing Sabre. Atcherley died later in a Meteor crash in Cyprus. (A.R. MacKenzie Col.)

North Luffenham provided 22 Sabres for the Battle of Britain fly-by over London. On October 8 F/O Paquette was noted as hospitalized after pranging his motorcycle (in the Air Division, automobiles and motorcycles would cause more casualties than aircraft). On Ex. Ardent's final day (October 12) F/L Kelly led a 1 Wing intercept on RAF B-29s over East Anglia. *Aeroplane* magazine of October 17, 1952 reported on the conclusion of the UK's biggest postwar air exercise to date:

> In all, the attacking and defending aircraft in Exercise Ardent flew about 6000 sorties, without major accident. The finale was a mass attack on London by more than 100 Canberras, Lincolns and Washingtons [B-29s of which the RAF had 87], which were intercepted by a large number of jet fighters. Previously, there had been attacks against airfields in East Anglia and the metropolitan area by RCAF, USAF, Dutch and Royal Navy aircraft... The exercise had been most valuable for Bomber Command, and the use of the Canberra permitted new operating methods and tactics to be tried.

No.1 Wing celebrated its first anniversary at North Luffenham on November 14, 1952. Included in the festivities was a show by the 410 Squadron team of F/L Nichols and F/Os Cinnamon, Bentham and Robb, followed by a solo flying display. This was reported in the *Aeroplane* of November 28, 1952: "The four Sabres were followed by some rather breath-taking, strong-arm aerobatics by Flight Lieutenant E.D. 'Dean' Kelly of No.441 (F) Squadron. His tight turns and vertical pull out from a low-level fly past must have severely strained his G-suit. Flt. Lt. Kelly is 32 and is one of the 'older' members of the Fighter Wing, the pilots' average age being about 25 years." On December 11, 1952 a Meteor arrived at North Luff to fly a photographer to shoot a formation of 441 Sabres. In the week after Christmas the wing was busy with a major air defence practice - Ex. Fabulous. It even flew on New Year's Day 1953, although duff weather limited 441 to 4:10 hours. Things improved next day with 35:30 hours: "Four sorties of bomber affiliation flown with a B-29 as target." Rotten weather continued to mid-January 1953, keeping pilots grounded, but giving them time to study for exams. On January 10 each 1 Wing squadron launched eight Sabres for mock strafing at North Luff, giving base defence forces some practice.

On January 25 there was a mock "invasion" of North Luff. RAF Hastings dropped paratroops, while Meteors beat up the flightline and hangars: "At noon the war was officially over. The verdict of the umpires was that the aerodrome had been successfully defended." To put things into perspective, however, the paratroop commander pointed out that a para-drop in daylight was scarcely normal and would be considered poor tactics in wartime. On January 27 there were lectures from Canadair tech reps. Such good training kept 441 in top form. The Soviet block knew how well prepared NATO was and how its pilots flew almost as much as they pleased. Meanwhile, their own MiG-15 pilots flew little and were poorly motivated.

Sabre versus Meteor

Reviewing the record, one might ask how realistic were the mock battles waged by the RCAF. These took place with a remarkably free hand. Royal Flight aircraft (which carried members of the Royal Family) were considered "off limits" as targets. In the early-to mid-1950s, however, a Sabre pilot's most elusive "foe" was another Sabre. The Gloster Meteor, often met, was looked upon as fairly easy meat, although a well-flown

Dating to 1943, the Meteor was obsolete by the time the Sabre reached the UK. Even so, it equipped many RAF Fighter Command squadrons into the 1950s. Norm Bigg of 441 photographed this Meteor 7 trainer *circa* 1955.

Meteor could give a green Sabre pilot a run for his money. No.1 Wing's diarist said as much in an entry for April 10, 1953: "The exercise was designed to simulate Korean theatre conditions and worked out in the usual way, with virtually no Meteors managing to get good shots at Sabres. The Sabre still has things all its own way against a Meteor, as long as it is flown by a competent pilot." On April 14, 1953, however, British pilots achieved a tactical advantage over the Sabre, which (in saving face) 1 Wing blamed on sloppy work by controllers.

One of the 25-foot wingspan Brooklyns gliders sometimes used as gunnery targets instead of flags. (via Bill Bain)

In early May 1953 several "Rat and Terrier" exercises were flown in conjunction with the Royal Observer Corps, Meteors being the usual targets for 441. The diary describes the sortie of May 16: "The exercise was quite successful, with an interception in nearly every sortie. All interceptions were at altitudes of about 50 to 100 feet, and concentration was needed to keep out of the trees." In a "Rat and Terrier" of June 20, 441 claimed 17 Meteor kills.

Silver Fox pilot F/O Ron Clayton had a memorable experience with a target tug Meteor on the RAF range at RAF Acklington. Here the boys from "North Luff" fired at a variety of targets, including the usual flags, but also gliders towed by Meteors. On February 18, 1954, while flying Sabre 19153, Clayton put a bullet through an outer wing panel of the Meteor. Four days later, during a reconstruction of the incident, he re-enacted his manoeuvres in a 2-seat Vampire with a RAF pilot watching everything. In February 2003, Ralph Annis reminisced about another Meteor/Sabre happening from North Luffenham days:

The Korean War was well under way when 441 Squadron arrived in England. Those were quite the times, with talk about whether Canada would send 441 to Korea, provide the US with Sabres, send some RCAF Sabre pilots to Korea, etc. It would have made far more interesting history today, had the squadron gone! Meanwhile, the RAF also wanted to get into the fray, so made arrangements with the RCAF to conduct trials between the Meteor and Sabre. Our Wing was tasked to fly some comparative air combat trials against Meteor 8s from the Central Fighter Establishment at West Raynham. We would cover the high-G trials from ground level to 1500 feet. Naturally, our section was led by Dean Kelly, with me as his No.2.

At this time most of us were inexperienced fighter pilots, knowing little about the vertical yo-yo, or much else, for that matter. I was typical, having about 80 Sabre hours. For the trials, we were up against the RAF's best fighter pilots. We made four flights on June 16, 1952, three from North Luffenham, then we stopped at West Raynham. In our morning briefing, we had it drilled into us that each wingman would stick tightly to his section lead, protecting his tail. We succeeded at this, and it certainly was a challenge staying with Dean - he pushed the G-limit all the way. The only relief came when I called another bogey, and he would reverse his turn. Meanwhile, the Brits were not maintaining elements, so we were outnumbered immediately by 2 to 1.

At afternoon tea at West Raynham, we reminded the Brits that formation integrity was part of the trial. Then we briefed for the final sortie, which was to be at zero feet, going head on along one of the canals that ran into The Wash. Off we went, formed up, then came out of the north, throttles bent full forward. Suddenly, there they were - four Meteors coming straight at us. Closing at 1000 knots, things were happening in split seconds. I picked a target, gave the trigger a squeeze, got a few frames of cine film, and pulled up to avoid colliding. But the Meteor pulled up too! A quick expletive, then I pushed forward for another squirt and pulled away, as the Brit did the same. The miss distance was pretty skinny! Again, the Meteors split up, but so did we, flying one-on-one, and more or less holding our own against the best in the RAF. We "lost", but learned something from this - the RCAF went on to rule NATO skies for the next decade.

Ultimately, the RAF sent no Meteors to Korea - perhaps their trials with 441 Squadron helped with that decision. Instead (as with the RCAF) RAF pilots served in USAF squadrons in Korea, usually on Sabres. The RAAF, however, equipped 77 Squadron in Korea with Meteors. In this they learned a bitter lesson - a Meteor was no match for a MiG-15.

Night Flying Capers

January 27, 1953 was set aside for night flying. This was a big deal for Sabre pilots: "Night flying was laid on and commenced at 1800 hours. The aircraft flew singly on a cross-country to Watford and Sculthorpe, with a bright moon and high cloud to make the trip relaxing. Fifteen pilots made the trip and flying ceased at 2200 hours. Daily total: 32:45 hours." Such exercises later made NATO all-weather CF-100 crews chuckle. They would mock their little Sabre buddies for night flying only by the full moon, using well-lit cities as their navigation cues, then scooting home as soon as fuel gauges started to dip. Of course, Sabre drivers got their revenge, usually by bouncing CF-100s by day, then splitting their sides as they guzzled beers, while viewing CF-100s in their gun camera film. The Swordsmen also had great fun with the CF-100, branding it "Aluminum Crow", "Lead Sled" and "Clunk". Holding their ground, the all-weather boys would redouble their scorn. Occasionally they would have their own cine film, showing some hapless Sabre caught in their sights. One day a CF-100 pulled along side a Sabre. The Swordsman asked what the Clunk planned to do next. The reply? "Surrender now, or we'll explode!" This was all part of the RCAF spirit, something that everyone knew was non-existent in Soviet squadrons, where party commissars would admonish (if not banish) anyone for so much as smiling outside the context of the great (and pitiful) Communist cause.

The unfortunate 1st anniversary cake with Jack Ecker, Don Hanson, Ray Jolley, Murray Neilson, Bill Gill (Andy MacKenzie's successor), Dean Kelly, Norm Ronaasen, Les Bentham and Steve Atherton. (Jean Ecker Col.)

A visit by 441 pilots to the Bristol factory on January 28, 1953 brought a comment about the massive Brabazon transport, then being developed. The boys figured that this monster could carry the entire 441 establishment with room to spare. Next day, F/O Villeneuve made the longest 441 trip, taking a Sabre non-stop to the Orkneys and back in two hours. On the 30th F/L Kelly had a famil flight in a Venom at West Raynham. In the first week of February the wing contributed manpower for dyke-building in a local neighbourhood inundated by a flood. Duff weather on the 11th gave time for ground school: "Pilots watched training films all morning and talked to the IAM representatives [RCAF Institute of Aviation Medicine in Toronto] ... making suggestions for improvement in the safety equipment." On February 16 runway lighting was off for repairs, so flying control was aided by flares fired at the runway's end. This was a flop, since the flares caused too much smoke. One Sabre lost orientation for a few moments, nearly wiping out the flare crew! On the 20th the Silver Foxes celebrated their first anniversary in the UK by laying on a fancy cake, but the diarist had a sad result to report: "Unfortunately, disaster overtook the cake on the way down from the mess, when F/L Hanson took a corner too sharply."

Korean War

The RCAF closely followed news from Korea, where Sabres were fighting MiG-15s. Although exchange pilot F/L J.A.O. Levesque had seen Korean action in 1950-51 (see *The Canadair Sabre*), Canada at first was too busy getting NATO squadrons organized to get more involved. In March 1952, however, a scheme began whereby a few RCAF pilots were attached to USAF Korean units on 50-mission tours. The stated intention was to train tactical leaders all of whom, intially were wartime veterans. Meanwhile, F/O Claude LaFrance, a graduate of the first postwar RCAF pilot course, then instructing at Chatham, found himself well down the list for Korea. He explained to his CO that he was the only instructor without operational experience, and asked how that

S/L Andy MacKenzie, Maj James Jabara and W/C R.T.P. Davidson during Jabara's 1 Wing visit. (A.R. MacKenzie Col.)

The MiG-15 and MiG-17 would have been NATO's adversary fighters in any 1950's war. This MiG-17 warbird was at Griffiss AFB, NY in July 1990. (Mike Valenti)

knowledge was going to be passed on, if the "old sweats" hogged all the Korean postings. LaFrance made his point, got the job, shot down a MiG and earned an USAF DFC (see H.A. Halliday, "In Korean Skies", *Roundel*, December 1963 and January 1964). LaFrance later flew with 441 at Marville.

Only 22 RCAF Sabre pilots flew operationally in Korea. Lacking direct contact with the air war, Sabre pilots at home devoured whatever they could, even second hand. On March 12, 1952 those at North Luffenham were enthralled by a lecture from USAF Major James Jabara describing his battles with MiG-15s. On October 28 there was a raucous farewell at 1 Wing for Korea-bound S/L MacKenzie. He departed on November 6, but on December 5 came news that he was missing. The 441 diarist lamented, "All members of the squadron are living in the hope that future good news of his whereabouts will reach us." Eventually, word came that MacKenzie had become a victim of friendly fire - his USAF wingman had mistaken a Sabre for a MiG-15! MacKenzie would spend two years in Communist captivity, much in solitary confinement as the only RCAF Korean War Sabre casualty. For December 29, 1952, 441 noted: "W/C Davidson, who has just returned from Korea, visited the pilots room and imparted a few words of wisdom on the air war in that theatre." Davidson, another wartime veteran, had flown 51 Korean missions.

When S/L Andy MacKenzie got home from North Korea, AFHQ sent him on a speaking tour of Sabre wings. In October 2002 W/C Duke Warren recalled of this:

For his tour of the Air Division, Andy had an F-86 to get around. At the time I was instructing at the Luftwaffe's Sabre OTU in Oldenburg. Since Andy and I were good friends, he came up to visit. I invited him and Erich Hartmann, the leading Luftwaffe ace of WWII, over to our house for lunch. They had never met, but Andy knew Erich's reputation, and Erich, who had been a Soviet POW, was interested in meeting a recent prisoner of the Communists. As I recall, their conversation went something like this:

(Andy) Those bastards put me in solitary confinement and I nearly went crazy. Never saw anyone, food pushed through the door, light on all the time. Were you ever in solitary?

(Erich) For most of ten years.

(Andy) Ten years! How did you stand it?

(Erich) It was the only way to stay alive. It was warm, they fed you and the trees didn't fall on you.

Erich then explained how the Russians forced their POWs to work cutting trees in Siberia. With no safety rules, people often were injured, which was tantamount to a death sentence. If a POW couldn't work, he wasn't fed, and the barracks were unheated. Food was so scarce that nobody could help you.

Exercises, Flypasts and R&R

The more Sabre pilots flew, the better they became at their trade. Thus, at 441 Squadron the training intensified through early 1953, in spite of stormy weather. A diary entry of March 12, 1953 notes: "For the first time in some weeks, formations of four were flown on 'lurkin' exercises, always popular with the pilots, in which the skies are searched for Meteors, Canberras or anything else willing to play games." On March 18 the Silver Foxes toured Martin Baker, maker of ejection seats. Next day, while attacking a 439 Sabre, F/O Peter K. Cranston, crossing behind somebody, lost a drop tank in wake turbulence. The tank did not fall cleanly, but tore pieces from the wing, so that Sabre was out of commission for some time. On March 25 the diarist noted, "During the morning, pilots posed for photographs to be displayed in a squadron 'rogues gallery'. Several people made use of the skeet range." Such photos were taken routinely by the station photographic section. As to skeet shooting, it was important in keeping a pilot's gunnery sharp. On the range

Andy MacKenzie, Duke Warren and Erich Hartmann during their Oldenburg get together. (via Douglas "Duke" Warren)

The three North Luffenham squadrons (441 nearest, then 439 and 410) practice a mass formation for the Coronation fly-past. Of 441's 19163, '164, '134 and '151, the former went down at sea. While flying it on May 17, 1954, 1 Wing COpsO W/C W.F. Parks disappeared at sea. (Flight 27953)

pilots fired shotguns at clay pigeons flung aloft by a spring mechanism. The point was to blast the speedy little targets before they hit the ground. On March 31 F/O Paquette finally returned to flying after his motorcycle prang. Meanwhile, 441 was frequently firing at towed flags. Results were poor, less than 10% hits being typical.

By this time 441 was visiting the new RCAF bases on the Continent. F/L Kelly and F/Os Branch, Ronaasen and Haverstock overnighted at Zweibrucken on April 21, 1953. Many such trips were made to attend parties. There were other R&R locations, some more popular than others. Diary entries don't always say "party time", but one can guess about an entry such as that for October 23, 1953: "F/Ls Burns and Kelly, F/Os Paquette, Ronaasen and Jolley took off in the Expeditor at 1255 hours to spend the week-end in Copenhagen." Danish beer and Danish blondes (who knows for sure about the order) were always on a NATO fighter pilot's "to do" list.

Naturally, every fighter pilot in the UK wanted to try the Sabre. Check rides often were given, as in April 1953 when W/C Shields and S/L Murphy of the RAAF flew with 441. This would have been good experience for the Aussies, since they soon were to add Sabres to the RAAF inventory. When five Chipmunk pilots visited North Luffenham on April 28, F/O Villeneuve showed them what the Sabre could do. Then, five 441 pilots each had a Chipmunk ride. Besides daily routines, through April and May 441 did much formation practice (to say nothing of polishing and painting Sabres), getting ready for the Coronation flypast.

In the end, the summer of 1953 would prove historic by any definition, starting on May 21 when HRH the Duke of Edinburgh visited North Luffenham. The 441 team performed, as did Dean Kelly with a solo show. June 2 brought the great Coronation fly-past over London. Of 168 aircraft, 24 Sabres of 439 and 441 squadrons represented the RCAF. The diarist wrote: "The weather could hardly have been worse, with a 1000-foot ceiling and heavy rain showers. Still, from all reports the formation was quite good." These festivities permitted Canada to strut on other fronts, as when RCN Seafires and Avengers appeared at the June 15 Spithead Naval Review. Meanwhile, history was made on June 2-3 when RAF Canberras, one flown by RCAF exchange pilot F/L Steve Gulyas, rushed Coronation film across the Atlantic for immediate viewing in North American theatres. Late in June, 441 still was engaged in post-Coronation celebrations.

On June 13, 1953 a diary entry causes one to wonder: "F/O Gaudry flew to Horsham St. Faith today for an aerobatic display. There are reports of a Sabre interrupting the England-Australia test match in Nottingham at the same time, but this obviously must have been a mistake." Talk about hilarious (and there was no mistake)! On June 17 G/C Hale announced new pass standards in gunnery: 22% air-to-air, 35% air-to-ground. To help shame his pilots into shooting straighter, Hale allowed some non-pilot personnel to view their cine film. Scores gradually improved, a note of November 3, 1953 stating, "F/O Haverstock achieved 37% ... the highest attained yet."

Pilots on any RCAF squadron normally had secondary duties, i.e. other than flying Sabres. Sometimes these were welcomed, sometimes not, but the jobs had to be done. For July 1, 1953 these duties at 441 were:

Pilot	Duty
F/L Atherton	Operations officer
F/L Benson	Squadron fund, intelligence officer
F/L Burns	Sports officer
F/L Ecker	Operations training board
F/L Hanson	Public relations officer
F/L Simmons	Accident prevention officer, squadron artist
F/L Turner	Instrument officer, entertainment officer
F/O Branch	Monthly reports (ground), ops time board
F/O Brine	Education officer
F/O Fine	Canteen officer
F/O Gaudry	Aircraft recognition
F/O Haverstock	Navigation officer
F/O Jolley	Cine assessor, pilot attack instructor
F/O McDonald	Historical reports, safety equipment officer
F/O McIlraith	Barrack officer, publications officer
F/O Ronaasen	Photo officer
F/O Villeneuve	Monthly reports (air)
F/O Williamson	Flight room supervisor

Canberras B.6s of 139 Squadron over Lincolnshire in 1956. (Flight via Garnet Ovans)

Through the summer of 1953 air firing days at 1 Wing involved one aircraft from each squadron designated as a "tow ship" operating from RAF Coltishall. The range was over the North Sea, 35 miles northeast of Cromer. Pilots detailed for air firing would rendezvous with the Sabre target tug, and proceed to shoot up the drogue (as per cine footage). After a sortie the tow pilot returned to base. As he made a slow pass across the field, he opened his speed brakes, where cable and drogue were stored. The target kit then fell away to be retrieved, so that hits could be counted, something that always kept the pilots in suspense (a tally was easy to make since the bullets painted red, blue, etc. left their marks on the flag).

Large scale exercises gradually increased as with Ex. Coronet (July 27-30, 1953). The 441 diary described "Coronet" as providing "... training for AAFCE in their offensive support and defensive roles, and for related national air defence forces and anti-aircraft artillery. Our aircraft will simulate raids of high level jet bomber formations against selected targets in 2nd ATAF and 4th ATAF areas." On this exercise 441 simulated high-altitude bombers intruding into defending areas. Pilots had to refuel their own aircraft at Fürstenfeldbruck, Germany. Nevertheless, on the first and second days no 441 sorties were intercepted. On the 29th some competing Sabres came close but, on the 30th, 441 again evaded their pursuers.

Ex. Momentum followed on August 15 - 23, 1953. The scenario seemed to be based on the assumption that the Third World War was going to be a re-run of the previous one, only faster. Phase I had the "enemy" occupying bases in East Germany. Phase II had them as far west as the Rhine River, and in Phase III they occupied all of Northwest Europe. Fighters in Britain would thereafter "repel" enemy attacks in a sort of trans-sonic Battle of Britain. For August 16, 441 flew 47:55 hours, claiming 9 enemy aircraft destroyed, 2 probables and 1 damaged. The Silver Foxes stood down on the 17th and played only a minor role in events on the 18th, when they deployed to RAF Horsham St. Faith. Now they roared back as Phases II and III developed. From Horsham on August 22 - 23, 441 flew high-level sorties against Canberras.

High Fliers

While the RAF maintained that its Canberras were immune to interception, RCAF pilots claimed 20 "destroyed". Of the Canberra, former 441 pilot Bruce Burgess recounted in 2002, "We could catch them if we were undiscovered - we certainly could in a Mark 5. But if they saw us at altitude, all they had to do was make a gentle turn and they were away safely." (Flight had confirmed this in an October 1952 "Ardent" report: "... several Sabres reported that their quarry [Canberras] jinked away at the crucial moment with a higher rate of turn than the Sabre could itself muster, even with its 'all-flying' tail.")

Flight reported especially about how many "Momentum" Canberras, simulating Soviet intruders, penetrated Fighter Command's defensive screen. This was distressing, since NATO suspected that the Soviets likely had a similar jet bomber. What if these could get through so readily to hit UK targets with nuclear bombs? *Flight* gives an informative "big picture" of Ex. Momentum. It was an exciting exercise in which 1 Wing Sabres had their part to play in a mix of hundreds of participants:

During the first phase ... the UK air defences were subjected to very frequent and widespread raids, starting with attacks by single, low-flying Douglas B-26s operating from the 4th ATAF bases in Southern Germany. Between 2100 and 2200 hours on the first evening, 12 Canberras operating singly from bases in Denmark and the 2nd ATAF area flew in from the North Sea at between 40,000 ft. and 43,000 ft., simulating atom bomb attacks on some airfields in Scotland and East Anglia. Several Canberras were intercepted by Meteor and Vampire night fighters.

Medium-sized formations of Canberras followed up the attack against principal cities; then, small groups of Lincolns and Washingtons flew over London and Portsmouth, and later Coventry and Birmingham, with many interceptions reported. Soon after first light, high-flying B-45 jet bombers were intercepted by 2nd ATAF Venoms, based for the exercise at Ouston, near Newcastle. At the same time, Meteors and RCAF Sabres intercepted other F-86s and F-84s from 4th ATAF, simulating high-altitude jet bombers over the Thames Estuary.

Coastal convoys from Portsmouth and Harwich were given Meteor escorts against intensive attacks by Fleet Air Arm Attackers, Wyverns and Sea Furies, which in all cases were intercepted before they reached the convoy. Other Meteors attacked some of the F-84s and F-86s of the 4th ATAF which attacked airfields and other targets in East Anglia, but the F-84s were considered to have made successful dive bombing attacks on some occasions.

Canberras continued their sorties in small formations, and interceptions were reported by Meteors of No.616 Sqn., R. Aux. A.F., and Meteors of a regular squadron based in Cambridge. Edinburgh was twice attacked in daylight by Canberras flying at over 40,000 ft, and a small formation of F-86s crossed the coast at Hastings and passed over London with Meteors in pursuit.

In February 2003 Ralph Annis of 441 recalled another Canberra anecdote involving North Luffenham Sabres:

Before the RAF introduced its V-Bombers, one of our regular scrambles was to intercept Canberras coming in from the Continent. The Canberras usually were at about 40,000 feet over the North Sea

- they weren't very speedy. On one intercept, we got some good film on a pair of Canberras. I advised our formation that we make a good search, since there usually were three Canberras. A few minutes later I spotted him quite wide at 3 o'clock.

Since he was painted all white, our other pilots also had trouble picking him up. If you took your eyes off him for a second, he seemed to disappear. We all slid over for a closer look (in those days before the air-to-air missile, the only "radar" in the typical day fighter was the Mark One Eyeball). While our radio discipline usually was good, this time we were busy passing comments about this "disappearing Canberra". We wondered if our comments had been duly recorded and passed on to Air Ministry for, when the V-Bombers appeared, they also were all-white. We later heard, however, that this scheme was needed to reflect the flash from an exploding A-bomb.

On August 20, 1953 G/C J.D. "Red" Somerville took command of 1 Wing from G/C Hale. That same day F/O Les Benson had some trouble in 19158 on 441's last sortie of the day:

As the flight was preparing to shoot on the flag, Benson's aircraft flamed out. He immediately started a glide from 9000 feet toward land about 30 miles away. Six minutes later at 2500 feet, five miles off Cromar, Benson bailed out, parachuted into the water and clambered into his dinghy. He signalled that all was well to F/L Kelly, who had remained with him from the time of flame out. Kelly then went to the nearest ship and fired his guns to attract its attention. After 40 minutes Benson was picked up by the ship "Adam Beck" from which he was transferred to an RAF rescue launch and kissed soil again at Yarmouth.

G/C Somerville, a wartime RCAF night fighter pilot, was a greatly respected postwar figure. The "groupie" was noted for his sense of humour, something that led to this brief news item (publication unknown):

No.1 RCAF Fighter Wing at North Luffenham are trying a new method calculated to reduce flying accidents. A goat is involved. Once a month the statistics for aircraft accidents are studied, the squadron with the worst accident record is ceremonially awarded a live and very un-military goat. The pilot committing the worst flying error is given custody of the animal with full military honours at a Station parade.

The hapless pilot who wins the goat for the month must personally make sure that it is properly fed and quartered, a duty which effectively eliminates week-end leave passes. The ambition of the station commander, G/C J.D. Somerville, DSO, DFC, is to be left with the goat on his hands at the end of the month, and no accidents to worry about.

Apart from exercises 441 reported some off-beat events in this period. On July 27, 1953 Capt Ben Fryiklund of the Royal Swedish Air Force was checked out on a Sabre. Two days later, again with 441, he became the first "Supersonic Swede". Another visitor was Lt Bert W. Mead, RCN, who reported on September 1, 1953 for a week of flying (he previously had flown Sabres at the RCAF Winter Experimental Flight). Early September involved practicing for the Battle of Britain Flypast, which took place over London on the 15th, S/L Gill leading: "The flypast was led by a Hurricane and a Spitfire flying at 185 kts in close formation. 240 jets followed." On September 19 North Luffenham held an open house for 35,000 visitors. Hollywood star Gary Cooper was on hand, and spent the night in the Officers' Mess.

To sharpen standards, the Air Division now began putting Sabre pilots through T-33 instrument training at Zweibrucken. F/L Dean Kelly left for "Zwei" to take the month-long course on September 21. On the 28th several 441 "old timers" were posted to No.1 Overseas Ferry Unit, being formed at St. Hubert under S/L Bob Middlemiss. F/Ls Benson, Ecker, C.R. Simmons and Walker, and F/Os Gaudry, McDonald and McIlraith were named. The OFU would become one of the RCAF's more notorious units. Its pilots, who always would get their Sabres and T-33s safely across the pond, earned a reputation (of which they were proud) of being ill-behaved party animals.

On October 6 F/O Heron had a flame-out and force landed in a field. For the rest of 1953 life at 441 included few remarkable events. On the last day of the year the diary noted, "A good flying day. Many squadron personnel away on New Year leave, but all serviceable aircraft were kept busy in the air all day. Daily total: 18:40 hours. Monthly total: 278:45 hours."

Last Year at "North Luff"

For January 1954 bad weather would hinder operations. As late as the 15th the diarist was reporting, "A very strong wind, gusts to 60 knots caused flying to cease at 1400 hours." Four days later F/O Fine landed at RAF Watton with a dead engine. His nose wheel collapsed on touchdown, causing considerable damage. On the 26th the pilots wrote their aircraft recognition exam. This subject remained important - in war a Sabre pilot had to be spot-on in recognition before firing on a target.

On February 1 and 2 the squadron was unable to take off for gunnery at RAF Acklington due to icy runways. On the 3rd, North Luffenham was open, but not Acklington. The latter finally was cleared by hand-shovelling (even the runways)

Sports were an integral part of squadron life. Here, 441 enjoys some volleyball. (A.R. MacKenzie Col.)

Each 441 squadron photo showed some new faces. Previous ones were missing, fellows having been posted or, sometimes, lost in accidents. This group dates to February 1954 at North Luffenham. Standing are F/L Dean Kelly, F/Os Abbott, Don Myles, Pete Cunningham, Jim Johnson, Bernie Eburn and Harry Klein, S/L Bill Gill, F/O "Mick" Fikowski, F/Ls Ray Jolley and Neil Burns, and F/O D.D. "Dave" Mills. In front are F/Os Jim Webber, Jim Raine, D.E. Bradley, Malcolm "Mac" MacGregor, Don Bergie and Ron Clayton, F/L Steve Atherton, and F/Os Ken Branch and Len Fine. Of this crowd Bradley, Cunningham and Fine later were lost in accidents. (Ray Jolley Col.)

on the 4th, so 441 got away. For the following days cruddy weather blanketed Acklington. Only after January 16 could 441 get in any serious flying. During this camp both flags and towed gliders were used as targets. On February 24 all Sabres flew home. Soon 441 was back at its routines, practicing intercepts and gunnery, formation and instrument flying, doing airshows, attending lectures, keeping on top of sports and entertainment, etc.

April 30 to May 2, 1954 the Silver Foxes took part in "Rabbit Trek", an escape and evasion exercise. Participants were dropped off miles from North Luffenham, then tried returning without being picked up by "the enemy". Only a few evaders made it all the way. The rest were apprehended, incarcerated and interrogated. Sometimes during an E&E exercise a pilot would return with a black eye, or other signs of rough handling by over-zealous MPs.

Since late 1953, unfortunately, 441's diarist was offering few details or colour in his entries - it appears that someone new had taken over. But one tidbit appeared on May 12, 1954: "The squadron pilots played 410 (F) Squadron pilots softball, defeating them 18-0." Ex. Dividend (July 17-29) kept 441 busy with daily totals as high as 60+ sorties. A new type of gun camera, however, proved disappointing, with many intercepts going unconfirmed due to poor film results. In the end the following successes were confirmed: Sabres killed - 17 plus 4 probables, Meteors - 10/3, Vampires - 10/0, F-84s - 9/2, Canberras - 6/3, B-45s - 5/1, Hunters - 1/0.

For August 1954 the 441 diary notes rocket firing on the range at Tichwell, 15 sorties being flown on the 17th. August 31 was a red letter day: "A concentrated effort made today to put squadron flying time over the monthly 500 hours ... A complete training programme was flown with the exception of actual firing exercises, making it the best flying day of the month... Visibility was such that the majority of squadron pilots got the best aerial view of United Kingdom of any they had seen so far. Daily total: 49:35 hours. Monthly total: 515:55 hours."

By November the weather again was turning. For the 10th: "The weather was again poor, but good enough for air-to-ground firing early in the morning and six sorties were flown." Also on this day, F/L Dean Kelly made his first flight in the Hunter at West Raynham. Friday, November 12 was a day to let one's hair down - "In the evening the squadron held its annual ball in the NAAFI building and a good time was had by all." There is no explanation in the diary, but for the next two days the only comment is "Squadron stood down."

On November 17, with frost on the runway, Kelly flew the early weather flight. He deemed conditions satisfactory and 23:20 hours were logged before flying gave way to afternoon sports. On the 21st F/O Raine couriered a part via Sabre to Prestwick for a North Star that was grounded there. The 28th proved to be 441's last day of flying at North Luffenham: "Squadron officers assembled in the morning and had a group photo taken... we are now without aircraft until reaching 3 (F) Wing, Zweibrucken, Germany."

F/O Ian R. McDonald shows his flying kit to Hon. George Drew, Canadian High Commissioner in London during an October 1, 1952 VIP visit. G/C Hale is on the right, S/L MacKenzie looks on. (441 Squadron)

Two types on which an RCAF fighter pilot "hopefuls" like Ian McDonald trained in the 1950s - the Harvard and the Expeditor. (CF)

S/L Duke Warren presenting Andy Mackenzie with a commemorative painting of the "Checkerboard" nag. 50 years later, Andy's wife, Alison, took this "update" photo.

Silver Fox Career

Born in Montreal on August 27, 1928, Ian Russell McDonald joined 401 (Aux) Squadron in 1947 as an airman, but later was picked by his CO for pilot training. This commenced at 1 Manning Depot in Toronto, then McDonald joined Course 9 at Centralia, flying initially on January 4, 1949 in Harvard 2782. He soloed on February 8, advanced to the Expeditor on July 22, finished his course on August 22, then attended Air Armament School at Trenton. All through his training McDonald's friend from 438 (Aux) Squadron, Jean Rivest, was his shadow. Now they returned to St. Hubert with their commissions, the Vampire being next on their agenda. F/O Bob Ayres gave a thorough ground school then, on November 10, 1949, McDonald flew Vampire 17021. W/C J.F. "Stocky" Edwards signed off his log book at the end of the course, which included 15 Vampire flights. McDonald now rejoined his squadron mates on 401. In November 1950 McDonald transferred to the RCAF Permanent Force and took a fighter refresher course at Chatham. He and his course mates then became the initial cadre of 441 Squadron under S/L Andy MacKenzie. It was no secret that 441 was destined for North Luffenham. For now, however, it still was working up on Vampires. By this time McDonald had some 400 flying hours.

McDonald first flew the Sabre on July 30. Through this period he was getting to know his squadron mates, young pilots like Don "Big Steve" Atherton, Les Benson, Gar Brine, Pete Cranston, Jack Ecker, Jean Gaudry, Bob Haverstock, Ray Himmelman, brothers Bob and Don Simmons, Fern Villeneuve and others. He quickly logged a dozen Sabre transition flights, then came several delivery flights from Canadair to 441. Finally, McDonald joined his fellow pilots in ferrying Sabres to Norfolk, Virginia, where they were craned aboard HMCS *Magnificent* for the UK. On October 22, for example, McDonald flew 19185 to Norfolk via Wilmington. Meanwhile, 441 continued with routine training to keep the pilots "on the ball". On November 6 McDonald flew a sortie with Bob Haverstock, who somehow lost an underwing tank along the way. On December 13 McDonald and two squadron mates delivered three Sabres from Cartierville to Bagotville, likely for 413 Squadron, then forming in "Bagtown" under S/L J.D. Lindsay.

While busy with official activities, 441 kept up its "social" activities - all good fighter pilots in those days had to drink as well as they flew! Great skits always seemed to be part of this life, and 410 pulled off one of the best at 441's expense. One evening some of the fellows, Mike Doyle and Grant Nichols included, "borrowed" an old nag from a farmer, painted its rear end in 441 checkerboard pattern, and led it into S/L MacKenzie's office. In the dead of night some AC2 on security heard a din along the hangar line and peered in the CO's window. The poor fellow was terrified when, there in the murkiness, he came nose to nose with a horse! In the morning the CO showed up to find his office in a mess. Word soon got around and even the AOC of Air Defence Command, G/C MacBrien, came over for a look. The usually taciturn groupie burst into laughter!

A December 19, 1951 flight with F/O Dean Kelly proved interesting for F/O McDonald. That day Kelly took him up in 14681, one of the T-33s on loan from the USAF. At 28,000 feet they flamed out, started down and were at 9000 before Kelly got a relight. All in a day's work, they probably figured, if they even gave it a thought. McDonald soloed in '681 on December 29. For the month he logged 6:20 on the Sabre, 2:35 on the T-bird - there still wasn't much flying going on. On January 2, 1952 McDonald noted for a T-bird flight, "First ride with the boss." Sad news came on January 6 - Jean Rivest had been killed in a Vampire crash.

For January 11 McDonald tabulated his jet time: Vampire 95:05 hours, F-86 - 44:45, T-33 - 10:10. Also in McDonald's log this day is this note: "Ceased flying at RCAF Station St. Hubert on 11th January 1952 on transfer to North Luffenham, England on 13th February 1952." The squadron now embarked for England and soon was starting work-ups at "North Luff". McDonald flew first in 19160 on March 3 - "Sector recce and QGH" (QGH being a controlled descent through cloud). Pilots immediately started doing readiness. This entailed two Sabres sitting in the 441 dispersal throughout the day, armed and ready to scramble. A pilot would spend two hours in the cockpit, then be spelled off by the next fellow on the schedule. The action slowly increased: March 11 - "Saw 24 Meteors over East Anglia", March 17 - "Saw 8 Vampires, 4 Meteors and 4 Sabres (US) over East Anglia", March 22 - "24 plane Wing do. Saw 29 B-29s", March 25 - "Low level map reading and local". For the month McDonald flew 11 times for 12:30 hours. On April 7 he noted his first UK night flying. On the 16th he took part in a fly-past honouring a visit from the Chief of the Air Staff, A/M W.A. Curtis.

On May 15, 1952 McDonald towed 441's first drogue target. Next day he did the squadron's first air-to-ground firing from North Luffenham. A nav exercise operated to Rhein Main (Frankfurt) on May 26 in 1:20 hours, thence to Fürstenfeldbruck (Munich) in 0:55, a low-level effort with Kelly, Himmelman and Ronaasen. The boys overnighted at "Fursty", then flew home next day in 1:35 hours (a good go for a Sabre 2 with "jugs", or underwing tanks). On July 11 McDonald was in a 441 gaggle to Chièvres, Belgium, flying 19183. The plan was to join in a fly-past over Brussels honouring NATO. Things went well, but not exactly as planned, for this was the time that Dean Kelly "boomed" the proceedings.

More routine activities continued, McDonald doing fighter affiliation with B-50s on July 18. A coastal recce of August 17 likely was a weather flight. As to "adversaries" over the UK, 441 found many. Although slower, as McDonald recalled, Meteors and Vampires could out-turn a Sabre. If inattentive in a tail chase with one of these, a Sabre pilot could find himself out of airspeed. Without some air underneath his wings, this could be dangerous. On the other hand, aggressive Vampire pilots could over-stress their

Jack Ecker, Bob Simmons and Buzz Neilson at 1 Wing. Then, others with their Silver Fox friend in the background - Andy MacKenzie, Ralph Annis, Pete Cranston and Steve Atherton. (Jean Ecker, 441 Sqn Cols.)

Jack Turner, Bob Haverstock & Don Williamson ready to scramble! (Remi Paquette)

machines. In at least one case a Vampire tore itself apart while tangling with a Sabre. Ian McDonald found the Venom (based on the Vampire, but more powerful) a challenging opponent.

On October 4, 441 joined in Ex. Ardent, one of the first grand-scale NATO air exercises. To October 12 F/O McDonald flew eight GCI "Ardent" sorties. Targets usually were Meteors coming out of Europe, simulating Soviet bombers. Whenever recovering from such sorties, McDonald put the GCA operators to work. For him this was the way to go - use all available resources and get good at them. Others, whether lazy, unsure of themselves, or prone to "macho" behaviour, preferred doing it all VFR. On a sortie of January 29, 1953 in 19168 McDonald noted, "Low flying over Belgium and Netherlands. Saw 6 Meteors from 56 Squadron." On January 21 he and his mates were beating up North Luffenham to let the base defence force practice on high speed targets with their Bofors guns.

Jack Ecker, Gar Brine, Don Williamson, Steve Atherton, Jean Gaudry, Don Hanson Bob Simmons in a jovial 1952 scene from North Luffenham. (Remi Paquette)

Before leaving North Luffenham in December 1954, 441's officers assembled for a final photo. Behind are F/Os Malcolm MacGregor, Dave Mills, Harvey Davidson, Nory Nishimura (armament officer), Harry Klein (in front of Nory), Don Bergie, Jim Stacey, Bob Cockburn, Jim Raine, Bernie Eburn, Dave Bradley, D.H. "Don" Myles and Jim Johnson. In front are F/Ls Neil Burns and Russ Armstrong (EO), F/O Alan Lockhart, F/L Dean Kelly, S/L D.R. Cuthbertson (CO), and F/Os Morley White, Len Fine, Ron Clayton and Norm Ronaasen. (D.H. Myles Col.)

On February 2, 1953 F/L McDonald was tour expired. Flying with 441 had been a fabulous time, but now he packed and boarded the SS *Ascania* for home. Soon he was at Trenton for the flying instructors course, then beginning a tour instructing NATO students at 4 FTS in Penhold. First he was on the Harvard, then the T-34. After a flight in Harvard 3141 of July 12, 1955 F/L McDonald left the RCAF, his log book showing 1670:25 hours. He now settled in Montreal with his family. Before long he dropped by Canadair, enquiring about work. Ken Ebel, a senior management type soon got McDonald some connections, and he started work in F-86 and T-33 technical support.

Through chief pilot Bill Longhurst, McDonald would get the occasional flight, starting with Ian McTavish in the CL-41 on March 28, 1961. In 1973 he became the assistant to chief pilot Doug Adkins. This period in his career began with a flight of April 9 in CL-215 CF-TXH. Henceforth, McDonald was much involved in CL-215 development. Sometimes he also flew the CL-41 chase plane, or the Turbo Mallard, which served Canadair's VIP fishing camp north of Lac St. Jean. As the Challenger developed, he joined that program. By the time he retired in August 1990 Ian McDonald had logged some 1000 hours on the CL-215, 4000 on the Challenger. Now he and his wife Joan settled in Orleans, near Ottawa.

F/O Norman Bigg at "North Luff"

In 1951 Norman Bigg finished high school and joined the RCAF. Serving first as an aero engine mechanic at Centralia, one day "out of the blue" he was singled out for pilot training. This began at Centralia, F/L Ainsley taking him aloft in a Chipmunk on October 10, 1952. Soon finished with the 25-hour primary flying course, Bigg progressed to FTS and AFS at Portage la Prairie, then to MacDonald for gunnery, all this being done on Harvards.

Late in 1953 F/O Bigg was posted to the OTU at Chatham. There he first flew the Sabre (19416) on December 16, finished his course, and was posted to 441 Squadron at North Luffenham. Bigg would leave the regular RCAF in 1959 to join 411 (Aux) Squadron at Downsview, there to spend 12 years, first on the F-86 and T-33, then the Expeditor and Otter. Meanwhile, he had joined Air Canada in 1966, starting on the Viscount and serving to 1991, by when he was a captain on the Boeing 767. In January 2003 Norman Bigg reminisced about 441 days:

In May 1954 I was part of a 441 contingent aboard an RCAF North Star. We began at St. Hubert, refuelled at Goose Bay and Prestwick, then reached North Luffenham. All the time we were squeezed into uncomfortable canvas seats and crammed in among baggage and a spare jet engine. Naturally, my personal kit did not arrive at the same time as I. Although we had only landed on a Wednesday, there was little time to adjust to our new home - on Friday I was thrown off the back of a lorry on an escape and evasion exercise. It wasn't long before a buddy and I were chased from a ditch by a patrol, then pursued over hill and dale in the darkness. For some time I parallelled what I thought was a canal, looking for a bridge to cross. Finally, I realized that this was no canal at all, but a rain-slicked road. Moonlight shining on it had tricked me.

Eventually, I found a place to sleep, then awoke to an incredible sight. I was on the grounds of a well-manicured estate, with countless rabbits scurrying about. By this time I was sore and hungry, and losing that "esprit de corps" that we were supposed to have. I set off again, this time down a country lane - I was tired of thrashing through hawthorn hedges. Before long, a police car came along and I was "arrested", delivered to the Army, stripped, searched and thrown into a cell. Later, I was led into a cozy office with a fire place. I was interrogated by a kindly old fellow, who offered me tea, a cigarette and a chair, if I would tell him what I knew. Since I had only been in Blighty for a few days, I had little to offer.

Happily, the E&E exercise ended the next day and we got on with normal duties. I made my first flight on squadron on April 26, 1954, taking up Sabre 19142. At this stage, however, I was considered a sprog at 441 until the next junior pilot came along. On my first sortie it was a real battle hanging in with my Lead and not making an ass of myself. After surviving the first part of my initial exercise, Lead called me in to close formation. He then put me in line astern and proceeded to try to shake me off. Then he popped his speed brakes and pulled into cloud. I followed, but quickly rolled onto my back to get back into the clear. In this mayhem, one of my wings sliced the top few inches off his tail.

I heard no more of Lead, so thought that I must have killed him. Once I was in the circuit, however, I saw a crowd around a Sabre on the ramp. As I turned final, my Sabre started to shake. Then I noticed a chunk on metal stuck in my leading edge. When my slats deployed, this FOD fell away. I landed safely, but the episode shook my confidence. For a while I had a hard time doing 4-plane aerobatics. In the aftermath, S/L Cuthbertson spoke to each of us separately. He gave us a hard time, but nothing went on our records. Failing all else, the CTechO now had a good "hangar queen" from which he could rob parts.

When it came to Sabre pilots, Dean Kelly was our best. It was only Dean who could dazzle the Royal Family with such amazing aerobatics. His favourite manoeuvre was to take off, then hold his Sabre on the deck, while cleaning it up. Next, he would dive out of sight into a valley, then pull into a loop, doing a roll off the top. We wondered how he avoided stalling at the top. All he had to say was that you had to "catch the flick at the top", before your Sabre stalled out.

When it came to navigating in poor weather, the area around North Luffenham was tricky - there was such a myriad of roads and railroads from which to choose! The best way to get home after an exercise was to descend over The Wash, pick up a particular canal, then follow it to a well-known smokestack. Then you knew that you were nearly home. Otherwise, you would use GCA, a very reliable system, when it was working.

F/O Norman Bigg while at North Luffenham. Like many such pilots on Short Service Commissions, he left the RCAF after five years to fly for the airlines. (Bigg Col.)

A view heading into the town of Marville as shot by Norm Bigg.
Also, a photo by LAC John Meuse of 1 Wing HQ and surrounding facilities.

CHAPTER 9

On To Marville

Good-bye "North Luff"

Late in 1954 No.1 Wing left for the Continent, but its new home in Marville, France was not ready. Thus did 410 Squadron temporarily squat at 4 Wing, Baden-Soellingen, 441 at 3 Wing, Zweibrucken, while 439 would follow in April 1955 to Marville. Because the move crowded all facilities, unmarried officers were sent on leave until the end of December. When it came time for 1 Wing to leave North Luffenham, there were regrets all around. Britain had been a friendly, familiar country which had become more comfortable as the vestiges of wartime austerity faded. At an official level, in February 1955 Britain's Secretary of State for Air, Lord De L'Isle and Dudley, wrote to the Honourable Ralph Campney, Canada's Minister of National Defence:

> Just over three years ago we welcomed back to this country the first units of the Royal Canadian Air Force stationed here since the end of the late war. The RAF station at North Luffenham was then handed over to No.1 Fighter Wing. These were the first fighter squadrons sent to Europe by the Canadian Government as part of the generous contribution which Canada makes to the strength of the North Atlantic Treaty Organization.
>
> The RCAF has been doubly welcome as partners in NATO as well as in the Commonwealth. On my own visits to North Luffenham I have admired the way in which officers and men have made themselves at home among us and have made lasting friendships in the neighbourhood.
>
> I know how welcome you have been in Fighter Command, where your squadrons have made a most efficient and valuable contribution to the air defences of the United Kingdom.
>
> Now, as the last of you leave, many of you to join the Canadian squadrons now deployed on the Continent, I offer you in the name of the Air Council and Her Majesty's Government our thanks for the exemplary way in which you have upheld the great reputation of the RCAF and our best wishes for the future.

Those from 441 arriving at Zweibrucken found it unfinished, so everyone chipped in where possible. The diary notes for December 28, "Space for squadron operations was allotted at 434 (F) Sqn dispersal. Acceptance checks are now being done on new Sabre Mk V aircraft for the squadron." On January 3, 1955 F/L Fine made the first 441 Sabre 5 flight. Working up on the Sabre 5 (16 of which soon equipped 441) was done cautiously, beginning with a mandatory hour on the T-33. There also were lectures, especially about the Orenda engine, and local conditions and procedures - West Germany was not England. Foul weather came with January and February, so the diary is replete with volleyball and basketball scores. Courses abounded, including flight safety back in Canada (F/O Mills), skiing in France (F/O Myles), E&E around Bad Tolz (F/O McIlraith) and current affairs (F/O Pigot). Many from the squadron attended the world hockey championships being held in West Germany, where Canada beat Russia 5-0. On March 9, 1955 F/Os Bergie, Johnson and Webber flew to Marville with Sabre 5s for 439 Squadron ("the first Sabres to land there.")

When he was CO of 441 (1956 - 59) S/L Lou Hill took this wide view of 1 Wing, Marville.

Commencing on March 9, 1955, 441 would fly into Marville for a day's work, then return to Zweibrucken each evening. Finally, on March 28 all 16 Sabres flew to Marville to stay. G/C J.D. Somerville welcomed them, and they held their first Marville party in the mess that evening. Even so, things were a bit rough: "As the runway at Marville is not completed as yet, we can only fly between ... 1200 and 1330, when the workers are having their dinner, as well as all day Sunday." The base was also short of refuelling bowsers, so commuting between Marville and "Zwei" continued until mid-May.

On April 6, 441 moved into its hangar. The big excitement on the 16th concerned five Sabres diverting to Grostenquin, when a disabled RCAF Bristol Freighter obstructed the runway

A 441 Sabre 5 in the earliest 441 Marville colour scheme. This machine ended its days as a pilotless drone with Flight Systems. On July 25, 1981 it was shot down over the White Sands missile range in New Mexico. (Norm Bigg)

for several hours. In this period the Air Division began painting over its lovely Sabre colour schemes, the diary for April 25 noting, "F/Os Eburn, Davidson, Clayton and Pigot flew four aircraft to Hooten Park [near Chester] to be camouflaged." Most Sabres now looked alike except for tail colours, although these could be garish.

The "Air Div" operated as a single force during Ex. Carte Blanche, held June 20-28, 1955. For this exercise some 3000 NATO aircraft conducted a simulated atomic war exercise. Involved were 12 RCAF squadrons flying nearly 2500 sorties. Some aircrew were billeted in Maginot Line bunkers or fortifications dating to the Franco-Prussian War of 1870, while others lived under canvas in conditions evocative of the Normandy campaign 11 years earlier. "Carte Blanche" also marked the first time that Canadian airwomen were deployed in field exercises. The intensity of operations on this occasion is suggested by F/O Ron Clayton's 441 Squadron logbook:

A typical "Carte Blanche" scene, where squadrons could be deployed to marginal airfields. (CF PL82263)

Date	Sabre	Time
June 23, 1955	23323	1:25 hours
	23229	1:00
June 24, 1955	23314	1:15
June 25, 1955	23339	1:15
June 26, 1955	23109	1:20
	23045	1:25
June 27, 1955	23337	1:05
	23337	1:10

The RCAF's fleet of Bristol Freighters (137 Transport Flight) supported 1 Air Division. Based at Langar (near North Luffenham), the Bristols flew weekly "skeds" to each wing, and special flights as needed, e.g. moving men and cargo to and from Rabat and Decimomannu for gunnery. To their horror, Sabre pilots sometimes were pulled off squadron to do a stint on the Bristol. AI navigator F/L Ted Simkins took this photo of "9699" at Marville. It served 1955 - 67, then was sold to Wardair of Yellowknife, and now belongs to the Western Canada Aviation Museum in Winnipeg.

Zulu Alert

An important Air Division tasking was "Zulu Alert", a description of which appears in a 441 December 20, 1955 diary entry: "A draw was held to determine which pilots would go on Exercise Zulu ... a 'hot gun' alert done one week in six at Zweibrucken. Ten pilots and aircraft are required..." Zulu

Zulu Alert at 3 Wing. A flight of 441 Sabres on 5-minute standby near the end of the runway. Then, the tents where pilots and servicing crew waited. On most Zulu shifts at least one 2-plane section would be scrambled on a practice GCI exercise. (Don Syms)

pilots normally stood by with a section of four Sabres at 10-minute readiness (i.e. to be airborne within that time) and one at 30-minute readiness . There were frequent practice scrambles, sometimes against NATO aircraft, although unit diaries and pilot logs rarely give any details. The 441 diary for August 1957 makes this brief reference: "Our droguing was interrupted in the middle of the month by the inevitable Zulu. Fortunately, the weather was above average and we managed about 30 sorties a day throughout our commitment." For the same month F/O Ron Hayman's log records the following for a 441 Zulu period:

Date	Sabre 6	Time Aloft
August 8	23636 Zulu	1.10
	23556 Zulu	0.40
August 10	23432 Zulu	1.20
	23555 Zulu	1.20
August 11	23556 Zulu	1.15
	23512 Zulu	1.30
August 12	23578 Test flight	1:05
August 13	23687 Zulu	1.25
	23512 Zulu	1.15

Also from the December 20, 1955 diary is this Zweibrucken banter: "Several married personnel were chosen [for Zulu duty] but, as the alert includes Christmas, this was looked upon as somewhat of a hardship. Very generously, the single men (stout fellows) offered to replace the married men for a small consideration. This is to be in the form of a case of Baccardis abetted by sufficient Coca Cola... the offer was accepted. S/L Cuthbertson and ten single men will defend the bastions of the free from the communist hordes from 21Dec. to 28 Dec." The diarist reported that on Christmas Day the pilots enjoyed a sumptuous dinner in their tent at the end of the runway at Zweibrucken. "A large time was had by all", is how he summarized the

Ron Hayman flying BT-667 on August 22, 1957. This Sabre 6 served the RCAF from June 1956 to March 1963. (Tom Gigliotti)

affair. Guests included the squadron Other Ranks, who had accompanied 441 to Zweibrucken, and four nurses. The station commander and 434 Squadron CO also dropped by for a Christmas beer.

The next mention of Zulu is a cryptic one of January 30, 1956: "Today we once again journeyed to Zweibrucken to perform the onerous duty known as Zulu. Enough said!" During March 1956 Zulu a live scramble is mentioned: "One section intercepted a USAF T-33 which had violated the Austrian border." Although Zulus usually were at regular intervals, sometimes a squadron was excused for such other duties as gunnery in Sardinia. This meant that

S/L Donald R. "Cuppy" Cuthbertson was one of the RCAF's best-liked postwar characters. Having joined the RCAF in 1941, he instructed, then flew Spitfires with 416 Squadron (2 Luftwaffe aircraft destroyed). Based at Goose Bay after the war, he excelled in search and rescue. For this he received the Air Force Cross. Cuthbertson succeeded S/L Gill as 441 CO (1954 - 56), then commanded the Overseas Ferry Unit at St. Hubert. (CF PL58031)

No Sabre wing could operate without its GCI people - the airmen and airwomen who controlled all fighter operations, guiding interceptors to their targets, then bringing them home. In The Canadair Sabre, controller Bob Durnan, whose original artwork is shown, explains the importance of his trade.

another squadron had to take up the slack. When 439 was absent in March 1958, 441 did Zulu Alerts in the first and last weeks of the month. In October 439 again was in Sardinia, so 441 stood sentry in the first and third weeks that month.

In second-guessing the Cold War, it is easy to forget the real tensions that existed. Depending on events (as with Berlin), people on both sides of the Iron Curtain could be nervous in varying degrees. Such a case occurred in March 1957, when 441 Zulu Sabres were scrambled after a bogie at 64,000 feet - likely a CIA U-2 spy plane. The diary notes: "Needless to say we didn't catch him." With other happenings such as the Cuban missile crisis, Cold War stakes reached new danger levels, so the role of the RCAF in NATO was ever more crucial. A Zulu scramble of June 26, 1957 would have been taken most gravely. That day four "Zulu" Sabres from 2 Wing intercepted a "bogey" soon ID'd as a Soviet Il-14 transport, off track while en route to Zurich. The Canadians escorted it to Swiss airspace. Three 1959 Zulu entries from the No.1 Air Division diary are chilling reminders of how jumpy even professionals could be:

October 14: *Two Canadian sections of four aircraft were diverted from a practice to a live scramble on a track in the Buffer Zone. After the interception the track was identified as a West German T-33 which had unintentionally crossed the border.*

October 22: *Information received from 4 ATAF concerning a message said to have originated from the Chief Controller of the Russian Sector of Berlin that there had been too many border violations lately and that further violations would be acted upon by the Russians.*

October 27: *Strongbox Sierra from Zweibrucken was ordered to scramble "live" on a track originating from East Germany. The section of four F-86s intercepted the track at 0931Z and identified it as two F-100 type aircraft of the USAF.*

Scramble Tales

In May 2003 John L. MacArthur and Gary Corbett recalled some scramble incidents from 441 days:

When standing alert during Europe's long and usually wet winters, we occasionally would have to start our aircraft to "blow the cockpit". This procedure would keep moisture from accumulating, then freezing our controls when airborne. On starting the engine we would close the canopy and pressurize the cockpit. The ground crew would open a small port at the bottom of the Sabre and any excess moisture would be expelled.

In preparation for a scramble some pilots would leave their 'chutes in the cockpit, ready to jump into them. Others preferred to sling them over a drop tank under the wing, donning them before climbing into the cockpit. Occasionally, someone would keep his 'chute dry by leaving it in the nose intake.

One rainy day four pilots, including 441's OC, W/C Blake Smiley, DFC, dashed out to blow their cockpits. As they fired up their Swords, W/C Smiley heard a horrible clanging sound. Shutting down his engine, he realized too late that he had left his 'chute "up the spout"! Scratch one Orenda 14 engine...

Several incidents occurred while on Zulu in the ORP. In one case the alert crew was in their bunks when the hair-raising klaxon blared. Scramble! Being spring-loaded to the scramble position, one gung-ho young Sabre jock awoke from his sound sleep. In leaping from his bunk, he took a wrong turn, crashing head first into a concrete wall. Only a section of three got airborne that day...

One day we had a visit from RAF Staff College - the students were to observe a scramble and quick turn-around. At the door of the ORP they were greeted by the klaxon's blare as four eager pilots careened to their steeds. In the process more than one of the RAF brass got a bit tarnished as the Sabre jocks stampeded through the group.

The Sabres were parked in front of the ORP with power units plugged in. As the pilots strapped in, the dignitaries stood in the hangar door to witness the efficiency of our operation. F/O Gilkinson was No.3, F/O Gary Corbett his wingman. Gary, sad to say, had a "hot start". As happened in such a case, his Sabre belched a big tongue of flame right back into the astonished assemblage. That really got their attention, but the show wasn't yet over.

Our VIPs next proceeded to 441's hangar to witness the quick turn-around after the scramble. As the four Sabres taxied in, the groundcrew, ever eager to impress, clambered to refuel them. The drop tanks should have been empty, or nearly so. However, they had been fuelled earlier - in the cool of the previous night. By the time they scrambled, the tanks had become pressurized as the day warmed. In a quick-turnaround "hot refuelling" is normal. That means that the pilots keep their engines running. Now, as the drop tank caps were removed, fuel came spurting out. With JP4 spilled all over the ramp, the Sabres taxied off. Happily, they did not turn this embarrassment into anything worse!

On another Staff College visit we scrambled from the ORP and fired up, as the groundcrew pulled the power cables and waved us off. The first element rolled, then called for our element to follow (a 3-second interval). Wanting to demonstrate 441's superior skill, F/O Yakachuk rolled at one second. In the spirit of the moment I tucked in beside him with his wingtip practically in my lap.

Just airborne and retracting the undercarriage, I had a problem - my Sabre started to roll slowly left towards Yak. Still slow, I had to ease back on the throttle. Passing Yak's tailpipe, I had rolled 90 degrees and still had little aileron control. Yak's jet wash worsened my roll as I headed for the quick turn-around area, from where F/L Barry Gartner and F/O Arnie Matthews were taxiing. They told me later that they were certain they were about to make the acquaintance of St. Peter. Finally, free of the jet wash from the lead element and Yak's Sabre, I regained control. Yak and the others, concentrating on their own flying, hadn't even noticed my predicament.

Christmas Away

In any year Christmas throughout the Air Division was a unique blend of Canadian and European experiences and traditions. There was, for example, likely to be more wine and fewer cranberries served than in Canada. While families might have Canadian-style dinners in the PMQs, single men were more likely to range over Europe, often gravitating to Swiss or Austrian ski slopes. Drizzle and slush were more likely than a truly "white Christmas", but mistletoe could be obtained free (almost by the wagon load). Diplomacy and public relations dictated sharing with European neighbours, and a press release described 1 Wing's community work in December 1960:

Forty girls from a Sedan orphanage will attend a Christmas concert at 1 Fighter Wing, Marville, France, December 18, and will be given dinner on the base as well as gifts. The Wing will serve dinner on Christmas Day to 40 members of the nearby Montmedy Old Folks Home and donations will go to needy families in the farming area of the base. Firemen from the Wing have collected and repaired toys to give to children of needy families and the Wing's airwomen have raised money to buy a washer and spin dryer as a Christmas present for a Sedan orphanage.

Marville Pilot

F/O Norman Bigg made the move with 441 from North Luffenham to the Continent. Of these times he recalled in 2002:

In 1955 the RAF took back North Luffenham and 1 (F) Wing moved to Zweibrucken for three months, while Marville was being readied. At this time I had a Volkswagen, so had to get it over to Germany. With Al McIlraith keeping me company, I set off for Dover to catch the Calais ferry. During the crossing, Al and I passed the time drinking wine. The ferry eventually docked and we drove off, me clinging to the left side of the road, as if we still were in England! Suddenly a big lorry rounded a corner and roared down upon us. This sobered me up in a hurry and I swung right and pressed on towards Brussels, much chastened.

Although "Zwei" was a bit crowded, we got on famously with the three squadrons there. The night of our departure for Marville, the Wing put on a great party. In anticipation, the station posted guards to thwart hijinks. In the morning, however, 3 Wing awoke to find "441 SQN" painted across the width of the runway. This could be seen from 40,000 feet, just like a neon sign! There was hell to pay for this, S/L Cuthbertson having to drive to Metz to explain to the "big boss", A/V/M Hugh Campbell.

The first squadron at Marville was us - 441. Although there was mud all over the place, we succeeded in holding a party and throwing empty bottles through most of the windows, thus christening the Officers Mess. Next day S/L Cuthbertson was again on his way to Metz! The squadron had to ante up for repairs. It was worth it, as the cry arose, "Who owns this mess? 441!"

We swore that Marville was the worst place for an RCAF airfield. First of all, the locals seemed to be living 400 years behind the times. Except for "Pop's" restaurant, there was nowhere to hang out. Thus did the bar in our mess become the magnet for the single pilots, school

French school children, parents and teachers during a squadron tour. (441 Sqn)

Even these days, bravado remains a big thing when it comes to the "mystique" surrounding any group of professional warriors. Like it or not, being a good drinker has always been part of this mystique. While not much allowed any more, a lot of old time fighter pilot lore and memorabilia to do with the subject is still around to cheese off the PC crowd. (CANAV Col.)

While few in the air force bother with airplane pictures, RCAF padre Les Corness was an avid photographer. While at 1 Wing on July 22, 1963 he took this great "set up" shot of Sabre 23675.

teachers and nurses. "Not too bad a deal", in retrospect! Weekends were for married folks to join in and long parties ensued. Pilots standing early morning alert would get their sleep "wherever". After one memorable party, a 4-plane section was brought up to 2-minute warning, i.e. pilots in the cockpit. There we sat - time dragging and it was hopeless trying to stay awake. Then came a scramble and three Sabres taxied out and roared into the sky. The fourth? There it sat, the groundcrew pounding on the aircraft, trying to rouse the dozing pilot!

One could expect the unexpected on any fighter operation. On one sortie from Marville, I had a starboard elevator disengage in flight. But the Sabre was rugged simplicity - it was designed to remain controllable, regardless. Another time a fairing ripped off in flight, damaging my stabilizer. Worst of all, one day I got separated from my section while dog fighting. Using the ADF (automatic direction finder) to find Marville, I headed home, but the ADF only led me into a thunderstorm. Figuring to survive this predicament, I let down in claggy weather. Low on fuel, I squawked mayday. USAF GCI came up, directing me to 2 Wing Grostenquin, just off my port wing. With 200 pounds of fuel I was in a jam, but strove to keep cool. I tightened my straps and pulled up to gain some bail-out altitude. Just then I looked down to see 8000 feet of USAF Étain runway. I set up for a quick landing (no permission), came in, then flamed out on the taxiway. The USAF colonel who met me was ready to have my head - his base was off limits in some kind of nuclear scenario. The colonel saw how shaky I was, and sent me off to Ops, where the fellows plied me with bourbon. Soon they sent me home - a 12-mile hop!

I count myself as one of the lucky ones from those Cold War years. Many others lie at rest in Choloy Cemetery near Metz. In due course I went home aboard a Cunard liner. In December 1957 I was at work at Downsview. There I finished my RCAF days as an Air Reserve support officer on 411 Squadron. My last exercise was a formation flypast at the CNE airshow. Ironically, I landed back at Trenton with my nose gear u/s and cocked to the right. Off the runway I went - that Sabre was a write-off and a crane from 6 RD soon carried it away to be scrapped. After the weekend of airshow flying, we left our five Sabres at Trenton "for disposal". A sad ending to such a magnificent era. We shall never see its equal!

What someone once called "Don Myles' empire" - Scottish Aviation's hangar at Prestwick where Sabres and CF-100s were overhauled and tested, and where an RCAF acceptance pilot was always on detachment. The Sabre 6 in the middle is BT-495. Taken on RCAF strength on June 24, 1955, it served until June 3, 1963, then went for scrap (Scottish Aviation purchased Sabres from the Crown each for about $100). (Scottish Aviation)

A Year in the Life ... 1956

The diary for January 4, 1956 notes that F/O Don Myles was posted to Scottish Aviation in Renfrew (near Glasgow), Scotland, to be RCAF acceptance test pilot there for six months. On January 20, 441 ferried 12 Sabres to Renfrew for overhaul, but this didn't mean that the test pilot was always busy, for aircraft only came off the refurbishment line every so often. Myles would be lucky to fly 10 hours a month. This left him with spare time, enough to meet a bonnie local nurse, whom he later would marry (a dozen years later Myles would return to 441, this time as commanding officer on CF-104s).

The diarist in this period deserves credit for his many informative entries. He notes on February 16 that USAF "F-86Hs are now seen quite often, and are a bit more difficult to handle than the Fs". On March 22 he recorded, "We learned today that F/O Eburn who, on leave in England, had gotten married. This is a severe blow to the remaining single men." On March 27 the squadron intercepted RAF Valiant bombers, "something new on the local scene." Next day he noted, "Although 4 (F) Wing have slightly better aircraft, we are having moderate success in intercepting them." Yes, there were Sabres, then there were Sabres!

On May 15, 441 began another E&E course, this one around Marville. For the 18th the diarist wrote, "The escape and evasion ended today and the unshaven, unwashed, undaunted troops were coming in all day. Others were driven back from the prisons at Verdun and St. Jean." In this period 441 was breaking in a new engineering officer, F/L Casley, himself a pilot. The Silver Foxes decided to make him a full-fledged Sabre jockey, this being noted on May 22: "F/L Casley ... did his first trip in the Sabre today and is now swept back and shaken." Having an EO flying Sabres was very unusual, since EOs rarely were pilots. But Casley had flown Mosquitos in Burma during the war with 82 Squadron. Postwar he was at AFHQ as project officer for of the Orenda engine, then joined 441. One day he and S/L Cuthbertson agreed that he should fly the Sabre. He began with a few hours on the T-33, then advanced to the Sabre, on which he eventually logged about 140 hours.

Weather permitting, Air Div pilots (usually the single ones) liked to head off on weekend R&R, finding their ways across Europe in Sabres, T-birds and Expeditors. These forays might end up in the squadron diary, although the wording sometimes is a bit mysterious. A June 22, 1956 note states, "F/Os Cockburn, Clayton, Bradley and Westphal left today for Copenhagen. F/O Cockburn complained bitterly about giving up his weekend for a training trip." The following Monday the diarist entered: "The four errants returned from Copenhagen. F/O Cockburn was noticeably placated. Normal flying in progress. Sorties: 50. Daily total: 46:20."

On August 9, 1956 tragedy again struck 441, dampening squadron spirits. That day F/O Ray

F/O Claude LaFrance while a sprog pilot *circa* 1950. (CF PL48390)

Sabre 23583 during NBCW training circa 1958. In this exercise it was being cleansed of radiation following nuclear contamination. Then, 23557 in a nice pose at Marville. (441 Sqn)

Lambert died in a car accident. On the 20th more grim news: "F/O Dad Bradley, one of the oldest and best party types in the squadron, was killed under unknown circumstances while flying an aircraft on an air test." About this time the first Sabre 6s were turning up at Marville. For August, 545:15 hours were logged.

For September 11, 1956 there is a diary reference to F/L Claude LaFrance. Having begun on Vampires, he had fought MiGs in Korea, instructed at the Sabre OTU, and now was on 441. From August 1 to 31 LaFrance had been on exchange with Escadrille 2/2 at Dijon. There he logged 33 flights (32:20 hours) in the Mystère IVA. To LaFrance the Mystère was underpowered and short on manoeuvrability. To him the RCAF still had NATO's best day fighter - the Sabre 6.

September brought Ex. Whipsaw with more rip-roaring action for 441. On the first day (26th) the diarist reported: "Everyone rolled out of the pit at 0415 hours, finished the usual early morning necessities, strapped on their Junior G-men cannons and took off for the airmen's mess for breakfast. With duff weather the first section didn't get airborne until 0715 hours, but from then on we flew steadily all day. We had several dog fights with Meteors, Hunters and the odd Venom... we had a section of four standing by all night in the hangar for a possible scramble... Sorties: 63. Daily total: 91:15 hours." The latter suggests that at least some sorties were with large underwing tanks (RCAF Sabres used either 100-Imp. gal. or 166-Imp. gal. tanks). "Whipsaw" ended on the 28th.

With November 1956 the 441 diary became a brief monthly summary, all the good details being lost forever. A mention in the December report notes of a Zulu scramble: "Our first scramble after four days of no flying turned into a live. The complete section made a successful interception on the bogie, which turned out to be a Scandinavian Airlines aircraft." Also in December F/O Bob Cockburn was posted to the Empire Test Pilot School at Farnborough; and S/L Fisher handed 441 over to S/L Lou Hill.

CHAPTER 10

Gunnery

Rabat

Once at Marville, 1 Wing did its gunnery training at Rabat-Sale, a French air base in Morocco. There, nature usually guaranteed excellent flying weather. The Silver Foxes first deployed to Rabat on November 10, 1955. Next day the diarist began: "Pilots ... spent the morning cleaning their barracks and delousing beds and bedding." They flew 32 trips for 50:40 hours. For the 12th: "Flying commenced at 0730 hours and ceased at 1710 hours. 19 flags were airborne, as we operated on a 30-minute schedule. The day finished with 77 sorties for 51:10 hours. The pilots are operating a 24-hours-on, 24-hours-off schedule. A bus is provided in the afternoon to take off-duty personnel to Temarra Beach for swimming. The Hotel du Chellah (American Officers' Club) is open to our use and most have found it a pleasant spot. There are also several local institutions, among them the Belima Hotel, La Nuit de Paris, etc. which are getting some play."

Training on this deployment emphasized the gun sight, which had three modes. A note for the 18th stated, "Scores are showing much improvement as pilots gain more experience." Naturally, there could be snags in daily ops. Fuel was a problem, shortages sometimes cutting into flying. Operations also could be curtailed, if the Sultan was using the airport. Low ceilings or sand storms also could restrict flying. For the 30th the diarist noted: "Weather again below limits. Same program - cards, sleep, food, cards, arguments."

November 24 produced a bit of drama at Rabat. Late in the afternoon F/O Peter Pigot, aloft in 23206, declared an emergency. His starboard tire had blown in the wheel well, rupturing hydraulic lines. Although his nose and port gear deployed, the starboard gear remained up. Pigot bounced the Sabre several times on the runway, trying to shake down the errant gear, but without success. Finally, pulling hard turns to use "G" forces, he obtained "three greens" on his panel, indicating that all wheels were down and locked. Pigot landed safely. (The loss of a colleague always stunned the Air Division. There were far too many such tragedies. Thus was 441 in mourning a few days later on December 3: "Members of the squadron were shocked

A post card view of the French colonial city of Rabat. In 1955 Sabre pilot F/O Bernie Curran sent this card to Madeline McMillan in Ottawa. Then, a Syd Burrows (434 Sqn) snapshot taken *circa* 1955 in Rabat's souk district.

today to learn of the death of F/O Pigot. Pete was a passenger on a Bristol which pranged on approach at Marville. Six other passengers were fatally injured." A funeral was held on the 5th, then Pigot's remains were taken to his family in Manchester.)

Outside Rabat air base, Morocco was seething with unrest. The French had removed King Mohammed V, replacing him with the more pliable Mohammed VI. Then they faced such unrest that they had to restore the original monarch. Norman Bigg of 441 Squadron witnessed the exile's return to Rabat. RCAF personnel were confined to base until French authorities restored order in the streets, but matters only got worse. The old king's supporters took fearful revenge on those regarded

105

Great 441 flightline scenes at Rabat, first with Armée de l'Air Mistrals (French-built Vampires). BT-059 served the RCAF only from December 1953 to March 1954, then joined the Luftwaffe as BB-143. Sabre 23314, leading in the second view, returned to Canada to finish its air force days at Chatham. It then was sold to Flight Systems in the US as N8687D. (Don Syms, Al Lockhart)

Don Syms, Jim Webber and Jim Fikowski yukking it up at Rabat.
(Don Syms Col., Larry Sutton)

Life at "RCAF Station Rabat". In 2003 Don Syms, who took this photo, noted: "When a squadron arrived here, everything had to be cleaned. All the mattresses were taken outside and powdered with DDT to get rid of all the creepy-crawlies."

A mob of 441 types pouring over the latest flag during a "Trophy Shoot"; then something really "candid camera" from Rabat!
(Don Syms Col., Larry Sutton)

"Flight ops" at Rabat as shot by Roy Smith.

A tortoise mascot or two seemed to be the thing to have around while in Rabat. Here a pair of the speedsters bears down on the finish line during their own competition. (Bernie Curran)

The gunnery flag/drogue/banner was anchored in a Sabre's speed brake well, then towed aloft, and let out on several thousand feet of wire. (CF PL84732)

as French collaborators (i.e. any who openly had supported Mohammed VI).

For the most part these disturbances were played out away from Canadian eyes but, as they travelled by bus, RCAF personnel were accompanied by armed guards. Side arms were carried in the vehicles, and men were issued "goolie chits" (trilingual - Arabic, English, French) hoping that such documents might protect them from hostile locals, who scarcely differentiated between French and Canadian uniforms. Nevertheless, in November 1954 F/O Arnie Hoogen of 422 Squadron, "out on the town" in Rabat's Arab Quarter, was waylaid and severely beaten. Rescued by a patrol of gendarmes, he was rushed to hospital. With grave injuries Hoogen was invalided back to Canada, his air force days over. Moroccan unrest, complicated by revolt in Algeria, eventually obliged NATO to relocate gunnery training to Sardinia.

Chadburn Trophy

Sabre wings competed annually for the Chadburn Trophy as proof of their marksmanship. Named for RCAF wartime fighter ace Lloyd V. Chadburn, the trophy was instituted in 1955 and only retired when CF-104s (without guns) replaced the Sabres. The trophy was awarded about every 16 months to that wing whose squadrons had registered the highest marks in two successive gunnery meets, a meet being conducted every eight months.

In the absence of air-to-air competition with other air forces, a weapons exercise was about as exciting an event as could be anticipated. Only one squadron was involved at a time, so there was no direct day-to-day competition, but the scores of pilots and squadrons were calculated and circulated like baseball statistics. Occasionally, a target flag was so thoroughly mauled that it was impossible to determine a score. Occasionally, an entire flag would be lost. On August 25, 1960, for example, F/O Jack "Kiwi" MacArthur shot one off its cable, He then ran into it, damaging his Sabre. Jack "The Snake" Riley did likewise next day, even though his gun sight was u/s. In 1956, 441 was blessed with an enthusiastic historical officer. His August 3 description of a trophy shoot is almost as evocative as a hockey play-by-play, with the home team surging from behind to win:

> Well, this was the big day for the whole squadron. Everyone was in the briefing room at 0630 for a short talk by F/O Tinson on the trophy shoot. The weather was clagged in the first part of the morning, but it finally cleared and at 0925 the first section fired up and got away. They came back with a roughly 65% flag. The general mood of both pilots and groundcrew was a terrific gaiety. Our second flag came back with almost as good a percentage as the first. However, the squadron average kept getting lower as each flag dropped a couple of percent. We also had some bad luck as a few of our top shooters had unserviceable sights and got low scores. However, we still had a good chance of being top squadron in Air Div.
>
> Then "A" Flight took over and old faithful S/L Admiral [S/L Cuthbertson] came through with a remarkable score of 74%. The boys went wild because it was our boss that did it and another record for the biggest and best of them all - 441. The Checkerboard had done it again. As the afternoon wore on, tension began to mount as things were getting rather close. Then finally the last flag came which could make or break us. The boss and most of the pilots and a large number of the ground crew were out at the end of the runway waiting for the flag to drop. S/L Cuthbertson was the first to spot this tow ship on its way home. There was a lot of sweat from the people on the ground as the tow aircraft made its final turn that brought it in line with the runway. Then came the drop and a mad scramble

A crowd of 441 officers and airmen at Rabat in the mid-1950s. (441 Sqn.)

for the flag. One look and we could tell by the large number of red splotches that 441 just made another record, the highest trophy shoot in Air Div. F/O Sanche was the hero of the day as he came through with a lovely 81. Needless to say there was quite a party in the evening, which spread from the Elmo Grabi house to the American Officers Club, France-American Club and who knows where else. Another memorable day in the life of 441 Fighter Squadron and we're sure there will be many more.

F/O Ron Clayton's log is one man's record of this event. His entries, though not detailed, indicate something of the pace created by these exercises. Having flown to Rabat from Marville via Istres and Rabat on July 23, 1956, Clayton noted his flying:

Date	Sabre	Sortie	Time (Minutes)
July 23	23221	AA*	40
	23326	AA	30
July 24	23231	Tow	40
	23309	AA	45
	23212	AA	35
July 25	23309	AA	45
	23212	AA	30
July 26	23188	Tow	30
	23188	AA	50
	23221	AA	30
July 27	23183	AA	30
	23229	Tow	30
	23019	AA	55
	23221	AA	45
July 28	23019	AA	45
	23221	Tow	45
	23221	AA	55
July 30	23038	AA	40
	23019	AA	40
	23326	Tow	45
July 31	23326	AA	60
	23188	AA	30
	23233	AA	45

* air-to-air

Rabat Memories

In March 2003, 441 alumnus Norman Bigg recalled a few anecdotes from Rabat days:

A typical day at Rabat began in the early morning. This allowed us to get in all our gunnery sorties before operations had to be curtailed, as the heat of the day took over. For any given sortie, one Sabre was designated to tow the gunnery flag. The flag was stored in a speed brake panel, from which it would be let out on a tow wire. After a section of four Sabres had finished firing on the range, which was over the Mediterranean, the tow pilot dropped the flag over the field, then landed.

The flag was retrieved and brought over to Ops, where all the holes were tallied. It was simple to count the holes, since the bullets we used were coded in coloured wax. As a bullet passed through the flag, it left its tell-tale colour. Naturally, there always was a lot of interest in the scores. The question always was, who was the best marksman in the squadron.

On occasion, the tow pilot would miscalculate and drop his flag outside the airfield perimeter. Now there was a rush among the local inhabitants to see who could get to the flag first - it was a case of "finders keepers". The lucky scavenger got to sell the wire and fabric from the flag in the bazaar (in the dead of night the same Rabat entrepreneurs even would cut down telephone wire to "recycle" in the bazaar).

Death by Misadventure

On July 18, 1956 the Silver Foxes had another foray to Rabat, the first departure being via North Star. "Those aboard had the usual enjoyable, quiet time", wrote a sardonic diarist. Weather delayed arrival of the Sabres. On July 21 it was written, "Everyone is getting a little cheesed off from lying in the beautiful sun and swimming all day, as again the word is 'No Sabres'. We made a report ... that we were being disturbed by aircraft flying over our rest camp. Every time we heard a jet, we were afraid it was a Sabre." The party ended with the arrival of the Sabres next day. On the 26th, 80 sorties were flown for 57:45 hours. Two days later Jerry Westphal scored an unheard-of 95% on the flag.

On August 1 G/C D.J. "Blackie" Williams, 1 Wing station commander, with his pilot, F/L Bob Carew of Air Div HQ in Metz, were due to visit 441 at Rabat. They departed Marville in T-33 21077 but, after their ETA had passed, 441 began to worry. A Sabre was dispatched on a recce to Gibraltar. There it was learned that the T-bird had crash-landed there. Although Williams and Carew were safe, the rest of the story was of disaster. In January 2003 Bob Carew told Larry Milberry how, after refuelling at Istres for Rabat, they had suffered a total electrical failure - instruments, radios, heat, fuel pump, everything was down. They headed for "Gib", but it was a dicey approach with an iced-up canopy. Without radios, there was no way of Carew calling "Mayday", but he assumed that local RAF radar would have them. They orbitted down, got onto final, then noticed that the barriers used to stop local traffic for landing aircraft, still were up. A large bus

As squadrons travelled to and from Rabat, they normally passed Gibraltar. Don Syms took this outstanding view showing a 441 Sabre carving by "The Rock".

appeared in front of the T-bird, but passed just in time. Then the crew felt a bump and landed hard.

The bump, it turned out, came when they knocked a Spaniard off his bicycle. Since the cyclist had been killed, manslaughter charges were brought against Carew and Williams. Eventually, a Spanish court settled the matter. Testimony proved that the timing for this emergency couldn't have been worse, for the RAF had its radar turned off for maintenance - just when it was urgently needed. In the end the court saw this as a case of death by misadventure, so the Canadians were exonerated.

Decimomannu

When Rabat became untenable for NATO, Decimomannu on Sardinia became the NATO weapons range. An Italian Air Force base, "Deci" had an 85-man RCAF Air Weapons Unit to "provide support, direction, and control for 1 Air Division squadrons which are deployed ... for air weapons exercises in accordance with 1 Air Division Headquarters training syllabus." The RCAF base itself was at the airfield, 12 miles north of Cagliari, Sardinia. Visiting squadrons were billeted some five miles away. The Italians were responsible for security, flying control, search and rescue, fire protection and crash assistance. The RCAF lodger unit took care of messing, administration and technical assistance. Visitors would find Deci cheerful enough, although AWU personnel, who stayed longer, found it a bit claustrophobic. A ritual practiced by all squadrons passing through was to contribute to local charities, either with lire or treats. During a February 1960 visit, 441 donated toys and chocolate to the Decimomannu School for Underprivileged Children. When 444 passed through in April 1960 it made a like donation.

Canadians began arriving at Deci in April 1957, the Silver Foxes paying their first visit in September. The AWU had no energetic diarist. He reported the historic first Silver Fox visit in two entries: September 18 - "441 (F) Squadron from 1 (F) Wing commanded by S/L Hill arrived at the AWU with 33 officers and 101 airmen to begin Exercise Weapons Fire IV", and October 2 - "441 (F) Squadron returned to 1 (F) Wing after two weeks at the AWU." If the AWU seemed unimpressed with 441, the squadron was much more effervescent in its own account. It had done intense training and cine exercises in anticipation of the trip. In September 1957 the 441 diarist wrote:

This was the month we hoped would show the results of all our hard work on the flag. 439 Squadron consented to take our Zulu for us and we pressed harder still in our efforts to become proficient marksmen. When the middle of the month rolled around, it was felt by all that the aircraft and pilots were in good shape to meet the Sardinian challenge. Tank tests completed, and bathing suits packed, the squadron roared off to Deci on 17 September.

Our first good news on arrival was that the range was closed due to NATO Naval exercises. Thus, 441 dejectedly climbed into their "camera platforms" and shot some more film for two days. Finally the signal arrived clearing us to fire and away we went - on fixed firing. The results are too horrible to record here. Undaunted, our heroes turned up at work Saturday for another go - and the weather clogged in.

At least Saturday turned out beautifully and the boys forgot their troubles on the beach. On Monday the squadron attacked the flag with vengeance and ended the day with about 17 flags and over 20 percent. With this precedent, the squadron went on to finish its required radar missions with a squadron average of 24.36 percent. Congratulations to all the pilots and groundcrew who made this possible. A special bouquet to our high man, Bill Mitchell, who also obtained a 91.5 percent on one flag.

Lou Hill views of the Deci flightline in 1958. Then, a general overview of Deci with 441 ready for action.

Ron Hayman in an experimental partial pressure suit circa 1958. Hayman recalled: "The suit was uncomfortable, particularly when compared to the comfort of the full-pressure type which we borrowed from the USAF some years later for a CF-104 high-flight project." (Hayman Col.)

A Chuck Winegarden photo showing 441 just arrived at Deci. Drop tanks have been removed to make the Sabres more fun to fly. Then, Jack Folkins' photo shows how the flag was like a pilot magnet while being assessed.

A good time was certainly enjoyed by all. Cagliari offered many attractions, and our skin-diving enthusiasts certainly capitalized on the wonderful weather and diving conditions. September ended with our stay in Sardinia just about over.

The records did not identify individual pilots or flying times, but Ron Hayman's log demonstrates the intensity of flying. From September 18 to October 2, 1957 he logged six sorties towing targets (most lasting an hour, three of them on September 30) and 18 sorties firing (with triple sorties on the 23rd, 24th, 25th, 27th and 28th). All but one of the shoots involved 45 minutes aloft. On six occasions he recorded his scores, which ranged from 48% to 58%. On his next Deci visit (May 7 - 19, 1958), Hayman towed six times (five trips in one day) and fired 14 times, scoring a high of 68.5%.

The squadron's visit in February 1960 (a Chadburn trophy shoot) also was memorable. They must have scraped together every available Sabre, for the historical report mentions 25 aircraft making the trip on the 10th. But all did not go smoothly - as of February 11 some ground personnel and equipment had not caught up with their squadron. The pilots spent the day doing cine practices, but lost an aircraft when F/L Ron MacGarva

October 1962, following another AWU deployment (the squadron's last with Sabres), 441 earned the highest gunnery score ever achieved by an Air Division squadron -37.7%. As 441 Sabres faded, 1 Wing's publication *Arrowhead Tribune* reminisced about Deci days in its August 31, 1963 issue:

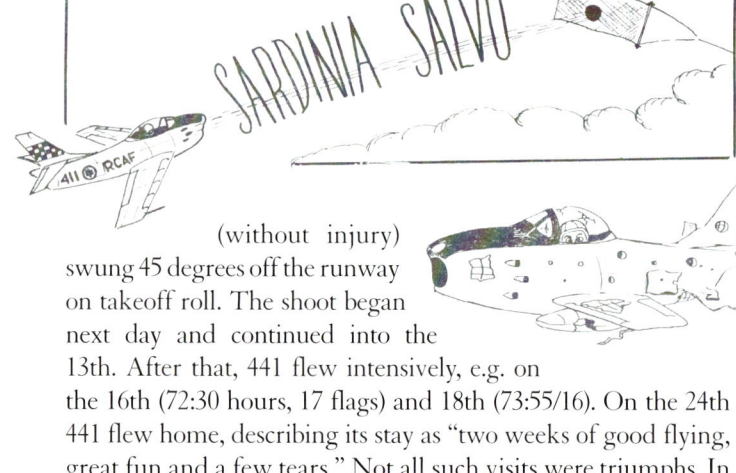

(without injury) swung 45 degrees off the runway on takeoff roll. The shoot began next day and continued into the 13th. After that, 441 flew intensively, e.g. on the 16th (72:30 hours, 17 flags) and 18th (73:55/16). On the 24th 441 flew home, describing its stay as "two weeks of good flying, great fun and a few tears." Not all such visits were triumphs. In August 1960 the Silver Foxes returned to Deci for another trophy shoot. Their scores over the two days were dismal. Yet, in

Silver Fox pilots pose with their spear guns before some Sardinian snorkling: Tom Crane, Jack Folkins and Ken Moreash. Behind are Don Syms, Bill Mitchell and Buster Kincaid. Note Deci's bare bones officer quarters. (Folkins Col.)

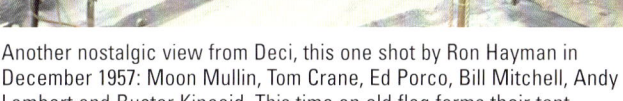

Larry Sutton and Larry Spurr at the train station in Deci. Then, Jock Gouley, Curt Barlow (EO) and Larry Spurr with a local Sardinian. (Nan Baggs Col.)

Another nostalgic view from Deci, this one shot by Ron Hayman in December 1957: Moon Mullin, Tom Crane, Ed Porco, Bill Mitchell, Andy Lambert and Buster Kincaid. This time an old flag forms their tent.

F/Os Carl Bertrand (left, behind), Doug Howlett (left, nearest), Ron Duffie and Mike Diss lounge in an old gunnery flag doubling as a hammock. Jack Reilly is nearest on the chair. (Chuck Winegarden)

Aside from the operational aspect of this twice yearly trip to Sardinia, it was a welcome relief from the ever-present Zulus at Marville, and seemed to be sort of a regular holiday by the Mediterranean Sea. It was true that the climate would be hot and tropical during the summer, damp and miserable in the fall, and downright cold and uncomfortable in the winter. Bedding seldom dried out, hamburgers were made from old donkeys ... Off-duty hours though, presented an opportunity to board an Italian bus and go into the capital city of Cagliari. There one could eat spaghetti, drink Chianti, shop for sweaters, lie on one of the nicest beaches in Europe, and acquire a marvelous sunburn ... Try to picture a few airmen and place them laying about in the dress of the day. This usually consisted of a dusty pair of boots topped by a pair of heavy gray wool socks, fatigue pants cut at various lengths, yellow, blue or white T-shirts, all shielded by a pith hat that could have the name or initial of every character who has worn it since the camp originated. All this and more, guarded night and day by the ever-trustworthy Italian guards, who impressed you with inexperience, irresponsibility and general carefree attitude that would sober you up at the sound of the bolt of his rifle being repositioned.

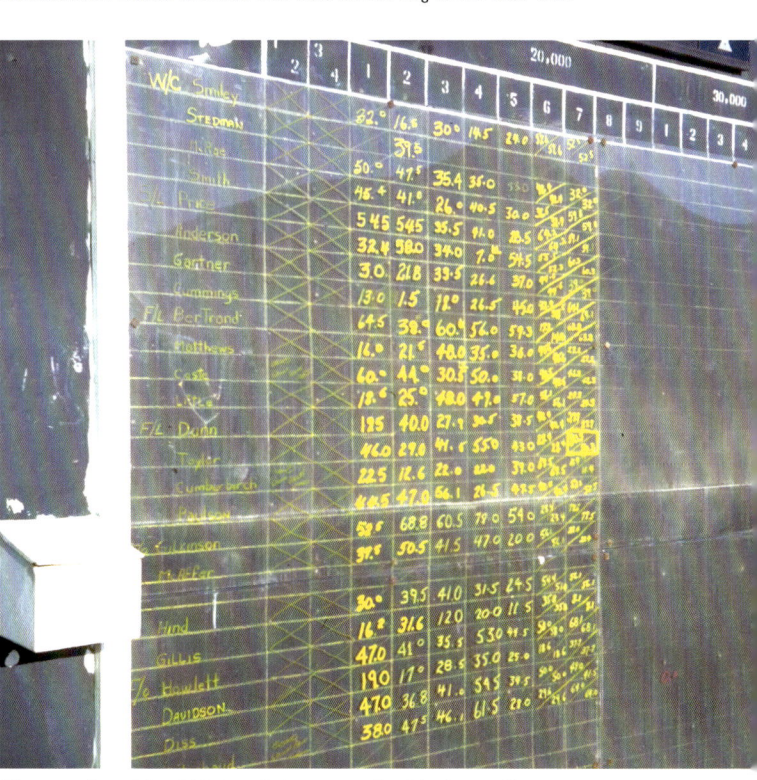

The scoreboard for 441's last Sabre camp. By this time, tallies were credible. F/O Don Gilkinson scored best with 71%. (Carl Bertrand)

The Guynemer Trophy

As much as wings competed for the Chadburn Trophy, the plume in everybody's hat was the Guynemer Trophy, named for a First World War French flying legend. Georges Guynemer had begun the war as a mechanic, remustered to pilot, flew in 600 aerial combats, was shot down seven times, and destroyed 53 German aircraft. He was last seen on September 11, 1917, attacking an enemy aircraft. His obituary in *L'Illustration* of October 6, 1917 read: "He was neither seen nor heard as he fell, his body and his machine were never found. Where has he gone? By what wings did he manage to glide into immortality? Nobody knows, nothing is known. He ascended and never came back, that is all. Perhaps our descendants will say: He flew so high that he could not come down again." A fighter pilot could have no greater model, so the gunnery trophy, which the RCAF "owned" for several seasons, was perfectly named.

RCAF Sabre units pooled their resources to field all-star Guynemer Trophy teams, but not until 1958 did an RCAF squad capture the prize at Cazaux, near Bordeaux. The sense of triumph was diluted by the fact that a USAF team had withdrawn from the competition. Nevertheless, *Roundel* of October 1958 ran their picture with a short story under the heading "Air Gunnery Champions". Team members were F/Ls William H. Norn (439 Sqn), Ron MacGarva (441, team captain), and Clifford J. Henry (422), and F/Os David Barker and Robert S. Paul (who was the meet's top individual marksman). The following year at Cazaux the RCAF again captured the trophy. This time *Roundel* (October 1959) ran a longer story and posed the whole team - five pilots, 31 ground crew - against the backdrop of a checker-tailed Sabre. The "Air Div" diary exalted what really was a victory for all Canada:

> Canada's NATO Air Division for the second consecutive year won the coveted Guynemer Trophy, emblematic of live air-to-air gunnery supremacy within the seven-nation NATO Command of Allied Air Forces Central Europe. In addition to capturing the trophy, the Canadians swept individual scoring honours, taking the first three places. The top score of the meet was posted by F/O David Barker, a 23-year old Sabre pilot from 4 Fighter Wing, Baden-Soellingen, Germany, whose hometown is Lakeview, Ontario. Taking second and third individual scoring places were F/L William Norn, 25, of No.1 Fighter Wing, Marville, France, from Calgary, and F/L Alfred McDonald, 31, of No.3 Fighter Wing, Zweibrucken, from Barrie, Ontario. F/L Ron MacGarva, 37, from Balmoral, Manitoba, the RCAF team captain, received the trophy presented by General Leon Johnson, USAF, Deputy for Air at Supreme Headquarters Allied Powers Europe.

The fifth pilot in the team this year was F/O W.J. "Bill" McArthur of 422 Squadron. F/L Norn, being 439, at least would have been on speaking terms with the Silver Foxes. The 40-odd groundcrew (from various squadrons) were led by S/L W.H. Casley and F/O Frank R. Jefferson. The RCAF had a right to crow about this year's results. Half-way through the 2-week, 8-team competition they held a commanding lead over the USAF's second-place 32nd FIS. MacGarva, anxious that his men might be complacent in the second half, tersely announced, "We still have three difficult exercises remaining and the competition isn't over by any means until the last gun is fired." Pilot enthusiasm was matched by that of the groundcrew who, dressed in natty white coveralls, meticulously performed their tasks.

The RCAF again took the Guynemer Trophy in 1960 and 1961, but it wasn't getting any easier as the Sabre aged. Even though it was on its way out in 1962, it surely is to the RCAF's credit that the Guynemer remained within the Air Division's grasp. Competing that year at Leeuwarden, Holland, the RAF took top team honours with 1563.5 points (maximum possible: 2400 points). Second was the RCAF with 1522.0, third was Belgium, then came the Netherlands, Germany and Norway. F/O C.A. "Chuck" Winegarden made the highest individual

Ron MacGarva's photo of the Guynemer flightline at Cazaux (near Bordeaux) in 1959. Checkerboard Sabres head the line, then come others from 439, 434, 422, 439 and 444.

score for the 2-week competition - 454.5 (second was RAF F/L Highton with 427.5). Winegarden's score was the highest ever in the history of the competition. For his good efforts he received the Prince Bernhard Award. Following the awards, Air Marshal Hugh Campbell, RCAF Chief of the Air Staff, cabled Air Div HQ: "Four firsts and one second in five years is a record that will be hard to equal. You can be justifiably proud of such a feat. Please convey my personal congratulations to the aircrew and groundcrew who participated in this year's competition for their splendid effort."

The 1959 RCAF Guynemer team: F/O Bill "Kiwi" McArthur (422), F/O D.J. "Dave" Barker, F/L Ron MacGarva (441), F/L Alf McDonald (434) and F/L Bill Norn (439). Top score among individual competitors went to McArthur, with Norn and McDonald second and third. Then, MacGarva accepting the Guynemer Trophy from USAF General Leon Johnson. (MacGarva Col., CF PL122710)

The RCAF's 1962 Guynemer team at Leeuwarden: F/L Carl Bertrand (441), F/O Burnell "Bernie" Reid (421 Sqn), F/O Douglas Dargent (444), F/O John Swallow (434) and F/O Charles Winegarden (441). Not shown are F/L Larry Spurr (444) - team gunnery leader, and F/L Russ Challoner - team captain. (CF PL147015)

in Trenton. In 1953 young Winegarden earned his pilot's licence through an Air Cadet flying scholarship. In 1957 he enlisted in the RCAF as an airman, training as an admin clerk. Posted to Trenton, he soon remustered to pilot with the blessing of his boss, G/C Bert Houle. Winegarden started on Chipmunks at Centralia, advanced to Harvards at Moose Jaw, then earned his Wings on T-birds at Gimli. Sabre OTU came next, then his posting to 441 in 1959, initially under S/L Lou Hill.

BT-759 of 441 at Cazaux as a USAF B-57 target tug fires up in the distance using a cartridge start. Alf McDonald noted of the Guynemer: "Each pilot flew three trips. Each trip he carried 100 rounds in two guns only, and was allowed two passes on the drogue." (MacGarva Col.)

Prince Bernhard presents F/O Winegarden with the Guynemer trophy honouring the pilot scoring highest in the 1962 competition. (CF PL147000)

Once again, superb training and top young pilots like Winegarden explain everything. Who were they, what did they accomplish, and how did they end? Here is the case of F/O Winegarden. Born on February 27, 1936, he grew up first in Saskatoon, where his father was an airman. The family then moved to Montreal, where Mr. Winegarden worked on Cansos at Canadian Vickers. After the war he served at 6 Repair Depot

The highlight of Winegarden's tour came at the Guynemer meet, then he instructed at home for seven years on the T-33. Next was an exchange with the USAF in Texas on the T-37 and T-38, an HQ tour at St. Hubert, CF-5s at Cold Lake (434 Sqn), then came Winegarden's final posting - Hercules at 435 Squadron 1976-79. Thereafter, he flew on Civvie Street - the "Herc" at NWT Air, corporate aircraft with Business Flights

Sabre 23667 gracing NATO skies in a near-perfect side view. First flown at Cartierville in June 1956, '667 soldiered on with 441 to March 1963, when it went for scrap in Prestwick. (Folkins Col.)

At Deci in November 1958 — 441 Sabres with 23428 heading the line. (Folkins Col.)

F/L Henry "Hank" O'Mara of 441 during free time at Deci in 1958. Hank was one of thousands of veterans who rejoined the RCAF as postwar "retreads". Most did so with reduced ranks, some with gallantry decorations even going down to be LACs. Most then worked back up, often to fly. Hank's is a fascinating case. Raised on Kingswood Rd. in east-end Toronto, he belonged to the "Flying O'Maras". Four O'Mara boys became wartime pilots. The eldest, Earl "Red" O'Mara, instructed in the BCATP, where he earned the AFC. Ray, who flew Beaufighters with 211 Squadron in the Far East, won a DFC. Hank instructed on Tiger Moths at Goderich, where one of his students was Larry Spurr (later his boss on 441). Howard got his Wings late in the war, then served in the postwar USAF. Younger brothers Bill and Ted earned flying licences postwar, and sister Rita was a WD. Hank was a greatly respected 441 flight commander in Cold War days. (Folkins Col.)

F/O Keith "Casey" Chapman, 441 Sabre driver, at Deci in 1958. Then, the 441 emblem painted on the wall in Deci's pilot lounge. (Folkins Col.)

Spare tires and brake parts on the Deci flightline in 1959. (Leo Lalonde)

Leo Lalonde photographed the frightening aftermath of F/O D.H.G. "Don" Barnes' fatal crash at Deci on November 20, 1958.

of Calgary, then a 13-year stint with Transport Canada. In 2003 Winegarden celebrated 50 years of flight (with some 22,000 flying hours) and still was current on Learjets and King Airs. A highlight from this period was his time with "Willy's Bandits" - Adlair of Cambridge Bay, NWT. There he flew Willy Laserich's famous Learjet, for years the only jet based in the Canadian Arctic.

Typical "Fighters of the 50s" against which "Air Div" Sabres regularly fought. First, the Hawker Hunter with its aesthetic lines. Then, a pair of Luftwaffe F-86K all-weather interceptors, and an Armée de l'Air F-100 Super Sabre. (Hawker Aircraft, Harry Tate, Armée de l'Air)

Some Fighters of the Fifties

Type	Length/Span	Max Weight lb	Max Speed mph @ sea level	Guns/Cannons+	Engine/Pounds Thrust
Canadair Sabre 6	37'6"/37'1"	17,600	710	6 x .50 cal.	Orenda 14 7275
Convair F-102	68'4.66"/38'1.5"	32,000	825 @ 36,000	AAMs/rockets	P&W J57 11,700^
Dassault Ouragan	35'2.25"	15,000	584	4 x 20 mm	H-S Nene 5070
Dassault Mirage IIIC	43'10"/27'	22,150	1350 @ 36,000'	2 x 30 mm + AAMs	SNECMA Atar 9370^
Dassault Mystère IVA	42'1.75"/36'5.75"	16,535	696	2 x 30 mm	H-S Verdon 7710
Dassault Super Mystère	46'1"/34'5.75"	22,050	743 @ 43,000	2 x 30mm	SNECAMA Atar 7495^
DH Vampire F.B.6	30'9"/38'	12,400	548 @ 30,000	4 x 20 mm	DH Goblin 3350
DH Venom F.B.4	33'/41'8"	15,830	597	4 x 20 mm	DH Ghost 5150
Fiat G.91	34'2.5"/28'2.5"	11,365	668	4 x .50 cal.	BS Orpheus 5000
Gloster Meteor F.8	43'6"/37'2"	17,350	592	4 x 20 mm	2 x R-R Derwent ea. 3600
Hawker Hunter F.6	45'10.5"/33' 8"	23,700	715	4 x 30 mm	R-R Avon 10,050
MiG-15	36'3.25"	14,225	668	1 x 37, 1 x 23 mm	Klimov VK-1 5950
MiG-17	38'/36'	14,500	650	3 x 23 mm	Klimov VK-1 5950^
NA F-86	37'6"/37'1"	20,200	656	6 x 50 cal.	GE J47 6100
NA F-100D	54'3"/38'9"	34,800	864 @ 35,000	4 x 20 mm	P&W J57 11,700^
Replublic F-84F	43'4.75"/33'7.25"	28,000	695	6 x 50 cal.	Wright J65 7220
Republic F-84G	38'1"/36'5"	23,525	622	6 x 50 cal.	Allison J35 5600

+ all types also carried underwing ordnance

^ plus afterburner

"Homeric" and other Escapades

Young men in general, and fighter pilots in particular, sometimes like to pose as rakish ne'er do wells, even if the jaunty exterior hides a decent young man. Squadron records occasionally hint at their boisterous antics, but the "wink-wink" nature of the entries may indicate either more or less than meets the eye. The 441 diary describes some typical mischief connected with Ex. Momentum of August 1953: "After a dance, a drink and a bite to eat in Norwich, our pilots had a thrash with the Horsham pilots in the mess." This would have been a typical fighter pilots piss-up. No decent citizen would care to have witnessed the goings-on, e.g. "F/L Slim Walker wrote out the squadron number backwards on the ceiling." Next day the Canucks departed, but soon were back: "Over Horsham they peeled off and came straight down. With nine loud bangs the squadron bade the traditional farewell to Horsham St. Faith." For two

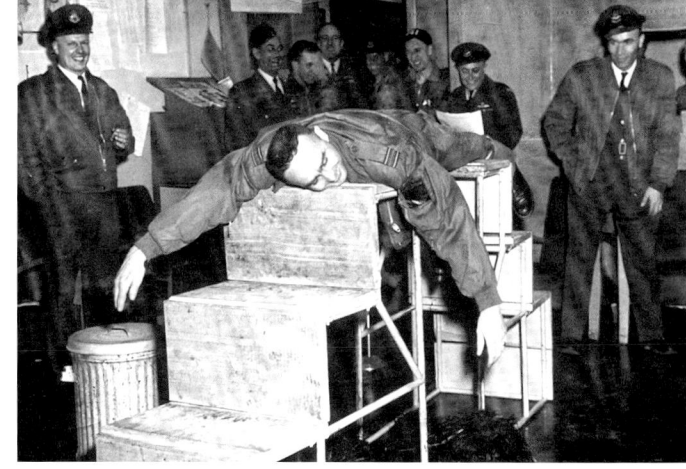

In this squadron skit, S/L Lou Hill "takes the cure" for sinus trouble - deep breathes as the aroma rises from the pile of cow dung below! (441 Sqn)

The fun never ended at 441. Chuck Winegarden is seen doing his best Julius Caesar at a squadron toga party. Then, the Silver Foxes behaving themselves (for a change) at the 1957 Christmas dance. Finally, some zany Silver Fox makes a spectacle of himself in the mess - nothing new! (Carl Bertrand, 441 Sqn)

days 441 stayed on the ground, supposedly to tend its aircraft. More likely this was to let groggy pilots deal with booming hangovers.

If all an author does is consult the official records for his material, he misses a great deal of good history, i.e. what he'll retrieve from interviews, log books, photo albums and scrap books. Thus did a good story come to light on January 28, 2003 during a conversation between Larry Milberry and Ralph Annis (Andy MacKenzie later confirmed the story). One evening at North Luffenham, Steve Atherton was playing the piano in the mess. A fighter pilot with musical talent? One might wonder, but there have been many, and blessed was the squadron having one. Along the way that night S/L Andy MacKenzie accidentally dropped his lighter into Atherton's piano. When MacKenzie was unable to reach it, the boys gathered around and flipped the piano. Sure enough, out came the lighter - along with the piano's innards. By now it was clear - this skit had gone too far. Now it had to spin itself out to a logical ending. Out the door went the piano to be set alight. As everyone cheered and sang, F/O Don Hanson had to be restrained from driving his car into the funeral pyre.

These days a fellow's air force career could come to a screeching halt, should he instigate or encourage such a skit. After all, some poor sod's tender feelings might be hurt, and charges of harassment (or whatever) might ensue. In 1952 at North Luffenham, however, the CO, proper Cold Warrior that he was, led the way. As to the station commander, he would have had a hearty laugh when he got the details next morning (in case he hadn't been present the night before to

More of 441 circa 1958: Kurt Barlow (EO) with pilots Roy Barnes, W.H. "Bud" McLeod, Larry Sutton, Danny Lambros, "KC" Chapman, Larry Spurr, Scotty Campbell and the CO, Lou Hill. (Larry Sutton Col.)

they were weathered out at Marville, ran low on fuel, so put in at Reims. Here, some weird activities ensued. The local Mystère pilots supplied the Canucks with some francs and flying suits, then the fellows set off to terrorize the neighbourhood pubs. In due course they had to make themselves scarce, the diarist giving only a hint of all this: "What happened after the order to scatter was given, we shall probably never know, dear readers. Even if it was known, I would undoubtedly have my honourary Reims Star taken away, if I put anything in writing. How everyone managed to safely make the trip back to Marville is still a mystery that shall go down in the history of aviation. Well, at least in the history of 441 Squadron." The diary entry for July 12 concludes the Homeric/Reims story:

This day's flying was mainly used for doing large tank tests in preparation for the approaching flight to Rabat. Another section of four were scrambled to pay a return visit to Reims with several bottles of grog and to repay borrowed money to the French boys. (Must keep up these foreign relations you know). However, F/O Moreash had to be substituted in the section, as some of the originals were still recuperating from the 10th and 11th. It was touching to see the Canadians hand over

Neil Burns (right), subject of the infamous "Homeric" beat-up, earned a DFC flying Spitfires with 442 Squadron. Here he is in 1965 with John Greatrix, a 441 CF-104 alumnus. In this photo both were stationed at AFHQ. (Greatrix Col.)

cheer on the proceedings). Endless such true stories do not appear in formal reports, so official historians choose to pooh-pooh them. Anyone familiar with RCAF mess life, however, appreciates the value of such great "heritage and history" anecdotes.

During an exchange to a Belgian base in August and September 1955, 441's diarist described a weekend stand-down as an opportunity to "go sightseeing and indulge in other activities". (This exchange was cut short when all squadrons were ordered back to Marville because of a polio epidemic. F/Os White and Stewart of 441 were diagnosed with the disease. The Belgian squadron that had gone to Marville during 441's absence, was quarantined there for a month.)

On July 10, 1956 the 441 diarist noted that "one of our fightinist fightin' brothers [F/L Neil Burns] sailed from Le Havre aboard the *Homeric*". To honour Burns, who was Canada-bound for a new posting, S/L "Cuppy" Cuthbertson, F/L Thomas N. Crane, F/Os Don Bergie, Jacques Sanche, Don Syms and Jim Webber hatched a plan to beat up the *Homeric*. The diary continues: "Now far be it from me to say the boys beat up the S.S. *Homeric*, but it wouldn't be surprising if the people aboard said ship remembered the 10th of July and the sign of the checkerboard for quite a while... A day later the unholy six returned with wild and hairy tales of their escapade." They did not, however, go straight home. En route,

Whenever possible a fly-by was arranged for any 441 member's wedding. Here, F/Os Mark Constantine, Norm Guay, Doug Howlett and Bill Lynn bring this formation over the 1 Wing chapel in honour of Jack and Gloria Folkins on June 11, 1960. (Folkins Col.)

the grog to the Frenchmen and a more touching sight when the Frenchmen pinned the Order of the Reims Star on the three pilots who had participated in the exercise. They then found it fitting to decorate F/O Moreash as an honorary member, something of which he shall always be proud. The four then took off, made a low pass over Reims air base in box formation, thus writing fini to Operations Mons Star.

In January 2003 Don Syms recalled the *Homeric* escapade:

The exercise did not go quite as planned. We had checked ship sailing times and expected the Homeric to be at least 30 minutes out to sea. It wasn't, but we did our flypast anyway. I'm not sure how many passes were made, but I do recall avoiding cranes and other harbour installations. For our return the weather at Marville had gone well below what was forecast, so we had to divert. Besides that, our low-level exercise over LeHavre had eaten into our fuel, so we had to find an airport in a hurry. We got the weather for Reims - 7000 overcast with good visibility. With Cuppy leading, we did a radar-vectored, cloud-breaking procedure, then found that the ceiling really was less than 1000 feet! Our vectors had us flying up a valley with the hilltops on either side buried in cloud. After landing, we were directed to a French fighter squadron. We exchanged our "G" suits for some general purpose flying suits and proceeded to entertain and be entertained by the local flyers. My memory still is foggy as to those goings-on.

The nuttiness carried on at 441, a diary entry of July 16 stating, "F/L Crane was the only one to get airborne today. It seems that he had to get a uniform pressed, or some such thing, at 3 Wing." Squadron records are peppered with references to other skits. In June 1957 F/L Crane spent three weeks at Dijon, flying Mystères. On his return the unit noted that he had been very active at Dijon in Franco-Canadian "foreign affairs", adding, "Whether what he did was a hindrance or a help we'll probably never know." The partying went on apace, one October 1957 entry noting, "Two sections spent a riotous night at 4 Wing and were still under the weather on arrival back at Marville. Tut, tut, boys."

for the Sabre, a chore for the sluggish F-84F. Although F/L Neil Burns had approved the 441 "greeting" at Florennes, it was the CO, S/L "Cuppy" Cuthbertson who had to do the explaining to A/V/M Godwin at 1 Air Division HQ. As one of the Silver Foxes put it, "That drive from Marville to Metz to see the AOC was all too familiar to Cuppy." To keep readers scratching their heads about 441 and its shenanigans, another great diary entry is that of October 4, 1960: "F/Os Lynn, Howlett, Yakachuk, McRae returned from their Munich Beer Fest today after a weekend of cementing relations with der Deutch." The fellows had flown into the nearby German base at Erding, then spent the weekend whooping it up at Oktoberfest. In 2003 Don Syms admitted to another nutty skit:

One night in September 1956 I was scheduled for a navigation exercise. After I had done my external checks and settled into the cockpit, one of the servicing crew climbed the ladder to ask if I would "bomb" our American friends at Étain AFB, a bit south of Marville, with a load of single sheets of toilet paper. I agreed, and with a few hand signals and

Pilots recalling their Sabre days sometimes boast of incidents that did not make it into the historical record. One might treat these tales with some caution or play it safe and accept them at face value. Such shenanigans might have been so outlandish, that the most liberal-minded squadron historian could not bring himself to record them officially. Examples? It is true that Silver Fox pilots visited 3 Wing one day and left an enormous "441" painted on the runway. But did they really paint the Base Commander's black staff car in a checker-board pattern? Or break into the Officers Mess at North Luffenham to steal frozen pheasants that were being kept in the freezer for some special occasion? Yes, it all happened!

In a typical 441 skit F/L Claude LaFrance was on an exchange at Florennes, Belgium from August 29 to September 4, 1955. There he was irked by a Belgian officer, bragging of the forthcoming delivery to the BAF of F-84Fs. Finally, "les Belgiques" could go supersonic. The official delivery of the F-84F was to include a sonic boom. Ticked off with all this talk about the F-84F (a real "dog" if ever there was one - F-84 pilots even agree), LaFrance hatched a plan with his fellow pilots. So did it transpire that, on the day of the ceremony, F/O J.A.E. "Al" McIlraith happened to be leading a section of four clean Silver Fox Sabres above cloud near Florennes. Minutes before the F-84F was to perform its trick, the four Sabres put their noses down and, one by one, produced thunderous "booms" - a breeze

The Soviets were not the only ones who built massive, ugly housing projects. Here are some of Marville's PMQs (permanent married quarters) in the 1950s. Eventually, RCAF NATO wings had all the good facilities. In this 1 Wing pool scene are Pat Lambros and daughter Kim (left), and Nan Spurr with daughters Deb and Jane (Nan Baggs Col.)

shouting back and forth with the servicing crew, they stuffed my speed brake wells with packages. I departed, cleared off tower frequency and headed south at low level on a nice clear night.

After maintaining a listening watch on Étain's tower frequency and assuring myself that there was no circuit traffic, I crossed the airfield in a southerly direction in order to deliver my load over the built-up side of the base. Gauging my "bombing run" as closely as I could, I popped open my speed brakes and released the load. I don't know how accurate the delivery was, but there were tales of USAF airmen armed with pointed sticks going around the next day picking up thousands of little squares of toilet paper!

Silver Fox Wives

While most air force wives enjoyed their time overseas during the early Cold War, life was not always a piece of cake. They and their children were far from home and sometimes living in makeshift quarters. Those at Marville in the early years recalled that their apartments could get so frigid that they warmed their hands over electric toasters. With husbands busy flying, there was little time for normal family life. One wife put it succinctly - "There's one thing we all understood - the air force came first." Yes, it was a man's world. After all, those hot-shot Sabre pilots were helping save the Free World from the Communist hordes!

In that era wives stayed home. By RCAF regulations they could not be employed, so they were stuck "making do" on the mothering and social scenes. Except on designated "mixed" occasions, they were not even allowed into the Officers Mess, where husbands and boyfriends gathered after a day's flying to re-enact their daring escapades and, all too often, to over-indulge. Drinking and driving was commonplace and, with Marville's PMQs 12 miles from base, there often were road accidents after a night in the mess.

Some 441 wives putting on a skit in the Officers Mess at Marville. Marg Laidler is on the left, Nan Spurr on the right wearing the crash helmet. Then, three "blonde bombshells: Tes O'Mara, Fay Milne and Helen Gourley. (Nan Baggs Col.)

There could be a lot of the tension associated with catering to their fly-boy "hubbies", raising children, and keeping up with so many other like-it-or-lump-it demands. Thus, to help keep their sanity, wives formed groups covering a hundred and one activities - babysitting, cooking, sewing, acting and music, education, etc. The story of those 441 Squadron wives is a book waiting to be written - will someone dare step into that minefield! In April 2003 Larry Spurr's wife, Nan, recalled her days at Marville with all their "pluses and minuses":

When we first arrived at 1 Wing, the PMQs were not ready for occupancy. As a result, most of us lived on the economy in France or Belgium. Those who arrived first, got the best places. Eventually, we moved into PMQs, but most of our furniture had not yet arrived. We made do with furniture borrowed from the barracks on base. Because there were still no curtains or drapes, we were issued blankets to hang over our bedroom windows (which happened to look over a huge parking lot). From outside, our windows certainly didn't look very tidy.

In spite of everything, we were extremely happy to be in PMQs, for now we had hot water, modern bathrooms and kitchens, and central heating. A PMQ had four floors each with eight apartments. Each floor shared a washing machine in the basement. Our first winter turned out to be one of the coldest in French history and, lo and behold, the PMQ heating system malfunctioned. I well recall the night that Tes O'Mara and I sat warming our hands over a toaster! Over the years we had many a laugh over that!

In Air Division days the Canadians were infamous for their huge cars. Cadillacs, Buicks, Lincolns and Chryslers proliferated. Larry and Nan Spurr drove this mighty Buick. Then, a view of 1 Wing families on a camping trip in the French Riviera. (Nan Baggs Col.)

Another oddity in PMQs was the garbage chute running from the top floor to the basement. Believe it or not, by yelling down the chute, we could communicate with our neighbours. We also could always tell who was having a party by the sound of bottles crashing down the chute.

We didn't do much shopping on base in the early years. After all, we were 12 miles from the base. Instead, we got to enjoy shopping in the local village shops and markets. We also had shopping privileges at any USAF base exchange, and any "BX" always was very well stocked. Unfortunately, the PMQs were without public telephones, a real disadvantage, especially if there was a medical emergency. However, there usually was a doctor at home in his PMQ and he would be happy to help. Since the men were away in Rabat or other places for weeks at a time, wives had to have current driver licences and cars.

One year we officers' wives put on a show that was a parody on the Broadway musical "Damn Yankees". That was a great deal of fun and so successful that we were invited to perform it at other Wings. Going "on the road" was a lot of fun, not to mention a real boost to our egos. All things considered, most of us enjoyed our tours overseas. It was hard to leave, when the time came.

CHAPTER
Training, Exchanges & Prangs

A Sabre pilot's training began long before reporting to squadron, where it continued on a daily basis. Every man's experience was different, but Ron G. Hayman of 441 Squadron is a typical example. Born in 1931, he joined the RCAF Auxiliary in 1952. He learned to fly Harvards at 3 FTS in Claresholm, Alberta, soloing on November 7, 1952. He described that 20-minute flight in a word - "Yikes!" His logbook subsequently hinted at small secrets. Of a March 18, 1953 flight he wrote, "Attempted formation - Phil, Paul and I - that was close !" From Claresholme, Hayman moved to 2 AFS at Portage la Prairie, followed by a session at 1 PGS at MacDonald.

Early in November 1953 Hayman joined 400 (Aux) Squadron in Toronto. By mid-February 1954 he had logged some 350 hours in Harvards. Finally, he was introduced to the Vampire. There followed two years as a "weekend warrior", switching between Harvards and Vampires (with an occasional T-33 flight), scrambling in air defence exercises against USAF B-36s and B-50s, and no foul-up more serious than the day he did a fly-by at Elmira, Ontario (he should have been over Elora, some miles away). Then, as Hayman described it, a Regular Force recruiter offered a wonderful opportunity - "Sign here and in six months you'll be flying Sabres in Europe!" This may have been a recruiter's ruse - in August 2002 Ron Clayton recalled an identical offer to induce his departure from the Auxiliary.

Having joined the Regular Force in February 1956, Hayman took a Harvard refresher course at Centralia, then returned to 2 AFS for further T-33 training. Most of August was spent at Uplands on T-33s then, on August 26, he reported to Chatham to meet the Sabre. First came two simulator sessions (the "sim" was little more than a Sabre cockpit wired for mock emergencies - a far cry from today's simulators that imitate noise, motion, even G-forces). Two local T-bird trips followed then, on August 31, it was time to fly the Sabre. Combat and gunnery tactics soon were introduced. Meanwhile, Hayman flew cross-country navigation exercises in T-33s. A major event was taking Sabre 23269 to St. Hubert on October 29, 1956, practicing a 16-aircraft formation fly-past, then taking part in a ceremonial fly-past over Ottawa the next day. As 1956 ended, Hayman tabulated his RCAF flying time:

Type	In 1956	Career Total
Vampire	128:10	187:45
T-33	180:10	268:35
C-45	27:05	29:25
Harvard	34:00	643.35
Sabre	71:45	71:45

Gunnery intensified in early January. Given that targets were towed at a slow 200 knots, it was possible to register many hits. Hayman's best day was February 9, 1957, when he scored 60.3 percent. Chief Flying Instructor W/C "Duke" Warren signed him off on January 11, 1957. With nearly 82 hours on Sabres, F/O Hayman was ready for overseas. As of February 27 he was flying at 441. The squadron diary noted his arrival - "Ron is a refugee from the reserve forces and finally realized that he wanted to do some real flying." On March 30, 1959 he was posted to "Air Div" HQ. While with the Silver Foxes he would run his Sabre time to 862:40 hours.

Combat Readiness

When a Sabre pilot reported to squadron, he began with intensive "phase training" to familiarize him with NATO and "Air Div" routines, and bring him to operational readiness. The syllabus was refined over time, but the essentials remained. If not completed within 70 days, the whole phase training process was to be repeated. It all began with "area indoctrination" a comprehensive ground school conducted by the Wing Instrument Flight (WIF). Normal operating areas were briefed, with emphasis on radar control, "fixer nets", navigational aids, and lost and letdown procedures. Next, one of the flight commanders lectured on flying regulations, including "Air Div" and Wing flying orders and procedures. The Wing meteorological officer briefed newcomers on European weather conditions.

The flight commander, or an experienced pilot, next gave instructions in emergency procedures - what to do in case of fire on the ground or in the air, engine and electrical failures, air starts, compressor stall recovery, and failures involving hydraulics (e.g. brakes or control surface emergencies). Also covered were ejection and forced landings. There were intelligence briefings, a visit to 61 Aircraft Control and Warning Squadron, a quick Sabre technical training course, and visits to flying control and GCA units. Next, a flight commander or senior section lead went into the Sabre's ground and air handling characteristics, pilot responsibilities on the ground, pre-flight and cockpit checks, start procedures, and taxi, takeoff and shut-down. Airmanship also included "Air Handling" (takeoff, throttle, speed brakes, undercarriage and flap operations, heating, ventilation, landing and overshooting). Flying orders and regulations included a description of the aerodrome, obstructions, safe heights, prohibited areas, local signals and RT procedures. Pilots finally completed a written test on which they had to score 90% before the squadron would let them into a Sabre.

Flying instruction followed a series of steps in which the aircraft, instructor, and nature of the lesson were all defined. Exercises 1 - 15 covered "the making of a Sabre pilot":

Ex.1: *Sector recce - done in a T-33, supervised by a WIF instructor. Visual recce of the normal flying area to familiarize a pilot with airfields and landmarks useful as nav aids.*

Ex.2: *Familiarization, WIF T-33. Instrument famil with emphasis on radar control, fixer systems and local letdown aids. Letdowns at one or two other wings might be included.*

Ex.3: *Instrument flying, WIF T-33. Practice instrument flying with further famil of other wing or USAFE letdown procedures.*

Ex.4: *Instrument flying proficiency check (if required). Supervised by OC WIF, squadron CO or flight commander. Check aspiring pilot during instrument climbs, unusual attitudes, GCA approaches, overshoot procedures.*

Ex.5: *General practice, T-33. Not mandatory, but additional sorties might be authorized to correct weaknesses. Sorties monitored by CO and OC WIF.*

Ex.6: *At last - fly a squadron Sabre, supervised by an experienced pilot. Climb to 35,000, general famil, beacon letdown and GCA landing.*

Ex.7: *Sabre famil with section lead as the chase pilot. Climb to 40,000, beacon letdown, GCA. Deliberate overshoot and re-entry for a normal circuit and landing.* The degree to which a pilot was watched and debriefed may be gauged by notes from March 17, 1960, when F/O Ronald A. Duffie was in phase training. His instructor wrote, "Flew wing on take-off. Held position initially, dropped back mid-way through climb by killing speed on turn (debriefed). Led let-down and full stop GCA (visibility no good for normal circuit). Did OK."

Ex.8: *Still with the section lead, climb to 45,000, sector recce of other bases - ADF (radio compass) homings, practice forced landings, circuit re-entry and landing.* Duffie went through this on March 18 and was assessed: "Climbed to 45,000, dropped back badly, initially. Did not actually get into position until 42,000 (debriefed on this). Unable to carry out sector recce and PFL [Practice Forced Landings] because of undercast. Did individual aerobatics. Let down. Cloud break and pitch. No difficulties. "

Ex.9: *Sabre famil. Lead took new man through take-off, power climb to 48,000, supersonic dives, aerobatics at 20,000, ADF homings, VHF letdown, full stop under GCA.*

Ex.10: *Two-plane element training. Instructor as section lead with the new pilot as wingman. Climb to 35,000 and 48,000, practice station keeping, turns, breaks, simple tail chase using cine gun, air fighting (when pupil was ready). New pilot led the return to base for final GCA letdown and full stop. This phase could go through several sorties.* Duffie did it in seven from March 21 - 28. Assessment for March 21 reads: "Dropped back a couple of times in climb, otherwise OK. Station keeping throughout turns and during some air fighting reasonably good. RT trouble near end of trip (No. 2 receivers u/s). No Bingo - didn't call air control - he should have." Next day the assessing officer was critical of another aspect - alertness: "Take off and climb satisfactory... Lead had two a/c at 6 o'clock for about one mile and No.2 did not see them. Very mild hassle with CF-100".

Ex.11: *Wingman 2-plane check supervised by squadron or flight commander.*

Ex.12: *4-plane section. Section leader flew as No.1 or No.3 with new pilot as wingman. Having climbed to 40,000 - 48,000 feet, the pilots did station keeping, turns, breaks and tail chases using cine gun and air fighting when pupil was ready. Concluded with ADF or beacon let-down and GCA approach.* Duffie flew at least four such sorties April 13 - 19. F/L J.N Guay, assessing officer on the 13th, wrote: "Pilot flew as No.4. Takeoff and climb all right. Good position during battle

The 1 Wing auto club was popular in Sabre days. Here is 441 pilot Jack Folkins with his 1955 Mercedes-Benz SL300, which he had purchased in 1958 for $4000. He brought the beauty with him when posted to Chatham in 1961, then sold it a year later for $5400. The second view shows the SL300 "wings extended" and beside Hugh Grasswick's Porsche. (Jack Folkins Col.)

A scene at the annual 1 Wing race day, where contestants competed on the taxiways and runways (which had to be closed to air traffic). Marville's station commander, G/C Blackie Williams, thought that this was a great idea. One year, when he learned that the Comet was due in on race day, he simply arranged to have it diverted to 2 Wing! (Jack Folkins)

Pilots of 331 RNoAF and 441 squadrons during an April 1961 exchange. Then, a typical Norwegian Sabre at RAF Leuchars in 1963. (441 Sqn, Wilf White)

More Exchanges

RCAF exchanges with other NATO units were frequent and fun. An exchange might involve deploying for only a day or weekend, or for a week or two. The objectives were straightforward - general training, strengthening inter-airforce operability, and building camaraderie. If, for example, 441 visited a Dutch F-84 base, this gave the Dutch hands-on experience servicing Sabres - refuelling, topping up fluids and

formation at any altitude. Fell back too far during air fighting. Failed to notice two attacking aircraft till they were in range. Good close formation on let down and GCA, but a bit poor on overshoot. Pilot was debriefed on air fighting position and looking around. Good trip except during air fighting." On another sortie F/L McLeod described Duffie: *"Flew as No.2, take off climb and formation flying good. No hassle. Landed at 3 Wing. Average trip throughout."* McLeod was critical on another sortie: *"Flew as No.4. Take off, climb and formation okay. Had one close call with No.3 while passing under. Passes much too close. 3 pulled up to avoid a potential mid-air. Debriefed on this. Flew a good wing position on 4 and GCA."*

Ex.13: *Wingman check, 4-plane formation with flight commander No.3, new man No.4. Broad lesson objectives: "Sortie shall require wingman to perform manoeuvres which will enable the Flight Commander to judge new pilot's ability as 4".*

Ex.14: *Section lead No.3, pupil No.4. Review of previous training with emphasis on weaknesses.*

Ex.15: *Combat ready check. Squadron CO or deputy in lead: "This check shall include such manoeuvres as Squadron Commander considers necessary to prove the pilot is combat ready."* Duffie flew Ex.15 on either April 20 or 21. Assessment: *"F/O Duffie flew in the No.4 position and flew his position quite well. His look-out is average and the only fault in the air was flying just a bit wide. On the let down he had difficulty tuning the beacon at ER and overshot 10-15 miles. Debriefed. F/O Duffie is considered combat ready to fly No.2 or No.4 positions."*

oxygen, re-arming, all the little details right down to putting on intake plugs and pitot tube covers, and helping pilots strap in. Meanwhile, pilots would be exchanging information about their respective aircraft and tactics, firing on the local range, and dogfighting - Sabre against F-84. At day's end they would be getting to know each other at the bar, at a BBQ, or "on the town". Thus was NATO kept strong from Norway, across the UK, and down as far as Turkey. If the Cold War ever turned hot, NATO would be able to fly and fight to one basic standard. Should 441 ever be rousted from Marville in war, it could continue the fight from any other available base.

While on exchange, RCAF pilots occasionally had the chance to fly in the back seat of a hosts' aircraft, e.g. a Danish F-100F or a two seat Meteor. Flying solo in an unfamiliar single-seater was verboten for obvious reasons. In an interview with Hugh Halliday on May 15, 2002, however, Claude LaFrance related an exception. In the course of his 441 tour, he attended the RAF Fighter Leader Course at West Raynham. There he checked out on the Hunter, which he found pleasant to fly, but limited. The Hunter had been introduced without dive brakes, something that would be rectified on later marks. Another problem was that the Hunter might flame out when the cannons fired - gun gasses could stifle the engine. When RAF Hunters later visited Marville, LaFrance was allowed to fly a sortie. While taxiing, he spotted two hotshot 441 pilots watching from the sidelines, practically begging for a chance to try the Hunter. As he passed them, LaFrance whipped off his oxygen mask to flash a grin at the envious pair.

Exchanges abounded at 441. In August 1958, for example, the squadron visited 256 Squadron (RAF, Meteor N.F.11s) at Geilenkirchen. This enabled the Sabre jockeys to get in some rare air-to-ground sorties, since the Brits had a range at Nordhorn. The diary for 1960 notes most 441 exchanges for that year, beginning with a regular exercise with the French known as "Tuesday Scrimmage" (not always held on a Tuesday). On January 5 F/Os Bruce Donald, Norm Guay, Malcolm McRae and Dennis Paproski (the diarist referred to them as "lucky boys") headed off to Creil, France on a "Tuesday Scrimmage". The usual thing was for a section (four Sabres) to depart for whichever base, meeting "enemy" Mystères enroute for some air fighting. Everyone then would land for fuel and lunch. The Canadians always were bug-eyed at how the French pilots casually sipped wine with their meal! Finally, everyone would roar off for another fight, after which 441 usually went home. On April 26 F/Ls Carl Bertrand, Bruce Donald, Bill Lynn and Barry Morris flew to Cambrai for "Tuesday Scrimmage". For May 5 it was held at Dijon.

While 441 would be busy at Deci in February and August of 1960, March included exchange activity. On the 15th four RNoAF F-86F Sabres arrived at Marville for two days of air fighting on Ex. Tall Timber. A later such RCAF - RNoAF exchange was held starting on October 4, 1961, 441 heading far north to Oerland, near Trondheim. Don Gilkinson was on this do. Flying for him commenced on the 5th with two "famil" trips, to get the lay of the land (i.e. mountains and fjords). After dark he flew a trip northward - any such flight would have been watched closely by the Soviets. On the 6th Gilkinson had two low level sorties, plus a GCI trip. Targets would have been RCAF or Norwegian Sabres - it didn't matter. On the 9th he flew with some mates up to Bødo to tour some RNoAF hangars built into the side of a mountain (a fellow would land, then taxi through a blast door into the mountain). Weather curtailed flying for the 10th and all Gilkinson had to do next day was a couple of air tests. He and Lorne Coste flew home on the 14th via Kastrup, Denmark, Coste's Sabre being u/s.

On July 18, 1960 F/L Stacey, and F/Os Grasswick, Gilkinson and Bertrand left for Rimini, Italy (via Istres) on Ex. Southern Bello. Arriving on the 19th, they did some air fighting next day, then were home on the 22nd. The challenge was not great for the Canadians, since the Italians were flying Sabre 4s, hand-me-downs from the RAF. Something else was that the Italians were rather hard up. They did their best to show their visitors a good time, but the 441 lads helped with the expenses. For September 27 that diarist noted that "The boss and Ron MacGarva flew to Skrydstrup in Denmark to look over the base we are to deploy to in Oct." On October 5 W/C McLachlan, flight commanders F/Ls Ken Stacey and "Jamie" Jameson (a Brit enrolled in the RCAF), plus F/Os Doug Howlett, Bill Lynn and Malcolm McRae flew to Skrydstrup to begin a week long deployment. Other pilots rotated in later, the last getting home on 14th. On the 18th F/Os Bruce Giffin, Ellis, Hugh Grasswick and Doug Howlett flew to Rygge, Norway for "Tall Timber".

Some 441 pilots visiting 96 Squadron (Meteor N.F.11s) at RAF Ahlhorn, Germany. Some time during this exchange the Brits thought that it would be a laugh to deface one of 441's "Checkerbirds". (441 Sqn)

When a RAF squadron visited 441 *circa* 1956, the pilots suffered their own humiliation. Check out the fancy new markings on their Hunter! (Don Syms)

A March 25, 1960 diary entry notes that F/L Morris and F/Os McRae, Yakachuk, Hackett, and Porco departed for the USAF F-100 base at Wethersfield northeast of London. This was for another kind of exchange - strictly cultural (one of the fellows categorized the trip as "a jolly"). From Wethersfield they got to London on the "40 - 40" train - a 40 minute ride, just time for the fellows to polish off a "40 ouncer" of their favourite liquid. For the weekend of April 25 - 28 F/Os Gilkinson, Lynn and Porco went to Copenhagen in T-33s. On November 8 the diary notes: "F/Os Les Hackett, Ken White, Clancy Sheldrup and F/L Ken Stacey flew into Spangdahlem air base to tee up a party with the boys from the 59th squadron, who were stationed at Étain last year." Yes, both the flying and the partying were intense on a squadron like 441. There certainly was no room for the faint of heart - it was war!

March 20 - 29, 1962 the Silver Foxes, F/Os Mike Diss, Don Gilkinson, Bill Lynn and Rogers Smith included, were on exchange with the Luftwaffe at Wittmund. Gilkinson's log shows: high battle formation on the 21st, two such trips next day, the same on the 26th, a "co-op" mission on the 27th (RCAF and Luftwaffe Sabres), two more high battle formations on the 28th, then home next day. Included on the social side during this exchange was a good thrash aboard a German naval vessel. On March 13, 1963 F/Os Bertrand, Cummings, Diss and Matthews were off to Bødo, Norway (one of the last 441 "Tall Timber" exchanges). Next day the diary reported that the fellows "blew in from the Arctic ... According to all war stories, plus the haggard appearance of the four pilots, it was a very successful trip. Norwegian hospitality is really the very best!"

In January 2003 Silver Fox alumnus Bill Lynn noted a few exchanges from his log book. October 9 to 13, 1959 he was at Aalborg then, on April 26, 1960, was part of a section visiting Cambrai - "I recall the French pilots wining and dining us at lunch before the scheduled air fight. I guess we made it home OK." October 5 to 11, 1960 Lynn was with some squadron mates on an exchange to Skrydstrup. On August 4, 1961 he was back at Cambrai on a Tuesday Scrimmage. "Maybe looking for more wine," he wondered 41 years later! While flying 23554 low level to 2 Wing on September 10, 1962, Lynn recalled that, "En route I felt an unusual jolt, which I soon realized was my port drop tank departing the aircraft. Never heard of it again."

In May 2003 John MacArthur recalled some further exchange and R&R anecdotes:

> Some of our deployments were to St. Hubert, Belgium, which was our emergency base should Marville ever be attacked. We also had exchanges with the German Air Force at Ahlhorn, and with the Norwegians at Bødo. There the "Norskis" greeted each of us at the cockpit with a shot of Aquavit (shenanigans followed in the Officers Mess). In contrast to such wintery trips, we sometimes ventured south to Rimini to fly with the Italian Air Force.
>
> Landing one day at Florennes, Belgium we were quite astounded at the sight of a huge wild boar penned up behind the Officers Mess. Someone explained that the emblem of the local squadron was a boar and that this big fellow was their mascot.
>
> Weekend trips often were taken with a section of Sabres, if the boss could be talked into it, and Zulu was not being held. We would visit

Other NATO fighters against which 441 trained 1952 - 63: Dutch F-84Gs and German Sabre 5s. (Harry Tate)

From March 20 to 29, 1962, the Silver Foxes visited Wittmund to train with JG.71 "Richthofen". Those in RCAF uniforms are Rogers Smith, Andy Anderson, Bill Lynn, Don Gilkinson, Mike Stedman, Ken Stacey (over Stedman's left shoulder) with Mike Diss in the cockpit. (via Don Gilkinson)

various spots, favourites being Copenhagen or Aalborg in Denmark. RAF Manston was popular, since it was close by train to London. In the fall of 1961 F/O Don Gilkinson and I took a T-bird to Munich for Oktoberfest. F/L Barry Gartner and F/Os Gary Corbett, Doug Howlett and Dave Cummings joined us as a section of Sabres. Our plan was to have a beer in each of the 21 tents that were set up. We started in the Lowenbrau tent, but some officials came along and asked us to move. When we explained that we were RCAF fighter pilots, however, we were asked to stay. Soon we were introduced to Robert Strauss, the West German Defence Minister, and spent the evening drinking with him and his retinue.

The Flight Commander

The flight commander had some of the toughest responsibilities on a fighter squadron. Father figure and joe boy were just two of his many uses. His daily tasks included passing the CO's orders down, keeping the flying schedule tight, detailing pilots for such things as Zulu Alert or squadron exchanges, assigning experienced pilots for a new boy's phase training, generally making sure that everyone was measuring up to combat ready standards, and holding the fort if the CO was absent. Any time that a pilot might be slacking off, the flight commander would be on his case, perhaps getting him some extra training or, in a rare instance, even recommending that a fellow be grounded. His duties went right down to getting joed to organize parades and a fighter pilot liked nothing less than a parade. Parades were as bad as the paperwork, and there was plenty of that for the flight commander, including writing up the annual "R211s" - personnel reports for each pilot.

Like many officers F/L Claude LaFrance wore two hats - flight commander and instrument flying officer. The latter entailed checking the instrument flying capabilities of each squadron pilot. His task, as he put it, was "to inform, brief and caution." He also spent much time monitoring the quality of controllers, particularly during GCA operations. One problem was the reluctance of pilots to ask for help when needed - requesting a "fix" smacked of admitting to failure. The

Sabre BT-530 lies where it crashed sans pilot on May 2, 1957. F/O H.A. Davidson ejected, but too low to survive. Then, BT-580 after a bad-weather landing at Marville. F/O Tom Koch rode this one out OK. (via: Jim Lyzun, Tom Koch)

controllers themselves were known to the pilots by numbers and, when weather turned bad, the best controllers frequently came on duty, whether scheduled or not. Pilots could identify by the numbers who was calling the instructions and, from experience, also knew who were the best. LaFrance noted that, in really tense circumstances, "If you got a good one, you knew you were in your mother's arms."

Sabre Prangs and other Mishaps

The Canadair Sabre, which lists all Category "A" RCAF Sabres accidents known to 1986, yields the following for 441 Squadron:

Date	Aircraft/Details
June 12, 1952	19189 - Engine failure - wheels-up dead-stick landing in a potato field; S/L A.R. MacKenzie unhurt.
October 31, 1952	19116 - Chatham, undershot, F/O Stuart A. Millar unhurt
December 5, 1952	19185 - North Luffenham, landed short, F/O Kenneth Alan Branch safe
August 20, 1953	19158 - Off Cromer, fuel exhaustion, F/O Les Benson ejected over sea, safe
October 6, 1953	19167 - North Luffenham, F/O Jean "Sonny" Haran unhurt (engine flamed out, force-landed in a field)
November 26, 1953	19152 - Wells, England, F/O Harold Klein ejected from spin, safe
May 17, 1954	19163 - North Sea, failed to return to base, W/C Walter Franklin Parks lost
June 23, 1955	23302 - Marville, stalled turning on final, F/O James H. Johnson safe
August 20, 1956	23654 - Dived in near Rheims; F/O David Eldred Bradley killed
May 2, 1957	23530 - Flameout at 21,000 feet, attempted dead-stick landing at base; ejected at 400 feet; F/O Harvey Archibald Davidson killed
February 10, 1958	23556 - Fire warning, ejected at 40,000 ft. near Angele, F/O R.K. Moreash safe
February 27, 1958	23659 - Flame-out, caught fire, crashed on taxiway, Étain Air Force Base, F/O Tidball safe
March 24, 1958	23436 - Engine trouble, ejected near Rhein-Main, landing in the Rhine River, F/O Larry Sutton safe
November 18, 1958	23491 - Fuel exhaustion, ejected near Frankfurt, Ex. Soft Spot; F/O Jack Folkins safe
November 18, 1958	23519 - Fuel exhaustion, ejected near Frankfurt; Ex. Soft Spot, F/O Norm Guay safe
November 20, 1958	23555 - Crashed at Deci, F/O Donald Hugh George Barnes killed
December 12, 1959	23590 - Marville, crashed in fog at base; F/O Thomas Koch safe
November 9. 1960	23497 - Marville, crashed on takeoff, F/O Ronald Alan Duffie killed
August 10, 1963	23593 - Controls seized at 30,000 feet, ejected at 10,000 feet, F/O Jack Arthur Davidson safe

Pilots by alphabetical order (* indicates KIFA): F/O Donald Hugh George Barnes*, F/O David Eldred Bradley*, F/O Kenneth Alan Branch, F/O Les Benson, F/O Harvey Archibald Davidson*, F/O Jack Arthur Davidson, F/O Ronald Alan Duffie*, F/O Jack Folkins, F/O Norm Guay, F/O Jean "Sonny" Haran, F/O James H. Johnson, F/O Harold Klein, F/O Thomas Koch, S/L A.R. "Andy" Mackenzie, F/O Stuart A. Millar, F/O R.K. "Ken" Moreash, W/C Walter Franklin Parks*, F/O Larry Sutton, F/O Larry Tidball.

There were a hundred and one hazards of which fighter pilots had to be aware any time they flew a mission. Commenting generally, someone on 441 complained in 1953 of how, during daily exercises, there simply seemed to be "too many fighters" and "many near mid-air collisions." This reflected the human side of safety - keeping a sharp eye was vital. But there also were technical glitches.

Although the safety factor in the Air Division generally was high, sometimes a day did not end well - from time to time 441's diary had to report prangs or lesser accidents. These would shock pilots into a greater appreciation for staying alive. The squadron's first Category "A" prang (i.e. aircraft written off) occurred on June 12, 1952. That day S/L Andy MacKenzie was leading a section of four Sabres from North Luffenham. They were 42,000 feet over The Wash when, out of the blue, MacKenzie's engine started vibrating, then quit. Down he came, with his wingman, F/O Don Simmons, sticking close. Mackenzie's first action was to try a relight, but this resulted in a great blast of flame from the exhaust. Simmons quickly advised his boss not the try that again!

In January 2003 MacKenzie recalled that he was feeling somehow groggy as he glided lower and lower. But at 5000 feet, with Mother Earth quickly rising to meet him, Mackenzie's surreal mental state suddenly vanished. He spotted an open field, lined up and made a smooth belly-landing, startling a farmer working with a pair of horses. The Sabre skidded then bounced onto a roadway, coming to rest with little more than a few bumps and scrapes. MacKenzie stepped down onto the wing, lit a cigarette and waited.

By this time North Luffenham had been alerted and G/C Hale was soon on his way in a staff car. First to reach the scene, he agreed with MacKenzie that a very good parking job had been done - the salvage crew would have little trouble getting the Sabre disassembled and back to base. On later inspection, the J47 engine in 19189 was found to have digested itself. What with fire damage and airframe overstressing in the landing, the aircraft was written off. All was not lost, however, for 19189 would serve 441 for some time as a handy source of spares.

Another dicey occurrence was on March 17, 1953: "F/O Annis, while on a low-level navigation exercise, collided with a large bird, which shattered the canopy and spread blood and feathers all over the cockpit. Annis was saved from injury by his crash helmet ... He landed his aircraft [19163] at Brize Norton, a B-50 base, and a ground crew was dispatched by road with a new canopy." In another adventure (April 16, 1953) the diary notes how "F/O Branch had a bad moment when a Harvard flew through the formation as it was returning

The ugly mess after Sabre 23436 crashed on March 24, 1958. In such cases the Canadian government made restitution to the property owner from his losses. (Larry Sutton Col.)

to base, and narrowly missed him." On May 17, 1954 the situation was far worse. That day F/L Dean Kelly took off with W/C Parks, the wing's new COpsO, in a scramble over the North Sea. Somehow, Parks became separated and failed to return to base, no trace being found of him. A memorial service was held on June 21.

On July 21, 1955 F/L E.L. "Len" Fine crashed 23109 on approach to Marville. The diarist commented only that Fine "went to hospital with an injured back." In fact, this was a serious prang, Fine being trapped in his burning Sabre. But F/O R.G. "Bob" Morgan of 416 Squadron, and LAC Harry J. Waters rushed to the scene, smashed the canopy and hauled Fine out. This later resulted in George Medals for the rescuers. (F/L Fine was not so lucky on March 9, 1959, losing his life that day in a T-33 crash near Gimli.)

Larry Sutton, a former Air Cadet from Winnipeg, joined 441 in 1956. His would have been a routine 441 tour had it not been for a mission of March 24, 1958. That day Sutton was air fighting with other Sabres, when his oil pressure began to drop. He declared an emergency, requesting "pigeons" (bearing and distance) from USAF control to the nearest airport. Advice was slow to come, then RCAF "Yellow Jacket" control in Metz gave a course to Rhein Main. Meanwhile, Sutton had shut off all but essential electric power, but to no avail - his engine seized and the controls froze.

Out of options, Sutton ejected at 15,000 feet. All went well as he descended in clear weather. Then he spotted high tension

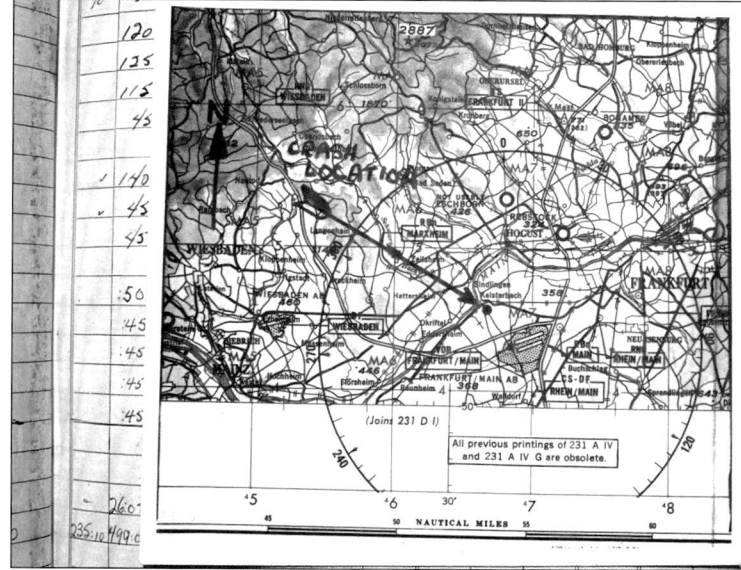

A map showing where 23436 went down near Frankfurt Main Airbase. Then, F/O Sutton's membership card in the Caterpillar Club as awarded by Irvin Air Chute, Ltd. of Fort Erie, Ontario. (Larry Sutton Col.)

wires and the Main River. He escaped the wires, but plunked into the middle of the river. Once he surfaced and discarded his 'chute, he swam ashore, not far from Kelsterbach. A helpful farm boy on the river bank took Sutton to his place, poured him a cognac, ran a hot bath, and got him dry clothes. Eventually, a USAF helicopter ferried Sutton to Rhein Main, from where he returned to Marville via T-33.

Sutton later instructed on Sabres at Chatham, then flew the CF 104 at Cold Lake. One day he heard of an exchange instructing Luftwaffe F-104 students at Luke AFB, Arizona. He mentioned his interest in this job and, to his surprise, got it. He had his first F-104 flight at Luke in July 1966. In later years he had tours on the Chipmunk, Tracker, at NDHQ and with the UN in the Middle East. In other 441 excitement, a February 1958 diary entry noted: "We hit the jackpot this month in losing two of our aircraft. F/O Moreash bailed out successfully not far from the station with a suspected engine fire, and F/O 'Moon' Mullin just barely force-landed a burning Sabre at Étain airforce base before the whole aft section fell off. We're very fortunate that neither pilot suffered any injuries other than the odd bruise."

By mid-1958, sad to say, 441's monthly reports had shrivelled to one or two short paragraphs. November's report refers to "the loss of two a/c for 441" with no further details. Research identified these as Sabres 23491 and 23519 (neither with underwing tanks), with F/Os Jack Folkins and Norm Guay. They had run short of fuel on the 17th after taking part in a no-notice NATO exercise. As the exercise waned, instead of returning to 1 Wing, as briefed, Folkins and Guay were diverted to 3 Wing, but they didn't pick up the 3 Wing beacon. Instead, they were decoyed by another beacon in the area. Upon breaking out of the clag, they spotted the Rhine, but nothing else looked familiar. With fuel running dry, they got some altitude, reviewed their bail-out procedures and ejected.

Soon Folkins was spotted by a forest ranger and picked up by a German Mojave chopper. Since he had been hurt crashing through trees on landing, he was hospitalized for a few days. Landing near a highway, Guay was taken to a nearby hotel for a few drinks. Next he was driven to the USAF base at Weisbaden, given the once-over in the base hospital, and released. Folkins later faced a board of enquiry, but was exonerated once the circumstances were made clear (besides the details noted above, he later learned that there were strong high-level winds about which he and Guay had not been advised).

On August 20 it was much worse for 441 - F/O D.H.G. "Don" Barnes, younger brother of Sabre pilot F/O Roy Barnes of 441, crashed fatally. Don had joined 441 as a pipeliner from Chatham in April. He had been No.2 in a 4-plane section arriving at "Deci". The leader had begun his turn to land, when No.3 saw Barnes raising his wheels and closing his dive brakes. When interrogated, he replied, "My power is stabilized at 60 percent and I cannot do a thing about it." Flying abreast, No.3 saw the canopy go and waited for the ejection, despite the low height. Instead, the Sabre nosed down, hit the ground and exploded.

In some instances the circumstances of fatal crashes were obscure. High speed impacts left little from which to reconstruct events. In the case of F/O D.E. "Dad" Bradley the sequence of events was described in a signal to Air Division HQ:

Pilot was authorized for an air test acceptance check by Acting Squadron Leader at 1440Z. Aircraft was clean. Aircraft was airborne 1505Z and request for climb heading was made to the WO Tower shortly after take off. No further RT contact was made after pilot acknowledged climb heading of 360 degrees magnetic. Weather at time was 3000 feet broken, visibility 15. At 1600Z Wing Operations

Jack Folkins recuperates after his prang. Then, a typical "hero shot" of Jack in the same period. (Folkins Col.)

The funeral at Choloy of four Sabre pilots killed on March 2, 1956. Many RCAF members from the Cold War era lie in this cemetery, having died in plane, auto or motorcycle crashes, or of natural causes. (Todd Pomerleau Col.)

informed Yellow Jacket and Passport Controller that aircraft was overdue. At 1635A a call was received from a civilian who stated that an aircraft had crashed at 1545Z in the vicinity of Aure. Crash truck was dispatched to the scene of the crash at 1800Z when positive area of the crash had been confirmed. At 2000Z WSECO [Wing Security Officer] called from scene of crash and stated that the aircraft was burning 20 feet in the ground....The guard party was dispatched to the scene of the crash at 2000Z. Cause of accident obscure. Investigation continuing.

As to F/O Harvey A. Davidson's loss, the casualty message from No.1 Wing to Air Division HQ said it all:

F/O Davidson was leader of Checkerboard X-Ray Section detailed to carry out cine work against towed flag. Section was airborne at 0821Z. Aircraft climbed out to rendezvous with tow aircraft but, just previous to gaining tow, X-Ray Leader advised that his sight was unserviceable and advised No.3 to take lead. He left formation without any further transmissions. At 0836Z X-Ray Leader reported to tower flameout over Marville at 21,000 feet, unable to relight and tower crash action was taken. Pilot did not advise any circumstances that might have affected flameout, or why unable to relight, or how many relight attempts were made. Tower advised pilot that field was cleared for his emergency and advised of landing conditions. At 0841Z pilot advised that he was changing his forced landing pattern from Runway 12 to 30. At about 2 to 300 feet over 439 hangar on downwind on Runway 30 pilot advised that unable to make forced landing and was ejecting. Just prior to this he was observed starting gentle bank turn but then rolled out. Pilot ejected 0842Z. Personnel on ground saw canopy and seat eject and pilot separate from seat, but chute was not seen to open. Aircraft was in landing configuration and continued to glide straight ahead until it crashed approximately 2 miles away... Automatic parachute was not connected nor had ripcord been pulled... It is my opinion that this very experienced Sabre pilot misjudged his forced landing pattern and professional pride induced him to stay with aircraft down to dangerous altitude. The fact that he did not have his auto chute connected was stupid as, even at the altitude at which he ejected, there was a good possibility that his chute would have opened. This wing is considering having ground crew observe pilot hookup in Sabre and T-33 aircraft with orders to refuse to start until all safety equipment is properly attached. During Zulu scrambles pilots will be required to state, "Safety equipment connected", during radio check.

Apart from these circumstances, Davidson's loss was particularly cruel. After losing interest in medical school and drifting from job to job, he had been inspired to join the RCAF (an older brother had served overseas during the war). On enlisting, he wrote, "I now feel certain that the Air Force offers all that I want. Not only will I have the chance to serve my country, but I will be able to establish myself in the rapidly expanding aircraft industry in Canada, either on a military or civilian basis." His stay in Europe should have ended six months earlier, but he had obtained an extension, since his fiancée had her own tour to complete.

As during the Second World War, committees moved in after a death to sort out personal effects, including automobiles. The inventories reflect the lives of young men living full (if Spartan) lives far from home. That for F/O Bradley (a bachelor who was obviously a keen photographer) included three cameras, flash equipment, films, 55 records, photo albums, a slide projector, record player, one squadron plaque, four souvenir scarves, two radios, a cribbage set, three beer steins, three civilian suits, 24 ties, one service blue tunic, four pairs of service blue trousers, one service summer tunic, four pairs of summer service trousers, and two battle dress tunics. Being on a Short Service Commission, he had no mess kit, and among his possessions were only six books, including an atlas and a dictionary.

There can be no doubt that RCAF tradesmen on Sabres delivered outstanding service, yet a small oversight could have grave results. Such an incident involved 441 Sabre 23501. As reported in the July/August 1961 edition of *Flight Comment*, a technician doing an engine start was seated in the cockpit. Suddenly, an electrician on the wing tapped him on the shoulder and pointed to smoke pouring from the tailpipe. The engine was quickly shut down. It transpired that the tailpipe dust plug was still in place. This had not been noticed, since the red streamers normally attached to the plug were missing. Had they been, either airman would have been alerted. As it was, the aft section of '501 had to be replaced. Flight safety incidents occurred right into 441's final months on the Sabre. On February 21, 1963, for example, the squadron diary noted that:

Icy runways and taxiways kept us on the ground until afternoon. Four Norwegian F-86Ks and a T-33 diverted from Soellingen with a very low fuel condition, one gauge was showing well below zero on shutdown! F/Os Howlett and Anderson had a close call - met the departing Comet head on about two miles off the end of the runway. The F-86s were on final GCA and the Comet had just taken off.

CHAPTER 13

Sabre Days Waning

The rapid expansion in early years of the Air Division had sparked rivalries between squadrons and wings. Senior wings delighted in showing off to new arrivals. As 441 alumnus Bruce Burgess recalled, "1 Wing Sabres beat up 2 Wing until they learned their business - then 2 Wing regularly beat up 3 Wing, and so on." It was the best air fighting practice available, since NATO Allies mainly were flying inferior fighters. But the natural edge enjoyed by the Sabre could not last. Swept-wing Mystères offered more of a challenge than Meteors, but even they were underpowered against Sabre 6s. However, in the course of Ex. Fox Paw of October 1955, with air battles fought over London and East Anglia, 441 reported difficulties: "The pilots found that when flying with tanks, the Sabre has a difficult time with the Hawker Hunter." Then, in June 1956, 441 noted that "F-100s (USAF) are seen more and more often and are very rapid machines. Oh well!" Even so, a Super Sabre could not match a Sabre 6 in a turn.

While the 441 diary had its periods of neglect, in March 1959 it again was being well attended. An interesting note of March 5 refers to the West Germany - Czechoslovakia buffer zone: "S/L Lou Hill with F/O Ellis did a small cross-country trip in the buffer zone, while under 'close control'. The buffer zone has been moved further west." Another time in the same airspace Tom Crane, Jack Folkins, Murray Lepard and Ken Moreash, flying from 3 Wing, tangled with some F-100s. Moreash did a barrel roll over the F-100 Lead, who was not impressed about being hassled. It turned out that contrails first spotted by 441, and later assumed to be F-100s, really were MiGs scrambled to intercept the Sabres. All in the 441 section were disciplined, except Folkins, who was under phase-training.

Ex. Top Weight ran April 13-16, 1959. For the 15th 441 flew an amazing 116 sorties for 145:35 hours, the diarist noting, "Everyone is very tired after the day's work." The worst problem for 441 was a bird strike suffered by F/L Danny Lambros. For October 2 the diary mentions a Sabre - CF-100 flypast at Metz for a local "Canada Day" celebration. The next day's entry reads: "F/O Ron Hayman was married today and the fly-by done by 439 Sqn was timed very well. A small party went to Verdun and terrorized their Mess for the night." On October 21 there was a lecture about the forthcoming CF-104, which would replace the Sabre in the Air Division. This was the first mention by 441 of the new type. As a sign of the times, "Air Div" HQ decided late in 1959 that Category "B" Sabre crashes (serious but "fixable" damage) would no longer be repaired. It would be another four years before the Sabre era closed, but people already were sensing that the "glory days" of the RCAF Air Division were done.

November 1959 brought "the woxof blues" - crappy weather. For the 23rd: "Clamped right in. Nil flying. Sports were in order for the day." 24th: "Didn't turn a wheel all day." 25th "Went on Zulu but did not fly because of weather." It cleared on the 26th and there was night flying, the diarist noting, "It was a good night as nil accidents occurred." Next day cloud was noted from 800' to 38,000', so it was another day for sports, cards, etc. Another weather-related entry was December 18: "Nobody got lost coming back from England." Meanwhile, postings in and out were regular, typical of those noted at 441 being on April 15, 1960: "F/O Lambert left for Penhold to fly yellow monsters. Au revoir, Andy." May 18's was a nifty entry: "We were off Zulu at noon. Had two scrambles. Exercise Bend Over was called for the afternoon." Explanation? G/C "Blackie" Williams had the whole station picking up rocks from 1 Wing's 9-hole golf course, located between the runways. Monthly flying for May totalled 643:15 hours, with 585 sorties. Another wedding took place - F/O Paproski on June 25. The diarist notes: "W/C McLachlan, after being caught while on E&E, was released from the Sedan prison, so he could give the bride away."

Dominion Day (July 1, 1960) was a holiday, but the diarist still had a comment: "F/O Barry Gartner was promoted to F/L. Should be good for a free party." The fellows always had their priorities figured out. Exercises continued, whether "Tall Timber" or "Southern Bello". For the Air Division, the training still was the best, its pilots the most capable and fun-loving, and its aging Sabres still ready to take on all comers. This said, 441 was obliged to admit to a poor effort at Deci in August 1960 - 14%: "One of the poorest shows our squadron has ever made."

Air Div Hockey

In May 2003, Jack MacArthur (441 Squadron 1959 - 62) reminisced a bit about hockey in the Air Division:

Hockey was important throughout the Air Division. Each base had a team, so did each squadron, and Base Operations. Games even drew spectators from the local French populace. Competition usually was intense and Air Force police were always in attendance to keep an eye out for over-zealous players or fans.

In one game where 441 was battling the team from HQ in Metz, our boys were having a tough time with a physically bigger team. The refs could not seem to find their whistles when Metz was flagrantly punishing us, but were quick to call anything against the Checkerboards.

Suddenly, a hulking Metz player pounced on one of our guys. Carried away by emotion, and emboldened by my thermos of hot rum, I charged down from the stands to help. Just as I was going over the boards, an Air Force policeman grabbed my raincoat, but I kept going.

By this time the fracas had turned and our player was on top. Seeing that the ref was about to intervene, I pinned his arms behind his back. Suddenly things were quiet again, and I released the ref who, by now, was pretty steamed up. Red-faced, he turned to heave the offending player from the game, but couldn't do much when he found that he was facing a fan. The whole thing ended peacefully.

The 1961 441 "Air Div" team (light shirts) fending off the opposition. Then, the standard team photo . (441 Sqn)

"Fini"

In October 1962, 441 Squadron attained the highest ever Air Division gunnery score at Deci - 37.7%. On a sad note the wing diary continued to mention various funerals, usually of airmen killed on the roads and buried at the nearby cemetery at Choloy. One of 441's last references in Sabre days to R&R is that of March 29, 1963. That day F/L Gilkinson and F/Os Diss, Gillis and Pirie headed for a weekend in London via RAF Manston. They were reported home on April Fools Day, "looking just a little haggard, though they aren't saying very much."

While the RCAF was loath to admit that the Sabre 6 was obsolete, a 441 diary entry for April 10, 1963 is revealing: "One section of four was bounced by a section of Belgian Meteors; its nice to see that someone is even more obsolete than the good old Mark VI." Of the same sortie, the diary noted: "441 aircraft heard an American calling Laon on guard frequency just before he went in like a dart in the centre of Vouzier airfield. No word from the pilot but, from the looks of the hole in the ground, there isn't much hope." One might also see how the old Sabres were holding up (not very well) from the unit diary of July 1963: "Squadron exchange to 724 Squadron, Royal Danish Air Force, Skrystrup. Many good parties, but flying limitations made the exchange next to useless as far as flying went. Some low level sorties flown in Denmark. Seven aircraft broke seven elevator hinges in one mission. Not one aircraft was over-stressed!"

Conversion of RCAF squadrons to CF-104s left the Silver Foxes increasingly isolated, logistically. On March 19, 1963 F/L Gartner of 441 blew a tire on landing at 3 Wing. There were now no Sabre repair facilities at Zweibrucken, and he had to stay the night. Meanwhile, minor failures, notably of

The Golden Hawks selected Sabre 6 No.641 from 441's inventory. In later years it was displayed in a Trenton, Ontario park, where it was photographed in August 1970. Today, 23641 belongs to the RCAF Memorial Museum in Trenton. Several Golden Hawks were 441 alumni. The team's 1960 edition included: (front) F/Ls J.T. Price - 4 Wing, Ralph H. Annis - 441, and D.V. "Dave" Tinson - 441, and (behind) F/O W.C. Stewart - 434, F/Ls E.J. "Ed" Rozdeba - 439 and J.D. McCombe - 434, and S/L J.F. "Fern" Villeneuve - 441. (Larry Milberry, CF PL64728)

Another view of the famous 441 hangar at Marville. (Leo Lalonde)

One of the last 441 "family" photos was this one taken in 1962. Standing are Lorne H. Coste, Arnold G. Matthews, M.W. "Mike" Stedman, Gary H. Paulson, A.H. "Hal" Taylor, D.W. "Dave" Dunkerley (Armament Officer), Michael J. Diss, Barry L. Gartner, Jack Reilly, J.W. "Bill" Hind, James A. Anderson and J.E.R. Robichaud. Seated are Jack MacArthur, D.A. "Dave" Cummings, K.L. "Ken" White, D.W. "Doug" Howlett, M.A. "Mike" Little, Don Gilkinson, Carl Bertrand, W/C D.A.B. Smiley, DFC (CO), L.C. "Les" Price, K.R. "Ken" Stacey, P.R. "Pete" Cumberbirch, Murray Dunn, J.A. "Jack" Davidson, Rogers E. Smith and P.C. "Gus" Gillis. After 5-year RCAF "short service commissions", many from this group joined the airlines. Jack Davidson, Gus Gillis, Doug Howlett and Arnold Matthews went to TCA/Air Canada. By the time he retired, Howlett's log showed 27,850 flying hours. Lorne Coste briefly was with TWA. He next was heard of flying cargo for a Detroit company, then faded from the scene. Jack MacArthur went from 441 to instruct on Harvards, then crop dusted in Saskatchewan, before joining American Airlines. Ken White flew for United Airlines. Bill Hind moved to the T-33 instrument flight at Cold Lake, flew Hercules at 435 Squadron, then King Airs for Syncrude in Edmonton. Jack Reilly left the RCAF to become a dentist. Others stayed in the air force. Dave Cummings worked in telecom before instructing on Tutors, then in the USAF on T-37s and T-38s. Later, he flew Kiowas and Twin Hueys with 427 Squadron, and finished his career in NDHQ. Don Gilkinson flew CF-104s with 421 Squadron, then served in NDHQ. Rogers Smith and Barry Gartner became test pilots. Smith spent years with NASA at Edwards AFB, and in 2003 was in flight test on the Eurofighter project in Germany. While on his ETPS course in the UK, Gartner had to eject one day from a Scimitar fighter. He splashed down off a beach crowded with bathing beauties, so was quite the hero as he waded ashore. In their long air force careers, Carl Bertrand and Les Price rose to Brigadier General rank. There also were some casualties from this 441 group. Mike Diss left Sabres to instruct on Chipmunks. On July 27, 1965 he and his student, OC J.K.W. Lomax, died in a crash near Centralia. Roby Robichaud perished in a CF-101 accident. While at RCAF Staff School in Toronto, Gary Paulson lost his life in a traffic accident. Mike Little ended badly, murdered while in South America. (via Jack MacArthur)

generators, were reported more frequently. For April 16, however, came a cheery note: "Rumour has it that a Luftwaffe F-104F had its tail waxed by the Checkerboards." On April 26 two 441 Sabres visited Cambrai to battle the French: "Intercepts between Super Mystères and the Mk.VIs are always a challenge for both sections, as the aircraft perform very differently. A pleasant lunch at Cambrai makes the trip all the more enjoyable." On May 14 the Golden Hawks again came looking for some nice Sabre 6s. The diarist approved: "It is nice to see some F-86s getting a new lease on life."

Come June 1963 and 441 Squadron's diary again fades, with one dull paragraph being the best that its scribe could muster. Mercifully, 441 served its last Zulu Alert in July and was finally stood down in September. The Starfighter generation which followed might differ, but Ron Hayman's summary of the RCAF in its Sabre days is shared by many: "Never since then have we reached that pinnacle of elitism." For September a comment mentions how Sabres were "being jugged to go to Prestwick." There they would be cut up for scrap - sold, according to rumour, at less than $100 per jet. Staff was being dispersed, some of the pilot postings being S/L Price to RAF Staff College, F/L Hind to Cold Lake, F/L McAffer to 439 Squadron at Marville, F/O Little to Bagotville, F/O Pirie to instruct at Centralia, F/L Gartner to CEPE in Ottawa and F/O Diss to instruct at Portage la Prairie. A final note (August 10): "F/O [Jack] Davidson bailed out of Sabre 23593 with slight injuries." He had seized controls at 30,000 feet, held on to 10,000, then got out. On September 17, 441 delivered its Sabres to Prestwick. The final Checkerboard entry for the day was simple - "Hours 216:50 for month. Fini."

At Marville in 1960 some decent 441 fellows adopted these wee foxes, which the locals had wanted to kill. LAC MacPherson is shown with his new friends. (Leo Lalonde)

An RCAF scene at Marville showing the local shepherd who kept his flock busy trimming the grass between the runways. Then, the Sabre 5 on display in 441 colours at Royal Military College in Kingston Ontario. (CF PCN1972, Larry Milberry)

It's All Over When ...

Musing one day in 2003, Bill Lynn of 441 reminisced about those great days of his youth from start to finish:

> When I arrived on 441 Squadron in January 1959, the Sabre was still "cock of the walk" in Europe. I enjoyed hearing the war stories about waxing opponents' posteriors from 50,000 feet. Somehow the steeds I flew, however, did not seem inclined to seek that rarefied level. By the time I left 441 in January 1963, that famous cockiness was on the wane.
>
> My first exposure to the "new world order" came one day over Bitberg, home to some F-102 Delta Darts. Normally, those hot USAF machines shunned us, but the day did come ... and it was rather a shock to this cocky young Sabre jock. There was what looked to me like some giant UFO turning inside me with a lethal lead - I was already a goner. "Oh mygawd," I thought, as I headed for home. What tremendous performers were the delta F-102 and its successor, the F-106.
>
> In late 1962, when our Sabres were already flying off to Sword purgatory at Prestwick, I was maintenance test pilot at Marville. One day, after flying a standard sortie, I decided to see if the clean Sabre 6 really could reach 50,000 feet. As we struggled our way up the last thousand feet at full throttle, fuel approaching minimum, a French Mirage pulled alongside. The pilot waggled his wings, kicked in the afterburner, and did a barrel roll over us. Heading for home, I felt a lump in my throat as the now familiar image of a Sabre pilot putting a bullet into his good and faithful steed floated through my mind.

Andy and Alison MacKenzie look over memorabilia in the Leif Erickson Room while visiting 441 in 1999. The occasion was the change of command that saw LCol Billie Flynn's hand over to LCol Steve Whitley. (Larry Milberry)

When the futuristic Lockheed F-104 Starfighter first flew in February 1954, nobody could predict that it would become one of aviation's legendary jet fighters. Here (opposite) is the first Canadian-built RCAF Starfighter. Aircraft 12701 spent its days in test and development with CEPE. It's seen on rollout day at Canadair in Cartierville, Quebec in March 1961; in Palmdale, California, where Lockheed test pilot Glen "Snake" Reeves flew it initially on May 26 ('701 had reached Palmdale in the back of a C-130); and, above, at Cold Lake during trials with the Vinton camera pod. The first CF-104 flights in Canada took place at Cartierville on August 14, 1961, when "Snake" Reeves flew '704, and Bill Kidd of Canadair flew '703. (Canadair 25308, 29092, CF PL140754)

CHAPTER 13

The Starfighter Years

A New Role in NATO

When it phased out the Sabre and CF-100 in 1962 - 63, No.1 Air Division relinquished its historic interceptor role. This change followed a December 1957 NATO decision to equip with tactical nuclear weapons. Prime Minister John Diefenbaker signed the NATO agreement for Canada, opening the door for a new RCAF mission - nuclear strike. In the same period, Diefenbaker's Conservative government agreed to new NORAD commitments, and orders were placed for equipment worth $685 million. These weapons systems (Starfighters for NATO, Voodoos and Bomarcs for NORAD, and Honest John rockets for the Army) made sense only if armed with nuclear warheads.

Addressing a joint sitting of the Canadian Senate and House of Commons on May 17, 1961, John F. Kennedy had commented: "Geography has made us neighbours. History has made us friends. Economics has made us partners. And necessity has made us allies." Unfortunately, as time soon would tell, the reality of this simple, practical view did not sink in with Prime Minister Diefenbaker. Initially having accepted a nuclear policy, he now changed his mind, refusing the warheads essential to Canada's new equipment. This waffling became embarrassing when the first RCAF Bomarc base opened in February 1962 with missiles that had no warheads. Then, during the Cuban Missile Crisis of October 1962, RCAF Voodoos were on high alert (level "DEFCON 3"), but their conventional weapons would have been next to useless had WWIII erupted.

When Diefenbaker suggested that there never had been a Canadian nuclear commitment, American officials contradicted him. Of this Desmond Morton wrote in *A Military History of Canada*, "It was tactless, insensitive, and absolutely true." On the same topic, Peter C. Newman wrote in Renegade in Power: The Diefenbaker Years: "All this military hardware had been acquired and then allowed to become useless for one reason - John Diefenbaker could not make up his mind to arm the weapons." Little wonder that there was no love lost between "Dief" and John Kennedy (or his successor, Lyndon Johnson).

By early 1963 Diefenbaker's indecision about nuclear warheads, and other crucial matters caused a Cabinet rift. Influential Conservatives talked of ousting their boss. In the House of Commons on January 25, Diefenbaker made an unintelligible statement alluding indirectly to nuclear policy, while suggesting that God would protect Canada. This disheartened the Hon. Douglas Harkness - in February he resigned as Minister of National Defence. Within days the Diefenbaker government fell in a vote of non-confidence.

As he campaigned for re-election in 1963, Diefenbaker accused Washington of trying to turn Canada into "a nuclear dump". Meanwhile, he toured the country, wooing rural voters, while running down big business and alienating urban voters. Not surprisingly, the Liberals under Lester B. Pearson won the election. They accepted nuclear warheads, so the RCAF now had the teeth to perform its duties. (Pearson, a Nobel Peace Prize recipient, had his own reservations about nuclear weapons. He hoped to re-negotiate the RCAF's role, but this would not happen for some years.)

Enter the Starfighter

While the politicians were squabbling over nuclear policy, the RCAF was evaluating fighters that might suit its new role in NATO. The choice came down to the Grumman F-11F-1F Super Tiger and the Lockheed F-104 Starfighter. Of these almost equally capable aircraft, the F-104 came out on top. In 1961 Canada ordered 200 CF-104 Starfighters to be built under licence by Canadair in Cartierville, near Montreal.

First flown in 1954, the F-104 holds a well-deserved place as one of history's great fighter aircraft. While books, articles and Web sites cover it well, for anyone wishing the Canadian story, the key printed sources are David Bashow's *Starfighter: A Loving Retrospective of the CF-104 Era in Canadian Fighter Aviation 1961 - 1986*, and Robert McIntyre's *Canadian Profile - CF-104 Starfighter*. Both are out-of-print, but copies may be found in libraries, or on Internet used book sites. For the full CF-104 story, readers should go exploring - this book is but the tip of the iceberg, even as far as 441 is concerned.

The first CF-104 was delivered on March 28, 1961, and 427 "Lion" Squadron, the first operational unit, was activated sans warheads at 3 Wing, Zweibrucken on December 17, 1962. Seven more squadrons formed as quickly as pilots were trained and aircraft were delivered. Even at this point, however, politicians and senior RCAF officers were being less than frank in describing the destructive power of Canada's new strike/attack squadrons. In November 1963 A/V/M D.A.R. Bradshaw, 1 Air Division AOC, described the CF-104 as "a small airplane which obviously cannot carry a tremendous size bomb". He failed to mention, as John Clearwater points out in *Canadian Nuclear Weapons: The Untold Story of Canada's Cold War Arsenal*, that one such bomb packed the power of a WWII 1000-bomber raid! Indeed, the smallest nuclear bomb slated for the CF-104 would have been almost as devastating as those that levelled Hiroshima and Nagasaki.

In November 1962 CF-104 12797 toured France and West Germany to let the Air Division see its amazing new fighter. For PR purposes a photo shoot was arranged with a Sabre, CF-100 and T-33. The last of 200 CF-104s for the RCAF was handed over by Canadair on September 11, 1963. Canadair also built 140 F-104Gs, the last being delivered in September 1966. These 140, paid for by "Uncle Sam", went to NATO and other friendly countries. (CF PL147902)

Qualifying to Fly

On November 14, 1963 A/V/M Bradshaw went before a Parliamentary Committee to describe the demands of the Air Division's new role:

Each pilot must attain, and then maintain, a combat ready status to meet the high standards laid down by 4 ATAF and the RCAF. He must also satisfy the stringent nuclear and safety criteria dictated by the USAF. Finally, he must be able to fly his aircraft at very low level, over devious routes, day or night, and in all weather up to distances of 200 to 600 miles, and then deliver his weapon with pinpoint accuracy. He must then return safely to his base.

In contrast to our Sabre pilots, who flew in formation at great height with one or more other aircraft, assisted by ground radar for interception and navigation purposes, the strike pilot must carry out his mission alone, usually at low level and without any outside help. Therefore it becomes dramatically clear why the strike pilot must be so highly trained and have such a high degree of initiative and determination if he is to be successful in his task.

At first the RCAF was loath to trust Starfighters to hot young pilots, so the initial pilot cadre was of experienced men. This policy, however, could not go on indefinitely. Speaking the same day before the same committee as Bradshaw, G/C Donald C. Laubman described the typical CF-104 pilot as being 33 years of age, married with 2.5 children, and with 3600 flying hours - 2200 on jets and 225 on the CF-104. Adding to the theme, on April 2, 1962 A/V/M W.R. MacBrien, AOC Air Defence Command, informed those pilots selected for Starfighters and Voodoos:

The RCAF is currently engaged in re-equipping Air Defence Command and the Air Division with the most modern weapons systems available. Some 66 CF-101Bs and 200 CF-104s are being acquired for this purpose.

The complexity, performance and cost of these weapons systems has materially increased compared to those which they replace... it has been necessary to select extremely competent pilots for the operation of the new aircraft. Those selected can be considered an elite group, the individual members of which have been carefully screened to ensure their complete suitability...

It has been forecast statistically that a significant number of the new aircraft will be wasted during 1962 as a result of accidents. Experience shows that transition to new high-performance aircraft normally involves an increase in hazards to flight safety and that extraordinary care must be taken in this respect if losses are to be minimized.

We are now faced with the dual objectives of achieving the transition as quickly as possible and avoiding unnecessary wastage of our resources in the process. You have been selected to take part in this programme as the result of a highly selective personnel policy designed to meet these objectives; the selection being based on a creditable personal record of outstanding ability. Your new assignment will prove to be interesting, but it will also be demanding of your best efforts and will require a high degree of self-discipline and responsibility.

It is my belief that if everyone concerned with the operation of Century Series aircraft by the RCAF takes a professional attitude toward his responsibilities, and is conscious of the need for safe flying practices, the forecasts of the statisticians can be proven wrong. This goal can only be attained if every individual contributes conscientiously toward it and I, therefore, will expect your personal support in our collective effort to derive the maximum in combat capability from the resources available for our use.

The average age of a CF-104 pilot declined after 1965, as graduates emerged from OTU. Nevertheless, the complexity of training had subtle effects on rank patterns in overseas squadrons. In the Sabre era a squadron was commanded by a squadron leader and seldom had more than five flight lieutenants. Most pilots were flying officers on Short Service Commissions (5-year terms). CF-104 squadrons were led by wing commanders, while squadron leaders and flight lieutenants proliferated. As of December 1978, for example, 441 Squadron had a lieutenant-colonel (LCol Remi Saulnier), 5 majors, 10 captains and only 3 lieutenants.

"Widow Maker"

CF-104 pilots always were aware of the risks of their chosen profession. Weather could close in unexpectedly, birds could be ingested with frightening results, and the thought of bailing out at 500+ knots was unnerving. Of some 750 Canadians who would fly the CF-104, 37 would die in accidents (seven while ejecting), while 84 would eject successfully. To the press and public, the CF-104 became a "widow maker". This impression was reinforced by the Luftwaffe's high F-104 accident rate - 269 aircrew lost over the years. One CF-104 pilot pointed out that fatalities often occurred on solo missions. In such cases, pilots sometimes "pushed the envelope", especially in weather. Had they been responsible for a wingman, they would have been more attentive.

Nonetheless, Canadian pilots quickly came to love their work and shunned the widow maker reputation invented by the media. Their view was the opposite - what they loved about the CF-104 was its intoxicating power and performance. Even Minister of National Defence Edgar Benson agreed. Following a CF-104 ride in March 1974, he asked, "What the hell was I doing in the army, when this is so much fun?"

CF-104 Basic Specifications

Wing span (minus tip tanks)	21' 11 1/4"
Wing area	196.1 sq. ft.
Length	54' 8 7/8"
Height	13'5"
Wing root chord	12' 11 7/8"
Wing tip chord	4' 10 3/4"
Wing dihedral	10°
Horizontal stabilizer span	11' 10 1/8"
Basic weight	13,940 lb
Max permissible landing weight	17,200 lb
Fuel (internal)	841 Imp. gal.
Fuel (tip tanks)	142 Imp. gal.
Fuel (pylon tanks)	162 Imp. gal.

Recce Starfighters over France circa 1965. The Starfighter typified the problem of Cold War strategy. Its very presence in NATO meant that the RCAF in Europe had an excellent chance of being wiped out in any Soviet nuclear "first strike", should things turn nasty. Conversely, these aircraft could be part of a NATO first strike. No.1 Air Division, thereby, was principally a deterrent force. NATO's air element later became a conventional force in the hope that a European war might remain non-nuclear - a policy dubbed Flexible Response. But the strategic assumptions associated with the role were questionable, and delivering a few 750-pound conventional bombs with exotic aircraft like the CF-104 seemed incongruous to some critics. (Larry O'Brien Col.)

CF-104 Squadron Evolution

Squadron	De-activated F-86	Activated CF-104	Role	Disbanded
6 OTU/417	N/A	10-61	OTU	1-7-83
427	15-12-62	17-12-62	S/A	1-7-70
434	15-1-63	8-4-63	S/A	1-3-67
444	1-3-63	27-5-63	S/A	1-4-67
422	15-4-63	15-7-63	S/A	1-7-70
430	31-5-63	30-9-63	S/A	1-5-70
421	31-7-63	2-12-63	S/A	31-10-85
441	1-9-63	20-1-64	S/R	1-3-86
439	1-11-63	2-3-64	S/R	30-11-84
CEPE/AETE	N/A	1959*	Test & Development	21-10-83†

*First CEPE pilots fly the F-104 in the USA.
†Last CEPE project flight, Capt Gerry Nicks flying 104847 at Baden re. LN33 nav system software upgrade.

Prime Minister Lester B. Pearson, who chose to break the nuclear conundrum created by John Diefenbaker, visits Marville on January 17, 1964. He and his party are looking over a CF-104 recce pod, the others being W/C Bob Edwards (CO 441 Sqn), G/C A.F. Avant, DSO, DFC (Commander 1 Wing), A/V/M D.A.R. Bradshaw, DFC (AOC 1 Air Division), and F/L Don Francis (1 Wing photo officer). (CF PL149879)

Recce Role

Although nuclear weapons were central to No.1 Air Division, they were secondary to 441 and 439 squadrons which would specialize in photo reconnaissance. While most NATO "photo recce" aircraft (Canberra, RF-84F or RF-101, etc.) had internal cameras, the RCAF opted for the Vinton Vicom reconnaissance pod hung beneath the fuselage. Designed to RCAF specifications by Computing Devices of Canada, the pod housed four 70-mm cameras giving forward, side-oblique, and vertical coverage. Cameras were wired to data recorders which, in turn, were linked with the inertial navigation system. Each could expose as many as eight frames per second.

The RCAF mission was to photograph targets in case of war in Europe, then do follow-up runs to assess strike damage. This would have been hairy business. Firstly, NATO bases like Lahr would have to endure the initial onslaught of Soviet nuclear weapons. Then, strike and recce CF-104s would have to get to and from their targets in the face of deadly enemy (and friendly) ground and air threats. Would there even be a home to which to return? Somehow, most people in NATO didn't think that it ever would come to this, so 1 CAG continued routinely with its duties.

Training on the CF-104

Every trainee's experience on the CF-104 was special in its own way, that of 441 Squadron CO, W/C James F. Dunlop, DFC, being typical. A wartime Lancaster pilot (166 Squadron), he rejoined the RCAF after the war, becoming one of its so-called "retreads". Dunlop hadn't flown a fighter until the Sabre OTU at Chatham in October 1956. Graduating in the following March, he was posted to 434 Squadron, serving there to May 1959. Next, he had staff positions at Air Division HQ in Metz and AFHQ in Ottawa, then commanded the radar station at Armstrong, Ontario.

Dunlop began CF-104 lead-in training at the Sabre Transition Unit on August 2, 1964. At "STU" students flew

W/C J.F. "Jim" Dunlop, DFC, would command 441 Squadron in 1965 - 68. (CF PL141900)

140

CF-104s on the flightline at Cold Lake in the early years of 6 (ST/R) OTU. This is where instructors first built their hours on type, and began training new pilots. Students initially were experienced fighter pilots. Eventually, however, came the "pipeliners" - young fellows who recently had graduated from flying training. (Ken Orr)

Sabres on low-level navigation and bombing exercises, then advanced to 6 (ST/R) OTU at Cold Lake. Dunlop started there on November 27. In this era OTU training was in strike/attack only, pilots destined for recce duties being trained later "on the job" at 1 Wing. Thus, Dunlop's experiences at Cold Lake reflected the syllabus bias. His flying times on course (November 1964 to May 1965) were:

Aircraft	Day (hours)	Night	Total
CF-104D Dual	31:20	4:55	36:15
CF-104	50:55	9:30	60:25
Simulator	-	-	21:40
T-33	26:30	6:45	33:15
Instrument T-33	16:55	-	16:55
Navigation "DC-104"	7:20	-	7:20*

* The "DC-104" was a nickname for needle-nosed Dakotas "Pinocchio", "Woody Woodpecker" and "Dolly's Folly". Officially these were NASARR, or North American Search and Ranging Radar, Dakotas.

In an OTU academic syllabus that totalled 3000 points, Dunlop achieved:

Topic	Available Marks	Dunlop's %
Aircraft Handling	200	93.4
Radar	100	94.8
Nav Systems	100	92.9
TAC Evaluation, Written	900	89.5
TAC Evaluation, Oral	1700	90.1

Before a Tactical Evaluation Board, Dunlop presented a detailed tactical evaluation ("TacEval") briefing. He had been given a scenario for which he was required to analyze and select the route and tactics. In this he demonstrated above-average knowledge of navigation and radar systems, making full use of these in planning his mission. All aspects of intelligence, escape and evasion, weapons delivery and return to base were briefed. The Board did not agree with all Dunlop's proposed tactics, but felt that he had made sound arguments to justify his decisions.

On 80 day/night OTU sorties Dunlop had no difficulty adapting to the CF-104. His Sabre experience was evident in formation flying and aerobatics, although he temporarily had difficulty establishing his glide path on GCA approaches. Under the heading "Visual Weapons Training" and "Radar Training" the assessment noted:

In the visual weapons phase W/C Dunlop readily acquired a sound knowledge of the delivery techniques and made consistently good progress... During the visual CPM [combat profile mission] training, some initial problems were apparent during the portion of the run-in between IP [initial point] and TRP [timer reference point, or "tickle point"]. At the same time W/C Dunlop was subjected to more than the usual number of LN3 [navigation system] faults, aircraft malfunctions and No Spot Bombs [likely when Mk.106 practice bombs were duds, i.e. giving no smoke on impact]. Despite these setbacks he steadily improved and, in both Long Range Missions, achieved excellent results. His professional approach to the pre-flight planning phase of the CPM was a contributing factor to his success in these missions... W/C Dunlop made satisfactory progress during the radar bombing phase and qualified in all deliveries. He displayed a good working knowledge of the radar and navigation systems during Radar CPMs, and his en route navigation techniques were quite well organized. Basic instrument flying was good, and the weapon delivery phase satisfactory, with a possible tendency toward a late pickle.

In July 1965 Dunlop returned to the Air Division as CO of 427 Squadron, then commanded 441 from September 16, 1965, until posted to 1 Wing HQ in November 1968. To January 7, 1969 he recorded his postwar flying types and times: Expeditor - 351 hours, Sabre - 578, T-33 - 703, and CF-104 - 428 (81 hours in the previous year).

Recce in the Syllabus

By 1968 the 6 OTU syllabus finally included reconnaissance. As with strike, recce involved precise navigation on fast, low-level missions. The experience of Maj Paul Manson shows how training had evolved. A former 440 Squadron CF-100 pilot, he attended STU from September to November 1966, logging some 51 hours on Sabres, 31 on T-33s. He began at CF-104 OTU with some T-33 "famil" and "nav" exercises. On January 12, 1967 he was introduced to the CF-104 Operational Fighter Tactical Trainer, a basic simulator. "OFTT" involved on February 28. He would log seven of these before flying a solo radar nav trip (March 19). Periodically, he would have a 2-hour OFTT session.

Recce students spent hours in ground school, mastering the "Essential Elements of Identification" - studying bridges, microwave towers, vehicles, guns, buildings, etc., so that one could glance at something flashing by, but remember it in detail. Once competent, a pilot could note as he blasted along: "A microwave tower, approximately 200 feet high, five dishes on top, six vehicles at the base".

In this period the Cold Lake range had few mock targets, so many sorties were flown to targets as innocent as a pipeline pumping station, or a hockey arena. Students received a brief description of a target, along with its "lat-long". They planned their missions, drawing routes onto maps, dividing them with tick marks into 1-minute intervals. Each leg was flown with a stop watch from one turning point to the next. There were many of these, for numerous points were red-circled. In war they might have been enemy SAM batteries, but in Canada they more likely were such things as turkey and mink farms. As such, there was danger of provoking a lawsuit from an irate farmer!

With his final OTU flight of May 21, 1967 Maj Manson was posted to 441 (having begun his course as a squadron leader, he emerged as a major - CF unification had occurred on February 1). Upon leaving Cold Lake for Marville, Manson's log showed (in hours):

Maj Paul Manson with 441 Squadron at Marville in 1968. (CF LR68-356-1)

P/O Paul Manson receives his Wings from A/V/M Bryans (AOC Training Command) at RCAF Station MacDonald, Manitoba on August 13, 1957. (CF PL107208)

an hour that day, two 2-hour sessions on the 23rd. Manson flew the CF-104 on January 26, going up for an hour with Maj A.R.H. "Tony" Bosman.

From the beginning, OTU instructors emphasized low-level flying, most missions being at 500 feet. Students soon concluded that, in a European war, anti-aircraft defences would be so daunting that they would be flying even lower. Manson soloed on his fifth mission (January 30). Next day he exceeded Mach 2. Formation flying followed and, on February 5, he was solo on a 4-plane mission. His first radar nav sortie (in a dual) was

Month	CF-104D	CF-104	T-33	OFTT
January	14.3	4.5	3.1	5.0
February	11.3	6.8	9.7	6.0
March	8.1	14.8	22.0	4.0
April	8.7	20.9	18.3	2.0
May	3.2	9.5	3.8	4.0

CHAPTER 14
Supersonic at 1 Wing

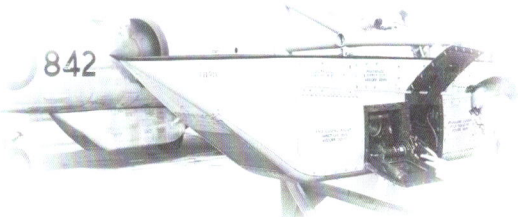

An early Marville scene with Starfighters 12755, '845, '898 and '747. A photo interpreter ("PI") would note the signs of construction, and the earlier stage of development at Marville compared to the aerial view from page 154. (Vic Johnson Col.)

W/C Bob Edwards, who joined the RCAF in 1947, served to 1976. Having retired as BGen Edwards, he settled in Calgary, working there with Ken Lett in corporate aviation. (441 Sqn)

Early Days

Re-activated on January 20, 1964, the Silver Foxes were led initially by W/C Robert M. Edwards, AFC, CD. The first 441 commander without wartime experience, he had joined the RCAF in 1947. His Air Force Cross dated to the Korean War when he had flown North Stars. He later flew CF-100s with 440 Squadron at Zweibrucken. While there still was a chance there, he arranged through Ken Lewis and John Ursulak at "Zwei" to check-out on the Sabre 6. In this way he finally got to fly supersonic. In exchange for this favour he was expected to get a CF-100 flight for one of 4 Wing's Sabre pilots. Edwards took a quick rear cockpit check from his navigator,

"Recce birds" in echelon right formation near Marville. Of these aircraft, Maj R.W. Porter of 441 ejected from '859 on August 27, 1980; F/O J.W. Holmes of 441 lost his life in '729 on January 18, 1968; S/L M.R. MacGregor of 430 Squadron ejected from '748 at Lahr on May 21, 1967; while '737 went to the Turks in 1986. (John Greatrix Col.)

then gave the front cockpit to his friend. Unfortunately, things went badly. The Sabre pilot lost control while taxying, and the CF-100 ended in a ditch. Station commander G/C Berg investigated the circumstances, but Edwards got off the hook. As he wrote in August 2003:

> G/C Berg was not at all pleased to find out that I had been in the back seat but, even before the smoke had cleared, I had been promoted to Wing Commander and made OC designate of 441 Squadron (the irreverent wisdom in the RCAF was that the best way to get promoted was to write off an aircraft). I reported to Chatham on April 8, 1962 for the Sabre Transition Unit. My fellow course mates were destined for 441, making for a good deal of camaraderie, and the weather was as glorious as it gets in the spring in New Brunswick. Yes, those were good days to be in the RCAF. Besides the joy of flying the Sabre, one perk that we enjoyed was the chance to use the T-33 on weekends to visit other parts of our great country. By the end of May at the STU I had flown 47:20 hours on the Sabre 5, and 33:20 on the T-33.
>
> After a leisurely drive across most of Canada, I next reported to Cold Lake and 6 Strike/Reconnaissance OTU on June 16, 1963. There were 17 of us on course, mostly 441 people. During our first week a senior pilot was killed in a CF-104 crash. A few days later a Dakota went into Pierce Lake, killing all on board. This was disconcerting, but it didn't dampen our enthusiasm for long.
>
> I flew my Mach 2 trip on 10 July. Canadair soon hosted a party in the mess where we all received our silver Mach 2 pins. One highlight for me on course was dropping a 2000-lb "shape" pretty well on time and on target. At our graduation, the OC, W/C Ken Lett, presented me with a CF-104 model inscribed "For achieving the highest standard on Course 7, 6 ST/R OTU". My time at OTU totalled 84 hours on the CF-104, 77 on the T-33.
>
> Most of us now took a Yukon from Trenton to Marville. We arrived on December 13 to be welcomed by G/C A.F. Avant (1 Wing Commander), W/C H.E. "Joe" Bodien (COpsO), S/L E.L. Arnold (former 441 OC) and others. Meanwhile, few of us could spell reconnaissance without a dictionary and, since it would be weeks before a CF-104 even reached Marville, we did our flying at 4 Wing. We also visited Air Division HQ and several American, French and German recce units, to learn as much as possible about the recce business. No.439, our sister squadron at 1 Wing, led by S/L Jack Frazer, arrived by the end of February 1964, but we still only had one CF-104 at Marville. This was quite a problem as we struggled to get operational.
>
> Our friends at AFHQ suggested that a 441 contingent visit Shaw AFB in South Carolina for the USAF photo recce course. I accompanied F/Ls Breffitt, Coulter, Gardiner and Willet on the 2-week trip in mid-April. The course covered photo-recce equipment, its operation, and the tactics needed to get the best results. Back in Marville we were busy setting up an operations complex that included mission planning and film processing facilities, and getting to know our photo recce pod. This remarkable piece of equipment hung on the centre-line bomb rack and housed four 70-mm Vinton cameras, two shooting obliquely to each side, one vertically and one forward. Each had an electrically-activated door, which opened when the pilot selected that particular camera. The forward-facing camera was well-protected by glass that could withstand a bird strike at 500 knots.
>
> A/V/M Bradshaw visited 1 Wing early in 1964. Along with the usual pep talk, he declared that we had to be "combat ready" by the end of the year. That was a tall order, but the wing eagerly accepted the challenge. G/C Mussells, 1 Wing Senior Staff Officer, was especially supportive of our efforts. As more equipment began arriving, we flew our first photo recce missions. These were mainly over France, but sometimes further afield. For nearer targets the mission profile would be "lo-lo-lo", while "hi-lo-hi" was for more distant targets. Such exercises often were dubbed "Photo Site", but we were

When 441 moved to Lahr, squadron ops were in an old dog kennel. Here, F/Os Bobby Joe Hart (right) and Sky King work on the chimney. They were checker-boarding it lest anyone not be certain whose kennel it was! (Sky King Col.)

gearing up for eventual participation in "Royal Flush", an exercise involving all NATO photo recce units (even France, which had withdrawn from NATO in 1963). Our pilots also practiced bombing on the range in Sardinia to keep up our offensive skills should they be needed.

Our first real challenge was an Air Division TacEval late in December 1964. We passed with flying colours, so were "combat ready". Now we were required to hold a 15-minute Quick Reaction Alert 24 hours a day. When a delegation from SHAPE visited 1 Wing, however, they learned that we had no night photo recce capability. We explained that it seemed pointless to hold QRA after dark. A/C/M Huddleston of the RAF agreed, and night QRAs ended.

Another event was something that affected morale. On February 15, 1965 the new Canadian flag was introduced. It soon replaced the Red Ensign on the tails of our aircraft. Gradually, we accepted this, but the taking down of the RCAF pennant, so revered since the air force was established in 1924, was not good news in this period. When W/C Bodien returned to Canada in October 1965, I took over as COpsO. W/C Dunlop now smoothly took over at 441. In my new job I remained closely involved with 441 and 439, and was at the forefront when we moved the wing to Lahr in 1967. Subsequently, I attended RAF College of Air Warfare in 1968, was promoted to Colonel and appointed Base Commander of Uplands. This ended a pleasant 7-year tour in 1 Air Division.

NATO reconnaissance missions placed a premium on knowing European geography. Targets of opportunity were welcomed, be they tanks or nudist colonies. A standard exercise saw a 441 pilot checking out three targets, plus a general "line search" along a designated railway, canal, etc. Accurate

A detailed view of Marville in the mid-1960s. Top right is the main base complex with the trailer park at the far right. A flock of 439 and 441 CF-104s is parked on the north marguerite. The 1 Wing photo operation sits beside the hangar (top left). Four more CF-104s are across the runway (lower left), the home of the Wing Instrument Flight. At the Air Movements Unit (top right) are seven Dakotas, a Yukon and a Bristol Freighter. Bottom right is the base aircraft maintenance engineering section. (Bill Van Oene Col.)

Cpls Stan Coe and Vic Johnson work on a recce camera pod at Marville. The 441 diary notes: "March 1964 saw the squadron live up to its name - Reconnaissance. The first photo pod was installed on old faithful '854 and W/C Edwards took the first photos 3 March 1964. Many passes were made over the airfield ... [this] produced considerable noise and, after two weeks, it was requested that we might find other stationary targets in lieu of the 1 Wing hangars. They had served their purpose well as everyone had gotten a few photo trips and the photographs taken were of very good quality." (Vic Johnson Col.)

A recce pod ready for installation on 12854. Following an April 25, 1969 bird strike, Capt Reg White of 439 ejected from this aircraft. (441 Sqn)

navigation was critical but, from 500 feet, touring Europe was no easy task. The route often was thick with haze and without such ready landmarks as lakes, which characterized Canada. Certainly there were towns, but these looked much alike at 500 knots. Thus did one use his "smarts" in getting around. Paul Manson recalled that tree patterns were as valuable as geographic features in determining location. He recalled one favourite 441 target - a Dutch building with "LUST HOTEL" emblazoned on the roof.

Even with sophisticated cameras, a recce pilot was expected to jot down visual observations (the "Mark I Eyeball" still had a use) and, if necessary, radio his findings. Notes were recorded on a card, the little boxes on which were ticked off as necessary - a check beside "armoured vehicles", a scribbled "25", if that was the number, etc. Vic Johnson, the editor in 2003 of *Air Force Magazine* in Ottawa, was an early 1 Wing photo tech. His reminiscences appear in Starfighter. Here are a few edited bits:

At the height of the recce program 1 Wing had almost 100 photo techs. We were fully integrated as tradesmen so, besides photo duties, were expected to work on line servicing, in snags, in repair and overhaul, or wherever else we might be needed. We adapted well and enjoyed the operational lifestyle. Occasional deployments to other NATO bases made life even more interesting.

At Marville we used four large moving vans converted into photographic labs. A 3-ton truck was parked alongside each van in which our photo interpreters debriefed pilots following their recce missions. As to film, we processed miles of it over the years. Those were the days before environmental concern, so we simply incinerated any film that wasn't required.

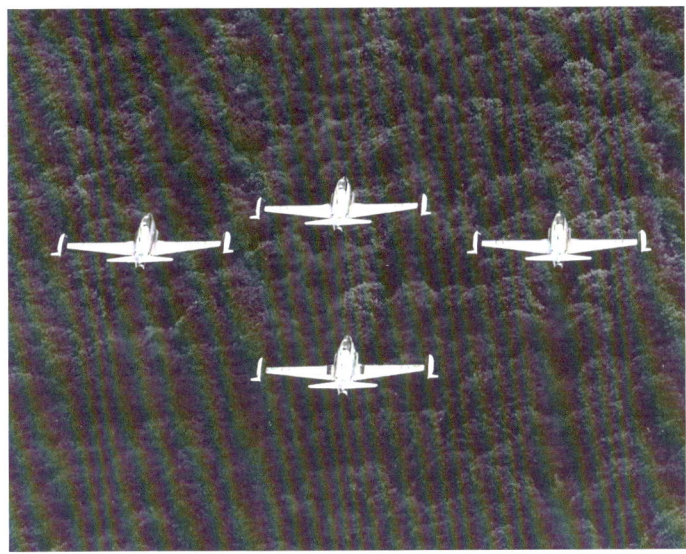

Wing Instrument Flight T-33s low-level from Marville *circa* 1965, then 133450 refuelling at Baden on March 19, 1978, by which time the "WIF" was the "GIF" - Group Instrument Flight. From Sabre to CF-18 days, Starfighter pilots kept up their instrument flying skills on the T-33. (Bill Van Oene Col., Larry Milberry)

Tactical Evaluation

On a daily basis it was essential that each 441 member be in top form, and that everyone knew that he was - trust and confidence went hand in hand. Through the TacEval system, every pilot was individually evaluated on joining his squadron and, yearly, thereafter. In the case of 441's CO, he was trained by 439 (and vice-versa). This was the equivalent of a Sabre pilot's phase training. Thus, when LCol Bruce Burgess took over 441 in early August 1969, he first logged 7.9 hours in a T-33, getting familiar with the area around Lahr. Then came 50 hours on CF-104s, completing the required CPMs and nav exercises under 439's eye. It was October 2 before he commenced flying with 441.

Nothing sharpened a squadron as much as its initial "TacEval". This meant drilling and practicing for what would be a mock 24-hour war, where one's every move was evaluated. At 441 this happened on December 15, 1964. Suddenly, Marville was invaded by umpires with notebooks and stop watches, timing and observing as groundcrew scrambled to ready aircraft, and pilots roared off on missions. By day's end the Silver Foxes had flown 21 sorties (26:15 hours) with everything going like clockwork. As of January 4, 1965, 441 was committed to a stand-by status in NATO's order of battle.

Even though it had few aircraft at first, 441 kept busy working up exercise profiles. Missions flown were either "Low-Low-Low" or "High-Low-High". The former meant flying all the way at about 540 KIAS and 500 feet (or lower). The latter, heading for more distant targets, began with a burner climb to 30,000 feet. Then the pilot descended to the deck for his mission, before zooming back to altitude to "RTB" - return to base. With a pod and tip tanks, a CF-104 climbed to about 27,000 feet outbound, but RTB'd at 40,000. Here is a CF-104 nicely "down in the weeds" and coming up on a typical photo recce target - the antenna at the pilot's 12 o'clock. (John Greatrix Col.)

These Rhine River locks would have been a prime target for Warsaw Pact strike fighters in any European conflict. (David Huddelston Col.)

These photos typify the countless thousands processed by 1 Wing Photo Section. F/O D. Huddleston of 439 photographed these bridges on December 27, 1964. To keep training as realistic as possible, recce pilots sought new targets at every chance. (David Huddelston Col.)

In early 1943 RAF photo recce Mosquitos photographed this dam - the Eder, near Kassel, Germany. On the night of May 16/17 of that year, 617 Squadron Lancasters attacked the Eder, along with the Möhne and Sorpe dams. They breached the first two, causing calamitous (if short-lived) damage. In the mid-1960s, 1 Wing recce pilots, no doubt in awe of the great deeds of 617, sometimes would visit the historic dams. (Red Morris Col.)

A 1 Wing image of the Canadian war memorial at Vimy, France. Then (opposite), 12898 over the cemetery and memorial at Verdun, another WWI battlefield where many Canadians died. Inherently, photo recce was dangerous work. On June 25, 1968 aircraft '898 was on a mission with Capt A.S. "Al" Andree of 439 Sqn at the controls. The weather was claggy as Andree radioed to his FAC (forward air control) pilot. He reported finding a hole in the cloud, through which to descend. Nothing further was heard, but the wreckage of '898 soon was spotted on a hilltop 35 miles from Frankfurt. (David Huddleston and Vic Johnson Cols.)

NATO Hawk missiles in the field during a Cold War exercise. The lack of camouflage made the Hawks easy recce pickings.
(David Huddelston Col.)

CF-104 12860 screams by a Black Forest communications site. This aircraft later was sold to Norway, only to be lost in a flying accident. (Red Morris Col.)

On this photo run the target was not quite simulated - it's an East German MiG-17 that had defected to West Germany. (Bill Van Oene Col.)

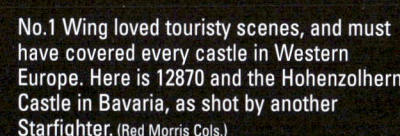

No.1 Wing loved touristy scenes, and must have covered every castle in Western Europe. Here is 12870 and the Hohenzolhern Castle in Bavaria, as shot by another Starfighter. (Red Morris Cols.)

TacEvals came "out of the blue" once or twice a year. Squadron and 1 Wing records duly noted them, but barely. An uneventful exercise was preferable to one marked by unforeseen incidents. National TacEvals were conducted by Canadian authorities, usually commencing with a mass recall of personnel to test mobilization preparedness, followed some weeks later by three days of flying with missions assigned by 4 ATAF. NATO TacEvals tested the whole formation, from Air Division HQ, down through wing and squadron levels. Everything was scrutinized, from maintenance and servicing, to combat performance and HQ communications. In 2003 Larry Crabb recalled the importance of the TacEval, known as "Snowballs", during his period as 441 CO at Baden:

> How happily we in the Starfighter world forget those monthly "Snowballs" that always seemed to happen in the middle of the night. During this era in the Cold War, 70% of our people had to be available on 3-hour recall - "24/7", all year 'round. The TacEval challenged the level of everyone's readiness, although it put a real

Royal Flush

NATO squadrons contended in Exercise Royal Flush, to see which could fly the tightest recce missions and produce the fastest intel results. Scoring was based on complex formulae assessing accuracy and detail of film, along with information reported after "eyeballing" the targets. "Royal Flush" had begun at Lahr (then a French base) in 1956. In the 1960s competitions pitted 2 ATAF (Belgium, Germany, Netherlands, UK) against 4 ATAF (Canada, Germany, USA with France as a guest member). The winning formation received the Gruenther Trophy, named for former Supreme Allied Commander Europe, USAF General Alfred M. Gruenther.

Initially, "Royal Flush" squadrons flew from home bases. In three days, each pilot had to fly three missions, each covering three targets. There were "opportunity" targets such as troops,

A 441 Starfighter at Baden on April 17, 1978. Beyond are typical HASs - protective structures that usually were advertised as being bomb- and NBCW-proof, points that never had to be proven either way during the Cold War. In the 1991 Gulf War and the Kosovo air campaign, however, many HASs were easily destroyed by direct hits. (Larry Milberry)

> strain on leave and training courses. Our "fan-out", by which participants were recalled to base from all the villages around Baden-Soellingen, was extremely effective.
>
> Our squadron's wartime location was in the bunkers and HASs at Lahr (a HAS, or hardened aircraft shelter, was designed to withstand a certain amount of battle damage, and to filter NBCW contaminants). When the hooters went off for a "Snowball", the ground crew uploaded the weapons as "fragged", and loaded each single-seat Starfighter with 600 rounds of 20-mm cannon shells. The pilots then accepted the weapons and the aircraft, the live bombs were downloaded, then we deployed to Lahr. Meanwhile, the maintenance officer and squadron warrant officer had despatched flatbeds of equipment to Lahr, to be ready for the aircraft as they landed, then "turn" them for continuous operations, just as if war had been declared. All this had to be done for local, national and NATO TacEvals. One of the most impressive things about a "Snowball" was how beautifully our ground crew always performed!

A CF-104 returns to the tarmac after a "Royal Flush" mission. Then, a photo tech dashes for the processing lab, clutching the precious film. (441 Sqn)

vehicles, missiles; and fixed targets such as buildings and bridges. Umpires deducted points according to complex rules affecting aircrew and ground personnel. A pilot, for example, had to overfly his target at 500 and 1000 feet, make one pass only, and avoid turns exceeding 90 degrees within five kilometers of the target. He also had to arrive within a specific time block. Failure to comply was penalized.

Umpires considered four phases, including teamwork among pilots, photo technicians and servicing personnel. First was the "In Flight Report" - a radio call by the pilot detailing within 90 seconds as much as he could about his targets. Next was the "Mission Report" - an intelligence report prepared within 30 minutes by the pilot and a photo interpreter using 9 x 9-inch target prints (unloading cameras and processing film had to be done speedily, prints had to be ready within five minutes). Photographic quality also was judged (photographic contrast and sharpness, no developing or printing flaws, etc.). Finally, points were awarded for target coverage, e.g. whether a target had been photographed from appropriate angles. Double points were awarded for superior coverage of "opportunity" targets.

Capt Bill Turnbull plans a "Royal Flush" mission. For the 1968 competition, he placed 4th in 4 ATAF individual honours, while 441 was judged 4 ATAF's best recce squadron. (441 Sqn)

1 Wing did poorly in its debut "Royal Flush" of 1966 but, in 1967, 439 Squadron came second, 441 third. F/L Kenneth R. Mowbray was 4th in individual standings. After "Royal Flush" missions of May 14 -16, 1968, the Silver Foxes were judged 4 ATAF's best recce squadron, with 439 second. Capt W.D. "Bill" Turnbull was top "Air Div" pilot, and he placed 4th in 4 ATAF individual honours. The Silver Fox team included Majs W.A. "Bill" Van Oene and E. W. "Ernie" Gardiner, Capts Bill Turnbull, Bruce Arnott, H.A. "Herb" Sievert, Ken Mowbray, Philip C. "Zorba" Engstad and H.A. "Bobby Joe" Hart, and Lts Ronald B.W. Tomcheck, T.W. "Ted" Lewis, Jim Jones and Lyle A. Gainsford.

In 1969, 441 and 439 repeated its one-two finish in "Royal Flush XIV". Of 108 pilots participating, Capt Scott Clements of 439 ranked first, and the 441 "PI" team was "Best in Class". A "Royal Flush" tradition held that the last roll of film delivered by any squadron had to be run from the aircraft by the unit CO. At Royal Flush XIV this was done for 441 by LCol Paul Manson, after his last of three sorties on May 20-21 (his log for May 20 shows a trip of 1.1 hours in CF-104 12865 and, for May 21, two in 12859 of 1.2 and 1.4 hours). The media made sure to cover such high profile NATO competitions. Sentinel, the voice of the Canadian Armed Forces in that era, told the story of Ex. Royal Flush XIV in its October 1969 issue. Bill Turnbull later summarized his memories:

"Royal Flush" veteran Bill Van Oene. (441 Sqn)

The big event for all recce squadrons in the Central Region was the annual Royal Flush competition. In its original form, each squadron competed from its home base. Under the rules, 70% of a unit's Combat Ready aircrew had to compete. Many umpires were required at each base and at selected targets - in the air or on the ground. Many army formations were asked to put units in the field under camouflage, specifically for the exercise. As I recall, every participating crew was to fly three missions of three targets each over the course of the 3-day exercise. At least three of the nine targets flown were to be "army". Fixed targets were usually of the pinpoint variety, but the army targets might be "fragged" as a pinpoint or a line search. In later years, a "strip search" was introduced. Here, the target was considered to lie somewhere within a narrow rectangle a few kilometers long. Over time, the emphasis on army targets increased. These were certainly the most challenging to aircrew and PIs.

For the day missions, all pilot visual reports were radioed to home plate. The PIs had to complete all of their target reports and print annotations within 30 minutes of aircraft shutdown. A squadron had a target list to work with and was free to select the number of targets it needed within areas of suitable weather. Once an aircraft was airborne, its mission was scored. If no results were obtained due to bad weather or technical malfunction, too bad - the mission scored zero. The pressure was on aircrew, groundcrew and PIs alike, and the flying pace was reasonably intense, especially if weather cut into available time. In that sense, it was a good exercise.

When 1 Wing first competed in Royal Flush, its squadrons, not surprisingly, came last, but, by 1968, we were starting to win. That

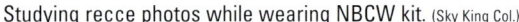
Sky King (441 Sqn), Guy Fabi (439), George Kirbyson (441) and Bobby Joe Hart (441) brief for a "Royal Flush XV" mission in 1970. (Sky King Col.)

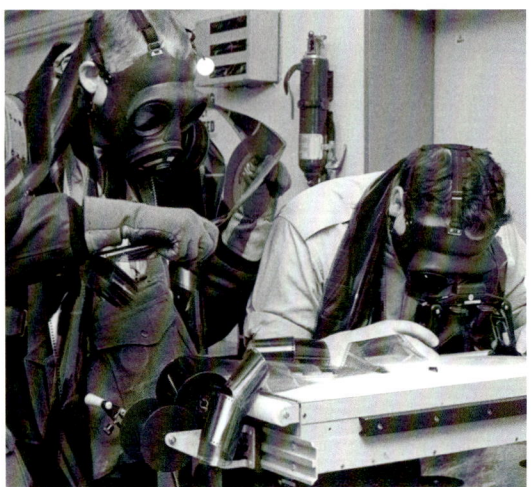
Studying recce photos while wearing NBCW kit. (Sky King Col.)

year I placed fourth overall and 441 won first place. That was also the year we hosted the awards ceremony in Lahr. The following year, 441 and 439 were first and second.

Policing the "big base" version of Royal Flush was a problem, and accusations of cheating were rampant. One air force did particularly well at finding its own national army targets which, in our experience, were seldom on plot. Moreover, that air force's visual reports invariably matched their army's submitted solutions, even when the targets were heavily camouflaged or hidden in woods. Collusion was suspected. With such a large target list, umpires could monitor only a few targets. Thus, multiple passes at the same target, forbidden under the rules, were unlikely to be detected.

Because squadrons did not necessarily fly against the same targets and, because they perceived wide variations in the marking standards, there were debates over the results. With the large number of targets flown, team scores were probably a good "on average" indication of proficiency. But, if you happened to be based in an area hampered by weather, when others were not, or if you received more than your share of poorly plotted targets, or if you happened to have several targets scored by a harsh marker, then you had some grounds for complaint.

Beginning with the 1970 competition, the modus operandi changed. Squadrons sent hand-picked teams to a single base where all flew identical missions. The numbers have become a bit hazy with time, but I believe each team comprised four crews and aircraft plus a spare machine. Limitations were placed on the number of groundcrew. Most targets flown were deployed army units. Much greater emphasis was placed on night capability. That year 439 Squadron won the day competition, but the handwriting was on the wall for day-only units. We wanted to get into night reconnaissance, but had to convince Ottawa to buy us an IR line-scanner. In my view we had the other essentials - an all-weather navigation system and the techniques developed by our confrères in the nuclear strike game. All we needed was a sensor, but this was not to be.

The busy scene in 1 Wing's photo section during Royal Flush XIII. PIs study their film and pilots wait around for results. W/C Dunlop is at the front left. (Bill Turnbull Col.)

Royal Flush XIII personnel wait at Marville for the last 1 Wing recce flight of the day to land: Ted Lewis, Bruce Arnott, Brian Castledine (1st pilot squatting on left), Ron Tomcheck, unknown USAF, Herb Sievert, unknown RCAF, Ken Mowbray, Gord Wallis (sitting on curb), John Duncan, Ross Brewer, Bill Van Oene, unknown RCAF and Ernie Gardiner. (Bill Turnbull Col.)

John Greatrix notes of this photo: "AFCENT day-recce competition, "Royal Flush" 1968. 441 Squadron won against the USAF, German Air Force, RAF and French 'guest' squadrons. Here are the 441 champions. On the left by the tip tank is Ken Mowbray with Charlie Paul and Ken McLeod on his left. Phil Engstad and Bill Turnbull are next, with Bobby Joe Hart and Bill Van Oene in front. Col Bob Christie, 1 Wing Commander, is in the cockpit. Behind on the right are Bruce Arnott and Ted Lewis, then Herb Sievert with Gord Wallis and Jim Jones ahead of him. In front are Ron Tomchek (leaning on the nose) and Ernie Gardiner. (John Greatrix Col.)

Vic Johnson, who joined the RCAF in 1959, trained at Camp Borden as a photo tech. He served to 1965 with the RCAF Photo Establishment at Rockcliffe, then at 1 Wing until 1969. Later postings included AETE at Cold Lake, DND public affairs, and six months in Bahrain during the 1991 Gulf War. When WO Johnson left the military, he took over the editor's desk at *Air Force Magazine* in Ottawa. (CANAV Col.)

Royal Flush Photo Tech

Vic Johnson recalls the efforts of the photo techs when the "Royal Flush" pressure was on:

As soon as a Starfighter shut down, the film magazines were rushed (on foot) to the processing crew, as the umpires eyed their stop watches. A machine was used to load the rolls of film into special spiral reels, then the film was hand-developed in our specially-concocted "soup".

Against all the laws of photo chemistry, we had boosted the temperature of our chemicals to 90°, while the manufacturer's specs stated 68°. Any more heat and the emulsion would have melted right off the film. Our film normally took 10 minutes to process, but our "liquid dynamite" shaved off a minute.

After a quick fix bath the film was hastily washed, dipped in alcohol, then spun dry in a powerful Sirocco dryer that duplicated a mini hurricane. It then was passed to the photo interpreters for initial assessment. The PIs selected negatives for printing, then passed them back to the darkroom where enlargements were printed and developed using a rapid processor. At every stage we were honing procedures - every second saved meant an extra second for photo interpretation.

Meanwhile, the PIs were debriefed by the pilot, then prepared a written report about what the pilot had seen. Target information was annotated onto the photos, and the negatives and reports were sealed in an envelope and handed to an umpire. Total time from engine shutdown? 30 minutes.

The mobile film labs and PI vans at 1 Wing circa 1965. In the aerial view they are beside the mission planning building. (Vic Johnson Col.)

"A great gang to serve with", commented S/L John Greatrix about this 1969 edition of 441 at Lahr. Standing are Sky King, Jim Jones, Keith Adlard, Lyle Gainsford, Jim Pfaff, Ken McLeod, Paul Manson (CO), Amos Pudsey (Base Commander), John Greatrix, Charlie Paul, Dan Orr, Rod Ellis and Pete Rawlings. In front are Jim Cratchley, Ron Doyle, George Kirbyson, Ted Lewis, Herb Sievert, Phil Engstad, Ken Mowbray, Bobby Joe Hart, Marc Dumontet, Neil Kleinsteuber and Jim McKay. (441 Sqn)

Decimomannu

Since 439 and 441 also had to maintain bombing proficiency, like the strike squadrons they used Decimomannu for weapons practice. W/C Edwards and F/L [Bob] Porter paid 441's first CF-104 visit there on September 28, 1964. Henceforth, at 2-week intervals a few pilots trained at Deci. An RCAF Air Weapons Unit document describes what was happening: "During the period 1 January - 31 December 1964, operational flying was carried out at the AWU in accordance with 1 Air Division Operation Order "Sardinian Salvo". CF-104 pilots deployed from 1 Air Division Headquarters and from 1, 3 and 4 Wings to carry out weapons training with the aim of qualifying or re-qualifying to SHAPE standards for the delivery of nuclear weapons. During the period a total of 194 squadron pilots, seven OFTT and seven tactical evaluation pilots were so qualified."

In a typical case 441's S/L John Greatrix was at Deci from May 12-23, 1969. His exercises included dropping the BDU-8 training shape (a dummy "nuke") on a night radar bombing sortie. The occasional ability of the recce squadrons "to wax the fannies" of their strike buddies on the range caused some grief among the latter. As 441's Bruce Burgess explained in a 2002 conversation with Hugh Halliday: "Every now and then we would get a bulls-eye and piss them off." As to flying conditions at Deci, LCol Dave Burt recalled that the heat could get so intense that flying would have to be curtailed.

With the termination of Canada's nuclear strike role in 1971, and the limited tactical air-to-ground facilities of Deci,

Starfighter '660 scorches across the Decimomannu bombing range in strike mode and where it belongs - on the deck. (CF IL70-53-10)

1 CAG terminated deployments there in May 71. In 1980, however, BGen Manson and his staff were able to lay the framework for a return to Deci, where the Germans were to accommodate us at their air weapons facility. In the forefront of the project was 441 under Larry Crabb, and with Major John David doing much of the "grunt work". In 2003 Crabb recalled this period:

With a mixed bag of aircrew from each squadron participating, I led the first exercise ("Sardinia Salvo 81") back to Deci in February 1981. Our main efforts were in air combat manoeuvring (ACM), most trips being with tip tanks removed. I also flew two trips on the Capo Frasca range during this deployment. There I had my eyes opened with the 20-30 knot crosswinds where one would almost have to aim at the next strafe panel to allow for bullet drift! Everything you have read about the Italian base and the air traffic control in the 60s and 70s was still true. "The base she's a closed", was the dreaded call, since your alternate without tip tanks was the adjacent taxiway.

Danes and Canadians during a 1968 exchange with 729 Squadron at Karup, Denmark. In front are pilots Don Hill, unknown RDAF, Lyle Gainsford, John Greatrix, Dal Uldahl (RDAF CO), Ron Chercoe, Gord Wallis, Ken Mowbray and Jim Jones. Then, 729 RF-84F subsonic recce birds at Marville for the Danish part of the exchange. Republic sold some 700 RF-84Fs to the USAF and NATO partners. (John Greatrix Col., 441 Sqn)

Exchanges

As in Sabre days socializing and business were joint objectives of unit exchanges. Describing a 1983 exchange with a Spanish squadron, 441's diarist noted the purpose as being "to exercise the concept of interoperability through the exchange of ideas, techniques and procedures." The same applied in 1984 with respect to visits with Italian and Greek units. "Interoperability" implied training for a variety of contingencies, the most immediate being the speed with which one Allied base could refuel, re-arm and re-launch aircraft from another. In reconnaissance this involved handling an unexpected arrival, downloading film, processing it and reporting the contents. In the days when it was not just pilots who were expected to be flexible, groundcrew had to service visiting aircraft, and staff officers learn where to direct intelligence findings. Little of this could be taught from a manual, so exchanges were vital. Meanwhile, "downtime" with one's allies was guardedly described by 441 (following a 1983 visit to Norway) as "mutual social activities to promote understanding and camaraderie between NATO partners". This concept appeared in other reports. A 1984 visit to Greece had "various social activities" which "allowed both Greeks and Canadians the chance to deepen their understanding of each other."

Of this photo from the Karup exchange, John Greatrix noted, "441's Gord Wallis looking over shipping in the Kattegat Strait". (John Greatrix Col.)

The Silver Foxes were on exchange August 3-12, 1976 to 1 Marinefliegergeschwader at Schleswig. Standing are Bob Endicott, Jim Maurstad, Jack Orr, Dave Owen, German pilot (G), Rick Wall, Phil Murphy, Judge Wenham, Bruce Reid, Gus Youngson, Ian Struthers, G, G, unknown Canadian and Clark Little. In front are Jim Gale, G, John Hutt, G, George Landry, G, Mike Major (USAF) and Pat Barrett. This CF-104 (104892) was lost on June 4, 1982, Capt Kerry G. Cranfield of 417 Sqn ejecting OK. (CF BS76-0937)

Some 441 Starfighter Exchanges

July 1966 - 4 Hunters of 2 Sqn, RAF (Gütersloh, Germany) visit 1 Wing for 10 days.

August 1966 - 7 Silver Foxes to USAF 1st TRS, Alconbury (UK) for 2 weeks.

August 1, 1967 - 6 CF-104s to RAF Upper Heyford with the USAF 18th TRS (RF-101s). The 18th paid 441 a return visit.

August 1968 - 6 CF-104s to Karup, Denmark. Missions to photograph Soviet and Warsaw Pact vessels, and 15 "H-L-H" missions flown to central Norway. "Despite complaining about physical exhaustion and depleted bank accounts", wrote 441's historian, "the pilots of both squadrons agreed that the training value and social life of the exchange was an outstanding success." After a similar exchange a year earlier, 441 had commented about the RDAF RF-84F, known for its sluggish performance, that those living near the ends of the runways would do well to remove their TV aerials for the duration of the exchange!

August 1971 - 8 CF-104s to Leuchars, Scotland with 43 Sqn (Phantoms). The Brits later visited Lahr where "many ales were quaffed and many stories told."

May 23 -31, 1974 - 718 Sqn RNoAF brought 6 NF 5s and a C-130 to Baden. June 6-15 441 visited 718 at Sola. Laurie Hawn about this exchange in Der Kanadier, this excerpt covering the Norwegians' first day at Baden:

It was a fine warm day as Major Egil Omdal led his gang into Soellingen... All were met in the cockpit with a cool bottle of brown bubbly... Many more cool bubbles were enjoyed by all in the squadron's beer garden, followed by a steak and sojourn to the mess to continue the serious business of exchanging ideas.

Enough ideas were exchanged by about 2 a.m. and the gaggle proceeded to Mrs. Best's little boy's house for some eggs on the floor and a chaser. The next day was not so sunny.

Wednesday [24 May] the Norskies began learning what it's like to navigate without lakes and with towns. They were ably (?) assisted by the odd clever Canuck in the back seat who was greatly enjoying an airplane that turns.

August 3-12 1976 - 8 pilots and 6 CF-104s to Schleswig, near Hamburg, to train with 1 Marinefliegergeschwader (1 Sqn/1 Naval Air Wing) flying F-104Gs. 441 flew 59 range and nav missions, dropping practice bombs on boat-towed targets. On an early mission the 1 MFG lead of a marine recce had to abort, leaving a Canadian unfamiliar with the area to take over. The CF-104 had no radar altimeter, making low-level flying in the Baltic hairy (German naval F-104 pilots visiting 1 CAG felt nervous flying over forests). Captain Bob Endicott's logbook offers a survey of flying during this exchange:

Date	CF-104	Route/Time
August 3	104761	Soellingen-Schleswig/1.3 hours
August 5	104761	Splash Target/1.3
August 5	104845	Air/Sea Demo/1.0
August 9	104805	Low Level Navigation, Simulated Attack/1.3
August 9	104815	Low Level Navigation, Simulated Attack/1.0
August 10	104705	Bombing Exercise ("BX"), Terschelling/1.3
August 11	104806	A/S Demo, Splash Target/1.2
August 11	104761	BX, Vlieland (1.3 hours)
August 12	104761	Schleswig-Soellingen/1.2

Other exchange friends of the 1960s - USAFE RF-101 Voodoos at Marville, and a French Mystère. (441 Sqn, David Huddelston Col.)

1977 - Exchange to 10 Sqn (F-104S) at Grazzanise Air Base, near Naples. The squadron historical report gives an overview:

While deployed 441 Squadron flew bombing and strafing missions to Brindisi Range ... and low level navigation missions to such places as volcanic Mount Etna in Sicily and Mount Cassino of World War II fame, south of Rome. Socially, all personnel were fascinated by tours of such places as Pompeii, the Isle of Capri and Naples. Members of the squadron returned with a warm feeling of friendship and understanding of the job performed by our NATO partners in the south.

April 25 to May 4, 1979 - To Schleswig:

On 25 April 79 six CF-104s and one CF-104 Dual flew from Baden-Soellingen to 1 Naval Air Wing at Schleswig to exchange with 1 Squadron of the German Navy. The ensuing ten days and nights provided a valuable exchange of operational doctrine and tactics. 441 Squadron and 1 Squadron flew over 50 sorties with a loss of only one sortie due to an aircraft unserviceability. During the entire exchange not one ground or air incident occurred, which again points to the extreme professionalism displayed by ourselves and members of 1 Squadron ... squadron pilots fired the CRV-7 rocket on Splash targets towed behind destroyers in the Baltic and North Seas... 441 Squadron participated in surveillance missions over the Baltic Sea, showing Canadian presence in seldom travelled airspace. Bad weather days were spent discussing the "ideas" and "tactics" via the medium of briefings on our respective roles.

September 25 to October 3, 1979 - return visit by 1 Sqn:

On 25 September, 1 Squadron, 1 NAW deployed from Schleswig with six F-104G aircraft to commence Phase II of the squadron exchange. During the ensuing nine days the weather was superb and only two missions were lost to unserviceabilities. The highlight of the

Capt Gerry Bayles of 441 starts 104716 at RAF Coltishall during an exchange there with 54 Squadron. Then, he gets airborne for the local range with a CRV-7 practice pod and centreline practice bomb carrier.
(Gerry Bayles Col.)

flying phase was a two-day mini-gun [competition] which was won by the two Squadron Commanders. A very busy social program included such activities as a car rally, hockey game, and skeet shooting. The climax of the nine days saw 441 (F) Squadron and 1 NAW Wing becoming sister squadrons.

August 15-28, 1980 - 7 CF-104s to Soesterberg, Netherlands to work with 32 TFS (USAF, F-15 Eagles) and a Dutch Hawk SAM battery. Six 441 pilots enjoyed familiarization rides in F-15s. During this exchange Maj R.W. "Bob" Porter ejected following a catastrophic flap failure.

June 1-10, 1982 - 11 CF-104s to 54 Sqn (Jaguars) at RAF Coltishall. Reasonable flying weather and extensive use of British air-to-ground ranges, while "the social calendar was filled with successful events." Also on the exchange was Maj Gorm Jensen 441, whose log shows a typical week.

Date	Aircraft	Route	Time
1	104739	Baden-Soellingen to Coltishall	1.1
2	104739	Holbeach Range	1.0
3	104716	Holbeach Range	1.0
4	104787	combat training [CT] and flypast	1.2
7	104716	CT	1.3
	104653	CT + famil ride for G/C Nash	1.4
8	Jaguar "GT"	famil ride + CT with Capt Pedersen	1.5
	104749	Holbeach Range	1.1
9	104716	CT	1.3
10	104749	Coltishall to Baden-Soellingen	1.2

August 17-26, 1982 - 54 Sqn to Baden for low-level and mini-gun competition missions with 441.

April 1983 - To 338 Sqn RNoAF. Dave Burt recalled how, since the main runway was being repaired, they operated from a 75-foot wide taxiway. Accompanied by an RNoAF pilot in a CF-104D, he did low fly-bys of several Norwegian airfields, then hit the afterburner to impress his passenger. Probably the person who best remembered this sortie was a sailboat operator, whom they beat up at Mach 0.98.

June 18-28, 1984 - 8 CF-104s and 54 personnel to Rimini, Italy to fly with 102 Gruppo (F-104S). Much was learned from working over unfamiliar terrain and ranges. 441 reported high serviceability during a full flying program. LCol Betts described the exchange as one where Canada's best fighter squadron was hosted by Italy's best, in the best possible location.

October 12-21, 1984 - 6 CF-104s, 9 pilots, 33 ground crew to 334 Sqn, Hellenic Air Force (Mirage F-1s), Tanagra Air Base, Greece. DACT and weapons practices at the Amnerlone Range.

May 28 to June 7, 1985 - 15 Sqn, RAF (Tornados) from Laarbruch, Germany deployed to Baden. September 3-13, 1985 the Silver Foxes took 9 CF-104s and 60 personnel to Laarbruch, where they operated over the flat terrain of north Germany and used the Nordhorn Range.

718 Sqn RNoAF (F-5s) visits 441 in May 1972. In front are Al Young (441 CO), Maj Umdal (718 CO) and Wally Sloan (441 DCO). The five in the middle (and the man behind Undal) are Norwegians. Then are Joe Molnar, two Norwegians, Dave Burroughs, Larry Best, Laurie Hawn, Tom Henry, Ken McCrimmon, Don Paxton, Gord Ball, Rick Parent, Walt Luedemann and Bob Kadonoff. The story is told of McCrimmon who finished on Sabres with some 994 hours. Nobody thought that this was fair, so one day some buddies hoisted him into the Sabre mounted at the Baden main gate. There he stayed for the time needed to qualify as a 1000-hour Sabre man. As to LCol Young, he had joined the RCAF in 1950. He was an armourer with 441 at North Luffenham, then remustered to pilot. He flew Sabres with 416 and 430, before converting to the CF-104. (Larry O'Brien Col.)

For 1 CAG the Canadian-made CRV-7 was the best air-to-ground conventional rocket. While its predecessor, the 2.75" rocket of the 1950s, was unpredictable as to what it might do in flight, the CRV-7 flew straight, steady and fast. Here, salvoes of CRV-7s head for the target. The scenario dates to June 7, 1985 when Gerry Bayles, Bert Doyle, Wally Peirson and Jim Sullivan of 441 were on the Baumholder range in West Germany. Going straight out is Sullivan's salvo, while Bayles' is on the left. 441's good work this day moved the German commanding this army-air force exercise, BGen Vollmer, to write to Col Dave McIntosh of 1 CAG: "By their precise weapons delivery on the target under marginal weather conditions they [441] have demonstrated high skill and proficiency. They thus have increased the reputation of the 1 CAG, as well as the confidence in our common capabilities... my thanks to everyone concerned." (Gerry Bayles)

Gerry Bayles joined the air force in 1969. After graduating from military college, he earned his Wings in 1974, instructed at Moose Jaw into 1979, then moved to '104s. He was on 441 from 1980 - 83, spent a year at Base Flight, then returned to 441 for 1984 - 86, finishing the CF-104 era with 1157.5 hours on type. His final CF-104 touchdown came at Diyarbakir, Turkey, where he delivered 104810 on March 19, 1986. Bayles later flew EW Challengers with 414 and 434 squadrons, then left the CF in 1995 for a career in civil aviation. (441 Sqn)

441 "boys and girls" (Bob Endicott leaning on the mast) at sea with NAW 1. At 8 knots this vessel had her railing at the water line. Much schnapps and beer was enjoyed by all during this June 1981 "cultural exchange". (Larry Crabb Col.)

This is to certify that

CAPT D. BURT

suitably humbled the other pilots of the Silver Fox Squadron by placing first in the

COMBINED JAGUAR & CF-104 SECTION

of the 441 Fighter Squadron Mini-Gun competition held

IN CONJUNCTION WITH 54 SQUADRON RAF

23 - 24 AUGUST 1982

While not meaning to detract from this not inconsequential achievement it is, however, apparent to all concerned that the aforementioned pilot's performance does shed some doubt on his moral fibre and standard of ethics.

Signed:

Witnessed:

A memento of 54 Squadron's exchange to Baden of August 1982. Then, 441's Harry Chapin being hog-tied by some 54 Squadron types who must have taken exception to his pants. (via Dave Burt, 441 Sqn)

Starfighter '761 of 441 on exchange to 9 Stormo at Grazzanise, not far from Naples/Vesuvius. (441 Sqn)

The opening round of a piano burning at Baden. (441 Sqn)

Ted Delanghe greets some 54 Squadron Jaguar types at Baden-Soellingen for a 1978 exchange. A cool can of Lowenbrau seems to be doing the trick for the Brits! This exchange was an eye-opener, giving the Silver Foxes a chance to see the Jaguar's "moving map" and "HUD" (head-up display) technology. (CF BS78-743)

Silver Fox piano-burners on exchange in 1975 with 14 Squadron at RAF Bruggen: Jim Maurstad, Gus Youngson, Ian Struthers, Laurie Hawn, John Hutt (CO), Bruce Stott, Ted Lee and Pat Barrett. The piano burning skit arose after the boys had been whooping it up in the mess. Everyone was familiar with the RAF tradition of smashing a piano to smithereens (rule: pieces had to be small enough to pass through a toilet seat). Then, the evidence would be incinerated. This gang destroyed the Brits' piano, assuming that it was a clunker. However, it was a rental needed that week for a recital. Before leaving Bruggen, 441 had to make restitution, which explains why LCol Hutt has his pockets pulled out. At Bruggen the Silver Foxes also were introduced by the Brits to the "the ring of fire" skit. As a few fellows stood in the mess in a blur of beer and babble, some mad RAF type would ring them with lighter fluid, then throw in a match. Instantly (if momentarily) would the amazed fellows be surrounded in leaping flames! Before long, 14 Squadron visited Baden. There they torched 1 Wing's piano and all was well (except that the fire was set on the base commander's parking spot, which then needed re-paving). (441 Sqn)

Maj Mike Nicholas on exchange at 1 Wing. (441 Sqn)

The damaged wingtip of Nicholas' CF-104. (441 Sqn)

First CF-104 Exchange Officer

In preparing for its new role, 441 could draw on experience from elsewhere. Thus did USAF Capt M.C. "Mike" Nicholas become 441's first exchange pilot. Born in 1931 and raised in Ogden, Utah, Nicholas joined the USAF in 1955. After basic fighter pilot training, in 1956 he was posted to the F-86D/L with the 337th FIS at Westover, Massachusetts. In 1958 the 337th became one of the first squadrons with F-104As. When tensions soared between the Nationalist and Communist Chinese, the 337th deployed to Formosa, so it was an exciting time to be on squadron.

In 1960 Nicholas moved to the photo recce world, flying the RF-101 from Toul, France, then at Ramstein, Germany. Next in his career came 1 Wing. In July 2003 he recalled how this came about: "In August 1964 I got a call from the officer assignment branch at 17th Air Force at Ramstein, telling me of the opening. The 17th had received a message from Washington to send someone to Marville to assist the RCAF with its new recce program. I jumped at the chance and was accepted."

Both 1 Wing squadrons would profit from Nicholas' experience. Eight months afterwards, 441 pilots were giving him a run for his money. Now he moved from training individual pilots to flying squadron TacEvals and hunting for suitable routes/targets that Starfighters might visit. With new routes the deal was that each squadron would send pilots out to try it. Whoever fell a bit short had to buy the beer in the mess that night.

One day, while scouting for a new route, Nicholas looked up to see his view blocked by another airplane! He took evasive action, but there was a crunch - he had collided with an RAF Canberra. Both pilots kept control and recovered at Grostenquin, where their aircraft were repaired. Mike Nicholas recalled that the board of enquiry looking into this incident was complicated. After all, an American, flying a Canadian aircraft based in France, had collided with a British aircraft over Germany, both pilots then landing in France!

Nicholas, who had been sent to 1 Wing for only six months, was delighted when asked by S/L Jack Frazer of 1 Wing to stay another six months. When he finally left 1 Wing in 1965, Nicholas instructed on RF-4Cs at Shaw AFB. In 1967 he was posted to Southeast Asia, where he flew 120 RF-4C combat missions, most over North Vietnam. Various ground tours followed until 1978 when LCol Mike Nicholas retired to go into business in California. As to his stay at 441? On that his memory is clear: "That was the most enjoyable year of my 24 years of active duty. I cannot say enough about the hospitality and great reception I received, and the willingness of the RCAF to accept my guidance."

Mike Major, born in 1940 in Ellensburg, Washington, served with 441 from 1975 - 77. A 1962 graduate of the USAF Academy, he earned his Wings at Williams AFB in August 1963. Following the basic gunnery course at Luke AFB, he joined the 50th TFW at Hahn Air Base, West Germany. In 1965 he was posted to the 3rd TFW flying F-100s at Bien Hoa, Vietnam where, in 12 months, he logged some 300 combat missions. Now he returned home to instruct on F-104s at the Fighter Weapons School at Luke AFB (1967 - 70). From here he served at TAC HQ at Langley AFB, Virginia, did post graduate studies, then had a posting to the TAC Air Warfare Centre at Eglin AFB, before returning to Southeast Asia, flying F-4s from U Dorn, Thailand. In 1975 Major attended Canadian Forces Staff College in Toronto. The following year he took a T-33 refresher course at Chatham, the CF-104 refresher course at Cold Lake, then joined 441. Major would thoroughly enjoy his exchange, which offered lots of challenging flying, and less structure and control than on a USAF squadron. Yet, whatever the task, it got done well at 441. As Major put it in 2003: "I was certainly impressed with the professionalism, airmanship and attitude of everyone I encountered during my Canadian exchange. It was a rewarding experience from both a career and personal perspective." In 1977 Major joined the 8th TFW flying F-4Ds at Kusan Air Base, Korea. Later, he commanded the 309th TFS (F-4Es) at Homestead AFB, Florida, attended the Air War College at Maxwell AFB, Alabama, had a Pentagon posting, then (1983 - 84) became Vice Wing Commander of the 8th TFW, flying F-16s at Kusan. When he retired from the USAF in 1985, Colonel Mike Major was flying F-16s from Bergstrom AFB, Texas. By this time he had some 4000 hours on high performance jets. From Bergstrom he joined Northrop in Los Angeles to work on such projects as the YF-23 and B-2.
(via M. Major)

C.D. "Doug" Barton joined the USAF in 1965, his first flying tour being as an EW navigator on B-52Hs at Homestead AFB, Florida. In October 1969 he earned his pilot's wings at Laughlin AFB, Texas, then flew F-4s with the 417th TFS at Holloman AFB, New Mexico, and the 34th TFS in Thailand. Of 278 combat missions flown with the 34th, that of October 6, 1972 was especially memorable. Operating that day with F-105 Wild Weasels, Barton was tapped by a MiG-19. As the fight developed, he dove steeply, pulling out low at 8+Gs. As fortune had it, the feisty MiG on Barton's six then flew into the ground. Following Southeast Asia, Barton instructed in the F-104 program at Luke AFB. When he heard one day that there was an exchange available in Canada, he jumped at it. "I had both hands up when the call went out for a volunteer", is how he put it in 2003. His involvement in Canada began in June 1977 with a refresher course at 417, then he began his tour as OpsO at 441. One of the great things about 441 was the opportunity to fly regularly and in a less structured organization than usual. He appreciated how a Canadian CO could take responsibilities and make decisions that, in the USAF, only a higher-up would touch. Finished at 441 in 1980, Barton served at Ramstein with the 7055th Operations Squadron, which was responsible for certifying pilots and weapons loaders, and for augmenting the nuclear and conventional roles. In this role he occasionally returned to 1 CAG during TacEvals. There he always was welcomed with an "open cockpit", should he care to log a CF-104 trip. Barton returned to the United States in 1984 for a final assignment at Red Flag, Nellis AFB. Then he left the USAF in 1988 for a career as a high school mathematics teacher in Nevada.
(via C.D. Barton)

Hunters and Starfighters

In July 2003 Sky King (RCAF) and Peter Riley (RAF) recalled the fun of exchanges, especially one week when 2 Squadron RAF visited from Gütersloh:

A 2 Squadron Hawker Hunter shows its great lines, then formates with a CF-104 flown by Sky King during the July 1966 exchange. (via Gorm Jensen and Nigel Walpole)

(Sky King) *Squadron exchanges were highlights for any pilot on an overseas posting. The opportunity to experience social adventures with another culture in yet another land, to share war stories of epic proportions and, if lucky, to fly the other guy's machine, was not to be missed.*

Danish exchanges were popular, not because of the RF-84, but more for Aalborg's many tourist attractions. As for the RF-84 its fame was the way it would roar off down the runway, then disappear as a blotch of smoke in the distance, the pilot battling for flying speed and altitude.

Then there were the Americans and the monster they flew - the RF-101. And its pilots? Most had completed a recce tour in Vietnam. Whenever we spotted one of them wearing his "100 Combat Missions" shoulder patch, we were in awe.

When it came to exchanges, the favourites for me were the Brits. Having British ancestry, I immediately accepted this motley crew as family. In their midst I felt surrounded by a group that had been type-cast for a Battle of Britain movie.

The Brits flew the Hawker Hunter. This was definitely a pilot's aircraft, having the lines of a beautiful lady and the tail of a shark. Perfect! On July 12, 1966 I had the pleasure of flying a Hunter T.7 at Marville. F/L Riley gave me the pre-flight briefing. Not much to that - "Awright then, once I get the beast started, you have control." Then came an aside - "Steering can be a wee bit tricky, mate." No kidding! Who designed this thing, I wondered. Somehow I got us into takeoff position. Away we went, but I immediately headed for the grass. Overcorrect, then head for the grass on the other side of the runway. Flashes of my first flight in a Chipmunk at Centralia years earlier did not help my concentration. Finally I got things squared away and we were airborne. "Well done," says good old Riley, smirking behind his mask.

Airborne was glorious, made easy with 10,500 pounds of Rolls-Royce thrust. More than enough power for rambling low across the French countryside. Loops were a breeze. At the top of one I was reminded of the day at Farnborough that the RAF Black Arrows demo team completed a formation loop with 22 Hunters!

On return to base we did a few "rollers" and closed patterns, then did a full-stop and taxied in. Again, the lovely Hunter becoming a handful for this neophyte pilot, so I quickly told my host, "You have control." Later in the day it was my turn for hospitality, taking F/L Riley up in a Starfighter. Taxying out in 12633 was a treat that only a Hunter pilot could appreciate, for we had nosewheel steering! Our exhilarating takeoff was immediately followed by the trademark afterburner climb. I think that F/L Riley was rather impressed by the whole experience.

(Peter Riley) *I had already flown two low-level sorties in my Hunter F.R.10 (well, as low as we were allowed in France). Then I flew a third in a CF-104 flown by F/L "Sky" King. We spent most of the trip doing aerobatics and finished with a Tacan recovery. Sky lived up to his name, showing off the CF-104's excellence in a straight line, whether horizontally or vertically, although it seemed to shudder any time we applied back pressure on the stick. Of course, it could easily out-run us, but it was no match for a Hunter in manoeuvrability at low level. I much enjoyed this memorable flight with a most outgoing and affable Canadian.*

Also in 2003 RAF Hunter pilot Nigel Walpole (F/L Riley's CO) put down a few memories from the days when 2 Squadron trained with 441:

At this stage my memory about 441 is rather vague, except about some excellent flying, and even better drinking. When I took four of my 2 Squadron Hunter F.R.10s to Marville in the summer of 1966, 441's boss was W/C Jim Dunlop. Two of his ace pilots whom I recall were "Sky" King and "Melton" Mowbray.

Something that we quickly learned from 441 was that the CF-104 could out-run us, even though we had a 600-knot "dash" speed. We flew all our sorties in pairs, Hunters and Starfighters leading in turn. While this tactic was frowned upon by the USAF (operating RF-101s at nearby Laon), we RAF and RCAF types saw eye-to-eye on it.

One thing where we did envy 441 was in the support available to pilots, as in the way that NCOs helped with mission planning. We RAF types, in contrast, had to do such tasks ourselves.

Our exchange to Marville was a one-way affair, since our runway at Gütersloh, Germany was a bit too short for the CF-104. Nonetheless, all was not lost, for we invited 441 over one weekend for some first-class "socializing". About that time, no one seems to remember much. All things considered, there proved to be a positive "recce synergy" between our two squadrons.

Our view at 2 Squadron about "Royal Flush" was different from other participants. To us it was a wretched academic competition that took far too much time away from operational training, certainly from our gunnery. After all, we were a "fighter recce" squadron, so had to be sharp at 30-mm firing, besides photo recce. "Royal Flush" could bring out the worst in human nature and, as we at 2 Squadron recall it, may have caused more acrimony than harmony in NATO. Of course, some good would come from it, but too many did little else but train for "Royal Flush". As I recall, the RCAF did very well at this competition, and sometimes bailed out the Americans in 4 ATAF.

Leuchars - August 1971

In August 1971 the Silver Foxes visited 43 Squadron, then flying Phantoms at RAF Leuchars, Scotland. This exchange would include one of the great 441/Starfighter skits. The "chief culprit" involved was 441's DCO, Maj W.S. "Wally" Sloan. He had begun as an Ordinary Seaman in the RCN in 1950, but remustered to aircrew. As was the RCN practice in that era, he won his Wings with the US Navy. Sloan rose to command a Banshee squadron, eventually amassing some 1250 hours on type. Meanwhile, he had the chance to fly some high-performance US Navy fighters, the Demon and Skyray included. He also had a tour at NAS Oceana logging some 250 hours on the F-4. Following Canadian Forces re-unification, he moved to the Starfighter, later was base test pilot at Shearwater, then retired from the CF in 1976 for a career in research at the Technical University of Nova Scotia. In August 2003 Sloan reminisced with Ted Lee about the Leuchars exchange:

After the proverbial meet and greet, where we held our own during the drinking stage of things, much was said about the merits of the CF-104. As the night progressed and things started getting a little blurry, I commented to the effect that an orangutan with a 10-minute briefing could fly a CF-104. Naturally, all was said in jest, but some 43 Squadron wit reminded me next day about my boast. He explained how his squadron commander fit the category that I had described, so the game was afoot.

The weather was no screaming hell, with rain and a 200-foot ceiling, but W/C Martin was keen to go. Since the dual was u/s, off we went in a pair of single-seaters. I chased the winco and we broke out of the soup at about 20 grand. W/C Martin then proceeded to wring out the 104, with me hanging on for dear life. By then the possible far reaching consequences of him bending the aircraft were starting to gnaw at my conscience. No matter, since the next thing was to follow W/C Martin down through cloud, flying formation while madly checking airspeed, altitudes, etc. I think that was when I lost the rest of my hair. We made it back to Leuchars, although there were bursts of power and some evasive manoeuvres on final approach.

I was familiar with the big, heavy US Navy Phantom with its high sink rate. The Brits had taken this basic design and made it even more of a pig with their own mods. So, when 43 Squadron offered to let us fly their Phantoms from the front seat, I was reluctant to let my young charges "have a go". They chided me for that, but got over it. The whole exchange to Leuchars proved to be great fun.

In 2003 Larry Crabb looked back on another NATO exchange concept - the "sister squadron":

Besides our routine exchanges, some of us also had "sister" squadrons. We at 441 were affiliated with German Naval Air Wing (NAW) Squadron 1 in Schleswig-Holstein. Such relationships were more informal, and especially social. In each case we were exposed to

Maj Wally Sloan during "naval air" days at Shearwater. The RCN was at least as nuts as the RCAF when it came to shenanigans, so no one is surprised at the Leuchars skit. Sloan came to 441 with a great deal of experience. Besides being a leading Banshee pilot, he had a US Navy exchange with VF-101 squadron in Key West. There he flew the F4D Skyray, F3H Demon and F9F Cougar (the Skyray was the most accident-prone USN jet fighter). In 1962 Sloan moved with VF-101 to Oceana, Virginia, to instruct on the F-4 Phantom. In one year he became the high time USN Phantom pilot on the east coast, logging some 250 hours. (via W.S. Sloan)

A PR photo of NATO fighters circa 1965. Clockwise from the RAF Javelin (top centre) are a USAFE F-105 Thunderchief, RCAF CF-104, Belgian F-104G, French Mirage, Luftwaffe F-104G and Dutch F-104G. In this period, when it replaced the F-84 and F-86, the F-104 dominated on the NATO fighter scene. (CF PCN 4993, Bill Van Oene Col.)

Where hundreds of RCAF dependents were housed in the 1950s - 60s - the 1 Wing PMQs at Longuyon, a few kilometers from the base. (Bill Turnbull Col.)

the other fellow's customs, traditions and operational capabilities. When 1 Squadron came to Baden, we would teach them curling, and our odd brand of hockey, with players each wearing one skate and one running shoe. This was a real hoot which everyone enjoyed immensely!

For one exchange, 441's pilots brought along their wives. To really impress us, the Germans took us out on a 33-meter sail boat, a thing of beauty with teak decks, which had belonged to Herman Goering before the war. A sail boat, on which the CO even had his ticket, was not as strange as one might think on a German squadron. After all, NAW pilots trained initially as sailors, before starting flying.

Family Life

No.1 Air Division and No.1 Canadian Air Group functioned in a half-forgotten age of "family values." Wives and children were officially tolerated, but not exactly welcomed. Single or childless women might work temporarily, but "working mothers" were practically unknown. Counselors sometimes advised wives that pilots should not be burdened with domestic worries when they came home, meaning that the overseas wife bore more responsibility, alone and in silence, than even her Canada-based counterpart.

With boyfriends, husbands and fathers often deployed, women drew together in their respective communities. The expression, "it takes a town to raise a child" had added meaning where family doctors were few and fleeting. Any woman who did not know how to drive was handicapped. Sandy Castledine, a veteran of two overseas tours, recalled that authorities seldom appreciated or thanked women for their contributions. Yet, when exchanges were on, and visiting personnel were to be welcomed, it was the military wives who organized the entertainment, prepared food for massive pot-luck dinners, and played gracious hostess. Meanwhile, the men partied, talked shop and, far too often, "got plastered". That the women were patronized and undervalued is demonstrated by a riddle posed in 441's historical record for August 1971: Q. What has a worn out body, red eyes, no co-ordination and an angry wife? A. A pilot after an exchange.

But there were perks, even for dependents. A European tour was not exactly a 30-month vacation but, in an age when trans-Atlantic air travel was still exotic, such a tour offered opportunities for weekend travel to cities founded before Columbus. Even pilots took 30-day leaves that permitted trips to Italy or Spain. Sandy Castledine recalled one time when her

Marville CF-104s on PR duty for Family Day at the USAFE base at Étain on May 24, 1965. Note all the folks plugging their ears as the recce '104 scorches past. Of these fighters 12757 (left) later went to Denmark, '737 went to Turkey, and '859 crashed in Holland. (David Huddleston Col., CF BS84-2193)

husband was deployed for 10 days to Sardinia. Rented off-base accommodation was available, since two enterprising NCOs had invested in a villa. Normally, families stayed home during "Sardinia Salvo", but Sandy managed to fly there and back with two small children aboard an RCAF Bristol Freighter. It was hardly luxurious, with uncomfortable seats and cargo strapped down everywhere. While the Bristol took five hours, Sabre and Starfighter pilots flew the same trip in 90 minutes. Fortunately, neither Sandy nor the children got airsick. Once there, the experience was marvelous:

> Every morning Brian would drive us to a beach, then go off to do his thing in airplanes. We were always the first to arrive but, when he picked us up at the end of the day, he would find us surrounded by Italians - not just spread out along the beach, but clustered in close to us. Our children were blonde, and these people, who were very dark, believed that blondes were especially lucky. They wanted to be near, even to touch the children to a degree that sometimes made me nervous.

Throughout the NATO years, service weddings were memorable affairs, with dress uniforms and flypasts. One such event is described in 441's May 1969 historical report: "The ceremony was executed in the bride's home town ... The boys, dressed in boards and belts, were ready with swords to form a guard outside the church but, when they came out, they found another guard already formed." This party, evidently skiing comrades of the bride, were dressed in T-shirts and raggedy jeans! In another 1969 case, as a new bride departed Lahr for Cold Lake, she was repeatedly warned by pranksters that she would have to get used to parkas and snow-shoes, and learn how to hook up a dog-team to mush to the corner grocery store.

If the RCAF made great demands on families, it did offer benefits that were impossible to measure. Twenty years after Canadian forces left Europe, former "service brats" (children who grew up on bases such as Lahr) maintain contacts and friendships forged in a world that was half-European, yet uniquely Canadian. Children were reared in cosmopolitan environments, not only mixing with Canadians of all descriptions, but with a host of Belgians, French, and Germans. Schools, following the Ontario curriculum, attracted highly motivated teachers, who competed for employment in Europe. Moreover, although a man's life revolved around his work, that career and its accessories could fascinate his offspring. On October 15, 1965 F/L Castledine wrote a newspaper item describing a visit by junior pupils to 1 Wing Operations:

> Out of the fog which shrouded 1 Wing last September 23rd charged over 600 school children, aged 5 to 8 years. Having escaped their routine of classroom activities, these refugees from PMQs were the guests of 439 and 441 Recce Squadrons, or more specifically, F/Ls Lowery and Castledine, who acted as talking encyclopedias, answering the barrage of questions put forth by the bug-eyed children.
>
> The onslaught started at 9. A.M. and continued uninterrupted, save an hour for lunch, until 3 P.M. when the last bus returned its load of newly educated Junior Schoolees to PMQs. During this time the children were invited to view the cockpit of the CF-104 and give its exterior a closer inspection. An engine mounted on a dolly was also present for their examination along with a parachute and oxygen mask. S/L Van Oene added to the atmosphere with a few high speed passes.
>
> A word of appreciation must be interjected here to our three dauntless bus drivers who made no less than thirteen round trips to PMQs during the operation.
>
> The school teachers who accompanied their classes to the display are all to be complimented on their organization and control of the children, which certainly assisted the two officers attending the aircraft. The children themselves were well behaved and asked a number of intelligent questions for their age. Indications that their visit was appreciated have been flowing into the squadrons in letter and painting form, i.e. "It was my very first look. I got a good look at the 104s." and "It is themendous how small the wings are. There are a lot

of buttons in it. I like everything about the plain ispecially the insection seet. It sure can go fast." (unabridged).

The squadron also appreciated the opportunity to stoke up the fires of a child's naturally inquisitive mind. Thank you for your interest; the pleasure was ours.

The *Arrowhead Tribune*, 1 Wing's magazine from Marville days, gives glimpses of service life as seen "on the line" and in the PMQs. A section headed "The Mart" offered cars, trailers and other items for sale, as personnel returned to Canada. The issue for August 31, 1965 included a 1961 Ford Falcon for $700, a 1964 Volkswagen with 55,000 miles on the clock - $1025, another with 34,000 miles - $950. The distances travelled by the two '64 "Beetles" in a year suggests something of their owners' passion of travelling Europe. In the same issue a Hoovermatic washer was offered at $60.00, a GE vacuum cleaner at $10.00, while bicycles were $2.00 - $5.00.

The *Arrowhead Tribune* for September 16, 1966 devoted space to a forthcoming curling season and the winding up of the years' golf tourneys. The same issue ran the program schedule for Canadian Forces radio programmes (5.30 p.m. to midnight four days a week, longer hours on Saturday, Sunday, and Monday). Included were recordings of CBC programs ("Assignment" and "Cross Canada Playhouse"), but a surprising number of programs were produced by the RCAF itself - "Air Division Kid's Show", "One Wing Teen Show", "Music From Marville", "Music From Metz", etc.

One thing that often bedevils civil-military relations is alcohol. On this topic authorities knew enough not to bank on Canadian self-restraint during the Cold War - some 60 RCAF Military Police at Lahr made that clear. A Lahr newspaper account of September 1967 noted, "Traffic offenses are punished by the Canadians very severely - more severely than by us." Other efforts, such as German-Canadian Friendship Clubs, promoted harmony. A July 1969 story described how a discarded telephone pole had been converted into a totem pole by Canadian students at Lahr's base school. Nevertheless, the matter of aircraft noise was routinely discussed throughout the period. One letter complained of "unbearable stress" caused by low-level Starfighters - civilian tolerance of military aircraft gradually eroded as the Cold War stagnated.

On the one hand it may be argued that the very presence of Canadian families at Lahr and Baden-Soellingen indicated how remote the Soviet threat was deemed to be. Even so, every Wing had a contingency plan for speedy evacuation of dependents to Canada, should war threaten. These plans included marshalling the commercial airlines. TacEvals included assessment of how well 1 CAG organizations were prepared to implement such plans.

Gerry Bayles and Rick Wilson of 441 escort school teachers on a Baden base tour. (David Huddleston Col., CF BS84-2193)

CHAPTER 15

Pulling up Stakes

Downsizing and Changing Roles

The mid-1960s coincided with chilling relations between France and NATO. President Charles de Gaulle was increasingly assertive of French sovereignty, and resented that the NATO nuclear weapons on French turf were under American control. He was determined that there should be no such weapons in France, other than those of his own force de frappe. This led to many NATO units moving elsewhere.

Tensions with the Canadians were understated in Europe, but they still were present. De Gaulle promoted Quebec sovereignty in international affairs, for which he was criticized by Ottawa, especially after his infamous "Vive le Quebec libre" speech in July 1967. Strategy and politics, therefore, meant that 1 Wing must leave Marville and 1 Air Division HQ leave Metz. For the Silver Foxes, moving day was March 28, 1967. Lahr, Germany would be their the new home. A key figure during this operation was 441 CO, W/C Jim Dunlop. His superior, G/C Robert G. Christie, subsequently wrote on July 14, 1967:

> Based on past personal experience with this officer, I selected him in February for the overall planning and conduct of the advance party on the relocation to Lahr. In every respect W/C Dunlop demonstrated my confidence in him was warranted. Since the time for the move was very short (less than one month) and impossible communications made it essential for him to use his excellent background and judgment as his guide, except for infrequent contact, he was on his own. The move required extensive contact with reticent French senior officers under exasperating conditions. Nevertheless, W/C Dunlop showed remarkable restraint, a high degree of diplomacy and, above all, was thoroughly successful. He spent long hours in arranging for improved messing and recreational facilities for the airmen and this, combined with his personal example of devotion to duty, encouraged the men to achieve previously unheard of goals. With the final move of the wing to Lahr in April, W/C Dunlop then became OC Rear Party and, again, demonstrated exceptional ability in dealing with innumerable problems associated with over 1000 families separate from their husbands and fathers.

The move to Lahr was memorable for all concerned. In the preceding weeks Marville wives had been proceeding with "Operation Manless", keeping the community running to the last minute. Domestic tasks became more complex, e.g. the wing laundry closed in early March and a Metz contractor was substituted. To help families with house hunting, primers were printed in German, e.g. phrases like "Furnished", "Unfurnished" and "Living Room" became "Mobeliert", "Unmobeliert" and "Wohenzimmer". Before departing, the Canadians made the rounds of the local villages they had frequented, and many a tearful farewell was made. Totem poles, carved by Chief Simon Baker of Vancouver, were presented to Virton, Belgium and Longuyon, France. At a March 10 mess dinner Chief Baker became an honorary Silver Fox.

Good action at Marville as '737 lands. (Bill Van Oene Col.)

On the day appointed for the move, a convoy headed out, every vehicle packed to capacity. German border officials waved them through ' no one remembered any car being inspected. However, the arrival at Lahr was fraught with difficulties. Although 1 Wing had been hurried out of Marville, its new quarters remained occupied by French forces and their dependents, who had been stationed there for years under former postwar Occupation agreements. Because they were on foreign soil, so thereby drawing extra pay, the French military was in no hurry to go. Photo tech Vic Johnson recalls this era:

Our new barracks were decrepit, unheated, there was no hot water and holes in the concrete floor served as toilets. W/C Dunlop reacted by "hitting the ceiling", then he stormed off to do battle with the French base commander. Soon we had improved quarters.

We immediately began preparing for the arrival of 439 and 441. Since the French Air Force still occupied the base, however, we were allotted only one dispersal area, or "marguerite". We soon had the place operational and 439 was first to show up. It immediately refuelled and flew several sorties. Thus, photo recce didn't skip a beat between Marville and Lahr.

Meanwhile, trucks were rolling in around the clock from France, and being unloaded at all hours by the same people running flying operations. There was a bit of a setback in July, when the French ordered all Canadians occupying Lahr married quarters to vacate the premises. Camping trailers and tents were the only options until autumn, when more permanent accommodations were available. Happily, there was good weather in the meanwhile.

We Canadians adapted quickly to Bavaria. The weather was better than in northern France, and the local people soon realized that we were not the bunch of drunken lumberjacks that a French disinformation campaign had led them to fear. We were welcomed and would enjoy many years of outstanding German hospitality in one of the most wonderful regions of Europe.

The 1 Wing memorial totem pole at Longuyon. (Bill Turnbull Col.)

In late 1969 more changes were in the wind as the Liberal government prepared to downsize Canada's military. Ottawa's feeling was that Europe now was militarily capable enough to get by without Canada. Besides, Ottawa felt, NATO had too much influence over the years on Canadian foreign policy. Meanwhile, France was becoming impatient with Starfighter missions over its territory, particularly when a pilot departed from his flight plan. On March 3, 1970 five CF-104s had just taken off for Moulins, when controllers informed them that they were not cleared to fly in France and must leave. The historical report noted: "We complied. Evidently the violations accumulated, and variations from flight plans incurred during recce hi-lo-hi mission profiles in three years, have finally disturbed the French military in Paris, who ordered their radars to reject Canadian hi-lo-hi flights. Our flying liberty in France had been virtually unlimited ... and [this was] too good to last." It was no great surprise when Ottawa announced that 422, 427 and 430 squadrons would disband. Lahr would close as an operational wing, and its recce squadrons relocate to Baden-Soellingen, joining 421 Squadron there. A March 19, 1971 memo headed "Last Recce Pilots on 441 Squadron" lists LCol Bruce Burgess, Majs Pete Caws, Ken McLeod and Red Morris, and Capts Keith Adlard, Jim Cratchley, Marc Dumontet, Rod Ellis, Terry Elphick, Bobby Joe Hart, Sky King, George Kirbyson, Neal Kleinsteuber, Dan Orr, Charlie Paul, Jim Pfaff, Herb Sievert, and Lts Gord DeJong and Ron Doyle.

The new plan was that 439 would continue in recce, while 421 and 441 would fly nuclear strike. In 441's case this became effective on May 1, 1970. In a kind of recce denouement Capts B.J. Hart (441), George Kirbyson (441) and Guy Fabi (439) were 1 CAG's 1970 Royal Flush pilots, Sky King being the team training officer.

On July 1, No.1 Air Division disbanded and was replaced by No.1 Canadian Air Group, part of newly-established CFB Europe. On the same day 422 and 427 squadrons disbanded, leaving 441 as a composite of 422, 427, 430 and 441. "The CAG" now comprised 439 (ST/R), 421 (ST/A) and 441 (ST/A). Further change came with a government White Paper of August 1971 announcing that Canada finally had negotiated its way clear of nuclear commitments. The last CF-104 nuclear alert was held on December 31, 1971. As of January 1, 1972, 441 and 421 assumed a conventional weapons attack role. With the new job came a fresh round of training, pilots returning to Cold Lake for a conventional course. This included the Vulcan cannon, which was fitted into all single-seat CF-104s. Reflecting on these changes, *Der Kanadier* reported on January 6, 1972:

On the surface, the change in role will not be too apparent. The skies of Baden will continue to resound with the inimitable whine/howl of the Starfighter, and 421 and 441 Squadron personnel will remain unchanged. There will, however, be significant differences. The USAF personnel of Detachment 3, whose responsibility it would have been to assist Canadian Forces in their nuclear strike role, will leave Baden shortly, greatly missed by all individuals and sections fortunate enough to have known them. The alert system known as QRA will disappear, and along with it some of the better-known Baden institutions as Fleetfoot and, and course, the QRA dogs, bywords in ferocity.

("QRA" was the Quick Response Alert, which had been associated with nuclear capability. Detachment 3 was the USAF agency providing immediate oversight of the "nukes". The Americans had always exercised tight control over the storage of these devices to the extent that, if armed with them, aircraft were virtually immobilized until a real war erupted. A Starfighter carrying an A-bomb could not even be towed, unless cleared from the highest NATO level.)

When 1 CAG adopted the conventional attack role, there was much experimentation in tactics. All NATO air forces were involved, with much attention given to America's Vietnam experience. The problem was to determine what was applicable from that theatre. It was agreed that low-level flying was still the most suitable tactic for Europe but, now that the potential target was an armoured division and the weapon an iron bomb, the lone Starfighter would give way to the 8-plane, mass attack. These could be broken down into 2-ship elements, usually paired line abreast in battle formation for double attacks and mutual support. Whether "double attack" was realistic can be argued, as it needed almost constant radio contact between aircraft. That might not be possible in a war with simultaneous communications saturation and jamming. Meanwhile, the conventional role meant loading a CF-104 with ordnance (not external fuel tanks), so range was traded for bombs. Maj Bob Endicott described the mass attacks as being "a lot of fun, but a lot of work". On such an exercise, participating squadrons took off from Baden (sometimes also from Lahr), then followed timed routes to target. Only after the attack would they merge into a big formation to sweep over the target that they had just (theoretically) clobbered.

Army Co-op

"Conventional" re-organization thrust 1 CAG into more intimate contact with Canada's NATO land forces 4 Canadian Mechanized Brigade Group at Lahr. This worried the army, which had moved in the late 1960s from north Germany to communities around Lahr that looked upon the military a bit more suspiciously. The troops were also now on bases where air force culture flourished. While 4 CMBG saw airfields with immense vehicle parking capacity, the air force saw army equipment as a source of FOD (foreign object damage). Along with the organizational shuffles, 4 CMBG lost its newspaper, The Beaver. Now, the airforce-dominated *Der Kanadier* seemed to run a different cartoon every week ribbing the army.

CF-104s sometimes flew exercises with 4 CMBG, perhaps supporting it, perhaps opposing it. In September 19-24, 1971 came Ex. Gutes Omen, the first major German exercise involving 4 CMBG after its move south. "The CAG" flew about 70 sorties per day, "enemy" airfields being attacked by formations of 12 to 20 CF-104s, but an army history describes "Gutes Omen" without mentioning the air element. In its 1979 historical report, 441 noted its work in Ex. Certain Sentinel (January 30 ' February 7) as "Close Air Support missions in support of Army Corps throughout Central and Southern Germany." Units of 4 CMBG played an "invading" (enemy) role. Ex. Coldfire, staged almost yearly, also saw CF-104s attacking ground targets. Apart from the flying, "Coldfire" drills checked on how well units communicated with each other and with higher command ("lateral and vertical command experience", as 1 CAG HQ called it). One of the more detailed accounts was submitted by 1 CAG for "Coldfire 84" of September 13 - 28: "This annual flying exercise forms the air contribution to the 'Army Reforger' series of exercises, and contributes significantly to 1 CAG training. 1 CAG aircrew flew missions against realistic targets in both the Battlefield Air Interdiction role and the Close Air Support role. The opportunity to exercise wartime procedures in conjunction with army formations is a key element of this NATO exercise." ("Reforger" stood for "Return of Forces to Germany" and included reinforcement of European-based formations from North America.)

While many exercises differed only in detail, others were conducted according to complex scripts. Ex Certain Sentinel, for example, proceeded according to a "Reforger" scenario. Other exercises were distinctly air-oriented. Ex. Datex of April 11 - 13, 1978 was a series of simulated air attacks on France, testing its air defences. Capt Bob Endicott logged three "Datex" sorties (3.4 hours) on April 12, typical for 441 pilots. Unhappily, the 1970s witnessed closer budgeting of resources. Paperwork seemed to be growing more complex, and accountants more miserly. A sign of the times was an entry in 441's historical report for March 1970:

> As the fiscal year draws to a close, we were told on the 18th that only 90 hours per squadron remained until April. The flying program became pitifully small until only Gord DeJong and chase pilot were flying, aside from the Royal Flush people, who got 30 hours from the General. At this time Air Division made a panic decision curtailing all flying to non-USAF and non-Canadian bases due to fuel bills. The next day the Comptroller-General discovered that the information upon which the General had acted was erroneous, but the decision held to the end of the month. Trips to Turkey and Greece (several), after many hours of planning and being diplomatically cleared, were cancelled. It's beginning to be difficult to "grin and bear it."

Policy Changes

Years after his career as a 441 recce pilot, Bill Turnbull analyzed the way in which Ottawa abandonned its NATO recce commitment and shrank 1 CAG to a nearly effete operation:

> Shortly after Pierre Trudeau became Prime Minister, he initiated a comprehensive review of defence and foreign policy. We worked hard to sell our presence in Europe, but had the feeling that no arguments were going to affect the predetermined outcome. The Europeans may have had the same feeling. I recall one visit by the NATO parliamentarians, when the Dutch representative, during his address, burst into tears and pleaded for Canada to remain in Europe. Dutch experience arising out of WWII presumably lay behind this outburst.
>
> I was told that a Canadian parliamentary delegation left Europe convinced that Canada should maintain the status quo. Its chairman reportedly showed a certain duplicity in submitting a report which ran counter to the group's agreed position.
>
> Regardless of what might have made sense at the time, Canada chose to reduce its commitment and to co-locate the Army Brigade Group with the Air Division in southern Germany. The air component reduction was advertised as 50%, i.e. from six squadrons to three, but squadron UE (unit effectiveness) was reduced at the same time. Consequently, the immediately available forces in theatre fell from 108 aircraft to 36, which was more like a two-thirds reduction.

Bill Turnbull of 441 took this photo, showing the magnificent view over the Alps that amazed Sabre and Starfighter pilots for many years as they passed to and from Deci. Flying '808 this day was Chris Harvey-Clark of 430 Squadron.

Canada also stated its intention to get out of the nuclear strike business. Our staff officers at 4 ATAF recommended making the remaining squadrons all fighter bomber. This meant an end to the recce role, and was stupid for several reasons. Firstly, it meant abandoning the hard-won expertise of our pilots and PIs. Secondly, it had the effect of getting the Canadian air force out of the reconnaissance business, a shortcoming that persists to this day. Thirdly, it greatly increased the cost of doing business, since all of the CF-104s had to be retrofitted with the 20mm cannon, and weapons stocks had to be acquired for three, rather than, say, two squadrons.

Frankly, I was never surprised at the recommendations of our own people, who were all day fighter-turned-strike pilots for whom reconnaissance was not a manly activity. I have never been able to figure out who they thought was going to provide them with their targeting information. If you ask that question today, you will still get a blank stare. History shows that inferior forces, armed with superior intelligence, often won battles. If people ignore the lessons of history, does that mean they haven't read history or can't read?

Diary Snippets ' 1971 Squadron Log

In the early 1970s diary keeping at 441 was in decline. The only daily record seems to have been a hand-written log, in which any fellow might scratch a few comments. These 1971 excerpts (in italics) tell something of squadron life, although it is not always easy to decipher handwriting or cryptic references:

January 21 *Morning trumpet at 0445Z hrs. Exercise time! Set up the a/c and stand by. Wx WOXOF, revert to 15 min. alert. Wx pickin' up, back to cockpit alert. Wx goin' down and runway pretty slick. Back to 15 min. scramble. LCol Oxholm [421 Sqn] led 7-plane attack on Soellingen air base.*

January 26 *Met briefing 0615Z. Routes, plus one 4-plane. Best, Heathe, O'Brien, Bartram. Great armed recce mission. 4-plane box fly-past at Memmingen, then individual conventional attacks on Memmingen air base at the request of Memmingen Ops. 3 or 4 passes each ' watch the Mach!*

January 27 *A dazzling dissertation on 104 hydraulic systems and sundry other items presented by our newly-elected (?) full-time Ops officer, Stanley Mooers. Maximum squadron attendance was acquired, no sweat... Walt Ludey and Eric Thurston round flag to Lakenheath.*

February 2 *Met briefing CAV-OK. A/c forecast ... what aircraft? Worked with max of 4 birds all day. 11 sorties, shut down at 1730, very disgruntled. Maybe tomorrow!*

February 4 *Top Gun 1971. Merv brought us in at 0530Z for briefing. Guess what the wx is? A/c? 4 with dispensers, 2 without + 6 for Top Gun. 0830Z ' Top Gun 1971 cancelled until March 26. After some discussion by all strike pilots ... decided that the 7 a/c would be split 441 - 421. Wx deteriorated ... with advice from "Sputnik" and "Frau Baker" decided to shut 'er down for the day. All 441 pilots retired to the bar.*

February 26 *Kurv got out of T-33s by taking Maj Holmes to Prestwick... Nite flying till 1900Z, then shut 'er down by downing a few brew with the line servicing boys.*

March 2 *Snowball. LCol Ox wasn't too happy when his efforts to launch 421 Sqn just before the alert came to a grinding halt when one of his fellers on the first launch took the barrier and closed the runway for one hour. (April 6-8 all aircraft were grounded for a special inspection on the wings, then came Easter weekend, so flying did not recommence until April 13.)*

April 14 *Alert recommenced 0645Z, wx CAV-OK. Mass launch 0715Z, alert terminated 1015Z. Squadron continued flying during*

Some 1971 Silver Foxes: Gord Ball, Jack McLean, Carl Stef, John David, Don Paxton, Rick Parent, Bill Bain and Larry O'Brien. Then, squadron members at Baden-Soellingen in the spring of 1974. Standing are mission planning Cpls Bob Schell and John Mansfield, then Capts John Croll, Wally Wright, Jim Maurstad, Dave Bligh, Bill Card, Laurie Hawn, Clark Little, Bruce Stott, Gus Youngson and Ted Lee. In front are Capt Tom Henry, Maj John Glover, Capts Dave Burroughs and Joe Molnar, LCol Don Myles, Maj Clancy Sheldrup, Capt Jack Orr and Maj Bob Kadonoff. (Larry O'Brien and Don Myles Cols.)

afternoon. Bob Kadonoff and Al French successfully completed their TacEvals, so they can go into the Q at 1530Z.

April 20 *Brief 0545Z, wx CAV-OK, on state 0645Z. Highlight of the day was a 20-plane attack on Diepholz/SLN 008/230 nm. (The diary reveals that in this period, although 441 was in the nuclear role, it was also flying conventional strike training missions.)*

April 22 *Guess which squadron set the range on fire ' 421 clanks another one! After taxing the sqn's flexibility in scheduling to the maximum, we finally got two sqn 4-plane sections for bombing at Suippes ... the Pussy Cats got to and from the range, but you can sure tell they weren't strike trained!*

April 23 *Stan Mooers and Carl Stef off to Deci, Gibraltar for the weekend. Ray Dunsdon and Larry B. (T-33) diverted to Ramstein in the morning as Soellingen was closed for 45 min. when Don Slimman went off the east side of Runway 04. No damage. Postings are coming in: Choppers Dale Anderson 408 Edmonton, Stan Mooers 427 Petawawa; CF-104 Ray Dunsdon 417 Cold Lake, Dave Bartram 417 Cold Lake; desk man Maj Dobson ADC HQ North Bay. (For a pilot leaving the CAG in this period, the flying postings offered might not suit his ambitions. As Stan Mooers recalled in 2003, his options included instructing at 417 in Cold Lake, at 2 FTS in Moose Jaw, or in the US on T-37s, or doing something different ' helicopters. He wasn't keen on instructing, so opted for the latter. It was a decision that he never regretted. He was proud to be associated with 427 with its famous reputation from wartime, Sabre and CF-104 days.)*

April 30 *Section to Suippes 0800Z, conventional section frag, FAC mission. Another section to Suippes at 1100Z. "Bullseye" Best dropped two laydown shacks and, not to be outdone, "Hat Trick" Heathe did the same. Quit flying at 1200Z. All pilots to Beer Bust at 1300Z.*

May 10 *14 a/c on the line. Launched all aircraft including 2 duals, with re-launches on most before 1100Z. LCol Wightman is back and selling Mirage a/c to anyone who is interested. Apparently, he and the group who went to Paris to visit Dassault, were wined and dined and treated in royal fashion.*

May 25 *Maj Bain's ground training program recommenced: gruntmobile recognition, defensive driving movie. Three visitors from 4 ATAF gave an informative briefing on ECM.*

May 26 *Stan Mooers and Dale Anderson 1000 hrs 104 time. Good show!*

June 2 *Still not getting near enough a/c. Maj Young seems to be appearing with frequent repetition around the squadron (2 trips today, even a nite trip). Keen to fly and looking forward to his new job as sqn boss. Col Wightman's off to Lahr to have tea with the General.*

June 24 *Plenty of aerodynes, even OpsO flew. Paxton heads for Italy and promptly violates French airspace ' flight plan screwed up. Walt finally finishes semi-annual T-33 requirements. (A stag that night left many a 441 driver with a sore head the next morning. Little flying was done, allowing 421 to start its schedule a bit early. The final comment on the 25th was, "All Foxes looking forward to "Schoolies Beer Call", so back they went at it right away! The "schoolies" were the 1 Wing teaching staff, which always included some single girls. No bachelor fighter pilot in his right mind would miss a "schoolies" bash.*

July 5 *Ops ' Kadonoff, wx CAV-OK in haze. 7 singles, 1 dual. After the first launch the fleet rapidly diminished. Quit flying early so we would have a/c for flypast during the handover ceremony. At 1500 local LCol Young took over from LCol Wightman in a dazzling ceremony including a 9-plane flypast.*

July 20 *No flying. Squadron baseball game with 421. At the end of the 7th the score was 12 all. Due to a fluke of luck 421 scored 1 more run to win the game. A rematch is definitely in the wind.*

July 23 *Dave Burroughs experienced compressor stall and was forced to punch out approx. 45 nm NE of base. Fell out of his tree on landing.*

August 9 *BX at Siegenberg and conventional training. The newees [Capt Sheldrup, Lt Bligh] are into phase training with routes and formations. The troops going [on exchange] to Leuchars are completing last minute planning.*

Another great 441 scene. Stan Mooers leads with Larry O'Brien on his left wing, Dave Anderson outside and Eric Thurston nearest. (Larry O'Brien Col.)

CHAPTER 16

Flight Safety

Squadron Losses

Flight safety was hammered into all CF-104 students. Nice as it was to fly, their new machine was a handful, especially in its low-level environment. One manual, under the heading "Critical Emergencies", stressed that, should a grave emergency arise, action had to be taken "immediately and instinctively, without reference to written check lists". Unfortunately, in spite of constant safety training, 441 would lose some pilots over the years. F/O Jerry Holmes struck a house during a January 18, 1968 low level photo mission. The telegram sent to his father by AFHQ had echoes of wartime communications:

> Deeply regret to confirm information already conveyed to you by Flight Lieutenant Walsh Protestant Chaplain Forces Winnipeg that your son 605 043 389 (86429) Flying Officer Jeremy Wayne Holmes was killed as a result of an aircraft accident 15 miles west of Gent in Belgium at approximately 10.30 A.M. local Belgium time on 18 January 1968. As Canadian Government policy prohibits remains or ashes being shipped to Canada internment will be in the Royal Canadian Air Force Cemetery, Choloy, France. Details of funeral arrangements will follow immediately they are received. Please accept my deepest sympathy.

On April 3 1968 Capt Ronald C. Archibald, a 14-year veteran of the Regular force, flew into a hill during a low-level recce. The preliminary report summed it up: "This man was the pilot of a CF-104 which crashed into a hillside while making a final run on target. The apparent cause of the accident is reported to be restricted visibility. There was no evidence of an attempt at ejection, and no report of an in-flight emergency."

Born in 1936, Archibald joined the Air Cadets at age 14. From May 1953 to September 1954, while at Mount Allison University, he was associated with the reserves. Having joined the Regular force, he trained on the CF-100, serving on 425 Squadron. A tour followed at Air Defence Command HQ. In 1964 he took a refresher flying course at Portage la Prairie, then attended STU and 6 OTU. In June 1965 he joined 441, where his non-flying interests included being the Entertainment Officer in the Officers Mess, coaching children's hockey, dabbling in military history, travel, amateur radio, and automobiles. As of December 1967 this experienced pilot had flown CF-100s (1045 hours), C-45s (126), T-33s (794), Sabres (64) and CF-104s (662). For 1967 he logged 248 hours on CF-104s, 23 on T-33s. His last assessment, written on August 14, 1967 by his flight commander, S/L E.W. Gardiner, is telling:

F/L Ron Archibald, then Starfighter '740, in which he was lost. Archibald's widow subsequently donated a trophy in her late husband's memory, to be presented to 441's top pilot in "Royal Flush". (Bill Turnbull Col., Canadair 30710)

During the reporting period F/L Archibald has proven himself to be an above average pilot. He demonstrated this by his high standing in the 1967 Royal Flush reconnaissance competition.

He has always shown a willingness to give his full support to any squadron or station venture. During our move from Marville to Lahr it was necessary to institute a self-help program to make our present facilities livable. F/L Archibald was always ready and willing to undertake any task large or small.

He is considerate and goes out of his way to help the younger pilots on the squadron. He was recently appointed Deputy Flight Commander on my flight. In this capacity he has proven himself to be a capable and willing assistant.

F/L Archibald is a happily married man, and he and his wife are enjoying their European tour. They are both good ambassadors of Canada. He is definitely recommended for promotion.

On the same day the squadron CO, W/C J.F. Dunlop, wrote:

F/L Archibald is a first class officer and pilot who turns his hand to any task, often without being assigned and can be relied upon to do a good job. He is forever offering his services to people with problems, service or otherwise and, because of this trait, has more contact with airmen than many other pilots. He has proven to be steady and reliable, with a flair for social activities. He is particularly well-liked by his fellows. He is ready for promotion."

Adding to the praise, Base Commander G/C R.G. Christie noted on August 28:

Fully concur. F/L Archibald promotes harmony in any group with which he comes in contact and, in addition to his Service duties, has been most active in Wing youth programs. I consider this officer to be a part of a small group of superior young officers whom I can always depend on for support of most difficult assignments. Well qualified and highly recommended for promotion.

Lt Roman "Ron" Fetchyshyn struck the top of a hill on November 6, 1969, ejecting a fraction of a second too late. Apparently, he had been crossing a valley, rather than using the standard procedure of following its course, while searching for his target (a shack which was also a turning point). Born in 1946 in Hamburg to Polish refugees. Fetchyshyn's family emigrated to Canada. The young man joined the RCAF in January 1967. Like Holmes, he was a "pipeliner" - 441 was his first operational unit. Following survival training, he was described as "A cheerful enthusiastic worker who put a lot of effort into the course". At Cold Lake, following a slow start, he routinely exceeded minimum course requirements.

The death of Lt Fetchyshyn was poignant. His father, more fluent in Polish than English, came to Lahr, anxious to bring his son back to Canada. LCol Bruce Burgess had to explain that government policy did not permit this, and he recalled the older man's grief and disappointment about this. Mr. Fetchyshyn subsequently visited the cemetery at Choloy several times and endowed the mess with several gifts. Lt Fetchyshyn was the last 441 member buried abroad in accordance with DND policy, which had stood for decades. So long as air travel and transport were difficult, and so long as foreign cemeteries, supervised by the Commonwealth War Graves Commission, ensured proper maintenance of graves, the system had been workable.

For several years, however, Michael Forrestall, Conservative Member of Parliament for Halifax, had been quietly campaigning for the repatriation of Canadian military casualties. His campaign had become more pointed following a disastrous fire aboard HMCS *Kootenay*, after which some men had been buried at sea and others in Britain. It was also becoming evident that, as Canadians played "peace keepers" in some of the most dismal of global backwaters, it would become increasingly difficult to ensure the dignity of graves abroad. Without fanfare, the Canadian forces adopted the policy of casualty repatriation in the early 1970s. (See House of Commons *Debates* for October 28 and November 4, 1969. On December 15 Minister of National Defence Leo Cadieux stated that casualties abroad for all services included: 1956 - 38, 1960 - 33, 1964 - 25 and 1969 - 27. All had been buried abroad with the exception of 27 at sea, 25 whose bodies were not recovered, nine who died in the United States and were returned to Canada, and one serviceman drowned in England and returned to Canada for burial owing to "an administrative error.")

The last Silver Fox fatality was Maj Gerald L.A. Hermanson. His career also reflected much of the postwar air force experience. Born in Saskatoon in July 1941, he had joined the RCAF in October 1960, training as a radio navigator. He flew in Maritime Command (405 Squadron), logging 2625 hours in the Argus, plus time in Neptunes and RAF Shackletons. He remustered to pilot, qualifying for his flying badge in March 1969, then he instructed at Gimli. After four years, Hermanson progressed to Starfighters. By this time the STU was defunct, students now beginning with a fighter lead-in course on the CF-5. Hermanson logged about 100 CF-5 hours, then passed easily through the CF-104 course. He was promoted to major while on course, then joined 441, but his arrival posed some problems. As one superior observed, "Major Hermanson is new both as a major and in tactical flying operations." He was not initially assigned tasks commensurate with his rank. Nevertheless, Hermanson's proficiency as an instructor, plus his staff skills, enabled LCol D. Myles to find a niche for him. In March 1975 Myles wrote:

Major Hermanson is a Training and Standardization Officer on 441 Squadron and in this capacity he is responsible for ensuring that all training commitments are carried out, that training records are accurate and up to date, and that standard flying procedures are employed by all squadron personnel. In addition, he is required to maintain a progressive level of personal efficiency in the CF-104 attack role.

In the five months that Major Hermanson has been on squadron he has completed his indoctrination training and will in the near future commence upgrade training to element lead status. This training has been conducted in the less-than-ideal European weather environment and with the added difficulty of an imposed flying time reduction. Despite this and the recognized fact that CF-104 attack operations in Europe is the most demanding flying role in the Canadian Forces, his background and flying ability have enabled him to progress favourably in this role. There is every indication that, as further experience in this role is acquired, he will continue to develop into an above average attack pilot.

Major Hermanson has demonstrated that he has the knowledge and interest that is necessary to successfully carry out his duties in Training and Standardization. These duties have been completed in an above average fashion and I believe that, with his Training Command background and with further experience on squadron, his contribution in the area of squadron supervision will also be of an above average level.

This officer has a congenial nature, and he and his wife are active participants in all squadron and mess social functions. In summary, Major Hermanson is a capable officer who has the potential that will allow him, with further experience in the CF-104 attack role, to become a valuable asset to the squadron.

On the morning of February 12, 1976, during a low level radar navigation training mission in adverse weather, Hermanson crashed fatally into a hill. His loss was keenly felt, especially since he left behind a wife and four children.

Choloy Cemetery near Meurthe-et-Moselle, France, where some 323 postwar RCAF/CF members and dependents lie at rest. The earliest burial among them appears to have been that of LAC J.C.A.G. Furois, a tech on 413 Squadron, whose funeral was on May 8, 1953. Also in Choloy are some 59 Canadian airmen lost during WWII. (441 Sqn)

"UAV" Starfighter

In September 2003 Larry O'Brien described a 4-ship 441 training mission that returned to base missing one Starfighter:

On July 23, 1971 I was conducting a Section Lead standards check. The mission included Capt Gord Ball #1, Capt Eric Thurston #2, Capt Dave Burroughs #4, with myself #3. We briefed, departed on Runway 22, joined up over the Schwarzwald, then set course eastbound at 450 knots and 1500 feet AGL. When Gord called for it, we eased out into 2-element battle formation. Just then, however, Dave reported a problem. I immediately closed up on him, but he was losing speed and altitude. As we passed below 300 knots, I put on take-off flap. Dave was still clean and I noticed his aircraft (104804) go into "kicker" a couple of times. He radioed that he suspected a compressor stall.

At 900 feet AGL I ordered Dave to bail out. At that moment, as I sat just off his right wing, his canopy flew off, followed immediately by Dave at the end of the blazing plume of his rocket seat. This was my cue to back away to a safe distance. I now directed Gord to climb and transmit the Mayday, and Eric to spot for Dave's chute, as I watched for the wreckage. Then came a surprise - '804 now was accelerating away. As I lit the burner to catch up, I realized that its engine had re-lit and was in full "mil" power. I formed up on '804, which was at 800 feet, right wing 10° down, nose about 5° down, speed 500 knots and on a course towards a village about five miles ahead.

At this time I recalled stories of Tempest pilots tipping the wings of V-1 "Buzz Bombs" during WWII to knock them off course, but this idea faded as we fell below 200 feet at 580 knots. We hurtled by the village at 50 feet. I moved to a safer distance, just in time to see Dave's aircraft hit the roof of an old garage on the edge of town, then crash in an open field. Just before impact I had rolled inverted to observe the most spectacular fireball I had ever seen. At the same instant I heard Eric's comment - "Holy sheepshit!". I couldn't have put it better myself.

After a slow recce pass over the village to spot for other damage, I got my flight back together and we returned to base. As soon as the Base Commander, Col Kaufman, had debriefed us, we proceeded to the Mess for therapy. Meanwhile, Dave was taken to the base hospital for inspection. His injuries were minor - a compression fracture to the back. We were so pleased at this that we headed for the hospital, carried Dave out on his mattress, deposited him on the Mess bar, and had him buy us a round. He was not impressed by all this, so we eventually carried him back to hospital.

Happily, no one was injured when Dave's Starfighter crashed. Later we heard that some damages were paid to a farmer for crop damage. That reminded me an a common saying in West Germany in those days - "If you would like your own F-104, just buy a hectare of land and wait. One is bound to drop in sooner or later." The accident investigation later determined that '804 had suffered a compressor stall. The procedure in such a case was to retard the throttle to the engine shut-down position, then push it to "full military" power, while hitting the ignition switches. Dave would have done all this, but didn't have the altitude to wait around for the results.

The last time I saw Dave, he was flying by the CNE grandstand inverted at about 550 knots during the Toronto airshow. I've got to tell you, it brought a tear to my eye.

There were at least six instances of Silver Foxes escaping after trouble developed. The first was F/L "Sky" King. During a Baltic recce off the Danish coast on July 18, 1967 his Starfighter swallowed a bird and lost power. In a flash King knew that he had to get out. A Danish Sea King helicopter, piloted by Ova Steele, an officer who had been on the same Wings course as King, effected his rescue 25 minutes later. The next incident involved CF-104D 104663. Following engine failure on October 7, 1970, both occupants (Maj William Bain, Capt L. O'Brien) ejected. The squadron historical report describes their adventure:

While on a normal training mission under the control of a Forward Air Controller, '663 was commencing a fourth pass at a conventional target in the neighbourhood of Darmstadt, when the engine was observed to run down. Air starts were attempted without success and Larry O'Brien bailed out of the rear seat first. Following his ejection, Major Bain observed that he should pull up to avoid hitting a town and, after doing so, he also bailed out successfully. The aircraft impacted on the side of a hill and no one was injured in the

The J79 and other pieces of Sky King's CF-104 (ejection seat included) after being dredged from the Baltic Sea. Then, Sky with his rescuer, Ova Steele. (Sky King Col.)

Bain and O'Brien receive souvenir "D" rings from safety systems tech, MCpl Rita Patry. (CF-BS71-197)

Strange sights over the village of Rueck, West Germany on October 7, 1970. Below left, smoke rises after 104663 crashed, then Maj Bill Bain parachutes to earth. He and Capt Larry O'Brien had to get out when a throttle control failed. A local farmer snapped the photos. (Larry O'Brien Col.)

area. Larry O'Brien strained his back a little on the ejection and Major Bain received a few minor scratches. Both pilots were returned to Soellingen via helicopter in relatively good spirits. It was later determined that a malfunction had occurred with respect to the main fuel control unit, causing the aircraft to lose power.

This prang was followed on December 11, 1974 by the loss of 104715 after what likely was a catastrophic bird strike. Thus did Capt G. Youngson join 441's "Conscientious Ejectors". In September 2003 Larry Crabb recalled another such event:

In August of 1980 I led an 8-plane of CF-104s headed for a 441 Squadron exchange with the 32 TFS at Soesterberg, Netherlands. There it was great to experience to fly in the F-15s and exchange ideas and tactics with our USAF counterparts. While on this deployment, on August 27 I led a 4-plane bombing mission to the Vliehors air-to-ground range near Terschelling on the North Sea. At some point while I was downwind on a 100-foot, level-bombing run at 540 knots. Just as Rob Porter (#3) was about to pickle his bomb, I heard the tower exclaim that something had come off Rob's Starfighter. At the same moment, I saw his aircraft disintegrate as it hit the water.

I instructed the other two aircraft to orbit high, as I rolled in and overflew the crash site. I was almost sick with despair as I reported to the tower that I saw nothing. Meanwhile, the tower advised that a Dutch rescue helicopter was inbound. It was a very long couple of minutes waiting, as they searched. Then, to our great relief, we heard, "They've got him!" I yelled, "How is he?" After a pause, came word that the chopper crew thought he was OK - they had him aboard and

Several CF-104s were damaged and a few lost after low level bird strikes. In this case it was the CF-104 that came out the winner after an altercation. (CF 77-0305-9)

he was cussing like mad! It was unbelievable that Rob had been able to get into the rescue harness by himself. He was aboard the helicopter six minutes after the crash bell sounded, and being rushed to hospital in Leeuwarden.

The ejection had shredded Rob's flying suit, and dislocated one arm. He was bruised all over, especially from the parachute harness, which left ugly blue welts. Otherwise, air blasting under his visor had snapped his helmet back, cracking his skull and cutting his chin. Rob soon was medivaced by Hercules to our hospital in Lahr, and soon

Maj Rob Porter, who ejected from 104859 on August 27, 1980. (CF BS79-357)

104865 after Dave Trask's dicey landing. After a stint in the repair shop, it survived its 1 CAG days to fly with the Turks. Then, Capt Trask being hosed down on the occasion of his 1000th CF-104 hour. (441 Sqn)

was back with us at 441. Meanwhile, 1 CAG was able to dredge sufficient parts from the sea to determine what had happened. A leading edge flap had come off Rob's aircraft on the run-in at 540 knots, causing an extreme rate of roll. Rob thinks he pulled the ejection handles as he was going inverted and ended up coming out on the top of the rotation. Until the case was closed and NDHQ was satisfied that this was a one-time incident, we were restricted to 450 knots.

In a final 441 prang, on June 16, 1983 Capt G.W. "Gerry" Bayles, was struck by a ricochet during a weapons exercise in 104830. The shell was ingested by his engine, resulting in a compressor stall and in Bayles ejecting.

Not all incidents meant bailing out. On December 4, 1969, Capt Willy Floyd hit a large bird, which thoroughly battered his photographic pod, and obliged him to seek haven at a German base. While on an earlier posting with 427 Squadron, Floyd had collided one day with an eagle. Luckily, when he saw the bird coming, he had advanced his throttle. The eagle was ingested by the engine and spit out the tailpipe in charred bits. Floyd returned safely to base. After tours with 427, 441, 417 and as a maintenance test pilot, he finished his air force career with some 2500 hours and 2300 strap-ins in the CF-104.

On April 25, 1980, Capt David H. Trask earned a "Good Show" from the DND's flight safety magazine *Flight Comment* (1980 No.4). Its account illustrates how a professional pilot handles an emergency:

Captain Trask was tasked on a low-level training mission in a CF-104. Approximately five minutes after take-off, a loud bang was heard. Initially suspecting a bird strike, Captain Trask had his aircraft checked visually by another local aircraft, which revealed that the right nose gear door was open and part of the door bracket broken. Normal landing gear extension resulted in the two main landing gears extending normally, but the nose wheel extending only a few inches. Re-selections using positive and negative G along with touch-and-go landings were tried in an attempt to extend the nose gear. Emergency landing gear procedures were then employed; however, the nose gear remained up.

Having followed all checklist procedures Trask was then faced with the choice between a controlled ejection or a nose-gear "up" landing, a procedure rarely attempted in the CF-104. Captain Trask professionally assessed the situation and, since conditions were favourable, elected to attempt the landing. He burned fuel down to a minimum, completed an approach, and slowly lowered the nose to the runway as he flamed out the engine using the main fuel shutoff. The aircraft came to a halt on the runway and suffered only minimal damage.

Captain Trask demonstrated excellent technical knowledge of aircraft systems and emergency procedures, a calm professional manner and outstanding flying ability during the emergency. His professional skill prevented the loss of an aircraft, damage to civil property and possible personal injuries.

Post-ejection ... John Greatrix with Cold Lake station commander, G/C Bill Vincent, Starfighter OTU CO W/C Ken Thorneycroft, and Army medical officer Claude Morin. Then, the all-too-frequent last remains of a CF-104 - the smoking hole where 12736 ploughed in. (Greatrix Col.)

Cold Lake Ejection

In 2000 John Greatrix described his ejection of November 4, 1967. At the time he was doing his type conversion at Cold Lake, prior to joining 441:

I was just one of many tremulous creatures who, at one second, was flying one of the most exciting airplanes in the world, and, at the next, was strapped to about 26,000 pounds of assorted metal with the gliding characteristics of a grand piano. At the time, I was flying formation bomb runs on one of our targets. Pudge Marshall was on my wing with a dual. In his back seat was a photographer shooting my runs at various stages. After the pictures were taken, Pudge and I split and I stayed on the range to see if I could raise my score to a low average.

On my final low-level run at about 500 KIAS there was a heart-stopping bang. I flamed out, as my aircraft vibrated excessively and started to porpoise - my control dampers had failed.

John Greatrix at home in Winnipeg with author Larry Milberry in 2001. (Greatrix Col.)

At about 300 KIAS I regained some control, pulled up and ejected. The only adverse result was that my right knee resembled a watermelon in size.

Within an hour, darkness settled in. Sad to say, my SARAH (search and rescue homing equipment) beacon proved to be u/s. However, I knew a search would soon be under way if, for no other reason, that I had a rather large outstanding bar bill in the mess. Sure enough, W/C Ken Thorneycroft, OC of 6 (ST/R) OTU and G/C Bill Vincent, Cold Lake base commander, had an air search going immediately. Bill Ross and Al French, flying a T-bird, saw my flares and led a Dakota in to orbit my position. Jim McDiarmid then arrived in his SAR helicopter, shone the spotlight on me and the neighbouring moose and wolves, then winched me up. We soon were back in Cold Lake, but too late for TGIF. The young airman who had packed my chute received the biggest bottle of rye I could find.

Once he had graduated, Greatrix joined 441 at Lahr, where he first flew the CF-104 on February 6, 1968. From August 24 to September 11, 1970 he again was at Cold Lake, this time for the conventional weapons course. He last flew a Starfighter on

BGen Ken Lewis and 441 CO LCol Al Young fly "Triple Pig" in happier times. No.1 CAG policy allowed NATO and 1 CAG staff officers such as Lewis to do proficiency flying. Larry Crabb recalls: "While posted at 4 ATAF HQ, Lloyd Campbell and I tried to get down to Baden every two or three weeks to keep proficient on the CF-104, and in touch with 1 CAG operational doctrine. This also helped our credibility with our NATO counterparts." (441 Sqn)

"Triple Pig" after its prang. Then, what remains of it at Cold Lake's Tri-Town Museum in May 2003. Turbo Tarling contemplates the restoration job. (via Ted Lee, Larry Milberry)

April 25, 1971, taking 104661 on a 1.8-hour trip. Now he was posted to the Instrument Check Pilot School in Winnipeg. This offered much good T-bird and Dakota flying. On March 26, 1975 Greatrix made his last air force flight in Dakota 973, then joined Transport Canada as an inspector, something that involved flying on the King Air and DC-3. For three years he was with ICAO helping to establish and improve visual aids standards at international airports. His last assignment was as Canada's Air Navigation Commissioner at ICAO. Greatrix did some private flying after retiring April 1989, his final log entry being for Cessna 172 C-FPCZ on October 26, 1999.

End of a Hangar Queen

By 1975 Starfighter 104666 was known around Baden as a bit of a hangar queen. "Triple Pig", they called it. On March 5, 1975 Capts L.E. "Ted" Lee and Ian Struthers rode the old clunker to its demise. In 2003 Lee described what happened (for Ian Struthers' version, see David Bashow's book, *Starfighter*):

It was a cool and clear Tuesday, so I was fairly certain that our bombing trip to Suippes would be a go. I was looking forward to sitting in the back seat to give Ian some cues on keeping position around the range pattern. On many a day visibility on the range was so bad that it was hard to see the aircraft ahead, and I knew how easy it was to get completely lost in the pattern.

I had flown a unit checkout on "Struts" the night before. Having seen his strong performance, I was expecting an easy mission and a chance to do a little sightseeing along our route. We were No.4 and the wind dictated a "finger right" takeoff on R22. That put us on the extreme right of the runway. Even with the CF-104's short wing span, our wingtip was less than 10 feet from the runway edge as we lined up.

The crucial part of the formation takeoff for a 4-jug dual with a centreline MN1A bomb dispenser was to get the throttle up to the top end of the sector afterburner range on lead's initial call to light the 'burner. Then, you had to get it to full uniform when the next call came. Struts did that perfectly and we were right in position as our speed mounted.

We went by the line speed marker (about 140 knots) in good shape, then rotated at 195 for liftoff. As the takeoff attitude was set, there was an obvious (but not familiar) noise. From the back seat I observed fragments of the right tire thrown forward - a blown tire! Oh well, that was no big problem - we'd carry on, burn off fuel for a while, then land on a flat tire. Struts, however, being locked onto Lead on his left side, had set the throttle to idle, figuring that we had a compressor stall.

I thought, "This is no time to be fooling around with the throttle." So I reached up and pushed the tail hook "Down" button. From our outer position on the runway, Struts did a great job of getting us down on the runway centreline. The 'chute was out, we were decelerating, and had alerted the tower. From my perspective, as we approached the arrester cable, the aircraft began drifting right. As we left the asphalt and went onto the concrete to the side of the runway, I wondered if we would snag the cable or just miss it.

At this point I wondered about ejecting, but we were at 100 knots. "Zero altitude" minimum safe ejection speed, however, was 90 - not a big enough cushion for my liking. As we rocketed over the concrete, I was pretty sure I saw the throttle slip to "Off". I figured that Struts felt we would snag the cable and was shutting things down before we left the runway. Without engine power we had no nosewheel steering, so could not correct our right drift. Struts, however, didn't know that our right tire had blown. As he braked, and we slowed from 195 knots, there was so much drag that we were being pulled inexorably right.

In the end we missed the cable, although our right drop tank hit the cable stanchion bang on. At that instant, all 1200+ pounds of JP4 fuel went up. To the folks in the tower it must have looked like a napalm tank hitting. We ploughed ahead on the grass, slithering sideways as our undercarriage dug in. Man, what a ride!

As we stopped, I saw some flame under one wing. From the front seat, straps were flying everywhere as Struts egressed. Finally, I realized what I, too, should be doing! I pulled the handle to fire my canopy,

Of Canada's 200 single seat CF-104s and 38 two-seat CF-104Ds, about 100 were lost while in Canadian service. Others crashed later with operators such as Turkey. In this Cartierville view of 12704 being towed, of the Starfighters beyond, the first four later crashed (all the pilots ejected safely): '765 had a bird strike while on an August 19, 1969 mission from Cold Lake (Capt G.F. Ball), '764 crashed from Cold Lake on November 1, 1963 (F/L C.W. Gehman), '734 was F/L Sky King's aircraft, and '762 flew through trees during a June 9, 1981 mission from Baden (Lt K.G. Cranfield). Not surprisingly, the CF-104 acquired a nasty reputation, even though many accidents were related to human, not technical, problems. (Canadair 31273)

but nothing happened. Gradually, I realized that this is how the system worked. There was a brief delay, a sequencing that was timed to any ejection from the front cockpit. But those few seconds seemed an eternity just then, causing a bit of panic. My canopy soon did fire, then I saw Struts going over the side and landing hard on the ground.

Next, I realized that the canopy was still obstructing my egress. With no slip stream to carry it away, it just came back down over the cockpit. I had to stand on the seat (parachute still on), muscle the canopy upwards, then slither out. Struts and I now stood off at a safe distance, waiting for the fire fighters to arrive. Soon there was a great flurry of activity, with the fire being foamed down and the wreckage otherwise secured.

When we initially had called our abort, the control tower sounded the crash bells. That got the fire fighters moving and also alerted Ops, which called tower for some details. The controller was just watching "666" go up in a fire ball, so reported, "They just blew up", and hung up the phone. It took a bit for Ops to appreciate what really was going on. Struts and I soon were in the base hospital for a check-up. All seemed normal, except that my blood pressure was quite slow in returning to normal. Soon a Board of Inquiry was held to look into the accident, but life gradually returned to normal. All was well, except for poor old "Triple Pig".

Sea Survival and E&E

Periodically, every fighter pilot took a sea survival course. In 1982, when Dave Burt did so, the program involved boat and wet suit drills. Then he was taken out into the Baltic, para-sailed up to 1000 feet, and released. Once in the water he struggled into his raft, then spent two hours "practicing boredom" and fiddling with his emergency radio. The hardest part was when a chopper arrived to complete the exercise by winching him aboard. That's when he learned that the best thing was to go limp and let the hoist crew do everything.

Burt also remembered Operation Zipper-Zip ("Zipper" and "Zip" were nick names for the CF-104). This was an escape and evasion exercise which

Capt Gord Zans does parachute/sea survival training during Op. Bikini, a 441 Danish exchange of the early 1980s. (Zans Col.)

Dave Owen

Bruce Arnott

Gord DeJong

Bruce Reid

A 1 CAG military policeman "captures" CF-104 pilot during escape and evasion training at Baden. (CF)

Burt, in 2002, described simply as "How to freeze your ass off." E&E training (described in the Sabre chapters) has been standard air force training for decades, but the one experienced by Burt was botched. He and several other aircrew in flying gear and carrying maps were bussed to a swampy area and dropped off. The object was to cross several miles of terrain without being caught. Several "safe houses" were available. The army and 444 Tactical Helicopter Squadron began the search, but not enough men had been assigned for this. When it was clear that nobody was being caught, the rules changed - the safe houses were no longer safe. Burt and a companion, smelling trouble, avoided the safe houses, but suffered through a cold, rainy night. Concerned about hypothermia, they found the house of a German friend. Here they spent their second night partying like any resourceful fighter pilots.

Bill Card

Some 441 alumni suffered accidents on later tours. Capts Dave Owen, Bill Card and Bruce Reid were lost while instructing at 417 Squadron. Capt Gord DeJong died while flying with the Snowbirds. Bruce Arnott was killed while instructing on Tutors. (441 Sqn)

Bill Card's grave site in the old Anglican Cemetery in Cold Lake. (Larry Milberry)

Bob Endicott (3rd from right) having logged his 1000th CF-104 hour. In his cheering section are Rob Porter, John David, Bobby Wade, Luc Trepenier, LCol Larry Crabb, Dave Owen and Ross Betts.
(CF BS76-0229, Larry Milberry)

CHAPTER

Profiles and Events

A Career on Starfighters

A Cold War pilot's years on the Sabre and Starfighter invariably were his best. Reminiscing in 2002, R.J. "Bob" Endicott did not argue with this. His log book opens on January 29, 1960 with the comment: "Commenced flying training at Centralia." Some 24 years later his last air force entry was on July 31, 1984, and showed a 2-hour T-33 flight from Chatham to Ottawa. Between those dates he logged 197 hours on piston-engined types, 1552 on turbo-props, and 6052 hours on jets. Along the way there were the milestones and events that characterized an aviator's life well lived - first solo February 18, 1960 - 15 minutes, first Harvard solo April 1, 1960 - 15 minutes, then his first jet flight - November 30, 1960, 1:35 hours in a T-33, followed by his first jet solo on December 2, 1960. After CF-100 OTU at Cold Lake, Endicott drew an overseas posting at 419 Squadron, commencing in August 1961. In March 1963 he was assigned to 2 Wing Instrument Flight. He moved on to Tutors at 1 FIS at Portage la Prairie in August 1965, then instructed at 1 FTS at Gimli from November 1965 to April 1968.

At this point Endicott was handed a choice posting. The USAF, bogged down in Vietnam and short of instructors, turned to Canada for help. Unlike in 2003, when Ottawa refused to help the US to oust Iraqi tyrant Saddam Hussein, in the 1960s Canada loaned some 75 qualified instructors to the USAF. As of May 1968 Capt Endicott was in Texas, converting to the T-37. Three months later he was instructing students in basic jet flight. This lasted until July 1971, by when he had logged 894 T-37 hours. There followed a tour in 1971 - 74 with 414 Squadron, North Bay, then came the CF-5 OTU with 434 Squadron from September to December 1974. Endicott began converting to the CF-104 at 417 Squadron on December 17, 1974 with navigation exercises in the T-33. He first flew in a CF-104D on January 27, 1975 (Maj D.R. Graham instructing), soloed on type on January 30, then joined the Mach 2 Club next day. In his log, missions were tersely entered as "Radar Nav", "BFM 1", "ACM 1", etc. He finished OTU on June 9, 1975 with 133:40 hours, 102:10 on the CF-104.

Endicott joined 441 on July 22, 1975. All the usual flying ensued - seemingly endless sessions in mission planning, then flying "canned" routes to simulated targets, hour-long trips to various ranges for gunnery, bombing and rocketry, exchanges with other NATO units, ceremonial flypasts, breaking in new pilots, etc. On January 13, 1977 Endicott logged his 5000th flying hour with a trip in 104739. His log by now was crammed with cryptic entries, many of which not even he could recall years later. A 1976 Siegenburg Range bombing exercise was recorded as: "Mar 3 - CF-104 - 806 - Bx Siegenburg - 1.2". Next day he recorded: "Mar 4 - CF-104 - 829 - Strafe Suippes - No.3 - DNCO - 1.2".

Bx" was the standard entry for "bombing", "DNCO" meant "duty not carried out" (something must have occurred en route, perhaps a technical glitch or weather), while "1.2" indicated a mission of 1.2 hours. In August 2002 Bob Endicott outlined a typical day's work for a CF-104 pilot:

> A day at the office started with a weather briefing at 0800. A short emergency procedures review followed, along with an intelligence slide show to test our skills identifying friendly and enemy military hardware. Next, the daily schedule was checked. Some lucky guys would go to the range. That required little pre-flight preparation, since range trips were along "canned" routes. Otherwise, a fellow could be stuck with a simulator trip or, even worse, a back seat T-33 instrument training flight "under the bag". Not so bad would be a slot on a 2- or 4-plane "CT", or combat training mission.
>
> A 4-plane mission began with planning for a low-level (500 feet agl) nav trip around Germany. En route the pilots would be attacking

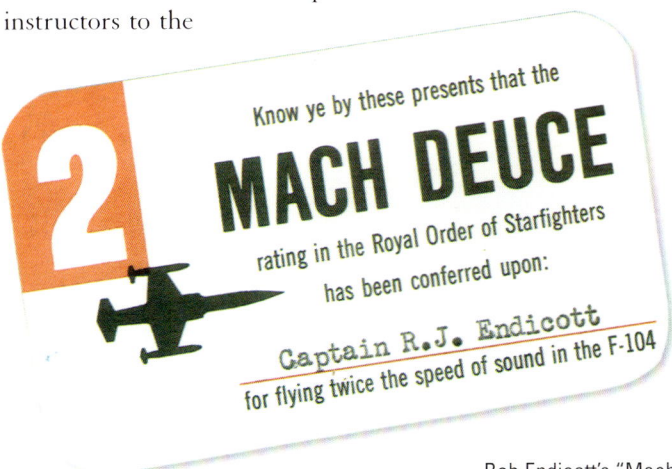

Bob Endicott's "Mach Deuce" membership card. (Endicott Col.)

three "equivalent targets" (bridges, missile sites, etc.). Lead and No.3 (lead of the second element) did the planning, while No.2 and No.4, whose sole purpose in life was "to start up and shut up", usually sat around playing ace-deuce.

In the mission planning section some experienced NCOs helped put the trip together - cutting strips from the appropriate maps, then assembling and gluing them, drawing on routes, etc. Our maps either were 1:250,000 for general navigation, or 1:50,000 for the run-in to each target. Headings and timing were marked along the route, plus such reminders as safety heights and restricted flying areas. Maps were folded and placed in order of use, the 1:250s to sit under the pilot's left thigh, the 1:50s under the right. Maps were carried only by Lead and No.3. The wingmen were only there to double the simulated weapons delivery and to "check six" for the element leads, in case of attack by defending aircraft.

After the pre-flight briefing by Lead, the mission launched. Each element took off in close formation, 15 seconds between elements. Once airborne, battle formation was assumed at 450 knots, with No.3 about a mile line abreast to Lead, wingmen in echelon to their leads at 1500 feet separation. Lead pulled out the first 1:250 and navigated by running his thumb along the route, noting and correcting for heading and timing errors. When the first map was finished, it was dropped on the floor, the first 1:50 was pulled out, and the first run-in timed for 510 or 540 knots. This depended on whether there would be a pop-up on approach for a 10 degree dive angle, a level curve to the target, or a straight fly-through. The second element used a different tactic in its attack.

Just before attacking, the first 1:50 was tossed to the floor, the attack flown, egress completed and the next 1:250 grabbed for the second target. Ground speed fell to 450 and the process was repeated for ensuing targets. For the trip home, battle formation was resumed. Nearing base the section climbed, tightened up and formed into echelon, the first time since takeoff that it had been above 500 feet (other than the few seconds for pop-up). Overhead the base, Lead called the pitch-out, then each pilot peeled off, flew the downwind leg, turned final and landed in sequence. Typically, such a mission took 1:15 hours.

Normally, a mission was without incident, but there could be complications. The weather could go down en route, or visibility be less than desired, e.g. should the daily smog be especially high. A formation might be bounced by lurking fighters, forcing pilots to take evasive manoeuvres. Someone might call "bingo" fuel, his limit for a safe return to base, or there might be mechanical problems. Mission debriefing followed immediately after landing. This could be long and interesting, depending on how things had gone. One that finished as planned (not that common an event) meant a short debrief, with the fellows patting each other on the back. The not-so-successful trip took longer "to lay the blame" on any member of the section, except the one pontificating at the time. On one mission, late on a Friday afternoon, I had been the "guest" section lead, i.e. not being a current squadron pilot. The wingmen (No. 2 and No.4) were both senior officers, not so Lead and No.3. The "wingers" finally had their chance to voice their opinions. So long-winded were these two that the squadron OpsO locked up the squadron and departed to the Mess for beer call, leaving us to babble on.

Bob Endicott's 1000th Starfighter hour came on November 29, 1978. Soon afterwards he moved to 1 CAG HQ in Lahr. From there he logged occasional sorties, when not checking out unit personnel or navigation systems. On October 3, 1980 he clocked his 6000th hour. On July 30, 1981 he made his last overseas flight, taking up 104815. Some pilots might not admit it, but there is life after fighters. On September 29, 1981 Endicott was flying again - this time Twin Otters with No.4 Regular Support Unit at Namao. In January 1982 he joined 404 Squadron at Greenwood to fly the CP-140 Aurora for two years, before retiring from the military in March 1984. Continuing in civil aviation with City Express and Execaire, Endicott ran his total to 12,280 flying hours, before "calling it quits" in January 1997.

Judge Wenham

In 1966 Garth B. "Judge" Wenham was a young man working in Vancouver. On the street one day he spotted a poster in the window of the Canadian Forces recruiting office. Featured on the poster was a fighter pilot, helmet under one arm and looking heroic beside his CF-104. Wenham stopped to ask a few questions, and soon afterwards was in uniform and training at Central Officers School. Even before he began there, he had a broken hand, so wore a cast that went half way up one arm. As the course progressed, the recruits often amused themselves by holding Kangaroo Courts for various "infractions". Wenham had his own gavel, so usually served as the "judge" for such occasions. Henceforth, he always carried that nickname.

Following basic training, Wenham was posted to 2 FTS in Moose Jaw for flight training. There he was on one of the RCAF's "all-jet" courses. This was a trial to determine whether students, who hadn't been in an airplane of any kind, could be trained to Wings standards, beginning on the Tutor, finishing on the T-33. Wenham first flew on October 18, 1966, going up with F/O Ralph Isenor in Tutor '056. He soloed on November 24 and finished this phase on July 6, 1967. Next came the T-33, Wenham flying it first on August 4. After 280 hours on both types, he graduated in October.

From Moose Jaw, Wenham was posted to 3 AW (F) OTU at Bagotville for conversion to the CF-101. This course began on the T-bird, since a student needed 500 jet hours before advancing to the CF-101. Wenham started flying on November 27, 1967, but didn't get up in a Voodoo until May 16, 1968, flying that day in 17407 with Capt Len Couture. In July he began what would be a memorable tour with 425 Squadron. Besides all the standard exercises and alerts at Bagotville and Val d'Or, there would be frequent get-aways. In December 1970, for example, Wenham took a T-bird to Wichita to collect USAF Voodoo 57-0363 for ferrying to the overhaul facility in Greenville, South Carolina. This was part of the program whereby Canada swapped its "old" Voodoos (acquired in 1961) for "new" ones equipped with an IR missile sight.

Wenham's 425 tour ended with a flight in 101007 on July 11, 1972, then he put in a year at Cambridge Bay on the DEW Line. This was followed by a tour at 1 CAG Group Operations in Baden-Soellingen. This was another ground job, but Wenham still scrounged the occasional ride. On January 11, 1974 he went up on his first CF-104 ride with

The Silver Foxes with Starfighter No.824 in August 1976. Standing are Cpl Lorne Scott, Capt Sam Howard, Cpl Carl Keenan, Capt Ian Struthers, Cpl Bob Churchill, Capts Gus Youngson, Dave Owen, Clark Little and Judge Wenham, Lt Ted Bain, Capt Bruce Reid, Sgt Fred Olsen, Capt Rick Martin, Sgt Gary Rung and Capt Rick Wall. In front are Majs Dave Girling, Pat Barrett and Dale Purcell, LCol John Hutt (CO), and Majs Mike Major (USAF), George Landry and Jim Gale. When Judge Wenham had spotted that recruiting poster in 1966, he had no idea that the "hero" pilot featured on it was John Hutt. (Wenham Col.)

Maj John England in 104666 "Triple Pig". From the GOC he progressed to the CF-104 world, beginning with the CF-5 lead-in course at 434 Squadron. There he first flew with Capt Dave Penney on January 14, 1975. The course continued to March 26, then Wenham moved to 417, flying initially with Capt Clancy Sheldrup in the CF-104 in 104614 on April 21. He had his first Mach 2 trip on May 28 in 104784. For July, he logged 25.4 CF-104 hours, plus 2.0 in the T-bird. His last mission was in 104790 on September 3, 1975, then he was posted to 441.

Now, Wenham again flew the Atlantic - as was the routine in those days, this was aboard a 437 Squadron 707 service flight. After reclaiming his earlier digs in Hugelsheim, a short drive from Baden, he commenced flying on the T-bird on October 1. On October 21 Capt Bill Card took him up on a CF-104 famil ride in 104658. Soon Wenham was into the swing of things - for November alone he logged 20.9 CF-104 hours.

Each Starfighter pilot recalls a few "fun" highlights from his career. One of Judge Wenham's was the time 441 was on exchange with 10 Gruppo, then flying the F-104S at Grazzanise, Italy. At a local eatery, diners could order pizza by length. Naturally, it soon occurred to one of the Canucks - "Hey, let's get ourselves a 441 cm pizza!" And so they did.

Meanwhile, ops offered its own chuckles. At the morning launch, the Italian Air Force briefers would struggle with their English. Each day the fellow describing runway conditions would report, "And a grass a cutting eez in a progress". He didn't seem to have practiced too many more such English phrases. Wenham also recalled the social pace whenever 441 was on exchange with the RAF. Any celebration with the Brits could end in that great RAF tradition - trashing the Mess piano. Over the years, however, hosts had wizened up. If the RAF was at Baden, the Mess piano would be replaced with some expendable clunker bought locally for a few marks.

Another time Judge Wenham was in Winnipeg on the ICP Course. Everyone enjoyed the proceedings, especially Wenham, who got to fly his first "prop" plane - the ancient Dakota. For end-of-course each student got his "ICP" patch to sew onto his flight suit, but also a T-shirt designed by Wenham emblazoned with "The Douglas Racers". In late 1978 Wenham was posted to instruct at 417 Squadron. He then finished his 441 tour with a TacEval on December 14, 1978 in 104891. This was a requirement for 417 "IPs", each of whom had to maintain combat ready status. By this time Wenham's log showed 2635.9 hours, 829.6 being on the CF-104. He began his 417 tour on February 13, 1979.

Judge Wenham
AN ALBUM

Starfighter pilot Judge Wenham enjoyed photography as a hobby. First in this selection from his archives is a 1979 scene at Cold Lake. 417 Squadron, where all Starfighter pilots learned the basics, is shown taxying for an all-out effort, perhaps a mass attack exercise.

Just airborne and already passed 200 knots.

The Silver Fox mascot in a Baden scene from February 1978.

Duals '638 and '641 depart Cold Lake on a training sortie. When Canada retired the Starfighter in 1986, the surviving aircraft met various ends. Some 54 ('638 included) went to Turkey, where their operational days extended into the 1990s. Others (such as '641) became aircraft battle damage repair training aids. As such, student techs used them to practice skills like sheet metal repair (ABDR aircraft sometimes were purposely mangled, so that students could have realistic repair assignments). Other Starfighters went to museums in Cold Lake, Winnipeg, Trenton, etc. A few ex-RCAF/RNoAF aircraft ended in the US, flying as warbirds and civilian EW trainers into the 2000s.

A favourite view of the snaky Starfighter.

Aerial portrait of 104786 in April 1978.

Pilot and groundcrew busy getting '733 on its way from Baden, June 1978.

A 441 Squadron 2-ship blasts off from a slick runway at Baden.

Are We Having Fun Yet?

In the records from 441's early CF-104 days, F/O Ken Mowbray's name often occurs. Having been raised in Cartwright, Manitoba, he joined the RCAF in June 1962. His flying training was usual for the era - Chipmunk, Harvard, T-33 and in November 1963 he won his Wings at Portage la Prairie. Now he headed for CF-104 OTU. There, some of the 10 students on Course 14 were experienced fighter pilots. One of these was "Black Robbie" Robinson, who had flown CF-100s. Others were pipeliners. Soon, Mowbray was moving through the program - ground school, OFTT, first CF-104 flight (August 21, 1964 with F/L Tim Boyd in 12631), solo, Mach 2, exams, etc. He graduated on December 17, having logged 93:45 hours on CF-104s, 36:35 on T-birds.

As his course ended, several students realized that they would not be getting their Permanent Commissions. Mindful of their futures, Jack Heiszek, "Pete" Peterson and "Black Robbie" Robinson left the RCAF for airline jobs. George Ellerbeck and F.G. "Buster" Kincaid remained at the OTU to instruct, while the others were posted to 1 CAG: J.P. "Des" Desbiens (427 Sqn), Romeo Lalonde (439), Ken Mowbray (441), Ray Sawchuk (439) and Gord Wallis (441).

When F/O Mowbray joined 441 in February 1965 he couldn't wait to get into the job. In the following four years he would enjoy each of his 1000 (or so) strap-ins, takeoffs and landings in one of the world's hottest fighters. Even when hung over from the night before, such gung-ho young pilots wouldn't dream of missing a day on the job, whether on recce exercises, worming their way onto ceremonial flypasts, doing airshows - whatever was happening. In October 1966, following an all-out squadron competition, Mowbray was judged top pilot by his peers.

Many years later, Paul Manson remembered Mowbray as having a photographic memory - the kind of pilot who could study his maps, then fly a perfect mission without them, if required. Little wonder that he excelled in "Royal Flush". Besides the flying, Mowbray was singled out as a superior cook at squadron parties (a fighter pilot always had to be versatile). In June 1969 Mowbray was posted home to instruct on CF-5s at 434 Squadron. In 1971 he left the military for a 32-year career in commercial aviation. He flew charters for Mercury Flights of Edmonton, water-bombed with their A-26, then moved to CP Air. By the time he retired in May 2003, Ken Mowbray had logged more than 22,000 hours. Of those, his 1200 on the CF-104 were by far the most memorable.

A Pilot's Impressions

A graduate of Course 57 at 417 Squadron, Ted Delanghe served on 441 from 1977 to 1980. In April 2003 he recalled of those great times:

> When a CF-104 came out of major maintenance, it needed a test flight or two to ensure that all was well. One thing on the check list was a run to Mach 2. This was done without tip tanks. In that configuration, it's amazing how, from the cockpit, you really had to strain and pull yourself around, just to see the wingtips.

"Royal Flush" veteran Ken Mowbray. (441 Sqn)

Born in Chatham, Ontario in 1951, Ted Delanghe joined the Canadian Forces in 1968 as an RMC student in mechanical engineering. He earned his Wings on T-33s with 1 FTS at Cold Lake, then instructed there into 1976. He converted to the CF-104 and spent 1977 - 80 at 441. Delanghe then left the military for the business world. His interests in 2004 included media development and, to keep his hand in the low-level flying world, crop dusting on the prairies. (CF BS78-1185)

On a test flight from Baden on February 20, 1979, I departed southbound in 104716. Accelerating to 500 knots, I brought the nose up and around in a sort of roll-off-the-top manoeuvre, levelling at 30,000 feet in about 100 seconds. One item on the test card was a timed, straight and level acceleration from Mach 0.9 to 1.4. This had to be done in under 90 seconds for all to be correct. That's when the fun really started. With all that ram air coming in, and a decrease in the overall drag curve, the engine re-set to 104% max-rated RPM and began to push the aircraft quickly up to Mach 2. You had to throttle back in burner, so as not to exceed the Mach limit (which the CF-104 would happily walk right through). On such a run there was always a distinct feeling of being in the midst of a whole lot of kinetic energy. The Zip really did like to go fast in a straight line.

When it comes to flying characteristics, every aircraft has its pros and cons, and the Zip was no exception. An exceedingly stable platform, because of its high wing loading, it rode over all the bumps in the air on a rough day. There was none of the jostling you felt in any other aircraft. It gave the same feel as riding in a train - a small side-to-side motion, but not like riding a bumpy road in a car.

The visceral feel at low speeds (anything under 400 knots) was of being surrounded by a lot of mass in a small space. There was a certain heaviness until you exceeded 450 and the flaps were fully up. Then you felt comfortable, going from manhandling the airplane, to being able to really "rock and roll". The Zip wasn't exactly agile, like a CF-5, just solid and smooth. And any time you lit the burner, it was like a real firm push on your back straight through until you came out of burner again. The real secret to happiness was to keep the coals stoked, only slowing down to land.

It was a lot of work to maintain proficiency in the CF-104 in low-level navigation, ground attack, close air support and air defence. A typical day would see all members of the squadron gathering in the Ops room at about 7 a.m. for a formal weather briefing. Next, each pilot would be tasked by the Scheduling and Ops Officers. A usual part of the morning briefing also included covering a random aircraft emergency, and a series of slides showing various NATO and Warsaw Pact aircraft and ground equipment. This was vital practice for recce ID purposes.

By far the commonest type of 441 mission was the 4-plane ground attack sortie, or "CPM" - combat profile mission. The mission planning process took the full morning, including briefings. Next came the mission (1.3 hours on average), then an hour to debrief from start to finish. It was all quite intensive, taking lots of training, co-ordination and teamwork.

It's hard to imagine today, but in the late 1970s very few restrictions were imposed on our flying. A 4-plane would depart in two sections with Lead and No.3, then No.2 and No.4 in their respective slots in close formation. Once clear of the Baden air traffic control zone, the formation would call "QSY" to tower, indicating a change in frequency. For the next hour or so the Starfighters would fly very low around West Germany in tactical formation without talking to another air traffic control agency. Storming down their routes at 500 feet, or below, they would attack their designated targets - bridges, rail junctions, etc. We also visited a variety of practice ranges, whether Siegenberg near Munich (rocketry and bombing), or Pampa (Belgium), Suippes (France) and Munsingen (Germany) for gunnery. Sometimes there was extra fun, when we got to deliver live Mk.82 500-pound bombs, napalm or rockets.

In any year 441 participated in various NATO exercises, including a few rapid response and recall scenarios when we would deploy to Lahr for several days. Working from hardened aircraft shelters and flying in full NBCW suits, we would be tasked by 4 ATAF with any number of ground support and CAS missions. NATO's fall war games always were the biggest exercises. These were designed to test how well NATO could conduct integrated operations throughout the theatre. As such, orders might be delivered from an Italian HQ to some German command, which would pass them on to a Canadian squadron.

CAG was proficient in Nuclear, Biological, Chemical Warfare procedures. During a TacEval, everyone worked in an NBCW "bunny suit" and mask (as worn here by 441's Dave Burt). "Gas! Gas! Gas!" was the dreaded call that sent people scurrying to don their masks. NBCW kit was uncomfortable in the best of conditions, but truly miserable for line crew working on a blistering summer's day. (via D. Burt)

From the pilots' view, the training and skill exhibited by our ground crew (who by my time belonged to a wing organization, rather than to 441) gave us the confidence we needed. Their judgment on technical matters could always be trusted. It was not uncommon to start an aircraft, then find that something was not right. After a quick call to Ops by the pilot, the appropriate technician would be summoned to review the situation, and a "go" or "no go" decision would be made. If your aircraft was declared u/s, there usually was a standby available. Then the pilot would have to scramble to switch cockpits and still make the takeoff with his formation.

A great thing about a CF-104 wing was the lively, non-stop, social scene. Naturally, each squadron had its own definition of fun and its own collection of characters. In the late 1970s, the Silver Foxes had an especially zany crowd. The fellows were always ready to burst into their signature song, based on the popular C&W hit "It's so Hard to Be Humble". Our version went like this:

*"Oh, it's so hard to be humble,
When you're perfect in every way.
I just can't wait to get up in the morning,
And see 441 every day.
441 Superstars ... we're even better than you think we are.
441 Superstars ... We're even better than WE think we are!"*

During this time our major social convener was "Judge" Wenham. Besides being an experienced pilot, he was the instigator of many an unforgettable skit. Themes that he brought to the Mess included "The Incredible Poor Taste Party" and the "Come as You Were Party" (in which you had to arrive dressed exactly as Judge photographed you when you answered your door at 3 o'clock in the morning).

Great dining was available for us on both sides of the Rhine. Just across the border in France, for example, stood the Auberge de l'Agneau. Before long we had re-christened this spot The Garlic Pit. After all, this was where 441 revellers would consume great quantities of garlic-drenched cuisse de grenouille, schnecken and moules (frog legs, snails and mussels). After such an outing, it was no mystery to everyone in our small briefing room where we had been the night before.

One day in 1979 there was an unusual (and hush-hush) event at 441. All members of 441 were told to report to one of our maintenance buildings. No exceptions tolerated! There I was quite astonished to see one of our aircraft in the early stages of an unofficial (and unapproved) repaint. It was all the work of our new CO, LCol Larry Crabb who, in the spirit of a true leader, wanted to mark the event in grand fashion. So we all proceeded to help paint the aircraft in large black-and-white checkerboard squares. Next morning, LCol Crabb, as "Check Lead", taxied out in this CF-104, now in full regalia, with three standard CF-104s. They blasted off, with me chasing in T-33 133542. In my back seat was a photo tech named René. He got some wonderful photos that day over the Black Forest, past the Hohenzollern Castle and over Baden. Too bad, but we didn't have a camera on the controllers in the tower as we all scorched past! Another one of those days to remember that made life at 441 Squadron such a delightful experience.

CF-104 Gunfighter

The CF-104 was unsuited to dogfighting (the operative term by this time was "ACM" - air combat manoeuvring). Most fighters of the day, besides having better weapons and ECM, easily could out-turn a CF-104. Nonetheless, in 1972, 441 assumed a secondary air defence role. An AIM-9 Sidewinder missile installation was evaluated, but this would have required many modifications. Had 1 CAG proceeded with the project, it would have split the squadron into a too-small fighter force and a too-small strike force. Thus did the 20-mm Vulcan cannon remain the CF-104's sole armament for aerial combat. Any ACM would have to be done close in.

Dave Burt described some 1982 ACM as "interesting" e.g., taking 10,000 feet to execute a loop, going over the top at 160 knots. At the Deci range he did ACM with F-4s and F-15s, pulling 7Gs with a "clean" jet. Unless the weather was bad, the F-15s routinely beat up on the CF-104s. Ted Delanghe also was there in 441 air defence days:

Line personnel (servicing and maintenance) were the unsung heroes of 1 CAG who kept Canada's CF-104s flying 1963 - 86. Here is "B" Crew of "441 Servicing" in June 1982: MCpl Pelletier, MCpl Morin, Sgt Pettipas, Cpl Thomson, MCpl Smith, Cpl Baker, Pte Cameron, Pte Laurie, MCpl Johnston, Cpl Thomassin, Pte Bertrand, Cpl Grogan, Cpl Morrison, MCpl Gaudreault and MCpl Lewis. The Turks eventually wrote off 104795 in a flying accident. (441 Sqn)

The only airspace in southern Germany designated for restricted military air-to-air practice was directly above our base at Baden-Soellingen. Unfortunately, this zone was for subsonic ACM only, and the CF-104 just wasn't comfortable doing subsonic ACM. Nonetheless, practicing in the air-to-air role kept that expertise intact, even though our pilots were humbled at the sight of USAFE's first F-15s overhead. Even so, in the true fighter pilot spirit of never crying uncle, we free-roving Canadians could get in our licks. Unlike the Americans, who usually were radar-vectored on departure, in my period we were on our own. As such, we occasionally would just "sit and wait", orbiting near Bitburg, as the F-15s departed under radar control. Then we would bounce them from behind with the element of surprise in hand, but it didn't take long to realize that you didn't hassle with these guys. They could easily out-turn a CF-104, getting on your tail in no time flat. Thus, our policy was simple - "One pass, haul ass!"

In another technological area, in the 1970s advances in weapons control systems were rendering the CF-104's older gyro-stabilized "iron" sight obsolete. Head-up display (HUD) technology with its highly capable electronics provided a dramatic leap in target acquisition and in bombing/gunnery accuracy. With this in mind, if Canada was to remain in the forefront in the fighter game, new aircraft and systems were needed. Soon the hunt was on to find the best replacement for the CF-104.

By Capt Gordon Zans' time on 441 (1983 - 86), the squadron flew air superiority exercises over southern Germany with NATO AWACS. In these dying days of the CF-104, the aircraft remained ill-equipped for ACM, his cannon still being a pilot's primary weapon for close-in fighting. While the CF-104's best piece of electronic kit since the early 1980s remained the Litton LW33 nav system/weapons computer (used to get a pilot precisely "from A to B"), by now 441 also had RHWR - a radar homing warning receiver to alert a pilot should an opponent get a radar lock-on. Unlike more modern fighters, however, the CF-104 had no built-in chaff/flare counter-measures or ECM pods to help evade the enemy. To get around this, 441 devised a Rube Goldberg effort, which Zans described in 2003: "We could use a 'one-time' envelope of chaff fitted (one each) into the speed brake wells. By cracking open our speed brakes, the envelopes would be released into the slip stream. They then broke apart, giving two bursts of chaff. It was a last-ditch effort about which we had no illusions." For ACM 441 also might carry a pod of CRV-7 rockets. These could be fired to decoy an opponent, obliging him to break or run, since he couldn't be sure what he was facing.

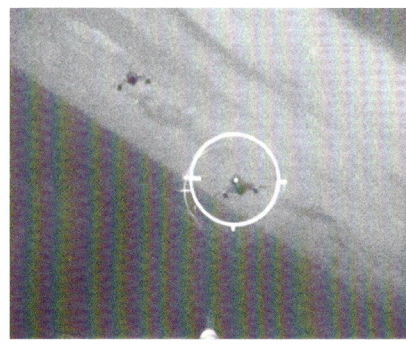

Proof that it sometimes worked! This CF-104 gun camera film shows the pipper on the canopy of a French Air Force Mirage. A lucky day for 441! (Larry O'Brien Col.)

Other than their radar controllers or AWACS friends directing them and warning of threats, RHWR and the "Mark One Eyeball", 441 pilots had to count largely on experience, instinct and Lady Luck to stand a chance of surviving in an ACM scenario. If worse came to worst, odds were that their best chance against something like a MiG-21 would have been to cut and run.

Starfighter Colour Schemes over the Decades

AN ALBUM

Over the decades Canada's Starfighters wore three basic colour schemes - (1) natural finish with white wings and red horizontal tail (2) khaki overall (3) two-tone camouflage above with grayish undersides. This squadron line-up typifies the first scheme as used at Cold Lake and at 1 CAG in nuclear days. Then, 6 (ST/R) OTU Starfighters at Uplands on June 11, 1967. (CF, Larry Milberry)

Khaki Starfighter 104842 wears 441's trademark while at RAF Wildenrath on June 6, 1978 for "Tactical Air Meet 78". (Siegfried Wache)

104733 and '762 in the spiffy trim worn on "Team Canada" Starfighters for the 1976 NATO Tactical Weapons Meet held at Twenthe, Holland. In 1986, '733 went to Turkey, but '762's days were cut short. On June 9, 1981 Lt Kerry Cranfield of 421 Squadron ejected from '762 after flying through trees. (Siegfried Wache)

A Cold Lake-based Starfighter in standard "natural" finish. The photo was taken by the Airborne Sensing Unit CF-100 over Saskatchewan in the summer of 1972.

104751 at Baden on March 1, 1986, in the final scheme worn by 1 CAG Starfighters. (G. Lang)

Some CF-104s carried commemorative paint jobs, including these 441 "Checkerbirds". The first appeared in the late 1960s carrying bogus tail number 104441, while 104880 came later during Larry Crabb's days as CO. (CANAV Col., 441 Sqn)

The 441 Checkerbird leads 439's "Tiger" and 421's "Red Indian" Starfighters during a photo shoot late in 1 CAG days. (Gordon Zans Col.)

Special Events

Other than a fighter squadron's annual flying activities, in the course of a year much else occurs. Some of these events are historically significant. One such in 441's annals had to do with its emblem - the Silver Fox. On December 15, 1967 Sky King arrived from Canada with "Rene", a live animal. The little fellow got considerable publicity in the German press and the city of Lahr even provided a cage. He was named for Rene Werls, the Wing's most popular and endearing bartender. The squadron also kept a stuffed silver fox. In 1976 LGen W.K. "Bill" Carr noted this tattered specimen and had it replaced.

More serious was the presentation of 441's Colours in May 1973 by HRH Prince Philip, Duke of Edinburgh. Then, in 1978 came the commemoration in London of 441's wartime role. This took place at St. Clement Danes, the official church of the Royal Air Force. On April 30, 1978 a copy of the unit's badge, implanted in the church floor, was unveiled. Among those attending was A/V/M J.E. Johnson, who had led 144 Wing and the Silver Foxes 34 years earlier.

No history of the period would be complete without reference to relations between the Canadians and their hosts. A scrapbook of clippings retained by the Directorate of History and Heritage in Ottawa, covering 1967 to 1969, provides a snapshot of life in Lahr. The move there was followed almost immediately by celebrations marking Canada's Centennial, and the Germans were impressed. German and French officers mingled with RCAF personnel and civilians. A German band played, but the presence of a Canadian pipe band, resplendent in bearskin head gear (on a cruelly hot day) fascinated a local reporter, who noted: "On a large table was an equally large marzipan cake on which the Canadian provinces were marked out in different colours. Air Vice Marshal Lane was the first to 'demolish' this masterpiece. Then, little by little, Canada was devoured... At the end a squadron of jets soared above the city."

1000 Hours

A prestigious milestone for a Starfighter pilot was reaching 1000 hours on type. In 1967 Capt Brian Castledine was the first Silver Fox to attain this honour, done while flying between Marville and Lahr. Having qualified on Sabres, he already had his "Mach Busters" pin from Chatham, and his "Mach 2" pin from Cold Lake. In 1968 Majs Van Oene and Gardiner became the second and third on 441 in the 1000 Hour Club. Such events were occasions for a party at which the qualifying pilot was presented with a plaque, usually from a representative of Lockheed. However, few received such a reception as LCol K.R. Betts on June 6, 1984. While taxiing in from an

The Church of St. Clement Danes on the Strand in London. Then, an interior view showing the hundreds of Commonwealth unit badges imbedded in the floor. The 441 badge is shown. (Church of St. Clement Danes, CF BS78-1043, '037)

A/V/M Johnnie Johnson accepts a silver fox memento from 441 CO, LCol Remi Saulnier, as Capt Ian Struthers looks on. This was during the St. Clement Danes event of August 30, 1978. (441 Sqn)

Of this March 1969 photo at Lahr, Romeo Lalonde of 439 notes: "These fellows are all 1 Wing 'time hogs', each having flown 1000 hours on the CF-104 (I had received my own 1000-hour plaque on June 11, 1968). In the front row are Phil Engstad (441), Gary Sanderson (439), Bob Garry (439) and David Huddleston (1 Air Div HQ, ex-439). Behind are Gerry King (439), me, Ken Mowbray (441), Ted Lewis (441), Bob Nicholson (439), Gorm Jensen (439), Gord Wallis (441), Scott Clements (439) and Bobby Joe Hart (441)." (441 Sqn)

A 1000-hour moment. LCol Larry Crabb (above) gets doused following his big day on July 30, 1979. Then, a sopping Mike Hoch is congratulated by LCol Ross Betts and Capt Bob Johnson. (441 Sqn)

afternoon mission, he was advised by groundcrew that his brakes were "hot" (smoking), so he should proceed to the hot brake area. Among CF-104 pilots, hot brakes were regarded as a sign of ham-handedness, a situation unflattering for any pilot. What followed is described in the "Foxes Lair" column in the June 13, 1984 edition of Der Kanadier, Lahr's base newspaper:

> Lieutenant-Colonel Betts managed to turn around and taxi, looking straight ahead and not closing the nozzle beyond the three position, to his notably isolated and somehow diminutive parking space. Upon his arrival, to add to his growing chagrin and, may we even venture, embarrassment, the fire trucks were laying in wait with blue lights flashing.
>
> On the marshaller's signal the boss gratefully shut down and climbed out, already envisaging the snickers at the Ops desk. Then the sting. The fire trucks opened up their water cannons and scored direct hits, soaking our leader to the core. You could see the steam rising as he cooled, and the light bulb illuminating over his head. You see, it was an elaborate ploy. Welcome to the exclusive 1000 hour club.

Dave Trasks' 1000-hour scene from 1980: Ross Betts, Doug Barton (USAF), Larry Crabb (CO), Rick Gelinas, Dave Ghyselinckx, Trask, LCol Willy Anderson (439), Doug Erlandson, Ian Struthers, Rob Porter, "Mex" Tremblay and Cpl Sandy Anderson (admin). (CF BS80-833)

Canada Day and Bombs Awry!

It seems that 441 members have an endless supply of great "war stories". These are most likely to come to the surface at squadron alumni get togethers, especially as the beer flows and the clock ticks beyond midnight. Larry Crabb tells two good 441 tales:

As my tour as CO 441 drew to a close, our Base Commander, Colonel Jack Frazer, gave his permission for me to lead an unusual formation for our Canada Day open house of June 20, 1981. I planned a 17-plane line abreast, gear down, lights on pass over the Rhine at 90 degrees to the runway and crowd. "Ajax Force", including the three squadron COs, were briefed. The marginal weather was emphasized on the route north up the valley past Ramstein, to the west of Zweibrucken, and then across France to Baden. Take off was calculated to include two orbits over the base to pick up our four sections.

As we proceeded north, weather prevented us from getting out of the valley. As the "pucker factor" rose, I used mental dead reckoning to calculate orbits in the valley. At the right moment I flew south along the Vosge mountains with two Sections on each side.

As we rolled in on the very short run-in to Baden, everyone got into position line abreast, slowed, dropped the gear and flicked on the lights. We crossed the Rhine and passed overhead 15 seconds late on TOT! Past the crowd, gear up and peel off at 3-seconds intervals to line up on the runway from opposite ends with burners going. Pass head-on at 600 knots and pull vertical (unfortunately through overcast). Needless to say, air traffic was busy recovering us all. It was an exciting and a fitting end to Canada Day...

Each year 1 CAG put on flying displays for visiting groups such as the Staff College tour. For October 1980, 441 Squadron was tasked to lead a combined 12-plane mass attack on a target (a junked car) positioned between the runway and taxiway to impress a large group of "schoolies". John David, and the Weapons Office calculated that if each aircraft pickled twice carrying a "slick" and a high-drag smoke bomb, we could have 24 bombs smoking on target.

The attack was on time, and the display impressive! Unfortunately, all hell broke loose the next day, when they went to recover the bombs, finding some outside the perimeter fence, and a bomb in the rafters of the old scramble hangar at the end of the runway, which was used by the flying club. No one had paid attention to the ricochet effect of a slick bomb hitting the hard surface from 100-feet and 450 knots. I guess since they didn't want to fire our three squadron COs, the issue quietly went away.

Father and Son

In 2003 Larry Crabb recalled an occasion that left a special impression:

In Baden days 441 traditionally sponsored the local Air Cadets. During my tenure as CO we provided the squadron with several dedicated instructors, Bob Endicott and Mark Hollman included. In April 1980 we arranged several flights in the T-33 and CF-104 for deserving cadets. My choice was to fly with my son, FSgt Darren Crabb. Then, in June 1980 I inducted Darren into the Canadian Forces, and he was off to start his military career at Royal Roads Military College in Victoria. When Darren returned to Baden for Christmas, we again flew, this time on December 23 in 104653. OCdt Darren Crabb subsequently was posted to 441 Squadron for OJT in the summer of 1981. He went on to become a Tutor instructor at Moose Jaw, CF-18 pilot (421 Squadron), CF-18 instructor on 410 Squadron, then the Air Liaison Officer with the Army in Calgary. While there, he left the CF and was recruited by the Royal Australian Air Force. He was posted to Williamstown, NSW to instruct on Macchis, then was on an F-18 Squadron.

Following his RAAF contract, Darren joined an executive jet firm which also had a warbird museum at Temora, NSW. There he flew everything from the Tiger Moth to the Spitfire, A-37D and Vampire. In a reversal of roles, he took me up in an A-37D during an air show at Temora in April 2001. It was great to fly with my son again, doing aerobatics and some impressive low-level manoeuvres.

LCol Larry Crabb with his son, OCdt Darren Crabb, then on OJT at Baden. On December 23, 1980 they flew together in 104653. (CF BS81-1492)

Squadron Highlights

AN ALBUM

Events formal and informal add vitality to a squadron. Always a highlight is the Change-of-Command ceremony. The presence of senior officers and VIPs, the squadron marching behind its Colours, speeches, the signing of documents, a perfectly-timed fly-past, and some good partying have always typified this event. Here, LCol D.L.J. "Larry" Crabb passes command of 441 to LCol C.W. "Willy" Wilson on July 9, 1981 at Baden. BGen Paul Manson, a former 441 CO, signs the official documents in the presence of the squadron mascot. (CF BS81-1542)

For the Myles-Hutt ceremony, the CAG Commander, BGen Theriault, decreed that there would be no Starfighter fly-past (his view was that fly-pasts were wasteful of scarce resources). Not to be deterred, the Silver Foxes instituted "Plan B" by which Ian Struthers, George Landry and Gerry Hermanson rented light planes from the local flying club. Led by Struthers, the formation came low over the Change-of-Command garden party, as LCol Hutt chatted with BGen Theriault. While the new CO appreciated the little gesture above, the CAG Commander was less impressed. Here, the somewhat hilarious formation of Cherokee, Cessna 172 and Cessna L-19 passes overhead. (441 Sqn)

The document by which LCol John Hutt took over 441 from LCol Don Myles on May 23, 1975. 1 CAG Commander, BGen G.C.E. Theriault, oversaw the proceedings. (CF BS75-0816)

LCol Larry Crabb of 441 led this smoking, thundering affair - a Change-of-Command fly-past for 439 Squadron *circa* 1980. (441 Sqn)

The presentation of awards to a unit as a whole, or to deserving individuals, is always important in squadron life. Here, BGen "BR" Campbell presents 441's LCol Wilson with 1 CAG's 1981 "Top Gun" award. This honour, instituted in 1965 to recognize precision bombing, originally was known as the Bradshaw Trophy. (CF BS83-1023/1)

Mid-summer 1977 and the Silver Foxes celebrate another win: George Landry, Gus Youngson, Jim Gale, Rick Wall, Mike Major, Bob Endicott, Bruce Reid, Remi Saulnier (CO), Bob Wade, Ian Struthers, Rick Martin, Ted Delanghe and Phil Murphy. (CF BS77-1018)

MCpl Glen Hupe, a 441 mission planner, receives his CD medal from LCol Ross Betts in 1984. Sgt Tom Pieroway, NCO i/c Mission Planning, looks on. Then, in August 1985 Betts himself receives the first clasp to his CD (after 22 years of service) from Baden Base Commander, Col A.M. "Al" DeQuetteville. (Ross Betts Col.)

441's lounge always has something going on, adding to the casual good times on the squadron. Here the Silver Foxes honour their "putzfrau" (cleaning lady). Rosa was celebrating her 20th year at Baden. (Ross Betts Col.)

Anniversaries are always important in squadron life. Here, former COs Bruce Burgess, Walt Niemy, Al Young and Paul Manson attend 441's 30th anniversary. (441 Sqn)

Occasionally, 441 would top off a VIP's visit with the flight of a lifetime in the CF-104. This jovial crowd came together in honour of famed Canadian ski champion, Nancy Greene, who flew this day with Maj Gord Hatch (at her left elbow). LCol Betts and Base Commander, Col Dave McIntosh, are on Greene's right. (Ross Betts Col.)

Larry Crabb recalls a special time: "Besides unlimited cocktail parties, the New Year's Ball, etc., each year 441 held a family Christmas party. At the appointed time the kids would be ushered outside to meet a CF-104 bringing Santa Claus in from the North Pole. What a thrill, and even pilots such as Harry Chapin made sure he got to sit on Santa's knee to ensure that the old boy was aware of his wish list." (Ross Betts Col.)

More great fun, this time for the alleged grown-ups. Doug Erlandson describes the proceedings: "Traditionally, a few days before Christmas the Wing would shut down for an afternoon to celebrate the festive season. Most units would stay put, while the flying squadrons made the rounds to wish everybody the best of the season. I remember this foggy occasion about 1981. Fog meant no flying, an early start to the party, and a happy crowd, as is evident in the photos." Included on the party wagon are Doug Erlandson standing left, Chris Tuck seated on Doug's left, George Izzard second from right nearest, Gerry Bayles (striped turtleneck) and Rob Porter beyond George, and Harry Chapin (far right). (441 Sqn)

CHAPTER 18

Starfighters Fading

441 Squadron Make-Up, July 1983

Commanding Officer	LCol C.W. Wilson
Flight Safety Officer	Capt D.C. Burt
Deputy CO	Maj G.W. Hatch
Operations Flight Commander	Maj C.D. Tuck
Operations Flight	Capt G.W. Bayles
	Capt D.P. Wilson
	Capt N.M. Nowosad
	Capt M.A. Holmes
	Lt G.P. Zans
Tactical/Weapons Flight Commander	Maj M.J. Savard
Tactical/Weapons Flight	Capt H.C. Chapin
	Capt R.P. Martin
	F/L T.L. Hammond, RAF
	Capt J.P. Sullivan
	Capt D.J. Anderson
Training Flight Commander	Maj B.M. Doyle
Training Flight	Capt J.P. MacNeil
	Capt R.I. Johnson
	Capt M.J. Hoch
	Capt W.J. Wolff von Wulfing
Squadron Adjutant	Capt D. Squires
Squadron Clerk	Cpl A. Jones
Squadron Mission Planners	Sgt C.P. Aucoin
	Sgt R.W. Moug
	Sgt T.W. Pieroway
	MCpl R.E. Hurst
	Cpl E.C. Denbeigh

Into the 1980s No.1 CAG was the smallest player in the NATO air combat Order of Battle. Nonetheless, standards and spirits remained high. "The CAG's" 50 or so CF-104s were ready to fight - two squadrons on the flightline, a few aircraft in reserve. The pilots were, as always for Canadians, the "best of the bunch" and flew their hearts out, always reaching or exceeding the NATO standard of 240 hours a year, when few other NATO fighter squadrons could boast that their pilots were meeting the mark.

The last 441 CF-104 era CO to serve a full term was LCol Ross Betts. A native of Toronto, he had joined the RCAF in 1963, initially as an RMC student. Having finished his studies, he began flight training on the Chipmunk at the PFS in Camp Borden. There he flew initially on August 3, 1967, and was done the course on September 7 after 27 hours. His training continued at Gimli, where he was introduced to the Tutor on September 28, then to the T-33 on the following April 1. Just as he was getting into the advanced course, however, Betts progress came to an abrupt halt. On May 30 he was on a flight into Thunder Bay with Capt Don Sharkey in T-bird 21184. As they departed for home, however, their armament door flew open. This was a known T-bird snag that sometimes had fatal results.

In this case, the aircraft was operating from a short runway on a hot day - not an ideal scenario for an emergency. The outcome was not pretty - the T-bird crashed at the end of the runway. The crew survived, but the aircraft was on fire. Unable to free himself, Betts contemplated his options. They were simple - stay put and fry, or pull the ejection handle. As flames spread into the cockpit, he ejected, coming down in his seat in a swampy patch, but still alive. A local man, Mr. Leppich, and his son, Peter, rushed over, the burly son hauling Sharkey from the plane. Other help quickly arrived and the two pilots soon were in hospital.

Betts, who had burns and fractures, recovered over a period of several weeks. He returned to flying on July 24, and progressed to his Wings. Posted to the Voodoo OTU at Bagotville, he spent some weeks on the T-33 getting his 500 jet hours and his "green ticket" (instrument flying rating). It was April 1969 before he began Voodoo simulator training. Finally, on May 20 Capt Earl McCurdy took him up in Voodoo 17478. The course continued to July 17, then Betts was posted to 425 Squadron, where he flew first on August 11.

Besides all the normal and interesting routines of a Voodoo squadron, from October to December 1970 Capt Betts was at Tyndall AFB on the Interceptor Weapons School course. There the emphasis was on tactics and weapons, and most flying was on F-101s. While at Tyndall, Betts twice fired the Genie rocket - the Voodoo's primary air-to-air weapon. On August 3, 1972 he flew his final 425 mission, going up in

Starfighter '880 in the maintenance hangar at Baden in 1978. It later was resplendent as a 441 "Checkerbird". (Larry Milberry)

101003 with Capt Pellow. Now he returned to RMC on the faculty, although he also was able to complete a Masters degree in mechanical engineering during this period. Three years later, he began his studies at Canadian Forces Command and Staff College in Toronto, then returned to flying. First came a Tutor refresher at Moose Jaw, flying initially with Maj Ed Rozdeba on August 27, 1976. Next, he did the CF-5 course with 419 Squadron, starting there with Maj Jake Miller on September 29. This ended on April 6, 1977, by when Betts had logged 110:00 hours on the CF-5.

On May 12, 1977 Maj Betts had his first CF-104 ride, Capt Lloyd Campbell of 417 Squadron taking him up on May 12. For Betts this would be a short course - 72.7 hours on the CF-104, 9:00 on the T-bird, before he left in September for 441 Squadron at Baden. There he first flew the CF-104 on October 28, 1977. His tour would mirror those described earlier, except that there was more ground attack and less ACM than in previous years. Betts was tour expired in June 1980, by when his log showed just under 700 hours in the CF-104. He next spent four years with 4 ATAF at Ramstein and Heidleberg. Following this he was promoted and given command of 441. He did a brief refresher course with 417, then began again at 441 in August 1983. The squadron continued with its usual tasks over the next two years, although there were some off-beat events. In May 1984, for instance, a flight of CF-18s arrived at Baden on a familiarization visit. On one of their missions they teamed with 441 in a mass attack on the Luftwaffe base at Memmingen, south of Augsburg.

In 1985 LCol Betts handed over command of 441 to LCol George Adamson, who would have the task in 1985 - 86 of winding up 441's NATO era. Following this tour LCol Betts remained a year at Baden as Base Operations Officer. In this

LCol George Adamson led the Silver Foxes at the end of the Starfighter era. (441 Sqn)

time he had a final opportunity to fly the CF-104 - August 8 - 9, 1986 he ferried 104747 to Turkey as part of a 2-ship with Maj Gord Hatch. On the 8th they departed Lahr, refuelled at Gioia de Colle, then overnighted at Bandirma, Turkey. Next

205

day Betts delivered '747 to Diyarbakir in eastern Turkey, having logged 6.2 hours en route. By this time his log book showed more than 1300 hours on the CF-104. Soon after this he was promoted and posted home for a year at National Defence College in Kingston. From 1987 - 89 he was Commandant of Royal Roads Military College in Victoria.

On June 26, 1987 Col Betts attended ceremonies at Cold Lake that brought 441 Squadron back to life, this time with CF-18s. Following Royal Roads, he was at NDHQ as Director of Air Requirements. In that period DAR projects included the EH-101 helicopter, the North Warning System, and the North American Air Defence Modernization project. The latter involved studies into establishing a number of CF-18 Arctic FOLs - forward operating locations. From 1993 - 96 Col Betts was in Washington as the Canadian Air Attaché, after which he retired from the Canadian Forces to pursue a consulting career in Ottawa.

The CO Looks Back

In September 2003 Ross Betts looked back on his days commanding 441 Squadron:

Getting command of a CF-104 squadron was like a dream come true - the top prize in a fighter pilot's career. A CO knew that, had always aspired to the job, and now it was his. By the time he got the nod, a fellow was in his late 30s or early 40s. He knew that other challenges lay beyond, so how did he know that this posting was the ultimate? Well, it was a feeling, although one that might not be fully appreciated until years had passed. The main thing was that, for now, the job belonged to him. It would be great fun, although there would be no escaping the work (and stress) that "came with the territory". Looking ahead, the new CO knew that he could prove his mettle only by living up to the responsibilities bestowed upon him. In this way he would not let down those who had passed on the torch over the decades, from Hurricane, Spitfire and Sabre days.

The best part of the CO's job was flying the CF-104 in the Cold War and NATO setting. This was serious, exhilarating business. What a rush it was to strap on "the missile with a man in it", then lead a 4-ship around Europe at 500 knots just above the treetops. What else impressed? The unparalleled talent of our Starfighter pilots, from flight commanders and squadron supervisors; through mass attack, section and element leads; to the greenest pipeliners. Each of them had wanted from the start to be a fighter pilot, and had come out at the top of the Canadian Forces' rigorous training system. We all know that '104 jocks had their differences, rivalries and idiosyncrasies but, at day's end, you could not work with a better bunch. The same went for those superb non-flying squadron mates - our maintainers, mission planners, "admin" folks, and others who supported the operation. They were good!

There were collective worries about our chosen profession, safety being one. Heaven knows that our aircraft had its reputation. Although dearly loved by all who flew and maintained it, the Starfighter was decisively unforgiving should attention waver for even an instant. Then there was the work load. For a squadron pilot, it was a full-time effort being a section or mass attack lead, getting in his 240 annual flying hours, keeping his green ticket current, passing his TacEval, participating in exercises and deployments, and holding a list of secondary duties.

The CO had to meet all these demands and also "run the place". Primarily that had to do with the operational mission. That was intricate business, with ceaseless planning, training, budgeting, reporting, etc. Taking an equal amount of time were human resources issues. In this regard the CO was a role model to any young, first-tour pilot. While the new boy might consider the CO "old enough to be my father", the CO knew better. He wasn't all that old to start with and he, too, had much to learn.

Other "HR" matters for the CO included annual performance evaluation reports - formal written assessments, or "PERs", done for each of his staff. One's PERs had a lot to do with future postings and promotions, so writing them was a serious responsibility. Recruiting also was a concern. The CO was looking for the best new talent available, but so were COs in all other CF-104 squadrons. The CO also had to deal with the military justice system and summary trials, family life issues and crises, and career managers, with whom he would collaborate in securing good, new assignments for tour-expired personnel. Otherwise the CO strove, through a variety of social events and other activities, to create a sense of cohesion and harmony to make 441 the best in the business.

Operationally, besides our primary ground attack mission, 441 had a secondary NATO role of day/VFR air defence. If the truth be known, in air defence we had only a rudimentary capability with our M61 cannon. On paper this would be supplemented by AIM-9 Sidewinders that, supposedly, would appear from USAF stockpiles if it ever came to a shooting war. Meanwhile, we trained for the mission and were prepared to give it our best.

Of Baden-Soellingen's three squadrons, 441 was the one designated to deploy to Lahr should war loom. How many times were we obliged to practice this mission in the dead of night and in marginal flying conditions! Our groundcrew were heroes in these exercises, rousted as they were from their beds in the dead of night by the dreaded "Kanadische Snowball Alarm". They always came through, more often than not having to load our vehicles in rain or mist, then disappear down the autobahn to be in position at Lahr and ready for war operations when the first Starfighter landed. In my years on squadron, 441 always rose to such challenges.

The following snippets have popped to mind at random from a memory overflowing with anecdotes that could fill a book of their own:

The howl of the J79's inlet guide vanes during engine run-up prior to an early morning launch.

Friday night in the Officers' Mess, a weekly ritual in the back bar to swap yarns. Bartenders René and Bob dutifully collected one DM per gross bier. Then would come dinner in the dining room under Johanna's careful supervision. She always supplied fresh eggs to "initiate" any invited guests at the Silver Fox table. Some hardcore 441 member then would demonstrate our custom of sucking a raw egg through an old sock, or variations on the theme. Guests would be "invited" to partake.

Often, with little advance planning, a crowd of us would pile into our cars and race across the Rhine, through the lonely border check point, and into France to enjoy a variety of gourmet haunts to feast on frogs legs, snails and steak moutard. The Garlic Pit was but one of our favourite places.

After a lengthy moratorium, in the early 1980s we re-negotiated our way back to Decimomannu for periodic "gun camps". There we were introduced to the capabilities of the instrumented Air Combat Manoeuvring Range for mock air-to-air combat. This included firing our M61 cannons at flags towed by Canadian T-33s. There always was time for after hours "debriefings" over calzone and red wine down the road at the Lorelei restaurant.

The 2-week winter survival course given by the French Air Force in Meribel and Val d'Isère. People wondered why downhill skiing was thought to be so important for fighter pilots (something to do with lead-deflection shooting, I think).

Squadron exchanges with our German sister squadron at Schleswig. Battle formation during anti-shipping exercises with them over the "fish bowl" of the Baltic Sea (without a radar altimeter). Awaking one morning at Tanagra, Greece to find that we Canadians were alone - our hosts had deployed overnight to forward locations in response to some tension with their friends, the Turks. Splash targets towed by high speed boats. The Danes taught us about them. The targets sent up a huge plume of water, so were easy to spot miles away. Range rules at sea were flexible, so long as one's nose was not pointed at the tow boat. This was an awe-inspiring way to test the long-range capabilities of our new CRV-7 rockets. Norway and the time our hosts underhandedly one-upped us at our raw eggs skit. Two Silver Fox "Eggmeisters" each were challenged to down a Norwegian egg. It was an ugly scene, for they were fed sea gull eggs, which our hosts had been preparing by incubating them for weeks atop a hot water radiator. Rimini and the Italian '104 pilot who, dripping in sweat after a mass attack flown in duff weather, was heard to complain, "Training witta you-ah Canadians is like-ah going to war!"

And let's not forget the wives and families. They did not come over to Southern Germany without a lot of sacrifice. The ladies often left behind careers and other responsibilities in Canada, to face a new set of challenges as to language, culture, housing, transportation, schooling for the kids, and taking care of business alone, when their husbands were away on exercises or deployments. They were the glue that kept 4 Wing together and running smoothly.

With the CF-18 scheduled to re-equip Canada's NATO squadrons, 439 Squadron stood down in November 1984, followed by 421 in the following October. While most 1 CAG pilots now were posted home to Canada, some joined 441, allowing us to preserve a credible NATO operational commitment. These additions, formerly friendly rivals, came to us in great style and were truly welcomed. The transition was smooth and they contributed much.

In my experience it was 441 that generally took the lion's share of kudos in 1 CAG competitions, and got the highest ratings on annual NATO TacEvals. We flew aggressively, safely, effectively, and were the squadron to beat.

Checkers! Checkers! Of Starfighters and Phantoms

RCAF postwar involvement with the Luftwaffe began when Germany was cleared by the Occupying Forces to re-establish its military. Re-formed in September 1956, the Luftwaffe chose the Canadair-built Sabre for its primary day fighter. Canada provided 75 surplus Sabre 5s, then 225 new Sabre 6s. A cadre of RCAF instructors was posted to Oldenburg to help the Germans establish a Sabre OTU - "Waffenschule 10". These men stayed on to instruct until the Luftwaffe became self-sufficient, a story that is covered in The Canadair Sabre.

In later years a number of Canadian Forces men had Luftwaffe exchanges mainly on F-4s and Tornados, while Germans flew CF-18s at Cold Lake. One of those involved was Gordon Zans, whose parents had emigrated to Canada from West Germany after the war. Gordon was born in Hamilton, Ontario in 1958. In 1972, however, his family returned to West Germany, settling in an area frequented by low-flying NATO fighters. Any time one of these roared over, Gordon got day-dreaming about being a fighter pilot, especially if he could fly the F-104. Intent on making his dream come true, in 1979 he visited Lahr and enlisted in the Canadian Forces.

The following January, Zans was in officer training at CFB Chilliwack. Soon he advanced to Portage la Prairie for primary flying training, beginning on Musketeers on October 21, 1980. Moose Jaw followed, Zans' first Tutor flight being on April 24, 1981 with Capt Gino Tessier. This course took Zans to

The last of many 6 (ST/R) OTU/417 Squadron Starfighter courses was No. 8203 of November 1982 - May 1983. Standing are Lt Harry A. Mueller, Lt Gordon P. Zans, Capt D.V. "Dan" Dempsey, Lt R.A. "Rich" Lancaster and Lt Craig R. Halliwell. Seated are Maj M.R. "Mike" Spooner, Capt J.L.R. Denis "Murk" Mercier and Maj B.M. "Bert" Doyle. (Gord Zans Col.)

Lt Gordon Zans while a member of Course 8203 at 417 Squadron. (441 Sqn)

February 17, 1982, when he qualified for his Wings, having logged 202.6 Tutor hours.

By this time Zans was on track for fighters and posted to 419 Squadron, beginning the course on April 27 with a flight in CF-5 116820 with Capt Ferguson. The 419 course continued to August 24 and totalled 107.5 hours. Now came what every Canadian fighter pilot "wanabee" dreamed of - a first flight in the CF-104. For Zans the date was December 6, 1982, Capt Kevin Vaillant showing him some of the CF-104 basics. The course, which included 90.3 hours on the CF-104, ran to April 19, 1983. Since Lt Zans topped his course, his reward was a familiarization ride with Maj Charleton in CF-18 188904. This was a great opportunity, for the first CF-18s had just arrived in Cold Lake.

From OTU, Zans was posted as a pipeliner to 441 Squadron at Baden-Soellingen. There he first flew in CF-104D '661 with Capt Gerry Bayles on May 17. Henceforth his tour reflected that of a typical Canadian flying in the NATO environment with standard route and range exercises, exchanges, airshows, TacEvals, etc. August 12 to 18, 1983, for example, Zans joined some squadron mates on an exchange with the Norwegians at Oerland. That was a good month for him - 27.6 CF-104 hours, another 1.5 in the T-bird.

In this period 1 CAG often operated on the range with the OV-10 Broncos of the US Army 704 TASS. Its OV-10s provided FAC (forward air control) during run-ins to bomb. Another periodic exercise was "Ample Gain", whereby a CF-104 section would land at another NATO base without notice. The object was to give other NATO techs training in refuelling and re-arming someone else's fighters. For October 17, 1983, Capt Zans was sent to Furstenfeldbruck for such "inter-operability" training.

Also great fun for anyone were exchanges with 441's sister squadron at Schleswig - 1 Marinefliegergeschwader (1 Sqn/1 Naval Air Wing). Zans first such exchange was in October 1983. Periodic visits to the range at Decimomannu also were a highlight. From November 14 - 24, 1983 he flew many range and ACM missions there. His first mission on the 15th was a 2-V-2 against F-16s. In the afternoon it was a 4-V-2 against F-15s. Next day he logged another 4-V-2. On one mission during this deployment, Capt Rob Martin scored two F-15s kills (as confirmed by ACM range instrumentation and/or cine film). On the 23rd at "Deci" Zans was on a gunnery mission against a towed banner (13 hits scored).

On December 9, 1983 came another typical mission from Baden - attacking a US Army Hawk missile battery. In May 1984 he was on exchange to Leuchars and Binbrook then, in June, was in Rimini, Italy training with 102º Gruppo, another Starfighter unit. From June 12 - 28 Zans logged eight sorties from Rimini, but there also was good fun on the side, the host squadron going overboard to keep the social calendar filled (to say nothing of quality time on the Adriatic beaches).

The life of a 1 CAG pilot was never dull. If he wasn't busy flying training routes, tearing up the ranges, doing TacEvals (once yearly per pilot, plus squadron and ATAF TacEvals), filling in the mandatory squares with such things as quarterly night flying, he was on the road. No sooner was Zans back from Rimini, for example, than he was off for a July weekend to Pferdsfeld in 104715. This was pretty well R&R - an airshow gig where '715 was on static display. On August 13, 1984 Zans, flying 104716, took part in a mass Ramstein fly-past honouring the Commander Allied Air Forces Central Europe. On August 24 Maj Fred Mueller passed Zans on his annual TacEval, following a sortie in 104658.

Another type of exercise was "Recall" (known in earlier days as "Snowball"). In this, the wing would be recalled to base. This usually began with an unwelcomed "wake-up" call at about 0300. When the phone rang, each man had to grab his kit, rush to the base and get to his post, whether he was a pilot, line tech, fueller, met briefer, MP, or admin type. Such a scramble could see 441 launched in its air superiority role to its secondary home, Lahr, where there were extra hardened aircraft shelters (Baden was short of HASs, with enough only for 421 and 439).

Another occasional exercise saw 441 suiting up in NBCW kit. For pilots this meant climbing into bulky "AR5" suits. Zans' log shows him doing this on March 13, 1985 for a mission in 104636. Awkward as the AR5 looked, he found it usable. His mission that day in '636 was logged as 1.4 hours. On April 19 Zans had his annual TacEval, this time in AR5 kit. Capt Marc Ouellet did that ride, giving Zans a pass.

Once a year in this period 441 attended gunnery camp at Leeuwarden, Holland. Zans was on one of these from October 2 - 4, 1984. These missions were brief - 0.7 to 0.9 hours, indicating the frequent use of normal throttle, plus afterburner (which guzzled fuel). For October 1984, 441 sojourned in Tanagra, Greece, although there were no missions with Greek fighters - they were on alert due to regional tensions. Thus did 441 make its own fun, bombing at the Abalone Range, or doing 2-V-1 or 3-V-2 ACM missions. The squadron flew home via Rimini (a social call on 102° Gruppo).

Every CF-104 driver seems to have logged some emergency or other, sometimes even a bailout. Happily, Gord Zans had nothing worse than a bird strike, plus a case of a u/s engine nozzle. The bird hit his jet on the windscreen after he had scabbed onto the Pampa range on March 25, 1985. The bird smashed through the nose, blood and guts obscuring the view ahead. Zans made a precautionary landing at Norvenich, near Cologne. Capt Dave Anderson came over in 104638 to take him back to base. An MRP from Baden repaired the damaged jet on site. For March 27, 1985 Zans' squadron was busy with a 20-mm mini-Top Gun competition. For this Zans flew four times for 4.4 hours. The task was to do air-to-ground at Siegenberg, but also to "hit" simulated targets en route. At day's end it was usual for the low scorers to buy the beer.

Even in these days of Starfighters waning, life at 441 remained exciting. So what that the first CF-18s were in the air and all sights were on replacing the CF-104. For those on 441 the future may have been uncertain, but there still was good flying to be done. For March 1985 Capt Zans logged an amazing 35.7 hours. Also in April he flew some missions supporting the NATO Tactical Leadership Program. These were from Jever and were "Red Air" (attacking) missions against TLP pilots flying as "Blue Air" (defending). By this time 441 was absorbing a few pilots from 421 Squadron, which had stood down in October 1985.

If the opportunity arose, Capt Zans would go along on famil flights with other NATO pilots. On June 6, 1985 he was in the back seat of a Dutch F-16 for a mass fly-by at Leeuwarden. On July 4 he flew chase on CF-18 Hornet 188786 (on his first nav flight in Europe, a Hornet pilot was required to have one of the "locals" squire him around the countryside). In July, Zans deployed to Rimini then, on July 20, was in a mass attack on the USAFE base at Bitburg, which was being "TacEvaled". As CF-104s poured in towards Bitburg, high level F-15s caught onto them. The Canadians pushed up the power to beat their adversaries with speed. In the process one of the pilots, while juggling throttle, burner, map, etc., punched off his tip tanks - a classic bit of "finger trouble". One tank demolished the (empty) rental car of one of the TacEval umpires.

The last time the CF-104 appeared in a TLP scenario was in December 1985, Capts Gordon Zans and Wally Niemi as course members taking part in this exercise from Jever. By now 441 was preparing to stand-down. On February 24/25, 1986 there were 12-plane fly-by practices. A few days later a big squadron reunion was held, and on March 1 the final fly-by went off smoothly, the pilots being George Adamson, Dan Dempsey, André Deschamps, Bert Doyle, Craig Halliwell, Bill Huckstep, Al Hunter, Harry Mueller, Kelly Kovach, Mike Savard, Ron Smith and Gord Zans (in 104815). March 12 - 13, 1986 Zans delivered one of the last of 54 ex-Canadian CF-104s to the Turks. For the occasion, Zans took 104735 to Diyarbakir. On April 14 he had his final CF-104 trip, going along with Capt Judge Wenham in 104661 on a local flight from Baden. Zans had logged 804.6 hours on type.

No sooner was Zans finished on 441 than a new opportunity arose - an RF-4E recce pilot exchange opened up in the Luftwaffe. This was ideal for Capt Zans, a German-speaking fighter pilot current on low level fighter operations. He applied, was accepted, and slid straight into the job. There was no OTU, so he immediately began training on his new unit, 511 "Immelman" squadron, based at Bremgarten, south of Lahr. He began with four sessions in the OFT (operational flight trainer), then flew initially on August 27, 1986. His crew solo (with a weapons system operator Maj Hergesell in the back seat) came on September 29 in RF-4E "35-38", after which routine operations commenced.

The move from CF-104 to RF-4 required some re-thinking for any pilot. Now there was that "guy in the back" to talk and listen to. A good back-seater was an asset. He did the flight planning, navigated and operated the recce equipment. But not all were equal so, to play it safe, Zans still carried maps for whichever the route. Then there was the equipment. No more cannons, bombs and rockets, but a load of electronics from

In November 1983 the Silver Foxes deployed to Decimomannu for weapons training. Here they display Gord Zans' banner that showed 13 hits after a shoot. Lined up are Chris Tuck, an "Intel" man, unknown, Rick Wilson, Willem Wolff von Wulfing, Dave Burt, Jim Kelly, Bob Johnson, Gord Hatch, Mike Hoch, Mark Holmes, Gord Zans, Neale Nowosad, Mike Savard, Ross Betts (CO), Rob Martin and John MacNeil. (441 Sqn)

recce cameras, to IR line scan (for low-level recces), and Side-Looking Airborne Radar used higher up to record such targets as armour miles inside the Iron Curtain.

As with any NATO squadron, 511 had regular deployments. There was an annual trip to the Coca low-level range in Portugal. For training in the wide-open spaces, there was Goose Bay, Labrador. Zans had one such deployment September 28 - October 13, 1987, when he flew 11 recce sorties. On the 14th he set off for home base on a 6.3-hour trans-Atlantic flight accompanied by two USAF KC-135s. Another periodic deployment was to Strasbourg, France; there 511 trained with a squadron of Armé de l'Air recce Mirage F.1s. On one Strasbourg trip Zans made five test sorties in NBCW gear (learning of Zans' experience with the AR5 suit, 511 had made him squadron NBCW officer).

Maj Zans had his last 511 flight on October 28, 1988. In two years he had accumulated 458.2 hours on the RF-4E. Replaced by Capt Ron Huzarik, Zans now spent June - July 1989 on a CF-18 "short course" at 410 Squadron, then served to 1991 at Lahr as TacEval officer. In this period the Gulf War threatened, and Zans was on the first Hercules into the Gulf region as part of a recce team determining potential CF-18 operating bases. Based for four months at coalition HQ in Qatar, he logged five Hornet proficiency trips in the days before hostilities erupted. From Lahr, he moved to Baden as Deputy WOpsO, but before taking up this slot, took the ICP course in Winnipeg, followed by his CF-18 upgrade at 410. The following year (1991 - 92) he was at Staff College in Toronto. He instructed at 410 Squadron from 1993 - 96, then spent four years as a NATO exercise planner in Ramstein. With the Berlin Wall down, he had the chance to plan and conduct exercises in some Warsaw Pact countries, and experience famil flights in such types as the Mi-8 helicopter and L39 trainer. In 2000 LCol Zans was posted to 4 Wing to command 410 Squadron, taking over from LCol Al Stevenson. This was preceded by a brief CF-18 re-certification in May. As CO, Zans would have two main jobs -- leadership and a busy training schedule.

Each winter 410 had an instructors deployment to some place like Eglin AFB or Tyndall AFB in Florida, or USMC Air Station Fallon in Arizona. This was Ex. Cougar South, an opportunity for the IPs to hone their advanced combat skills. In January 1994, for example, "Cougar South" at Eglin included many ACM missions, 4-V-4s, 8-V-8s, etc. Often using AAR (KC-130s), 410's IPs were able to squeeze a lot from each mission.

On March 22, 2001 Zans was honoured to fly one of 410's most famous wartime night fighter pilots - G/C R.D. "Joe" Schultz, DFC and Bar (8 kills). That evening 410 had Schultz at the head table for a Mess Dinner. In August 4 Wing hosted a flight of B-1B from the 128th ANG "Georgia Bones" Bomb Squadron. Some B-1B fellows were given Hornet rides. The squadron CO, Col Doehling, reciprocated by offering a ride to LCol Zans. On August 6 as they boarded B-1B No.'0124, Zans headed for the co-pilot's seat. "No you don't", said Col Doehling, and directed him into the aircraft commander's seat. What followed was the full, hands-on B-1B treatment, from low-level at 600 knots, to mountain flying, touch-and-goes, etc. -- 3.4 hours of fighter pilot heaven in a big bomber.

From August 8 - 13, 2001 LCol Zans led 410 Squadron to victory at the inaugural "Tiger Meet of the Americas" at Buckley Airfield, Colorado. There 410 pitted its flying, athletic and social skills against other "big cat" hemispheric squadrons. Another great opportunity was delivering the oldest CF-18 (188901) from Cold Lake to the National Aviation Museum. On October 17 Zans flew to Ottawa International Airport via Thunder Bay. Next day, with LGen Al Dequetteville (the first CO of a CF-18 Squadron and the first Canadian to fly '901) he made the short hop into Rockcliffe, landing on its foreshortened runway, equipped for the occasion with a mobile arrester cable system.

During the G-8 Summit in Alberta, Zans flew two Op. Grizzly sorties (June 25, 2002 in '793 -- 5.9 hours, and June 27 in '784 -- 5.7 hours). These were CAP missions (with AAR) covering the G-8 site against any possible aerial threat (9-11 still was fresh in everyone's mind). On July 5, 2002 (as he had done a year earlier) LCol Zans conducted the flypast for the Calgary Stampede. Four days later he flew his final sortie as 410 CO, taking up 188741 on a 1-V-1 mission. Upon making up his log after the mission, he noted his total air force time as 2875.4 hours, 804.6 on CF-104s and 1177.4 on CF-18s. He had finished his fighter pilot days with much satisfaction, 99% of his flying having been on high performance jets.

More skits, starting with the disappearing man act - perpetrated at Deci. Seen are Mike Hoch, Mark Holmes, Rick Wilson, Tom Hammond and Marsh Simpson (AWC). Neale Nowosad is here, too - stuck in the armoire for having done something to aggravate his room mates. (Gord Zans Col.)

Gord Zans, Dave Anderson and (underneath) Bert Doyle try to get a 1 NAW "Tornado" off the ground. (Gord Zans Col.)

Silver Foxes during some August 1983 boating with their Norwegian hosts from Orland: Neale Nowosad, Rob Martin and Dave Anderson. Then, from the same exchange, Silver Foxes having a beer or two with their hosts. (Gord Zans Col.)

Silver Fox CO LCol Ross Betts at a dinner honouring 441 during its October 1984 exchange to 334 Sqn, Hellenic Air Force. The Greek CO has just accepted 441's gift of a CF-104 print. Then, BBQ kings Mark Holmes and Mike Hoch during the same deployment to Tanagra, and the zapper designed for the occasion. (Gord Zans Col., 441 Sqn)

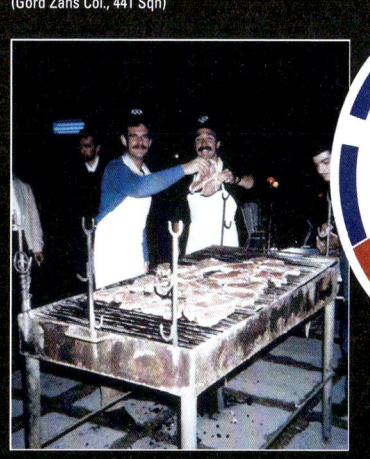

Gord Zans' reminders of 441 ACM days. First, a beat-up of the F-4 flightline at RAF Leuchars during a May 1, 1984 TacEval exercise. Then, an RAF F-4 in Zans' sights over the English Channel. (Gord Zans Col.)

Piano burning scenes in Gord Zans' day as F/L T.L. Hammond (RAF) was being honoured at the end of his 441 exchange. In front are demolition team members Neale Nowosad, Mike Hoch, Mike Savard, Tom Hammond, Don Squires (Adj). Behind are Gord Zans, Dan Dempsey, Craig Halliwell, Jim Sullivan, John MacNeil, Dave Anderson, Chris Tuck, Craig Richmond, Dave Burt, Rob "Clobber" Johnson and Gerry Bales. Then, Hammond opening the procedures. (441 Sqn)

The wreckers get down to business. As the Brits used to say, the piano is first "reduced to produce", set alight, then the party really goes crazy! (414 Sqn)

The final 441 line-up at Baden in the spring of 1986. In front are Maj Mike Savard, Capt Rich Lancaster, Capt Bill Huckstep, Maj Dan Dempsey and Capt Jim Sullivan. The first few in the cockpits are LCol George Adamson (CO), Maj Wally Peirson, Capt Dave Anderson, Capt Neale Nowosad, Capt Craig Halliwell, Capt André Deschamp and Capt Harry Mueller. (Gord Zans Col.)

Coming to an End

The "handwriting on the wall" for Canada's CF-104s came early in 1984. On January 11 the "Foxes Lair" column in *Der Kanadier* remarked on a forthcoming visit by "the F-18 talent scout agency ... referred to by the unimaginative as the career manager's visit." Capts Mike Hoch and John MacNeil were plucked from 441 to train on CF-18s. The new fighter represented a leap in technology over the CF-104, with computers, HUD, AAMs, and power, range, payload and manoeuvrability to spare. That spring a 410 detachment deployed to West Germany using in-flight refuelling.

The last CF-104s now began to fade, 439 Squadron going first in 1984. That October Capt Dan Dempsey of 439 flew 15 times for 17.1 hours in Starfighters 104658, '713, '737, '786, '806, '808. '865, and '899. His missions included to the ranges at Pampa and Suippes, a radar route, a local instrument training flight and several "TAC BAV" missions. He also had one session in the OFT instructing Lt Rich Lancaster in emergency procedures. On October 24 he had Dr. Mick Meyer in the back seat. On November 28, 1984 Dempsey was in 439's final flypast, a 1.3-hour trip in 104815. Of this he noted in his log, "The end of the Tiger CF-104 era". He and several other Tigers now joined 441 to finish up Canada's operational CF-104 years.

In October 1985, 421 Squadron also stood down, and things at 441 also were heading in that direction. Even so, there still was a lot of good flying taking place. January 1986 proved to be a great finish to Dan Dempsey's CF-104 career. That month he flew 21 times for 26.2 hours. Included in all this fun was a mass attack by 15 CF-104s on Bitburg. With LCol Tom Byrne in '636 on the 27th, Dempsey passed his 600th hour on type. On the Baumholder Range in '788 on the 31st he fired 22 CRV-7s in salvo.

On February 5 Dempsey flew '808 to RAF Coningsby to meet with the Red Arrows. This was a liaison trip, since he knew that he had been recommended to lead the Snowbirds. He logged his last CF-104 supersonic run in '808 on February 7, noting his top speed as M1.6, or 560 kts ground speed. Meanwhile, Dempsey was busy on the CF-104 stand-down committee, getting the commemorative book *CF-104 Starfighter 1961 - 1968* into print, and having aviation artist Dugald Cameron in Scotland produce two special edition CF-104 prints. On the 24th and 27th the Silver Foxes flew 12-plane practices then, on March 1, the final 441/CFE Starfighter flypast took place, Dempsey taking up '841. For the occasion the CO, LCol George H. Adamson, noted of the Starfighter era:

Canadian fighter pilots and their dedicated maintenance personnel have made a significant contribution to keeping the peace in Central Europe. Whether in the strike, reconnaissance or conventional strike role, we have maintained an excellent reputation amongst our NATO allies, while constantly striving to improve our capability to operate and survive in an ever increasingly complex and difficult

Silver Foxes of yore at the CF-104 close-out in 1986. The four behind are Keith M. Adlard, Ken Mowbray, Jim Pfaff and Ron Tomcheck. In front are Bob Christie, Sky King, Ron Doyle, Neal Kleinsteuber, Paul Manson, Herb Sievert and George Kirbyson. (Sky King Col.)

battlefield." The CO then paid tribute to those in the CF-104 community lost in accidents, and finished by eyeing the future: "The Starfighter is hanging up her spurs and making way for the Hornet era. However, I am confident that the order of Starfighter pilots will keep the memories and esprit de corps alive for many years to come.

The transfer of 54 serviceable CF-104s to the Turkish Air Force, which had been proceeding since January 11,1986, now accelerated at Lahr. On March 12 - 13 Dan Dempsey ferried 104865 to Turkey, going down in a gaggle with Harry Chapin, André Deschamps, Al Hunter and Wally Peirson. On the three legs of this operation he logged his final five CF-104 flying hours. The last of six ferry flights departed for Turkey on May 5. Now the Silver Foxes, who had set up shop at North Luffenham in March 1952 and been on the Continent since 1955, went home to Canada.

Silver Fox pilots and "Intel" staff at the end of the Starfighter era. Standing are: unknown, MCpl D. Smith, MCpl G. Hupe, André Deschamps, Dave Anderson, Mike Savard, George Adamson (CO), Dan Dempsey, Don Squires, Craig Halliwell, Gerry Bayles, Neale Nowosad and Harry Mueller. In front are Gord Zans, Wally Niemy, Kelly Kovach, Bill Huckstep, Jim Sullivan, Al Hunter, Wally Peirson, Rich Lancaster and Mark Holmes. (Gord Zans Col.)

The last contingent of 441 NCMs, March 1986. In front are Cpl R. Letness, Cpl J. Matthews, Sgt A. Halloran, Cpl J.C.Martin, MCpl D. Austin, Cpl J. Richkun, Pte R. Trepanier, Cpl A. Rogers, MCpl W. White, Pte K. Monk, MCpl P. Blouin and Cpl H. Anderson. Standing are MCpl M. Savard, Cpl R. Clowater, Cpl S. Cummings, Cpl R. Holliday, Pte F. Wiesman, Cpl P. Conroy, Cpl J.D. McCully, WO A. Anderson, Cpl D. Lloyd, Cpl K. Makins, Cpl N. Wafer, Cpl L. Nault, Cpl R. Ziegler, Cpl G. Rodrigue and Cpl W. Stoyles. Absent were Sgts R. Bergeron and M. Tracey, MCpls G. Hupe and D. Smith, Cpls J. Donegan, C. James and P. Laurent. (441 Sqn)

Sky King as a young Starfighter pilot at Marville does some "secondary duty". He's giving a cockpit tour to 1967 Miss Canada, Barbara Kelly. (441 Sqn)

Starfighter Pilot - A Retrospective

Garry "Sky" King, who grew up in Humboldt, Saskatchewan, joined the RCAF in 1959 as a Royal Military College student. In the summer months King trained on the Chipmunk and Harvard. He won his Wings on Course 6301 at Portage la Prairie in June 1964, coming away with the 2 AFS Flying Trophy. From November 1964 to February 1965, King completed the STU at Chatham, then was posted to 6 ST/R OTU. On March 26 he first flew the CF-104, going up with instructor Bob Saxberg.

Sky King joined 441 at Marville in September 1965 to begin what would become the longest uninterrupted 441 Starfighter tour. He would stay with the squadron until August 1970 and log some 1000 hours on type. King's career now followed a varied path, beginning with a 4-year posting in Operations at NDHQ. In 1974 - 75 he attended CF Staff and Command School in Toronto, then migrated into the transport world, first on C-130s with 435 Squadron, then as CO of 440 Squadron on Twin Otters. Thinking back to those days in 2003, King remarked about how the takeoff speed of a CF-104 was faster than the Twin Otter's top speed! But it was all great fun, at any speed.

While on 440, King one day flew A/C/M Sir David Evans, RAF, from Edmonton to Cold Lake. Their chat en route seemed to turn into more of a job interview, and LCol King soon found himself on Evans' staff at RAF Strike Command in High Wycombe. From here, in 1981 he was promoted and posted in Plans and Policy at 4 ATAF in Heidelburg, Germany. In 1983 he became Base Commander at CFB Trenton where, among other projects, he led the move to establish the RCAF Memorial Museum. For its opening in 1984 he invited A/C/M Evans to Trenton to officiate. In the summer of 1986 now-BGen King returned to 4 ATAF. Two years later he became Chief of Staff Operations at AIRCOM HQ in Winnipeg, from where he retired in 1990. Before long he entered the business world with his own aviation consulting firm, Skyworks Inc. In 2003 Sky King looked back on his 441 years flying the Starfighter.

It was a slice. In a historical sense some might say that it was a small, perhaps insignificant slice of a squadron's life. Yet, for the 441 Squadron pilots and families who were assigned a new role that they could not spell, in a land that they knew little about, their experiences would be indelibly inked forever in their hearts and souls. Granted, 441 Sabre pilots had ruled the air in Central Europe since 1954, but this was going to be different. Reconnaissance was different. Reconnaissance was low and fast, enemy ground orders of battle, photo vans, cut and paste, line searches, choke points, AMX VTPs, and Schutzenpanzer Kurz. It was in the mud and the murk of a strange land in an aircraft that preferred to purr at 35,000 feet. It was Recce.

For seven years, 1964 to 1970, the RCAF/CAF was in the tactical reconnaissance business in NATO Europe. Canada's government of the day decided that Canada should contribute nuclear strike, reconnaissance, and attack air forces to NATO's Central Region using the CF-104 Starfighter. Thus began an incredible process of RCAF pilots, starting with the docile Sabre Transition Unit in Chatham, advancing to the intense six-months course at 6 ST/R OTU in Cold Lake, then moving on to their the squadrons No.1 Air Division.

The banter on course at Cold Lake was filled with excitement and anticipation. Strike or Recce? Everybody had a preference for the Starfighter squadron they wanted, and the role - or thought they did. To most they were just numbers and strange names in foreign lands. "Baden's the only game in Europe... strike role, the Kur Haus in Baden Baden, Fasching, Oktoberfest." ... "Give me Zweibrucken and 434 Squadron" ... "Marville and Recce ... Forget it! You can't kill anybody with a Brownie Starflash."

The great debate would continue undiminished for the life of both roles in Europe. No.1 (Recce) Wing would comprise 439 and 441 Squadrons and have an intense rivalry in the tactical reconnaissance business all their own, but they were absolutely united when confronted by a Strike puke from 3 Wing or 4 Wing. It made for healthy repartee on Friday nights and during weapons deployment camps at Decimomannu. But there would not be a winner. Each role had its appeal. But the recce squadrons did revel in new challenges on a daily basis, as mission planning provided fresh targets for each sortie. Recce pilots could boast that they never flew the same mission twice, while the Strike pilots led a predictable existence, plowing through the low level system on canned routes that they had long since memorized through countless repetition. The monotony was broken only with a semi-aerobatic munitions delivery routine (the "LADD" manoeuvre) prior to returning to base.

But, of course, reconnaissance was easier to explain to Moms, Dads and concerned elders of clans left at home: "So what will you be doing in France, Dear?" "Taking pictures, Mom." "That's nice, Dear. Make sure that you wear your heavy socks when you fly that starplane of yours." "Yes, Mom." That worked for a while, until the first Christmas, when all the new charges sent squadron Christmas cards home to relatives. Unfortunately, the highlight of the card was the squadron motto emblazoned so that no one could miss it - "Stalk and Kill." Whoa, did that get a reaction! Aunts and uncles from Gander to Victoria wrote in tomes expressing horror to their precious innocents. The following Christmas, our cards were less "offensive"..

We Learned About Flying From That

Through 1964-65 the Cold Lake mill continued to churn out Starfighter pilots for the NATO Wings, and 441 eagerly accepted its share. The system provided a curious mix of seasoned CF-100 and F-86 drivers (who had already "been there") and green pipeliners with shiny new wings on their tunics and fire in their bellies. This chemistry would prove to be a key ingredient to success in this new role. The seasoned pilots did their best to keep the lid on the youthful energy and inexperience of the "pipes." For some it became a full time job.

The graduates of Course 7 (6ST/R OTU) provided the nucleus of the new look 441 Squadron. W/C Bob Edwards officially accepted the baton on January 20, 1964 and made history six weeks later when he took the first aerial photographs from a CF-104 in NATO's Central Region. The hunt was on. 441 Squadron would be extremely well served by the cadre of leadership that crossed the Atlantic in turn over the next six years to take charge of the flamboyant Silver Foxes. W/C Jim Dunlop took over from W/C Edwards just in time to accept a healthy influx of new Course 17 pilots. He would spend the majority of his tenure working magic to keep his junior troops out of jail. This left the daily management to the quiet efficiency of S/L Bill VanOene (V-One), with S/L Ernie Gardiner naturally assuming the role of squadron whip. The cardinal rule on 441 was simple - "Don't mess with Ernie." A master of the understatement with little patience for the unprepared, he announced to a very lost pilot on a routine chase trip, that the river they had just crossed (completely missed by the distraught pilot) was "large enough to float the Queen Mary."

The Recce God continued to look kindly on 441 by sending G/C Bob Christie to be Marville's new Base Commander on hand-off from G/C Avant. An avid pilot, he quickly became a dedicated recce fan, and for the 441 "SMU" (single members union), a saviour. It was a slow Monday morning in the Base Commander's office that did not have to quell some kind of international incident, created by an SMU somewhere in Central Europe on the weekend. G/C Christie stick-handled his way out of many such touchy escapades. He also was greatly loved for his great directives issued to 441's single troops. Included were escort officer duties for Miss Canada, and for female entertainers on tour from Canada. Then there was the most legendary G/C Christie epistle of all - "During the renovations of the single officers quarters, all officers will be required to live together in the single female quarters. Your patience in these cramped living conditions is appreciated."

Since tactical reconnaissance in a modern theatre of operations was a new experience for the RCAF, the learning curve was steep. Pilots would return from missions with photos of military targets that they could not identify. The team went to work. Intelligence, mission planning, photo interpreters and aircrew worked feverishly to bring the squadron up to speed. The first time a wandering pilot chanced upon a Nike Hercules missile site, he reported sighting, "a bunch of pointee thingees laying beside several garages". The contrast of this sparkling bit of intelligence, to the precise report that would be filled out on the same site a very short time later, was indicative of the remarkable transition from neophyte to seasoned pro that was accomplished by the gang of dedicated recce troops at Marville.

Some recce pilots transitioned from the crystal clear and lonely skies of northern Alberta to the crowded, bleak skies of Central Europe more easily than others. Although the unswerving pride of the "zipper" pilot stood the test for the most part, many stories of panic while airborne trickled into the squadron lounge: "If I hadn't turned him around, we would have been in Salzburg for lunch," or "That's the second time this month that I've popped up in Frankfurt's traffic pattern," or "Hey Boss, what big city has a large tower in it that looks just like the Eiffel T... Oops!"

The incredible rush of flying low and fast over the convoluted, patchwork terrain of France, Germany and the Benelux gave the recce driver his daily bread. In an attempt to provide some sort of system to daily training in NATO airspace, a group of rocket scientists decided that 500 feet above ground was the low level operating altitude for all NATO fast jets flying tactical training missions. On any given day, several hundred of NATO's finest could be found thrashing around in the murk and haze of a particular region that was lucky enough to have marginal VMC conditions at 500 feet. Marvelous! Canadians, for the most part, flew lower. Incredibly, it was the safest place in Europe. Many a mid-air was avoided as CF-104s slipped underneath Phantoms, RB-66s, RF-84s, Canberras and others who were idly meandering along at the stipulated 500 feet, oblivious to how close death had been.

Daily training followed the weather. A favorite mission was a High-Low-High profile to Chateauroux in southwestern France mostly because you could sing the "Chateaux-roo-roo" song all the way there. On the downside for the unprepared, it offered some of the most challenging terrain in Europe. The hedgerow countryside of that beautiful region of France was a humbling experience to the most capable recce driver. For many, however, the ultimate intimidator was the Eiffel Mountains, and beautiful region of Germany east of the Grand Duchy of Luxembourg. The Eiffel was the home of the USAF at Hahn, Bitburg and Spangdahlem, the Luftwaffe at Buchel and Pferdsfeld, and the famous Formula One Nurburgring racing complex. Line searches were a special challenge. Tactical evaluation pilots loved to chase pilots on their check rides through this wonderfully sadistic chunk of real estate. Pilots having trouble navigating on good days prayed constantly for permanent poor visibility in the Eiffel.

Although not as unencumbered as the "no-rules" era of the Sabre, recce flying did enjoy the excitement and freedom of OAT (operational air traffic). The F-86 life saver, Yellow Jacket, the Canadian GCI site at Metz, was replaced by the infamous French GCI system manned by conscripts who spoke precious little English. Radar controllers with strange call-signs such as Calva Radar, Mazout, and everyone's favorite, Menthol Rouge (speaking marginally better English) were part of the daily challenge of peacetime training in France. It was a critical mistake to check in with, "Bonjour, Calva, comment ça va ce matin?" The language invariably became uniquely French despite the protests of an impatient pilot from Elbow, Saskatchewan. If asked a question they couldn't answer, which was the norm, the famous answer would be transmitted, "Stand by, I call you back." And of course, they would switch off their mike, have a large glass of vin de table, a healthy slice from a baguette and a tranche of camembert.

Everyone who flew in Marville, or later in Lahr, at one time or another became trapped somewhere in the low level environment in a weather box and was forced to plug in the after-burner and climb on top. In France it was impossible to consider getting a clearance from our lucid French friends. More often than not, it meant climbing through 35,000 feet of clag with nothing more than nerve and a basketful of luck. During the endless climb, the pilot would sub-consciously crouch down in the safety of his cockpit as if to offer

Starfighter 868 fitted with its recce pod poses near Marville. (441 Sqn)

a smaller target to the Air France BAC-111 that was trundling along airways from Marseilles to Paris. Eyes riveted on the dials, daring a glance outside at the gray that engulfed his precious aircraft, a quick prayer would be said to the Recce God, respectfully reminding him of the big sky theory. Once on top, our hero would recover quickly, plug in the Mike Mike Yankee TACAN (Marville), head for home and check in with Calva Radar as if he had been there all day. Of course Calva would acknowledge, because it was much too difficult for them to challenge appearing out of nowhere onto their radar screen, in English. They would simply come back with something like, "Roger, Sheckerboord forty-tree, we have yoo. Woood yoo like an eentercept from a French Mystère, ou peut-être woood yoo like to play weez Air Frawnce BAC cent-onze at trente milles pieds enroute to Paree, n'est-ce pas?" Incredible, but true.

And on the Ground

From the moment the pilots and their families stepped off the Yukon onto the Marville ramp after a marathon flight from Trenton, their lives changed. The men rushed off to their new home on the corner Marguerite (dispersal) on the base, leaving wives and children to cope with the PMQs in Longuyon or the special challenges of living on the economy. It was a challenge all round. This unlikely group of families, thrust together by the profession of their husbands and fathers, and the isolation of Lorraine, generated a special spirit and kinship that would flourish 6000 kms from home.

Work days would start with a drive in darkness and curious on-coming yellow headlights from Florenville or Lamorteau in Belgium, a sleepy wave to the French douanier at the frontière and a winding road to the base. The weather briefing would remind everyone that 4.3 miles visibility was a luxury, someone would answer the recce question of the day, then it was off to mission planning. After a day of cut and paste and the most exciting flying anyone had ever experienced, regardless of log book size, it was time for the Mess and an informal debriefing and exchange of the latest war stories, followed by a drive home in the dark and more yellow headlights.

For the most part families were left to fend for themselves. Pilots flew their Starfighters, went to the Mess, played fastball, hockey, or curling and went to the Mess. The wives did the rest - ran a household, shopped in strange stores and pointed a lot, listened to CFN Marville for news from home, went to the PX to buy things they recognized (Campbell Soup never looked so good) and, when "cleared solo", ventured to the huge American Army PX in Verdun.

Although Marville was in an isolated, depressed region of France, it was a Mecca for anyone even remotely interested in history. The daily drive to work for some went by Montmedy Haut, Louis XIV's old haunt and the scene of many a romantic weekend with Marie Antoinette. Verdun, a Roman city dating to 843, was the crossroads of countless invasions and the evidence remained, most visibly the bomb craters of the Great War adjacent to the roads, and the Ossuary of Douaumont where lie 115,000 unknown dead. The French appropriately referred to this region as the "Coeur de la France."

And who could forget that fabulous French cuisine! On arrival in Marville, rank amateurs in the world of degustation did not take long to forget Mom's overcooked roast beef and potatoes. Enter escargots de maison, coquille St-Jacques, truite meunière, steak tartare, danseuses de prairie. Strangely, it excites the palate when spoken in French. Unknown cafés and restaurants in the area became frequent dining targets. Names such as Juvigny, Rouvroy, Gaichel, The Rallye in St-Laurent, Damvillers, and the notorious Garlic Factory bring back a flood of delicious memories and Gevrey Chambertin at 15 francs a bottle.

But the undisputed winner was the Pfeiffeschof in Arlon, Belgium. It was special. For pilots who were in need of brownie points due to chronic wife neglect, or for single pilots on a heavy date, it was the Pfeiffeschof. When Mom and Dad came to visit, it was, predictably, the Pfeiffeschof. Monsieur Bley-DeBruyn created the magic in front of his guests on an open hearth proudly displaying around his neck his medal from the Culinary Olympics. The secrets of his fabulous sauces remained secure behind closed doors dans la cuisine. It was very special.

441ers worked hard and played harder, if that was possible. Moderation was not part of the vocabulary. Squadron parties, either at the Mess or on the economy, remain vivid in memory, blurred only slightly by that extra magnum of wine. The single troops stroked the married Foxes for a home cooked meal, which inevitably turned into a party that just wouldn't end. It was family.

In preparation for a particularly important date, an enterprising single Fox took pictures of the target restaurant, the Abbaye de Conque in Belgium, from his trusty zipper and had the photo boys prepare some 8x10 glossies for presentation at the appropriate moment. On arrival at the Abbaye, our hero presented the pictures to the maitre d' who just happened to own the place. The service became

VIP, the menu was abandoned in favour of non-stop courses suggested by the accommodating host, and the wine cave was tapped extensively, to the delight of the hopeful pilot and his most impressed date. At the end of the evening the staff lined up and the intrepid Fox was obliged to shake hands all round and make a small speech en français. An unexpected bonus came when it was announced that there would be no charge for the gourmet dinner and incredible libations. When this story broke on squadron, it started a rash of restaurant picture-taking and girl-impressing the likes of which you have never seen.

Pre-wedding stags were popular sport in Marville and Lahr. The single troops were slowly cut out of the pack by Canadian school teachers and femmes fatales from France, Germany and Denmark. The legendary Bobby Joe Hart unanimously won the grand prize for his stag, not only for his historic address to the assembly gathered in the Chateau Room in the Mess (move over, Winston Churchill or, perhaps, Danielle Steele), but also because the contents of his room in the barracks were relocated to the sand trap on the first green of the Marville golf course, with Bobby Joe in the bed, of course. The puzzled looks of the early morning golfers were only surpassed by the shocked awakening of Bobby Joe as he was forced to watch incoming golf balls land around him and knock the picture of his fiancee off the night table carefully arranged beside his bed.

The "schoolie" contingent added an essential je ne sais quoi to our euphoric life in Marville. Most were single, and acted more like CF-104 pilots than did CF-104 pilots! They were the first to arrive at the myriad of social functions and most often the last to leave. When the invincible schoolie, Jim Williamson, married maid Marion from the base hospital nursing staff, his stag also made history when a full length leg cast was applied by Dr. Merv Connery. The complicated operation was performed with great skill (assisted by a few Foxes) while Jim was quite comatose. When nature called, Jim fell out of bed on his beak, to be immediately revived with a healthy glass of wine by the Doc and his assistants. About the time that the majority of the Marville contingent had used up their last life, word came that 1 Wing was moving to Lahr. This had potential - a chance to do it all over again in Germany!

Au Revoir Marville, Guten Tag Lahr

After five years and seven months of continuous publication, the station newspaper, "The Arrowhead Tribune", published its final edition in Marville on March 17, 1967. Read religiously by the Canadians during the recce era, its passing was part of the closing down process of Canada's operation in France. Now known as "Der Kanadier", the paper would have a new look, but its singular purpose - to provide a 'warm and cozy' to Canadians living far from home - remained.

Since President Charles de Gaulle's historic announcement about ousting foreign military forces not under French control, NATO had been busy identifying new homes for the various headquarters and fighter wings from Canada and the U.S. Supreme Headquarters Allied Powers Europe moved from Fontainebleau, near Paris, to Belgium. USAFE's six recce and two transport squadrons shuffled off to England, disbanded or returned to the US. Canada consolidated some of its 1 Wing strike and recce forces at the former French base in Lahr in the Black Forest. No.1 Air Division HQ in Metz opted for a large French army caserne on Lahr's outskirts, a few kilometers from the airbase.

For the HQ staff, it would be tough to replace the imposing Chateau de Mercy in Metz. Although the chateau was only 60 years old, its grounds had a history dating to the 3rd century. The original chateau had been destroyed and rebuilt three times by the 16th century. A grand entrance hall, fabulous marble staircase, statues of Jeanne d'Arc and Chevalier Bertrand du Guesclin, and the Italian Trevi fountain facsimile, La Fontaine de Retour, had been a unique HQ environment for the RCAF. It would be as hard to leave this fantasyland as it would be for the Silver Foxes to leave their beloved Chateau Room in the Marville mess. It was an emotional day on March 28, 1967, as 441 packed up and flew, en masse to its new home. As the squadron formation bid adieu to France with one final low pass by Montmedy Haut and across the air base, another chapter in the illustrious history of the Silver Foxes ended.

As the winds of change continued to blow, 441 Squadron and its recce partners at 439 concentrated, establishing a new operation at Lahr. From the humble dog kennel days (the first billet for the fearless Foxes) to the palace (relatively speaking) on the other side of the base, the recce wing became operational in minimum time. Daily training now focused on Bavaria with its relatively good weather. The French village of Vitry-le-François was replaced by the magnificent Hohenzollern Castle, created by mad King Ludwig, as the most popular master check point for Starfighters out-bound into the target area. But the memories lingered. Good flying weather in France and the opportunity to exchange international pleasantries with our old friends from Menthol Rouge across the Rhine River continued to be the implicitly preferred training sortie.

By now, the Canadian recce wing had become a respected contributor to the allied air effort in NATO's Central Region. Pilots delivered the goods, and photo interpreters and intelligence specialists produced a superb final product. We were combat ready and proud of it. We were at the leading edge of a profession that demanded a finely-honed machine, and pilots in cockpits who danced a thin line between a most demanding type of precision flying and reckless abandon. It was Recce.

And on the Ground Again

The first wave of 441 Squadron lived briefly in a wonderful gasthaus, the Lowen in Dorlinbach buried in the wonderment of the Black Forest. This was temporary and the Foxes soon moved to the Schick Apartments in Lahr. This proved to be a major factor in quickly adjusting to the culture shock of the transition from France to Germany. In contrast to the isolation of Marville, the Lahr region had a wealth of diversions and natural beauty. Suddenly there was so much to do. As families settled in, some chose the idyllic countryside of the Black Forest, others found comfortable accommodations in Lahr itself. Mess life changed correspondingly. The new Black Forest Officers' Mess was co-located with 1 Air Division HQ in the caserne and definitely not convenient for our traditional daily debriefings. Besides, it was full of HQ staff weenies and a new phenomenon, the Canadian Army, recently transferred from the North German Plain. Debriefings and repartee were saved up for Friday nights, which did manage to survive the country transfer - some things remained sacrosanct.

Squadron personnel rotated back to Canada and new Foxes and families entered the scene. Mostly, it was business as usual for 441. LCols Paul Manson and Bruce Burgess commanded 441 in this period. The Foxes that served under them were the better for it, especially the predictable few who tended to stray on good days.

Royal Flushing

441 Squadron participated in six NATO Reconnaissance competitions, code-named "Royal Flush". This was a fiercely competitive annual event that pitted the best from every 2 ATAF and 4 ATAF recce squadron. The upstart Canadian teams from 439 and 441 boldly took on the old pros of the French, British, Belgian, German and Dutch squadrons in their own backyards. From its modest beginning in Royal Flush XI in 1966, to having the outstanding NATO recce team four years later in Royal Flush XV, 1 Wing showed that it had what it took to be the best. This record was achieved using an aircraft designed for high altitude, supersonic intercepts, not for grinding out line searches at 100 feet in the Vosges mountains. It was won with a rudimentary camera system that required ingenuity and skill to achieve target coverage. Pilot options were precious few - four or eight frames per second, and the grim knowledge that, even with all cameras blazing, 100% coverage of the target area was not in the cards. Success hung on pilot skill, lady luck and making magic happen in the photo vans. The photo interpreters, working under intense pressure to meet the 30-minute finished product deadline, would glue their stereo glasses to their foreheads and go to work. Often, pilots would return and report seeing nothing as they flew over the target co-ordinates, but still ran the cameras. Worried faces would change to elation thanks to our "PI" specialists and their uncanny ability to spot and identify heavily camouflaged military equipment buried in the trees.

Most Royal Flush participants upgraded their equipment to remain competitive, and gamesmanship became a factor with the home-based European squadrons covertly demonstrating masterful manipulation of the rules. The Canadian squadrons hung in with their simplistic 70mm Vinten camera system and complained to themselves about their competitors' questionable morals. Of course, the Canadians never cheated.

Royal Flush gradually changed from participants operating at home bases, to a single-base concept and small, hand-picked teams carrying each nation's colours. The final format created quite an atmosphere, since the "enemy" was now in full view, giving the Canadians a renewed determination to beat them at their own game. Permanently etched in memory is the sight of the USAF arriving in their fleets of Hercules, vans and other support vehicles. Contrast this to the Canadians arriving in two 5-ton trucks and their two tired-looking photo vans. Nonetheless, Royal Flush proved, yet again, that, as far as 441 was concerned, people made the difference. As in RCAF Sabre and CF-100 days, it was pilots and support personnel who ensured that Canada's reputation remain unchallenged - we always played to win, and most often did.

Hey Luigi!

During the seven years that 441 flew reconnaissance in Central Europe, it was also required to remain current and qualified at dropping conventional and nuclear weapons. Ottawa had an agreement with Germany and Italy to co-operatively fund the weapons training base at Decimomannu. Along with their Strike squadron counterparts from Zweibrucken and Sollingen, 1 CAD recce pilots were required to attend annual camps to qualify for various weapons deliveries. Pilots either loved or hated this sun-burnt piece of real estate in southern Sardinia, a short drive from the capital city of Cagliari.

Uttering the word "Deci" to anyone who has been there will generate animated conversation and anecdotes mainly focusing on our Italian hosts. Mixing Italian air traffic control, airbase support, weapons range controllers and German, Canadian and Italian pilots and airplanes into the same environment made for most entertaining deployments. Camps normally lasted two weeks and involved pilots from all "Air Div" squadrons. Four-plane formations from the three Canadian wings would fly into Deci via Marseille and Corsica. Entering Italian airspace was a constant challenge that was often lost, as the temptation to call Roma Control "Hey Luigi" was too great. Pilots were billeted in barracks on the base complete with snake pit (bar) and squadron crests adorning the walls.

Royal Flush crews service a recce pod as a photo tech dashes to the film lab. Royal Flush pilots George Kirbyson and Sky King are inset. On '776's tip tank is an "F-4 Spook" zapper, applied by some F-4 type when nobody was looking. The Spook was the universal emblem of USAF F-4 units. (Sky King Col.)

A Marville-based CF-104 during an exchange in Norway. (411 Sqn)

Competition was fierce at Deci and, not unexpectedly, the recce pilots were under extra pressure to produce, since they weren't in the bombing business. They were razzed constantly as the "kill 'em with film boys". To the horror of the strike pilots, however, 439 and 441 pilots won the betting pots as best bombers more often than not. Skip bombing was a favorite all 'round, not only because it was the most fun, but also because the amused Canadians got to listen to the Italian range controllers call "skeepa heet", whenever a practice Mk-106 bomb made a skip hit on target.

Capo d Frasca Range was the scene of the action. On the west coast of the island, it provided a picturesque sight-seeing tour on every sortie and an ideal location to practice airborne weapons delivery. Downwind was flown over the sea, as was most of the run-in. Screaming by an old martello tower at 50 feet and Mach .85 was a rush that every zipper pilot loved. The range was manned by personnel who sounded like they were drop-outs from the French Calva Radar with Italian accents. It was a slow day that did not produce some incident, most often humorous, at the range. On one occasion No.4 in formation had dropped a bomb and almost hit the shack housing the startled Italian who was marking the scores and controlling the traffic: "Numbah Four, you go home, you-a-danger." "Roger Capo, Four is returning to Deci." Moments later, from Capo - "Number Four, thats-a-okay, you cumma back."

The Deci circuit was also a rich environment for free entertainment. The Italian Air force tended to shut down the entire airport operation on a regular basis without rhyme or reason. If there was a cloud in sight, Deci would probably be closed. As long as the tower controller could see the hills to the West, he tended to stay open - unless of course, his senora, Gina, had thrown him out of the house again - then anything could happen and usually did. One day Deci Tower transmitted:

"Attention all-a traffic. Attention all-a traffic. Da base is a close-ed. Da base is a close-ed. Da TACAN is a mechanical, its-a not possible." Another day four CF-104s waiting takeoff, complete with pilots boiling in their" poopy suits" in the summer sun, got to witness the following drama unfold: A German F-104 couldn't get his undercarriage down and had flown several passes by the tower to get a visual inspection. He was contemplating ejecting when, on downwind for the 10th time, he announced proudly that he had a 'three green' safe indication for his gear. He then rolled out on final, missed the main runway, and asked to return to initial via a closed pattern. Approved for this, the German raised his gear (if you can believe that!), accelerated to the end of the runway and pulled up in a beautiful wing-over. The four Canadians groaned and sweated. The German dropped his gear on down-wind, got a safe indication and landed without further incident.

It was a sad day when the Canadians pulled out of Decimomannu for the last time. Gone were the flying adventures of Capo d Frasca and the Deci circuit, sea survival training, Marty's hamburgers, 120 degree heat on the ramp, getting the aircraft hosed down after flying through the salt sea air, de-briefs in the snake pit, evenings in Cagliari, the Canadian Poetto, Sardinian screech, moules marinière, hepatitis, and God knows what else.

The AWU's sign at the gate at Decci, the famous pilots' landmark – the ancient Martello tower, then a CF-104 scorching along "on the run-up" to the Capo de Frasca range. (Sky King Col.)

The Great Paris Caper

"The Great Paris Caper" epitomizes the adventures of beloved Checkers in 441's halcyon days in Marville and Lahr. Ron Tomcheck ("Checkerboard 47") tells the story this way:

"While attending the Paris Air Show in 1967, Phil Engstad ("Checkerboard 43"), John Duncan (a navigator mission planner, who would go on to become a CF-104 pilot and establish several driving records of his own) and myself went out to the Tour d'Argent for dinner one evening. After a wonderful evening of incredible degustation, we left the establishment and were looking for transportation. We hopped into a taxi, but there was no driver in sight. After waiting a few minutes (actually 15 seconds), I slid into the driver's seat and departed with Engstad and Duncan howling in the back seat.

"Little did we know that the taxi's owner was 30 feet away buying a newspaper when he saw his livelihood departing the fix outbound. Also, unbeknownst to us, he hailed a cab and gave chase. They passed us several blocks later and slammed on their brakes in the middle of a busy intersection. They didn't stay there long before I drove both vehicles through the rest of the intersection. I told my passengers to take off and that I would handle the problem with my impeccable French. I was somewhat taken aback when I realized that the passenger in the taxi that I had hit, quite unceremoniously, owned the cab that I was driving!

"And now, the rest of the story... I went to jail in a nice little wagon with flashing lights and a siren. It reminded me of the Pink Panther movies. Once in jail, on a sweltering Paris evening, I soon tired of the frantic discussions between the police and cab owner. In this particular jail, there was a dog pound with about 30 pooches of various shapes and sizes making an incredible bruit. Wanting to get closer to these fine specimens, I made the mistake of opening the mesh door of their prison.

"On account of the Paris weather, the main door was propped open and my captured dogs were launching in every direction, but mostly out the open door. The two over-weight imitations of inspector Clouseau were frantically trying to stop them without success. With most of the animals gone, I think they were looking forward to seeing the last of me. After numerous phone calls, the detectives told me that, as a Canadian living in Germany and getting into trouble in Paris, I was not worth the paper work. I agreed to pay the damages and we bid our fond adieus. I made a mental note to write a thank you letter to President de Gaulle for having the foresight to get us out of France prior to our visit.

"Three months after the accident I still hadn't received a bill for the damages. It had been sent but, since it was mis-addressed, it floated around the postal system. The French tracked me down via the Canadian Embassy in Paris, Ottawa, the Judge Advocate General and, finally, the CO of 1 Wing Lahr. Wingco Dunlop wrote a memo on my behalf, never mentioning that I had stolen this poor man's cab. After reading it, I thought that I should be suing somebody for defamation of character. It was a masterpiece. Anyway, I paid the damages and we all lived happily ever after."

Last Call

Pilots will understand what follows. Hopefully others will enjoy the trip. Approaching home base in a 4-plane formation is always an exciting procedure to be a part of, or to watch from the ground. From "initial" to overhead the runway and the break, to rolling out on final and touchdown, pilots unconsciously give it a little extra. It is a proud business and fiercely competitive. It just wouldn't do to be tagged as the jock who was out of position at the break or had to overshoot because he blew it on final turn. A pilot's last Starfighter sortie with the squadron that has been home and family for five years, makes this ritual even more memorable:

"Fox formation, echelon left."

"Lahr Tower, Checkerboard Foxes, Initial with Four."

"Roger Checkerboard Foxes, call the Break."

"Foxes."

Feels good. No.2 and No.3 are nice and tight. The Boss is flying a smooth lead to-day. Here comes the break, hang in there, the pussy cats are probably watching.

"Foxes on the Break."

"Check, Foxes on the Break, call final with the gear."

"Foxes."

There goes Three - thousand and one, thousand and two. Now! Throttle back, turn, pull, IGVs tracking. Love that sound. Got

Three, spacing looks good. Roll out, drop the gear, check airspeed, three green... shake test. 200 kts, time to turn, full flap, momentary wing dance as bleed air kicks in. Lower the nose, keep turning, spacing still OK. Tighten the turn. Don't 'S' turn, not to-day, watch your airspeed. Roll out. Three's on the nose. Christ its turbulent! Dive under Three's wake, that's better. Feeling good.... final check.

"Fox Four, final with the gear."

"Roger Fox Four, you are cleared to land."

"Four."

Over the lights, airspeed on the numbers, approach lights rushing by. Threshold, runway button, hold it off another second. Kiss-kiss. Down, safe and sound. Lower the nose, deploy drag chute. Good chute, here's the cut-off.

"Four is clear."

"Check, Fox Four is clear."

Now a little jig and pop the chute on the grass - perfect! De-arming point, pins in, smile and thumbs up from Corporal Ron.

"Ops, Checkerboard 44 down in the green."

"Calling Ops, say again."

"Disregard, Ops."

"Ops checks."

Some things never change. Canopy open. Damn that fresh air feels great! Visor up, loosen mask, sweat feels strangely cool on the face. Arm on the canopy rail, nose wheel steering engaged, listen to the contented purr of the J79 at 67%. Feel the strange tranquillity of the moment after the incredible energy and motion of the past hour. Into the line, slow down, ground crew signals the turn, dead slow. Arms cross. Full stop.

Sergeant Jim signals shut down with a throat slashing motion and the throttle comes back around the horn. The beautiful bird spools down for the last time. It's over. Down the ladder slowly, reluctantly. Loosen parachute, take off the trusty spurs, a huge grin and an embarrassing hug from Jim. Walk to the shack, stop and take one final, fleeting, reverent look at the ultimate love affair. Life's a bitch. It definitely was a slice.

It wasn't just the guys who knew how to have a good time. Here are some of the 441 "Checkerbirds" in full support of the squadron. (441 Sqn)

441 Squadron officers' wives in 1983: Marlene Wilson, Anne Wolf von Wulfing, Jeanne Burt, Ginnette Rochefort, Susan Tuck, Carolyn Anderson, Carole Nowasad, Jane Hammond, Betty Ann Hoch, Vivian Peel, Hugette Savard, Joan Holmes, Penny Bayles, Jane Ann Sullivan and Helen Doyle. (441 Sqn)

441 Squadron Commanding Officers - Starfighter Era

CO	From	To
W/C Robert M. Edwards, AFC, CD	September 15, 1963	October 11, 1965
W/C James F. Dunlop, DFC, CD	October 12 1965	August 1968
LCol Paul D. Manson, CD	August 1968	July 13, 1969
LCol Bruce T. Burgess, CD	July 14, 1969	April 28, 1970
LCol Walt Niemy	April 29, 1970	June 30, 1970
LCol David P. Wightman	July 1, 1970	July 4, 1971
LCol Al Young, CD	July 5, 1971	August 2, 1973
LCol Donald H. Myles, CD	August 3, 1973	May 22, 1975
LCol John E. Hutt, CD	May 23, 1975	July 4, 1977
LCol Remi J. Saulnier, CD	July 5, 1977	July 5 1979
LCol D.L.J. Crabb, CD	July 6, 1979	July 9, 1981
LCol C. W. Wilson, CD	July 10, 1981	July 26, 1983
LCol K. Ross Betts, CD	July 27, 1983	July 31, 1985
LCol George H. Adamson, CD	August 1, 1985	March 1, 1986

441 Squadron Bases - Starfighter Era

Marville, France	September 15, 1963 to March 31, 1967
Lahr, Germany	April 1, 1967 to June 30, 1970
Baden-Soellingen, Germany	July 1, 1970 to March 1, 1986

Starfighter 104785 overseeing the Canadian section of the Soellingen cemetery (inset). With the closure of CFB Baden-Soellingen, the Base Commander, Col Lloyd Campbell, and the Burgomeister of Soellingen, agreed that '785 be moved to the cemetery, where Canadian pilots, airmen, and dependents lie at rest. '785 now was re-dedicated to the long-standing friendship and goodwill that exists between Canada and Germany. (Larry Crabb)

The McDonnell Douglas CF-18 Hornet has been the heart of 441 Squadron since 1987. May 25 - 26, 1994 ten Hornets crossed from Goose Bay to Scotland on Ex. Tartan Paladin for joint exercises, and to do some airshows and fly-pasts commemorating D-Day's 50th anniversary. Here are "Tartan Paladin" CF-18s en route over Labrador. Flying '781 is Maj John Roulston; beyond are Capt Gary Venman in '758 and Capt Steve Nierlich in '754. The special colours on '781 include D-Day stripes and "JE-J" code letters honouring W/C J.E. "Johnnie" Johnson, DSO and Bar, DFC and Bar, who often led 441 into battle while commanding 144 (RCAF) Wing in 1944. (Tony Cassanova)

CHAPTER 19

A New Start

Through the 1950s the main Cold War threat to North America was the Soviet bomber. Against it the US and Canada established a huge force of all-weather fighters and surface-to-air missiles, and such other defences as the Distant Early Warning Line, a chain of radar stations from Alaska to Baffin Island. Hardly was this system operational, however, than its usefulness was challenged. Instead of long-range bombers, the Soviets began amassing intercontinental ballistic missiles. As NORAD changed gears to face this new threat, bomber interceptor designs like the Avro CF-105 Arrow, North American XF-108 and Republic XF-103 were cancelled. Instead, both sides in the Cold War rushed to develop anti-ICBM missiles, although US – Soviet treaties would restrict their deployment. Later, the US began research into a space-based ABM system – "Star Wars".

Then came the threat of Soviet cruise missiles, sparking further NORAD initiatives. The US and Canada revamped the DEW Line, closing old sites, upgrading others and establishing new ones. The result was the North Warning System – 15 long-range and 39 unmanned, short-range radar sites. The first Canadian NWS site was operational in November 1987. The teeth in the system would be manned fighters at fighter bases like Elmendorf AFB and CFB Cold Lake. Interceptors based there would be deployable to remote Arctic FOLs – forward operating locations. Canadian FOLs were established in the NWT at Iqaluit, Inuvik, Yellowknife and Rankin Inlet. As part of the NORAD upgrades 441 Squadron re-formed with CF-18s at Cold Lake under LCol Ian "Struts" Struthers on June 26, 1987 (originally, 441 had been slated to serve in 1 CAG with NATO). CF-18s of 410 Squadron (also based at Cold Lake) flew overhead to welcome the newcomers, much as 410 had greeted 441 at North Luffenham 35 years earlier.

The New Fighter

In the early 1970s the light-weight Northrop YF-17 was competing for a USAF fighter contract. General Dynamics won that battle with its YF-16. Undeterred, Northrop teamed with McDonnell Douglas to modify the YF-17 for a 1500-plane US Navy/US Marine Corps competition. The winning design would replace such aging fighters as the A-4, A-7 and F-4. The YF-17 now evolved into the bigger F/A-18 Hornet and took the prize. Flown in November 1978, the first examples were delivered two years later.

A well-known 1982 PR photo from McDonnell Douglas in St. Louis at the time the first CF-18 was delivered to Canada. Then, an early CF-18 flown by Capt Pete Ten-Bruggencate of 409 Squadron. WO Vic Johnson took this photo on a 1986 mission from Baden-Soellingen. (CF NBC82-1548, ISC86-819)

The CF-18 gave Canada a "computer age" fighter. Its many advanced features included cockpit CRTs, seen in this great "over the shoulder" photo by WO Johnson from the back seat of a Hornet. The CRTs display all the data required by a pilot, whether airspeed, altitude, attitude, heading, "G", or a mass of data about targets and weapons. Should all else fail, a pilot still has a few "steam powered" instruments, such as the compass seen on the far right. (CF ISC87-587)

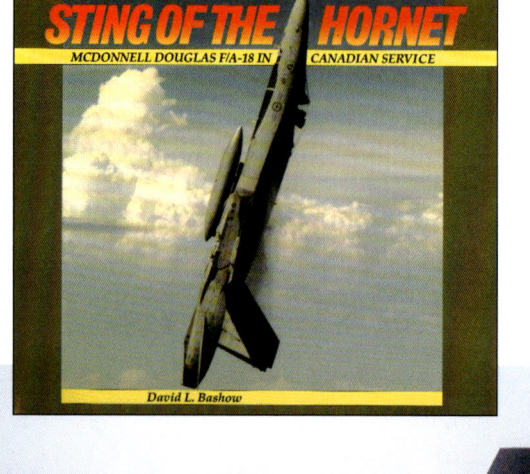

410 "Cougar" Squadron was the first Canadian unit to operate CF-18s. This early 2-seater was at Cold Lake on May 23, 1983. (Larry Milberry)

The multi-role F/A-18 attracted foreign interest, especially from Australia and Canada. It had come along just as Canada was seeking a replacement for its CF-5s, CF-101s and CF-104s on NORAD and NATO duties. Several types, including the F-16, F/A-18 and Tornado were evaluated during this "New Fighter Aircraft" program. Considering such details as a $2.34 billion fixed budget, and assurances of "industrial off-set" contracts for Canadian industry, in November 1978 the competition narrowed to the single-engine F-16 and twin-engine F/A-18. In April 1980 the F/A-18 was selected. An order was placed for 138 (including 24 two-seat trainers). The first "CF-18" reached Cold Lake in October 1982.

A key reason for Canada picking the F/A-18 was its twin engines. The NFA team always had insisted on this, knowing that NORAD duties meant patrols over the Arctic, and off Canada's Atlantic or Pacific coasts. Canadian crews always had enjoyed this insurance with CF-100s, then CF-101s. As far as NATO tactical operations would go, the Hornet's twin engine capability would be a plus in the low-level environment where bird strikes had claimed many single-engine fighters over the years, and where, in a conflict, fighters would be susceptible to ground fire. Far better two engines than one. Other Hornet features were air-to-air refuelling, a "glass cockpit" with performance and systems data displayed on user-friendly screens, APG-65 radar that could select targets as far as 80 miles away, and multi-mission weapons capability – air-to-air missiles, a 20-mm gun, bombs and rockets. For the Canadian version there was also a 600,000 candlepower spotlight for identifying targets during night intercepts.

Canada's Hornets would be built by McDonnell Douglas in St. Louis, Missouri, but with considerable manufacturing input at such branch plants as McDonnell Douglas Canada, and Canadian General Electric. For all the Hornet technical details, readers should refer to an endless flow of data on the Internet, e.g. there are web sites for most Canadian and US Hornet squadrons. Readers also should track down a copy of *Sting of the Hornet: McDonnell Douglas F/A-18 in Canadian Service*.

CF-18 – Some Basic Specs

Length	56'
Wing span	40'4"
Wing span tips folded	27'5"
Height	15'3"
Empty weight	23,400 lb
Typical fighter mission weight	37,000 lb
Typical attack mission weight	52,000 lb
Ordnance load	13,000 lb
Max weight	56,000 lb
Max fuel (internal)	9400 lb
Engines	GE F404 each 16,000 lb thrust
Max speed	Mach 1.7
Approach speed	134 kts
Combat radius	500+ nm
Ferry range (no AAR)	1800 nm
Combat ceiling	50,000'
Approx. cost per unit	US$35 million

Opposite: Officers past and present at the 441 stand-up. Behind are BGen Bruce T. Burgess, Cols C.W. "Willie" Wilson and D.L.J. "Larry" Crabb, BGen Remi J. Saulnier, LCol Don Myles, S/L A.R. "Andy" MacKenzie, LGen McNaughton, BGen Wally Niemy, LCol Ian Struthers and LCol John E. Hutt. In front are Col Ross Betts, LCol George Adamson, S/L E.L. "Gene" Arnold, W/C Lou Hill, Col J.F. "Jim" Dunlop and BGen R.L. "Bob" Edwards. (CF CKC87-3734)

Getting Up to Speed

Once re-formed, 441 Squadron's main objective was to become operational as soon as possible. Adding to this challenge was that few pilots had much CF-18 experience – most were fresh from the OTU at 410 Squadron. Some were old hands from CF-104 or CF-101 days, but others were "sprogs" who had earned their wings on the Tutor at 2 CFFTS, passed the CF-5 fighter lead-in (FLIT) course at 419 Squadron, then advanced to the CF-18 OTU at 410 TAC (OT) Squadron.

CF-18 courses were designed for 26 students and ran for 5 ½ months. On paper, flying training boiled down to 43.8 hours of dual instruction, 27.7 of solo over a 78-day flying schedule, weather, serviceability and other commitments allowing. Ground school totalled 161 hours of academic/simulator instruction covering such topics as aircraft operating instructions, APG-65 radar theory, air-to-air weapons, intercept tactics (BFM – basic fighter manoeuvres, ACM – air combat manoeuvres), air-to-surface tactics (e.g. CAS – close air support), tactical weapons (bombs and rockets), and electronic warfare (EW).

It was some weeks before 441 had its unit establishment (UE) of 203 groundcrew. Meanwhile, for the first two weeks of July 1987 the pilots

LCol Ian Struthers (left) with LGen Don McNaughton, Commander Fighter Group (right) and Col Dave Kinsman, Base Commander Cold Lake, during 441's June 1987 stand-up at Cold Lake. Silver Fox "René" is in his place of honour. (CF CKC87-3735)

The officers of 441 Squadron with LGen Don McNaughton in July 1987. Behind are Capts McFarlane (EO) and Rich Corver, Maj Bob Wade, Maj "Red" Luke (EO), Capt Beswick, Maj Stu Holdsworth, LGen McNaughton, LCol Ian Struthers, Maj Jack Orr, Lt Gorth (EO), Capts Hollis Tucker, Rob Chapman, René LeBlanc and Jim Christie. In front are Capts Graham Sinclair, Luc Savoie, Michael Erickson, Bill Ryan, Guy Sawchuck, Lts. Bruce Miller (IntO) and Serge Beaulieu, and Capts Curt Johnson, Dave Burton and Dave Deere. (CF CKC87-3736)

Some 1987 event at 441 with CWO Dan Cameron front and centre. From the left the others are Capts Lief Erickson, Curt Johnson, Bruce Beswick, Guy Sawchuck, Rob Chapman, Maj Stu Holdsworth, Capt Hollis R. Tucker, LCol K.I. Struthers (CO), Serge Beaulieu, James Christie, Capt Bill Ryan, Maj Bob Wade, Capt Bruce Miller (IntO), Capt Dave Burton and Maj Jack Orr. (CF CKC87-3392)

Original 441 NCMs. Standing are Pte Mike Wright, Sgt Dave Ralston, Pte Gilles Gallant, Sgt Claus Grendys, WO Dave Allison, Pte John Nicholson, Pte Sharon Daley, Pte Steve Brum and OCdt Billard. In front are Sgt Jim Marshall, Sgt Dave Dove, Lt Dave Gorth, WO Rick McCollum, Sgt John Morgan, Pte Tess Cousineau and OCdt Owens. (CF)

were busy with DACT (dissimilar air combat training) with visiting USAF F-5Es, and doing cross-country missions. Combat ready training commenced on July 13 with lectures until month's end, when CRT flying began. Even so, with only five combat ready pilots the number of missions was limited. Most flying (443 hours in July) was for general proficiency. There also was some cross-country flying, including to Yellowknife and Inuvik to verify airfield conditions. By mid-August all pilots had completed day CRT, and night CRT commenced.

Now came more realistic exercises, such as a Tactical Air Support Maritime Operations/Air Defence Exercise (TASMO/ADEX) in September. For this 441 deployed to Comox to fly "missile profiles" (mock attacks) against Canadian warships. Later that month came Maple Flag XX, a large-scale fighter exercise at Cold Lake involving the CF,

441's first DACT was against USAF F-5E Aggressors. This typical F-5E was at Cold Lake for Maple Flag in May 1987. (Larry Milberry)

RAF and USAF. Maple Flag had evolved from a USAF concept. During the Vietnam War, the US calculated that 90% of its air losses occurred during a crew's first 10 missions. To rectify this, "Red Flag" came into being at Nellis AFB,

Something familiar to CF-18 pilots — trailing an AAR tanker before moving in for fuel. Here, Capt Dave Burton of 441 approaches a 437 Squadron 707 tanker during a 1989 Alaskan exercise. (Burton Col.)

Nevada. A realistic war game, Red Flag put fighter pilots through rigorous training; soon the USAF was reaping the benefits. From 1977 onwards, NATO air forces joined in Red Flag. The following year Canada suggested a similar exercise for Cold Lake, where rolling hills, pine forests and lakes were more akin to the topography of Central Europe. The Canadian version became Maple Flag, an annual event in which 441 would participate. For the third week of Maple Flag XX 441 provided four pilots.

Next came another TASMO/ADEX (October 8-9, 1987). More ambitious was an air refuelling exercise (October 18 - 20), when six Hornets flew to Elmendorf AFB, Alaska to qualify 12 pilots in day, night and tactical air-to-air refuelling from 437 Squadron Boeing 707 tankers. This was supplemented by Alaskan Air Command briefings on northern fighter operations. From October 27 - 30 the squadron participated in Ex. Quick Talk, flown in support of 1 Canadian Brigade Group, Calgary. This saw 441 firing live weapons at CFB Wainwright. On the historical side of squadron life, LCol Struthers had taken a CF-18 to St. John's, Newfoundland in July for a reunion of 125 Squadron personnel. The first such get-together in 40 years, this was a chance for the "old boys" to view the Hornet. Lamont Parsons of 125 later wrote to LCol Struthers:

A short personal note to thank you for the tremendous contribution you have made to our reunion last weekend. We never dreamed it would be such a success. Your bringing in one of your CF-18s was the icing on the cake. You not only attracted the press coverage that is always nice to have on such an occasion, but showed the general public and us old fogies that the Canadian Armed Forces is still top line.

On November 1, 1987 the Silver Foxes were designated as "limited combat ready". On November 3-5 they participated in Ex. Keynote along with 414 (EW) Squadron, whose ET-33s and Falcons offered lessons in how to counter targets capable of "spooking" an interceptor with electronics and chaff. For November 17 - 25 there was DACT with F-15s of the 54th TFS visiting from Elmendorf.

Early Ops — Life in "the Q"

Since 1955 Comox has had a proud heritage in postwar air defence. Initially, CF-100s based there with 409 Squadron were "on alert" 24 hours a day. From 1962 the squadron flew CF-101s, then was deactivated in 1984. Alert duties resumed in 1987 with rotating detachments of 441 and (later) 416 Hornets. Those were the days when anyone with 441 or 416 was never sure where he might wake up — Cold Lake or Comox. Hornet tech Bill Mitchell of 441 once pointed out: "None of us could complain that we were in Cold Lake too long, since we were spending so much good time in the Q in Comox." In 2003 Maj Dave Burton recalled 441 Hornet days in the "QRA" (quick reaction area, or "the Q") Comox:

I logged my first 441 CF-18 flight to Comox in August 1987. This was the start of a pattern that would see most of us spending one week of every month holding NORAD alert on the West Coast. Our boss, LCol "Struts" Struthers was keen to ensure that everyone knew that we were now in the neighbourhood. His plan included such "practical"

A CF-18 on alert in the QRA at Comox. Weapons are typical for the NORAD mission — AIM-9L Sidewinders on the wingtips and AIM-7 Sparrows underwing. (CF CXC89-2236)

training as approaches into any conceivable alternate airport, but to us this was merely an opportunity to ensure that the skiers on Mount Washington knew we were there. Somehow, the "higher ups" didn't see it that way.

Pilots would volunteer to ferry a CF-18 to Comox from Cold Lake, but quickly would disappear when the dreaded "Herc" trip to Comox was even hinted at. When flying hours were plentiful, Comox was a glorious opportunity to log time. Four pilots working alternate days, or three pilots working two days on and one day off typically would fly two trips per day on alert. Our maintenance crews did superb work each and every day to keep the two primary alert CF-18s and one spare serviceable. A close second to the great flying was the added benefit of having no secondary duties, nor the other paperwork evils for which most fighter pilots have no time. Days off meant a host of activities that were not available in Cold Lake – golfing in December, downhill ski runs longer than 30 seconds, and no spouse-imposed mess curfews. Neither was flying the best fighter in the world out of Comox too much of a hardship.

Unfortunately, the realities of military life contributed to many missed birthdays, anniversaries, even Christmases. Moreover, we were all reminded of our own vulnerability with the tragic losses during Comox missions of Lief Erickson in 1988 and Hollis Tucker in 1990. I know that to this day their spirit lives in each of us. Nonetheless, we soldiered on doing our part 24/7, 365 days a year, while our families managed without us in that time-honoured military tradition of absent loved ones.

Air defence exercises, weapons controller training, dissimilar air combat missions, and joint naval and airforce exercises were some of our predominant Comox mission profiles. Primarily, life in the "Q" meant being ready to scramble on a moment's notice. At the sound of the horn, an outside observer might use the adjective "chaotic" to describe our preparations to get airborne. To us and the groundcrew it was a well-practiced and choreographed sequence of events. It had to be, in order to get from a sound sleep to being airborne in roughly seven minutes. Everyone involved had memories of pilots struggling into their one-piece rubber "poopy" suits. Simultaneously cranking the engines, watching the groundcrew and strapping in by feel, hadn't changed since CF-100 days. Neither had the feeling of climbing on top of the cloud layer and suddenly seeing the stars, as if for the first time. Of course, memories of Comox are as varied and rich as the individuals who flew and worked there. My personal memories are lasting, but the real essence of 441 Squadron is captured in the exceptional men and women who call it home.

In 2004 Graham Sinclair of 441 also recalled QRA days:

Being a NORAD squadron, 441 enjoyed the task of defending the West Coast with a pair of armed CF-18s on 5-minute alert status in the Quick Reaction Area at Comox. Typically, three aircraft, four pilots and support staff would be deployed to the Q from Cold Lake. The crews would decide whether or not they would work 24- or 48-hour shifts. One way or the other, the off-duty crew always had lots to keep them busy – golfing in summer, skiing in winter, etc. Meanwhile, crews on alert and awaiting a scramble had time to relax and even catch up on some movies – our ground crew offered four movies (with popcorn) every night.

Q duty also could be quite a burden to the squadron, with pilots having to spend one of every three or four weeks on alert. Some of us, however, really enjoyed the occasion to concentrate on some excellent flying training, without the distractions of daily squadron life. A Comox deployment meant the chance to spend lots of time debriefing and analyzing a sortie, and really getting into the manuals to learn as much as possible about our great new flying machine.

Shift change in the Q began by "cocking" a Hornet. For this, power was applied, systems and weapons checked, and all the switches placed just so to ensure a rapid start. Every shift would bring a practice scramble, and it didn't take long before we were all very fast at getting airborne within minutes of the horn sounding. We could do this even though we had to don our awkward "poopy suits" (immersion, or sea survival, suits) any time we would be flying over the Pacific.

Flying twice a day, we normally did an intercept mission in the morning. This allowed us to hone our skills using our radar, and also

Supporting 441 and 416 on QRA and FOL duties were ATG's Hercules. Here a "Herc" prepares to depart Cold Lake for Comox. (CF CKC88-2998)

Hornet '775 firing up in the Comox QRA. (Mike Valenti)

A 441 Hornet 2-ship (188777 nearest) on a QRA mission skims past some typical West Coast scenery. (CF CXC95-857)

provided training to the GCI controllers based in North Bay. In the afternoon we would do a BFM hop or maybe a visual navigation flight up the West Coast. Sometimes we would fly down the mountain valleys to see how well our radar could ground-map. Sometimes we'd even check out Mt. Washington. Any skiers or mountain climbers out there usually could count on seeing a couple of CF-18s "up close and personal". All things considered, the Q was a good time for all. It made us feel operational and that we really were contributing something valuable in the defence of North America.

Early FOL Deployments

Canada's first FOL deployment was completed by 410 Squadron in September 1987. The first for 441 was during Ex. Amalgam Chief (December 6 - 12) when 4 Hornets, 6 pilots and 40 groundcrew deployed to Inuvik. This item by Capt Jim Stewart in *Flight Comment* (1990, No.5) describes FOL activity:

Asleep in the hotel, the Alert crew is awakened by the phone: "Scramble, scramble". It is three o'clock in the morning, and the crew is on one hour air defence alert at 441 Tactical Fighter Squadron's FOL, Inuvik, NWT. Pilots and ground crew scramble out of bed, dress and run to the duty vehicle, which has been left running all night to prevent freeze-up. The outside temperature is -45 degrees C with a wind-chill in the neighbourhood of 2100 watts/square metre; typical for January.

Twenty minutes pass as the crew drives to the airport contemplating what lies ahead. On arrival the pilots are briefed on the mission while the groundcrew tow the aircraft from the hangar onto the small, ice-covered ramp. Within minutes, engines are started and four aircraft are taxiing. With a 6000 foot runway, a JBI of .45 and an arresting gear system which may be degraded by the severe cold, the aircraft prepare for take-off. There is little room for error, as the runway is 150 feet wide and lead must start his take-off roll while No.2 is still taxiing down the near side of the runway. Number two then takes off

441 on deployment to Inuvik in 1997: a wide view of the FOL, a Hornet taxis out, then two lightly-laden Hornets back-tracking on the runway for takeoff. (CF CKC97-176-25, '176E12, '176F7)

into ice fog conditions, created by lead's engine exhaust. All four aircraft get airborne into the "black hole" and are vectored out over the Beaufort Sea, some 450 miles north of Inuvik. Canadian NORAD Region controllers, based in North Bay, direct the two flights of two toward what is believed to be a Soviet reconnaissance aircraft. The mission is to intercept and identify and the pilots are "pumped", having little regard for the fact that they are flying over one of the most hostile environments in the world, where there is virtually no search and rescue capability within hundreds of miles should unforeseen problems force an ejection.

The winter Arctic is formidable and offers, perhaps, the greatest challenge to the military flying community. Most members of 441 Squadron have completed the Arctic Survival course. However, it is of little consolation when you know you would be on your own, with little help from the "outside world" (military SAR is at least four to five hours away, on standby in Namao). The equipment carried in the CF-18 seat pack and on the pilot falls decidedly short of what is provided on the survival course. There is, however, a SKAD [survival kit - air droppable] kept in Inuvik which can be loaded onto a CF18 and dropped to a downed pilot in an emergency. The equipment in this kit would greatly improve one's chances of survival, provided you did not freeze during ejection, were not injured on parachute landing, or did not land in five feet of snow.

Arctic Survival

NORAD's concern in the 1980s being Soviet manned bombers and cruise missiles, CF-18 pilots would be flying more than ever over Arctic terrain. Opening several FOLs emphasized this commitment, so it was vital that pilots train in Arctic survival. Such training was not new. The RCAF had pioneered in it since the 1920s and, following WWII, established a survival school at Resolute Bay, NWT. It even developed special Arctic survival clothing and equipment (G/C Frank Phripp of the RCAF Winter Experimental Establishment describes this work in *Sixty Years: The RCAF and CF Air Command 1924 - 1984*). In 2004 Graham Sinclair, in a light-hearted mood, recalled his Arctic training:

Arctic survival training was mandatory at 441 Squadron. Nobody looked forward to the course, but we all understood that it was a good thing. Thus, in February 1988 I found myself stepping off a Hercules in Resolute Bay, about to begin a week of adventure in "Crystal City". Appropriately, a blizzard welcomed me and the other 23 uninitiated.

After a couple of days of skills training and acclimatization, our first real test began – build an igloo, then survive in it for two days. Working in the cold, the "buddy system" was essential. I was paired with an Aurora navigator, a big guy who used to play professional football. Given his size, and my innate need for the finer comforts in life, in spite of a warning from our Inuit directing staff we agreed that our igloo should be slightly oversized.

Our igloo building efforts soon fell behind the other white bumps sprouting on the ice around us, and I sensed that all was not right with my partner. I wondered why he was stumbling around like a zombie with an ice block under his arm mumbling "Go long, go long!" Before I knew it, he was pulled from the game and I never saw him again. That left me solo with half an igloo to build.

By now I regretted my idea about building for comfort, but pressed on and finally put the cap in place as darkness fell. All I could see by this time was a yellow glow emanating from each of the other igloos. Without doing the final chinking, I crawled into my igloo and started my "kootlick" – a 4 by 2 piece of cloth soaked in a tray of lard. Simon, one of our Inuit instructors, came by to inspect my handiwork. He warned about the lack of chinking and that I likely would be frozen to death by morning. Simon realized that I was out of energy, so offered to finish up my chinking. Outside he went with his big machete-type knife. Soon I could hear him clambering over the igloo and chinking away. Meanwhile, I stripped down to my combat sweater, got the kootlicks fired up, and made some hot chocolate.

Sitting on my snow bench, I began to think that life wasn't so bad after all. Then came a reality check – Simon suddenly came crashing through the top of the igloo into my "cold well". There we were – face to face and Simon with his big knife between our noses. He began to laugh hysterically, as I tried to figure things out. My hot chocolate was spilled in the cold well and above were the stars. I soon came to my senses and started laughing, too. Then I dressed and we went outside to start on a new igloo, this time a bit smaller than the first. Simon went home after I got settled in, but returned later with a family photo album. One picture showed his son at age 12 standing by his first polar bear kill. By this time Simon and I had become good friends.

Arctic survival training at Resolute Bay. First, a general scene of igloo building. Then, Dave Deere, Rob Chapman and Serge Beaulieu with their famous instructors, Simon and Levi (who had himself been born in an igloo). (441 Sqn, via Rob Chapman)

Rob Chapman, also a member of 441's original Hornet pilot cadre, has his own recollections about Arctic survival training at Resolute Bay:

As 441's lead scheduler, I received a call one day from LCol Struthers to come into work. As the CO he had been tasked to send all 441 pilots for Arctic survival training. I think it was a Sunday afternoon, and by the end of the day the entire QRA schedule had been re-written for the next three months to allow for the training. In groups of four or five we attended Arctic survival. I'll never forget when the rear-loading ramp of the Herc opened in the Arctic night in Resolute. Virtually every day the temperatures were at or below minus 40°C with winds in excess of 30 kts.

Our first few days were spent in the comfort of the Resolute Inn from where we took day trips learning how to build igloos. Then, the Survival School directing staff, along with our Inuit instructors (Levi and Simon), headed out about five miles to "Crystal City" to train. We spent our first night in a tent which "comfortably" slept four or five. This, of course, was after spending the day erecting the tent. Next day we tried our luck at igloo building. An instructor could build one by himself in about 45 minutes; the rest of us, well, most never did finish without their help. The next two nights were spent in the igloo in 2-man teams. During this stay, we also built a snow cave. After two nights in it we were deemed to have "survived" in the Arctic, so returned to the Resolute Inn in a Bombardier tracked vehicle. By this time we all looked like we had placed second in a chain-saw fight. Our faces were chaffed, wind burned, scabbed and frost-nipped almost beyond recognition.

441 Rock Stars

As operationally focused and intense as life was at 441 in its early days, there was a good balance to it. Partying abounded, of course, and the squadron even had its own rock stars. In 2004 Graham Sinclair recalled those times:

Soon after standing up the squadron, three of us decided to form a rock band, with Luc Savoie on guitar, Dave Deere on bass and me on drums. Naturally, we were the "Checkers"! On weekends we would get together to jam, mostly doing "oldies but goodies", but also some current hits. Quite often we would alter lyrics to relate to squadron personnel and events. We did one tune called "Radar Love" that was about scrambling out of the Q in Comox on a dark and dirty night.

The highlight of our short rock career was 441's "Checkerbash" of September 1987. What a night! Morale was booming and the old gymnasium packed with Silver Foxes and their spouses. Everyone was in black-and-white, with the check motif dominating.

We played three sets that night – 20+ tunes and we rocked the house down. We were hardly the best band that 441 had ever heard, but we were theirs. Our CO, LCol Ian Struthers, resplendent in his checkerboard blazer, was so ecstatic that night, that he authorized the band for a cross-country training mission anywhere

Hornet drivers Luc Savoie, Graham Sinclair and Dave Deere hammer it out during 441's September 1987 "Checker Bash". (Sinclair Col.)

in North America. We didn't hesitate in taking him up on this, and two weeks later could be found, 441 Checkerboard flag flying high beside us, sunning on a California beach.

"Media Heroes"

In its early years the CF-18 was favourite material for the media. After all, everyone was conscious of the image epitomized by Hollywood's Tom Cruise in "Top Gun". While pilots sometimes catered to these notions, they usually explained that a "hot-shot" pilot would be seen as a loose cannon, more likely to be court-martialled than promoted. Nonetheless, in a January 5, 1988 Winnipeg *Free Press* item, Steve Mertl reported of 441's CO:

Ian Struthers is a high priest of a very exclusive religion. Clear-eyed and firm-jawed, his blond hair closely cropped, Struthers looks exactly like the typical image of a fighter pilot ... Except that Struthers pilots Canada's CF-18 Hornets, and Top Gun was a paean to the cult of the United States fighter jock. "Actually, it was fairly close," Struthers says of the film. "There was a lot of Hollywood involved in the movie, but the bravado, some of the spirit, some of the aggressiveness, is a reality."

Struthers, who at 39 still looks too boyish to be a lieutenant-colonel, doesn't quite conform to type. Married and with a 16-year old son, the sportiest thing about his ground-bound life is a vacation camper. His wingman, Lieut. Serge Beaulieu, is another story. The 25-year old Quebec City native races motorbikes and owns a sports car. He got hooked on fighters after his first ride in a jet trainer. "I was so impressed by the rush, by the way those things handle. It really did turn me on."

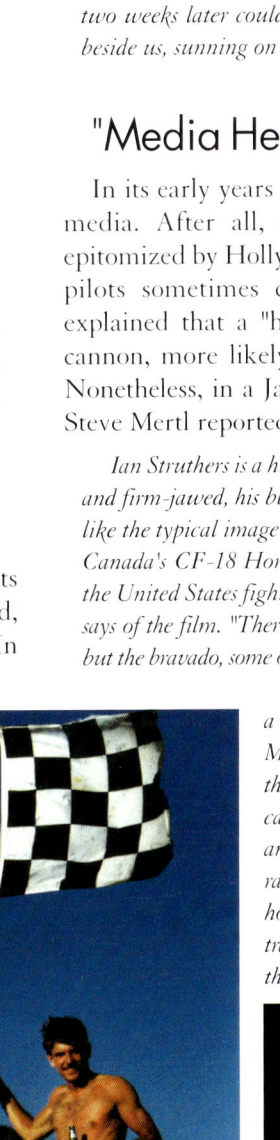

A couple of weeks later and 441's band was roughing it on the beach in California. (Sinclair Col.)

LCol "Struts" Struthers suitably attired at the bash, with air traffic controller Suzanne Sinclair. (Sinclair Col.)

Two of LCol Struthers rough and ready (and sometimes unruly) fighter jocks — René LeBlanc and Serge Beaulieu. (CF CKC89-4002)

The CO's ceremonial role includes officiating at promotions, medal presentations, squadron highlights, etc. Here, LCol Struthers joins Maj Tim Strocel, and Capts Dave Burton and Serge Beaulieu on the occasion of Maj Jim Christie (centre) passing the magic 1000-hour mark on the Hornet. (CF CKC87-5180, CKC88-4135)

Other Happenings

In 1987 the media was all over the news that Canadian women would be eligible to fly jet fighters. Of the original candidates Dee Brasseur would fly with 416 Squadron, Jane Foster and Kim Reid with 441.

Predictably, from the beginning the women were in the media spotlight. They could make few moves without being interviewed, photographed, analyzed, even criticized. While each would contribute to her squadron, they had relatively short fighter pilot careers.

The Cold War still remained real in 1987, although there were hopes for better things from a man called Gorbachev, and Russian phrases like "glasnost" and "perestroika" were entering the global vocabulary. Nevertheless, a few "peaceniks" remained up-tight about American cruise missile tests over the Arctic and Cold Lake's Primrose Lake weapons range. Protesters demonstrated outside the base, and attempted to infiltrate the range. It was not just pacifism that drove them, since others of these perennially grumpy people distrusted Prime Minister Brian Mulroney and his coziness with Washington.

December 6 - 20, 1987 saw three 441 pilots deployed on Ex. Combat Archer at Tyndall AFB, Florida. The main USAF air intercept training base, Tyndall was a "sun and fun" retreat that would become a kind of second home for 441. Not only

In 1988 CWO Dan Cameron of 441 received his CD/2 medal from LCol Struthers. The CO considered "Chief Cameron" an indispensable leadership figure, to whom NCMs and officers alike looked for advice and moral support. Raised in Grenville, Quebec, Cameron joined the RCAF in 1957. After training as an aero engine tech at Camp Borden, he served in Comox for seven years, working mainly on Lancasters and Neptunes. In 1964 LAC Cameron was posted to 4 Wing on CF-104s. Then, in 1967 he, his wife and four children moved to Trenton on a 10-year posting. In 1977 he joined AETE in Cold Lake and by 1982 was MWO Cameron and the EO at Base Flight (T-33, Dakota, Huey). He was posted to 442 Squadron in 1984, then to AIRCOM HQ in Winnipeg in 1986 before being made 441's Chief in 1987. CWO Cameron left the military in 1990 to retire in Comox. (CF CKC88-7038)

During Ex. Combat Archer a 441 Hornet cuts loose over the Tyndall air weapons range with an AIM-7. (CF RS88-7915)

In re-establishing itself, 441 began connecting with its alumni. Here, LCol Struthers looks over some wartime memorabilia with 441 Spitfire pilot Hugh Ritchie at a 1988 reunion. (CF IOC88-161-3)

December 23, 1986 and one of two Soviet Bear "F" maritime patrol bombers is intercepted off Newfoundland by 425 Squadron CF-18s on a "Cold Shaft" scramble. Making the dawn intercept were Maj Richard "Bross" Brosseau and Capt Chris Hadfield. In May 2004 "Bross" recalled how he and Chris had scrambled from Bagotville and flown to Gander (1.3 hours) for fuel. They departed ASAP to find the Bears over the Atlantic in a loose echelon about a mile apart. Flying in 188727, "Bross" went in on the first Bear. Chris, flying 188714, took the "intel" photos, and did the close-up ID on the second Bear. Finally, they waved at the Russians and returned to Gander after a 1.4-hour mission. Refuelled again, they were off for home and another 1.7 hrs in the log book - all in a day's work for a Hornet pilot. The first ever CF-18 Bear intercept occurred on June 11, 1985, when Chris Hadfield and Eric Matheson of 425 scrambled after a pair of Bear "D's. (CF)

was this a chance to go against USAF F-15s and F-16s in DACT but, occasionally, to fire missiles at target drones. Tyndall used two types of drones on its Gulf of Mexico range. Radar-guided AIM-7 Sparrow missiles were fired at full-scale North American QF-100 Super Sabres; heat-seeking AIM-9 Sidewinders were aimed at sub-scale Ryan drones. Missile warheads were replaced with a telemetry package that relayed data to ground stations.

The QF-100 operated at 350 to 750 knots at 2000 to 25,000 feet. Dodging missiles, it could pull four Gs. Even before fighters got airborne from Tyndall, a T-33 would confirm that a 10-mile corridor over the range was clear of boats. For a "Combat Archer" mission a QF-100 would execute defensive manoeuvres, while the pursuing fighter would try to score programmed near-misses. Usually, the drone would return to base but, should a QF-100 be damaged, it could be remotely destroyed in flight. The smaller Ryans parachuted to land or into the Gulf for recovery.

Ex. Lightning Strike

"Lightning Strike", which began on January 18, 1988, was a joint army – air force exercise. Early on in the scenario, CF-18s taking part from Cold Lake could not deploy forward until Special Service Force troops had "captured" their base. At that stage 441 set up at Inuvik. On one FOL mission Capts Curt Johnson and Graham Sinclair, flying a combat air patrol 180 kilometers north of there, intercepted some "enemy" A-10 ground attack fighters with their refuelling tanker. Johnson later boasted: "We smoked 'em twice. This is one of the few parts of the world where you can come low out of the sun. Not only were the A-10s surprised, but they were also unescorted and are not built to tangle with multi-role fighters like the CF-18." During Ex. Sweetbriar in February 1950, 410 Squadron had deployed Vampires to the Yukon. Much was learned about Arctic operations but, decades later at Inuvik, some of the same issues lingered for 441. Techs found that working in sub-zero temperatures remained brutal work, no matter how much "progress" had been made since 1950.

On February 5 three Lightning Strike CF-18s (LCol Struthers, Capts W. "Bill" Ryan and Hollis Tucker) scrambled on a 2.5-hour mission to intercept two Soviet Bear-H bombers over the Beaufort Sea. Alaskan F-15s had begun this intercept but, as they reached their maximum range, the Hornets took over. The Bears never overflew Canadian territory, their closest approach being 290 km off Shingle Point, Yukon. This was the first Canadian intercept of Soviet aircraft in the Arctic, and marked the fourth time in seven days that the North Warning System had detected intruders. While the Bear could launch cruise missiles, and an F-15 or CF-18 could easily destroy such a bomber, care was taken by both sides not to provoke. Such scenarios, in which each side was testing the other's defences, had more to do with the Cold War's elaborate rituals.

Following 441's intercept, this message was sent by BGen Remi Saulnier, Deputy Commander of NORAD in Colorado Springs and a former 441 CO: "My compliments to you and your Silver Fox Squadron for your achievement on the night of 4 Feb 88. As the Command Director on duty in the NORAD Command Post, it gave me great satisfaction to witness the first interception of a Russian Bear off our Arctic coast by Canadian fighters. That this event was made possible by the exceptionally fine work of 441 TFS was doubly satisfying. Well done and continued success."

CF Fighter Group's 1989 annual historical summary reported on Bear intercepts by CF-18s. Soviet Naval Bears had been detected routinely since 1970, when Voodoos equipped Canadian NORAD squadrons. Soviet Strategic Air Services Bears had begun appearing in 1984, first in the North Atlantic, then over the Beaufort, which became their principal "playground". In 1987 there were 11 Bear intercepts in that area, eight in 1988. But, by 1989 there were only two Bear intrusions into Fighter Group's domain, both being over the Atlantic. This coincided with the collapse of the USSR, after which Bears rarely tested NORAD. Another sign of the times was a "hands across the borders" visit in May 1992 by two Bears to the USAF B-52 base at Barksdale, Louisiana. A few years earlier such openness would have been unthinkable.

More Adventures

Having joined the Canadian Forces in 1974, Rob Chapman trained first on helicopters, then flew a tour on Sea Kings with 423 Squadron. In 1980 he was posted to Moose Jaw to instruct on Tutors. For a bit of a lark he applied early on for the Snowbirds. To his surprise he was invited for the annual try-outs and was accepted. For 1982 - 83 he flew as Snowbird No.7. Chapman's next posting was as executive assistant to Col Scott Clements, Base Commander Cold Lake, then he won his slot to train on the Hornet, then flew with 441 Squadron from 1987 - 89.

Later postings found Chapman instructing at 419 on the CF-5, working at AIRCOM HQ in the Directorate of Flight Safety and instructing on the King Air at Portage la Prairie. In 2004 he was with 1 CAD in Winnipeg. While doing a desk job there, he retained his King Air ticket. As *Fighter Squadron* was nearing completion in 2004, Capt Chapman submitted a few anecdotes from the early days of 441 on Hornets:

In the Beginning

In the beginning 441 was dedicated to the air defence role. We didn't do a lot of air-to-ground flying – only when we had to meet training objectives. Even then, while at Cold Lake there wasn't really a lot of flying to be had, since many of the aircraft were reserved for Combat Ready Training, if not for Willy Tell work-ups. So, if you wanted to fly, you had to go to the QRA in Comox. From there virtually all missions were over water and involved GCI training for the Air Weapons Controllers in the Underground Complex – the NORAD "Hole" in North Bay.

At the end of each intercept from the "Q" we were allowed to "mix it up". Needless to say, every pilot involved got exceptionally good at BFM/ACM. In those days, we did not have the integrated plumbing in the cold water immersion suit to allow for the G-suit to be worn with, but underneath, the immersion suit. We were granted permission to use one or the other. Most 441 pilots chose the immersion suit. So, all of our over-the-water ACM battles were fought without G-Suit.

The other discipline that all 441 pilots excelled at was air-to-air refuelling. We refuelled from every type of tanker you could imagine. The other type of flying we got good at was transiting back and forth from Comox and Cold Lake, including the very occasional step climb to (and brief cruise at) FL550. Oops! Did I say FL550? Sorry, I meant to say FL430. Yeah, that's right, FL430. (By the way, you can't see the curvature of the earth at FL550).

As part of ongoing training we had to attend and pass the "High Sustained G" course at the Defence Civil Institute of Environmental Medicine in Toronto. I volunteered to take the centrifuge training and I'm glad I did. I'm proud to report that I didn't "G-LOC" (G-loss of consciousness) and still have the video tape to prove it. In those days, the final grading profile was 8-G for 15 seconds without a G suit. Others took the training, but, I hear, some required extra training ... if you know what I mean.

The remaining skill set for we Hornet pilots was the ability to consistently engage the arrester cable, whether one of the mobile arrester gears at the FOLs, or the normal one, permanently installed at Cold Lake or Bagotville, or at a Deployed Operating Base like Comox or Goose Bay. I think this was a pretty straight-forward operation. That said, there was one engagement that I witnessed. Two pilots in a dual, were practicing a cable engagement on R04 in Cold Lake as part of CRT. I had just landed on R13 L and was on the parallel taxiway looking towards the approach end of R04. I had full view of the arrestment and what I saw next watered my eyes.

The cable engagement was slightly off-centre and I think the pilot in command was a wee bit fast. The cable yanked the Hornet sideways, then started to aggressively drag the aircraft backwards. If memory serves, this cable had less play than those on the parallel runways, so the pull-back was more positive. The hook dug into the asphalt and, with some side and rear motion still happening, the Hornet reared up, pivoting sideways on the hook. I saw its entire topside. The missile rail must have been inches from the ground. Then the Hornet plopped down properly, and came to a complete stop. The ground crew had to dig the hook out of the asphalt and then disengage the aircraft from the cable. In my opinion, the crew would have been justified in ejecting. They didn't and, fortunately, everything worked out well.

Other Flight Safety Occurrences

It shouldn't come as a surprise that we had the occasional flight safety occurrence. After all, the majority of 441 pilots were new to the fighter world, and all were new to the Hornet. A typical flight safety incident occurred one day as I was sitting in the QRA front office in Comox overlooking the dispersal area. Two Hornets had just started and were taxiing for take off. One of the pilots elected to use just a bit too much power and blew out the window of the office with his jet exhaust! This happened about two seconds after I had ducked under the table.

In a second incident I was taking off with a triple jugged Hornet, enroute from Cold Lake to Comox. Shortly after getting airborne, I heard "Bitching Betty" make an aural caution: "Bleed Air Left, Bleed Air Left". I thought, "Jeez, that is only supposed to happen on the ground during the pre-start checks!" Then I heard "Engine Fire Left, Engine Fire Left!" I shut the engine down, activated the fire extinguisher, then turned back towards base. Fearing that I might still be burning, and not wanting to open the dump valves, I elected to pickle the tanks over the water. The centre line jettisoned, as did the right wing tank, but not the left. I made some other switch selections and, finally, the left tank came off. By then I was over land, but there was no damage reported below. I recovered via an approach-end arrestment, wrote up the jet as unserviceable, got another jet, and headed off to Comox. The unserviceable Hornet took some nine months to repair – there had been a raging fire in the engine compartment, causing extensive damage.

Maj Dave Burton ready to fly a 441 photo chase mission from Cold Lake on May 25, 1998. (Larry Milberry)

AI Nav to Hornets - A 441 Pilot

A member of 441's initial CF-18 pilot cadre, Dave Burton, spent his boyhood in Ottawa. In 1980 he joined the Canadian Forces, training first at the Air Navigation School in Winnipeg, then taking the AI navigator's course at 410 Squadron in Bagotville. Next, came a tour on Voodoos with 416 Squadron in Chatham. These were exciting times, but all good things come to an end – 416 folded in 1984. Having logged some 900 Voodoo hours, and with a Bear intercept to his credit, Capt Burton now cross-trained to pilot. He began pilot training on the Tutor in Moose Jaw, his first log book entry being on February 27, 1985. His final "clearhood" check ride was flown with Capt Dan Trynchuk on December 4. Course graduation saw Capt Burton receiving the City of Moose Jaw Honour Graduate trophy, and the Province of Saskatchewan trophy for flying proficiency. Having already had his father present his navigator Wings, Capt Burton's dad, a retired flight sergeant, now proudly presented his son with pilot Wings.

After holding over for some months at Moose Jaw in H-Flight, Burton advanced to 419 Squadron for the fighter lead-in course, his first flight being in 116825 with his CO, LCol Lloyd Campbell on May 9, 1986 (Campbell later became Chief of the Air Staff). The CF-5 course carried on to December 18, by when Burton had 92.6 hours on the CF-5, many flown with his instructor, Maj Bart Wickham, himself a former AI navigator and a squadron mate of Burton from 416 days.

Capt Burton now joined his CF-18 course, which would form the original 441 pilot cadre. Students included a few pipeliners, such as Serge Beaulieu and Luc Savoie (classmates on Burton's Wings course), former 442 Buffalo pilots Guy Sawchuk and Bruce Beswick, some ex-CF-104 pilots, and ex-AI navs Dave Burton and René LeBlanc. As they trained, the rest of 441 was getting the hangar and shops ready for operations. Capt Burton began his course with a January 13, 1987 mission in 188924 with his instructor, Capt Tom Sabean, another ex-416 squadron mate. He soloed in 188773 on January 27. The course proceeded normally and, following all the prerequisite class and flight simulator sessions, plus 75.4 hours flying, Burton graduated on May 29, then joined 441.

June was spent getting set up and enjoying all the fun of the official 441 stand-up bash on the 26th. Capt Burton first flew with 441 on July 3 – a 1-V-1 DACT mission in 188774 against a visiting F-5E Aggressor. August 14 to 19 he completed his first alert in the "Q" at Comox. On a November 1987 deployment there, Capt Burton logged the following trips:

Date	Mission	Time (hours)
16	Transit from Cold Lake	1.5
16	ACM* 2-V-1	1.2
17	ADEX◊	1.6
18	AI#	1.6
18	ACM	1.7
20	ACM	1.0
21	LL Navᵝ	2.0
22	ACM	1.1
23	Transit to Cold Lake	1.3

*air combat manoeuvring - ◊air defense exercise - #airborne intercept - ᵝlow level navigation

In September, Capt Burton took part in Maple Flag XX, flying on the "Red Air" side and mainly intercepting "Blue Air" intruders. No sooner was Burton back in Cold Lake from a Comox deployment on November 23, than he had a back seat ride in an F-15D flown by Capt Ray Broyhill of the 54th TFS visiting from Elmendorf. From May 11 - 14, 1988 he had his first FOL deployment at Inuvik. There he flew two low-level, 1.6-hour missions on the 12th with the CO, then had a scramble on the 13th and 14th, each for 1.8 hours. Flying low level over the featureless snow-bound tundra proved to be a new experience. Burton's Comox mission of May 30 in dual 188925 was with fellow pilot Capt Chris Sponder in the back seat, Sponder's job being to take PR photos of Hornets with mountain backgrounds. May proved busy, Burton logging 36.7 hours. In June he flew in Maple Flag XXI, his mission of the 18th being a 2-V-2 against two US Navy F-14s. Besides general duties, from June - September 1988, 441 was training for Ex. William Tell at Tyndall AFB. On September 12 Capt Burton took Lt Paul Kissmann on his first Hornet ride (Kissmann later would excel as a Hornet pilot, test pilot and CO of 433 Squadron).

After WT-88 life at 441 returned to normal, Capt Burton's log in this period showing a range of missions. In December he was at Portage la Prairie where 441 gave a few back seat "motivational" flights to students training on Musketeers. On January 2, 1989 Burton's passenger on a 1.4-hour mission at Comox was Maj John Melson, a Maritime Group pilot more used to the Aurora than to the confines of a fighter cockpit. For the occasion Melson got a good ride on a 2-V-2 mission.

February 21 - 22 Capt Burton was with 441 at Eielson AB, Alaska for AAR training with a 437 Squadron 707. In March came the opportunity to drop live 500-lb Mk.82 bombs on the Jimmy Lake Range at Cold Lake. Maple Flag and Ex. Amalgam Chief followed then, on May 23, a 441 detachment flew to Bermuda for joint naval – air training. The positioning flight (5.3 hours in Capt Burton's case) was direct from Cold Lake accompanied by a 437 Squadron tanker. Burton returned to Cold Lake on the 31st aboard the 707. He flew his last 441 trip on June 20, then joined 410 to instruct, flying there first on July 4, 1989.

Compared to the fast-paced existence on an operational squadron, life as an instructor was predictable. Nonetheless, things rarely were dull. On June 6, 1991 Burton surpassed 1000 hours on the CF-18. For the 29th, with Capt Jeff Beckett in his back seat, he led a firepower demonstration, one of the events as 410 celebrated its 50th anniversary. Promoted to major, his tour ended with a mission of January 17, 1992. Now the inveterate fighter pilot began two years with 425 Squadron at Bagotville. Finished there in June 1994, he began a ground tour as an Exercise and TacEval officer with AIRCENT HQ at Ramstein AFB, Germany. There he was involved in the "Partnership for Peace" program, whereby Western forces began the planning process for bringing former Warsaw Pact nations into NATO. In that period Maj Burton travelled to several former "enemy" bases, observing first-hand the life of fighter pilots from the other side of the Iron Curtain.

Maj Burton now attended CF Command and Staff College, then returned to 441, this time as DCO under LCol Billie Flynn. He first flew with his old squadron on August 7, 1997. As a practical fighter pilot, he didn't find that much had changed since leaving eight years earlier, although most pilots, inevitably, now were young. The Hornet remained familiar, the only things really new being that FLIR (forward looking infra red sensing) and the Maverick missile had been introduced. Some typical activities for Burton in this period were deployments to Luke AFB in December 1997 and March 1998, and a May 2 - 15, 1998 one to Holloman AFB, New Mexico to fly against each other and against F-4s of the Luftwaffe FWIC. Also, in May 1998, 441 flew in Maple Flag as Red Air.

Maj Burton's last 441 trip was a KC-130 AAR mission of July 29, 1998. By this time his log showed 2091.2 hours total flying time, with 1750 on the CF-18. Posted now to 1 Canadian Air Division HQ in Winnipeg, he was promoted to lieutenant colonel, heading the "A3 Fighter Readiness" shop. To LCol Burton, however, this now seemed a good time to launch a new career. In April 2000, therefore, he joined Air Canada as an A320 first officer; but Air Canada soon was in lay-off mode. Being low on the seniority list, Dave Burton saw that Air Canada was a bit of a career gamble. He decided to return to air force life in 2003, initially as a staff officer at CF College in Toronto.

Pilots get ready for the May 25 mission: Maj Burton and Capts Venman and Soroka do their pre-flight paperwork. Someone once said that a crew should not take off until the weight of the paperwork equals that of the airplane. Then, everyone just before stepping to their jets: Larry Milberry, Jan Reudiseuli, Gary Venman, Dave Burton and Kirk Soroka. Finally, a sight to make any 441 pilot smile — Hornets joining up. (Larry Milberry)

CHAPTER 20

William Tell

As a new NORAD squadron 441's first trip to Tyndall AFB for Ex. William Tell was a benchmark. "Willy Tell", a biennial event, was the USAF's premier air-to-air weapons meet. With its motto "Train to fight, and fight to win", its goal was to provide a realistic environment where squadrons would compete, using the full range of air-to-air skills and resources. The meet first was held in 1954 at Vincent AFB, Arizona, where it was the air-to-air rocketry phase of the Third Annual USAF Weapons Meet. That year F-94s took first and second places over F-86s and F-89s. In 1955 overseas squadrons first took part. Nine squadrons were involved in 1956. The meet moved to Tyndall in 1958, when the first Air National Guard units competed, and the first guided missiles were fired. Florida ANG F-86Ds recorded Willy Tell's first perfect score that year.

Each year brought something new at Willy Tell. For 1965 there were 16 teams, including the first from the RCAF (Voodoos). On account of the Vietnam War there were no further meets until 1970, when weapons loading and air weapons control categories were added. Henceforth, the Ryan BQM-34A and -34F subsonic and supersonic drones were used as targets. In 1974 the USAF was startled when all three categories (flying, weapons loading, AWC) were won by the ANG. A further advance in drones came in 1978 with the use of full-size PQM-102s – retired F-102s converted to drones. As the last of these was shot into the Gulf of Mexico, the QF-100, QF-4 and QF-106 took over in their turn. In 1980 the B-52 and F-111 were added to the "intruder" phase of Willy Tell. In 1982 the 20-mm gunnery competition was introduced for the F-4, F-106 and F-15. "Willy Tell 86" was the last time for F-106 teams. Into the early 1980s Canada entered a Voodoo team, although results usually were spotty. The CF-18 first competed with "Willy Tell 86", Team Canada that year being 425 Squadron from Bagotville.

Several units comprised Team Canada for "Willy Tell 88": 441 and 42 Radar from Cold Lake, the Radar Control Wing at CFB North Bay, and 65 personnel from various other Cold Lake units. Beginning in June, 441 began WT-88 work-ups, with Profiles 1 and 2 training being done at Comox from June 14 - 20, followed by air-to-air gunnery in Cold Lake, and

The first appearance of the CF-18 at Willy Tell was in 1986, when 425 Squadron formed Team Canada. Here, judges scrutinize 425's weapons loaders on October 18, as they service 188714's 20-mm gun. (Larry Milberry)

239

Canadians at Tyndall for "Willy Tell 92" gather on October 20 for an informal "photo op". Their Hornet is being judged in the weapons load competition. Team Canada this year was a composite Cold Lake group including many non-flying 441 folks, but only one 441 pilot. (Larry Milberry)

Capt Burton flies 188778 during a photo mission over Niagara Falls. This took place while 441 was in Willy Tell work-ups at Niagara Falls Municipal Airport, NY. Such a skit today would get a Hornet pilot crucified on the spot. (via Dave Burton)

ECM training at Ex. Copper Flag at Tyndall AFB from July 11 - 15. On the 17th the team flew to Niagara Falls, NY to train with the 136th FIS (F-4s) until the 24th. This included weapons training over a Lake Ontario range. Team member Capt Dave Burton flew eight missions in this period, one a photo session over Niagara Falls on the 21st. August 22 - 27 "Team Canada" was at Elmendorf for DACT with USAF F-15s. On the 29th, the team departed southbound, routing via Ellsworth AFB (South Dakota), Tinker AFB (Oklahoma), Tyndall AFB (Florida), NAS Cecil Field (Florida) to Ellington Field (Texas), where it spent two days training with the 147th FIG (Texas ANG, F-4s). Illustrating how busy the Willy Tell team was is the flying total for the month in Capt Burton's log book – 46.2 hours.

Finally it was Willy Tell time and Team Canada set off for Tyndall. For this event, pilots Majs Stu Holdsworth and Bob Wade and Capts Dave Burton, René LeBlanc and Hollis Tucker, planned two skits – this being the way CF fighter squadrons always used to do things. Firstly, they dressed not in regulation kit, each man instead being decked out in his formal mess kit. Then came their arrival show at Tyndall, which was based on Bob Wade's "high alpha" solo Hornet demo. Viewed as a single ship, this was always impressive for an airshow crowd. In Dan Dempsey's book *Tradition of Excellence*, Wade described this manoeuvre from the point in his 1986 routine where he completed a 360-degree/325-knot turn:

Having just arrived at Tyndall for WT-88, Canada's pilots, brewskis in hand, pose in their "flying suits": René LeBlanc, Dave Burton, Bob Wade, Stu Holdsworth and Hollis Tucker. Then, the team looking a bit more operational the next day. (Burton Col., Larry Milberry)

I re-entered from stage left at 200 feet above ground in level flight. Reducing speed to approximately 100 knots and a flight attitude of 28 to 33 degrees angle of attack, I could demonstrate the superior low-speed handling characteristics of the CF-18. This was my signature manoeuvre, and one that could not be duplicated by any other fighter. I would complete a 360-degree level turn in front of the crowd at this angle, and appear to be hanging in the air by a thread. It was not difficult to fly, as one simply maintained attitude with stick pressure, and altitude with thrust. The turn was actually accomplished with rudder, since the fly-by-wire system washed out the ailerons at 25 degrees angle of attack.

The crowd loved the high alpha manoeuvre, and it convinced the world that this jet had a slow speed capability second to none. The advantages in a gun fight were obvious. Upon completion of the 360 degree high alpha turn, and back at centre stage, I selected full afterburner and pulled the nose up to 80 degrees of pitch...

For WT-88, 441 came up with a new high alpha "look" – five Hornets line abreast flying across the field at 100 knots, then breaking off to land. Next, to the amazement of those lucky enough to see 441's October 8 arrival show, five pilots in tuxedos stepped down from their jets. Greeting them were 441 maintenance personnel in plaid shirts and toques, while several pretty 441 "hostesses" handed each pilot a glass of champagne. What a zany arrival, except for one snag – the USAF general commanding Tyndall hit the roof. So ticked was he at Team Canada's stunts, that he was tempted to tell the Canadians, "Gas up and get the hell off my base!" Eventually, however, he relented, and 441 settled into its quarters to make last-minute plans for Profiles 1 and 2 to be flown the next day.

Profiles 1 to 5

Twelve squadrons took part in "Willy Tell 88" from October 6 - 23. Each would fly five profiles guided by its own AWC team. For missile profiles P1 and P2, live weapons were fired at drones by each pilot (four pilots per team, plus a spare). A pilot would identify his target to the weapons controllers about two minutes back, before the fighter's initial point (IP), although the pilot did not commit to an attack until he heard "target hot" from the range control officer. He then fired his AIM-7 Sparrow head-on at the drone. Passing the target, he turned to fire his AIM-9, by when the drone was evading. There was always a chance that an AIM-9 might hit the drone, especially its wingtip heat-generator. In 2004 Dave Burton recalled the challenge:

From a personal standpoint, Profiles 1 and 2 were unforgettable. First of all, receiving the clearance to fire seemed painfully slow. In part, this was due to the need to ensure that the range was clear of air and water craft. Once a pilot had a radar lock during P1, and was cleared to fire, it was a matter of waiting for the optimum fire control, computer-generated solution, then pulling the trigger. For "Willy Tell 88" the range would be at about 10 nautical miles with a closing speed of about 900 knots. Having never fired a missile in a theatre of war, it seemed that my closing speed roughly equalled my heart rate!

Squeezing the trigger, then waiting for the AIM-7 launching off its rail seemed to take forever. In that instant I even had time to wonder if something had gone wrong with my missile. In fact, it was gone in a flash, and accelerating ahead in a billow of smoke. Just then my target began a programmed barrel roll, designed to prevent a direct hit. Now my focus was on maximizing the ability of my radar to hold a solid track of the target.

A miss within select distances during P1 determined one's score, Zone 1 scoring the highest, and so on. My AIM-7 scored in Zone 2 – even though all seemed well in the cockpit, the missile had lost target acquisition in the final moments. However, there was no time to worry, as the immediate task was to acquire the target visually for the P2 phase, pass above and abeam it, make the prescribed radio calls, and again listen for the calls for clearance to manoeuvre and fire.

Points would be allotted for minimum time to AIM-9 launch, plus for the missile's tracking. Although the CF-18 could come up with a fire control, computer-generated firing solution, in training we had determined that a faster missile launch could be achieved by not waiting for the computer. Instead, we would fire as soon as a distinct tone was heard in our headset (the tone was generated by the AIM-9 once it acquired a heat source).

Position and speed were critical to ensure the optimum start point from which a max-G, slicing turn could be initiated once cleared to manoeuvre. We were trained to do all this, while visually acquiring the target, but were assisted by a strong dose of adrenaline. For P2 I saw my target at about a mile. I called 'visual' and was cleared to manoeuvre upon crossing abeam the drone. I rolled quickly to establish the plane of my turn directly into the target's projected path, selected afterburner, and pulled a maximum 7.5G turn. Through about 120 degrees I started to get a missile tone. As my nose came up, the tone became a loud squeal, indicating a solid missile lock onto the heat source. Instantly, I pulled the trigger.

The AIM-9 leapt off my right wing. However, as the target continued its 4-G slicing turn, I lost sight of my missile as it arced right in what appeared to be the wrong direction. I sensed immediate defeat! Then, to the left, I saw my QF-100 target explode. "Hornet 2, splash one" were my sweet words of victory, as the first target drone of WT-88 plunged into the Gulf of Mexico. Maximum zone points were assured and, once I had landed came the news that I had executed the turn-to-trigger squeeze in a record minimum time. Respectable team points and an experience never to be forgotten, and this was only Day 1!

For Profile 3 pilots fired 20-mm cannons at a towed target. Firing had to occur at a precise moment, or the shooter was disqualified. Aircraft attacked in pairs, Lead firing, while No.2 made a tracking run. They then reversed roles for the second pass. For P4 a team launched all four jets to counter a mass attack, where the intruders used ECM and chaff, and appeared at various levels. In WT-88 the targets were 4 B-52s, 5 Learjets, 4 FB-111s, 1 T-33 and 2 F-16s. Defenders had to identify their targets visually on this 40-minute mission, and the scenario included a "friendly" aircraft in the midst of the attackers. The latter had to be identified, and saved from "friendly fire", while enemy aircraft had to be taken out. Each defender was allowed four simulated shots. For WT-88 the highest P4 score was the 1st TFW's 9750/10,000. Teams scrambled for P5 in pairs against four bogies at different altitudes and locations on the ACMI range. From the moment of scrambling, an interceptor had only 10 minutes to get airborne,

Some "Willy Tell 88" participants. First, the 441 Squadron flightline coming alive as Hornets flash up for an early morning mission. (Mike Valenti)

William Tell 88

There was nothing more exciting for the aviation fan than a stroll down the Willy Tell flightline. Here, F-16s of the 474th TFW crank up at WT-88. This was the first year at the meet for the F-16. Based at Nellis AFB, the 474th's flew in the utility role, doing morning weather recces, range sweeps, and intruder missions for Profile 5. (Larry Milberry)

An F-4 of the 136th FIS, NY ANG. This was the Willy Tell swan song for the F-4. (Larry Milberry)

Georgia ANG F-15As of the 116th TFW based at Dobbins AFB near Marietta. (Larry Milberry)

North Bay's 414 Squadron T-birds flew EW missions in WT-88. Note the ersatz Soviet markings. Along with civil Learjets, the T-birds jammed fighters, making life miserable for pilots on intercepts, and for weapons controllers trying to get their own day's work done. (Larry Milberry)

WT-92 Team Lead, LCol Laurie Hawn, with pilots Pierre "Mo-Mo" Morissette, Emile Calderon, Marcel Major, Jim Stuart and B.J. Ryan with their staff car, a 1968 Plymouth Fury. By "special arrangement" a USAF C-5A carried the Fury as far as the Stewart AFB, NY. Then LCol Hawn and Capt Eddie Haskins drove it on to Tyndall. Haskins described his team's objectives simply: "Naturally, the first goal was to bring home all the trophies. Failing the first, we vowed to make sure that everybody knew the Canadians were here." The Fury was part of the plan. (Larry Milberry)

Team Canada armourers heft an AIM-9 to the flightline. (Larry Milberry)

Signing out jets just before stepping to the flightline for an October 19 mission: Stuart, Morissette, Major, Ryan with Cpl Wayne Erskine. Then, the same fellows post-mission with team medical officer, Maj "Doc" Fever. (Mike Valenti)

Pilots await the "Go" sign after scrambling for their P4 mission of October 20. Then, QF-106 Delta Darts in the overhead break after a P4 mission. (Mike Valenti)

Hornet '735 taxies on an October 17 mission. Once the pilot reached the "last chance" position near the end of the runway, the armament techs removed the missile safety pins, making them "live". (Mike Valenti)

Team Canada watching as their CF-18 is judged during the WT-92 ICT on October 20. (Mike Valenti)

Let 'er burn! Great after-hours fun typified any Willy Tell. For 1992 Team Canada was quartered in a beach house. Outside, volley ball seemed to rage day and night. In this case the Canucks are in full flight, while some of the beach house furniture is used to cheer up the scene. Adding to the spirit, most teams also put on some first-class grub in the Officers Club. The 1st FW from Langley came with crabs, the 120th from Montana served buffalo burgers, while the 18th FG from Kadena offered sake-soaked shrimp. (Mike Valenti)

WT-92 judge Maj Dave Burton with 441 fan Mike Valenti. (Larry Milberry)

More good action at the WT-92 scoreboard. (Larry Milberry)

recovered at Tyndall, one was marshalled to the ICT area to be readied for a "quick turn-around". All went well until an AIM-7 refused to mate with the airframe, and Team Canada scored a fifth in the ICT/Static Weapons Load categories.

On Day 2 Team Canada's maintenance team scored a perfect "1000" in having its five Hornets ready for the P1 launch, but poor weather saw the mission scrubbed until Day 3. Team Captain, Maj B.J. Ryan, had a technical snag after takeoff, so was replaced by Capt Calderon. The team came within one second of a first in P1, tying for second behind the 36th FW. On this profile Maj Major downed a Ryan drone with an AIM-7.

QF-100 Super Sabres were replaced in this year's P1 by more expendable BQM-34As. Competitors would "accidentally" shoot down five Ryans this year. Also on Day 3, Team Canada flew P3 – its mass raid/area defence mission. Backing up the pilots was the GCI team – Capts Tony O'Keefe and Joe Richardson, plus TSgt Bob McMickle and SSgt Cliff Cook, the latter two being USAF. P3 rules demanded that each of the 16 targets be visually ID'd before the "shoot-down". This was important – nobody cares to destroy a "friendly". Of 16 intruders, Team Canada accounted for 15, a low-level B-1B escaping. The Hornets got a third on P3, the Canadian GCI team a second.

Team Standings Willy Tell 92

Place	Unit	Type	Base	P1	P2	P3	P4	Total
1	18 WG	F-15C	Kadena	9675	1778	10,000	9120	30,573
2	1 FW	F-15C	Langley	9800	1356	9300	8820	29,276
3	33 FW	F-15C	Eglin	9450	1674	10,000	7840	28,964
4	Canada	CF-18	Cold Lake	9800	1274	9300	7310	27,684
5	36 FW	F-15C	Bitburg	9825	1964	9300	6500	27,589
6	120 FG	F-16A	Great Falls	9550	2382	8600	5500	26,032
7	125 FG	F-16A	Jacksonville	9355	1560	9300	5500	25,715
8	102 FW	F-15A	Otis	9600	1338	8000	6400	25,338

Air Weapons Controllers			Maintenance Teams			Weapons Load Team		
Place	Unit	Total	Place	Unit	Total	Place	Unit	Total
1	1 FW	9325	1	18 WG	3927	1	18 WG	2760
2	Canada	9000	2	33 FW	3917	2	1 FW	2630
3	10 WG	8950	3	102 FW	3915	3	102 FW	2600.5
4	120 FG	8500	4	120 FG	3881	4	125 FG	2560
5	33 FW	8450	5	36 FW	3872	5	Canada	2535.5
6	125 FG	8425	6	Canada	3661	6	120 FG	2416.5
7	102 FW	6625	7	125 FG	3584	7	33 FW	2319
8	36 FW	6075	8	1 FW	3534	8	36 FW	2030

The final day was for the exciting P4. When the scramble horn sounded, pilots and groundcrew raced across the tarmac to their Hornets. Engines were winding up within seconds and the two elements (Ryan/Stuart and Major/Morissette) were on the move as soon as the marshaller flashed his "Go" sign. The Hornets quickly rose into their designated CAP (combat air patrol) zone, each element to await four QF-106 targets. Of these, seven were splashed. Major/Morissette would end the week in fourth place among the 16 competing elements.

Willy Tell Judge

Dave Burton describes his duties as a WT-92 judge:

While serving as Ops Officer on 425 Squadron, I had the opportunity to become a judge in WT-92. Having experienced WT-88 from the pilot's seat, I quickly accepted the offer. After all, this would allow me to help ensure some competitive fairness within my small sphere of responsibility.

The judges arrived at Tyndall a few days before the competition. We soon got acquainted with each other and with the rules and procedures of the judging to follow. Teamed with a USAF counterpart, I was responsible for aircrew judging during P3 – the mass attack. Our task was to validate kills using head-up display (HUD) tapes. Should a tape prove inconclusive, there were other means by which we could validate kills and award points. Other P3 judges were responsible for the Air Weapons Controllers, aircraft turn-arounds, etc.

Each defending pilot in P3 had enough "ammunition" to kill 4 of the 16 intruders. There also was a "friendly" aircraft in the engagement zone, so pilots were busy making each shot count, while not hitting the "friendly".

Liaison between judging staff and competitors was forbidden. Even so, it was not difficult to feel proud of each Canadian kill, and disappointed when we fell short. Watching in real time, I mentally urged our team on to the last target, but it was not to be. When the judging was over, I was left with the impression that WT-92 had been fairly run, even if it was slanted towards a USAF modus operandi.

For "Willy Tell 96" (October 21 - 27) Team Canada again was a composite group, mainly from 4 Wing, which contributed 56 personnel including 441 pilots Maj E.R. Boyd and Capts A.M. Mirza and Steve Nierlich. This year the Canadians won seven trophies, "Top Team" included. Capt Nierlich came away as "Top Gun", having scored 3262.57 points to his USAF runner-up's 3235. (An RMC graduate, Nierlich had joined the Canadian Forces in 1986, earned his wings in 1991, then joined 441. In 1997 he left to instruct with 410, then took a NATO posting at the Tactical Leadership Program in Belgium.) Since 1958 no team had so dominated at Willy Tell. Once home Team Canada was summoned to Ottawa for formal congratulations in the House of Commons. Team Canada CO, LCol Marc Ouellet, received a Chief of Defence Staff Commendation for his team's effort.

LCol Marc Ouellet, Team Lead WT-96, brings his troops home with the gold. (CF)

CHAPTER 21

A Changing World

LCol Terry L. Hunt assumed command of 441 on July 6, 1989. In this period, 441 would see a shift in global trends, the main event coming in 1989 when Eastern European communist governments began toppling. Symbolizing developments was the appearance of two MiG-29s on a peaceful mission over North America. It all began with a Fighter Group tasking for the 441 Comox Detachment to escort two MiG-29s, flying south from Russia and Alaska to take part in the Abbotsford International Airshow on the weekend of August 7. Since this was the first time that the Russians had allowed their fighters to participate in any Western airshow, there was much interest in the event. As to which pilots would fly the escort, the CO, LCol Struthers, let his boys know that this tasking must not interfere with QRA operations. In 2004 Rob Chapman recalled of this: "As the squadron crew scheduler, I knew that a QRA rotation was hard enough to cement as it was, without introducing a short-notice curve ball. No change to our schedule was to occur; whoever was on alert that day would do the intercept." In 2004 Bob Wade recalled the whole episode:

Commanding 441 when the first Soviet jet fighters visited Canada was LCol Terry Hunt, shown presenting 441 pilot Capt Bill Ryan with his CD. Having joined the Canadian Forces in 1968 as an ROTP candidate, his first flying posting (1974 - 78) was on Voodoos at 416 Squadron. He flew with the Snowbirds for two seasons, then returned to Voodoos at 409. Later postings were to the USAF Air War College at Maxwell AFB and NDHQ in personnel, before taking over 441 in 1989. After a NORAD tour at McCord AFB, Washington, LCol Hunt retired from the military in 1993. (CF CKC89-5296)

Air force photographer Cpl D. Schoenenberger captured these views as 441 escorted the MiG-29s to Abbotsford on August 5, 1989. (CF CKC89-5730, '5682)

On August 5, 1989 the MiG-29s (single seater "315", two seater "304") were escorted from Russian airspace into Alaska by USAF F-15s. The following afternoon four F-15s and an AWACS escorted them to the Canadian border. Then, as the QRA Det Commander at Comox, I led our escort of CF-18s, the three "hot" QRA aircraft. My aircraft was a dual, with Capt Hollis Tucker in the rear seat. Capt Rob Chapman flew as No.2, while Maj Stu Holdsworth flew the third CF-18, a dual with photographer Cpl D. Schoenenberger in the back seat. Lacking tanker support, we were configured with external

When the MiG-29s reached Abbotsford, fighter pilots for miles around wanted to have a look. Canadians in this mob scene are Bill Huckstep (441) in the cockpit then, standing in front, are Col Dave Jurkowski (Base Commander Cold Lake), Al Bennell (441), Hollis Tucker (441), Craig Richmond (441), Mark Stowe (419), unknown USAF, LCol Terry Hunt (CO 441), Maj Marc Ouellet (419), Maj Bob Wade (441), MiG pilot Roman Taskaev of the Mikoyan Design Bureau, and two unknown USAF. (via Bob Wade)

Mike Valenti's photo of MiG-29 "315" at Abbotsford on August 8, 1989.

tanks, so had enough fuel to loiter for about 15 minutes in the rendezvous area along the Canada - Alaska border, then complete the escort to Abbotsford and return to Comox.

The launch from Comox was under NORAD GCI control and allowed for direct routing at optimum altitudes. Arriving at the border we entered a hold to await the package flying south. Handover to AWACS was accomplished in our first orbit and we soon had the package visual at about 15 miles. Flying north, I led the CF-18s into a stern intercept behind the package at about one mile. The F-15s then broke and headed back to Elmendorf.

The MiG-29s were operating under a civilian IFR flight plan and should have been communicating with Vancouver Centre for clearance through Canadian airspace. Remaining under AWACS control and not monitoring civilian frequencies, we remained astern of the MiGs. After about 15 minutes the MiGs climbed 2000 feet and appeared to be about 20 degrees right of the airway that I anticipated they would follow. I queried AWACS about this, got no explanation, so tuned my second radio to Vancouver Centre to determine the reason for the routing change. Vancouver Centre was happy to hear from me, since they had had no communications with the MiGs since they had entered Canadian airspace. I advised AWACS of this, then closed up to the left of MiG No. 304.

Fighter Group had directed me not to talk directly with the MiGs, and to avoid close formation with them. Now I could see both MiG pilots watching me closely. The navigator in "304" had a high level chart opened and appeared to be searching for information. Meanwhile, the pilot pointed to his helmet ear piece and gave me the thumbs-down signal. He then raised his palms upward, indicating a radio receiver failure. I advised Vancouver Centre and requested clearance for the MiGs to proceed direct to Abbotsford. This was approved and now Vancouver Centre could predict where our formation would be heading. Using hand signals, I then directed the lead MiG to turn about 40 degrees left on a rough track direct to Abbotsford.

Now the MiG navigator showed me the palms of his hands – he didn't know his position. We were in bright sunshine at 37,000 feet, but this would change in about 200 miles as the cloud tops would be above our altitude. I was concerned that the MiGs would have problems upon entering cloud lacking radio and navigation aids. I advised AWACS that I would take the lead of the MiG formation, and switch to civilian air traffic control.

Another concern was that the MiG pilots were company test pilots, and I wasn't sure how proficient they would be at flying close formation in cloud. On the other hand I was confident of my own pilots holding formation. Now I pointed at the lead MiG pilot, patting my right shoulder to indicate that he should now fly close formation on my right wing. He slid nicely into position, followed by his No.2. I quickly realized that all was well – the Russians were good pilots, holding position with great finesse, even in turbulence. I called my own wingmen into echelon left formation and we proceeded south as a 5-plane formation.

Using hand signals, I now requested the remaining time in minutes that the MiGs had fuel to fly. The answer was within 10 minutes of the time needed to reach Abbotsford. I advised ATC, requesting priority handling over other traffic for descent and approach. With approval from Abbotsford we began descent about 80 miles out, penetrating 30,000 feet of cloud before breaking out at about 5000 feet agl. I cancelled my IFR clearance about 10 miles back from Abbotsford, and switched to tower frequency.

With tower's approval we flew down the runway in a 5-plane formation, then completed a climbing right turn to the downwind for the runway. I indicated to the lead MiG that he break away and land. He gave us a little salute, then entered a steep diving turn towards the runway. The MiGs flew low and fast over the end of the runway, then executed a battle break and landing. As soon as the MiGs were on the ground with their drag chutes streaming, I put my wingmen into a 5-second trail formation. We passed over the taxiing MiGs in burner and began a steep climbing turn back to Comox. Another great day in the life of a fighter pilot! A delegate from the Russian Embassy later called me in the QRA to thank us for our assistance. Little did I know how that thank you would affect the next year of my life.

That weekend at Abbotsford, Maj Wade flew in MiG-29 "304" with Maj Valery Menitsky, sharing the controls for 12 minutes. Every fighter pilot in the West suddenly couldn't wait to hear about Wade's flight, so he was sent on a year-long road tour, speaking about the MiG-29 to squadrons in the US, UK and Western Europe. Fellow Silver Fox pilot Craig Richmond later described this as "the ultimate fighter pilot gig and we CF-18 pilots were envious beyond belief."

Further Escorts

For all the smiles and handshakes with its old enemy, NORAD still kept an eye on the declining USSR. In Ex. Amalgam Chief of May 15 - 20, 1989, 425, and 441 squadrons flew in the fighter role, supported by 437 tankers and 414 ET-33s, plus USAF units with B-1s, F-111s, etc. Too bad, but whoever compiled Fighter Group's annual historical report had little to say about "Amalgam Chief", other than the odd-ball comment, "It allowed for real time deployment and employment of Fighter Group Headquarters resources in a NORAD scenario to and for dynamic implementation of pertinent plans." In September 1989, 441 flew in "PACEX 89". In part, this involved two US Navy carrier groups moving up the west coast; eight 441 Hornets provided opposition to some 90 USN fighters.

In 1990 Hornets from Cold Lake escorted Russian fighters during PR visits to North America. First came some Su-27 Flankers, then some MiG-29s. In both cases the Soviets entered North American air space at Elmendorf AFB, met first by USAF F-15s, then by five 416 and 441 CF-18s led by 441's Capt Craig "Richmo" Richmond. Capt René LeBlanc of 441 led the next leg – Comox to Winnipeg, but departure from Comox was delayed – the Russians needed airline-type fuel, not military grade, so a supply had to be delivered from Vancouver. The escort from Winnipeg was provided by 433 Squadron of Bagotville. Craig Richmond recalls of this exciting activity:

As the Cold War faded in the late 1980s, one interesting happening was the unprecedented arrival in North America of Russian fighter aircraft on tour. Bob Wade led the first MiG-29 escort in 1989, earning a flight in a 2-seat MiG-29. Then, in June 1990 I was lucky enough to fly in two escorts. On June 12 I was part of a 441 Squadron 4-ship that escorted Su-27 Flankers from Elmendorf to Comox during their first visit to the West. Naturally, we all were very keen to fly with the mighty Flanker, a massive air defence fighter that we respected as a formidable adversary.

After a spectacular arrival at Elmendorf, the Flankers refuelled and taxied out with some F-15s, as we CF-18 types (I had Capt Al Bennell in my back seat) trailed along the parallel taxiway – a big mistake! For reasons unknown the Russians quickly took the runway and, without waiting a moment, took off and climbed like bats out of hell. Everyone else followed as fast as possible, liberally using afterburner (and fuel) for about 150 miles before we caught up with the wily Flankers. From there the mission went routinely, all of us landing at Comox. There we refuelled and flew back to Cold Lake, while the Russians overnighted at Comox before carrying on.

On June 27, 1990 I was detailed to lead a formation of 441 and 416 CF-18s escorting two MiG-29s, also to Comox. Flying a dual, I had Capt Brad Sinclair in my back seat. In Elmendorf I received a telephone call from

As MiG-29s "304" and "315" approached Ottawa from Winnipeg on June 28, 1990 one of their escorts, flying 188791, was 433 CO, LCol Ray Levasseur. Here, in a classic WO Vic Johnson photo, the CO holds position on "315's" wing. Then, the MiGs arriving in the rain in Ottawa. (CF ISC90-2168, Larry Milberry)

LGen R.W. Morton, Deputy Commander of NORAD. That in itself was unusual, since NORAD generals usually don't phone captains. "Captain Richmond," he said, "under no circumstance will the MiGs leave first! Understood? Get them to Comox without incident." I replied, "No problemo, Sir", and arranged to get to the runway first, no matter what. (I didn't know whether or not the F-15 folks had been chastised for the embarrassing Flanker tail chase, but they didn't fly with us that day.)

Where the Flankers had lots of fuel, we soon realized that the MiG-29 did not. As I gave the mission briefing, I had to dicker with the Russians about climb speed. They also were unhappy that Anchorage ATC required a 270° climbing turn, before turning south, while they wanted a quick right turn towards Comox. The non-pilot Russian "translator" in the back of the lead MiG listened to my patient explanations for about 30 minutes, relaying in Russian, while the pilots kept shaking their heads and muttering "nyet". With time pressing, I put on my best Kamloops beef-fed grin and asked, "So, is everybody happy with the plan?" The MiG pilots shook their heads and started pleading with the translator, who abruptly held up his hand and shouted, "SHTO!". He took a long drag on his cigarette, slit his eyes and, in a Hollywood-thick Russian accent, said, "Da – we are happy with the plan." You can guess in which part of the Soviet government he worked!

I camped out on the runway 20 minutes early, my wingman and I blocking as much concrete as possible, just in case. Our departure was uneventful. It was a long trip south – about 2 1/2 hours, and we watched the weather (and the MiGs) closely. About an hour into the flight the translator asked if we could stop for fuel at Sandspit, in the Queen Charlottes. While this was pretty good intelligence about the MiG-29's range, there was no way that we could land at such a small, isolated airport. We pressed on to Comox, where the ceiling was no worse than on a typical winter's day in Europe, so I figured that the big 7-plane Vic would make for an impressive arrival show. We joined up in cloud and, when we broke out, I led a nice pass down the runway. As I pulled up, I thought, "That wasn't too bad. Why not do another?" Then, suddenly there went the MiGs! They had spotted the runway and dropped right out of the middle of our formation like bricks. Guess they were pretty well sucking fumes by then! Next day the MiGs pushed on to meet an engagement at the National Capital Airshow in Ottawa.

More glasnost ... Ukrainian Air Force MiG-29s at the Edmonton airshow on May 16, 1992. (Larry Milberry)

441 escorts two of Russia's mighty Su-27 Flanker long-range interceptors during the mission led by Maj Craig Richmond. (CF)

CHAPTER 22

Squadron Losses

On the night of April 4, 1988 a small fishing boat was anchored off Vancouver Island as a storm lashed the region. Apprehensive, the boat's sole occupant asked the Rescue Coordination Centre in Victoria for a heading to open water, but RCC first needed an accurate fix. Conditions made it inadvisable to despatch a Buffalo or Labrador from 442 Squadron at Comox, so RCC asked the NORAD Regional Operations Control Centre if a CF-18 from the Comox QRA could be used. Approval was granted. Two 441 CF-18s took off at 0207 hours on April 5. Capt Guy Sawchuk orbited at 23,000 as a radio relay, while Capt Michael "Lief" Erickson descended to find the vessel. The minimum safe altitude issued by the ROCC had been 10,000 feet over land, 2000 over water. Capt Erickson descended to 2000, located the vessel using radar and DF equipment, then overflew it, gave a position report, then made a second pass to confirm the fix. Soon afterwards he disappeared from radar – he had crashed into a 2300-foot rise on Vancouver Island's Brooks Peninsula.

Capt Rich Corver of 441. Then, the stained glass window that honours him. Created in 1990 by Andrea E.W. Simpson, the window graces 441's heritage room. The inscription reads, "Captain Rich Corver. Because I fly, I envy no man on Earth."
(via Rob Chapman, Larry Milberry)

Investigators concluded that Capt Erickson had been aware of the peninsula and its hills. He had flown a track parallel to the main shoreline, and current winds ruled out drift as a factor. His radar altimeter enabled him to maintain height over the sea, but the steep slope would have allowed only a momentary warning at low level. In fact, his inertial navigation system was in error by about five to seven miles, suggesting that the CF-18 was further from land than it was. Having flown the same machine the previous day, Erickson had reported this snag. Some in the CF-18 community later voiced concern at his aircraft not being 100% serviceable, while others were bitter about the decision to use a CF-18 on such a mission.

Another 441 Comox incident had a happier ending. On December 24, 1988 two CF-18s led by Capt Richard Corver scrambled for a practice intercept. After some 30 minutes No.2 called for a "knock-it-off", stating an oxygen problem. Corver requested a re-join vector and tried to determine what was wrong. He quickly saw that things were deteriorating – his wingman was on the verge of unconsciousness and had begun a steep dive from 17,000 feet. Corver alerted No.2 and, once the errant Hornet levelled, he insisted that autopilot modes be used. He also ensured that emergency oxygen procedures were followed, and No.2 gradually recovered. On the 100-mile flight home, Corver informed ground of their progress and handled radio traffic. *Flight Comment* subsequently reported: "Captain Corver's presence of mind, knowledge of aircraft systems and strong leadership during this difficult emergency contributed directly to its successful conclusion."

With January 29, 1990 came further heartbreak at 441. That day Capt Corver himself was one of three pilots taking off from Inuvik during an ALCM (Air Launched Cruise Missile) test. At 0757 hours his Hornet suddenly crashed off the end of the runway. *Flight Comment* (No.1, 1990) later reported:

> CF188726 took off from Inuvik Airport in support of Exercise Slow Scan in the dark early morning hours. Witnesses on the ground saw the aircraft in an approximate 30 degree nose high after-burner climb. Thirty seconds after take-off a fire ball was reported 2.5 nautical miles from the departure end of the runway. Attempts to establish radio contact with the accident aircraft were unsuccessful. Ground personnel were despatched to the scene and confirmed that the aircraft had crashed. The pilot sustained fatal injuries.
>
> Ground personnel from CFB Cold Lake, working in extremely arduous conditions, recovered approximately 70 percent of the aircraft wreckage. Initial findings indicated that the aircraft impacted the ground wings level in an approximate 30 degree nose down attitude. Examination of the ejection system indicated that ejection had not been initiated. To date there is no evidence of a malfunction of any of the aircraft systems. Recovery and salvage teams returned to Inuvik in May to re-sweep the wreckage area when the snow cover had melted.

Tragedy struck 416 Squadron a few months later when, on April 4, 1990, Capt Pierre Trottier lost his life. In a compact flying community, a death in one unit hurt all others. Everyone at 441 grieved along with 416 at Capt Trottier's loss. Then, on April 22 Capt Hollis Tucker of 441 lost his life in 188772 while 21nm west of Brooks Peninsula, Vancouver Island. *Flight Comment* (No.3, 1990) provided an account:

> While conducting air defence intercept training off the west coast of British Columbia, a CF-188 was vectored by the Regional Operations Control Centre to the northern edge of the Sea Fox Training area. After acknowledging a heading change, the aircraft was seen on radar descending some 20,000 feet. It was last observed on radar through 7000 feet. Attempts to establish radio contact both by ROCC and the lead aircraft proved unsuccessful.
>
> The lead aircraft [Capt Craig Richmond] was vectored to the missing aircraft's last known position and, once on scene, spotted wreckage in the water. There was no bail out tone heard or parachute seen. Two days after the crash, HMCS Saskatchewan deployed a long term beacon to mark the location of the crash site. After many unsuccessful attempts, recovery efforts were postponed.
>
> Finally, in mid-June, after having sailed through the Panama Canal from the East Coast, HMCS Cormorant was joined by Pisces IV, a submersible from Energy, Mines and Resources Canada. A survey of wreckage was completed and various aircraft components were retrieved in almost 4800 feet of water. Finally, Pisces IV, on behalf of the crew of Cormorant, left a plaque on the ocean floor as a memento to the pilot killed in the accident.

Capt Hollis Tucker in his Hornet August 4, 1989 while on a QRA deployment in Comox.
(Mike Valenti)

Such accidents were bound to raise questions. With the House of Commons Defence Committee meeting soon after Capt Tucker's loss, the news magazine *Alberta Report* ran a May 7, 1990 cover showing a CF-18 and the headline "Widowmaker II". The story speculated about the CF-18 accident rate being inordinately high, and wondered if pilots were being overwhelmed by the flow of data generated in the cockpit. It was agreed that CF-18 pilots were getting ample experience, flying some 240 hours per year, while USN/USMC pilots were averaging 220 and the NATO minimum standard was a mere 120. At the heart of the matter, it seemed to *Alberta Report*, was the balance to be struck between safe operations and meaningful ones. For its part, until it had more facts, Air Command opted to modify Hornet operating limits by increasing minimum altitude and air speed for some exercises."

"Fuji" Punches Out

A. R. "Fuji" Day had joined the military in 1985 as a "Mil-Col" student. He earned his Wings at Moose Jaw in August 1990, completed the FLIT at 419 Squadron, then was sidelined doing OJT at 416, awaiting his Hornet course. Finally, he passed through 410 and was posted to 441. On June 15, 1995 the Silver Foxes deployed with seven aircraft and 52 personnel to Klamath Falls, Oregon for DACT with USAF F-16s. Flying 188713 that day, Capt Day was No.2 in a DACT 2-ship, lead being Luftwaffe exchange officer Capt Bernhard Tantarn. The plan was that Day would supervise Tantarn on an element lead upgrade sortie but, some 90 seconds after takeoff and just before entering cloud, Day lost alternating current power in a double generator failure. *Flight Comment* (February 1996) described what followed:

> The pilot separated from lead, remained below cloud, then rejoined lead approximately 14 miles southeast of the field. Lead coordinated with Seattle Centre to orbit below cloud while planning the approach. As they began their straight-in approach to Runway 32, approximately seven and a half minutes into the flight, "Hornet 2" lost all battery power and the aircraft flight controls reverted to mechanical (MECH) mode [i.e. the only flight controls being the horizontal stabilizer, connected directly to the pilot's stick]. At one and a half miles on final at 250 feet the aircraft departed controlled flight and the pilot ejected. The aircraft crashed in a farmer's wheat field and sustained "A" category damage. The pilot received minor injuries during the parachute landing.

Without electrical power, Day made a flapless approach for which there were no recommended speeds in CF-18 AOIs or checklists. A preliminary estimate suggested that, on approach, he was 50-60 knots below the required speed. As such his flight controls failed, and he entered an uncontrollable right roll. As to his "minor" injuries, in 2003 Day noted: "These included four crushed vertebrae and a badly-twisted ankle." He later instructed at 410, and had a Hornet exchange in Australia. Another 441 mishap in this period involved 188935. Upon landing in poor weather at St. Hubert on May 27, 1994, it left the runway. Capt Kim Reid was uninjured, but '935 needed costly repairs.

Tragedy struck the CF-18 family again on June 28, 2004. While on a USMC Hornet exchange, Capt Derek "Crush" Nichols (441 from 1999-2001) crashed fatally as his squadron (VMFA-122) was landing home at MCAS Beaufort, South Carolina after an Ex. Clean Hunter detachment in Denmark.

255

Hornet Pot-Pourri

Having begun in with 410 in 1982, CF-18s eventually operated at Cold Lake – 409, 410, 416, 441, AETE; Bagotville – 425, 433; and Baden-Soellingen – 409, 421, 439. As postings came and went, pilots often moved from one squadron to another. Many from 441, for example, have instructed with 410, served in Bagotville, etc. In the first of these photos the Lynx emblem on the tail identifies 188798 as a 416 Hornet. A Desert Cats veteran, it's seen at Cold Lake during 416's 50th anniversary celebrations in September 1991. (Larry Milberry)

The Bagotville flightline on April 12, 1989 — mainly 425 Squadron Hornets ready to fly during "Fighter Meet 89". (Larry Milberry)

From 1984 - 93 Canadian Hornets helped defend NATO from the Soviet threat. In this March 13, 1987 scene at Baden-Soellingen a Hornet gets set for a mission. Seen (right) on the same day is a 439 mission with Capt Ken Gerhard leading Capts Kirk Leuty and Chris Grasswick. (Larry Milberry)

With the collapse of the USSR in 1989 - 90 the Cold War faded. In the resulting "peace dividend" era, Canada repatriated its forces after more than 40 years in NATO. Here, 1 CAG Hornets, including 439's "colours" jet, head home from Germany during Op. Rhine Prosit of January 1993. They were refuelled en route by a 437 Squadron 707. (Larry Milberry)

CHAPTER

More of the Nineties

Concerns about CF-18 safety soon were eclipsed by Iraq's invasion of Kuwait in August 1990. Canadian forces began to deploy to the Persian Gulf later that month, first with ships (Op. Scimitar), then with an Air Task Group, which became part of the larger venture, Op. Friction. Although two 441 pilots (Capts Gerry MacKinnon and Brad Sinclair), and six 441 Other Ranks (CWO H.J. Cormier, MCpl W.G. Ten Eyck, LSgt R.L. Fletcher, and Cpls R.J. Campton, D.B. Marta and I.J. Stewart) served in the Gulf, the greater part of the air contribution was from CF Europe. Capt MacKinnon later contributed to the unofficial history of the operation. On one sortie he carried eight 500-pound bombs, but it seemed that he might have to return to base in Doha with his ordnance. Finally, a forward air controller vectored him and his partner, Capt Paul Regli, to a 6-km long Iraqi vehicle column, which they bombed from high level. In this period NORAD defence responsibilities still had to be discharged, although training for William Tell, etc. was deferred. After all, the "real thing" was on in the Persian Gulf.

January 14, 1991 views from the Persian Gulf War, as the US-led coalition was on the brink of its final push against Iraq: "Desert Cats" Hornet '758 ready at Doha for a CAP mission, a pilot conferring with his ground crew, and armourers getting set to upload an AIM-7. Finally, Capts Jeff Beckett and Van Peterson wash their dishes in the mess tent in Doha. Although Iraq soon capitulated in 1991, the US chose not to finish off dictator Saddam Hussein. In March 2003 came another US-led campaign, but without Canada's help. Saddam quickly got the heave-ho, but drawn-out guerrilla warfare ensued. (Larry Milberry)

"Roach"

In July 1991 LCol Pierre Rochefort assumed command of 441 Squadron. Having joined the Canadian Forces in 1973, he earned his Wings at age 19 at 1 FTS Cold Lake on November 15, 1974. Now he was posted to Trackers at 880 Squadron in Shearwater. That Rochefort got to be a crew commander by age 22 shows what a great opportunity 880 Squadron was for an ambitious young pilot. From here (and already with 2000 flying hours) Rochefort was selected for the CF-104. He began with the 6-month CF-5 FLIT course, advanced to the CF-104 OTU, then was posted to 441 at Baden-Soellingen in March 1981. Next he served in the TacEval shop at 1 CAG, and was OpsO at 421 for a year. In 1986 he converted to the CF-18, then returned to the "new" 421 in Baden-Soellingen.

Col Rochefort officiates at the opening of a display honouring wartime CO S/L George U. Hill. The venue is 441's history centre, the "Lief Erickson Room". Presenting his father's material is Wally Hill, an Air Canada pilot. (CF CKC92-515-16)

CF Staff College followed for Rochefort in 1988, then came the inevitable NDHQ slot – from 1989 - 90 was in the Directorate of Air Operations and Training. In this period DAOT was swamped with projects following a run of fatal CF-18 accidents. Rochefort himself worked in a cell known as the Human Factor Working Group, tasked to understand these mishaps. In the end there was little to say, since the accidents invariably were related to human failures of one kind or another. In the same period DAOT was busy with Gulf War affairs, so there were few quiet days on the job.

In July 1991 LCol Rochefort took over 441 Squadron. Following this, he attended the USAF Air War College, finishing with a Masters Degree in June 1994. He now was assigned to NDHQ in the Chief of Force Development bureau, e.g. working on White Papers. In 1995 he left the military to spend several years with Bombardier, initially with the company's CF-18 group. Finally, in 1998 he established his own consulting company in Ottawa, Cirrus Research Associates. By the time he had left flying, Rochefort had accumulated some 5000 flying hours, including about 1000 on the CF-104 and 1200 on the CF-18.

With Friends Like That

Following a 1992 DACT exercise at NAS Miramar, California, 441's scribe penned a 5-part series for Cold Lake's base newspaper – *The Courier*. A few excerpts from this "dramatic" travelogue illustrate the great fun that fighter pilots can have at their own expense. For better or worse, this particular deployment (and its aftermath) took place during LCol Rochefort's tenure at 441:

> *Deployments invariably allow squadron members to get to know one another, frequently much better than they would like. Small idiosyncrasies are noticed and rapidly become almost unbearable annoyances... One day while sitting in the van and waiting for "Doogie" [Capt Grant Pagdin] to arrive (he was late, what a*

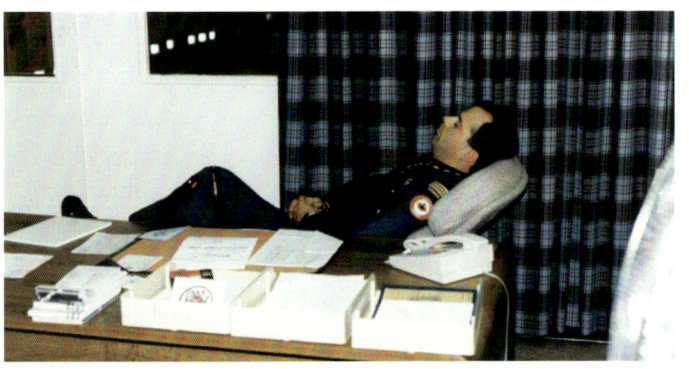

Check six, boss! One of LCol Rochefort's pilots, Capt Kim Reid, couldn't resist snapping off this shot of the CO hard at work!

An informal 441 "family photo" from about June of 1993. In front are: MS St-Jacques, Maj Rick "Ziffer" Zyvitski, Capt Sylvain Lavoie, Capt Kim Reid, Darlene Dunn, LCol Pierre "Roach" Rochefort, unknown, Capt Jeff "Squeeze" Young, Capt Chad "Chico" Sylvester, LS Fletcher (Int NCM), unknown IntO. In the middle are Capt Steve "Spaz" Roberts, Maj Chris "Timber" Forrest (SAMEO), PO Kean (Int NCO), Maj Jim "Jimmy-D" Donihee, "Debbie", Capt Jeff "Snake" Jacques, Maj Rick "Relic" Boyd (DCO), Capt Brad "Sinc 2" Sinclair, Capt Jeff "Eggs" Benedet, Capt Dave "Merk" Mercer, Sgt Muriel Runge (NCO i/c OR), unknown AdminO, Capt Ken "Willy" Williamson, Capt Jean "Guido" Guilbault, Capt Jim "Duff" Stewart, Capt Darren "Kaak" Cockell. Behind are Capt John "Spanky" Argue, Maj John "JR" Roulston, Lt (USN) Maurie "Moby" Leland, Capt Mark "Turf" Lawrence, Capt Alex "Fuji" Day, Capt Kurt "Salad" Saladana, Capt Mike "Woody" Woodfield. (441 Sqn)

surprise), "Sinc" [Capt Brad Sinclair] sprinted into the barracks reception area. One of the guys commented that Sinc had a funny leaping stride when he was excited. After several minutes discussion it was decided that he pranced in a way that would make a male hairdresser's heart flutter.

When Sinc returned, he was needled by his friends, so who needs enemies? He attempted to mask his embarrassment by clearing up several days litter that had accumulated in the van. At this point someone else commented that Sinc seemed to have some sort of obsessive compulsive neatness disorder. Showing their usual sensitivity, his comrades pounced upon him like jackals onto a sick zebra. Sinc, of course, took the only acceptable option and ridiculed someone else in an unsuccessful attempt to divert the unwanted attention.

At the beginning of the deployment, "Kaak" [Capt Darren Cockell] came close to getting his call sign changed to "Echo". This was because he had a tendency to let his mind wander while participating in a conversation. When he would join the discussion, he would invariably repeat what someone else had already said. This had previously been attributed to loss of hearing, but Kaak disproved that theory by undergoing an audiogram and ear cleaning. By the midpoint of the two-week exercise, he was frequently falling behind by almost half of a conversation. While this proved confusing, the problem was minimized by appointing a designated summarizer, who would keep track of the conversation and periodically bring Kaak up to speed...

Amazingly, during the two weeks spent in California there were very few incidents where Canadians found themselves in uncomfortable positions. At first the Canucks were leery of driving on the freeways, having been spooked by the large number of drive-by shootings reported in the area. Their minds were put at ease after they experienced the driving abilities of several of the pilots. "BB's" [Capt Reid Johnson] theory of defensive driving was simply to be the fastest vehicle on the road. Anything going fast enough to keep up would be easy to spot. Any car actually capable of keeping up would also be too close to the ground to get a clear shot through the van's windows. "Salad" [Capt Kurt Saladana] had a different approach. By continuously and randomly changing direction and speed, he employed a jinking defence. Combined with his habit of ignoring red lights, this proved highly effective. Unfortunately, the jinking method triggered loud whining noises from the interior of the vehicle, which usually prevented Salad from getting behind the wheel.

Jamming also proved highly effective. Luckily, the squadron was equipped with both active and passive type jammers. If "Duff" [Capt Jim Stuart] or "Woody" [Capt Mike Woodfield] had consumed any type of solid or liquid within a 24-hour period, they could emit an overpowering, caustic vapour capable of stripping chrome off a trailer hitch. Just by cracking the windows of the vehicle while either of these two walking methane factories was in the active mode (i.e. always), no other car or truck would close nearer than three lanes and 10 vehicle lengths. While effective, especially after a meal of Mexican food and beer, these active jammers had a debilitating effect upon the occupants of their own vehicle. They also killed all birds within a 200-foot radius and, simultaneously, defoliated the green sward along the freeways.

"Jimmy-D" [Maj Jim Donihee] was the sole example of passive jammer. Primed by only several ounces of highland nectar, he would press a repulsive, hairy visage against the window. This would result in scaring drivers of any nearby vehicles into losing control, as their panicked passengers, chalk faced and screaming, tried to scratch out their own eyes in a futile attempt to destroy even a memory of that hideous sight.

Over the years various 441 personnel distinguished themselves as Snowbirds, or in other demo flying. At Comox on April 5, 1990 are Snowbirds/441 alumni Rich Lancaster (team member 1990 - 91), Les Racicot (1989 - 90) and Dave Deere (1994 - 95). (Mike Valenti)

While the defensive driving methods were condoned by local police forces, legal action was threatened if the Canadians did not immediately cease all jammer operations. To limit future use, several laws and mandatory sentences were legislated into effect by a special emergency meeting of the California State Legislature. If Duff and Woody ever returned to California, they must restrict their diet to only bland foods. Anyone caught providing either of them with Mexican food was to be summarily executed...

The Mid-Nineties

For 1993 the usual 441 Ex. Checkerboard South gave way to Ex. Chynx South at NAS Miramar from January 28 to February 13. A 416/441 effort (five jets each), 441 was represented by 19 pilots, a maintenance officer, a logistics officer and 33 NCMs. Teaming with 416 was necessary due to a lack of airlift from ATG, which was over-taxed in Somalia and former Yugoslavia. "Chynx South" DACT was against VFA-301 F-14s and other Miramar types.

In this period all Cold Lake units came under 4 Wing, a formation that had disappeared when the Canadian Forces left Europe. The "new" 4 Wing stood up on June 26, 1993 in the presence of such visitors as LGen

Fighter pilots distinguish themselves in many ways. Take these 441 coneheads for example – Curly Halliwell and Kelly P. Kovach. Rich Lancaster looks on. (441 Sqn)

In the spring of 1990 Canadian airmen participated in D-Day ceremonies in Normandy. Attending were the COs of the Canadian squadrons originally comprising 144 Wing: LCol Terry Hunt (441), LCol Gaston Cloutier (442) and LCol Ebby (443). Here they are at the monument at B.3 Ste-Croix-sur-Mer marking the first D-Day airfield used by 144 Wing. (441 Sqn)

The marker notes a starting date (for 144 Wing) of June 10, 1944. *The RCAF Overseas: The Fifth Year* explains: "On June 10th one of the hastily constructed landing strips between Ste. Croix and Ver-sur-Mer ... was ready for operation. The first RCAF pilots to use it belonged to Johnnie Johnson's wing which, after a sweep inland as far as Evreux, landed on the strip at 1400 hours to re-arm and refuel. For the first time since June 1940 ... British squadrons operated from an airfield in France." On June 15, 441 reached B.3 as a squadron, operated from there for a month. (441 Sqn)

units, were demonstrating Canada's ability to respond to a European crisis. The most striking Hornet from "Cold Fire" was 188781. In anticipation of forthcoming D-Day 50th anniversary celebrations, '781 carried 1944-style invasion stripes, 1950s-style roundels, and 441's checkerboard design. The letters "JE-J" bracketed the fuselage roundels – a tribute to 441's wartime wing leader, W/C J.E. "Johnnie" Johnson. On September 12 the squadron paraded at Bayeux, France to honour the 49th anniversary of D-Day, four Silver Fox Hornets flying overhead for the occasion. Another fly-past saw 441 Hornets over Calgary for the Grey Cup game.

October 15 - 30, 1993 eight 441 Hornets, 25 pilots, 50 groundcrew and others deployed for missile qualifications (Ex. Combat Archer) to Tyndall AFB. Then, testing 441's versatility, on the 19th Maj Jim Donihee and Capt Brad Campbell were scrambled southbound from Cold Lake. After refuelling at Offutt AFB, they pressed on to Tyndall, arriving after 4.3 hours airborne. They immediately completed a "combat turn", refuelling and arming within 30 minutes, so were ready to re-launch on an intercept mission. Instead, they stood down after a long day. On the 20th they flew an AIM-7 live-fire mission. During this "Combat Archer" 441 would fire four each AIM-7 and AIM-9, and fly DACT with F-15s and F-16s. Other 1993 exercises included "Maple Flag" in May, "Stalwart Ram" (CAS support of the Army at CFB Wainwright), "Keynote" (three EW exercises), "DACT VFA-301" (F-14s visiting 441 at Cold Lake, 441 flying 41 sorties October 2 - 9), and "MARCOT" (5 CF-18s and 8 pilots to Comox to train with the Navy).

Training and upgrading being a hallmark in any fighter squadron, it is no surprise that courses busied 441 in this period: Capt John P. Argue – Fighter Electronic Warfare and Advanced Radar, Capt J.L. Malainey – Fighter Weapons Instructor, Capt K.J. "Kim" Reid – Forward Air Controller, Capt S.G. "Steve" Roberts –

David Huddleston, Commander AIRCOM; S/L Robert Huson, whose RCAF service dated to 1935; and civilians Rene Werls, Robert Zanner and Johanna Joerger, who had been popular figures in bygone years at 4 Wing in Baden (Werls had been the bartender for whom 441's mascot had been named). One of the largest postwar Canadian military parades celebrated the occasion. As five squadrons marched behind their colours, 12 CF-18s (410, 416 and 441 squadrons), four CF-5s, four T-33s and two Huey helicopters gave an overhead salute. Ceremonial highlights at 441 in 1993 included LCol Pierre Rochefort passing command of 441 to LCol Marc Ouellet on June 30.

In August 1993 a detachment of CF-18s crossed from Cold Lake to Twenthe Air Base, Holland for Ex. Cold Fire 93, a NATO Central Region tactical exercise. The Hornets, drawn from all Canadian-based

Cold Fire 93" meant some good flying and some of the usual fighter pilot shenanigans. Here, the Dutch F-16 Tiger squadron at Twenthe torches a piano, ably assisted by some nutty friends from Canada – Marc Ouellet, Richard Brosseau and "Brez" Brezinski. Then, "doing Canada proud" – Marc Ouellet (441) and Denis Mercier (433) take up some idiotic challenge from the Dutch. (Ouellet Col.)

Tactical Leadership Program, Capt Terry Shortt, and Capt S.P. "Steve" Will – CF Staff School. New pilots joining 441 were Majs S.P. "Pat" Ellison and Marsh R. Pettitt, Capts D.J. Regenwetter, G.H. "Greg" Shepherd and Gary J. "Venom" Venman, and Lts B.D. "Brad" Campbell, A.M.A. Mirza and S.G. "Steve" Nierlich. Awards for the year

These photos give a taste of the many types with which 441 has flown in Maple Flag since 1987. Such realistic training ensures that Canada's CF-18 force is ready to undertake operations as required. Here, during a Maple Flag mission of 1997, 441 Hornets wear markings identifying them as "Red Air" players. (CF CKC97-7001, the rest by Larry Milberry)

included some 441 members receiving the Gulf and Kuwait medal, and the Canadian Forces Decoration (CD). As always, promotions occurred, including 16 Silver Foxes from private to corporal.

The squadron's 1994 annual report began: "441 TFS did not undergo any major changes in organization or function. We did, however, assume the role of Lead Squadron and, as such, our training was tailored towards being prepared for any unforeseeable contingency operation in the shortest possible time," the latter referring to what then was being touted as Fighter Group's "Vanguard", or

RAF Harriers at Maple Flag in June 2000. The Luftwaffe Transalls beyond also took part in the exercise.

F-111s from Cannon AFB, New M
F-111 and Tornado always were r
weeds" Maple Flag players.

For 1994 Ex. Checkerboa
Luke AFB, and the emphasis
element and section lead u
training). Several exercises we
(live weapons, FAC, etc.). A sp
Cold Lake fly-past of March
MGen Don Williams (Comm
"Dave" Bartram (Commander
May and June. On June 30 LC
441 to LCol Dave Burt.

An A-7 of the 125th FS, Oklahoma ANG from Tulsa at Maple Flag on May 13, 1992. Beyond are F-15Es of the 336th FS from Seymour Johnson AFB, North Carolina.

September saw six aircr
Ex. Ocean Venture. The Silv
December on Ex. Desert T

"rapid reaction" capability (3 Wing and 4 Wing swapped "Vanguard" duties every six months). 441 also set a new baseline in 1994 in aircraft maintenance that would be emulated by other squadrons. In this period 441 maintainers were busy with a mod to strengthen the Hornet's vertical stabilizers. This was accomplished in conjunction with civil contractors working on base.

establishment for the year total
increase over 1992 – up from 2
from the closing of Canadian F
hours in 1994 totalled 4770, 63
to-ground. Silver Fox pilots av
than USAF, USN or NATO fig

Luftwaffe MiG-29s, inherited by the "new" Germany from the GDR, at Maple Flag in June 2000.

the 1990s. Here is a Dutch ay 26, 1998. (All, Larry Milberry)

With the 1990s the concept of the "total" package expanded in Maple Flag to include transports. C-130 130324 of 429 Squadron (Aircraft Commander: Maj Ken Pfander) took part in 1993, simulating special forces and resupply missions. Here is a view from the cockpit during one of its missions. This was a rare occasion where a C-130 evaded all Maple Flag threats and returned to base "in one piece".

Left: AWACS is a traditional Maple Flag player. Here at Maple Flag are USAF and NATO AWACS.

A Maple Flag aerial view of May 13, 1992. Nearest are F-15Es of the 336th FS; then, A-7s of the 125th FS; an F-16 of the 309th FS, Homestead AFB, Florida; and CF-18s of various squadrons. Hangar 3 down the line is the home of 441.

"Coco" – CO Profile

Born on April 18, 1951, Marc "Coco" Ouellet was the son of an RCAF supply tech. In August 1970 Marc joined the Canadian Forces in Ottawa, then spent the next four years at Royal Military College. In the summer of 1972 he completed the Musketeer course at Primary Flying School in Portage. In 1974 he advanced to the Tutor at Moose Jaw, flying initially with Capt Jim Sorfleet on July 29. On September 6 he soloed, then finished with an April 1, 1975 mission with Capt "Cat" Beaulieu. Ouellet now was posted to 1 FTS in Cold Lake for the CF-5 course, his first flight being on May 7 with Capt Craig Furlong. The course involved 68 flying hours and ended on July 11.

On September 3, 1975 Ouellet began the instructor's course at FIS in Moose Jaw. He earned his instructor's category on December 3 and, five days later, flew his first student trip with Lt Brunet. Over the next two years he would train a host of new pilots including Eddie Campbell (later a Desert Cat with 439 Squadron), Bob Drake (to C-130s, later KIFA at Namao), Steve Green (later a CF-5 demo pilot), and Reg Decoste (to CF-18s). He also taught several Dutch students. In 1977 Capt Ouellet was selected by the Snowbirds, then commanded by Maj Gord Wallis (ex-441). Flying commenced on November 22 by when Ouellet's log showed some 1400 flying hours. Sadly, the team suffered a loss in this period. At an airshow at Grande Prairie, Alberta on May 3, 1978 the tail of Capt Gord deJong's Tutor separated, the jet crashed and deJong, also a 441 alumnus, was killed. A structural inspection followed, so the team didn't fly again until May 25. Capt Ouellet finished his tour in the fall of 1979, having logged 688.5 hours as a Snowbird. (To appreciate the full significance of the Snowbirds, one must read two glorious books: *Snowbirds from the Beginning* by O.B. Philp and Bill Johnson, and *A Tradition of Excellence* by Dan Dempsey).

On February 11, 1980 Ouellet began the 419 Squadron CF-5 fighter lead-in course going up in 116821 with Capt Roger Ayotte. The course finished on June 26, then Ouellet advanced to 417, flying first in Starfighter 104640 with Capt Cash Poulson on October 3. He soloed five days later, but soon had a problem. He broke his jaw playing hockey, so missed the ACM phase of his course. In January DCIEM in Toronto deemed him fit to fly, so he picked up his course in the ground attack phase. When the class graduated, Ouellet remained for ACM, flying 10 sorties from February 2 - 5, 1981. He left 417 with 67.9 hours on the CF-104 to join 439 Squadron at Baden-Soellingen. He flew the T-33 there on April 1, then the CF-104 on the 16th (T-33 sorties were essential to familiarize a new pilot with the local terrain, restricted areas, diversion airfields, etc. Eventually, a pilot would know the local geography like the back of his hand in order to navigate confidently at low level in any weather). The next two years for Ouellet were crammed with activity. On one weapons training deployment to Decimomannu (July 1 to 7, 1982) he flew 11 sorties. His log shows that ACM trips were short – with all the dogfighting, pilots constantly were in and out of 'burner, so rapidly used up fuel. Flights of about 0.7 hours were usual, while bombing missions lasted an hour.

Besides "Deci", the CF-104s visited NATO bases on exchanges. October 6, 1982, 439 was at Twenthe, Holland, training with Dutch NF-5s. Other than dogfighting, bombing and firing rockets, the competitors went against range targets with 20mm cannons. Naturally, such deployments brought out the best in the host squadron – there were plenty of good times in off hours. On this occasion the Dutch arranged a superb evening aboard a tall ship. With 439 being the "Tiger" squadron, another great tradition was Ex. Tiger Meet (in Ouellet's case at Kleine Brogel, Belgium). Here NATO squadrons featuring the tiger emblem would get together for flying and other fun.

OCdt Marc Ouellet while at RMC from where he graduated in 1974. (Ouellet Col.)

An almost monthly exercise during Canada's CF-104 era was Ex. Snowball, a practice alert and a full base recall. Groundcrew and pilots would don NBCW kit, weapons would be uploaded, and missions planned and flown. As to missions, the Litton LN-3 nav-attack system, dating from Canada's nuclear days, remained in service in the 1980s. It would be loaded with mission way-points before a pilot departed, then would navigate automatically from point to point. But the LN-3 was over-sensitive. This was not a problem during "nuke" days, when there was one big bomb pegged for one target – a little bit either way wasn't so critical. But, in the 1980s the mission was conventional and there could be several pin-point targets on one sortie. Excellence in manual map reading was essential and had to be done as a pilot was flying at 510 – 540 knots. Before Canada retired its CF-104s, the more advanced LN-33 system was fitted.

The highlight on any CF-104 squadron in this era was the TacEval. Whether at the national or NATO level, a TacEval critically measured a squadron's ability to function at 100%. For a TacEval a team of umpires from 4th Allied Tactical Air Force (USAFE), or Fighter Group (North Bay), would descend on the Wing with a team of umpires. The Wing and squadrons would come to maximum alert with aircraft fuelled, armed, launched and recovered without a glitch. The National TacEval was tougher than the NATO, and normally came first. In Ouellet's time 439 passed a national TacEval on February 14 - 16, 1983. Then, from April 11 - 13 the NATO team pounced on Baden. In the latter case Ouellet flew seven missions, each in a 4-plane section.

Capt Ouellet finished at 439 in July 1983, then became executive assistant to MGen Dave Wightman, Commander of CFE. They flew the T-33 and CF-104 as time allowed. As Canada re-equipped with the CF-18, an historic interlude occurred – the transfer of 54 CF-104s to Turkey. Many were fresh from overhaul at a West German contractor and were urgently awaited by Turkey, which was waging a war of attrition against Kurd insurgents. On May 7, 1986 six CF-104s departed Baden for the Turkish base at Diyarbakir, Marc Ouellet and Walt Pirie crewing 104638. They flew first to Brindisi and, next day, carried on to Ankara and Diyarbakir, where an acceptance ceremony was held. After some R&R, including a visit to Istanbul, the Canadians flew home on a 412 Squadron Dash 7.

Ouellet now took a Tutor refresher at Moose Jaw, then attended 419 Squadron to qualify as a CF-5 instructor. He flew there initially on August 27, 1987 in 116716. Something new in his fighter pilot career was aerial refuelling, his first "AAR" sortie being on October 14. Later that week he was in a CF-5 formation on a cross-country

Maj Marc Ouellet (front cockpit) and Maj Walt Pieri while delivering Starfighter 104638 to Turkey in May 1986. (CF BA86C-2322-25)

LCol Ouellet (left) takes over 441 Squadron in June 1993 from LCol Rochefort (right). Col Dave Bartram, Cold Lake Wing Commander, officiates. (CF CKC93-695-4)

AR exercise to Langley, Virginia in 4.2 hours. He stayed only eight months instructing, then moved to 419's "SWAT" desk – Standards, Weapons and Tactics. This involved developing a new course training standard. Meanwhile, Ouellet continued to fly the CF-5, training new instructors and doing student progress rides.

Maj Ouellet's 419 tour expired in August 1990, when he began CF Staff and Command College. Following this, he went on course to 410 Squadron, where he first flew the CF-18 on August 1, 1991 (118932 with Capt Dave Tower). Getting to 410 had not been easy for, as a senior major, Ouellet was more likely to have been posted to a staff job. But his CO's (LCol Fred Mueller) promise prevailed. On December 16, after 67 hours of training on the Hornet, Ouellet joined 416 Squadron as a flight commander. There he remained until July 1992, when he was posted to 4 ATAF in Heidelberg. As chief of the Attack Branch there, he was responsible for fighter doctrine and air campaign planning.

From 4 ATAF Marc Ouellet was promoted and named to command 441 Squadron. Since he did not believe that a new CO should just show up, then figure out how he was going to get up to par with his pilots, he argued that 410 should bring him up to combat ready status. He began his course on May 26, 1993 and on July 7 passed his combat ready check ride with Capt Van Peterson. He also believed that a CO should lead by example, meaning that he should fly. And that he did. For September and October, for example, he logged 26.6 and 30.4 hours. For March 1994 he flew 23 sorties for 31.1 hours. On March 12 he flew 3 missions for 3.6 hours of ACM and DACT. These are times that would have made a Sabre pilot jealous 50 years earlier when, as the old boys like to say, "Canada had an air force". March 1994 finished when 441 had 18 serviceable Hornets on the line, ready for a mass takeoff, range mass attack, and Cold Lake flypast. This nearly happened, except that two jets pooped out before takeoff. Sixteen Hornets from one squadron aloft at the same time, however, was impressive.

In May and June 1994, 441 was at RAF Lossiemouth for Ex. Tartan Paladin. The first thing that LCol Ouellet made sure about was for him to take the station commander, G/C Nigel Day, for a Hornet flight. From here, he led 441 Hornets on several UK flypasts, including on June 3 over Buckingham Palace. Another was planned for the Runnymede Memorial, but marginal weather and strict regulations imposed by UK ATC (which gave the Hornets one minute to do their flypast and wouldn't allow a practice run) resulted in the Hornets missing their target by a mile. Weather also forced elements of the D-Day flypast over Omaha Beach to cancel their appearance, 441 included. On the 13th 441 was in Evreux, a famous Normandy setting, to lunch with wartime heroes Johnnie Johnson and Danny Brown.

Back in Cold Lake 441 returned to normal. On August 16 Col Bartram (Wing Commander), LCol Ouellet, Maj Cash Poulson and LCol Gordy Todd made up a 4-ship for a "Quick Draw" exercise. The idea was to see who could score the highest on the Jimmy Lake Range with rockets and bombs. After 1.5 hours Ouellet had excelled at the bombing, Todd with rockets. A few beers in the bar would have followed, so that each pilot could boast about his prowess. For August 1994 LCol Ouellet logged 25.7 hours, showing that he had not relented in his quest to fly a Hornet more than a desk.

In August there also was an Alaskan deployment to Eielson AB – Ex. Cope Thunder. Flying from there on August 23, LCol Ouellet had Cpl Boivin in his back seat. Near Northway, along the Alaska - Yukon border, Boivin had just pointed out the old wreck of an airplane in a lake below, when Ouellet caught something from the corner of his eye – it was a Snowgoose. Almost instantly "Bitching Betty" started to squawk about the left engine. Ouellet shut it down instantly and quickly landed on the marginal strip at Northway. Soon, Boivin squeezed into the engine bay to have a look – he returned with a handful of melted and shattered parts. Hornet '913 wasn't going anywhere until an MRP arrived to do an engine change.

For February 24, 1995 there was another push to get the whole squadron airborne, and this time it worked – 18 jets went out to the range, then returned for a formation fly-by. On June 15 the squadron deployed for DACT with the F-16 squadron at Klamath Falls, Oregon. But the day ended badly, with Capt "Fuji" Day's ejection. On the 23rd LCol Ouellet made his final flight as CO of the Silver Foxes. He now spent a year at the USAF Air War College in Alabama, then returned to Cold Lake as Wing OpsO. In this period he led the 1996 William Tell team, which brought home more honours and awards than any of Canada's previous Willy Tell teams. LCol Ouellet made his last flight at 4 Wing in Hornet '781 on July 31, 1998. He was then promoted and appointed Wing Commander at Moose Jaw, beginning there in July. He served to June 2000, when he was removed summarily from his command, following a minor incident at a mess dinner. Having no recourse, Col Ouellet chose to leave the military to pursue a career in the business world (eventually, he was cleared of the charges).

LCol Ouellet: Summary of Jet Flying Time

Type	Hours Flown
Tutor	2221
T-33	137
CF-104	724
CF-5	806
CF-18	773

Marc Ouellet leads during the June 6, 1994 Omaha Beach flypast commemorating the 50th anniversary of D-Day. Right wing is Al Stevenson, left wing — Wayne Karperian, slot — Tom Jackson. Too bad, but the flypast was "DNCO" when the weather closed in. Tom Jackson soon left the military to fly his uncle Bernie Jackson's Spitfire XVI. He lost his life in California on June 3, 1998, while flying the "Spit" in bad weather. (Ouellet Col.)

Fun on the Road

In 2004 Capt "Fuji" Day recalled a bit more about Ex. Tartan Paladin which, by the sound of it, was not pure drudgery:

In late May 1994, 441 TFS, as part of a combined 3 and 4 Wing effort, deployed to RAF Lossiemouth in Scotland. The mission was twofold: to participate in the celebration of the 50th anniversary of D-Day, and in a fortuitously scheduled Joint Maritime Course exercise. The deployment would last five weeks, with Canadian personnel divided into two groups. For the first period, half would take part mainly in D-Day parades and flypasts. After a swap-out, the second half, which included me, would fly in the exercise.

For the trip to the UK, we hitched a ride from Edmonton on an RAF L1011 that was re-deploying from Maple Flag to Brize Norton. After over-nighting there, we were picked up by a Canadian Forces Challenger and flown to RAF Kinloss. Then came a bus trip to Elgin (near Lossiemouth), where we soon discovered all the decent watering holes.

I'll never forget my first mission in Scotland. Apart from not understanding a word the tower was saying, I was cleared for a famil flight around the northern UK. This included a fly-by over the Isle of Jura – the place of my family roots. Having only the picture on the label of a bottle of "Isle of Jura" Scotch to go by, I eventually found my target below a break in the clouds!

A typical JMC mission consisted of deciphering a 200-page air tasking order to find our 4- and 8-ship taskings. We would take off to meet our bombing package, then escort it through the air-defence

LCol Ouellet with 441 wartime CO, S/L J.D. "Danny" Browne, DFC, in Normandy in June 1994. S/L Browne, who practiced law in Florida, was lost while flying his own airplane in December 2001. (Ouellet Col.)

The Boivin-Ouellet team who rode Hornet '913 into Northway, Alaska following a close encounter. The occasion here (June 1995) has WO Boivin and LCol Ouellet accepting a painting of "D-Day Hornet '781" by Cold Lake artist Wendy Boyd. (441 Sqn)

441 guys and dolls on New Year's Eve 1994. Behind are Jeff "Beck" and Lisa Beckett, Bernhard "Tarzan" and Chris Tantarn from Germany, Brad "Bundy" and Wendy Campbell, Rick "Relic" Boyd, Diane Pettitt, Steve "Bunt" Nierlich, Karen and Glen "Flaps" Phillips, Dr. Dan (former Hornet pilot) and Linda Morley. In front Theresa and Bill "Maggot" Rielly (US Navy exchange pilot), Cathy and Dan "Pig" Constable, Susan and Marc "Coco" Ouellet, Marsh "Swamp" Pettitt, Angie Nierlich, Steve "Snatch" and Leola Langille, Ian "Manic" and Helen McLean. (Ouellet Col.)

screen, and on to the task force of ships, over which we would fly as low and as fast as we dared. After we were off target, it would be a leisurely flight back to "Lossie", usually with a scenic flight down some loch or other to get us down to landing weight.

About half-way through this exercise, a few of us had a chance to hop on a Challenger for an overnight visit to 4 Wing's sister wing in Germany. There the wing commander met us and escorted us on a local tour, before we sat down to a fantastic dinner. "Sparglefest" was underway and not since then have I enjoyed such delicious asparagus.

The only other trip of note during this deployment occurred when the Challenger and two Hornets flew to Manchester for an airshow. Capt Gary Venman and I took a dual down for that event, which was strictly a static display for our three aircraft. We arrived in formation on this, our final weekend in the UK. As usual we enjoyed first-class hospitality – from a freshly-carved roast beef "snack" served in our hotel at 0300, to the airshow throngs swarming around our aircraft, we were treated like rock stars. Our trip home was aboard one of 437 Squadron's new CC-150 Polaris transports that was rotating Army personnel home from Bosnia.

Changing Times for a New CO

David C. Burt had joined the military as an RMC student in 1972. To his disappointment, upon graduation he was selected for air navigator, not pilot, training. After his basic nav course in Winnipeg, Burt advanced to the AI world, training on the Voodoo at 410 Squadron. In October 1977 he was posted to 409 Squadron in Comox. Before too long, however, he was relieved that his request for cross-training to pilot was accepted. Burt began flying in Portage la Prairie in July 1979, then worked his way through his Tutor, CF-5 and CF-104 courses, ending with a choice posting to 441 Squadron in Baden-Soellingen. That tour finished, in 1985 he went to work in 1 CAG HQ in the tactical evaluation shop. That spring he took a famil course on the CF-18 at 410 Squadron, then returned to 1 CAG, by then dual qualified on CF-104 and CF-18.

Following his 1 CAG years, Maj Burt took the 6-month course at Army Staff College in Kingston, Ontario. In January 1988 came the CF-18 OTU, after which he joined 416 Squadron. At the time 416 totalled only two officers in Cold Lake – himself and the engineering officer, Maj Chris Schofield (the CO designate, LCol Laurie Hawn, still was at AIRCOM in Winnipeg, and the first aircraft wouldn't arrive until November). Burt would spend 3 ½ years at 416, then he studied through 1992 at RAF Staff College. Promoted in this period, he was named to be the EA to LGen Huddleston and Clements, Commanders AIRCOM.

LCol Burt's dedication to the exacting EA role would pay off – from 1995 - 97 he had his dream posting as CO of 441 Squadron. Talking about this in 2004, he cited the highlight of it all – a Hornet mission on June 3, 1997 with 441 Spitfire pilot, Arthur Jewett. Their flight began with some gentle 1-V-1 interaction, but Arthur wanted more than, especially some vertical manoeuvring. Considering Arthur's age, Burt was slightly wary, so worked up gradually to about 4 Gs. Arthur, meanwhile, was loving every second, so away they went. When Burt gave his back seater the controls, Arthur soon got the hang of it, and when the time came to return to base, he instinctively turned the Hornet onto the right heading. While Arthur had had the flight of his life that day, the same went for LCol Burt.

Drastic budget cuts had hit all government departments in 1995, National Defence being shaken from Ottawa to the most remote units. At 441 aircraft establishment fell from 18 to 15, and maintenance shrank from 190 to 147 personnel, partly from down-sizing, but also because of trade structure revisions. That saw periodic checks on Cold Lake CF-18s, usually done by 1 Air Maintenance Squadron, pass down in November to the 441 level. A happier 1995 event was 441's nostalgic visit in May to its 1942 birthplace. Officially, the occasion was to help Sydney, Nova Scotia celebrate the amalgamation of various municipalities. During the same visit, the local Royal Canadian Legion branch arranged with the Silver Foxes for a salute over Sydney's cenotaph in honour of First World War hero, John Bernard Coak, VC.

As part of 4 Wing, 441 functioned within the larger formation. Thus did it behoove the squadron to be sensitive to political realities, including the need to win local support for forces national in scope, Maple Flag XXIX being a case in point. Scheduled for May 6 to June 15, 1996, the exercise was open to the public in that civilians were allowed to view proceedings from a picnic area just off base. MF XXIX also was the first time that Maple Flag was promoted by the local Chamber of Commerce. Something else reflected changing times – for the first time at Maple Flag visiting units (RAF, German, Dutch, US) were being charged $200 per mission – "cost-recovery" was becoming reality in the cash strapped forces (meanwhile,

LCol Dave Burt presents Sgt Weber of 441 with his CD on June 24, 1996. After 441 LCol Burt left the fighter world. By then his logs showed 480 hours as a Voodoo AI nav, 800 on CF-104s and 1400 on CF-18s. Now came a year in language training, then an NDHQ posting at the Directorate of Aircraft Requirements to work on the CF-18 Incremental Modernization Program. After five years at this, during which he was promoted to colonel and appointed director of DAR, Burt was proud to see the first IMP CF-18 enter service with 441 on November 3, 2003. By 2009 IMP should be complete, giving Canada a force of Hornets that will be equal in capabilities to the newest US Navy F/A-18Cs. (CF CKC96-390-2)

Canadians training in the US routinely were paying user fees of $750 to $1500 per sortie). Parallel with Maple Flag in 1996 was a public relations exercise dubbed "Target: Top Gun" which encouraged NATO to train more pilots at Cold Lake, particularly since key NATO/US training agreements were to expire in 2005. With officials from 21 countries visiting Cold Lake on the eve of Maple Flag, everyone from local townspeople to Premier Ralph Klein were on hand to shower the VIPs with Alberta hospitality (Klein even got a Hornet ride).

Meanwhile, internal concerns were affecting policy. When LGen John Boyle, as Chief of Defence Staff, visited 4 Wing in March 1996, he listened to many comments about service conditions. One was pay, another was the perennial issue of postings. By this time the CF annually was paying some $250 million to relocate personnel from base to base. However, the shrinking number of bases, and the tendency to develop so-called "super bases", now made longer postings more economic. When it came to postings, the trick, as always among NDHQ career managers, was to strike balances as to a member's expertise, enthusiasm, merit, etc., while considering the impact that postings have on family life.

Looking back on 1996, LCol Dave Burt noted in his annual historical report that night air-to-surface tactics had been introduced on the squadron. "This training has given 441 TFS an additional capability which no other Canadian fighter squadron possesses", he noted. Regarding "real world" operations, 441 stayed home through 1996, although two members were abroad as part of Canada's commitments in former Yugoslavia. Most squadron activities focused on the constant routine of training, and exercises that tested that training. Activities included: Ex. Arctic Fox, March 9 - 23, 1996 – 10 CF-18s and 88 personnel to Luke AFB for gunnery; Ex. Amalgam Warrior 96-2, April 7 - 13 – nine CF-18s and 79 personnel to the Inuvik FOL; Maple Flag 29, May 6 -June 14 – two cycles of air-to-air and air-to-ground training at Cold Lake (some missions lost to bad weather); Ex. RIMPAC (for Allies bordering the Pacific Rim), June 1 - 16 – six CF-18s to Hickam AFB, Hawaii to train with air and maritime resources of Australia, Canada, Chile, Japan, South Korea, and the US; Ex. Midnight Sun, June 24 - 28 – three CF-18s to Inuvik during a visit by the NORAD Commander-in-Chief.

LCol Marc Ouellet of 441 presents Capt Mike Mirza with a Commanding Officer's Commendation in 1994. (CF CKC94-240-5)

"RIMPAC 96"

In a *Roundel* article of July 1996, CF public affairs officer LCmdr Phil Anido described the AAR capability of the Hornet relative to Ex. RIMPAC 96:

The vast ocean and over 3000 nautical miles between their home at 4 Wing Cold Lake and Hickam Air Force Base [Hawaii] is too far for the 441 Tactical Fighter Squadron CF-18s to go on their own. So they depend on 8 Wing Trenton's 437 Transport Squadron Boeings to give them the legs they require... The process of getting the fighters to Hawaii was exacting indeed. There were five refuelling "brackets" over the Pacific; precise timing and accurate calculations were essential. A tanker departing from Lemoore Naval Air Station, California had 158,000 pounds of fuel aboard, and consumed 75,000 pounds itself. That left 83,000 pounds for three CF-18s assigned to the Boeing and, in fact, they were topped off with 44,500 pounds of fuel during a 5-hour, 18-minute mission. Refuelling was most frequent as they left the mainland behind but, once the formation was 1100 nautical miles off Hickam, it was assumed they could make it on their remaining fuel, although that still assumed there was no head wind.

"This is the first time we have crossed the Pacific to exercise with our RIMPAC allies," remarks Major Pat Ellison, the deputy commander of 441 Squadron, who led the first wave of three CF-18s. "It took us five and a half hours to cross 2200 miles of the Pacific, which really tests the limit of our safe recovery range to land."

Twice each day at RIMPAC the Boeings and CF-18s take off and rendezvous some 30 miles off the glorious sandy beaches in the exercise area. Just after taking off, as the Boeing banks to the right over Pearl Harbor, the white memorial to the USS Arizona and her sailors who were sunk by the Japanese is clearly visible... "A typical mission will see us at 45,000 feet in air-to-air combat alongside US F/A-18 Hornets and F-15 Eagles against Australian F-111s and other US Navy F/A-18s who are "attacking" friendly warships," says Lieutenant-Colonel Dave Burt, Commanding Officer of 441 Squadron. "In the afternoon we'll be at 500 feet strafing enemy shipping."

441 gets around. Techs Scott McNeil, Nick Kolotylo, Shantal Smith and Bill Chisholm are seen in front of the Capitol in D.C during a 1994 NAS Oceana deployment. Then, Silver Foxes over Hawaii during RIMPAC '96 (Via Bill Chisholm)

More Highlights

LCol Burt listed 35 non-flying courses taken by personnel in 1996, from aero medical training, flight safety, two courses on ground search techniques, aircraft battle damage repair, and the Air Force Battle Staff Course. Several 441 members received honours this year including 13 CDs, a CO's Commendation, a UN medal for service in former Yugoslavia (Capt G.H. Shepherd) and two NATO medals for service there (Capts J.L. Malainey and A.M. Mirza). LCol Dave Burt noted of his squadron at year's end: "As the lead fighter squadron for the Canadian Forces, 441 Squadron met and, in many cases, exceeded all established goals ... The most visible event ... was the overwhelming success of the 4 Wing team which took top honours at the William Tell Weapons Competition in Tyndall, Florida. Eighteen personnel from 441 Squadron were members of this team, including Capt Steve Nierlich, who captured the title 'Top Gun'." On February 21, 1997, Maj Jeff Beckett of 441 flew his 3000th CF-18 hour, the first Canadian pilot to attain this level.

Having flown his 3000th hour in the CF-18, Maj Jeff Beckett steps down from his jet at Cold Lake on February 21, 1997. Then, he poses with Capt Gary Venman, LCol Dave Burt (441 CO), Capt Steve Wallace, Maj Armstrong, Wing CWO Gilles Guilbault, Capt Yvonne Pritchett (Public Affairs Officer), Col Ron Guidinger (Base Commander) and CWO Tony Calderone. Beckett's interest in aviation began when he joined 167 Air Cadet Squadron in Owen Sound, Ontario. There he earned his gliding and powered flying licences. He joined the military in 1978 and, after completing the CF-5 OTU at 419 Squadron, spent 1981 - 84 on CF-5s at 433 Squadron in Bagotville. Next came an exchange on F/A-18s with VMFA-531 at USMC El Toro, California (the first Canadian on this posting). He instructed at 410 Squadron 1987 - 91. In October 1990 he was seconded to 416 for the first Gulf War, serving at Doha and completing 26 combat missions. Capt Beckett returned to Cold Lake in March 1991 and that summer began a 3-year tour in Fighter Group HQ in North Bay. In 1994 he joined 441, serving there into 1998, when he left military life, having flown some 800 hours on the CF-5, and 3340 on the CF-18. He joined Air Canada in September 1998 but, due to the merger of Air Canada and Canadian, soon was at the bottom of the seniority list. In 2003 he took a leave of absence to be airport manager in Owen Sound. (CF CKC97-079-1, '-3)

Ground Crew Recognized

Adventures also involve ground crew. In one case the central character was Cpl D.M. "Mike" Munroe, a 441 aero engine technician from Sussex, New Brunswick. As *Flight Comment* No.2 of 1997 reported, he was doing ground maintenance on a CF-18 in a hangar bay at Inuvik:

The hangars are equipped with an Automatic Foam Fire Fighting System which, without warning, started to discharge the full contents of fire suppressant foam while the engine run-up check was underway. Corporal Munroe immediately initiated engine shutdown procedures to prevent foam ingestion and began to egress the aircraft to exit the hangar. While evacuating he realized that the foam agent could seriously damage the cockpit's instruments and avionics. Corporal Munroe got back in the cockpit and closed the canopy until the discharge was complete, consequently saving the aircraft's cockpit instrumentation from damage and expensive repairs. Corporal Munroe's professionalism, poise and quick thinking during a very stressful and hazardous situation averted serious damage to both the engines and avionics of a valuable aircraft.

Another case of ground crew professionalism involved Cpl Leon Hynes, a 441 Airframe Technician. During a 1997 inspection he noted that an aluminum clamp had been installed in a wheel well, where a metal one should have been. Fire in the wheel well would have melted the clamp, causing a fuel leak. Further investigation showed that five of 441's 18 Hornets had improper clamps. A fleet-wide special inspection was implemented. *Flight Comment* (No.2, 1998) was generous in its praise: "Corporal Hynes' professionalism, dedication and utmost concern for safety prevented a potentially serious flight safety occurrence." The same issue reported another case of technical attentiveness, this one involving Cpl Rob A. Petsche:

During a routine AVS survey of a CF-188 cockpit during a periodic inspection, Corporal Petsche decided to further investigate a re-occurring heating problem with the R/H DDI. Although not part of the normal AVS inspection, Corporal Petsche removed the R/H DDI and inspected the cooling air duct. The air duct was almost completely clogged with FOD.

A further investigation revealed that 80 percent of squadron aircraft had FOD in the R/H DDI cooling air duct. A Special Investigation was immediately released by DAEPM. Corporal Petsche's follow-up investigation into what caused the FOD led to his submission of a UCR and a recommended solution. Corporal Petsche's excellent initiative and high motivation have helped prevent future flight safety incidents involving overheating and dust contamination.

CHAPTER

Hornet to Eagle

Exchanges are a long-time feature in the military. When a pilot from one unit spends a tour with a foreign unit, a great deal of data can be exchanged. Each side learns new and useful details about the other's operations, while enjoying some great camaraderie. Over the years many 441 pilots have been on exchange with units in the US, UK, Ge[rmany and] Australia. As early as 1952, 441 h[ad a] USAF Sabre pilot, and the CO i[n Korea,] S/L Andy Mackenzie, went to [fly] combat with a USAF Sabre [squadron. In] Starfighter times, several USAF [pilots flew] with 441 at Marville and Baden-S[öllingen. More] recently, Capt Graham Sinclair [flew an exchange] with the USAF.

Born in Ottawa on April 19, [1961, he joined the] Canadian Forces in 1980 as a Roy[al Roads cadet. In] June 1982 he passed pilot selectio[n at Portage La] Prairie. He continued his studies at [Royal Roads and] then began jet training at Moose Ja[w. His first flight, in Tutor 114121 with Capt Paul G[   ], a good time, since they usually we[re jumping through] basic hoops to get their Wings. [Many student pilots] would find their progress stymie[d by weather, staffing, and the training system [itself. Many] young pilots found their progress [delayed, but in] Graham Sinclair's case, he left M[oose Jaw and went] directly for CF-5 training at 419 [Squadron, Cold Lake.] On November 5, 1985 he flev[   ] with Capt Keith Esplen in 11[   ] proceeded through his course to gr[aduate on] December 9, 1986. Having logged 1[   ] on type, he joined Course 6 (26 st[udents) at] 410 Squadron.

After some ground school an[d sessions in the simulator, Lt Sinc[lair flew] Hornet 188916 with Capt Don Le[   ] January 19, 1987. In this period 410 [had] some of its Hornet instructor "o[riginals",] including Les Koski, Jake Or[r,]

Squadron (the FWIC is called the PhD of fighter courses). In November he logged 39.2 hours, a high for him for any month on the Hornet. His sortie of November 14 was an intercept controlled by an E-3 AWACS.

More flying took place on Ex. Slow Scan of January 23, 1990. That day Sinclair intercepted and tracked a USAF ALCM flying own the MacKenzie River Valley after being launched in the eaufort Sea area from a B-52. Flying 188781 at 500 to 1000 feet, his ob was to evaluate the Hornet radar against a small target. On anuary 26 Capts Sinclair and Dave Deere scrambled from Inuvik fter an unknown bogie. A NORAD GCI controller then sent the Hornets across Alaska, somewhat unusual, since USAF F-15s from Galena normally would have handled this intercept. Should the ogie continue towards Canadian-patrolled territory, they then ould hand over to the Hornets. This time, however, Galena had uch low temperatures that its F-15s were grounded. The Hornets acked down their target, a Soviet Il-18 "Coot" ELINT aircraft. inclair and Deere chose not to make a radar lock-on, for that would ave alerted the Coot to their presence. Instead, they edged up from ehind, then Sinclair pulled forward to illuminate the Coot with his spotlight. The startled Coot crew immediately peeled off and headed for Soviet air space. NORAD later surmised that the Coot had been on a mission to gather "intel" about US ALCM trials.

A poignant event occurred on February 3 when Capt Sinclair flew in the "Missing Man" formation honouring Capt Rich Corver. In March, he travelled to Colorado Springs in 188781 to take part in a NORAD change-of-command ceremony – a routine assignment, but one that ended with a funny twist. Since '781 was a working jet and had flown an air-to-ground gunnery mission that day, its nose was streaked

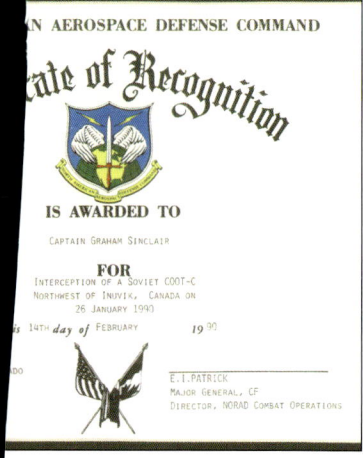

with 20-mm cannon shell residue. Because of this the USAF objected. After some discussion the matter was resolved when a USAF crew gave it a wash. March 2 - 4 Sinclair was with squadron mates Craig Richmond, Hollis Tucker and others at Great Falls for DACT with the F-16s of the 120th FIG. A B-52 and an EW Learjet also took part. In this period 441 was working up for "Willy Tell 90", Sinclair being a team member; but the Gulf War erupted and Willy Tell was cancelled. The focus turned to training for a Persian Gulf deployment, e.g. in October and November 441 did DACT with the 119th FIG at Fargo, ND. The Gulf War, however, ended, so 441 returned to NORAD duties.

By this time Capt Sinclair was the last of 441's Hornet pilot "originals" with the squadron. In this period, while he was eligible for a USN F/A-18 exchange at NAS Cecil Field, Florida, he stayed put, hoping for an F-15 exchange at Elmendorf AFB, Alaska, a slot then held by Capt Seldon Doyle. On January 16, 1991 Sinclair passed 1000 hours on the Hornet. In March he was part of a DACT exercise with the 43rd FS (F-15s) at Elmendorf. He flew his last 441 sortie in 188724 on June 21, 1991, an air-to-air mission that finished with a flypast back at base.

In August 1991 Capt Sinclair began his USAF exchange at the F-15 OTU in Tyndall. The course lasted to October 25. By then Sinclair had 38.4 hours on type. He then joined the 54th FS of the 3rd Wing (US Pacific Air Forces) at Elmendorf, where he flew initially with Capt Miller on November 13. Meanwhile, the Sinclair family adapted to the local scene, living off base and enjoying a busy social calendar in and around Anchorage. As to missions, the task was air-to-air (unlike 441 the 54th had no secondary tactical role). Sinclair found that the F-15Cs were not much more advanced than CF-18s. While they had a HUD (head-up display), it was certified for weapons only, while that in the CF-18 was also certified for instrument flying. The F-15C, however, outshone the Hornet in range. It also had more fire power: four AIM-9s to the Hornet's two, and 980 rounds of 20-mm ammunition to the Hornet's 580 (both types carried four AIM-7s).

Exercises at the 54th paralleled those at 441. On April 24, 1992, for example, Sinclair was doing DACT with F-16s and visiting RAF Tornados. On June 4 he was on a scramble against three B-52s. On July 7 the mission was air-to-air gunnery on a DART target towed by a civil F-86. For Ex. Tandem Thrust in July the 54th deployed to Luke AFB supporting F-15E Strike Eagles of the 90th FS, also from Anchorage. The 54th's task was to escort the 90th to Luke AFB, supporting the 3rd Wing's "Worldwide Mobility" commitment. Approaching Luke, the 54th had to fend off "enemy" F-14s. In August the 54th spent a week in Cold Lake.

While 441 operated from the Inuvik FOL, for Arctic training and operations the 54th had FOLs at remote Galena and King Salmon, Alaska. This duty was done on a weekly rotation with two F-15s. While 441 pilots at Inuvik flew daily, the F-15s rarely launched from Galena or King Salmon, except on "live" scrambles. Capt Sinclair's log shows deployments to Galena in June 1992 and King Salmon in September. In November the 54th sojourned to USMC El Toro to fight with F/A-18s. After 8-V-8 missions of November 19/20, Sinclair attained "mission commander" status at the 54th.

Capt Sinclair while on deployment at remote Galena, Alaska. (Sinclair Col.)

In March 1992 Capt Sinclair had a special deployment. On the 17th the 54th began a trans-Pacific mission to Misawa, Japan to support an F-16 wing on its annual OpEval. The primary mission was flown on the 23rd – 4 F-15s against 32 F-16s. On the 30th the 54th set off for home – six F-15s escorted by three KC-10 tankers. On that crossing Capt Sinclair piloted 79080 on a 6.7-hour flight. In January 1993 the 54th deployed to Tyndall for a missile shoot. On March 3, 1993 Maj Sinclair was involved in a special mission involving a Boeing 747. For this he received a "Pacific Air Forces Aircrew of Distinction" award for which the citation reads:

Captain Graham N. Sinclair distinguished himself with unparalleled airmanship as F-15D aircraft commander during a critical in-flight emergency of a civilian Evergreen International 747, 31 March 1993 at Anchorage International Airport, Alaska. Captain Sinclair observed fuel vapors and the subsequent departure of the number two engine from the 747 aircraft. Captain Sinclair responded in a professional manner by directing his wingman to a chase position on the right, as he moved to chase on the left. As the Japanese crew began experiencing extreme flight control difficulties, while quickly losing altitude, Captain Sinclair reacted in an expedient manner, relaying damage assessment to the mishap crew. Captain Sinclair continued to escort the 747 away from a densely populated area to a flawless landing at Anchorage International Airport. Captain Sinclair's quick thinking, skillful maneuvering at slow speed, low altitude, in turbulence and windshear helped save the lives of the 747 crew and millions of dollars in cargo and aircraft. Captain Sinclair reflects credit upon himself and the United States Air Force.

Having been promoted to major in April 1993, Sinclair completed his exchange with his sortie of May 8. By then his log showed 1996 hours total time, including 401.4 on the F-15C/D. At this time, as a result of software upgrades to the F-15 that were classified "Secret. No Foreign", the CF F-15 exchange ended. In June, Sinclair did a CF-18 refresher course, then spent three years as a flight commander with 433 Squadron. Next, he had a year in 3 Wing Operations, while flying with 425 Squadron. Maj Sinclair was Team Lead for WT-94, when Canada had its best ever Willy Tell finish. In 1996 he was attached to 2 Canadian Mechanized Brigade Group in Bosnia-Herzegovina, commanding a tactical air control party and serving as a FAC for the NATO Implementation Force. In 1997 he

The Sinclairs had three children during their air force years. Here, young Alex tries out his dad's office. (Sinclair Col.)

Graham Sinclair at home in Manotick, Ontario on November 10, 2003. He's with Bill Stowe who, half a century earlier, had flown Kittyhawks in Alaska and Spitfires over Europe. The backdrop is a print by Anchorage artist John Hume showing an Alaskan F-15 waxing a Soviet Su-27 Flanker. Great fun! (Larry Milberry)

was stationed in the COAC at Vicenza, Italy with Op. Deliberate Guard, supporting efforts in former Yugoslavia, then he returned to 3 Wing as Chief of Standards and Evaluation. In August 1997 he was posted to Mirabel as detachment commander at 4 Software Engineering Squadron, and doing acceptance flying of CF-18s coming off Bombardier's Mirabel overhaul/modification line. Projects on which he worked in this period included installation of a CF-18 GPWS (ground proximity warning system), and precision-guided weapons (PGM) upgrades. His tour ended with a test flight on 188910 of April 12, 2000, after which Maj Sinclair joined Air Canada on the Airbus A340, but later moved to CAE at Mirabel working in CF-18 software.

Phantom to Hornet

Over the decades Hornet squadrons at Cold Lake and Bagotville have hosted exchange pilots from the France, Germany, Holland, the RAF, USAF, USMC and USN. One of these was Bernhard Tantarn, who would serve with 441. Having joined the German Air Force in July 1983, he first completed basic training and officer school, then he passed his initial pilot training on light aircraft. In April 1985 he was posted to Sheppard AFB, Texas for jet conversion on the T-37 and T-38. In June 1986 he completed the F-4E OTU at George AFB, California, then upgraded to the F-4F with FBW36 at Rheine/Hopsten, Germany. He now joined 711 Squadron of FW71 "Richthofen" at Wittmund, flying F-4Fs, then instructed at 721 OCU on F-4Fs. From June to December 1992 Tantarn was at Holloman AFB on the FWIC. By now with some 1400 fighter hours, much of it instructing, he qualified for some sort of a "reward". He was offered a slot instructing at the F-15C OTU at Tyndall AFB, but had had his fill of training units.

Meanwhile, Tantarn was interested in giving his family some exposure to Canada, a country to which he had a special affinity – he had been born in North Bay, Ontario of immigrant German parents. In 1964, however, his father decided to take the family home to Germany. Thus, when an offer came for an exchange at 441 Squadron, Tantarn jumped at it. Soon after he reached Cold Lake, he met one of 441's sprog pilots, Kirk "Rambo" Soroka. In 2004 Soroka recalled meeting with "this awesome German exchange pilot". He just about split his sides when Tarzan introduced himself: "Glad to meet you, Rambo. I'm your friendly local Luftwaffe POW." In September 2003, Tantarn looked back on this period in his career:

Although my wife, Chris, was initially a little reserved about living in a small town "in the middle of nowhere" with six months of winter, she changed her mind rather quickly. We never regretted our decision and can honestly say that these were some of our best years.

I began at Cold Lake with a Hornet conversion course, then joined 441. To get to know our new friends, Chris and I planned a little German theme night at our place. Sad to say, however, Chris had broken a leg after stepping in a gopher hole. Instead of the party, she ended in hospital in Edmonton, and I ended up at home minding our three young children. My first official duty at 441 was to ask my new CO, "Coco" Ouellet, for three weeks of leave.

After a week, Chris was home and, on her first night, there came a knock at the door. In came Coco and his wife, Sue, with a huge flower arrangement. Then, one by one, came all the other officers with their wives and girlfriends, and all the food and drink for a great party! After that we were well taken care of by our 441 "family", while Chris recuperated. Nobody was going to starve at our house!

My memories of our three years with 441 are so numerous that they could fill their own book. One is of a March 1995 deployment to Luke AFB, Arizona. Ian W. "Manic" McLean flew down first, then I left a day before the rest of the squadron. I routed via Holloman to pick up some material from the GAF FWIC school, which would help us at Luke with our gunnery training. I departed next day and, after a pleasant flight over the Grand Canyon, landed at Luke at about 1100 hours. Manic met me and, since the rest of 441 was not expected until after lunch, we drove over to the Burger King on base. Just as we arrived, we noticed a USAF female MP who was

Bernhard Tantarn with Billie Flynn while both were flying the EuroFighter at Manching, Germany in October 2002. "Tarzan's" patches include Eurofighter, Phantom and CF-18. (Larry Milberry)

stunningly attractive. The fact that her blue uniform was a size too small did nothing to cool off our imaginations. "Look," I said, "she's even carrying her own handcuffs!"

We said "Hi", passed, had our burgers, then returned to the flightline in two cars to meet the incoming Hornets. Driving out onto the flightline, we were careful not to cross any of the dreaded security "Red Lines". Do that, and it's big trouble from the MPs. We knew enough to drive onto the tarmac only at the designated entrances. Then, just as our Hornets taxied in, I saw "her" again, this time on duty in her battle dress, and carrying a radio and an M-16 rifle. She came a little closer, speaking, but I couldn't get her drift with the Hornets making so much noise behind. So, I approached, but she yelled "Stop!", which I did.

Now I was looking into the barrel of an M-16. Manic, noticing this weird encounter, came forward, then the MP pointed her rifle at him. "Sorry, Tarzan. you're on your own," he said, then walked away. Suddenly two MP vehicles pulled up and I found myself in my little beauty's handcuffs – not what I had envisioned for those things! An old Master Sergeant took me away, with "my" MP as escort. Since the Hornets now were quiet, as we passed them, I looked up pleadingly at Coco, sitting in his cockpit. What I got was a wide grin and a good-bye wave from him! My reaction is not fit to print.

Soon I found myself spread-eagled uncomfortably against a wall, being searched, lectured and questioned, while "my" MP watched. It took 20 minutes for the cops to agree that I wasn't a Russian spy. The old "sarge" explained that the MP had not recognized my German flight suit and had called to me to show my ID. "I couldn't hear her", I explained. "So why didn't you get closer to her, so you could hear?" he wondered. Just then I saw that gorgeous MP getting into her car with a big smile on her face. That was the last we saw of her. It had been an interesting start to our deployment at Luke, but now it was down to the serious business of flying.

Another incident took place away up north – at Inuvik where we were on a NORAD exercise. On our final day there, the plan was to launch all six Hornets and return to base at Cold Lake using air-to-air refuelling. As I started my engines, however, a lot of smoke came pouring from my left cockpit console. I quickly shut down, egressed and was in a bad mood at the thought of being left behind. To my surprise, however, the technicians soon had my jet serviceable. I started up and everything seemed fine. Just before I taxied, the groundcrew asked if I would give them a fly-by on departure. Thankful to them for such good work, I decided to go for it. After takeoff, I turned back and, in full afterburner, made a knife-edge pass low in front of the hangars, rolled underneath, then headed for home.

Upon landing at Cold Lake, I was greeted by my flight commander Jeff "Beck" Beckett. He had a strange look in his eye, but didn't say anything. My curiosity got the better of me, so I asked him what was wrong. Beck smiled and said, "Nice fly-by, Tarzan, but your timing was off. Just as you flew by, I was on the phone to "Duds" [Ron Dudley] in the hangar at Inuvik. Consider yourself warned."

That was that, so I thought, but not quite. An hour later we were all in the squadron lounge, when the maintenance officer came in. In front of everyone he announced, "Hey, Tarzan, great fly-by, and great roll! Thanks from all the groundcrew up there! I just pulled the tape – 560 knots, 60 feet ... just great!" My CO's ears seemed to be getting bigger and bigger, while I was shrinking behind the bar. I got away with that one. Lucky for me, and for the fact that I was "only" an exchange officer.

How was it being a German fighter pilot on a Canadian squadron? Well, as to the pilots' mind set, attitudes and way they approached their business, the differences seemed minor. Of course, we employ slightly different tactics, but you'll find pros and cons on both sides as to that topic. Organizationally, however, there were differences. In Germany, a wing typically consists of two operational squadrons (e.g. FW71 has 711 Sqn and 712 Sqn). A squadron includes only pilots and some admin people. Maintenance and support are separate organizations. Below the wing level there are three groups: the "Flying Group" with a staff, the two squadrons and the flying control service; the "Technical Group" with a staff, the maintenance squadron and the repair squadrons organized by trade; and the "Base Group" in charge of logistics, transportation, medical, etc. There were advantages to this kind of organization during the Cold War, but things got complicated if you had to deploy. There were too many different units to co-ordinate. Having experienced operations at Cold Lake, I preferred the Canadian system.

Similar things were true for regular flying operations. In Canada, flying was based mainly on scenarios with certain objectives, and only a general outline of the specific amount of individual tasks. Squadrons were responsible for controlling the training, and prioritizing and weighing the benefits of smaller, individual deployments, versus training results.

In the Luftwaffe, continuation flying training, deployments and exercises were controlled and scheduled by German Air Force Command. The tasks that each pilot had to fulfill each year were described in the Tactical Training Program down to the specific details – intercepts (low, medium and high altitude), BFM, ECCM, etc. As long as the flying hours were available and the number of commitments were reasonable, this worked just fine, despite the dreaded bureaucratic accounting effort. But, due to circumstances that most NATO air forces have faced in recent years (budget cuts, downsizing, international commitments, re-organization, etc.), this system seemed more of a hindrance, lacking flexibility and favouring quantity instead of quality, since wings were obliged to fulfill their statistics. Training suffered because of this.

Chris, I and the children enjoyed our three-year tour with 441 so much, that we decided to stay in Canada. I arranged to transfer to the Canadian Forces, where I would continue flying Hornets. Unfortunately, only weeks before the final commitment, a family issue back in Germany forced us to reverse our decision. The door was not closed, however, and we still may come back to Canada some day.

In January 1997 Bernhard Tantarn returned to instruct at 721 Squadron. Then, in March 1998 he began his first staff job – a year in Air Force HQ on the Eurofighter project. In April 1999 he joined the German Air Force test and evaluation unit at Manching to fly the EuroFighter. This was the period leading to formation of the first Luftwaffe EuroFighter unit, the EuroFighter OTU. Meanwhile, as recently as 2003 he continued as an F-4F pilot with FW74 "Mölders" at Neuberg.

CHAPTER 25
441 in Task Force Aviano

Even though the Cold War was fading, the early 1990s had their own challenges – the Gulf War, the collapse of Yugoslavia, the horrors of Somalia and Rwanda, etc. Canada, ever anxious to be seen as an international player, volunteered its military to help in many such crises. At the same time, ironically, Ottawa was hamstringing the military with budget cuts which it described as "peace dividends" accruing from the post-Cold War years. Through the 1990s, for example, it reduced Canada's regular forces from 88,000 to 60,000. According to Chretien government spin doctors this was fine – think of all the money that taxpayers were saving. But these "savings" were a sham and the piper soon would have to be paid.

The breakup of Yugoslavia drew in the UN and NATO, but UN monitoring of hotspots seemed to do little to deter atrocities. At Srebrenica, UN peacekeepers handed over thousands of Bosnian muslims to the Serb military, which quickly slaughtered them. In the air, NATO patrolled no-fly areas and occasionally bombed Serb positions, but nothing seemed to bother Serb President Slobodan Milosevic. In 1997 tiny Kosovo now was threatened by Milosevic with ethnic cleansing so, before another round of Balkan genocide could go too far, NATO decided to act. A plan was devised to confront Serbia with an air campaign. NATO began concentrating air power at bases in Italy. On August 14, 1997 six 416 Squadron CF-18s flew to Aviano, Italy on a 3-month deployment. This was Op. Mirador, commanded by LCol Jim Grecco. "Mirador" was followed on June 24, 1998 by six CF-18s from Bagotville on Op. Echo, commanded by LCol Alain Boyer. Op. Echo became part of a grander NATO plan, Op. Allied Force. The CF-18 element, named Task Force Aviano (TFA), initially would enforce a no-fly zone over Bosnia-Herzegovina. Commanding TFA during the fighting was Col Dwight Davies (he was based in the Combined Air Operations Centre at Vicenza, a few miles south of Aviano). On the home front, TFA would be overseen by LGen Ray Henault and his second-in-command, BGen Dave Jurkowski.

Serbia's reckoning came in the spring of 1999 when it ignored a NATO ultimatum that its 40,000 troops and 300 tanks in Kosovo cease ethnic cleansing. An air campaign aimed at forcing Serbia's hand began on March 24. Strikes were made by aircraft from Belgium, Canada, Denmark, France, Germany, Italy, Norway, Spain, Turkey, the UK and the US. This was the first time in its 50 years that NATO had undertaken European combat operations. Op. Allied Force would continue for 78 days, its pace gradually rising. On April 9, for example, Aviano launched some 100 fighters against such targets as a Danube bridge at Petrovaradin, and a bridge on the Magura-Belacevac railway. At its height, TFA numbered 18 Hornets and 310 personnel (there would be two rotations during the war). With some 32 pilots available (about half of Canada's combat ready Hornet pilots) TFA usually was tasked for 16 daily missions. Targets included Serb airfields, army concentrations, communications centres, bridges and rail/road junctions. In the end TFA would fly

Hornet 188794 of 425 Squadron starts at Aviano on July 11, 1998, in the days before the big "Allied Force" push to crush Serb military might in Kosovo. '794 was on a multi-purpose patrol this day, armed with AAMs plus a PGM on the port wing. Then, 188785 of 433 Squadron at Aviano. (Larry Milberry)

Refuelling Hornet '744 at Aviano. (Larry Milberry)

A CF-18 tech at Aviano inspects the seeker head on a 500-lb PGM. Then, a typical stores arrangement showing PGM and FLIR pod; and a close-up of the FLIR pod. (Larry Milberry)

558 bombing and 120 CAP missions, deliver some 171 Mk.82 500-lb "iron" bombs, 241 GBU-12 (500-lb) "smart" bombs, and 120 2000-lb GBU-10 "smart" bombs, and log about 2600 combat hours. TFA pilots would lead half the missions in which CF-18s flew, an indication of the confidence placed by the Allies in the Canadians. ("Allied Force" missions would total 38,004 of which 10,484 were strike missions).

Mainly because Task Force Aviano war diaries remained classified by NDHQ, this book cannot begin to tell the TFA story. Generally, NDHQ is secretive about the details of Canada's involvement in such operations as "Allied Force" and "Noble Eagle". This contrasts to the US military, which has published a great deal of history about both operations, including a major book about "Noble Eagle" – *Air War over America*. For now, beginning with a profile of LCol Billie Flynn, TFA's "Balkan Rats" wing leader, this is what CANAV Books has to offer.

"Wing Leader"

While 3 Wing Bagotville launched Canada's action against Serbia, the main Task Force Aviano effort fell to 4 Wing Cold Lake under LCol Billie Flynn, 441 CO from June 1997 to September 1999. Flynn's would be a job not unlike that of (then) W/C Johnnie Johnson, who led 441, 442 and 443 RCAF squadrons into battle during Spitfire days. This brief profile describes how one man rose from officer cadet to command the largest Canadian fighter force to go to war in 55 years.

The son of R.J. "Bob" Flynn, a former "Air Div" Sabre pilot, Billie Flynn joined the Canadian Forces in 1976 as an CMR student. He began flight training in May 1978, then did some OJT at Cold Lake. There, on June 11, 1980, he had his first back seat ride in a CF-104, going up with Hptm Harold Reidel, 417 Squadron's Luftwaffe exchange officer. By the time he left Cold Lake, Flynn had scrounged 14 Starfighter rides, plus five in the CF-5.

In October 1981 Lt Flynn began his course at Moose Jaw, finishing on September 3, 1982 with 189.6 hours in the Tutor. Upon graduating, he was awarded the 2 FTS "Centennaires" trophy and selected as the first CF-18 pipeline pilot (even before the CF-18 had been delivered). Following a stint on T-birds at Base Flight Cold Lake, he began the CF-5 FLIT, flying initially on June 10, 1983 in 116831. One of his CF-5 trips would end badly. On December 23, 1983 he was on a cross-country to Westover AFB, Massachusetts with USAF exchange pilot Capt Mark Leeson. Upon landing at Westover, the CF-5 struck a snow ridge on the runway, collapsing the undercarriage. Flynn got out OK, but Leeson was severely injured (he recovered and later flew F-15s and F-117s).

Flynn now joined Course 1 at the CF-18 OTU, flying first with Maj Laurie Hawn on January 31, 1984. He soloed on February 3 (the first pipeliner to do so), and graduated on August 8 with 95.1 hours. He was posted to newly-formed 409 "Nighthawk" Squadron on August 15, 1984 and soon was busy with all sorts of activity – Ex. Cold Shaft at Gander, Ex. Copper Flag at Tyndall, QRAs at Bagotville, and AAR and ECM training. Deployed to Bagotville from February 19 to March 3, he flew 11 times – great excitement for any young fighter pilot.

Capt. Billie Flynn as a young CF-18 pilot with the "NightHawks" at Baden-Soellingen on March 13, 1987. (Larry Milberry)

The Leeson/Flynn CF-5 prang (CF)

In April 1985 Capt Flynn passed 1000 flying hours. On June 5, 409 departed for Baden-Soellingen, Capts Flynn and Motriuk crewing Hornet 188918. First stop was Goose Bay, a 4-hour AAR transit. Next day they made Baden in four hours. Taking a few days to settle in, 409 commenced local flying, Flynn's first mission being on June 19 to the Suippes Range in France. Now came all the usual exercises – ACM, low-level nav trips, night instrument flying, night low-level, DACT with F-15s and F-16s, etc. In August Capts Flynn and Breau deployed two Hornets to Jever Air Base for the Hornet's first air-to-air Tactical Leadership Programme course. In 2004 Flynn recalled: "We were humbled by how much the CF-18 community had to learn about air-to-air in the European environment. Our experience at the TLP led to significant changes in 1 CAG's tactical doctrine."

In May 1986 the Nighthawks passed their first NATO TacEval. June 2 saw 409 pulling a mass attack on Hahn. On July 31 Flynn did his "Lead Upgrade" trip. On a melancholy note, on April 10, 1987 Capts Flynn and Grasswick flew a memorial T-33 formation salute honouring Capt Paul Jones. Later that day he and Capt Bill Kelly flew a similar mission for Capt Jim Sorfleet. Jones and Sorfleet had died a few days earlier in a T-33 mishap.

For the 1987 airshow season Capt Flynn was the 1 CAG "demo" pilot. His first show was at Liège, Belgium on May 23, then came Aviano on the 31st. June 16 to 21 he made a big hit at the Paris Airshow. July 13 - 17, 409 was at Deci for ACM with F-4s and F-5Es. In October the squadron "crossed the pond" for Maple Flag XX. In March 1988 came an adventuresome deployment with Hornets 188729, '744, '796 and '798, this illustrating the intensity of training in early CF-18 days. Flynn's log book shows:

Date	Route	Mission	Time
14	Baden - Lossiemouth, Scotland	Transit	2.0
	Keflavik, Iceland		2.0
	Sondrestrom, Greenland		1.8
15	Goose Bay		2.0
	Bagotville		1.5
18	NAS Oceana, Virginia		2.2
19	Tyndall AFB, Florida		2.2
21	Tyndall	Combat Archer, fire AIM-7	1.3
		AAR, BFM 1-V-1	1.3
23	Tyndall	DACT 4-V-4 F-15s, AAR	1.7
24	Tyndall	BFM 1-V-1	0.9
25	Tyndall	DACT 4-V-4 F-15s	0.8
28	Tyndall	DACT 4-V-4 F-15s	1.2
29	Tyndall	ACM 1-V-1	0.9
30	Tyndall	DACT 4-V-4, EW T-33s	1.2
31	Tyndall - Offutt AFB	Transit	1.9
	Cold Lake		2.3

Back at 4 Wing on July 2 Flynn flew with the Frecce Tricolore then, in August, hit his 2000th flying hour. On December 18 he made his last flight as a Nighthawk, going up with Capt Jeff Beckett in 188922. He now began training at the US Navy Test Pilot School at NAS Patuxent River, Maryland. Flying commenced in a T-2 trainer on February 1, 1989. As the months passed, he flew many types including (chronologically) the Learjet, T-38, F/A-18B, Beaver, HH-65, Grob glider, F-111D, P-3B Orion, P-51D and NT-33A. Flynn tested the Mirage 2000B and other types during a November 1989 assignment in France. His course ended with a TA-4J mission of December 6. Along the way he had applied for astronaut training. Instead, however, he won a secondment to the 6512th Test Squadron at Edwards AFB, California.

Excerpts from Billie Flynn's logbook during TPS days.

Maj Flynn commenced flying at Edwards on February 1, 1990, going up in a T-38. In May he took the F-16 OTU, soloing on the 17th. Most of his flying, henceforth, was doing chase and target missions, and shake-down flights on new F-16s. He advanced to F-16 flight performance testing, e.g. jet wake and pitch oscillation, doing high angle of attack (AOA) and out-of-control trials, testing new engines, or evaluating performance with external stores. In this period Flynn became the USAF's most experienced "High AOA" test pilot.

In 1993 Maj Flynn was assigned to the Multi Axis Thrust Vectoring (MATV) F-16D program, a joint Lockheed-General Electric-USAF effort to assess the practicality of an expanded

Views of the MATV F-16D at Edwards AFB. (Larry Milberry, USAF)

manoeuvring envelope. The air force wished to determine the tactical advantages that an MATV nozzle could give a fighter at low speed (below 300 kts), where thrust vectoring can help a pilot point his aircraft more quickly. Such an edge could give a pilot an otherwise impossible kill, or let him manoeuvre away from an adversary.

The MATV F-16D had been in the VISTA program –variable stability, in-flight simulator test aircraft. It differs from a standard F-16D with its prominent dorsal fairing, beefed up landing gear, and spin chute housing. For MATV it had its standard exhaust nozzle replaced by an axi-symmetric vectoring exhaust nozzle (AVEN). Three actuators were installed to vector the nozzle. A vector electronic control digital computer was added to control nozzle actuators and afterburner. Following July 1993 tests at Fort Worth the MATV F-16D flew to Edwards, where the goal was to develop combat tactics against the F-15, F-16 and F/A-18. November 9 - 19, 1993 two pilots from the 422nd TES at Nellis AFB flew an operational assessment, including 1-V-2 engagements. By Christmas, 86 flights and 105 hours had been logged by 22 pilots. Maj Flynn flew the aircraft on August 17, 1993. This was the first time that it flew at more than 80° sustained AOA, and performed yaw pedal turns at that high an AOA, or at that high a vectoring rate. Related Flynn, "It was unique to have the opportunity to fly an airplane where no one had ever been. That mission truly expanded the envelope of flight." By mid-December 1993 Flynn had 20 MATV flights. The program ended on March 15, 1994 with the 100th flight. Subsequently, he flew NASA's HARV (High Alpha Research Vehicle) F/A-18, evaluating thrust vectoring. Included was 1-V-1 ACM with the thrust-vectored X-31.

Also at Edwards, Maj Flynn flew such types as the UH-1N "Twin Huey", T-34C, B-52 and F/A-18. His last mission was in an F-16A on July 27, 1994. He attended CF Staff and Command College in Toronto, then served at NDHQ in the Directorate of Aircraft Requirements, working on CF-18 future upgrades. This bureaucratic work would prove valuable for his next posting – commanding 441 beginning in May 1997. On July 22 LCol Flynn flew his first mission as Silver Fox CO, a trip in 188925 with Maj Jeff Beckett.

What followed was the best that Flynn could have hoped for. As usual, it was a life on the road. October 19 - 31 at Comox, for example, he flew 13 times on BFM, ACM, and naval exercises. On the 30th there was 6-V-5 DACT against F-16s then, on March 18, 1998, the squadron deployed to Holloman AFB for DACT. In May, 441 invited Canada's Olympic bobsled champions to Cold Lake. As part of the skit, LCol Flynn took his brother Clarke, a former Olympic bob-sledder, for a CF-18 ride. When 441 returned to Holloman in November, Flynn also visited NAS Patuxent River. There, he and Canadian exchange test pilot, Maj Mo Girard, flew an F/A-18 out-of-control demonstration for the US Navy TPS. Flynn flew a special sortie from Cold Lake on January 28, 1999, taking 441 Honourary Colonel David Graves on an introductory Hornet ride.

As LCol Flynn prepared 441 for what lay ahead, he wondered about how much training should go to NORAD, compared to NATO missions. With the world shaping up as it was, common sense told him NATO. He scheduled no 441 FOL deployments, and only two to the QRA in Comox. In October 2002 he recalled, "If we had had a NORAD TacEval in this period, we definitely would have done poorly." What Flynn now was emphasizing was coalition warfare scenarios and high level bombing (By this time CF-18 tactics had changed away from the low-level, CAS missions that had typified training since 1982, to high level missions using laser-guided "smart" bombs.) Flynn led his pilots on gruelling exercises, qualifying each on GBU-12 500-lb, GBU-16 1000-lb and GBU-10 2000-lb "smart" bomb delivery. They even simulated combat with gunship helicopters, which Serbian forces operated in large numbers. In time Flynn was convinced that of Canada's CF-18 community 441 was "the best of the best".

Balkan Rats pilots during LCol Flynn's command at Aviano. Standing on the wing are Capts Paul "Pepe" Prevost, Les "Kosmo" Racicot, Travis "Brass" Brassington, Eric "Slice" Kenny, Stephane "Yoda" Hébert, Maj Rich "Stitch" Foster, Capts Chris "Nomad" Larouche, Neil "Hoss" McRury, Ken "Flush" Welch, Rob "Crack" Carter, Joe "Sloth" Mahoney, Majs Rob "Hooker" Parker and Alain "Data" Pelletier. Sitting on the wing are LCmdr Mark "Fisk" Carlton, Capts Todd "Piper" Sinclair, Kirk "Rambo" Soroka, Pete "Homey" Homewood, Darwin "Mac" MacMillian, Ryan "Scrape" Stich, Alasdaire "Psycho" Clarke, Maj Pat "Roach" Laroche, Capts Siegfried "Use" Usal and Jason "Tubs" Regenwetter, Majs Tim "TJ" Jordan and Georges "Chicken" Bertrand. In front are LCol Billie Flynn, Capts Brian "Gyproc" Dunsterville and Brett "Laser" Glaeser, Majs Todd "Norm" Balfe, Capt Bill "Huck" Huckstep and Maj Steve "Swill" Will, Capts Brent "Sparky" Sparks and Dave "Prowler" Prowal, Maj Glen "Flaps" Phillips, Capts Jan "Trigger" Reudiseuli, Brent "Bing" Nelson and Paul "Frig" Frigault, and Maj Rob "Waldo" Martin. (CF CKD99-2024-07)

Kosovo Campaign

On March 19, 1999, a 441 Squadron advance party departed Cold Lake for Aviano. once complete, this rotation would replace 3 Wing pilots, ground crew and support personnel then on duty in Aviano. The advance party included Maj Murray "Forest" Carlson (DCO), Maj Glen "Flaps" Phillips (OpsO), Maj Rob "Hooker" Parker (Weapons and Tactics), Maj Steve "Swill" Will (Training), Maj Chris Ouellette (Maintenance), Capt Brent "Sparky" Sparks, Capt Jan "Trigger" Reudiseuli (Dutch exchange pilot) and Lt (N) Mark "Fisk" Carlton (USN exchange pilot). When combat began on March 24, the squadron had not completed pilot check outs. Flynn and Carlson initially were tasked to support the Combined Air Operations Centre in Vicenza, Italy, but both quickly returned to Aviano, where a change of command ceremony took place. Meanwhile, 441's other pilots had been integrated into operations and been wrung out over Kosovo.

Initially, there were many details about the deployment yet to be hammered out, as TFA prepared for uncertain days. In one case, since the duration of the Kosovo campaign was unknown, LCol Flynn recommended that personnel serve in theatre for two months, followed by two months of leave in Canada. This proposal was adopted. On April 11 Flynn and others from 441 joined in their first strikes against Serb targets. In 2004 Flynn reviewed this historic time:

> Task Force Aviano during Operation Allied Force was largely a 441 effort. We departed Cold Lake on March 19 with our advance party. We deplaned the Airbus a day later in our blue Canadian flight suits to be greeted by our 3 Wing comrades in US green camouflage flight suits. Tensions were spooling up and the unit was preparing for the inevitable first combat missions.

> I had brought with me eight of the best trained, most skilled 441 fighter pilots, men with "FWIC" (Fighter Weapons Instructor Course) and "TLP" (Tactical Leadership Program) experience. Some also had previous combat or Balkan theatre experience. All were experienced flight leads and, though I had briefed them to be mellow and humble, they were not all that good at containing their aggressiveness and excitement. They virtually overran their 3 Wing comrades, even before the war started

> Originally, we had planned to integrate ourselves with the 3 Wing unit, rotate them out at the end of their deployment, then take full charge of the deployment. The outbreak of hostilities put an end to that plan – 441 immediately was thrown into the situation and integrated as best as could be. Considering the range of experience, and the energy level of we newcomers, compared to our more wary predecessors, this did not work well.

> When I finally took command of the TFA detachment 17 days into the conflict, it was basically dysfunctional. The mix of 3 Wing and 4 Wing, from logistics to ground crew to pilots was not working. I tried bridging the gap between personnel from the two wings and from the five different CF-18 squadrons. While the majority of the leadership was from 441, I solicited a name for the deployed unit so that the collective "we" might find some middle ground, and bind the group for the duration of the war. The politically incorrect name "Balkan Rats", proposed by 441's Kirk Soroka and Brent Sparks, was the winner. Why rats? In the trailers where we were quartered, rats had eaten us out of house, home and computer cords. As well, since we always were short of the essentials to function as a deployed unit, we had to scrounge to make up the difference. Finally, that the DCDS and CDS did not like the name cemented its future.

The famous emblem under which the Balkan Rats flew in 1999. (Andrew Cline)

Hornets at War

Carrying a full weapons load (GBU-10s, AIM-7s and AIM-9s, plus external fuel, Hornet 188787 taxis for a mission, as a USAF F-16 departs to join its package bound for Kosovo. During Allied Force, Aviano normally was home to some 180 aircraft and, on one day handled 210, all on one runway! Then, '783 climbs out from Aviano already at 200 knots. Although a fully-loaded Hornet departed with eight tons of fuel, its first stop would be a tanker somewhere over the Adriatic. (CF CKD99-2067-08, '2082-01)

More great Aviano combat action – Hornet '794 taxis from its HAS, then gets airborne. (CF CKD99-2085-05, '09)

Mission Planning

At TFA the vital planning ritual took place each night before a mission. This involved the entire "package", each flying unit having representatives present. Targets would be briefed, weather checked, "intel" about air defences discussed, pilots assigned, etc. Every pilot had to be certain of his assigned target (e.g. the exact type of bridge or building), how to identify it, and just what the legalities were of hitting it. Typical targets (always bombed from high level) would be Serb barracks, vehicle parks, ammunition and fuel dumps, bridges and power plants. Those briefed also would learn which units were going in and in what order (the "flow" of the package). Normally there would be electronic jammers like the USN's EA-6B Prowlers, and "suppression of enemy air defence" (SEAD) types such as Luftwaffe ECR Tornados and USAF F-16CJs with weapons like the HARM (high speed anti-radiation) missile. SEAD forces obliged the Serbs to turn off their AAA and SAM radars, or risk these being pinpointed and destroyed. Packages also included "sweepers" – F-15s with AMRAAMs (advanced medium-range air-to-air missiles) forging ahead to clear Kosovo and Serbia of MiGs. Combat SAR helicopters always were present, along with their A-10 or F-16 CAPs. So was AWACS there, orbiting in the background, giving the big picture, reporting on tanker tracks, etc.

Aircrew had much to contemplate, but SAMs were foremost – 700 would be launched by the Serbs. Weather also was a concern. It

A CF-18 ready for the fight as EA-6 Prowlers of Electronic Attack Wing Aviano depart on an EW mission. As jammers of enemy radar, Prowlers were so vital to Allied Force that no mission would launch without them. (CF CKD99-2029-01)

might be fair, or not so fair. After USAF Capt Scott O'Grady was shot down above cloud by a SAM, a new rule was introduced – when above cloud, be at least 10,000 feet over "the tops". That way a pilot had a chance to spot a SAM and take evasive action. By the time a briefing was over, each crew had all the "gen", their particular call signs, tanker RV times, the AWACS situation, etc. Finally, everyone would talk over their roles in small groups, leads from various units would confer, and pilots would gather by unit to review final details.

An F-16CJ of the 363rd FW, Shaw AFB, Georgia taxies on an Allied Force mission. Its primary weapon is the HARM anti-radiation missile that seeks out and destroys enemy radar sites. AIM-120 AMRAAMs are on the wingtips, with Sidewinders inboard. Canada is adding the AMRAAM to its CF-18 arsenal. AMRAAM does not oblige a pilot to keep pointed at a target, as does the AIM-7 with its semi-active radar. A pilot can fire an AMRAAM, then turn to other business as it flies to its target. As to USAF units at Aviano, they were on the go day and night. Dan Leaf, a USAF "One Star" general himself flew 18 combat missions, and his colonels were flying all the time. If you weren't a tiger, Aviano was not the place for you. (CF CKD99-2050-04)

Air-to-Air Refuelling

Air-to-air refuelling in Allied Force was done several times per sortie. This ensured that each aircraft had enough fuel to transit to Kosovo, to avoid aerial traffic jams, for possible combat during ingress (or egress), for the strike itself, or for an unplanned diversion. Tankers were USAF KC-135s and KC-10s, RAF VC-10s, Italian 707s, French KC-135s, and Spanish KC-130s. Qualifying on a new type was an OJT affair. Average CF-18 mission length would be 4.5 hours. The longest (8.7 hours) was a daytime CAP over Skopje, Macedonia.

On a typical mission, aircraft would depart from various bases and climb out for their first tanker RVs. Flying in uncontrolled airspace, tankers normally were located by radar. Then night vision goggles would come into play (with NVGs a pilot can "see in the dark", pick up surrounding details, easily hold position, then close in to refuel). This is

"Rambo" following an Allied Force mission, then taking a walk for the photographer with fellow Hornet pilots Brian "Gyproc" Dunsterville (425), Dave "Prowler" Prowal (416), Ryan "Scrape" Stich (425) and Brett "Laser" Glaeser (441). ("Rambo" Col., CF CKD99-2000-01)

where the CF-18 was handicapped, for the Balkan Rats were the only fighter unit in the war lacking NVGs. Instead, they had to rely on their APG-65 radar and on the "Mark I Eyeball".

In 2004 Capt Kirk "Rambo" Soroka, who served with the Balkan Rats from March 24 to June 1, 1999, recalled combat operations over Kosovo and Serbia during "Allied Force". The material below is adapted from what he originally wrote in 2000 to describe a series of paintings that he had commissioned – the "Airpower for Peace and Freedom Collection". This material portrays the fighter pilot's experience in modern aerial warfare.

Capt Soroka had a unique background – having joined the military in 1983, he was first an infantry private in 3 PPCLI. He progressed to master corporal's rank and became a reconnaissance specialist, sniper and Infantry Section Commander. In 1989 he became a "Mil-Col" student at Royal Roads in Victoria, graduating in 1993 with a BA in military and strategic studies. During this period Soroka was selected for pilot training. He earned his Wings in 1993, graduated as a Hornet pilot in April 1997, then joined 441, serving there until August 2001.

Capt Soroka would fly 20 Allied Force operations. Typical was a mission of May 14, 1999 – a 4-ship with Capt John Hutt, Capt (RNLAF) Jan "Trigger" Reudiseuli and Maj Yves Tessier. Their target at first was to be airfield bunkers, but that changed to a Serb army base. Following takeoff at 0355Z, the Hornets flew to rendezvous with a French KC-135. After refuelling, they waited in a pre-planned hold over Albania, then pressed in at 0600Z for their target near Prizen through which Kosovar refugees were passing towards Albania, and in which were Serb Army concentrations. Each Hornet carried a pair of GBU-10s, six of which soon would be released. From a point five miles from target, all weapons struck home. In 2004 Capt Soroka reflected on other combat experiences, notably AAR:

Affectionately dubbed the "Iron Maiden" by fighter pilots, the KC-135 was the workhorse in AAR. Its refuelling system consists of a 28-foot boom plus 9 feet of rubber hose. At the end of the hose flies a 150-pound cast iron basket. To receive fuel, a pilot flies his refuelling probe into the basket, then manoeuvres so that the knuckle, which attaches the basket to the now bent rubber hose, has a 90-degree turn in it. That turn allows fuel to flow through the boom and hose into the CF-18.

The KC-135 is infamous for the unforgiving "kiss" that it can administer to any inattentive pilot. The basket can be tipped off into the slipstream, causing a violent pendulum motion that can cleave important sensors off a Hornet's nose, or leave gouges or torn aircraft skin. Whenever AAR damage occurred, our groundcrew were quick to adorn the plane with a painted probe under the right wing. Several aircraft carried these symbols.

At the outset of hostilities few CF-18 pilots had tanked from a KC-135, let alone at night. They knew how demanding refuelling was but, to do it at night from the KC-135 (about which they had heard so many horror stories), seemed just as dicey as going into combat. Returning pilots could smile at having survived their date with the "Iron Maiden". I was so tense the first time at night that, when the mission was over, my right arm and shoulder were simply exhausted. I guess that's what happens when you lift 50,000 pounds of Hornet into the basket and hold it there for five minutes!

Ironically, each sortie would appear to the untrained eye to have been completed with clockwork precision. On one occasion, where the Balkan Rats were tasked to bomb a petroleum site near Belgrade, two CF-18s had to divert to Split, Croatia. This came about after numerous fighters tried to intercept their assigned tankers simultaneously, overloading the single AWACS controller. Several aircraft already had arrived on the tanker, some with critical fuel. Thus did I and Capt Reudiseuli have to break off for Split. There our Hornets were surrounded by police, causing Trigger and I to wonder, "Are they friendlies?" We sure hoped so! Our welcoming party proved to be quite interested in the modern Allied fighters that had just dropped in. Several British troops soon arrived to assist us in securing our aircraft. We quickly refuelled and departed for Aviano.

The Push, Threats, Targets & Weapons

Once its tankers were left behind, a night strike package would marshal just outside the Kosovo border. This was SOP – standard operating procedures – since all aircraft had to be in place before a mission proceeded. CF-18 pilots have vivid memories of holding with a sky full of other Allied aircraft. Everyone felt uncomfortably close, while waiting for the signal or "push time" to proceed. The go-ahead would come from a FAC (forward air controller), usually an F-16 for night missions and an A-10 during the day. Now the stakes rose, as the package pressed into enemy territory. Most pilots would experience a rush of adrenaline whenever their missile warning system "lit up" when they were painted by Serb radar. Many also would report Serb SA-3 SAMs in flight. Happily, enemy defences proved ineffective – Serb fighters rarely scrambled, and SAMs nearly always were defeated by countermeasures. Although only two NATO aircraft would be shot down during Allied Force (an F-16 and an F-117, both pilots rescued) most pilots had a sense of caution about their missions, as suggested by Capt Soroka:

At first it was hard to believe that real bombs were being dropped to destroy real targets, and that real bullets were being fired back at us. When the F-117 went down, I thought the Serbs had been holding their cards close to their chest, so they could snag the big prize. I felt certain our next mission was going to see someone go down. The chance of being shot down or having to shoot down another aircraft was possible on every mission, and most pilots came to terms with this. As to being shot down in enemy territory, it was a great relief when both USAF pilots who parachuted into the former Yugoslavia were rescued by Combat SAR crews. After those guys went down, it wasn't hard to get our pilots to practice with their GPS, radios and other survival gear, and they gave their undivided attention during CSAR briefings.

It was at the "push" that entering combat became deeply personal. Allied aircraft then would extinguish any external lighting. This meant that a Canadian pilot no longer could see the rest of his formation, since he had no NVGs (night vision goggles). At this point he was essentially "alone". His next realization was of a "line in the sand" created by the urban lighting from bordering countries that were largely unaffected by the conflict. Kosovo, however, was in darkness due to a blackout, because the power grid had been disabled to interrupt communications with Belgrade. The whole experience was like crossing over into a black hole. The only light coming from the ground was from the AAA [anti-aircraft artillery, or "Triple A"] and burning buildings.

While enroute, or when approaching the target area, much AAA was observed. This was fascinating – it looked like long waving fans or snakes originating from the ground and ending with small white flashes. Pilots steadily manoeuvred to look straight down to avoid a round in the belly. Bursts of adrenaline or "dry mouth syndrome" were common. Besides SAMs and AAA, large flashes and secondary explosions would highlight a target area if other Allied aircraft were attacking the same target.

Pilots on missions in the north felt extra anxiety, since the well-equipped, highly-trained and combat-experienced Serb military had concentrated SAMs and AAA in an integrated air defense umbrella around their capital, Belgrade. Besides AAA and SAMs the Serbs also operated Galeb ground attack fighters, and MiG-21 and MiG-29 interceptors. Especially worrisome were the MiG-29s at Batajnica north of Belgrade. Therefore, unlike Kosovo or southern Serbia missions, the chance of being shot down and captured in the north was greater.

A Hornet over typical Kosovo terrain. On the ridge to the far right is a target just bombed by the Balkan Rats. Capt Soroka notes "This is the only known picture of Canadians in combat since Korea." (Soroka Col.)

Once in a target area, pilots had to be able to see their objective. At this stage, weather could affect a mission, since forward looking infra-red (FLIR) pods and laser designators could not see through cloud. At 10 miles a pilot's FLIR pod would designate his bombing point, and his bombs would be dropped automatically (4.2 miles being the maximum distance for a 500-lb laser-guided bomb, 5.2 miles for a 2000-lb bomb). During the campaign TFA would strike every known airfield in Kosovo and Serbia (Pristina, Batajnica,

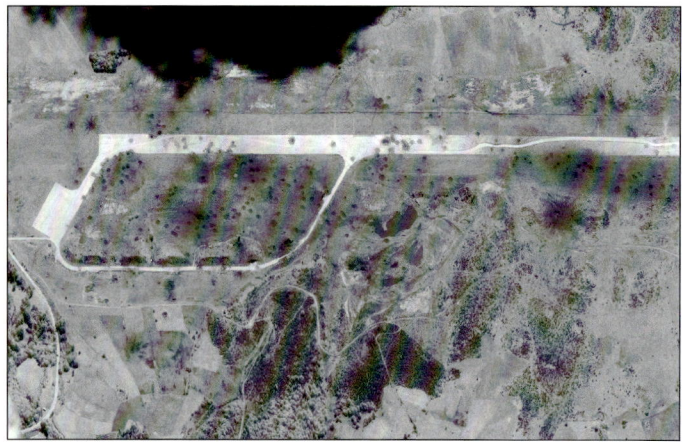

A post-strike damage assessment recce photo of Ponikve airfield, Serbia. Ponikve was struck frequently by everything from B-52s to CF-18s. Due to strict Canadian Forces policy about releasing photos, we had to turn to the US Department of Defense for these images. (US DOD 990601-0-999M-001)

The Batajnica aircraft repair and overhaul base in Serbia also was on the Balkan Rats "hit list". (US DOD 990413-0-0000K-001)

Obrva, Ponikve, etc.). As a rule the plan was to leave runways intact, while cratering taxiways and destroying airfield infrastructure. The fighter bases at Sjenica and Ponikve, however, were virtually destroyed. On one of his missions, LCol Billie Flynn noted six prominent bomb craters on an airfield, equally spaced at about 1000 feet along the runway. That computed OK – the USAF's B-2 stealth bomber carried 6 x 2000-lb GPS guided bombs on a typical mission. In the case of LCol Flynn's 14 BAI missions, on 6 he carried 500-lb "smart" bombs, on 5 – 2000-lb "smart" bombs, and on 3 – 500-lb "dumb" or "iron" bombs. Ultimately, he dropped almost 35,000 lb of ordnance, more than any other Balkan Rat.

As noted by Capt Soroka, TFA also bombed bridges, including some across the Danube: "A CF-18 2-ship normally attacked a bridge with 2000-pound laser guided bombs, aiming for both ends. This would send shock waves through the bridge and, where the two waves met, the bridge would collapse. Downed bridges prevented Serb army re-supply, and telephone wires routing through them would be severed when the structure collapsed. Thus, the Serbs' ability to give orders or co-ordinate SAMs, AAA sites, etc. in Kosovo was degraded, along with their morale and will to fight."

Aviano's Best

"Not a wheel could have turned without our ground staff", explained one Balkan Rats pilot, and no truer statement could be made. It was the technicians and other non-flying folks who kept Canada's Hornet detachments working smoothly at Aviano. This great scene shows many of these vital personnel who worked around the clock in all weather to make sure that Task Force Aviano had such a high CF-18 serviceability and "mission accomplished" rate. Standing across the fuselage of Hornet '770 are MCpl Brian Greengrass, MCpl Rita Duerr, MCpl Stanley Davenport, MCpl Tracy Constable, Cpl Wayne Hoskins, Cpl Pete Cardinal, Cpl Mike French. Around the cockpit are Cols Brad Ethier, Dave Barclay and Dave Jamieson. Seated across the top are Cpl Steph Dionne, Cpl Terry Gwynn, Cpl Mike Atkin, Cpl Linda MacDonald, Cpl Scott Trudell, Cpl Terry Lucy, MCpl John Piercey, Cpl Rob Petsche, MCpl Dave Greswell, Cpl John Meaney. Seated on the wing are Cpl Dave Farris, Cpl Karen Norton and Sgt Len Mainville. From the missile loader across to the tip of the AIM-7 are Cpl Dave McCorriston, MCpl Ron Pischke, Cpl Greg Ferguson, Cpl Ron Weiche, Sgt Greg Cryderman, WO Dave Wideman, Cpl Don Cornies, MCpl Pierre Dumont, Cpl Bernie Girard, Cpl Athanasios Mavridis and Sgt Mike Upham (arms folded). Standing from there are Cpl Craig Haire (dark glasses), Cpl Eric Braun, MCpl Ken McRae, Cpl Earl Howitt, Cpl Bruce "C16" Cassar-Torregiani, MCpl Reg St. Laurent, Cpl Doug Zylenko, Cpl Shane Smith, Cpl Ron Melnyk, MCpl Dave Norris and MCpl Don McRoberts. The others in front are Sgt Nicole Brosseau, MCpl J.C. Lessard, Cpl Bill Chisholm, MCpl Wayne Ohalaturnyk, CWO Bill Atkinson, Sgt Garth Schmidt and Cpl Frank Maher. (CF CKD99-2057-01)

Weapons loaders with Hornet 776. Standing in the rear are MCpl Daryl Shields, Cpl Mitch Kain, MCpls Don Perry and John Edelman, Sgt Frances Dagenais, Cpl Rob Wengal, and MCpl Bruce Chartrand. The others are Cpls Dan Marlow, Darren Broadwell, Aron Lehtinen, Don MacDonald, Guy Clark, Murray Anderson, Rob Williams, Andreé Jouan, Randy Arsenault, MCpl Gary Falardeau and Cpl Mark Rehbein. (CF CKD99-2088-01)

A tech pulls away the wheel chock, so Hornet '733 is free to go. Note the impressive row of mission markings. US servicing techs were interested in the chocks used by the Balkan Rats. Instead of their typical wooden ones (that can turn into FOD), the 7-foot by 2.5-inch nylon ropes used with CF-18s do the job simply and safely. (CF CKD99-2090-10)

MCpl Bruce Chartrand (416, nearest), MCpl Dan Perry (416) and Cpl Aron Lehtinen (441) mount an AIM-7 on a CF-18 at Aviano. (CF CKD99-2067-04)

Cpl Mitch Kain and MCpl John Edelman do the final armament checks on '753. Safety pins are being pulled and arming mechanisms set. (CF CKD99-2041-07)

Hornet '795 festooned in honour of the Toronto Maple Leafs who, at the time, were fighting their way through the National Hockey League post-season. Then, Aviano ball hockey fans Cpl Frank Mayer, MCpl John Piercey, CWO Bill Atkinson and a fourth unknown player in a face-off. (CF CKD99-2053-09, '04)

Besides hockey, raging volleyball contests were fought daily on the Balkan Rats courts. (CF CKD99-2115-03)

Pilot Profile — "Brass"

One of LCol Flynn's Balkan Rats was Capt Travis Brassington. Having been raised in Victoria, where his father was an air traffic controller, he first flew while a member of 676 "Kittyhawk" Air Cadet Squadron. As a cadet he earned glider and powered flying licences. Later he trained on the Musketeer at Portage la Prairie, then advanced to Moose Jaw, flying the Tutor there first on June 25, 1993. The following May he graduated at the top of the class.

Capt Travis Brassington looking fired-up after a mission as he signals "Shack!" – the sign for "bull's eye". (CF CKD99-2070-03)

Since there were few CF-18 training slots at Cold Lake for pipeline students, a lengthy wait followed at Moose Jaw in "H" Flight ("H" for "Hotel"). This was a good opportunity to get in some extra Tutor flying. Finally, in December 1995 Lt Brassington started his "FLIT" (fighter lead-in) course. Since 419 Squadron had been stood down, Canada had no adequate fighter lead-in trainer, so the Tutor filled in for the CF-5 until 419 Squadron later re-formed with BAe Hawks. Brassington's FLIT course lasted into March 1996, then he did some OJT at Cold Lake with Maple Flag. Finally, he got his 410 slot and, on July 26, 1996 flew the CF-18.

Having graduated on April 17, 1997, Brassington was posted to 441, then under LCol Dave Burt. He quickly discovered just how good life could be on an operational squadron, especially with deployments. That October, for example, "Brass" was at Holloman AFB, training with the Luftwaffe FWIC. On February 1, 1998, 441 provided four Hornets (Capts Travis Brassington, Paul Dimitriou, Leath Greenwood, Garry Venman) for a fly-past over Calgary honouring the Canadian Winter Olympic team. This was especially memorable since Capt Brassington's son, Riley, was born that same day.

March 1998 was typically busy at 441, including DACT at Luke AFB. That spring 441 also participated in Maple Flag. Meanwhile, the squadron was mindful of its upcoming tour at Aviano, so participated in a large-scale night bombing exercise at Hill AFB in Utah in September 1998, honing skills that would be needed in Kosovo. 441 returned to Holloman in November for more support of the German FWIC. Ex. Island Reach of February 1999 saw 441 in Comox, sharpening up for a TacEval, much of the emphasis being on NATO operational doctrine. Now, Capts Brassington and Les "Kosmo" Racicot were briefed to fly the first 4 Wing Hornets to Aviano (the 441 advance party had reached Aviano on March 20). Racicot, however, was redirected for duties in the Op. Allied Force Combined Air Operations Centre (CAOC) in Vicenza, near Aviano. This slightly ticked off "Brass" and "Kosmo", who had been planning a whiskey tour in Scotland, while en route. In a new scenario, on March 26, 2000 Capts Brassington, Brett "Laser" Glaeser and (spare) Maj Steve "Snatch" Langille departed 4 Wing for Goose Bay. On the 27th "Brass" and "Laser" pushed on to Iceland, escorted by C-130 AAR (435 Sqn), while "Snatch" returned to Cold Lake. On the 28th the two Hornets flew to RAF Kinloss, Scotland, thence to Ramstein, Germany. They reached Aviano on the 29th.

Next day "Brass" and "Laser" were scheduled for mandatory briefings in the CAOC. Tired from their trip, however, they overslept and had to be rousted from their beds. Once in Vicenza they were briefed about such things as the big strategic picture, the Rules of Engagement (ROE), and the legal facts of life, i.e. legal when it came to dropping bombs on which targets. Never before had something like "collateral damage" been so important as in this theatre. Meanwhile, the rest of 441 was positioning to Holland to support a NATO exercise that had been planned before the outbreak of combat operations. Exercise support subsequently was cancelled and the 4 Wing jets and most 441 aircrew then deployed to Aviano. It was April 4 before Capt Brassington operated from there, flying a night mission against a radio relay station. Airborne for three hours, he refuelled from a KC-135 before bombing the target with two GBU-12s. Upon landing, he was an official "Balkan Bat" – a CF-18 pilot who had flown a night mission.

Through his time at Aviano, Brassington would log 27 missions for 135 combat flying hours. His longest mission (May 12, 1999 – a 7.9-hour CAP) was flown with Capt Racicot. In 2003 "Brass" recalled some images from his Aviano tour. As to AAR, he usually found himself behind an RAF L.1011 – there always seemed to be a "Ten Eleven" nearby, flying its "racetrack" pattern and topping up fighters from a steady queue. When not bombing, he was on a CAP. On these his Hornet might be reconfigured with the FLIR pod downloaded and replaced with an extra missile. Although several enemy aircraft would be shot down by NATO fighters during the Kosovo air campaign, the nearest Brassington would come to CAP action was being vectored onto a bogie that turned out to be a civilian aircraft. Other memories included incomparable Adriatic sunsets that eased the boredom of an arduous mission. On May 5 Capt Brassington witnessed the only USAF F-16 to be lost in action take its SAM hit. Overall he compared Kosovo with a typical Maple Flag, except for the night missions, the accelerated pace, and the caution needed in the face of Serb defences.

"Brass" with some Balkan Rats sidekicks (all 441 except for one). Standing are LCmdr Mark "Fisk" Carlton (441's USN exchange), Capt Brassington, Capt Les "Kosmo" Racicot, LCol Flynn, Capt Rob "Crack" Carter and Capt Jan "Trigger" Reudiseuli (441's RNLAF exchange). In front are Capt Todd "Piper" Sinclair and Maj Georges "Chicken" Bertrand (416). (CF CKD99-2024-20)

Flaps and arrester hook down and carrying a formidable warload, a CF-18 lands at Aviano. The basic picture is all here – AIM-9s on the wingtips, PGMs underwing, an AIM-7 on the starboard nacelle, the FLIR pod on the opposite side, and "triple jugs". Occasionally, a pilot was obliged to return to base with such a load, the mission having been scrubbed at some point, even at the last second. Countless WWII RCAF Bomber Command log books carry the ideal entry for such a mission: "DNCO" – duty not carried out. In the second view, the photographer catches the Hornet moments later as it hammers onto the runway. (CF CKD99-2034-01, '02)

Balkan Rats with the PM. Standing are Capts Jason "Fudge" Paquin, Wayne "Karp" Karperian, Maj Murray "Forrest" Carlson, Capts Patrice "Cervix" Hervieux, Scott "Hen" Henson, Maj Shaun "Burner" Byrne, Capt Jason "Duke" Smith, Maj Georges "Chicken" Bertrand, Capts Leath "Lothar" Greenwood, Rick "Slick" Williams, Jim "Preston" Manning, Maj Brian "Mur" Murray, Capts Francis "Squint" Mercier, Chris "Nomad" Larouche, Miles "Milhouse" Selby, John "Nod" Totti, Lee "Midas" Vogan, Blais "Blaze" Frawley, Maj Steve "Swill" Will, Capt John "Jabba" Hutt. In front are Majs Neil "Gramps" McDermid, Yves "YVs" Tessier, Pierre "Tubbs" Ruel, Glen "Flaps" Phillips, LCol Flynn, PM Jean "da Big Boss" Chrétien, Col André Viens, Maj Steve "Snatch" Langille, Capts Dave "Prowler" Prowal and Jordan "Kato" Kirbyson. (CF CKD99-2105-10)

Snatch

Maj Steve "Snatch" Langille joined the Canadian Forces in Fredericton in 1987. He first trained on the Musketeer at Portage la Prairie in December 1988, flew the Tutor in April 1989 then, beginning in July 1990, was on his CF-5 course at 419. In January 1991 he began CF-18 training at 410, from where he graduated the following August, then was posted to 421 Squadron at Baden. When 421 disbanded in March 1992, Capt Langille served briefly at 439. With them he flew in Op. Rhine Prosit (Canada's remaining CF-18s leaving Germany for home). He then joined 441, during which tour he completed the FWIC course at 410. Next came a tour with 433 at Bagotville (for 1998 he was the 3 Wing Hornet demo pilot). In 2001 Maj Langille joined 419 Squadron to instruct Canadian and other NATO fighter pilots on the Hawk. In February 2004 he reminisced about Aviano:

The date was early May 1999, the time was just before 4 AM. As a wake-up call penetrated my sleep, it took a few seconds to remember

Capts Steve Langille (left) and Dave Wheeler flight plan at Baden-Soellingen during Op. Rhine Prosit, January 18, 1993. Both had been flying Hornets with 421 Squadron, but now were 439 "Pussy Cats" (421 having stood down). In 2004 Langille was instructing on Hawks at 419 Squadron, while Wheeler was commanding 410 Squadron. (Larry Milberry)

where I was and what I was doing here. The place was Aviano and I was about to start my second day of Operation Allied Force. I had been in theatre about a week, after flying a CF-18 from Cold Lake to Aviano. Having completed my first combat mission a few days earlier, I was ready for another. While the pilots scheduled for today's mission had been sleeping, others had been busy through the night, assembling maps and intelligence, and meeting with representatives from the other units in the mission "package" (to provide structure and control for any such operation, aircraft were grouped into packages to ensure mutual support and overall success). Today's package would number some 30 aircraft, including four CF-18s each carrying two 2000-lb laser-guided bombs.

The mission planners covered all issues affecting the package. Knowing our TOT (time on target), they could work back to create a timeline. They determined, for example, when we would leave our tanker to RV with the rest of our package. They then calculated the time needed to reach the tanker, and the time from take-off to tanker RV. With take-off established, finally they determined the timing for such essentials as mission planning and briefings, going right back to the pilots' wake up calls. With all this accomplished, the planners could hand the details to the crews flying the missions.

Getting Psyched Up

After acknowledging my wake-up call, I took a few precious minutes to collect my thoughts. I had been flying the CF-18 for almost 10 years, had trained throughout North America and Europe, was a graduate of the Fighter Weapons Instructor Course, and had that first combat sortie under my belt. I felt confident. Although serious and important thoughts, such as about my wife and kids back home, filtered through my mind, I laughed as I remembered the fighter pilot prayer of "Please Lord, don't let me screw up".

After meeting with the other members of my formation, we headed for the squadron to start our work day. Today I would be No.3 of a CF-18 4-ship within the overall package. Soon we were busy in the flight planning trailer. Our two wingmen, No.2 and No.4, would be responsible for preparing the mission log card and enroute procedures. Meanwhile, Lead and I took the target information from mission planning and began working out our detailed attack plan. Our targets were two bridges. Lead and No.2 would hit the first; I and No.4 would hit the second. After looking at the maps and talking to the Intel guys, we determined that the targets should easily be identified and were lightly defended.

Next, we combined our individual tasks and prepared for the mission briefing. Intel gave us an update on the situation and the Duty Ops Officer confirmed that our task had not changed. Lead began a thorough account of the mission we were about to fly. A lot of the material such as take-off, transit to the tanker, refuelling, etc. was considered "SOP", but there was plenty of information that gripped our attention. We focused carefully on how to react should enemy fighters or SAMs appear, and how we would find our target and employ our laser-guided bombs.

Getting It Right

In "Allied Force" there were serious legal issues, so military lawyers were part of mission planning. They were here to help us complete our missions, so as to never see the inside of a courtroom. A big concern was about bombing accuracy. Since we were using laser-guided bombs, we could achieve amazing accuracy, resulting in minimal collateral damage. The lawyers helped us look at our targets, and ensure that collateral damage would fall within our ROEs. Thus was a variety of "what ifs" carefully discussed during mission planning. For example, should we find our bridges just sitting there in the clear, the situation would be simple – attack and be on our way. But how did the ROEs address more complex scenarios, e.g. people and equipment on a bridge? Might those people be military, non-combatants, or whom? I would develop a respect for our legal staff, who helped us understand such issues.

On with the Mission

Finally, we began suiting up, something that was second nature. For a combat sortie, however, there were a few extra steps compared to a training mission. For one thing we "sanitized" our flight suits, removing all items except for our "name, rank and serial number". Also, each pilot carried extra combat survival gear that could come in handy if down in enemy territory. A 9-mm pistol was standard issue. Placing mine into its holster was another reminder that these missions were anything but routine. Finally came a last-minute brief by Intel, and a quick weather update from the Duty Ops Officer. Then we were driven out to our jets. For me this was when my nerves started working in double time. Even though I reminded myself that I was here to do a job, I couldn't forget that the enemy would be doing his best to spoil my day. Yes, there were a few butterflies but, having already completed one sortie, I knew they would fade once I strapped in and got my engines running.

Once out at the jets we stored our maps and equipment, then came the age old process – the "walk-around". What was interesting at Aviano was how such a routine could become one of my strongest memories. Although the ordnance adorning my Hornet were impressive (AIM-7, AIM-9, 20-mm cannon, FLIR targeting pod, and two 2000-lb laser-guided bombs), what stuck in my mind was the ground crew. Although we chatted back and forth as always, the conversation would come around to the mission at hand, and how busy we would be dealing with enemy defenses. We were well aware that just a few days before a USAF squadron down the hangar line had lost an F-16 to a SAM. On each of my combat missions my start crew made a point of shaking hands and wishing me a safe trip – they were concerned and wanted us all home safely.

After the walk-around I got comfortable in the cockpit and started the engines. Then, once we four were satisfied that all systems were working as advertised, we taxied to the arming point. There our techs completed the first step in arming our aircraft, ensuring that safety switches were in position to allow each weapon to function. Training with practice weapons this was no big deal but, with "hot" missiles, bombs, cannon, chaff and flares, it took longer. Next, we taxied to position and Lead and No.2 got airborne. It was now time for me to light the burners and get the show on the road. In a few minutes we joined as a 4-ship and headed down the Adriatic for about an hour to rendezvous with our tanker. Since our package was not the only one involved today, many tankers were airborne. With a quick word from our AWACS controller we received a radar vector and an altitude where we would find our tanker. As we approached, we could see many contacts on radar. After a few selections of our HOTAS (Hands on Throttle and Stick) controls, we spotted our tanker, a big Lockheed L1011. All around were other tankers with fighters in tow.

I was happy that we were going to "plug" into an L1011 and not a KC-135, for many a fighter pilot has been "slapped" by that lady.

Tanking usually took more than one "poke" per aircraft. After each of us topped up, we stuck by our tanker, awaiting our package RV time. Otherwise, we had a bit of extra time built in at the tanker, lest we encounter anything unforeseen. But all went as planned today. Lead had us rotate through the L1011 one more time to "top up" for, we all agreed, if we met enemy fighters or SAMs, we'd appreciate the extra time in afterburner that this last-minute gas would give.

The Real Deal

Once en route to our package RV point, each of us activated the master arming switch in the cockpit. Now, all that was necessary would be to select the weapon with our HOTAS control and press the trigger. As we checked in on the tactical frequency, it was clear that the mission was a "go", so we pushed towards our targets, assuming a tactical "card" formation, aligned as if in a square with a jet at each corner. With a couple of miles between each Hornet, we had enough room to maneuver if evading an incoming SAM. At the same time we were close enough to cover each other's 6 o'clock.

After crossing into Kosovo, the only indication that we were in enemy territory was the position of the aircraft symbol on our moving map on the centre computer console. From mission planning, we already had an idea of the location and type of defences arrayed against us. Thus did we select our altitude, speed and heading to avoid as many such threats as possible. Eventually, our package began to fan out, each element formation heading to its individual targets. Since ours were about 10 miles apart, we could stick together, enjoying mutual support almost to the end of our attack run. As we neared our targets, we conducted a detailed radar search– we didn't want to be surprised by enemy fighters, while dropping our bombs.

As we neared the bridges, we switched from air-to-air to air-to-ground radar mode and began searching for our target environment. The advantage of attacking a large bridge is that it normally spans a river. In this case, the river stood out on radar and we quickly spotted the first target. Next, we passed our targeting solution from the radar to the FLIR pod, which senses infrared energy and displays its imagery as shades of green on one of our computer displays. By now I had accelerated almost to Mach 1 – about eight miles a minute. I could see the target on my FLIR. I aimed at one end of the bridge, my wingman at the other.

The basic steps in our attack sequence now were complete. Still, in the final moments I began questioning whether or not I had made all the right selections. Yes... my master arm switch was "live". Yes... my laser was armed. Yes... everything looked right. I checked a third and fourth time before feeling sure that everything was perfect. Another part of my brain was processing the ROE. I had found the target, but now had to ensure that I met with my conditions for weapons release. After sanitizing the area below, I was sure that I had the correct target. In a flash my mind returned for a moment to the fighter pilot prayer, then I pressed the pickle button. The computer display indicated a release symbology and I felt 4000 pounds of bombs drop.

Now I had to ensure that the weapons guided to the aiming point. As I continued to close on the target, the clarity of my FLIR image improved. This allowed me to further refine my aim point, and continue to assess the ROE for compliance. Even at this stage I could, if necessary, steer the bombs off target into a safe area (the river would be handy). Suddenly, about 15 seconds from bomb impact, I noticed a dark patch on the bridge close to my aim point. I couldn't believe it, since everything had been going so well. I had only an instant to decide. As I was processing the information, I remembered from the Intel photos that the bridge had been targeted before. In that attack it had been damaged, so had a few small craters on its surface. As I analyzed my display, I saw that the dark patches were not vehicles or people, but the craters. I was now completely satisfied that I had met the ROE, and fine-tuned my aim point on the bridge.

Moments later my display blossomed – the bombs had struck. In a second or two my wingman's bombs also found their aim point and the target was destroyed. I quickly selected A/A on my radar, jinked through the sky lest targeted by AAA, and scanned my partner's Six. With a quick call to Lead of "Target destroyed", we selected 'burner and climbed away. As we headed for friendly territory, we all rejoined and egressed Kosovo at supersonic speed. As we crossed the border and selected our armament switches to "Safe", the reality that we had completed our objective started to sink in. Nonetheless, this was no time to get cocky and have a lapse of attention.

Home in One Piece

Soon we were back on the ground in Aviano. As we climbed out of the jets after four hours aloft, our CO was there to introduce us to a TV crew from back home wanting to interview a few pilots back from a mission. We were happy to help but, due to security, had to keep our helmets on with our dark visors down. Even so, I knew that my wife and family would recognize my voice and know that I was doing okay. By the time debrief was complete, 10 hours had passed since our day had begun. We heard through Intel that, although we hadn't seen any enemy activity (AAA is hard to see during the day), there had been plenty of radar and AAA action en route (it would be a few more days before I had the chance to see the "white trail in the sky" – a SAM searching for a fighter to sink its teeth into). Now we had a chance to eat, celebrate our success, and relax for a few hours before heading back to bed. Tomorrow was another day, another mission and another chance to tempt fate and do the job for which we had been trained. By the end of the war, I would be happy and relieved that everyone in Task Force Aviano got home safe and sound. We finished our Allied Force without a single loss.

A Tech Looks Back

In 2004 Cpl Bill Chisholm recorded a few memories of 441's early Hornet years, then of his own Aviano tour:

During the closure of Canada's bases in Europe, I learned of my new posting that was due to commence in 1993 – I would be joining 441 Tactical Fighter Squadron. On reaching Cold Lake, I was made to feel very welcome by my new squadron. What struck me right away was the great atmosphere in Hangar 3, 441's freshly painted home. It was evident just how high morale was in Hangar 3, compared to almost anywhere else on base.

Having spent 11 of my 38 years with 441, I can safely call the squadron my home, especially given today's shrinking Canadian Forces. There are people here with whom I had gone through basic training at Cornwallis in 1984, others from my TQ3 courses in Borden, and a few who were with me here in the 1980s at 410 Squadron, or at 421 and 439 in Baden.

I arrived in 1993 to a sad time – well-known 441 member, Joe Bogden, recently had passed away. Soon, however, I saw the spirit with which 441 celebrated his life. This showed itself in other ways, too, as with the first 441 sports day I attended – that was the first time I ever saw people try driving a golf cart up a tree! After 441 golfers Glen and Donny left the base, it was some time before the squadron was welcomed back to Cold Lake's "Palm Springs" course.

As an experienced IE Tech, it seemed like a lot of deployments came my way in a short time. In time 441 would show me the world from Hawaii to Italy. Many of our deployments were "firsts". I was on the first of many to Luke AFB, our first and only (so far) to NAS Oceana, Virginia, the first to Holloman AFB to train with the German Air Force, the first (and, hopefully, not the last) to Ex. RIM-PAC at Hickham AFB, Hawaii, and DACT with our sister squadron from Hill AFB in Utah.

It hasn't always been fun and games, as with those TDs to Las Vegas, courses in Ottawa, and weekend trips to Whitehorse and Salinas, California. There also has been severe weather to endure, and long hours in places like Inuvik, and at Comox to train for Op. Echo in Aviano. Along the way the Air Force implemented a trade restructuring in which many traditional trades disappeared. Through that ill-conceived plan I became a weapons loader.

Aviano in 1999 was the highlight of my career. While there I did some interviews with newspapers, radio and CTV. I distinctly remember telling the media: "I trained all my life to do just this." Hearing, only three weeks into Op Echo, that my wife was pregnant with our second child, made it really easy to make the CTV reporter cry. Another Aviano "war story" that we armourers like to re-tell is how, after slaving away to upload our Hornets with one type of bombs, someone would change the mission profile. Now we would have to "drop" the first weapons, then load new ones. It used to make our Commanding Officer cry when the armourers would claim that we had dropped more bombs in our first few weeks at Aviano than had the pilots!

Post-Aviano and 441 Squadron members gather for the presentation of the "PAS 23" painting. Standing are Cpl Dave McCorriston, Cpl Athanasios Mavridis, MCpl Jean Demarais, Cpl Leon Hynes, MCpl Ron Pischke, Sgt John Rose, Cpl Doug Zylenko, MCpl John Piercey, WO Greg Cryderman, Cpl Brad Ethier, Cpl Terry Lucy, Cpl Steff Dion, Cpl Joe Poirier and CWO Bill Atkinson. In front are Cpl Scott Trudell, Ardell Borgeois (artist from Kelowna), Cpl Chisholm and Capt Kirk Soroka. (CF CKC01-0225-06)

"PAS 23"

Protected Aircraft Shelter 23 at Aviano was our primary maintenance facility. There we stored our tools and shared some of the most memorable events of our lives. After the conflict a painting to commemorate this was commissioned. The painting captures the atmosphere on a typical day in Aviano during the first half of Operation Allied Force.

Since many bombing missions were carried out at night, we had to pay attention to detail at all times, particularly when we spun and parked two or three Hornets in an area no bigger than a kids' outdoor hockey rink. The well-lit PAS in the background was a welcomed shelter when doing major repairs. However, most of our work on "before and after flight checks", and on minor snags, was done outside in what seemed like a continuous downpour. Nevertheless, ground crew spirits were high and our dedication unquestionable. This became especially clear when, following two successive ground aborts by our CO, LCol Flynn, he was able to climb back into the quickly repaired original jet, and fulfill his mission.

Over the years 441 proved that it can be dropped into any situation and get the job done. We pride ourselves in being "spectacular on the road". Aviano was no different and it was 441 who gave the Balkan Rats their reputation (even though Task Force Aviano included many personnel from other CF units). Despite never-ending shifts, extreme weather changes, shortages of people, parts and bombs, with 2% of the combat aircraft available in theatre we succeeded in launching over 10% of all Allied Force bombing missions. All this was done from a 2-desk shelter on the side of PAS 23.

On Remembrance Day following the conflict I was invited to speak to a high school assembly about my experiences in Aviano. When challenged by a brash teen about my "6 month Italian vacation", I was quick to point out that many of us had spent more time in our rain gear in the first 6 weeks in Italy than we had in our beds. Standing in that rain on an active taxiway, waiting "to safety" the air-to-air missiles and/or unexpended bombs from our returning aircraft was no job for the faint of heart. I pointed out how our maintenance personnel had worked tirelessly to produce a staggering 99.4% aircraft availability rate, second to none among the Allies. Yes, the Silver Foxes had played an integral part in the success of Op. Allied Force, and made all of Canada proud by doing more with less than any other nation involved.

LCol Flynn Leads the Balkan Rats Home

Task Force Aviano CAP missions of June 1999 were a sign that the air war was near done – the Serbs were beaten, so the bombing had petered out. Then, even the CAPs subsided. By war's end the Balkan Rat with the most war missions was Maj Rob Parker, credited officially with 31.

Task Force Aviano and 3 Wing CF-18s following the July 1, 1999 Canada Day flypast. Then, Balkan Rats Hornet '770 taxiing at Ottawa airport on the same day, the nation's colours proudly flying. (Andrew Cline)

LCol Flynn leads the Balkan Rats 12-ship over Parliament Hill on Canada Day 1999. (Vic Johnson)

LCol Flynn gets a well-deserved "Welcome home, dad!" from his son Bret. The 4 Wing Balkan Rats had just landed home at Cold Lake. (Edmonton Journal)

Balkan Rats pilots in Ottawa for Canada Day. Standing are Capts Jordan Kirbyson, Jim Manning, Brad Williamson, Chris Larouche and Blaise Frawley, Majs Pierre Ruel, Georges Bertrand and Francis Mercier, Capt Lee Vogan, Maj Jason Regenwetter, Maj Anthony Ledsham and Capt John Hutt. In front are Capt Dave Prowal, Maj Yves Tessier, LCol Sylvain Faucher, LCol Billie Flynn, Majs Glen Phillips, Jean Guilbeault and Neil McDermid. (Andrew Cline)

Other high mission pilots were Maj Glen Phillips (28), Capt Travis Brassington (27) and LCol Flynn (25).

With the cessation of hostilities on June 20, 1999, Canada's presence in Aviano shrank and 12 of its 18 CF-18s flew home. On June 27 they departed in three formations. LCol Flynn flew in 188745 first to Kinloss in 3.5 hours, then to Keflavik in 2.8 and a night's rest. Next day they flew to Bagotville in 4.8 hours. On Canada Day, July 1, 1999 Flynn led 12 Hornets over Parliament Hill in a salute to the nation. Next day those destined to Cold Lake flew there via Winnipeg. In 2004 Flynn took a retrospective look at this period:

The greatest part of the return home story was the "coup" of getting permission to do the flypast over Parliament Hill on Canada Day 1999. As the war was coming to an end, Prime Minister Jean Chretien detoured from a European trip to visit the Balkan Rats. Knowing that a return of 12 Hornets was already being planned, I made a deal with Col André "Kermit" Viens, TFA Commander in Vicenza, an old 409 Squadron mate, and a superb fighter pilot. If I could convince the PM to invite us to fly over Parliament Hill, Viens would let me return to lead the formation. I set to work on the project as soon as the PM's party landed, first with his Chief of Staff, then with Mme Chretien and, finally, with the accompanying Members of Parliament. By the end of the visit, when I finally met the PM, everyone was on board. The PM heartily supported the idea that Canadians would be proud to see their CF-18s return from combat on Canada Day. On his way out to the Airbus the PM told the CDS, General Baril, of the plan. By all accounts, the CDS did not seem impressed by TFA's coup, and while there were naysayers in the various staffs at home, it was hard to turn down a direct request by the PM.

On 1 July 1999 I led 12 Hornets (with airborne spare) from Bagotville to Ottawa with as many Balkan Rats jets as we could muster. In the formation was LCol Sylvain Faucher, the CO of 425 whom I had replaced early in the Kosovo conflict. While it was a glorious day in Ottawa, I had good Intel not to be early over the "Hill". The final part of the ceremony included a choir of deaf children signing "O Canada" live on TV, and it was feared that the thundering Hornets would take away from this unique moment, should we appear in the middle of their performance. So, with remarkable luck, we screamed overhead 15 seconds late and everyone was happy. The Master of Ceremonies that day was astronaut Julie Payette.

My return to Cold Lake lasted less than 24 hours, but was one of the most poignant moments of the combat experience. My personal focus throughout my Aviano time was on again seeing my 5-year old son, Bret. Before each mission, as I sanitized my flight gear, I would remove his picture from my wallet and steel myself not to let the Serbs have a chance at me. The enemy was not going to prevent me from seeing my son again. On 2 July we flew six Hornets back to Cold Lake, stopping in Winnipeg for fuel. After a flypast there we landed at home. As I taxied in, I saw Bret among the welcome crowd in front of 441 Squadron, waving a Canadian flag. When I stepped off the ladder, he ran up and hugged me with roses in his hand.

Now that the Balkan Rats were safely home and the mission was accomplished, holding my son in my arms was a very emotional moment that brought closure to this incredible adventure. While the press was keen to speak with the aviators, I was more interest in playing with a my little boy. Later the press provided me with two photos of this unforgettable return: Bret's flag waving and the welcome hug. These now are mounted on a wall in my house, along with a Canadian flag that flew with me on every combat mission.

Unfortunately for father and son, I had to leave early next morning to get back to Aviano and finish my tour of duty. I returned home for good in late July.

LCol Flynn's War

Date	Hornet	Mission	Details	Time
April				
11	188770	CAS	No drop	4.1
13	188770	CAS	4 x Mk.82	3.6
17	188733	BAI	1 x GBU-12	3.0
19	188753	BAI	weather abort	3.3
22	188790	BAI	6 x Mk.82	3.5
28	188793	BAI	2 x GBU-12	3.5
30	188781	BAI	2 x GBU-12	3.3
May				
2	188733	BAI	weather abort	3.3
3	188795	BAI	4 x Mk.82	3.4
5	188790	BAI	2 x GBU-10	4.1
7	188780	BAI	weather abort	3.2
10	188733	BAI	weather abort	3.3
12	188733	BAI	weather abort	4.6
17	188733	BAI	2 x GBU-12	4.3
21	188795	BAI	2 x GBU-12	3.3
24	188746	BAI	2 x GBU-10	2.8
25	188776	BAI	2 x GBU-10	2.9
26	188785	BAI	2 x GBU-10	3.5
29	188789	BAI	2 x GBU-10	3.7
30	188789	BAI	no drop	2.8
June				
3	188785	BAI	2 x GBU-12	2.5
6	188795	CAP*		5.3
15	188798	CAP		4.2
17	188798	CAP		4.2
19	188793	CAP		3.5

*combat air patrol

In Retrospect

In 2004 LCol (Retired) Billie Flynn looked back on the highlight of his career as a fighter pilot:

In the end, what would stand out most when Task Force Aviano's job was done is the contribution of the officers, and men and women of 441 Squadron. They had led at every level during the deployment. The leadership, the stunning performance of the ground crew, the amazing efforts of our logistics personnel – all were the result of Silver Foxes turning up the heat. There did not exist another unit capable of performing at that level, sustained for that period of time. Unfortunately, they did not get the credit for their efforts in the long run. While the name "Balkan Rats" served us well, in the end I regretted that 441 Squadron and its superb people did not receive the recognition that they so richly reserved.

In Balkan Rats pilots. In front are Maj Neil "Gramps" McDermid (black cap), Capt Jan "Trigger" Reudiseuli, Maj Rob "Hooker" Parker, Maj Steve "Swill" Will, Capt Rob "Crack" Carter, Capt Lee "Midas" Vogan, Capt Travis "Brass" Brassington, Capt Brent "Sparky" Sparks (straw hat), Capt Daniel "Spoon" Dionne, LCol Flynn and Capt Chris "Nomad" Larouche. The Balkan Rats held their first reunion June 18 - 20, 2004 at Cold Lake. (CF CKD99-2097-29)

It Wasn't Perfect

Even though they would be viewed by their Op. Allied Force peers as top professionals, the Balkan Rats had their limitations, since the CF-18 was not fully "interoperable" for such a campaign. CF-18s were not "NVG" compatible, so missions were flown at a relatively higher risk. (NVGs, which cost only about $20,000 per cockpit, would not be evaluated on a CF squadron until April 2001 and would not reach service until late 2004).

Earlier (1990 - 91) Canada's CF-18s had gone to war in the Persian Gulf without the means to communicate with US Naval air defences. This equipment was loaned by the US and installed in-theatre. Gulf War CF-18s also lacked jam-resistant Have Quick-type radios and, in Aviano, still did not have them. Without such radios TFA pilots knew one thing for sure – the Serbs always knew they were coming. Meanwhile, all aircraft in a package had to use single-frequency, jammable radios if CF-18s were involved.

TFA reached Aviano with insufficient FLIR targeting pods – Canada had only 13 Nite Hawk "B" model FLIR pods, but 18 CF-18s. The Balkan Rats were able to borrow a few extra pods.

GPS in the CF-18 would have permitted greater FLIR pod precision, but TFA did not have GPS.

Canada did not have AMRAAMs in Aviano, only less capable AIM-7s and AIM-9s. The AMRAAM is superior to both in terms of speed, manoeuvrability, reliability and resistance to ECM. Its active radar guidance system allows a pilot to launch multiple AMRAAMs simultaneously and immediately go about other business. With the AIM-7, however, the attacking pilot must guide each missile to its target.

Task Force Aviano also was obliged to improvise at every turn. Logistical support was minimal and there were not enough bombs – TFA had to scrounge them from the Americans. Finally, by the time of the Kosovo air campaign, Canada had no aerial tankers, having earlier retired its Boeing 707 tankers. Since then, and until the delivery of its first of two Airbus tankers, Canada's CF-18s depended on its allies for strategic AAR.

Well Done, Task Force Aviano

Sixty-nine CF-18 pilots became Balkan Rats, i.e. by flying at least one Allied Force mission. That represented nearly the whole strength of Canada's combat ready fighter force. The Balkan Rats would lead half of the international packages where CF-18s were involved. Nevertheless, the Canadian public was (and remains) generally uninformed about Op. Echo and Op. Allied Force. LCol Flynn explained this to Hugh Halliday in August 2001:

The lack of recognition of the efforts of those people lies with the CF and the Air Force itself. We, the institution, kept the press out and the VIPs away, so that we could focus on our mission and as I would say, "Kick their asses and win the war". Colonel Davies expressly denied access to all but the key VIPs. I supported much of that but, in the end, no one knew what was going on, or to what level Canadians were sharing the brunt of the responsibility for the conduct of the air war. The PR people were so worried about the reaction of the Serb population in Canada, that they even tried to prevent public access to us in Ottawa on Canada Day after we landed from our post-war flypast over Parliament Hill. We should learn from this experience and be more intelligent about how we conduct ourselves in the future.

LCol Flynn was disappointed when only two Meritorious Service Medals were awarded to Canadians following Operation Allied Force. It was especially galling that only one medal went to an active line officer, Maj Rob Parker. Not one medal was accorded to TFA support staff. In his article "No Medals for Kosovo" in Airforce magazine (Summer 2001, some edited excerpts shown here), Flynn voiced his opinion:

> My men, who shouldered a greater responsibility in combat than Canadians have for decades, got nothing. Tell me when the last time was that a Canadian was allowed to plan and lead a mass strike into combat? Certainly this did not happen in the Gulf War (we were relegated to the back of the pack)... One of the greatest testaments to how well the flights were led is that we seldom allowed ourselves to get shot at. The Serbs were always up and ready, and often we attacked directly into the face of SA-6 and SA-3 surface-to-air missiles. I personally led a day mission to the main airport of Montenegro, where we stared right into the SA-6s. However, unlike our American friends, we kept our tactics and our flying focused, reducing, to the best we could, the opportunities for them to take shots at us.
>
> Many of our colleagues were not as lucky or smart. One of my fellow squadron commanders at Aviano got himself a parachute ride down and a helicopter ride home out of Serbia, leaving his F-16 behind, for not executing the prescribed tactics. One of our A-10 comrades returned from Kosovo minus one engine, then had to land in Skopje, Macedonia because he executed his tactics wrongly...
>
> I am very happy as a CO not to have had to accompany a body home from this conflict. I cite the brilliant airmanship and leadership in the air of my flight leads as a primary reason for our "no losses" record.
>
> While the Brits may have flown 1000 strike sorties, their share of the risk and danger was measurably less than ours, as you will see when you break down the types of missions flown, the kind of ordnance dropped, and Canadians' leadership positions during individual strikes. For example, the Brits dropped laser-guided bombs also. But virtually every time they used a "buddy lasing" technique. With this one aircraft would find the target and designate the desired point with its laser pod. The second or third jet then would drop its bombs and allow the first to guide the bombs to their target. In other words it took two or three aircraft to do the destructive work of one CF-18.
>
> CF-18 pilots carried two laser guided bombs per mission. Each pilot found the target with his FLIR and radar systems, designated it himself, then dropped and guided the weapon to its desired point of impact – without the help of a buddy. Meanwhile, the pilot had to evade detection by Serb SAMs, look out for AAA fire and, in many cases, continue to lead his mass attack formation through the target area and home. Most importantly for this conflict, the bombs had to be precisely guided to their impact point, since the collateral damage potential in civilian-populated areas was high.
>
> The CF-18 bombing record was better than most other nations. Considering the technological limitations of our bomb guidance units, and the relatively poor capability of the 4-power magnification of the FLIR pod, I think that this is remarkable. The workload was easily twice that of the 2-man Tornado (i.e. 4 aircrew versus 1) dropping the same number of bombs. Yet, in the Brit stats, all airplanes in the formation counted as strike aircraft, even though half dropped nothing. Imagine also that only the Canadians and Americans planned and led missions into Kosovo and Serbia proper ... The workload and leadership in the air is dramatically different when you are a Brit or French unit, flying in the middle of the pack, compared to the Canadian up front in his single-seat fighter orchestrating and executing leadership decisions about when and where to go, who turns back, who attacks what, how AWACS is integrated, what to do for all fall-out cases, and the list goes on. At no time did the Brits ever shoulder any of that responsibility. The NATO Package Commanders from the Balkan Rats did so all the time.
>
> I am very proud to have had the honour and privilege of commanding such fine men and women in combat. The record of the Balkan Rats is stellar. I doubt that we as an Air Force will again perform to such a high standard, in such difficult conditions, without having to pay a greater price in terms of human sacrifice.

Meritorious Service Medal

For his contributions during Allied Force, Maj Robert "Hooker" Parker received the Meritorious Service Medal. The MSM (Military) had been created in 1991 to honour Canadian Forces members for particular achievements, or for deeds covering a specified period). Parker had joined the Canadian Forces as a "Mil-Col" student in July 1982. After completing his studies, he followed the usual route for an aspiring fighter pilot, eventually finishing at 410 Squadron and joining 441 in January 1989. His career included a tour in Belgium in the NATO Tactical Leadership Program. There he was an air-to-air seminar leader covering such topics as building force packages. From the TLP, Parker returned to 441 where, at various times, he was SWATO, DCO and Ops Officer. Following Allied Force, by when he had logged some 2500 CF-18 hours, he attended CF

Maj Rob Parker, who received the MSM for a job well done in Aviano. (CF CKD99-2097-09)

Staff College in Toronto, then was posted to the "fighter shop" at 1 CAD HQ in Winnipeg. News of Maj Parker's MSM (M) was announced on November 30, 2000, the citation observing:

> Maj Parker served on Task Force Aviano from 20 March 1999 to 15 June 1999. During 31 combat missions that he flew as part of Operation Allied Force, he was frequently selected to plan, brief and lead NATO formations comprising over 40 aircraft from several nations. As the Weapons officer, he played a crucial role in the training and qualification of Task Force Aviano personnel in the use of a new weapon, in the midst of an intense, round-the-clock effort. Maj Parker's flying, supervisory and leadership skills were a source of inspiration to all. His exemplary performance brought credit to his unit, to the Canadian Forces and to Canada.

The CO Moves On

Following Aviano, LCol Flynn set his sights on a new career. With his command of 441 about to end, the prospect of an NDHQ career had little appeal. But something did – before Aviano, his friend Rogers Smith of NASA's Dryden Flight Test Center at Edwards AFB, had met with Ulrich Neuberger. A former Luftwaffe F-104 pilot and now a senior man with EuroFighter in

In this conflict the CF's hard-pressed military air lifters consistently performed at a peak. Here a 437 Squadron Airbus A310 disembarks at Aviano. (CF CKD99-2002-07)

Hornet 188753 with another typical Aviano backdrop. Note the FLIR pod along the port engine nacelle. (CF CKD99-2014-01)

LCol Billie Flynn with TFA commander, Col André Viens, (middle) and Col Duff Sullivan. The occasion was Flynn passing command of TFA to Sullivan. (CF CKD99-2125-06)

Balkan Rats Hornet 188731 in a wartime setting – HAS and PGMs. (CF CKD99-2085-08)

Ready for an Allied Force mission, LCol Billie Flynn does his walk-around. (CF CKD99-2010-01)

Hornet 790 awaits its mission, armed with PGMs and Sidewinders. Buckets collect drippings from the external tanks. (CF CKD99-2005-04)

293

Aviano presentations: BGen Dave Jurkowski presents Maj Glen Phillips with the NATO medal, and Col Bill Cleland, Commander 4 Wing, honours Capt Soroka with a "Commander Task Force Aviano Commendation". (CF CKD99-2111-02, '0141-64)

LCol Billie Flynn at Aviano with 441 HCol David Graves, then with Balkan Rats HCol Mirco "Mister C" Cossutto, proprietor of the Hotel Antares, where Balkan Rats pilots stayed during Allied Force. (CF CKD99-2074-05, ' 2078-24)

Armed for a CAP mission, Hornet '795 is shown in a great Balkan Rats action shot. Then, a Hornet slices by, caught by a sharp-eyed CanForces combat "photog".
(CF CKD99-2067-10, '2112-13)

Germany, Neuberger was looking for a test pilot. Smith put him together with Flynn, and an agreement soon was in the works.

On September 1, 1999 LCol Flynn led a wild 8-ship air combat fight from Cold Lake, then returned for a flypast over the flightline where 441 and guests had assembled for a change of command. Among the VIPs were three WWII and Korean War fighter pilots – Omer Levesque, Andy Mackenzie and Eric Smith (Mackenzie had commanded 441 in Sabre days). As the Hornets taxied in, all was ready for LCol Steve "T-Bo" Whitley to take command. After the handover, Flynn visited for a few minutes with his friends, then departed – he had a Munich flight to catch. Not too quick, however, for his boss and 4 Wing Commander, Col Jim Donihee, had something to inscribe in Flynn's log book: "Billie – an exceptional career. Your friendship, your drive, your abilities have contributed greatly to the accomplishments of our fighter force. All the very best on the next chapter of your life. Until next we meet."

On September 5, 1999 Flynn landed in Germany to begin his tour as a EuroFighter test pilot at Manching. Flying commenced with conversion to the Luftwaffe F-4F at Hopsten Air Base. Flynn next flew F-4s, chasing the EuroFighter in Decimomannu, then was on a project upgrading Hellenic Air Force F-4Es (e.g. F/A-18 radar, F-16C avionics, advanced weapons). On February 16, 2000, for example, he flew the HAF F-4E prototype for 1.6 hours on "Air to ground delivery evaluation". HAF proving flights ensued with the AIM-9L, AMRAAM, Taurus stand-off air-to-ground missile, etc.

LCol Flynn signs 441 over to LCol Steve "T-Bo" Whitley. The Wing Commander, Col "JD" Donihee (middle) officiates, as HonCol Graves looks on. (LCol Whitley's call sign originated from his days as a student pilot. As an avid young folk singer, he used to tell in song the story of a fictional Acadian bon vivant, Fred T-Bo.) (Larry Milberry)

Flynn converted to the Tornado in January 2000 at the German OTU at Jever Air Base. On March 13 he flew a Tornado for the first time, going up with Maj Schlägel. After several flights Flynn was not impressed by the outdated machine – even the HAF F-4E had more going for it. Finally, on April 13 he flew the EuroFighter at the BAe Test Centre in Warton, England – a 1.2-hour test mission in DA4 with BAe chief test pilot Paul Hopkins. Next came Cessna Citation training in Paris (April 17 - 26). On August 28, 2000 he soloed in DA1 – a 0.6-hour flight control test.

In January 2001 Billie Flynn was doing EuroFighter aero-medical tests with the RAF, beginning with some 9-G centrifuge runs. At Farnborough, Hawks XX327 and XJ100 had been modified for EFA 9.5-G helmet trials. On January 16-17, 2001 Flynn and USAF exchange flight surgeon and pilot, Col Brown of the Centre of Aviation Medicine, made three flights, including some CPM and

On the morning of his Change-of-Command ceremony, LCol Flynn took 441's 1982 Ford Bronco "staff car" onto a taxiway at Cold Lake to drag 1 AMS's pick-up truck driven by LCol James Doherty. (Larry Milberry)

VIPs at 441's historic Change-of-Command ceremony included WWII/Korean War fighter pilots W/C Eric G. Smith, S/L A.R. "Andy" MacKenzie and S/L J.A. Omer Levesque. They are flanked by Maj Jason "Duke" Smith, Larry Milberry and Capt Glaeser. (CANAV Col.)

The Change-of-Command flypast of September 1, 1999 as it passed over Cold Lake's beach front. LCol Flynn leads. To his right are Col Donihee with Hon Col Graves, Capt Travis "Brass" Brassington and Capt Kirk "Rambo" Soroka. Left are Majs Glen Phillips, Rob "Hooker" Parker and Steve "Swill" Will with Stu McIntosh of AETE. In the slot is Capt Les "Kosmo" Racicot. Flying chase was Brett "Laser" Glaeser with Larry Milberry.

LCol Flynn after the flypast with Col Donihee, HCol Graves and Maj Phillips. (Larry Milberry)

A ceremonial tradition – LCol Flynn is hosed down after his flypast. Here he assists USN exchange officer Jeff "Chef" Carlton. (Larry Milberry)

ACM profiles to 9-G. The task was to prove the multi-purpose helmet (with a helmet-mounted display, whereby a pilot can fly and fight without having to look inside the cockpit). Each EuroFighter helmet is tailored to the particular pilot, so has a slightly different centre of gravity. Beginning on March 24 Flynn deployed DA5 to the former Soviet MiG-21 base at Laage, by then the home of Luftwaffe MiG-29s. The purpose was EuroFighter multiple target radar evaluation using (on the same mission) 20 MiG-29 and F-4F targets; all were "shot down". Other flying done by Flynn in this period involved weapons evaluation, supersonic handling, flight control system development, and icing, engine and air-to-air refuelling tests.

On February 27, 2003 Flynn flew his last EuroFighter mission – a flight control test in DA1 up to Mach 1.9. Of this period he later recalled enjoying the low-level routes over Bavaria and along the German-Austrian border checking out snow (i.e. ski) conditions in the Alps. His work in Greece was another highlight. Flynn left the EuroFighter project at the end of March 2003 for a new opportunity with Lockheed Martin in Fort Worth, Texas. By this time he had flown the EuroFighter more than 100 times for 150 hours. He began flying at Lockheed Martin in June 2003, his first program being the new F-16E, but with the F-35 on the horizon.

Billie Flynn with his boss Ulrich Neuberger at Manching in October 2002. (Larry Milberry)

EuroFighters DA1 (Development Aircraft 1) and DA5 in the flight test hangar in October 2002. (Larry Milberry)

The groundcrew takes a breather as Billie Flynn settles into DA5 to do his pre-flight checks. (Larry Milberry)

Walk-around time – Flynn gets ready to fly DA5. (Larry Milberry)

With Flynn at the helm DA5 rockets off the runway at Manching. (Larry Milberry)

Aviators just can't get enough of that addictive flying stuff, and a place like Manching only makes them crazier than ever. Besides all its high tech activity, Manching also is home to the Willy Messerschmitt Museum, where one priceless possession is an Me.109G. Here, Billie Flynn listens as museum pilot Walter Eichhorn (who learned to fly in the 1950s with Central Airways at Toronto Island Airport) discusses Me.109 characteristics after giving the classic fighter a good wringing-out over the field. The crest on Flynn's jacket is that of the USN TPS. (Larry Milberry)

CHAPTER 26

Recent Times

The High War — An Outsider's View

Over the years many non-pilots have enjoyed flights in the Hornet. Often these lucky folks are squadron members, e.g. NCM techs getting an "appreciation" flight. Others are visiting VIPs, or media people reporting on squadron matters. One of those fortunate enough to have flown with 441 was Dave O'Malley, chief honcho at Aerographics in Ottawa. Having done the design work for Maj Steve Will's 1 CAD retrospective history, *Wings of Change*, Dave was thrilled to get an invitation for a back seat ride with 441. So it happened that in June 1996 he found himself strapping in for a flight of a lifetime. Once back to reality in Ottawa, he sat down to chronicle his fabulous experience. Here, then, is one of the best "Been there, done that" jet fighter articles ever written by an outsider.:

Every spring, NATO air forces send fighter elements to train in the unlimited and unsullied skies of Northern Alberta as part of Exercise Maple Flag. Here a myriad of operational training tasks occur under realistic conditions. Thus, to find myself strapped to a CF-18 just minutes from launching into those crowded skies was a dream come true.

Insulated beneath my Gentex helmet, I watched the silent choreography of the 441 Squadron tarmac readying for the launch of two sections of Blue Air into low, gray Alberta skies. Capt Steve Will – call sign "Swill", author and friend – was my pilot and

Prior to launch during Maple Flag 1996, Dave O'Malley is all smiles and a thumbs up. (John Vincent)

"Checkers One" section lead. I listened, relaxing, as he talked himself through his litanies, readying his fighter and his head for the coming battle. The minute I was plugged in, I had switched to cold-mike and his calming stream of technobabble came flowing through my headset. It reminded me of the old Latin mass – an unintelligible, magical litany instilling confidence in the uninitiated, while elevating the speaker to high priest status.

The practice of this cockpit chit-chat came from thousands of hours as an instructor on Tutors back at "the Jaw". There it was a training technique to get fledglings to verbalize and visualize each step and control input required to light the stove and fly the bird. The technique gets you to recognize your actions at all times, thus building

a foundation for situational awareness – the No.1 state of mind for the healthy operation of a CF-18. Talking to yourself at WalMart while pushing around a cart is considered sub-human; talking to yourself while strapped to 25 tons of bitchy, flying blowtorch is, well, easily understandable.

To get the sleeping fighter up and on-line, Steve negotiated a labyrinth of inputs and settings, button-punching and knob-twisting the mighty CF-18 to life. Inside my helmet, I could hear the beast awakening – a sing-song concerto of dings and pings, punctuated by Swill's Yeager-like mantra and Bitchin' Betty's sexy and understated warnings. Finally, Steve jabbed the wakening Hornet's left start button and the fighter whooped as a GE engine flashed up. Sitting out on the bleak, gray ramp, nailed bolt-upright to my ejection seat for 20 minutes, the jet had seemed lifeless. But, when engine No.1 came up, a rush simultaneously went through my headset, up through the seat of my pants, even carried on the diluted oxygen and sucked deep into my lungs. Now I could feel the life blood of the beast surging around me. Then came one more tortured whoop from No.2 – Hornet '925 was fully awake – and pissed-off. The access ladders were pulled away and the ground crew backed off, dragging the hawser chocks and showing respect for the fearsome power of the engines burning like a run-away pipeline beneath our seats.

Steve called to me to clear hands from the cockpit ledge and the big canopy dropped softly into place. At the moment of contact it seemed oddly misaligned, but the next second brought two large hooks up to engage pins on the canopy, pulling it down tight and forcing it back another inch to create a perfect seal. Steve snapped a look right, then left, checking aileron deflection. He nodded to the crew chief and gave the throttles a sharp nudge. 925 moved out of her place and swung left, loafing along the edge of the ramp as the others came up behind. Steve led his section down the taxiway parallel to the runway. The 441 boys were going hunting.

At the end of the runway the elements of Blue Air were assembling – fuelled, armed and anxious for the battle to come. Today it was the High War – a high altitude, high-risk engagement at 35,000 feet. We were Blue Air, the good guys, and part of an 18-plane air force sent north to the Primrose Lake Range to defend the skies, to hunt and destroy Red Air, an attacking force of 12 aggressor squadron F-16 Vipers from Nellis AFB. Using known MiG-29 tactics and weapons profiles, the Vipers carried their charade to the max, even painting their fighters in Eastern Bloc camouflage with red stars on the wings and tails. Blue Air, a mixed stew of eight CF-18s, four F-15Cs and six F-15E Strike Eagles, had only met at the morning briefing. They would, however, have the benefit of an RAF battle controller orbiting above the fight in a Boeing E-3D Sentry AWACS.

Ahead, the four F-15Cs wheeled to the left and rolled off the taxiway centre line to let us pass. Hellish gouts of heated air fumed from their engines. We rocked gently in their wash as Steve advanced the throttles to push on by for the set-up at the button of the runway. As section lead he took position on the left side of the runway. Our wingman, Hauptmann Bernhard "Tarzan" Tantarn, pulled his Hornet to our right and waited. The two other CF-18s of our section wheeled in behind. Steve busied himself with a last-second cockpit scan, glancing over to Tarzan who gave us a nod, his face no longer visible beneath mask and visor.

My anticipation was almost overwhelming for those last seconds before Steve lit the burners. I was now just seconds from living a life-long dream. I reached to the floor on my left and felt for the electric seat-height switch. I dropped the ejection seat to the lowest position taking the advice of my friend, 2Lt John Vincent, who said the closer I was to the centre of gravity, the less my head would be tossed around during ACM. Oddly, my heart seemed to slow, and I breathed easily the mixture of air and pure oxygen through my mask. I snugged my straps a little more and adjusted the brightness on my three CRTs though, to be honest, the straps were already tightened to the max and the brightness knobs tuned for full daylight. It just made me feel like I knew what I was doing – knob-adjuster at the pointy end of the stick, strap-snugger in the technowar.

Steve locked up the brakes, advanced the throttles and checked the power. The deafening sound of our mighty engines in full afterburner was almost completely muffled by my snug-fitting helmet. We rocked in place and I could feel a slight genuflection in the nose as the engines fought with the brakes. A look to the right, a nod and Steve released the breaks, sending us in one ultra-smooth, accelerating dash down the left of the runway with Tarzan seemingly glued to our right wing. The take-off roll was as smooth – no bumps, no left or right tracking, just one huge, powerful headlong rush to get our 25 tons of metal and gas into the air. Steve was still yakking away up front, calling out ground speed, looking for that magical number that meant it was safe to rotate and begin the climb. I stared at Tarzan's aircraft as we lifted into the air. The ground released us and Tarzan at virtually the same instant. I watched our winger's gear come up into the wells a split second after I heard Steve speak the thought in my headset.

I was where I always dreamed to be – wired, strapped and plugged into a front-line fighter lifting off from an operational fighter base on a serious mission. I let out a big howl from the privacy of my cold-miked hide-away. I pounded my knees and happily mumbled the F-word over and over. I was one happy camper. I switched to hot-mike and waited for a break to talk to Steve, who was taking his two-plane formation up through the first layer of low cloud. He continued talking to himself and chatted easily to me at the same time. The weather guys had briefed a 4000 foot cloud top, but we continued into the murk beyond that. Since taking position beside us on the runway, Tarzan had never moved more than a few feet from our right wing and, as we bumped our way through the cloud, it was even more important that he maintain this perfect relationship. If he were momentarily to lose sight of us in the cloud, we risked a mid-air.

Climbing through 8000, the gray soup brightened steadily, until we found ourselves skimming waist deep in the cloud tops at 10,000. We popped out and continued up in the clear air, but still beneath a cloud layer well above. Steve now turned briefly to our winger and tapped his helmet with a gloved hand. Tarzan took his cue for the break, pulling his nose slightly up, rolling his belly to us and peeling away in a sleek, sliding motion. Within seconds he was holding station in battle formation about a klick away, while the other 2-ship spread out to our left and slightly behind. We settled in the classic "Finger Four" fighter formation and pushed towards the exercise zone. Steve continued the climb as the upper cloud layer slipped behind us, revealing a deep blue sky with some broken layers of white stacked along the northern horizon. At 25,000 feet the cockpit was bathed in clear, radiant light. My eyes took in every detail – the rivets and knobs, the weathered paint on the LEX, the dazzle of minute scratches on the canopy, the stitching on my harness, the way the light reflected from iridescent fingerprints on the CRTs.

We now were climbing steadily on a heading to bring us over the area south of our ACM area. There we would turn MiG sweeps until contact was made with elements of Red Air. Steve would use the next ten minutes to get "in the zone", to go over the parameters and possibilities of the conflict ahead. But before he settled in, he demonstrated a snap roll for me at 600 knots. He brought the nose up slightly, then gave a deft right jab to the stick and we tumbled, corkscrewing through 360 degrees in about one second. So smooth, so fast. "Do it again, Steve!" This time I grabbed my palm-corder which I had stowed and held it in front of me, tight to the cockpit coaming. Steve repeated the slick roll, while I "Yahooed" from the back seat.

Enough fun. Now Steve settled down to business and called for "Coco" (LCol Marc Ouellet leading the second 2-ship on our left) to climb to "Check for cons". Right now, as we drilled holes in the clear air, no condensation trails were streaming aft of us though, certainly, somewhere up above us was a layer of colder air – the perfect medium to draw long, white chalk lines that could lead Red Air directly to us. Coco's job was to climb parallel to us and, while we watched, he reached that telltale layer. "Cons!" Steve radioed and the higher Hornet bunted over, descending to the formation, leaving only a short, 2-second blast of contrail. With the expanse of white cloud below, it was advantageous to take the highest air possible, so that we would not be silhouetted. But now we knew that our highest altitude was around 34,000. Any higher and everyone in the sector could track us visually from 50 miles

With all four jets spread across the same altitude, Steve took us into a right hand racetrack pattern. This was the MiG sweep, covering 50 miles of blue turf. He leveled on the back stretch and talked easily to me, all the while staying in contact with his section and the lone AWACS controller watching the battlefield from her vantage point miles away. With no bogies reported in the area, Steve held to the racetrack, turning back in the direction of the Bull. The steeply banked turns were gentle, with the sun's white light coursing shadows across our cockpit. Steve had yet to pull any G, but I anxiously awaited full deployment of my G-suit. There was however, a "speed jean" test button down to my left and I stabbed at it. Wham! The inflatable air bladders around my calves, thighs and waist popped, gripping my lower half in a firm, reassuring squeeze – a sensation not unlike a giant blood pressure cuff. I kinda liked it, and jabbed at the test button several times, wondering how I could get one for home use – who knows, maybe connect it to my "central vac" system.

Though AWACS had nothing yet to declare, Steve scanned the skies high and low and invited me to do the same, looking for any advantage over the enemy. To the north we could see several cons scooting along the tops of high cloud. "F-15s" snorted Steve in disgust, as he turned away to scan the south. I was not much help, and this was confirmed when my eyes picked out the dark, menacing shapes of two B-1Bs at our 2 o'clock low. "B-1s to the right!" I shouted, since Steve hadn't mentioned them. "Yeah, don't worry, they're not in this war" reassured Steve, "just returning to base". He probably had seen them 20 miles away on radar, spoken to the controller, and picked them up visually long before I had. Even so, I couldn't resist the thought, "Look Mom, I'm MiG sweeping".

On our next sweep Steve stiffened. AWACS was tracking three Bad Guys 40 miles off our nose and pushing through. I had turned down my radio at Steve's suggestion, to hear our intercom talk over all the radio chatter, so I never heard when the fight was on, but I sure felt it. As Steve shoved the throttles to afterburner, I could feel the rising acceleration as he rushed to join the fray. We were now pushing Mach 1, but I was unaware until Steve said "Feel that little bump?" "Uh-huh" "Well buddy, you just went supersonic!" Indeed there had been a slight nudge as we pushed through the sound barrier, but I wouldn't have noticed if Steve hadn't pointed it out. None of the buffeting and violent shaking reported by Yeager, just a slight sensation of being released. There was, however, total silence with only the sound of oxygen being pulled through my mask. We were leaving our own sound behind, but the airframe still vibrated with the synchronized high frequency buzz of two GE 404s. "Hey, John McQuarrie, eat your heart out" I thought, as Steve retarded the throttles and settled us down to Mach 1.2. In all the Hornet time my good friend and aviation photographer had, John had not gone supersonic.

I assumed that Red Air would smoke on through supersonic as well, so our closing speed would be in the neighbourhood of 1500 mph. Steve now was getting pretty pugilistic, weaving and bobbing his head like a prize fighter, shifting his shoulders and grumbling loudly. He knew there were bandits around and wanted to eyeball them. His head moved rapidly between his radar display and the big, menacing blue sky to our left. Radar showed elements of Red Air coming in hard from the west and probably to the south. Steve's spirit had changed dramatically over the last minute – from chatty aviator to a tightly wound techno-jock with an urge to kill. His breathing had accelerated and I felt his elevated excitement. The battle began.

They were here. Steve knew it, but he couldn't see them. He snapped the fighter hard over 100 degrees to port, looking straight down. Before I could even take a look, he concluded that there was nothing there, and Wham! Hard back level, then hard over right, "What the!" Scanning, neck muscles straining, "Whoa!", snap to level, Steve cursing now, head turning, anger boiling. "Got 'em! Tally ho!" What he saw, the position of the aircraft (wherever they were), their direction or something in the way they moved, caused an instantaneous reaction from Steve as he rolled back left 110 degrees, slamming the throttles to full burner and reefing the brutal power of the Hornet through a blood-draining, descending turn. Steve's years of training took over and, like the best athletes, he stopped deliberate thought and reacted, for if he took the time to weigh the possibilities, we were dead.

That was my first introduction to the world of high-G. No casual build-up here, just straight to the maximum 7.5 Gs, going supersonic. Steve held the G on for only three seconds, then decided his best move lay in the opposite direction. He "unloaded" as we descended, whipping the Hornet to starboard, pulling hard on the pole. Vapour boiled from the LEX on both sides, but the ship still seemed to make no sound. There was, however, that high-frequency rushing turbine vibration that rose and fell with the ferocity of the turns.

In the world of aerial combat, situational awareness is a much ballyhooed concept. "SA" is the ability to maintain control, knowing whether you're up or down, to understand where you are in space and where the bad guy is. It's the awareness of where your guys are and where you are going to be in the next five seconds, the ability to extend your beleaguered brain so far beyond the crushing weight of your own G-battered body, that you can visualize the arc and curve of your path through the air and where it will bring you in relation to your enemy's flight path. Beyond that, a pilot with good "SA" can play out the battle, even the movements of enemy planes not engaged, using only information from AWACS, radio calls from his comrades, and what he knows about the capabilities of his enemy. The Canadian fighter pilot trains to the highest possible such level – a pinnacle of mental excellence combined with Olympic-level athleticism that enables him to scan three CRTs, operate a radar screen from a cursor on the throttle, and monitor a head-up display while talking to other fighters in his section and to AWACS.

As far as my SA was concerned, it disappeared, vanishing into a swirling, crushing tumble where my confused mind channeled its efforts to maximum sphincter control. While Steve flew and fought up front, I gripped the handles on the cockpit sides and strained to maintain consciousness. It was fabulous, it was brutal, it was where I wanted to be, even though I didn't know where I was. From the next 15 minutes I remember only small fractured scenes with any clarity. The rest of the fight was a series of punishing high-G reverses and turns, negative-G push-overs and spine-compressing pull-ups. My vision traded sun for sky for cloud as Steve yanked and banked 925 through the sky in an effort to shake off closing Vipers and position himself for a missile shot.

Though I had supposedly pulled nearly four G's in Les Shockley's jet truck and even more in Greg Williams' Mooney somewhere over the Gulf of Mexico, and even though I fully understood the concepts of multiple gravities, tunnel vision and gray out, nothing could possibly have prepared me for the massive, draining crush of 7.5 Gs. I thanked god for the Hornet's G-limiting computer for, no matter how hard Steve rammed that stick into his stomach, the CF-18 would only give him 7.5. The F-16 has no G-limiter but it did have a slightly reclined seat enabling a pilot to load 10+ Gs, even though risking G-induced blackouts at critical points in a fight. Turn after turn I gripped the handles on Hell's roller coaster, felt the unholy snap of my G-suit squeezing my lower half, and grunted and groaned under the onslaught of stultifying loads and stomach-churning negative G bunts.

At the outset of the fight, the fighters engaged miles apart with missile shots that are the death blow of choice. Steve's initial hard turn was to avoid the greater WEZ (Weapons Effectiveness Zone) of the F-16. By notching 90 degrees, he was forcing missile shots to turn a corner, thus lengthening their track and rendering the shot less effective. During the ensuing furball, the fighters grappled, both pilots loosing missile shots, swapping angles and energy until the scuffle got in real tight – a knife-fight-in-a-telephone-booth kind of tight. I heard the electronic warble tone in my headset indicating that a Viper had us locked up. I held on tight for the evasive manoeuvre to come – a hard climbing right turn with Steve pounding the big red chaff button on the left side of his cockpit. Oddly, he continued to talk to himself through the entire battle, an endless conversation interrupted by radio calls and killer turns. "Check low right Dave – where the hell is he for god's sake? Tone! Tone! Grunt, grunt! Turning, Chaff! Chaff! Chaff! Roll back. Turning into him. Damn! Chaff! Chaff! Chaff! Is he back there? Comin' around. Grunt, grunt!"

To me Steve was fighting an imaginary adversary, for only once did I see any Red Air, and then I couldn't miss it. Steve was clawing his way round a left turn in full burner, punching out chaff, grunting to keep his wits and straining to see behind. My head was also locked behind, but only because that's the way I was looking, anticipating a right turn, when he pulled left. "Is he there? Is he there?" puffed Steve. "Hnnnnnnphhh, Hunnnph" groaned the old passenger, oblivious to any tiny spec that might be presently waxing our tail. Somewhere behind, a mile back and turning inside us, was an F-16 locked on and ready for the shoot-down. Steve sensed his immediate demise. Unloading, he rolled wings-level and yanked the stick back, simultaneously fire-walling the throttles. In two seconds we went from a hard left to full vertical, clawing for altitude on two cones of fire. We were vertical for only a few seconds, then the ship shuddered as if an anchor had been thrown out. Drifting upwards almost weightless, Steve pounded in a bootful of top rudder and the high-tech fighter hinged off the big right rudder input, skidding and yawing nearly 30 degrees a second. As we floated there, our nose swung down until we were looking at the cloud swinging into view below. Steve slammed the throttles again and we dove straight down in full burner, accelerating with gravity on our side for a change. Our nose wanted to pull us well through vertical, so Steve was two-fisting the stick back. Great clouds of white LEX vapour streamed past him, giving me the odd sensation that I was canoeing in white water.

Puffing and grunting as we pulled to keep vertical, my vision squished under the strain of big Gs. I emitted a gasping "WOW!" as the stunning image of a Russian-camo F-16 swept across our beam. He was no more than 300 meters off our nose and pulling hard to undercut Steve's surprise manoeuvre. The scene played out in slow motion for, as Steve hauled the nose up, he tracked the Viper as it tried in vain to not be where he knew he already was. The vision was immaculate – a Soviet-style blue-on-blue camouflaged F-16 with great wedges of angry white vapour blasting off his wing roots like steam shrieking from a locomotive. The scene was top lit by the sun, while the cloud below accentuated every detail. If I had only one thought at this moment, it was that the Gomer pilot knew he was dead. No tones here, no lock, just a switch to guns and the Gomer's perfect planform clawing its way into Steve's sights. No kill like a guns kill. Later, in the video room, the entire scene played out in black and white, exactly as I saw it, but with white HUD data showing 6.3 Gs and flashing "Cannon!, Cannon! Cannon!" as the Viper's left wing cut across the target box in the centre of the screen.

Dave O'Malley and Steve Will after High War exercise at Maple Flag '96. (John Vincent)

The fight itself seemed divided into three parts separated by two brief periods where Steve merely flicked and jinked around, itching for a fight. The guns kill on the Viper happened at the end of the second act, with about five minutes of punch-up still to go. We came out of the kill, pulling vertical once again. By now I was getting pretty green, but feeling pretty good about containing my corn flakes. I switched to pure oxygen and immediately felt the benefit of the cooling flow. Still, as a precautionary measure, I pulled the bayonet clip off the right side of my helmet and undid my mask, holding it on with my left hand. Then, of course, Swill cut a huge 7 G turn to the right causing the mask and my arm to weigh about 80 lbs. Now the mask was ten inches from my face and I struggled in vain to bring it back against the G. I wondered if there was breathable air in the cockpit at 15,000. Now, Steve unloaded and jammed the jet just as hard to the left, causing the mask and my arm to slam into my face. First chance I got, despite the growing nausea, I did the clip up, thinking there's no stomach muscle strong enough to toss anything against the forces Steve was subjecting my stomach to anyway.

Throughout the battle I could hear Bitching Betty warning Steve repeatedly. "Altitude!, Altitude, Altitude!" she admonished as we spiralled down. Though we were thousands of feet from the real hard deck, she'd been pre-programmed to warn us before we entered the lower altitudes. Thus, 20,000 was ground and Betty bitched at every spiralling descent. About 12 minutes into the scrum, Betty started bitching about the fuel state, calling "Bingo!, Bingo!" over the intercom right in the middle of Steve's last round with an F-16. On cue, a minute later, the sky was empty as the defeated Red Air beat feet for home.

The battle had rambled up and down 50 miles of Alberta real estate from 20,000 to 35,000 feet. The sky still sparkled with tumbling clouds of metal foil chaff floating down to the range. Thirty bingoed-out fighters, 36 sweaty aviators and one dizzy, puking back seater headed for home, joining up and sorting themselves out. The final tally was Blue Air – 12, Red Air – 2, with Steve getting a guns kill and Tarzan two with missiles. In the final analysis, we were grappling with three F-16s at the merge and one had notched north away from the action. In the fight we had tangled with and disposed of the other two, but the little Gomer who'd turned left was forgotten in all the hubbub. We had only one AWACS chaperone for the whole dance and she had plenty to do, so the forgotten Viper end-ran us, cutting back behind to shack two from Blue Air.

In Maple Flag exercises, pilots fly every profile from ground attack to combat air patrol to bomber interception. What they really want is High War action – the kind we had experienced. The High War was the true test of flying skills, aggressiveness and above all, the holy concept of situational awareness. As we settled down through the clouds with Tarzan snug on the wing, I had a few moments to think about it all – phenomenal skills of pilots like Steve Will and Bernhard

Tantarn, the levels to which they had taken the art of flying, the risks they took every day, the degree of training necessary to mitigate those risks. Fighter pilots are a cocky bunch. Today I understood why. That evening Steve and I ate a pizza. The next day I drove to Edmonton, stopping on the way to visit the world's biggest pirogie – considered a must-see by every fighter pilot at Cold Lake. Steve drove back to the war.

Father and Son

In many families where the father is a professional pilot, sons or daughters also pursue aviation. As a young man Roland Selby learned to fly while in Air Cadets. He next joined the RCAF and had a tour as a flying instructor. Many years later his son, Miles, also joined the air force, eventually qualifying on the CF-18 and winning a posting to 441 Squadron. As sometimes happens in such cases, the happy day came when young Miles was able to take his father for a flight in the mighty Hornet. In 2004 dad described that special day:

One afternoon while visiting in Cold Lake with our son, Captain Miles "Milhouse" Selby, he came home with the documents necessary to take me for a Hornet ride – 4 Wing Commander, Col William Cleland, and 441 CO, LCol Rob Thorneycroft, both had given their approval. Unbelievable!

A couple of days later I had a medical exam on base, then was checked out on the CF-18 ejection seat. The plan was to fly later that day, but during my seat check we began hearing news of bizarre events in New York City – it was September 11, 2001. No civilian dad would be joy riding in a Hornet that day.

Everything was on hold for some time, but I waited patiently. Finally came January 29, 2002, the day I strapped into a 441 Hornet for the flight of a lifetime – in the back of a Hornet being flown by my kid!

My own RCAF career was in training, then I spent 31 years in commercial aviation with CP Air and Canadian, starting on the DC-3, then progressing to the DC-8, 737, 767 to the 747-400. You can imagine the pride we felt watching Miles do what I had only dreamed of – flying fighters.

You might say that our flight that day was payback for the trips on which I had taken Miles to places like London, Frankfurt and Amsterdam. But together on the 29th, it was a different ride – we went higher (45,000 feet) and faster (M.1.54) than we had ever before flown together. Miles made the trip extra special by letting me fly the Hornet on my first ever supersonic ride. Another thrill was flying low across a frozen lake in afterburner into the setting sun behind "Chek 66" was an unforgettable thrill. Somehow, considering my age, it seemed all the more fitting that we had taken our flight in the oldest CF-18 still in service – No.902.

Roland and Miles Selby on the occasion of their father-son Hornet flight. (441 Sqn)

Airshow Memories

In February 2004 MCpl Bill Chisholm of 441 Squadron recalled a CF-18 deployment with a twist:

In our own way we all remember September 11 and the days following. In my case the horror of it all was tempered by an unusual deployment, beginning on the 14th. On that day 4 Wing would send two jets to an airshow in California. This seemed odd since, so far as we knew, North American airspace was still closed.

In the servicing blister at around 1000 hrs that morning I was wondering out loud who from 441 would be going in the back seat to the airshow (normally that would be another pilot). To my surprise our CO, "Thorney", snapped back, "You are! Can you be ready in an hour?" All I had to do now was to ask permission from my "boss" – my wife said that she didn't mind. To be on the safe side, I cleared things with my Warrant Officer then, equipped with a spare flight suit, a change of socks and underwear from my locker, and a credit card, I suited up.

After 410 OTS had two ground aborts of their specially painted "color jets", those guys jumped into two "plain jane" Hornets. Wolfgang "Ice" Plewnia, 441's German exchange pilot, and I finally rolled out behind 410 after a 2-hour delay. Our hop to Mountain Home AFB, Idaho was uneventful but, apparently, some young flight line guard was not informed of our arrival. He approached the aircraft too closely for my liking, so I warned Ice, "Watch him." Now, I had a chance to meet the rest of our team. What a surprise to greet Mark Riach, an ex-441 technician, ex-441 pilots Greg "Shep" Shepherd and Rick "Slick" Williams, and Tim "Red" Shopa, a 410 pilot with whom I had served during Air Cadets days in Yellowknife.

After refuelling, doing a quick AB check, and catching up on some 441 alumni news, we got back enroute to California. Ice mentioned that commercial traffic still was limited to big name cargo only. We were almost alone up there, and rarely able to get a fix on any aircraft in our corridor until well into California. As we neared Salinas, the 410 boys informed us that the ILS there was down (by this time we had become separated from the 410 jets, something to do with fuel, as I recall). With rain and darkness ahead, a VFR approach was ruled out, so Ice got busy flipping maps and looking for our alternate, Monterey Peninsula Airport, 20 miles to the west on the coast. Meanwhile, I observed that we were slowly losing altitude. Slightly annoyed at this, ATC asked what altitude they had requested Ice to hold. Ice brought us back to 6000, then had me hold it there, while he sorted out things for the Monterey approach and, before long, we were shutting down on the ramp.

The next obstacle to contemplate (over a beer in the "MillionAir" FBO lounge) was security of our trio of Hornets. Salinas had been expecting us and normal logistics were arranged for there, but now what? As is normal, checking out our surroundings, I browsed at the TV over the bar that appeared to be set on a weather channel. Cool – the channel had a live camera focussed on three Canadian CF-18s! No security problem after all. The airshow staff eventually showed up to take us to the Salinas Comfort Inn. The clerk at the reception desk there reported that we were the only visiting aircraft to show up.

Next morning, a little under the weather from some welcome basket wine, the pilots headed for Monterey airport, while I got over to Salinas to clear some parking spots, see to roping off, etc. Good thing that I did, as our area was littered with FOD. Show co-ordinator John Paul Jones gave me the personnel I needed to get the job done. We swept and walked the area just in time as two Hornets came in low and fast "out of nowhere". Salinas tower called "Slick", our airshow Lead, giving him some crop spraying intel – there was some fear that crop dusters might be used by terrorist, so ATC wanted anyone airborne to get on the ground ASAP. Our guys fudged around up there for a bit, squeezed in good beat-up, then landed. The diehard airshow fans really appreciated those CF-18 decibels, but it was interesting trying to keep them out of the way as the jets taxied in. Referring to their landing pattern antics that morning, Slick later commented, "After all, who were they going to send up after us?"

Due to September 11 the American military was so busy that we ended up being the only fighter at the show. If not for one National Guard helicopter, we would have been the only aircraft – period. The airshow staff had to scramble to get some entertainment for the expected 90,000 spectators (only a fraction of that actually showed). There were exotic cars and they even brought in a Hollywood dinosaur – "Robosaurus" could crush cars and shoot 20 foot flames from its mouth.

Naturally, we couldn't have been made to feel more welcome, than at Salinas. Almost every visitor was quick to tell us, "It's great that you all could make it!" We met an older gentleman who threw us the keys to his Chrysler Prowler retro sports car to join the parade by the stands. Because we were the only game in town, we had golf carts to take us to the VIP tent whenever the California weather required that we quench our thirst. A behemoth of a man, a self-declared Viking, had a bar set up across the wings of a biplane in the VIP tent. He, his wife and daughter quickly befriended us. Later, he took us to a local establishment that had a mechanical bull. As DetCO, Slick warned us against any bull riding – he wasn't going to leave anyone behind with broken bones. Nonetheless, fighter pilot that he is, Ice grabbed a cowboy hat from the bull's horn and planted it squarely on my head. "We don't work for 410, Bill, so giddy up." The good folks from the bar later sent me the video of Ice and me in flying gear trying to ride. The bull's controller took it easy until the eight second mark, then turned it up a notch or two on me. Somehow or other no damage was done, and that weekend after 9-11 turned out to be memorable for me in more ways than one.

"The Sharp End of the Stick"

In 2003 Garth Eichel, editor of the Victoria-based aviation magazine *Aviator*, visited 4 Wing to do research for a 441 feature story. Being steeped in aviation (his father was a retired Air Force general, his brother a CF-18 pilot, and himself a commercial pilot), Garth published the kind of story that readers enjoy. Here are a few excerpts from "The Sharp End of the Stick":

"Stalk and Kill." That is the indelicate and straightforward motto of 441 Tactical Fighter Squadron, and it suits the CF-18 Hornet pilots and crews of the black and white checker unit. In fact, the squadron takes pride in its politically incorrect credo for, despite the neutered language of our day, it is exactly what they get paid to do in the defence of Canada.

441 TFS is one of Canada's few "Vanguard" squadrons – those first to deploy in the event of a threat to national security. Unfortunately, a lack of resources and trained personnel can make maintaining this first line of defence a difficult task. As it stands, the fine line between operational readiness and irrelevance remains the dedication of those who serve in 441.

Well that's nice, but talk is cheap, and lip service does not cut it at 441. What the squadron truly wants is not expressions of appreciation, but the ability to do its job properly. In both the enlisted and officer messes, talk is not about wanting more acknowledgment, money or benefits, but what squadron members collectively refer to as an improved "quality of profession".

A Checkered Past

In wandering around 441's hallways and offices during my visit in 2003, one of the first things I noticed was the six decades worth of squadron photos – black-and-whites of wartime Hurricanes and Spitfires, and faded colour images of Vampires, Sabres, and CF-104s of Cold War days. Also on every wall are photos of the squadron's present machine – the CF-18 Hornet. But outnumbering airplanes photos are those of airmen, some of whom helped establish the combat reputation of Canadian fighter pilots during WWII, while others enhanced it after the war by standing ready for a conflict that never came. Then there are the portraits of who served recently, and so well, in the Balkans.

In former years the Canadian Air Force was a fighting machine with teeth. Fighter pilots flew and trained continuously, and were superb at what they did. They had reason to feel good about themselves and their profession. More recently, however, the fighter community has had flying hours and resources significantly diminished. The end result is not only a less capable force, but sometimes a group of pilots and techs who feel that their abilities and potential are not being realized. Yet, despite their frustration, members of 441 Squadron seem to have little interest in being anywhere else except where they are. A lot of that has to do with "The Boss".

Lead Dog

441 Squadron's Commanding Officer in 2003, LCol Rob Thorneycroft (call sign "Thorney"), was an experienced fighter pilot with Gulf War combat missions to his credit. With a fighter pilot's trademark moustache, flat top haircut, and the athletic build of a pilot accustomed to pulling punishing amounts of "G", Thorney looked the part of a fangs-in-the-floorboards fighter pilot. What distinguished him as a leader was not only an infectious smile and the energy to motivate people, but the lean and hungry nature of a straight-talking commander who preferred the hard seat of a fighter jet to a plush office chair. Unfortunately, like most of his pilots, Thorney found himself behind a desk all too often.

"The biggest challenge is getting people qualified on the squadron", he told me, with a hint of frustration creeping into his voice. "There's satisfaction that we are still in the game with the limited

Garth Eichel's June 2002 air-to-air of 441 Hornet '740 in 60th anniversary colours. The Hornet has been in Canadian service for more than 20 years. What is the general concensus about it by now? Anyone who had flown older generation fighters like the Starfighter certainly has long been impressed by its power, versatility and comfort. Yet, in spite of being a "pilot's airplane", not everyone originally adjusted in the early days. In 2002 former 441 CO, Billie Flynn, put it this way: "Not all the old sweats adapted to the Hornet. The true masters of this jet could be characterized as ex-long-haired, hippy kids who had grown up with electronic gaming experience."

resources we have, but we're just not getting the people and stuff we need." To make matters worse, the CO was concerned about the major airlines and civilian industry hiring away the squadron's most experienced pilots and techs.

Rising from his desk, he walked to the window, which faces the hangar floor, where four Hornets were undergoing maintenance. "This Squadron is here to go to war," he said. "Some people haven't thought about that in years." But the CO's exasperation didn't last long, and he concluded with relish: "The job itself is fantastic. It's the pinnacle of a fighter pilot's career to be the CO of a Tactical Fighter Squadron. Where do you go from here?"

The Troops

Perhaps the most impressive thing about the fighter pilots and crews serving under Thorney was their dedication of purpose. As if the squadron were a small company on the verge of going out of business, they shared his frustrations, but struggled to overcome the multitude of difficulties. No one, it seemed, wanted to let "The Boss" down. Sgt Scott Corley, 441 Squadron's senior aviation supervisor technician, believed that part of the problem facing the squadron was that, because they continually were proving that they could do more with less, the senior decision makers had come to expect that. "Meeting operational commitments is tough, but manageable," he noted. "It requires a lot more planning, the guys have to work twice as hard to get it done, but we still manage. The problem is this – our 'can do' attitude is like shooting ourselves in the foot."

Beyond obtaining parts, the biggest problem facing 441 maintenance, according to Corley, was getting techs qualified and keeping them on the squadron. "It takes up to four years to get those people trained," he explained. "Civilian industry is the big poacher – in the last three years half of our squadron has left to go work on civvy street."

Maverick Vs. Noodle?

Modern culture has always glorified fighter pilots, but the movie "Top Gun" really cemented the image of "Maverick" and "Goose" in the popular psyche. The question, though, is how much is fact and how much is fiction? Well first of all, regardless of their distinctive black and white checkered neck scarves, cryptic handles, and "HoooAhh" bravado, the fighter pilots of 441 TFS are far too ugly to be movie stars. And their ground crews generally consist of a single tech who steadfastly refuses to lurch around like a pansy making wild hand signals. But perhaps the biggest difference between fact and fiction is in the personalities of the pilots.

"Fighter Jocks" long have been regarded as arrogant, in-your-face jarheads, but at 441 you would be hard pressed to find any such jackasses. Despite their unfortunate call signs, individuals like "Millhouse", "Bender", "Migs", "Squish", "Loaf", "Bypass" and "Noodle" are a few of 441's first rate characters. They take satisfaction in being the world's most highly trained rednecks and use their unique brand of gunslinger humour and camaraderie to advantage as they struggle to keep the squadron operational.

If you were to follow any of these pilots through an operational day at 441, you quickly would discover how little resemblance there is between Hollywood and the demanding world of combat flight training and operations. For starters, there is nothing glamorous about the volumes of paperwork and secondary duties each pilot faces. And there is not much to rivet the senses, watching them spend hours planning a single mission. But, tedious as all this might be, there still isn't a surround-sound home theatre system that can duplicate the rush of a flight in a high performance fighter like the Hornet.

White Hat, Black Hat

Three hours prior to the afternoon launch "Squish", "Lothar", and "Migs" gather in the mission planning room to prepare a 3-ship exercise. On this particular air-to-air mission Lothar and Migs are to be "Blue Air" (the good guys) flying a patrol in defence of King Ralph (Klein) of "Beerland". Intelligence reports a hostile build up of "Red Air" (the bad guy) patrols by the rogue "Prince Bypass" in neighbouring "Squishistan". On this flight, Squish is instructed to play the adversarial role of Red Baron, and make life hard for the good guys.

When the exhaustive briefing is over, the three pilots head downstairs to collect their flight gear and get "dressed to kill". Suited up, they make their way to the operations room for a weather briefing where Bypass – a Dutch exchange officer – updates the situation and instructs them to "wear something nice". Each pilot then signs out his aircraft before proceeding out to the flight line, where dozens of Hornets are parked at 45 degree angles. Each pilot heads for his own machine, does a careful walk-around, then clambers up into the cockpit where a crewman waits to help him strap in.

Pre-start checks complete, each pilot lights up his pair of General Electric F404 smokeless engines. One by one the Hornets spool up with guttural howls, as their turbine blades suck more and more air for combustion. Upon ignition, the howl gives way to the high-pitch droning whistle of a fighter jet. Like a dream sequence, the exhaust from the three Hornets distorts the air behind them, blurring the image of every Hornet in its wake. Once the after start checks are complete, the pilots close their canopies, do a flight control check, and get marshaled off the flight line. With menacing grace, the three Hornets meander along the taxiways to Runway 31 Right. Migs launches first, followed shortly by Lothar, while Squish hangs back. As designated Red Air bad guy, he doesn't accompany the other two Blue Air Hornets. He has a bit of time to kill before he has to pounce on Migs and Lothar and, like any good fighter pilot who hasn't flown for a few days, he opts to shake out the cobwebs in the meantime.

Squish clicks the radio mike on his joystick and requests an unrestricted climb from tower on departure. Tower seems all too happy to oblige. Cleared for take-off, he taxis out to the button of R31R and completes his final pre-flight checks before standing on the binders and advancing the throttles. When all the digital numbers on the instrument panel have spun up to where they should be, his Hornet lurches forward initially like a drag racer, but with 32,000 pounds of thrust cracking and snarling out the tailpipes the Hornet accelerates from 0 to 350 knots in less than 60 seconds. Squish then pulls back hard on the stick, standing the Hornet on its tail in a 60 degrees nose-up attitude. 45 seconds later he is passing through 20,000 feet, at which point Squish rolls his jet on its back, giving a clear view of the earth below. "Nice day at the office," he says with measured satisfaction.

Just getting started, Squish does a "G" warm up. He accelerates back up to 500 knots and commences a series of 90 degree bank turns to left and right. Despite the six "Gs" heaving blood from his torso to his feet, he barely utters a grunt. In fact, he seems to thrive on the physical punishment that gravity delivers, as he continues carving up the troposphere for another ten minutes enroute to the combat area.

Once over "Squishistan" it was all business. Perched up at 20,000 feet, Squish began sweeping the horizon with his radar in search of Blue Air. Like a pinball wizard, he flicked a variety of buttons and scrolled through screens in an effort to lock up Migs and Lothar. However, just as everything was coming together, his radar started playing games. "Goddamn piece of crap," he cussed through the hiss of oxygen in his mask. After banging the screen with his free hand a couple of times, the radar snapped back to life as if on cue in a bad movie, and Squish resumed harassing Blue Air, who were approaching head on about 10,000 feet below with a 1000-knot closing speed. As they passed below they were little more than a pair of angry gray blurs. Squish quickly reacted, rolling inverted and pulling through to dive on them. He accelerated to catch up and his airspeed indicator soon showed Mach 1.3.

After an hour of tangling with each other, the three Hornets formed up for the return to base. Tired, but happy, the pilots opt for some fun on the way home – most of it inverted. Lothar had special reason to enjoy the return to base, as this was his last flight in the Air Force. Like so many other pilots, he had found that the military could not compete with the airlines – when the siren call came from Air Canada, he put in his release. Still, as grand as opting for airline life must have seemed, for Lothar the knowledge that he would never again mix it up in a high performance fighter must have seemed bittersweet. As such, he made the most of his last flight and proceeded to give one last, loud and dramatic fly by over the base to the cheers of the techs and pilots taking it all in. For those watching it was a pleasant distraction from the melancholy fact that one more of their own was leaving for "greener pastures".

Capt Paul "Squish" Umrysh of 441 Squadron. His enthusiasm for flying began as a boy in 614 Air Cadet Squadron in London, Ontario. There he earned his private pilot licence, and later completed a degree in mechanical engineering at Royal Roads and RMC. He received his Wings at Moose Jaw in 1996, then flew the T-33 in 414 Squadron to 1999, logging some 940 hours. In April 2001 he joined the esteemed company at 441. To the spring of 2004 Umrysh had flown some 850 CF-18 hours. Main activities at 441 that year included alerts in the Q at Cold Lake and Comox, DACT in New Orleans, "Maple Flag", "Combat Archer" (live missile shoot at Tyndall AFB), live bombing at Eglin AFB, and all the general fun of flying the impressive CF-18M. To Umrysh the "M" lives up to all the glossy PR brochures accompanying the program. The squadron was looking forward keenly to adding NVGs later in 2004, a CF-18M simulator in 2006, then a new IR missile to replace the AIM-9, and a helmet-mounted weapons sight. (Garth Eichel)

Pilot Profile – "The Boss"

Robert J. "Thorney" Thorneycroft, who commanded 441 from September 2001 to August 2003, joined the Canadian Forces on August 10, 1976. Beginning as a "Mil-Col" student at Collège Royale Militaire, he flew initially at Portage la Prairie in the summer of 1978. After graduating in mechanical engineering in 1981, he was posted in October 1981 to Tutors at 2 CFFTS, Moose Jaw. After completing his course in September 1982, he started work as a

Garth Eichel's view of "Checkerbird" '724 ready to fly, then Larry Milberry's shot of it departing for a May 2000 Maple Flag mission.

"pipeliner" instructor at "The Big 2". In 1987 he took the fighter lead-in course at 419 Squadron, then completed CF-18 conversion at 410. From here he was posted on a dream tour for any young fighter pilot – to 409 Squadron at Baden. During the first Gulf War of 1990 - 91 he spent three months at Doha in the Persian Gulf. His 409 tour ran to July 1991 when the squadron disbanded at the end of the Cold War.

From 1991 - 93 "Thorney" instructed at 410, then had a tour at Fighter Group HQ in North Bay as executive assistant to MGen Don Williams, then to MGen Dave Kinsman. He returned to Moose Jaw in 1995 - 97 to command "Apache" Flight at "The Big 2", then to be commandant of the Tutor FLIT in 1997 - 99. The FLIT took 3-months and included about 30 missions – BFM, ASM, AST, etc.

Sadly, all does not always go as planned in the air force. Thus, on December 10, 1998 Moose Jaw was shattered by the loss in a flying accident of Capt Michael VandenBos. Five days later Maj Thorneycroft led a flypast over Moose Jaw honouring the aspiring young Snowbird. On the 17th Thorney also led a flypast over Oshawa, Capt VandenBos' home town. In November 1999 he led a 13-plane Moose Jaw flypast for the close-out of the Flying Instructors School there.

Maj Thorneycroft now left Moose Jaw for the last time, his log book showing a phenomenal 4135 Tutor hours. He was then posted to RAAF Staff College in Canberra, then was promoted and named to command 441. In January 2001 he began his CF-18 refresher course at 410, then made his first flight with 441 on July 17. Now came two more great years on the Hornet, but with the additional honour of being "the Boss" of this incomparable squadron. Thorney's log again overflowed with fighter pilot highlights, although there was one day that he and everyone else wished had never come – September 11, 2001. From shortly after 0700 on that day everyone at 441 gathered in the squadron lounge to follow the

LCol Rob Thorneycroft with his wife Kathy and daughters Jordie (left) and Whitney. (Thorneycroft Col.)

horrible events unfolding in Manhattan. Within a few hours dozens of 4 Wing Hornets were armed, fuelled and ready for whatever orders might come.

Another historic event for Thorney came on November 19, 2001. That day with MCpl Thom Short in his back seat, he took Hornet '925 up on its 5000th hour. This was the first time that a CF Hornet had hit the 5000 mark. Since, in the post 9-11 climate, there remained a concern that kooks might try disrupting the G-8 Summit planned for Kananaskis, west of Calgary, Op. Grizzly was authorized in June 2002. The scenario saw 441, and 410 and 416 Hornets on 24-hour-a-day, AAR-supported CAPs. LCol Thorneycroft flew on the 25th (3.6 hours), 26th (6.4) and 27th (5.8). Of his CAP of the 26th the records show that he burned 32,000 pounds of fuel! Some 350 Hornet hours were logged by 4 Wing during the 92-hour G-8 Summit.

More sadness came to the fighter community in 2003. One of LCol Thorneycroft's FLIT students had been Capt Kevin Naismith. Thorney, 441 and everyone in the fighter world were shattered when, on May 26, Naismith of 416 lost his life while on a routine training mission. On July 31, 2003 LCol Thorneycroft strapped into Hornet '724 for his final 441 mission. Along with squadron mates Greg Bend, Chris Hamilton, Shawn Hartzell, Mark Laverdière, Kevin McNaughton and Mike Woodfield he headed out for some ACM. Mission accomplished, they returned to base for a 6-ship flypast, then Thorney made two solo fly-bys, landed and taxied in for a final, nostalgic time. On September 9 he took his release from the military, his log book showing by then a total of 6026 hours, nearly all on high-performance jets. The following week he began a new job at Westjet. Following ground school and simulator training in Calgary, on October 30, 2003 he flew his first day on the Boeing 737-700.

2002 Annual Report

Often since the 1980s Canadian air force squadrons produced annual historical reports that were "bare bones". Future historians will find little of value in such documents. Happily, for 2002 441 TFS submitted to the Chief of the Air Staff an informative summary of the year's efforts. In his preface LCol Thorneycroft reminded the reader that, with the events of 9/11 still vivid, the Silver Foxes put in a commendable year. Canada's fighter force remained on a state of alert, with CF-18s ready for anti-terrorist action at 3 Wing and 4 Wing, and at detachments from Comox to Trenton to Greenwood.

While 441 strove to meet daily objectives, there were difficulties. "The number of qualified personnel on squadron continues to decline," complained the CO. The problem was that, as seasoned techs retired from the CF, or were posted out, they usually were replaced by privates recently graduated from their "TQ3" courses at CFB Borden. "While the net result was a zero gain in personnel," wrote Thorney, "the overall effect ... as it has been over the past several years [was] a decrease in the number of qualified technicians." This reflected a particular problem, whereby seasoned techs were taking early releases to seek civilian jobs. This trend grew after Ottawa began contracting maintenance for such fleets as the Hornet, Polaris and Cormorant. Meanwhile, Bombardier was hiring techs from the military for its CF-18 operation at Mirabel. Complicating matters was how fighter pilots were leaving for jobs at Air Canada, Canada 3000, Cathay Pacific, Korean Airlines, Westjet, etc. As this was happening, the CF-18 OTU was graduating only 6 - 8 new pilots per year, compared to 26 in early years.

Another matter reported by LCol Thorneycroft was a shortage of aircraft. The squadron had a "UE" (unit establishment) of 15 CF-18s, a number which fell to ridiculously few aircraft on some days. To begin, two Hornets always were in periodic inspection. Three usually were committed to the QRA at Comox. This left perhaps 10 Hornets for daily training, but snags invariably had some of these unserviceable and spares were not always in stock. On a good day only five or

The flightline in front of Hangar 3 during Maple Flag in May 2003. Then, the CO – proud "owner" of his personal Hornet. (Mike Valenti, Larry Milberry)

six Hornets would be working. Nonetheless, for 2002 the Silver Foxes logged about 3000 flying hours.

In February 2002, 441 re-assumed Vanguard duties, taking over from 416. Vanguard was a 12-plane, 6-month NATO commitment wherein a squadron could deploy within a few days. Everyone involved had to be fully trained for the task. For pilots this meant being combat capable in the air, but also "up to speed" in such areas

Two-seater 188925 during a major check at 441 in May 2003. Then, techs inspecting a Hornet, and MCpl Thom Short at work in the refinishing shop. (Larry Milberry, Mike Valenti)

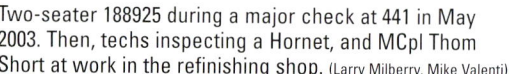

Pilots checking out their jets for a weekend cross-country trip. Capt Paul Umrysh, Maj Mike Woodfield, Capt Miles Selby and LCol Thorneycroft. The "OpsO" behind the desk is Capt Des "Deuce" Brophy. Then, Capt Selby and Maj Woodfield qualifying on the small arms range at 4 Wing in May 2003. The standard pistol carried by Hornet pilots is a 9mm Sig Saur. (Larry Milberry)

as NBCW, individual combat skills (e.g. small arms), first aid, even defensive driving. In August 441 handed over Vanguard duties to 3 Wing. On February 15 the squadron began its 2002 winter deployment at NAS Key West. The chief adversaries here were F-16s of the 466th FS from Hill AFB, Utah. For 441 the results were stellar, only four missions being scrubbed due to snags – another feather in the caps of 441's technical experts. At Cold Lake on March 21 - 22 the squadron joined in a multi-purpose exercise, flying four "strike" Hornets protected by four 416 "sweepers". Against this force were four 419 Hawks and two 410 Hornets. A USAF KC-135 provided AAR. In May 441 flew in Maple Flag in the air-to-ground mode.

For August 30 the 2002 report notes 441 playing "Blue Air" at Red Flag. About this the CO reported: "This particular Red Flag was truly a coalition exercise with participants including Israeli F-15s, Australian F-111s, Singapore F-16s, Italian Tornados and a number of USAF F-15 and F-16 units." Thorney concluded: "Each pilot had the opportunity to drop some live ordnance, including GBU-12s... the groundcrew, through their professionalism, hard work and positive attitudes, provided an amazing 93% serviceability rate throughout the exercise." Entries in the CO's own log suggest the intensity of Red Flag – from September 3 - 11 he flew six times for a total of 7.2 hours. The squadron left Nellis on September 14, but soon was on the road again, this time for DACT at Luke AFB from November 30 - December 14. The year ended with a few Silver Foxes stuck in the Q at Comox. Meanwhile, the highlight of 441's 2002 social calendar was a weekend-long 441 60th anniversary celebration. For the Key West and Nellis deployments the social event proved to be "Canada Night". For 2002, 441 postings (always of great interest on any squadron) included Maj Paul Kissmann to Montgomery, Alabama to attend USAF Air War College.

Thorney Looks Back

In February 2004 Rob Thorneycroft reminisced about his career as 441's CO:

The pinnacle of any fighter pilot's career comes when he is appointed to command a squadron, so it was with great pride and some trepidation that I began my tenure as 441 CO on Tuesday, July 17,

2001. It was a glorious day for a parade, which was followed in the evening with a BBQ, hosted by my wife Kathy and me, in our PMQ backyard. I awoke very early next morning (I seem to recall no sleep whatsoever) and headed to work to get organized for what I was sure was going to be an extremely hectic two years.

I arrived at work at 0615 hours, got a freshly brewed cup of coffee, sat down in my spacious new office, and didn't have a clue what to do! It dawned on me at that moment that I was ill-prepared for my new appointment. Thankfully, we had an APM (all pilots meeting) at 0800, which encouraged me to start thinking of the job at hand. From that point I launched into what was certainly the busiest, most rewarding two years of my military career.

As with any tour of duty, there are always a number of events that stand out. For me it was the terrorist attacks of September 11, 2001. I remember going in to work on a glorious fall day and watching in awe and horror as the events of that fateful day played out on CNN. Knowing the significance of this day, I penned my thoughts as they were happening:

"What a day! It is now 3:15 PM and there has been much activity here on the wing, and indeed, all over the world. At 9:00 AM EST, two hijacked airliners flew into the New York City World Trade Center Towers. About an hour later, both buildings collapsed! At about the same time, an unidentified aircraft flew into the Pentagon... The United States Armed Forces have been placed on Defcon 3. This state has not been declared since the Cuban Missile Crisis in the early 1960s. As a result we too have been placed on Defcon 3. This means that all available jets on the wing will be loaded with missiles and be ready to move out. We have already scrambled two aircraft on alert and have another two on RPI (Readiness Posture Immediate).

"We are also getting our aircrews ready to go with the jets if need be. There is a tremendous amount of work being done at the present time in order to get the jets ready. We (all available aircrew on the wing) had a special brief on NORAD scramble procedures over at 410 Squadron. There were at least 50 CF-18 aircrew in the briefing.

"There is an air of expectancy on the wing, if that is such a feeling one would get! In other words, everyone is serious about what has happened in New York and Washington, D.C. I had a quick briefing with all the folks on squadron. I tried to answer some of the questions they had. However, there was not too much I could tell them other than what CNN had announced. I do think it is important to make sure that everyone is informed as much as possible."

The scope and magnitude of these attacks was obvious, and the world changed forever on that day. For those of us on fighter squadrons in Canada, it began with increased readiness as part of our QRA duties. Following the USAF's lead, we began (and are still) holding QRA.

Deployments are an integral part of squadron life. These are either air-to-air or air-to-ground exercises which generally take place south of the Canadian border. The purpose is two-fold: these exercises test the squadron's ability to deploy aircraft, personnel and materiel to a foreign location, and allow aircrew to hone their flying skills in mock air combat training. In December 2002, 441 Squadron deployed to Luke AFB near Phoenix with ten CF-18s, 17 aircrew and 65 groundcrew. Over the next 10 days we flew an astonishing 118 of 118 sorties planned. This 100 % serviceability rate is testimony to the phenomenal work of the groundcrew. Valuable training was realized by all aircrew, and many important lessons were learned with respect to deploying aircraft, personnel and materiel.

As well as the operational significance of this deployment, two social events stand out. As we planned for the deployment, we learned that there was a USAF base hockey team at Luke AFB. A challenge was issued to the Canadians to bring their hockey gear from the "Far North". The game, played in the NHL's Phoenix Coyotes America West Arena, turned out to be a hard-hitting affair with the ultimate outcome favouring the Americans 7 - 3. Both teams then stayed on at the arena to watch some real hockey – the Montreal Canadiens playing the Phoenix Coyotes.

The second highlight was "Canada Night". In other words, 441 threw a party for its USAF hosts. Highlights included a BBQ, Moose Milk (milk, ice cream, Kaluha), Canadian beer and a variety of games to liven up the spirits. The feature game was "Beer Bungy", which involves wearing a harness attached to about 50 feet of bungy cord. While one end of the bungy is attached to this harness, the other is attached to some immovable object – a tree does the job. The rules are easy – strap yourself into the harness, walk forward stretching the bungy to near maximum length, chug-a-lug a beer placed on a cooler

441's somewhat wacky Phoenix hockey team. Across the back are Capt Kevin "Mac" McNaughton, MCpl Chuck "Bones" Mathews, Cpl Mark Prosser, Capt Mike "Migs" French, Maj Shawn "Loaf" Hartzel, Capt Mark "Happy" Laverdière and Maj Mike "Woody" Woodfield. Next are Sgt Guy Godin, Capt Brent "Laser" Glaeser, Cpl Bryce Culver, MCpl Jean Petit, Cpl Luc Fortier and Maj Rob "Crack" Carter. In front are Lt Mario Clement, Cpl Dwayne Petitte, LCol Rob "Thorney" Thorneycroft and Cpl Jason Tomiuk. (Thorneycroft Col.)

barely within reach, then go backwards ever so slowly. You record a point for your team if you do not spill any beer, or do not become a human projectile attached to the bungy.

After much frivolity the Canadians prevailed at "Beer Bungy", so some of their lost hockey pride was redeemed. Later, a few USAF personnel, who had not been successful in their initial bungy attempts, decided to tackle "Beer Bungy" on their own. One fellow strapped himself into the harness and, after directing his partner to place a beer on the cooler, took a full run ahead. What seemed very surreal from a spectator's vantage point was that this participant did manage to "touch" the beer – right before he was snapped back about 40 feet as the bungy cord recoiled!

"Pink Pussy" culprits at 4 Wing's main gate show off the chattels filched from the office of the "Missing Lynx" CO. Behind are Capts Chris "Hammy" Hamilton and Kevin "Mac" McNaughton, Lt (USN) Chris "Beeker" Myrah, and Capts Mike "Happy" Laverdière and Des "Deuce" Brophy. Across the front are Capts Reagh "Rage" Sherwood, Chris "Bypass" Bijdevaate and Dan "Poot" Mcleod, LCol Thorneycroft, Brehn "Noodle" Eichel and Maj Shawn "Loaf" Hartzel. (Thorneycroft Col.)

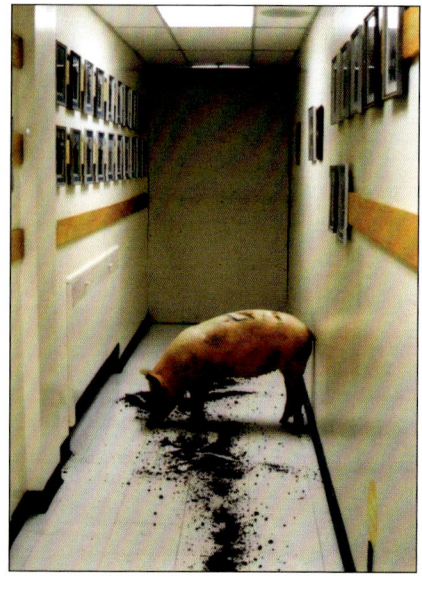

Operation Pink Pussy secret "WMD" doing a recce down 416's "wall of fame" corridor. (Thorneycroft Col.)

With inter-squadron rivalry being a big part of life at Cold Lake, 441's pilots one day felt obliged to conduct a retaliatory "raid" on our sister squadron, the venerable Lynxes of 416 TFS. The Lynxes first mistake was in making a "pin-up" calendar of our own brave pilots. This was after they had stolen the keys to our hangar and painted their own names on our jets. Then they made off with our hero pictures from the squadron briefing room, defaced them, and presented them back to us. We at 441 all agreed that enough was enough!

This explains why "Operation Pink Pussy" came about. First, we had to consider a number of important questions. What level of retribution should be directed towards 416? What time frame was ideal? What farm animal should be used, etc? It was amazing to see how fast "Operation Pink Pussy" came together. The final plan was brilliant. A raid under the cover of darkness would be conducted, as this would afford the highest element of surprise. There would be a 3-pronged attack to avenge the three previous attacks endured by 441. Finally, the farm animal picked was a pig, since this animal represented the same colour as the operation – pink!

With the precision of a well-oiled fighting unit, 441 launched its raid precisely at midnight on May 12, 2003. The three stages, which took two hours to complete, included: (i) the placement of the contents of 416 Squadron CO's office at the front entrance to the base (ii) redecorating the 416 Squadron Pilots' lounge in solid pink (iii) placing "The Pig" in the esteemed hallways of the Lynx Lair.

The response the following morning to our raid was totally unexpected. In direct contrast to the light-hearted nature in which the raid was conducted, the reaction at the wing was of anger and disappointment. How dare 441 do such a despicable thing to a sister squadron? How could a squadron expect a raid of this magnitude be taken as a joke? Well, in my opinion 441's raid should have been taken exactly as it was intended – as a good practical joke. However, as the Commanding Officer of these "ruffians", I did take full responsibility and ordered that all damages be paid at a cost of $139.40 per pilot for a bill of $2369.80! Every 441 pilot accepted responsibility for his actions and gladly paid his share.

One of my final 441 duties was a cairn dedication honouring a 441 Squadron pilot who lost his life while on a WWII mission. F/L William Walter Lindsay Brown was killed on August 13, 1944 after his Spitfire was hit by flak over enemy territory. In 2001 a northern Alberta lake was named in honour of F/L Brown. The squadron was approached by the 4 Wing cairn committee, and asked if it would raise funds to pay for the monument. A 441 committee was established and the funds were raised within three months. Dedication of the cairn took place on a glorious July 29, 2003. Some 30 personnel from 441, 4 Wing, and the Lac La Biche Royal Canadian Legion branch took part in a moving ceremony. Included was a flypast by two 441 CF-18s – a fitting tribute to a fallen comrade.

In my opinion the biggest difference between being in the military or being a civilian is one of liability. The average civilian does not sit around the office with his co-workers discussing the prospects of war, or the possibility of making the ultimate sacrifice for God and country! After 9/11 I felt it necessary to have frank discussions with all the pilots on 441. I was encouraged to find that not one of them would hesitate to put himself in harm's way if ordered to do so. This was why we train to be fighter pilots. Everything we do on a daily basis is geared towards going to war. In a tribute to a great friend and fallen comrade, I wrote the following – "The Fighter Pilot – in memory of Captain Kevin "Nasty" Naismith, who lost his life in a training accident on May 26, 2003:

> We are the Warriors of society
> While what we do may disgust and trouble some people
> It is these same people who want us to stand on guard for them
> We understand what we do and we love it
> When called upon by our government and country to go to war
> We willingly and anxiously go
> We train our whole careers for this very moment
> And during this training we must stay on the edge of being the killing machines we are

Silver Foxes present to dedicate the memorial honouring F/L Bill Brown: Cpl Pete Gould, MCpl Craig Spencer, CWO Hal Fuhr, Capt Brehn "Noodle" Eichel, LCol Thorneycroft, MWO "Bo" Boudreau and MCpl Ron Melnyk. Then, a detail of the momument itself. (Thorneycroft Col.)

We are willing to give our lives to fulfill these promises we make to society
And if this training takes us over the "line" occasionally
Get over it because we must keep this edge to be ready to fight!
And to win!
We are proud, we are warriors – we are fighter pilots!

My two years as Commanding Officer of 441 Tactical Fighter Squadron went by far too quickly. This tour of duty was unequivocally the pinnacle of my 27 years in the military. What touched me the most about this wonderful experience was the men and women of 441. They were the most professional people I ever worked with and I salute each and every one of them. CHECKER, CHECKER!!

Improved Hornets

The Aviano experience is a proud period in Canadian military history, stretching to the limit, as it did, the fighter fleet and the skills and commitment of all concerned. LCol Dave Bashow pointed out that Task Force Aviano owed much of its success to previous years of solid training, and had been formed at a time when CF-18 resources had not yet been degraded. In "Mission Ready: Canada's Role in the Kosovo Air Campaign" (*Canadian Military Journal*, Spring 2000) he observed: "Without further resources the fighter force risks being marginalized, which is the precursor to extinction."

Since the late 1960s the Canadian Forces were being squeezed by Ottawa. Oddly, while money was tight, official expectations remained high, even as morale suffered. As for the CF-18, it was proving to be less durable than hoped. First came structural integrity problems with the tail surfaces. In another setback, in October 1998 cracks were found in fuselage bulkheads. Fifteen Hornets were removed temporarily from the fleet. Meanwhile, as Canada was investing only marginally in CF-18

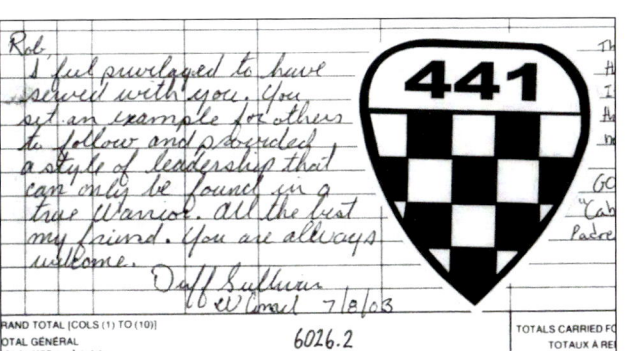

LCol R.J. "Rob" Throneycroft handing over command to LCol J.J.P. "Stammer" St-Amand on August 8, 2003. Officiating is the Wing Commander, Col C.S. "Duff" Sullivan, while Thorney's father, LGen (Ret'd) Ken Thorneycroft, is there in cardboard cut-out form (another 441 "first"!). Ken had never missed one of his son's career highlights so, unable to make this one, "showed up" vicariously, a skit that was the brain-wave of 1 AMS CO, LCol Kevin Yamashita. (Thorneycroft Col.)

One of the send-off messages inscribed in LCol Thorneycroft's log book. Then, his total air force flying hours by type, also in his log. (Thorneycroft Col.)

MILITARY HOURS	
CF-18 HORNET	1725.3
CT-114 TUTOR	4135.1
CT-115 HAWK	1.0
T-33 SILVER STAR	19.0
CF-5 FREEDOM FIGHTER	106.5
C-47 DAKOTA	1.3
F-16 VIPER	1.0
HARRIER	2.2
KIOWA	0.5
F-14 TOMCAT	1.1
CT-134 MUSKETEER	32.0
F-3 TORNADO	1.2
GRAND TOTAL	6026.2

upgrades, operators such as the US Marine Corps and Royal Australian Air Force were extending their Hornets with improved computers, communications equipment, and weapons systems.

Canada eventually got on board with the $1.2 billion CF-18 Incremental Modernization Program. This involves 80 CF-18s and will extend the useful life of the aircraft to 2017 - 2020. The first two Hornets (188793 and '939, dubbed CF-18M) were modified by Boeing at NAS China Lake, California, and tested there by AETE. With the lessons learned from Aviano, NDHQ now accelerated the IMP schedule. From January to March 2003 Maj Travis Brassington, Maj Tim Shopa and Capt Brad Williamson of 410's Fighter Operational Test and Evaluation Flight were at China Lake proving the two IMP prototypes.

IMP upgrades include: new mission computers, advanced US Navy operational flight control system improvements, liquid crystal cockpit displays, APG-73 radar allowing a pilot to track multiple targets, then to attack targets with AMRAAMs, HaveQuick II jam-proof radio, stores management system upgrade, missile approach warning system, IR jammer, helmet-mounted sight, ANAPX-111 IFF system, GPS (for accurate Nitehawk employment), chaff/flare system. Phase One of IMP in itself makes the CF-18 compatible in any future coalition scenario. In its 2003 annual historical report, 441 summarized the coming of the CF-18M:

> As early as Mar. 2003, aircraft from 441 Squadron were sent to Mirabel, Quebec for conversion to the CF-18M configuration. The number of available aircraft at the squadron slowly decreased until flying operations ceased on 17 Oct. 2003. On 3 Nov. 2003 LCol "Stammer" St-Amand flew the first 441 Squadron CF-18M sortie. The CF-18M looks very much the same as the Legacy aircraft. The only visual differences consist of the blade antennas of the Combined Interrogator Transponder (CIT), and some Global Positioning (GPS) antennas on the dorsal spine. The cockpit is similar to the Legacy version, except for a PMCIA card receptacle situated to the left of the ejection seat. Overall, serviceability has improved significantly since the 2002 report. This is due in part to the modernization of key systems and a focused approach at solving past maintenance deficiencies.

The Silver Foxes in 2003

Life on a fighter squadron, though never dull, tends to be predictable, but each year usually brings some noteworthy change. For 2003 the biggest event was the arrival of the first CF-18Ms. 441's annual historical report for 2003 describes on-going activities:

> The New Year was ushered in by defending North America from the Quick Reaction Alert (QRA) area in Cold Lake. This is a continuing task shared by 441 and 416 Squadrons at 4 Wing. The importance of this duty has not been lost on the members of the Silver Fox Squadron since 2001. QRA duties are still our number one task and, with a diminishing number of aircraft on the Squadron, it became an all-consuming task several times in 2003. Over the summer months, the Squadron would occasionally find 100% of its serviceable aircraft committed to the QRA. As 4 Wing transitioned to the CF-18M in 2003, Vanguard duties were assumed by 3 Wing Bagotville.

January 2003 saw 441 in Tyndall AFB on a "Higher Headquarters" mandated deployment. This exercise would demonstrate 441's readiness to operate away from its "MOB" - main operating base. Besides DACT missions with the host unit (95th FS with F-15Cs), the squadron took part in three "LFE" missions ("large force employment", i.e. packages). LCol Thorneycroft, and Majs Hartzell and Woodfield each had a chance to plan and execute LFEs. Only four sorties were lost at Tyndall due to aircraft unserviceabilities for a 97% serviceability rate.

During "Canada Night" festivities at Tyndall, 441 introduced their Floridian hosts to another zany bit of 441 culture – "Beer Bungee". In one case, beer bungee practitioner MCpl Al Chase was frustrated when unable to haul himself the 40 feet to the beer. This was maddening, since Cpl Michelle Masse, whom he followed in the competition, had

LCol St-Amand, CO of 441 in 2004. (CF)

made it with ease. Chase had to concede defeat, but must have shaken his head when he realized that the bungee cord had been wrapped around a palm tree twice before he was strapped in and, without that extra 8 feet, there was no way he could win!

Tragedy struck 441 twice in 2003. On March 6 Cpl David Farris lost his life in a highway accident. Maj Woodfield, as acting CO, stood the squadron down for the day. 441's yearly "Chiefs Vs Indians" hockey game later was dedicated as the David Farris Memorial Tournament in honour of David's love of the game. In May 2003 the squadron participated in Maple Flag. As 416 was short of pilots, so some from 441 were detached to the "Missing Lynx" to help them put a 4-ship together. It was on one of these trips that Capt "Mac" McNaughton of 441 watched as Capt Kevin "Nasty" Naismith of 416 crashed. Although he ejected, Naismith, a well-respected member of Canada's fighter community, did not survive.

Day 2 of Maple Flag was very blurry for most CF-18 pilots and 416 did not fly for the rest of the week. Maj Woodfield was forced to plan in a very somber mood, since Day 3 was his Mass Attack TacEval. Capt Naismith's funeral was held on April 30 at 4 Wing's J.J. Par Centre. LCol Thorneycroft led the flypast, while Capt MacNaughton flew the missing man position. There was not a dry eye in the crowd as MacNaughton pulled up into a cumulus overcast.

The Maverick air-to-surface IR missile – part of 441's arsenal. (Larry Milberry)

Following Maple Flag, 441 deployed to Comox to man the "Q", fly in Ex. Amalgam Warrior, and work with the Canadian Navy on a TASMO exercise (Tactical Support to Maritime Operations). For "Amalgam Warrior" a NORAD command and control exercise, EW Lear Jets simulated the hostile bomber force, accompanied by a Gulfstream with jamming capability to disrupt "the recognized air picture". One day during this exercise 441 flew 52 hours with their six Hornets – once again 441's techs had risen to the occasion. For this TASMO HMCS *Vancouver* and HMCS *Calgary* were on work-ups before deploying to the Persian Gulf, so needed to exercise their shipborne air defense controllers. 441 pilots took turns using their "Precision Guided Strike" capabilities against the ships, or played the role of ship defenders. This TASMO gave 441 exposure in using the IR-guided Maverick missile, and a new respect for the Navy's capabilities.

A USAF airman at a 441 bash has a go at "bungee beer". What the heck, eh! (Thorneycroft Col.)

LCol Thorneycroft flew his last hop in a CF-18 on July 31. Maj Shawn "Loaf" Hartzell "em-ceed" Thorney's retirement Mess Dinner, which his father, LGen (Ret) Ken Thorneycroft, attended. On August 8 LCol Pierre "Stammer" St-Amand took over 441 as it prepared to transition to the CF-18M and was nominated as 4 Wing's lead Vanguard squadron.

"Stammer"

A native of La Sarre in Northern Quebec, LCol Pierre St-Amand joined the Canadian Forces in June 1981. He graduated from RMC with a degree in electrical engineering, then trained at Moose Jaw, receiving his Wings from there in the summer of 1987. Next came fighter pilot training at Cold Lake, then Capt St-Amand served with 433 Escadron Tactique in Bagotville from 1989 - 1992.

Next, St-Amand instructed at 410 for a year, then spearheaded the formation of the Fighter Electronic Warfare Advanced Course. In 1993 he attended the Aerospace Systems Course in Winnipeg, then returned to 410 to instruct, and later established the Fighter Operational Test and Evaluation Flight (also at 410). Promoted to major in 1997, St-Amand became the first Officer Commanding FOTEF. Projects there included development of a laser-guided training round (that simulates a typical PGM), and the Maverick missile. In 1998-99 St-Amand was 410 SWATO and DCO.

In 1999 Maj St-Amand attended CF Staff College, then was posted to NDHQ in the Directorate of Aerospace Requirements. Upon promotion in the summer of 2001, LCol St-Amand became Project Director at DAR for the CF-18 IMP program. On August 8, 2003 he took command of 441 as it was re-equipping with IMP Hornets in November 2003. Squadron DCO in this period was Maj Rob Carter, who also had DAR/IMP experience, especially regarding NVGs and FLIR pods.

August and September were quiet months as 441's aircraft inventory decreased, although maintenance and operations were busy with CF-18M ground training. Meanwhile, 441 continued to hold "Q" in Cold Lake.

There was no flying at 441 in the last two weeks of October as pilots received CF-18M transition training – a week of groundschool in Cold Lake, a week in St-Louis doing "sim" training. Meanwhile, eight CF-18Ms were delivered and 441 maintenance used the down time to prepare the new aircraft. LCol St-Amand flew 441's first CF-18M sortie on November 3, 2003. Flying for the next two weeks consisted mainly of check rides and basic training, with emphasis on air-to-air tactics and NORAD mission profiles. Since 1 CAD required a NORAD Air Sovereignty Alert (ASA) "initial operational capability" for November 28, efforts focused on achieving the minimum capability elements of this mission. On November 28 LCol St-Amand recommended to the Commander 4 Wing that 441 be declared NORAD ASA capable. This milestone was approved. In December 441 deployed with five CF-18Ms to San Diego to support a Canadian Navy exercise, using this opportunity to test and validate new procedures, tactics and the sustainability of the CF-18M, while deployed.

The number of qualified 441 maintenance personnel on squadron continued to decline in 2003, although new privates with TQ-3 qualifications continued to arrive. These young personnel were welcomed, yet training so many new techs proved to be a limiting factor in 441's capacity to generate sorties. As 2003 closed, the Silver Foxes had achieved their goals for the year. However, real world events required them to deploy three Hornets to Winnipeg from December 22 - 26 in support of Op. Noble Eagle. As a test of 441's ability to respond to short notice taskings and deploy away, it passed with flying colours. This deployment effectively closed the year.

Through 2003 the squadron social calendar was busy. As usual, there were "spontaneous" parties, TGIFs at various messes, the Annual Mess Dinner, the Change of Command, Snowfest, Sports Day, etc. Mr Mark Little, newly appointed Honourary Colonel, joined 441 for its Christmas party.

Three top-notch Silver Foxes mourned in the 1990s - 2000s: Cpl Vic Vautour (Aug. 17, 1998), MCpl "Joe" Bogden (Dec. 18, 1992) and Cpl Dave Farris (March 6, 2003). (441 Sqn)

441 Squadron Commanding Officers — CF-18 Hornet Era

CO	From	To
LCol K. Ian Struthers, CD	June 26, 1987	July 5, 1989
LCol Terry L. Hunt, CD	July 6, 1989	July 2, 1991
LCol J.A. Pierre Rochefort, CD	July 3, 1991	June 29, 1993
LCol J. Marc Ouellet, CD	June 30, 1993	June 29, 1995
LCol David C. Burt, CD	June 30, 1995	June 26, 1997
LCol William A. Flynn, CD	June 27, 1997	September 2, 1999
LCol Stephen L. Whitely, CD	September 3, 1999	July 16, 2001
LCol Robert J. Thorneycroft, CD	July 17, 2001	August 8, 2003
LCol Pierre St-Amand, CD	August 8, 2003	

Aircraft of 441 Squadron

Type	Period	Max Power	Length	Span	Max Wt lb	Max Speed mph/M
Hawker Hurricane XII	1942-44	1x1300 h.p.	32'3"	40'	7360	330
Supermarine Spitfire IX	1944-45	1x1500 h.p	31'1"	36'10	9500	408
D.H. Vampire	1951	1x3100 lb s.t.	30'9"	40'	11,970	531
Canadair Sabre 2	1951-53	1x5200 lb s.t.	37'6"	37'1"	17,750	679
Canadair Sabre 5	1953-55	1x6500 lb s.t.	37'6"	37'1"	17,580	696
Canadair Sabre 6	1955-63	1x7440 lb s.t.	37'6"	37'1"	17,560	698
Canadair CF-104	1964-86	1x15,800 lb s.t.	54'9"	21'11"	26,800	M2.0
McDonnell Douglas CF-18	1987	2x16,000 lb s.t.	56'	40'5"	45,000	M1.84

This brass Silver Fox piece is typical of the hundreds of heritage items and souvenirs around 441 Squadron at Cold Lake. (Mike Valenti)

What does the future hold? In the era kicked off by the collapse of the old Soviet Union much has taken place in the world. Initially, there was the mad rush to cash in on the "peace dividend", as Western powers closed bases and disbanded fighting units. Then came 9-11 and the global War on Terrorism. No one knows what will come next. In a spirit of optimism, however, as its 2003 Christmas card 441 Squadron, perhaps "dreaming in Technicolor", envisioned itself driving EuroFighters around the skies. Well, for many years to come it will be driving CF-18Ms then, if anything, may have F-35s. All that in mind, 2020 and the F-35 are not all that far away. (Thorneycroft Col.)

Glossary

A/C/M	Air Chief Marshal		CF-104 nav trainer	LCol	lieutenant colonel	RAAF	Royal Australian Air Force
AAA	anti-aircraft artillery	DCDS	Deputy Chief of the Defence Staff	LEX	leading edge extension	RAF	Royal Air Force
AAFCE	Allied Air Forces Central Europe	DCIEM	Defence and Civil Institute of Environmental Medicine	LL	low level	RCAF	Royal Canadian Air Force
AAM	air-to-air missile			LS	leading seaman	retread	RCAF WWII veteran who returned to join the postwar RCAF
AB	afterburner	DEFCON	defence condition	Lt	lieutenant		
ABDR	aircraft battle damage repair	DetCO	detachment commander			RMC	Royal Military College
ABM	anti-ballistic missile	DEW Line	Distant Early Warning Line	M/G	machine gun	RNAF	Royal Netherlands Air Force
ACM	air combat manoeuvres	DF	direction finding	Maj	major	RNoAF	Royal Norwegian Air Force
ADEX	air defence exercise	DFC	Distinguished Flying Cross	MCAS	Marine Corps Air Station	ROE	rules of engagement
ADGB	Air Defence of Great Britain	DFM	Distinguished Flying Medal	MCpl	master corporal	RV	rendezvous
AdminO	administration officer	DNCO	duty not carried out	Me.	Messerschmitt		
AETE	Aerospace Engineering and Test Establishment	DND	Department of National Defence	MET	motorized enemy transport	SAM	surface to air missile
				MiD	Mention in Dispatches	SARAH	search and rescue homing equipment
AFHQ	Air Force Head Quarters	E&E	escape and evasion	Mil-Col	Military College		
AI	airborne intercept	EAC	Eastern Air Command	MP	military police	SEAD	suppression of enemy air defences
AIRCOM	Air Command	ECCM	electronic counter counter measures	MRP	mobile repair party		
ALCM	air-launched cruise missile			MS	master seaman	SFTS	Service Flying Training School
ALG	advanced landing ground	ECM	electronic counter measures	MSFU	Merchant Ship Flying Unit	Sgt	sergeant
AMRAAM	advanced medium-range air-to-air missile	EFTS	Elementary Flying Training School	MSM	Meritorious Service Medal	SHAPE	Supreme Headquarters Allied Powers in Europe
		ELINT	electronic intelligence (gathering)	MT	motor transport		
ANG	Air National Guard	erk	slang term for groundcrew	MTU	Mobile Technical Unit	SSgt	staff sergeant
AOC	Air Officer Commanding	EW	electronic warfare	MWO	master warrant officer	ST/A	strike/attack
AOI	aircraft operating instructions					ST/R	strike/reconnaissance
ASAP	as soon as possible	FAC	forward air controller	NAAFI	Navy, Army, Air Force Institute	STU	Sabre Transition Unit
ATAF	Allied Tactical Air Force	FIS	Flying Instructors School	NAS	Naval Air Station	SWATO	squadron weapons and tactics officer
ATC	air traffic control	flak	anti-aircraft fire	NATO	North Atlantic Treaty Organization		
AWACS	airborne warning and command system	flamer	MET that burned	nav	navigation		
		FLIR	forward-looking infra red	NBCW	nuclear, biological, chemical warfare	TacEval	tactical evaluation
AWC	air weapons controller	FLIT	fighter lead-in training			TAF	Tactical Air Force
AWU	Air Weapons Unit	FOD	foreign object damage	NCM	non-commissioned member	TASMO	tactical air support maritime operations
		FOL	forward operating location	NCO	non-commissioned officer		
BAI	battlefield air interdiction	FOTEF	Fighter Operational Test and Evaluation Flight	NDHQ	National Defence Headquarters	TD	temporary duty
BFM	basic fighter manoeuvre			NFA	New Fighter Aircraft	TFA	Task Force Aviano
BOpsO	Base Operations Officer	frag	an order or a "fragment" thereof	NORAD	North American Aerospace Defence Command	TGIF	Thank God It's Friday
BX	bombing exercise	FSgt	flight sergeant			TLP	Tactical Leadership Program
		FTS	Flying Training School	NT	Northwest Territories	TOT	time on target
CAG	Canadian Air Group	Fw.	Foche-Wulf	NU	Nunavut	TQ	technical qualification (course, e.g. TQ3)
CAOC	Combined Air Operations Centre	FWIC	Fighter Weapons Instructors Course	NVG	night vision goggles		
				NWS	North Warning System	TRP	timer reference point, or "tickle point". A point during a nuclear bomb delivery run just prior to the "pop-up", after which the bomb was released.
CAP	combat air patrol	GCA	ground controlled approach	NY	New York		
Capt	captain	GCI	ground controlled interception	OBE	Order of the British Empire		
CAS	close air support	gong	slang for a gallantry medal	OC	officer commanding		
Caterpillar Club	Membership accorded those who save their lives by parachute	GPS	global positioning system	OFTT	operational fighter tactical trainer		
				OFU	Overseas Ferry Unit	U-boat	German submarine
CAV-OK	ceiling and visibility OK	HARM	high speed anti-radiation missile	OJT	on-the-job training	UE	unit establishment (e.g. how many aircraft are assigned to a squadron)
CD	Canadian Forces Medal	HAS	hardened aircraft shelter	OpEval	operational evaluation		
CDS	Chief of the Defence Staff	HMCS	His/Her Majesty's Ship	ORB	Operational Record Book		
CEPE	Central Experimental and Proving Establishment	HR	human resources	OT	operational training	u/s	unserviceable
		HUD	head-up display	OTU	operational training unit	USAF	United States Air Force
CF	Canadian Forces	HWE	Home War Establishment	PER	performance evaluation report	USAFE	USAF Europe
CFE	Canadian Forces Europe	i/c	in charge	PFS	Primary Flying School	WAF	Women's Air Force
CFFTS	Canadian Forces Flying Training School	ICAO	International Civil Aviation Organization	PGM	precision-guided weapon	WD	RCAF Women's Division
				PGS	Pilot Gunnery School	WIF	Wing Instrument Flight
CFI	chief flying instructor	ICBM	intercontinental ballistic missile	PI	photo interpreter	WMD	weapon of mass destruction
CMR	Collège Royal Militaire	ICP	Instrument Check Pilot	pipeliner	an aircrew fresh from his Wings course	WO	warrant officer
Col	colonel	ICT	integrated combat turn			WOpsO	Wing Operations Officer
Cpl	corporal	IE	instrument electric	PM	prime minister	woxof	aviation weather term meaning: indefinite ceiling, zero feet, sky obscured, visibility zero, fog
CPM	combat profile mission	IFR	instrument flight rules	PO	petty officer		
CRT	cathode ray tube	ILS	instrument landing system	pop up	when a low-flying fighter suddenly pulls up to deliver its ordnance		
CRT	combat ready training	IMP	Incremental Modernization Program			Yellow Jack	RCAF GCI controller at Metz
CTechO	Chief Technical Officer			POW	prisoner of war		
CVSM	Canadian Volunteer Service Medal	INT	intelligence	PRC	Personnel Reception Centre		
		INT/O	intelligence officer	Pte	private	Zip	slang for CF-104
CWO	chief warrant officer	IR	infrared			Zipper	slang for CF-104
		ITS	Initial Training School	QRA	quick reaction area or quick reaction alert (also called "the Q")		
DACT	dissimilar air combat training, e.g. CF-18 against F-16	KIFA	killed in flying accident				
DAR	Directorate of Aircraft Requirements			R&R	rest and recreation		
DC-104	colloquial term for DC-3 used as a	LAC	Library and Archives Canada	R/T	radio telegraphy		

Bibliography

In researching *Fighter Squadron* many printed sources were used. Hugh Halliday referred to numerous paper and microfilm files held by Library and Archives Canada (formerly the National Archives of Canada) and the Directorate of History and Heritage, both institutions being in Ottawa; and from the Public Records Office in London, England. Since this is not an academic publication, these rarely are referred to specifically. Many uncatalogued paper files and albums held by 441 Squadron also were used, as was the personal memoir of wartime pilot Bruce MacKenzie, and the draft by Bob Lacerte.

416 Squadron History, Hangar Bookshelf, 1984.

419 Squadron History, 419 Squadron, CFB Cold Lake, Alberta.

434 Squadron History, Hangar Bookshelf, 1984.

Allison, Les and Hayward, Harry, *They Shall Grow Not Old: A Book of Remembrance*, Commonwealth Air Training Plan Museum, Brandon, Manitoba, 1991.

Bashow, David L., *Starfighter: A Loving Retrospective of the CF-104 Era in Canadian Fighter Aviation, 1961-1968*, Fortress Publications, Stoney Creek, Ontario, 1990.

Bashow, David L., *Sting of the Hornet: McDonnell Douglas F/A-18 in Canadian Service*, Canuck Publications, Ottawa, 1987.

Blatherwick, John, *Royal Canadian Air Force: Honours, Decorations, Medals 1920-1968*, FJB Air Publications, New Westminster, BC, 1991.

Boyne, Walter J., *F/A-18 Hornet: A Navy Success Story*, McGraw Hill, New York, NY, 2000.

Campbell, Donald L. *The JG.26 War Diary*, Grub Street, London, UK, 1998.

Clearwater, John, *Canadian Nuclear Weapons: The Untold Story of Canada's Cold War Arsenal*, Dundurn Press, Toronto, Toronto, 1998.

Dempsey, Dan, *A Tradition of Excellence: Canada's Airshow Team Heritage*, High Flight Enterprises, Victoria, BC, 2002.

Deere, David N., *Desert Cats: The Canadian Fighter Squadron in the Gulf War*, Fortress Publications, Stoney Creek, Ontario, 1991.

Foreman, John, *Over the Beaches: The Air War Over Normandy and Europe*, 1st-30th June 1944, Air Research Publications, Surrey, UK, 1994.

Frappé, Jean-Bernard, *La Luftwaffe face au débarquement allié*, Chateau de Damigny, Heimdal, France, 1999.

Gaddes, John Lewis, *We Now Know: Rethinking Cold War History*, Clarendon Press, Oxford, UK, 1997.

Government of Canada, *Debates*, October 28, 1969, November 4, 1969, and December 15, 1969.

Government of Canada, *Minutes of Proceedings and Evidence, Special Committee on Defence*, November 14, 1963.

Green, Bill, *The First Line: Air Defense in the Northeast 1952 to 1960*, Wonderhorse Publications, Fairview, Pennsylvania, 1994.

Green, William, and Cross, Roy, *Jet Aircraft of the World*, Macdonald & Co., London, 1956.

Griffin, John A., *Canadian Military Aircraft: Serials and Photographs 1920-1968*, Canadian War Museum, Ottawa, 1969.

Halliday, Hugh A., *Not in the Face of the Enemy: Canadians Awarded the Air Force Cross and Air Force Medal 1918-1966*, Robin Brass Studio, Toronto, 2000.

Halliday, Hugh A., *The Tumbling Sky*, Canada's Wings, Stittsville, Ontario, 1978.

Halliday, Hugh A., *Typhoon and Tempest: The Canadian Story*, CANAV Books, Toronto, 1992.

Jefford, W/C C.G., *RAF Squadrons: A Comprehensive Record of the Movement and Equipment of All RAF Squadrons and Their Antecedents Since 1912*, Airlife Publishing Ltd., Shrewsbury, England, 1988.

Jenkins, Dennis R., *F/A-18 Hornet: A Navy Success Story*, McGraw-Hill, New York, 2000.

Kostenuk, S. and Griffin, J., *RCAF Squadrons and Aircraft 1924-1968*, Samuel Stevens Hakkert & Company, Toronto, 1977.

Lamb, Gregor, *Sky Over Scapa*, 1939-1945, Byrgiscy, Someret, UK, 1991.

Lewis, Peter, *The British Bomber Since 1914: Fifty Years of Design and Development*, Putnam, London, 1967.

Lewis, Peter, *The British Fighter Since 1912: Fifty Years of Design and Development*, Putnam, London, 1967.

Maloney, Sean M., *War Without Battles: Canada's NATO Brigade in Germany, 1951-1993*, McGraw-Hill Ryerson, Toronto, 1997.

McIntyre, Robert, *Canadian Profile CF-104 Starfighter*, Sabre Model Supplies Publishing Ltd., Ottawa, 1984.

Middlebrook, Martin and Everitt, Chris, *The Bomber Command War Diaries: An Operational Reference Book 1939-1945* (revised edition), Midland Publishing Ltd., Leicester, England, 1996.

Milberry, Larry, *Canada's Air Force at War and Peace, Vol.1*, CANAV Books, Toronto, 2000.

Milberry, Larry, *Canada's Air Force at War and Peace, Vol.3*, CANAV Books, Toronto, 2001.

Milberry, Larry, *Sixty Years: The Royal Canadian Air Force and CF Air Command 1924-1984*, CANAV Books, Toronto, 1984.

Milberry, Larry, *The Avro CF-100*, CANAV Books, Toronto, 1981.

Milberry, Larry, *The Canadair Sabre*, CANAV Books, Toronto, 1986.

Milberry, Larry and Halliday, Hugh A., *The Royal Canadian Air Force at War 1939-1945*, CANAV Books, Toronto, 1990.

Molson, Kenneth M. and Taylor, H.A., *Canadian Aircraft Since 1909*, Canada's Wings, Stittsville, Ontario, 1982.

Morton, Desmond, *A Military History of Canada From Champlain to the Gulf War*, McClelland & Stewart Inc., Toronto, 1994.

Newman, Peter C., *Renegade in Power: The Diefenbaker Years*, McClelland and Stewart Ltd., Toronto, 1973.

Pickler, Ron and Milberry, Larry, *Canadair: The First 50 Years*, CANAV Books, Toronto, 1995.

Rawlings, John, *Fighter Squadrons of the RAF and Their Aircraft*, Macdonald and Co., London, 1969.

Robertson, Bruce, *British Military Aircraft Serials 1878-1987*, Midland Counties Publications, Earl Shilton, UK, 1987.

Sabre 5 & 6 Shortcuts, Canadair Sales Service Publication No.105, 3rd Edition, Canadair Ltd., 1957.

Saunders, Hilary St. George, *Royal Air Force 1939-1945*, Vol. III, "The Fight is Won", HMSO, London, 1954.

Shores, Christopher, *Luftwaffe Fighter Units, Europe 1942-45*, Osprey Publishing Ltd., London, 1979.

Shores, Christopher & Williams, Clive, *Aces High: A Tribute to the Most Notable Fighter Pilots of the British and Commonwealth Forces in WWII*, Grub Street, London, 1994.

Smith, David J., *Action Stations: Military Airfields of Scotland, The North-East and Northern Ireland*, Patrick Stephens, Cambridge, UK, 1983.

The RCAF Overseas: The First Four Years, RCAF Historical Section, Oxford University Press, Toronto 1944.

The RCAF Overseas: The Fifth Year, RCAF Historical Section, Oxford University Press, Toronto 1945.

The RCAF Overseas: The Sixth Year, RCAF Historical Section, Oxford University Press, Toronto 1949.

Watkins, David, *De Havilland Vampire: The Complete History*, Sutton Publishing, Stroud, UK, 1996.

Thetford, Owen, *Aircraft of the Royal Air Force since 1918*, Putnam, London, 1962.

Thetford, Owen, *British Naval Aircraft since 1912*, Putnam, London, 1962.

Wilkinson, Les, et al., *The Avro Arrow: The Story of the Avro Arrow from Its Evolution to Its Extinction*, Boston Mills Press, Cheltenham, Ontario, 1980.

Journal, magazine and newspaper sources: Air Force Association of Canada *Air Force: The Magazine of Canada's Air Force Heritage*, *Aircraft Illustrated*, *Air International*, *Alberta Report*, 1 Wing Marville *Arrowhead Tribune*, *Aviation Week and Space Technology*, Canadian Aviation Historical Society *Journal*, *Canadian Military Journal*, *Der Kanadier*, Edmonton *Journal*, *Flight*, *Flight Comment*, Grand Centre-Cold Lake *Sun*, *RCAF Roundel*, DND *Maple Leaf*, Saskatoon *Star Phoenix*, DND *Sentinel*, *The Aeroplane*, *World Airpower Journal*.

Library and Archives Canada references: RCAF File 60-1-59, "Aircraft - Manufacture and Development in Canada", RG.24, Vol.6179; RCAF File 19-7-83 Volume 7 "RCAF Current Plan, Programme of Activities, 1951-52 Fiscal Year", RG.24 Vol.5227; RCAF file 905-2/16, "Public Relations - Monthly Reports - 1 Air Division", RG 24, Volume 17,929; Microfilm C-12170 (Historical Reports, Air Defence Group and Air Defence Command); Microfilms C-12319 and C-12320 (Operational Record Books and Historical Reports, Nos. 125 and 441 Squadrons); Microfilm C-12414 (Historical Reports, 1 Air Division); Microfilm C-12415 (Historical Reports, No.2 Fighter Wing); Microfilm C-12419 (Historical Reports, Air Weapons Unit, Sardinia). Public Record Office references: Air 19/615, (official correspondence regarding North Luffenham); Public Record Office WO 208/3348 (evasion reports of G.E. Mott and A.J. McDonald)

Index

A Military History of Canada 137
A Tradition of Excellence 240, 263
AAA 279, 281, 287, 292
Aalborg, Denmark 164
AAR 229, 237, 238, 263, 267, 280, 284, 286, 287, 291, 307, 308
Abbot, F/O 91
Abbotsford, BC 251, 252
accidents: 14, 15, 18, 19, 73, 74, 78, 104, 105, 115, 126-130, 134, 139, 162, 175-185, 204, 236, 254, 255, 265, 275, 276
Adamson, LCol George 205, 209, 213, 214, 223, 227
Adlair 116
Adlard, Capt Keith 155, 170, 214
Aerospace Systems Course 313
AETE 154, 295
AIM-7 Sparrow 234, 235, 240, 246, 248, 257, 260, 271, 279, 285, 286, 291
AIM-9 Sidewinder 194, 206, 240, 246, 247, 260, 271, 279, 285, 286, 291
Ainsley, F/L 95
Air Cadets 175, 284, 302, 305
Air Canada 95, 238, 258, 268, 307
Air Force Cross 99, 143
Air Force Magazine 154
Air Transport Auxillary 54
Air War over America 275
air shows 276, 302, 303
air to air refuelling 229, 237, 238, 263, 267, 280, 284, 286, 287, 291, 307, 308
Airbus A310/CC-150 Polaris 293
AIRCOM HQ 215
Aistrop, Sgt 48
Alaska 229, 237, 264, 270-272
Alberta Report 255
ALCM 254, 270
Algonquin Regiment 48
"Allied Force" 274-294
Allison, WO Dave 228
AMRAAM 279, 280, 291, 312
Anderson, Carolyn 222
Anderson, Cpl H. 214
Anderson, Cpl Murray 283
Anderson, Cpl Sandy 199
Anderson, D.J. "Dave" 174, 204, 209-213
Anderson, Dale 174
Anderson, F/O 54
Anderson, F/O James A. 130, 134
Anderson, LCol Don 199
Anderson, WO A. 214
Ann Hoch, Betty 222
Annis, F/O Ralph 76, 81, 82-86, 89, 90, 93, 117, 127, 133
APG-65 radar 226, 227
APG-73 radar 312
Archibald, F/L Ronald C. 175, 176
Arctic survival 232, 269
Argue, Capt John 258, 260
Armstrong, F/L Russ 94
Armstrong, Maj 268
Arnhem 38, 39, 50
Arnold, S/L E.L. 144, 227
Arnott, Bruce 151-153, 184
Aroostock, NB 51
Arrowhead Tribune 168, 218
Arsenault, Cpl Randy 283
Atcherley, A/V/M R.L.R. 84
Atherton, F/O D.H. "Steve" 72-76, 82, 84, 86, 88, 91-94, 117
Atkin, Cpl Mike 282
Atkinson, CWO Bill 282, 288
Aucoin, Sgt C.P. 204
Auster aircraft 59
Austin, MCpl D. 214
Avant, G/C A.F. 140, 144, 216
Aviano, Italy 274-294
Aviator 303-305
Avro Canada types:
CF-100 70, 86, 103, 138, 142, 143, 175, 187
CF-105 Arrow 225
AWACS 251, 262, 270, 279, 281, 292, 299, 300
AWC 243
Ayres, P/O Bob 92

B-2 stealth bomber 282
BAe: Harrier 261, Hawk 285, 296
Bailey, Sgt Raymond W. 51
Bain, Lt Ted 189
Bain, Maj Bill 173, 174, 177-179
Baker, Chief Simon 169, 170
Baker, Cpl 194
Balfe, Maj Todd 278
"Balkan Bat" 284
Balkan Rats 275-294
Ball, Capt Gord 173, 177, 183
Barclay, Cpl Dave 282
Baril, Gen (CDS) 290
Barker Field 54
Barker, F/O David 112, 113
Barlow, F/L Kurt 111, 118
Barnes, F/O D.H.G. 115, 127, 129
Barnes, F/O Roy 118, 129
Barrett, Capt Lee 161
Barrett, Maj Pat 157, 189
Barton, C.D. "Doug" 163, 199
Barton, W/C R.A. 52
Bartram, Col D.W. 172, 174, 261, 264
Bashow, David 138, 183, 311
Batajnica airport 282
Battle of Britain 74, 84
Bauline, Newfoundland 18
Bayles, Capt Gerry 158, 160, 168, 180, 203, 204, 208, 212, 214
Bayles, Penny 222
Bayliss, Maurice 57
Bear bomber 235, 270
Beaufort Sea 270
Beaulieu, Capt "Cat" 263
Beaulieu, Lt Serge 227, 228, 232, 234, 237
Beckett, Lisa 265
Beckett, Maj Jeff 238, 257, 265, 267, 268, 273, 276-7
Beech Expeditor 75, 91
Bellerive, LAC G.C. 19
Bend, Capt Greg 307
Benedet, Capt Jeff 258
Bennell, Capt Al 251, 252
Benson, F/O Les 72, 73, 82, 84, 88, 90, 92, 127
Benson, Hon. Edgar 139
Bentham, F/L Len 75, 84, 86
Berg, G/C V.L. 144
Bergie, F/O Don 91, 94, 97, 118
Bermuda 237
Bertand, Pte 194
Bertrand, F/O Carl 111, 113, 124, 125, 134
Bertrand, Maj Georges 278, 284, 285, 289
Best, Capt Larry 172, 174
Beswick, Capt Bruce 227, 228, 237
Betts, LCol Ross 159, 186, 198, 199, 202-206, 223, 227
Bigg, F/O Norm 85, 95, 101, 102, 106, 108
Bijdevaate, Capt Chris 310, 313, 314
Billard, OCdt 228
Bligh, Capt Dave 173, 174
Blom, Maj Jelle 246
Blouin, MCpl P. 214
Bodien, W/C H.E. 144
Boe, F/L Bernard "Barney" 63
Boeing types:
B-29 69, 84, 85
B-52 163, 241, 271
B707 229, 237, 238, 246
B747 271
E-3 AWACS 262, 299;
KC-135 280, 281, 284, 286
Bogden, MCpl Joe 313
Bohemier Lake, Manitoba 66
Bohemier, WO Joseph Eloi 46, 66, 67
Boivin, WO 264, 265
Bombardier 258, 272
Borgeois, Ardell 289
Bosman, Maj A.R.H. 142
Boudreau, MWO 311
Boyd, F/L Tim 192
Boyd, Maj E.R. 249, 258, 265
Boyd, Wendy 265
Boyer, LCol Alain 274
Boyle, F/O H.V. 34
Boyle, LGen John 266
Boyle, P/O John J. 13, 16, 66
Bracken, Robert 53
Bradley, F/O D.E. 91, 94, 103, 104, 127, 129, 130
Bradshaw Trophy 202
Bradshaw, A/V/M D.A.R. 138, 140, 144
Branch, F/O Ken 88, 91, 127
Brannagan, F/O Thomas A. 25, 28, 29, 33-36, 62, 63, 67
Brantford, Ontario 48, 50
Brasseur, Capt Dee 234
Brassington, Capt Travis 278, 284, 290, 291, 295, 312
Brassington, Riley 284
Braun, Cpl Eric 282
Breau, Capt 276
Breffitt, F/L J. 144
Bregman, F/L Sidney 39, 51, 52, 54-59
Bremgarten, Germany 209
Brewer, Capt Ross 152
Brezinski, Capt "Brez" 260
Brine, F/O Garnet 72, 73, 75, 81, 82, 84, 88, 92, 94
Bristol Freighter 97, 98, 105, 167
Broadhurst, A/V/M 29
Broadwell, Cpl Darren 283
Brochu, F/O Leopold 29
Brochu, FSgt Armand G. "Gil" 29, 32, 34, 43, 63, 67
Brophy, Capt Des 308, 310, 314
Brosseau, LCol Richard 235, 260
Brosseau, Sgt Nicole 282
Brown, Cec 80
Brown, Col 296
Brown, F/L William W.L. 29, 31, 36, 41, 51, 310, 311
Brown, P/O G.F. 60
Browne, S/L J.D. "Danny" 25-27, 29, 30, 32, 33, 67, 264, 265
Broyhill, Capt Ray 237
Brumm, Pte Steve 228
Brunet, Lt 263
Brunton, P/O Norman 16-18, 20, 21
Bryans, A/V/M J.G. 142
Buckingham, 1Lt 61
Burgess, LCol Bruce 89, 131, 155, 170, 176, 203, 223, 227
Burns, F/L Neil 51, 88, 91, 94, 118, 119
Burris, MCpl Jamie 245
Burroughs, Capt Dave 173, 174, 177
Burrows, S.E. "Syd" 105
Burt, Col David C. 54, 155, 159, 160, 184, 185, 193, 194, 204, 209, 212, 261, 266-268
Burt, Jeanne 222
Burton, Maj Dave 227-231, 234, 237, 238-243, 246, 249, 284
Business Flights 113
Butler, Charles H. 15, 18
Butler, Harold 18
Byrne, LCol Tom 213
Byrne, Maj Shaun 285

Cadieux, Hon Leo 176
CAE 272
Calderon, Capt Emile 246-249
Calderone, CWO Tony 268
Calgary Stampede 210
Cameron, CWO Dan 228, 234
Cameron, Dugald 213
Cameron, Pte 194
Campbell, A/M Hugh 101, 112
Campbell, BGen "BR" 202
Campbell, Capt Brad 260, 261, 265
Campbell, Col Lloyd 182, 205, 223, 237
Campbell, Eddie 263
Campbell, Scotty 118
Campbell, Wendy 265
Campney, Hon Ralph 97
Campton, Cpl R.J. 257
Canada Aviation Museum 210
Canada Day 1999 289
Canadair 92, 138
Canadair types:
CF-104 136-223; CL-41 Tutor 188, 207, 208, 263;
Challenger 95, 160, 246;
CL-215 95;
F-86 Sabre 68-135, 138
Canadian Car and Foundry 12
Canadian Fighter Pilots Association 17, 23, 62, 79
Canadian International Paper 50
Canadian Military Journal 311
Canadian Nuclear Weapons 138
Canadian Profile - CF-104 Starfighter 138
Canadian Volunteer Service Medal 64
CAOC 284
Card, Bill 173, 185, 189
Cardinal, Cpl Pete 282
Carew, F/L Bob 108
Carlson, Maj Murray 278, 285
Carlton, Jeff 295
Carlton, LCmdr Mark 278, 284
Carr, LGen W.K. 198
Carter, Capt Rob 278, 284, 291, 309, 313, 314
Cartierville, Quebec 70, 136, 137, 183
Cartwright, Manitoba 192
Cashman, Leo 25
Casley, F/L W.H. 103, 112
Cassar-Torregiani, Cpl Bruce 282
Castledine, Capt Brian 152, 167, 168, 198
Castledine, Sandy 167
Caterpillar Club 15, 16, 128
Caws, Maj Pete 170
Cazaux, France 112
Central Airways 297
Central Technical School 54
CEPE 136
Cessna: Ce.172 201, L-19 201, T-37 187
Chadburn Trophy 107
Chadburn, Lloyd V. 107
Challoner, F/L Russ 113
Channel Islands 53, 56
Chapin, Capt Harry 160, 168, 203, 204, 214
Chapman, Capt Rob 227-8, 232-3, 236, 243, 250
Chapman, F/O Keith 115, 118
Charleton, Maj 208
Charnley, AC1 J.R. 70
Chartrand. MCpl Bruce 283
Chase, MCpl 312
"Checkerbirds" 222
Chellendor, Capt Scott 245
Chercoe, Capt Ron 156
Chester Herald 65, 66
Chiasson, Capt Dave 245
Chick, LAC 21
Chisholm, Bill 267, 282, 287, 288, 302, 303
Choloy Cemetery 102, 130, 133, 175
Chowen, F/O William R. 24, 31, 34, 41, 62, 63
Chowen, Mrs. W.R. 62, 63
Chretien, PM Jean, 285, 290
Christie, Capt Jim 227, 228, 234, 269
Christie, Col Robert G. 153, 169, 176, 214, 216
Churchill, Cpl Bob 189
Churchill, Prime Minister 17, 50
Cinnamon, F/O Garth 84
City Express 188
Clark, Cpl Guy 283
Clarke, Capt Alasdaire 278
Claxton, Hon. Brooke 74
Clayton, F/O Ron 85, 91, 94, 98, 103, 107, 121
Clearwater, John 138
Cleland, Col Bill 294, 302
Clement, Lt Mario 309
Clements, LGen Scott 151, 199, 236, 266
Clowater, Cpl R. 214
Clyde River, Scotland 78
CNN 309
Coak, John Bernard, VC 266
Cockburn, F/O Bob 94, 103, 104
Cockell, Capt Darren 258, 259
Coe, Cpl Stan 146
Cold Lake Museum 182
Cold War 69-273
Commonwealth Aircrew Reunion 23
Commonwealth War Graves Commission 28, 39
Computing Devices of Canada 140
Connery, Dr. Merv 218
Conningham, A/M Sir Arthur 28
Conroy, Cpl P. 214
Constable, Cathy 265
Constable, Dan 265
Constable, MCpl Tracy 282
Constantine, F/O Mark 118
Convair: F-102 239; F-106 239, 246, 247, 249
Cook, SSgt Cliff 248
Cooke, Doug 72, 82, 84
Copeland, F/L J.C. "Jake" 34-36, 39, 41, 48-50, 52, 55, 67
Copeland, June 50
Corbett, F/O Gary 100, 101, 126
Corley, Sgt Scott 304
Cormier, CWO H.J. 257
Corness, Les 102
Cornies, Cpl Don 282
Coronation flypast 88
Corver, Rich 227, 254, 255, 270
Cossutto, HCol Mirco 294
Coste, F/O Lorne H. 124, 134
Coulter, F/L Lyle 144
Cousineau, Pte Tess 228
Couture, Capt Len 188
Cpl Frank Mayer
Crabb, LCol Larry 155, 165, 166, 179, 180, 182, 186, 194, 197, 199-201, 203, 223, 227
Crabb, OCdt Darren 200
Craigmyle, AC 21
Crane, F/L Thomas N. 110, 111, 118, 119, 131
Cranfield, Capt Kerry G. 157
Cranfield, Lt K.G. 157, 183, 196
Cranston, F/O Peter K. 75, 82, 84, 87, 92, 93
Cratchley, Capt Jim 155, 170
Croll, Capt John 173
Crook, Jim 41
Crump, WO Peter 28
CRV-7 158, 160, 195, 207, 213
Cryderman, Sgt Greg 282, 288
Cuban Missile Crisis 137
Culver, Cpl Bryce 309
Cumberbirch, F/O P.R. 134
Cummings, Cpl S. 214
Cummings, F/O D.A. 125, 126, 134
Cunningham, F/O Pete 91
Curran, F/O Bernie 105
Curtiss P-40 13
Curtiss P-40 Kittyhawk 61
Curtiss, A/M W.A. 83, 84, 93
Cuthbertson, S/L D.R. 94, 95, 99, 101, 103, 107, 118, 119

D-Day 28-32, 224, 260, 264, 265
DACT 228, 229, 235, 237, 240, 246, 255, 258-260, 264, 269-271, 276, 277, 284, 288
Dagenais, Sgt Frances 283
Daley, Pte Sharon 228
DAR 206, 266, 277, 313
Dargent, F/O Douglas 113
Dassault:
Mirage 165, 195
Mystère 104, 119, 134, 158
Davenport, MCpl Stanley 282
David, Maj John 155, 173, 200
Davidson, F/O Harvey 94, 98, 126, 127, 130
Davidson, F/O Jack 127, 134
Davidson, W/C R.T.P. 83, 87
Davies, Col Dwight 274, 2910
Day, Capt A.R. "Fuji" 255, 258, 264-266
Day, G/C Nigel 264
DCIEM 263
de Havilland Canada 54
de Havilland types:
Tiger Moth 40, 51;
Twin Otter 215;
Vampire 69, 72-74, 92, 93, 235;
Venom 83, 94, 106
Dean, H.L. 20
Decimomannu (AWU) 98, 109-111, 114, 115, 155, 174, 208, 210, 215, 220, 221, 263
decorations 64-66
Decoste, Reg 263
Deere, Capt Dave 227, 232, 259, 270
DeJong, Lt Gord 170, 171, 184, 263
deKoninck, Tristan 269
Delanghe, Capt Ted 161, 192-195, 202
Delauney, Gaby 33
Demarais, MCpl Jean 288
Dempsey, Capt D.V. 207, 209, 212-214, 263
Denbeigh, Cpl E.C. 204
Denmark 124-126, 133, 156, 157, 164, 167, 177
Dept. of Industry, Trade and Commerce 50
DeQuetteville, Col A.M. 202, 210
Der Kanadier 157, 218
Derraugh, F/O Harold E. 39, 58
Desbiens, J.P. 192
Deschamps, André 209, 213, 214
Desert Cats 256, 257
DEW Line 188, 225
DFC 50, 65, 67, 73
Diefenbaker, PM John G. 137, 138, 140
Dimitrou, Paul 284
Dionne, Capt Daniel 291
Dion, Cpl Steph 282, 288
Diss, F/O Michael J. 111, 125, 126, 133, 134
Distinguished Flying Medal 64
Dobson, Maj 174
Doehling, Col 210
Doha 257
Doherty, LCol James 295
Donald, Bruce 124
Donegan, Cpl J. 214
Dorval, Quebec 74
Douglas Genie rocket 204
Douglass, SSgt Danny 245
Dove, Sgt Dave 228
Dowdy, F/O 32
Doyle, B.M. "Bert" 160, 204, 207, 209, 210, 214
Doyle, Capt Seldon 271
Doyle, F/L Mike 92
Doyle, Helen 222
Doyle, Lt Ron 155, 170
Drake, Bob 263
Draper, Bill 25, 41, 51
Drew, Hon. George 92
Driscoll, F/O Harry 75
Dudley, Ron 273
Duerr, MCpl Rita 282
Duffie, F/O Ronald A. 111, 122, 123, 127
Duisberg, Germany 56
Dumont, MCpl Pierre 282
Dumontet, Capt Marc 155, 170
Duncan, Capt John 152, 221
Dundee, Scotland 49
Dunkerley, F/O D.W. 134
Dunlap, A/V/M C.R. 74
Dunlop, Col James F. 140-142, 145, 152, 169, 176, 216, 221, 223, 227
Dunn, Darlene 258
Dunn, F/O Murray 134
Dunning, Bill 25
Dunning, F/O Boyd W. 64, 65
Dunsdon, Ray 174
Dunsterville, Capt Brian 278, 280
Dupais, Lucien 33
Duren, Germany 52
Durnan, Bob 100

Ebby, LCol 260
Eburn, F/O Bernie 91, 94, 98, 103
Ecker, Jack 72, 73, 75, 82, 84, 86, 88, 90, 92-94
Edelman, MCpl John 283
Edwards, BGen R.M. 140, 143-145, 216, 223, 227
Edwards, W/C J.F. 92
Eichel, Capt Brehn 310, 311, 314
Eichel, Garth 303-305
Eichhorn, Walter 297
Eldridge, Ron 18
electronic warfare 229, 260, 279
ELINT 270
Ellerbeck, George 192
Ellis, Capt R.E. "Rod" 155, 170
Ellis, F/O 124
Ellison, Maj S.P. 261
Elphick, Capt Terry 170
Endicott, Maj Bob 157, 160, 171, 186-188, 200, 202
England, Maj John 189

English Electric Canberra 84, 88, 89, 162
Engstad, Capt P.C. "Phil" 151, 153, 155, 199, 221
Erickson, Capt Michael "Lief" 227, 228, 230, 254, 269
Erlandson, Doug 203
Erskine, Cpl Wayne 247
escape & evasion 36, 91, 95, 103, 131, 184, 185
Eshott, UK 51
Eskimos 232
Esplen, Capt Keith 269
Ethier, Cpl Brad 282, 288
EuroFighter 261, 273, 295-297
Evans, A/C/M Sir David 215
Evans, Mr. T. 60
Evergreen International 271
exchanges 119, 123-126, 133, 156-166, 208-213, 269-273
Execaire 188
Exercises:
ADEX 228, 229, 270
Amalgam 231
Amalgam Chief 237, 253
Amalgam Warrior 267, 313
Arctic Fox 267
Ardent 84, 94
Bikini 184
Carte Blanche 98
Certain Sentinel 171
Checkerboard South 259, 261, 270
Chynx South 259
Coldfire 171, 260
Cold Shaft 275
Combat Archer 234, 260
Cope Thunder 264
Copper Flag 240, 269, 270, 275
Coronet 89
Cougar South 210
Datex 171
Dividend 91
escape & evasion 36, 91, 95, 103, 131, 184, 185,
Fabius 28
Fabulous 85
Fighter Meet 256
Fox Paw 131
Gutes Omen 171
Island Reach 284
Keynote 229, 260, 269
Lightning Strike 235, 269
Maple Flag 228, 237, 260-2, 266-8, 276, 308-12
MARCOT 260
Midnight Sun 267
Momentum 89, 117
PACEX 89 252
Quick Draw 264
Quick Talk 229
Rabbit Trek 91
Rat and Terrier 85
Red Flag 163, 228, 229, 308
Reforger 171
RIMPAC 267, 288
Royal Flush 145, 150-154, 164, 165, 171, 175, 176, 192, 219, 220
Sardinia Salvo 110, 167
Slow Scan 270
Snowball 206, 263
Southern Bello 124, 131
Stalwart Ram 260
Sweet Briar 235
Tactical Air Meet 196
Tactical Weapons Meet 196
Tall Timber 124, 125, 131
Tartan Paladin 224, 264-266
TASMO 228, 229, 313
Top Gun 172
Tuesday Scrimmage 124
Top Weight 131
Whipsaw 104

F-117 stealth fighter 281
Fabi, Capt Guy 152, 170
FAC 208, 260, 261, 271
Fahsholtz, Capt S.L. 245
Fairchild A-10 269, 281
Falaise 36, 37, 50, 56
Falardeau, MCpl Gary 283
Farris, Cpl Dave 282, 312, 313
Faucher, LCol Sylvain 289
Felhaber, F/L Bill 82, 84
Fellows, AC 21
Ferguson, Capt 208
Ferguson, Cpl Greg 282
Fetchyshyn, Lt Roman 176
Fever, Maj "Doc" 247
Fighter Factory 12
Fikowski, F/O "Mick" 91, 106
Fine, F/L Len 88, 90, 91, 94, 97, 128
Fitton, Len 48
flak 28, 37, 43
Fleet Finch 47, 48, 54, 60
Fleming, F/O J.W. 25, 27, 31, 32, 67
Fletcher, LS 258
Fletcher, LSgt R.L. 27
Flight Comment 231, 243, 255, 268
Flight International 243
Flight Systems 106
flight safety 236
FLIR pod 275, 281, 284, 286, 287, 291-293, 313
FLIT 255, 258, 275, 284, 306
Flood, Jimmy 51
Florennes, Belgium 119
Floyd, Capt Willy 180
Flying O'Maras 114
Flynn, Bret 289
Flynn, Clarke 277
Flynn, LCol Billie 135, 238, 275-297, 304
Flynn, Sgt 21
Foche-Wulf Fw.190 26
FOL 206, 225, 230-232, 235-237, 255, 267, 269, 271, 273
Folkins, F/O Jack 110, 118, 122, 127, 129, 131
Folkins, Gloria 118
Ford Bronco 295
Forest, Maj Chris 258
Forrestall, Michael 176
Fortier, Cpl Luc 309
Foster, Capt Jane 234
Foster, Maj Rich 278
Found, F/O Ron 74
Francis, F/L Don 140
Frappé, Jean-Bernard 36
Frawley, Capt Blais 285, 289
Frazer, S/L Jack 144, 162, 200
Frecce Tricolore 276
French, Capt Mike 309, 314
French, Cpl Mike 282
French, F/O Al 181
Frigault, Capt Paul 278
Fryiklund, Capt Ben 90
Fuhr, CWO Hal 311
fun and games 17, 18, 21, 52, 88, 92, 93, 102, 107, 117-19, 123-26, 131, 160, 189, 194, 203, 206, 207, 215-222, 246, 248, 258, 259, 283, 309, 310
Furois, LAC J.C.A.G. 177
Fürstenfeldbruck, Germany 89, 93, 208
FWIC 270, 272, 278, 284, 285, 286

G-8 Summit 210, 307
Gaines, Charles 51
Gainsford, Lt Lyle A. 151, 155, 156
Gale, Maj Jim 157, 189, 202
Galeb fighter 281
Galena, Alaska 270
Gallant, Pte Gilles 228
Gamey, P/O Thomas C. 25, 28
Gardiner, F/L E.W. 144, 151-153, 175, 198, 216
Garry, Bob 199
Gartner, F/L Barry 101, 126, 131, 133, 134
Gaston, LCol 260
Gaudreault, MCpl 194
Gaudry, F/O Jean 76, 81, 82, 84, 88, 90, 92, 94
GCI 100
Gehman, F/L C.W. 183
Gelinas, Rick 199
General Dynamics:
F-16 241-249, 262, 279-281, 284, 296, 300, 301
F-111 241, 246, 261
Genie rocket 204
George Medal 128
Gerhard, Capt Ken 256
German flying units:
1 Marinefliegergeschwader 157, 158, 208, 210
511 "Immelman: 209, 210
KG.51 39
Gerwing, C.F. "Clem" 17, 20, 21
Gestapo 26
Gibraltar 108
Gilbertson, S/L P.A. 54
Giles, Capt Paul 269
Gilkinson, F/O Don 100, 111, 124-126, 134
Gill, S/L W.T.H. "Bill" 86, 91, 99
Gilleade, FSgt 34
Gillis, F/O Paul C. 133, 134
Gilmartin, P/O John W. 13, 15, 20
Girard, Cpl Bernie 282
Girard, Maj Mo 277
Girling, Maj Dave 189
Glaeser, Capt Brett 278, 280, 284, 295, 309
Gloster:
Javelin 165
Meteor 82-85, 93, 124, 133
Glover, Maj John 173
Goderich, Ontario 48, 51
Godfrey, A/V/M A.E. 16, 17
Godin, Sgt Guy 309
Godwin, A/V/M H.B. 119
Golden Hawks 133, 134
Goldilocks 74
Goodin, LAC 21
Gorth, Lt Dave 227, 228
Gould, Cpl Pete 311
Gouly, F/O Jock 111
Gourley, Helen 120
GPS 291, 312
Graham, Maj D.R. 187
Graham, P/O Alex 25, 32, 60
Graham, Pam 60
Grant, S/L F.E. 61
Grasswick, Capt Chris 256, 276
Grasswick, Hugh 122, 124
Graves, HCol David 277, 294, 295, 296
Grazzanise Air Base, Italy 158, 160, 189
Greatrix, F/L John 118, 155, 156, 181, 183
Grecco, LCol Jim 274
Greece 159, 209, 211
Green, Steve 263
Greene, Nancy 203
Greengrass, MCpl Brian 282
Greenville, South Carolina 188
Greenwood, Leath 284, 285
Grendys, Sgt Claus 228
Greswell, MCpl Dave 282
Grey Cup 260
Griffin, F/O Bruce 124
Grogan, Cpl 194
Gruenther, Gen Alfred M. 150
Grumman types:
EA-6 Prowler 279
F-14 Tomcat 259, 260, 270
Goblin 13, 60, 61
Turbo Mallard 95
F-11F-1F Super Tiger 138
Guay, F/O Norm 118, 121, 124, 127, 129
Guidinger, Col Ron 268
Guilbault, Capt Jean 258, 289
Gulf War 210, 246, 257, 268, 291, 306
Gulyas, F/L Steve 88
gunnery 85, 89, 90, 91, 93, 131, 133
Guynemer Trophy 71, 112, 113
Guynemer, Georges 112
Gwynn, Cpl Terry 282

Hackett, F/O Les 125
Hadfield, Chris 235
Haire, Cpl Craig 282
Hale, G/C E.B. 61, 82, 84, 88, 90, 91, 127
Halifax, NS 47
Hall, S/L James D. 24
Halliday, Hugh A. 87, 155, 291
Halliwell, Lt Craig R. 207, 209, 212, 214, 259
Halloran, Sgt A. 214
Hamilton Aero Club 60
Hamilton, Capt Chris 307, 310
Hammond, Jane 222
Hammond. S/L T.L. 204, 210, 212
Hanson, F/O Don 72-75, 82, 86, 88, 94, 117
Haran, F/O Jean 127
Harkness, Hon. Douglas 138
Hart, Capt H.A. "Bobby Joe" 145, 151-153, 155, 170, 199, 218
Hartmann, Erich 87
Hartzell, Capt Shawn 307, 309, 310, 313
HARV F/A-18 277
Harvey-Clark, Chris 172
HAS 293
Haskins, Capt Eddie 246, 247
Hatch, Capt G.W. 204, 205, 209
Haverstock, F/O Bob 76, 82, 88, 92, 93
Hawk SAM 148, 159
Hawker types:
Hunter 70, 116, 123, 124, 125, 131, 164, 165
Hurricane 12-20, 23, 47, 48, 51, 54, 61
Hawn, Capt Laurie 157, 161, 173, 246, 247, 266, 275
Hayes, R.C. "Bob" 17, 18, 20, 21, 66
Hayman, F/O Ronald G. 99, 110, 111, 120, 131, 134
Head, LAC 21
Heasman, F/O George E. 37, 38, 41, 49
Heathe, Capt J.F. 172, 174
Hébert, Capt Stephane 278
Heidleberg, Germany 205, 215
Heiszek, Jack 192
Heligoland, Denmark 56
Hellenic Air Force 159, 295
Henault, LGen Ray 274
Henderson, Sir Athur 74
Hengeveld, M.H. 83
Henry, Capt Tom 173
Henry, F/L Clifford J. 112
Henson, Capt Scott 285
heraldry 64-66, 198
Hergesell, Maj 209
Hermanson, Maj Gerald L.A. 176, 177, 201
Heron, F/O 90
Hervieux, Capt Patrice 285
Highton, F/L 112
Hill, Capt Don 156
Hill, Cpl Mitch 21
Hill, P/O W.D. 21, 25, 34
Hill, S/L George U. 24, 26, 27, 35, 63, 258
Hill, W/C Lou 97, 104, 109, 117, 118, 227
Hill, Wally 258
Himmelman, F/O Ray 72, 75, 82, 84, 92, 93
Hind, F/L J.W. 134
Hindmarsh, F/O Harry 14, 15, 20, 676
HMCS:
Calgary 313
Cormorant 255
Kootenay 176, 270
Magnificent 71, 78, 92
Saskatchewan 255, 270
Vancouver 313
Hoch, Betty Ann 222
Hoch, M.J. 199, 204, 209-213, 246
hockey 132
Holdsworth, Maj Stu 227, 228, 240, 246, 250
Holliday, Cpl R. 214
Hollinger Mines 48
Hollman, Mark 200
Holmes, Capt Mark 172, 204, 210, 211, 214
Holmes, F/O J.W. 144, 175
Holmes, Joan 222
Home War Establishment 13
Homewood, Capt Pete 278
Honest John rocket 137
Hoogen, F/O Arnie 107
Hooten Park, UK 98
Hopkins, Paul 296
Hoskins, Cpl Wayne 282
Hotel Antares 294
Howard, Capt Sam 189
Howes, S/L H.A. 48
Howitt, Cpl Earl 282
Howlett, F/O D.W. 111, 118, 119, 124, 126, 130, 134
HRH Duke of Edinburgh (Prince Philip) 88, 198
HRH King George VI 84
Huckstep, Maj Bill 209, 213, 214, 251, 278
HUD 161, 271
Huddleston, Gen David 199, 260, 266
Hughson, Capt Mike 243
Humboldt, Sask. 215
Hume, John 272
Hunt, LCol Terry L. 250, 251
Hunter, Al 209, 214
Hupe, MCpl Glen 202, 214
Hurst, MCpl R.E. 204
Huson, S/L Robert 260
Hussein, Saddam 257
Hutt, Capt John 280, 285, 289
Hutt, LCol John 157, 161, 189, 201, 223, 227
Huzarik, Capt Ron 210
Hynes, Cpl Leon 268, 288

ICBM 225
Ilushin: Il-14 100, Il-18 "Coot" 270, Il-28 69
Incremental Modernization Program 266
India-Burma 2
Inuit 232
Inuvik, NT 225, 231, 232, 237, 255, 267-269, 273
Iqaluit, NU 225
Ireland, W/C E.G. 80
Irwin Air Chute 128
Isenor, F/O Ralph 188
Isralson, FSgt Glenn H. 61
Italy 158, 161
Ivens, Herb 17
Izzard, George 203

Jabara, Maj James 86
Jackson (Copeland), June 50
Jackson, Bernie 265
Jackson, Tom 265
Jaguar 261
James, Cpl J. 214
Jameson, F/L 124
Jamieson, Cpl Dave 282
Jaques, Capt Jeff 258
Jefferson, F/O Frank R. 112
Jensen, LAC Arnold B. 16
Jensen, Maj Gorm 199
Jever, Germany 209, 276, 295
Jewell, FSgt Jewell 51
Jewett, Arthur 50-54, 67, 266
Jewett, Joyce 53
JG.26 War Diary 28
Jim Donihee, Maj Jim 258-260, 295, 296
Jimmy Lake Range 237, 264
Joerger, Johanna 260
Johnson, A/V/M J.E. "Johnnie" 23, 25, 32, 34, 49, 51, 63, 67, 198, 260, 264, 265, 275
Johnson, Bill 263
Johnson, Capt Curt 227, 228, 235
Johnson, Capt R.I. 204, 209, 212
Johnson, Capt Reid 259
Johnson, F/O Jim 91, 94, 97, 127
Johnson, Gen Leon 112, 113
Johnson, President Lyndon 137
Johnson, WO Vic 146, 154, 170, 225
Johnstone, Alan "Johnnie" 25, 32, 36, 38, 40, 49, 55
Joint Maritime Course 265
Jolley, F/O John "Ray" 72, 75, 82, 84, 86, 88, 91
Jones, Capt Paul 276
Jones, Cpl A. 204
Jones, Lt Jim 151, 153, 155, 156
Jordan, Maj Tim 278
Jorgenson, Ken 75
Jouan, Cpl Andreé 283
Jurak, Anthony 57
Jurkowski, Col D. 243, 251, 274, 294, 294

Kadonoff, Maj Bob 173, 174
Kain, Cpl Mitch 283
Karperian, Capt Wayne 265, 285
Kaufman, Col F.J. 177
Kean, PO 258
Keenan, Cpl Carl 189
Kelly, Capt Bill 276
Kelly, F/L E.D. 75, 79, 80-86, 88, 90, 91, 93, 94, 95, 128
Kelly, Jim 209
Kennedy, President John F. 137
Kenny, Capt Eric 278
Kent, F/L R.E. 74
Kidd, Bill 136
Kimball, F/L Donald H. 21, 24, 25, 34-36, 38, 39, 41, 43, 51, 65, 67
Kincaid, F/O "Buster" 110, 111, 192
King Beaudoin 83
King Salmon, Alaska 271
King, AC1 R.L.S. 70
King, Ambrose 15, 18
King, BGen Garry R.J. "Sky" 145, 152, 155, 164, 165, 170, 177, 178, 183, 198, 214-222
King, Chesley 15
King, Gerry 199
King, Mrs. Miriam 18
Kinsman, Col Dave 227, 306
Kirbyson, Capt George 152, 155, 170, 214, 219
Kirbyson, Capt Jordan 285, 289
Kissmann, Maj Paul 237, 308
Klein, F/O Harry 91, 94, 127
Klein, Premier Ralph 266
Kleinsteuber, Capt Neil 155, 170, 214
Knaghjneum, Sgt 51
Knights of Columbus 19
Koch, F/L Tom 126, 127
Korean War 73, 75, 104
Koski, Les 269
Kosovo 274-294
Kovach, Kelly 209, 214, 259
Kusiar, FSgt Charles W. 16, 19, 20

Laage, Germany 296
Labert, F/O Ray 104
Lac la Biche, Alberta 310, 311
Lacerte, R.J. "Bob" 18, 44, 67
LaFrance, F/O Claude 86, 103, 104, 119, 123, 124, 126
Laidler, Marg 120
Lake, F/O Ronald G. 25, 27, 33, 38, 39, 49, 67
Lalonde, Leo 115
Lalonde, Romeo 192, 199
Lambert, Andy 111, 131
Lambros, F/O Danny 118, 131
Lambros, Pat 119
Lancaster, Lt R.A. 207, 212, 214, 259
Landry, Maj George 157, 189, 201, 202
Lane, A/V/M R.J. 198
Langille, Leola 265
Langille, Steve 265, 284, 285-287
Laroche, Maj Pat 278
Larouche, Capt Chris 278, 285, 289, 291
Laserich, Willy 116
Laubman, G/C Donald C. 138
Laurent, Cpl P. 214
Laurie, Pte 194
Laverdière, Capt Mark 307, 309, 310
Lavoie, Capt Sylvain 258
Lawrence, Capt Mark 258
Leaf, BGen Dan 280
Learjet 241, 246, 271
LeBlanc, Capt René 227, 234, 237, 240, 246, 252, 269
Ledsham, Maj Anthony 289
Lee, Capt Ted 161, 173, 183, 184
Leeson, Capt Mark 275, 276
Leeuwarden, Holland 112, 113, 209
Legrow, James S. 15, 18
Legrow, Reginald 15, 18
Lehtinen, Cpl Aron 283
Leland, Lt (USN) Maurie 258
Lemieux, Todd 314
Leonard, Capt Don 269
Lepard, F/O Murray 131
Leppich, Mr. 204
Leppich, Peter 204
Lessard, MCpl J.C. 282
Letness, Cpl R. 214
Lett, Ken 143, 144
Leuty, Capt Kirk 256
Levesque, F/L J.A.O. 86, 295
Lewis, BGen Ken 143, 182
Lewis, Capt T.W. 151-153, 155, 199
Lewis, MCpl 194
Lewis, Mr. 54
Lief Erickson Room 258
Linda Morley 265
Lindsay, S/L J.D. 92
Little, Capt Clark 157, 173, 189
Little, F/O M.A. 134
Little, HCol Mark 314
Litton radar 195
Lloyd, Cpl D. 214
Lockhart, F/O Alan 94
Lockheed 136
Lockheed Martin:
F-16 series 241-249, 262, 279-281, 284, 296, 300, 301
F-35 296
Lockheed types:
C-130 Hercules 231, 262, 284
F/CF-104 136-223, 263, 264
L.1011 284, 286, 287
T-33 62, 77, 108, 109, 121, 122, 138, 142, 144, 174, 204, 208, 229, 241, 242, 305
Aurora 188
Ventura 51
Logan, F/L 34
Lomax, OC J.K.W. 134
London, England 59
Longhurst, Bill 95
Longuyon, France 166, 169, 170, 217
Lord De l'Isle and Dudley 97
Lucy, Cpl Terry 282, 288
Luedemann, Capt Walt 172
Luftwaffe 125, 126, 139, 165, 207, 261, 262, 272, 273
Luftwaffe units
JG.26 28, 32
JG.2 32
JG.71 126
FBW36 272
FW71 272
FW74 273
721 OCU 272
Luke, Maj "Red" 227
Lundberg, Sten T. 15, 16, 20, 21, 66
Lynn, F/O Bill 118, 119, 124, 125, 135

MacArthur, F/O John L. 100, 101, 125, 126, 132, 134
MacBrien, G/C W.R. 74, 93, 138, 139
MacDonald, Cpl Don 283
MacDonald, Cpl Linda 282
MacGarva, F/L Ron 110, 112, 113
MacGregor, F/O "Mac" 91, 94, 144
MacIntosh, WO 20
MacKenzie, Alison 92, 135
MacKenzie, Bruce M. 16, 17, 20, 21, 24, 25, 32, 34-38,

41-43, 66, 67
MacKenzie, S/L A.R. "Andy" 72-76, 79-82, 84, 87, 91-93, 117, 127, 135, 227, 269, 295
MacKinnon, Capt Gerry 257
MacLean, Helen 265
MacLean, Ian 265, 272
MacMillan, FSgt Ross A. 25, 31, 67
MacMillian, Capt Darwin 278
MacNeil, Capt J.P. 204, 209, 212, 213
MacPerson, LAC 134
Maher, Cpl Frank 282
Mahoney, Capt Joe 278
Mainville, Sgt Len 282
Major, Maj Marcel 246-249
Major, Maj Mike 157, 163, 189, 202
Makins, Cpl K. 214
Malainey, Capt J.L. 260, 267
Manching, Germany 295-297
Manning Depot 17, 47
Manning, Capt Jim 285, 289
Manson, Gen Paul D. 142, 146, 151, 155, 192, 201, 203, 214, 223
Marlow, Cpl Dan 283
Marr, F/L 62
Marshal, Sgt Jim 228
Marta, Cpl D.B. 257
Martello tower 220
Martin B-57 113
Martin, Capt R.L. "Rick" 189, 202
Martin, Capt R.P. "Rob" 204, 208, 209, 211, 278
Martin, Cpl J.C. 214
Martin, F/L Ernest W. 46
Masse, Cpl Michelle 312
Matheson, Eric 235
Mathews, MCpl Chuck 309
Matthews, Cpl J. 214
Matthews, F/O Arnold G. 101, 125, 134
MATV F-16 276, 277
Maurstad, Capt Jim 157, 161, 173
Maverick missile 238, 312, 313
Mavridis, Cpl Athanasios 282, 288
McAffer, F/L George 134
McArthur, F/O Jack "Kiwi" 107, 112, 113
McCabe, F/O Eddie 46, 53
McClung, F/O Vernon F. 53
McCollum, WO Rick 228
McCombe, F/L J.D. 133
McCorriston, Cpl Dave 282, 288
McCully, Cpl J. D. 214
McCurdy, Capt Earl 204
McDermid Capt Neil 285, 289, 291
McDiarmid, F/O Jim 181
McDonald, A.J. "Alex" 20, 25, 33, 40, 43, 63
McDonald, F/L Alfred 112, 113
McDonald, F/O G.A. "Gord" 72, 75, 76, 82, 84
McDonald, F/O Ian R. 72, 82, 84, 88, 90-95
McDonald, Joan 95
McDonald, Mrs. Ellen 63
McDonald, P/O "Adj" 13, 19, 20, 67
McDonnell/McDonnell Douglas:
F-4 series 162, 163, 165, 209, 210, 211, 239, 242, 262, 272, 295, 296
F-15 159, 195, 229, 237, 239, 242, 243, 246, 251, 252, 269-272, 279, 299
F-101 158, 162, 164
CF-101 137, 138, 204, 237, 266
CF-18 54, 213, 225-314
CF-18M 305, 311
McFarlane, Capt 227
McGeary, SSgt 34
McGonigle, LAC 21
McIlraith, F/O Don 82, 88, 90
McIlraith, F/O J.A.E. 119
McIntosh, BGen D.F. 160, 203
McIntosh, F/O J.A. 39, 51, 51, 58, 97
McIntosh, Stu 295
McIntosh, Wesley H. 60
McIntyre, Robert 138
McKay, Capt Jim 155
McLachlan, F/O Percy A. 25, 27, 28
McLachlan, W/C H. 131
McLean, Jack 173
McLeod (Pattinson), Lynne 62
McLeod, F/L Henry W. 23, 28
McLeod, F/O W.H. 118, 123
McLeod, Maj 34
McLeod, Maj Ken 155, 170
McLeod, Capt Dan 310, 313
McMaster University 50
McMickle, TSgt Bob 248
McMillan, FSgt Alexander T. 63
McMillan, FSgt Osman 39
McMillan, Madeline 105
McMillan, Mrs. Ina 63
McNaughton, Capt Kevin 307
McNaughton, Capt Kevin 309, 310, 312, 313
McNaughton, LGen 227
McNeil, Scott 267
MCpl Ron Pischke, 288
McQuarrie, John 300
McRae, F/O Malcolm 119, 124, 125
McRae, MCpl Ken 282
McRoberts, MCpl Don 282
McRury, Capt Neil 278
McTavish, Ian 95
Mead, Lt Bert W. 90
Meaney, Cpl John 282
Melnyk, Cpl Ron 282, 311
Melson, Maj John 237
Menitsky, Maj Valery 252
Mention in Dispatches 50, 64
Mercer, Capt Dave 258
Merchant Ship Flying Unit 14
Mercier, Capt Francis 285, 289
Mercier, Capt J.L.R. 207
Mercier, Maj Denis 260
Meritorious Service Medal 292
Merritt, F/L 54
Messerschmitt Me.109 26, 56
Meuse, LAC John 96
Meyer, Dr. Mick 213
Middlemiss, W/C R.G. 61, 72, 73, 76, 90
MiG fighters
MiG-15 86, 87, 104
MiG-17 87
MiG-21 281
MiG-29 250-253, 262, 281, 296
Milberry, Larry 181, 245, 295
Miles Master 48, 51, 61
Millar, F/O Stuart A. 127
Miller, Capt 271
Miller, Capt Bruce 227, 228
Miller, Maj Jake 205
Mills, F/O D.D. 91, 94, 97
Milosevic, Slobodan 276
Milstead, Vi 54
Mirabel, Quebec 272
Miron, F/O 51
Mirza, Capt A.M. 249, 261, 267
Miss Canada 215
Mitchell, Bill 229
Mitchell, F/O Bill 109-111
Molnar, Capt Joe 173
Molyneux, F/O Kenneth S. 47
Monk, Pte K. 214
Monnette, P/O 67
Monterey, California 302
Montgomery, Field Marshal 38
Mooers, Capt Stanley 172, 174
Moore, F/L Leslie A. 25, 26, 28, 33
Moreash, F/O Ken 110, 118, 127, 129, 131
Morgan, F/O R.G. 128
Morgan, Sgt John 228
Morin, Claude, Capt 181
Morin, MCpl 194
Morissette, Capt Pierre 246 249
Morley, Dr. Dan 265
Morris, F/O Barry 124, 125
Morris, Maj Robin 170
Morrison, Cpl 194
Morton, Des 137
Morton, LGen L.W. 253
Motriuk, Capt 276
Mott, F/L Guy E. 13-21, 25, 32, 34-36, 39, 41, 43, 49, 55, 66, 67
Moug, Sgt R.W. 204
Mount Allison University 175
Mountbatten, Lord Louis 62
Mowbray, Capt K.R. 151-153, 155, 156, 164, 192, 199, 214
Mueller, LCol Fred 208, 264
Mueller, Lt. Harry A. 207, 209, 213, 214
Mullin, F/O "Moon" 111, 129
Munroe, Cpl D.M. 268
Murphy, Capt Phil 157, 202
Murray, Maj Brian 285
Mussells, G/C C.H. 144
Myers, F/O William J. 34, 35, 41
Myles, LCol Donald H. 91, 94, 97, 103, 173, 176, 177, 201, 223, 227
Myrah, Lt (USN) Chris 310, 313

Nadler, LAC 21
Naismith, Capt Kevin 307, 312, 313
NAS:
Cecil Field 240, 271
China Lake 312
Keflavik 243
Key West 308
Miramar 258, 259, 270
Oceana 261, 288
Patuxent River 276, 277
Whidbey Island 246
NASA 277, 295
Nash, G/C 159
NATO 69-223, 256, 271, 274-294
NATO units:
2 ATAF 150
4 ATAF 71, 100, 151, 172, 193, 205, 215, 263, 264
Nault, Cpl L. 214
NBCW 150, 152, 193, 208, 308
Neil, F/O John W. 34
Neilson, F/O M.B. 72, 74-76, 82, 84, 86, 93
Nelson, Capt Brent 278
Netherlands 165
Neuberger, Ulrich 295, 296
New Brunswick Power 54
New Fighter Aircraft program 226
Newfoundland 13-21
Newman, Peter C. 137
Nicholas, Maj M.C. 162
Nichols, Capt Derek R. 255
Nichols, F/L Grant 84, 92
Nichols, Ralph 75
Nicholson, Bob 199
Nicholson, Pte John 228
Nicks, Capt Gerry 140
Niemi, Capt Wally 209, 214
Niemy, BGen Walt 203, 223, 227
Nierlich, Angie 265
Nierlich, Capt Steve 224, 249, 261, 265, 267
Nijmegen 38, 39, 49, 65
Nishimura, F/O Nory 94
NORAD 225, 229-231, 235, 236, 250-253, 270
Normandy 30-41
Norn, F/L William H. 112
Norris, MCpl Dave 282
Norris, S/L Robert W. 13, 16, 20, 21, 24, 47, 61
North American types:
B-1B 246, 248
Harvard 13, 16, 48, 51, 54, 61, 73, 77, 91, 187
Mustang 46, 52, 56
Yale 60
Sabre 68-135, 138
F-86D 116
F-100 116, 125, 131, 235, 239, 244, 248
XF-108 225
North Warning System 206, 225, 235
Northrop 163
Northrop types:
CF-5 176, 189, 192, 205, 263, 268, 275, 276
F-5 228
Norton, Cpl Karen 282
Norway 123-125, 157, 159, 211, 220
Nowasad, Carole 222
Nowosad, Capt N.M. 204, 209-214
nuclear weapons 170
NVG 280, 281, 291, 305, 313
NWT Air 113

O'Brien, Capt Larry 172, 173, 177-179
O'Grady, Capt Scott 279
O'Keefe, Capt Tony 248
O'Malley, David 298-302
O'Mara brothers 114
O'Mara, F/L Henry 114
O'Mara, Tes 119
Ogilvie, F/L Noel 61
Ohalaturnyk, MCpl Wayne 282
Olsen, Sgt Fred 189
Omaha Beach 264, 265
Omdal, Maj Egil 157
Operation Allied Force 274-294
Operation Noble Eagle 275, 314
Operations:
Big Photo 73, 74
Echo 274-294
Leapfrog 71, 74
"Little Blitz" 31
Grizzly 210, 307
Hurricane 56
Market Garden 38
Mirador 274
Nimble Bat 71
"Pink Pussy" 310
Rhine Prosit 256, 285
Scimitar 257
Sea Lion 28
Orkney Islands 44, 46, 86
Orr, Dan 155, 170
Orr, Maj Jack 157, 173, 227, 228, 269
Ottawa 289, 290
Ouellet, Col Marc 208, 249, 251, 260, 261, 263-267, 272, 273, 299
Ouellet, Susan 265
Ouellette, Maj Chris 278
Owen Sound, Ontario 268
Owen, Capt Dave 157, 184, 186, 189
Owens, OCdt 228
Oxford University Press 50
Oxholm, LCol B.A. 172

Page, W/C Alan G. 39, 49, 63
Palmdale, California 136
Paproski, Dennis 124, 131
Paquette, F/O Remi "Rocky" 76, 82-84, 88
Paquin, Capt Jason 285
Paris Airshow 276
Parker, Maj Rob 278, 290-292, 295
Parks, W/C Walter F. 88, 127, 128
Parliament Hill 289-291
Parsons, F/O Lamont M. 13, 16-18, 20, 67, 229
Patry, MCpl Rita 178
Pattinson, F/L Harry 13, 17, 20, 60-62, 66, 67
Pattinson, Lynne 62
Paul, Capt Charlie 153, 155, 170
Paul, F/O Robert S. 112
Paulson, F/O Gary H. 134
Paxton, Don 173, 174
Payette, Julie 290
Pearson, PM Lester B. 138, 140
Peel, Vivian 222
Peirson, Maj W.G. "Wally" 160, 213, 214
Pelletier, Maj Alain 278
Pelletier, MCpl 194
Pelletier, Roy 75
Pellow, Capt 205
Perkin, F/O Reginald W. 46
Perry, MCpl Don 283
Persian Gulf War 210, 246, 257, 268, 291, 306
Perth, Scotland 48
Petsche, Cpl Ron 282
Peterson, Capt Van 257, 264
Peterson, F/L Pete 192
Petit, MCpl Jean 309
Petitte, Cpl Dwayne 309
Petsche, Cpl Rob 268
Pettipas, Sgt 194
Pettitt, Diane 265
Pettitt, Maj Marsh R. 261, 265
Pfaff, Capt Jim 155, 170, 214
Pfander, Maj Ken 262
Pferdsfeld, Germany 82, 208
phase training 121, 122
Phillips, Glen 265, 278, 285, 289, 294-296
Phillips, Karen 265
Philp, Col O.B. 263
Phoenix Coyotes 309
photo interpreter 172
Phripp, G/C Frank 232
piano burning 161, 189
Piel, André 34
Piel, Roland 33
Piercey, MCpl John 282, 288
Pieroway, Sgt T.W. 202, 204
Pigot, F/O 97, 98, 105
Piper Cherokee 201
Pirie, F/O 133
Pirie, Maj Walt 203, 204
Pisces IV 255
Pischke, MCpl Ron 282
Plewes, F/O Harry 38
Plewnia, Wolfgang 302
Plummer, F/L Lloyd 25, 27, 34, 35, 41
Plymouth Fury 246, 247
PMQs 119, 120, 166, 167, 217
Poirier, Cpl Joe 288
polio 118
Ponikve airfield 282
Porco, F/O Ed 111, 125
Porter, F/L Bob 155
Porter, Maj R.W. 144, 159, 179, 186, 199
Potter, Mr. and Mrs. 83
Poulson, Capt Cash 263, 264, 269
Prestwick, Scotland 103, 134
Prevost, Capt Paul 278
Price, F/L J.T. 133
Price, S/L L.C. 134
Prince Bernhard 112
Prizer, F/O E.L. 26
Prosser, Cpl Mark 309
Prowal, Capt Dave 278, 280, 285, 289
Pudsey, Col Amos 155
Purcell, Maj Dale 189

QRA 170, 229-231, 236, 237, 250, 254, 269, 277, 305, 307-309, 312
Quebec City 59

RAAF 88, 200
RAAF Staff College 306
Rabat-Sale/Rabat 98, 105-109
Racicot, Capt Les 259, 278, 284, 295
Raine, F/O Jim 91, 94
Ralston, Sgt Dave 228
Rankin Inlet, NT 225
Rawlings, Capt Pete 155
Raynor, F/O Art 75
RCAF Memorial Museum 215
recce 136-168
"Red Flag" 163, 228, 229, 308
Reeves, Glen "Snake" 136
Regenwetter, Capt Jason 261, 278, 289
Regli, Capt Paul 257
Rehbein, Cpl Mark 283
Reid, Capt Bruce 157, 184, 189, 202
Reid, Capt Kim 234, 255, 258, 260
Reid, F/O Burnell 113
Reidel, Hptm Harold 275
Reilly, Jack 134
René the Fox 227, 260
Renegade in Power 137
Renfrew, Scotland 103
Republic:
F-84/RF-84 119, 123, 125, 156, 164
F-105 165
XF-103 225
Résistance 32, 33
Resolute Bay, NT 232, 233
Reudiseuli, Capt Jan 238, 278, 280, 281, 284, 291
Reyno, W/C E.M. 54
Rhodes, P/O Ernest B. 13, 16
Riach, Mark 302
Ribble, Sgt 51
Richardson, Capt Joe 248
Richkun, Cpl J. 214
Richmond, Capt Craig 212, 243, 251-253, 255, 271
Riley, Bill 265
Riley, F/L Peter 164
Riley, F/O Jack 107
Riley, Theresa 265
Rimini, Italy 159, 208, 209
Rimouski, Quebec 74
Ritchie, F/L Hugh 40, 41, 235
Rivest, P/O Jean 92
RNoAF 123-125, 159
Robb, F/O Al 84
Roberts, Capt Steve 258, 260
Robichaud, F/O J.E.R. 134
Robinson, "Black Robbie" 192
Rochefort, Pierre 258, 260, 264
Rochefort, Ginnette 222
Rodrigue Cpl G. 214
Rogers, Cpl A. 214
Rogers, Rev. Silas G. 18
Ronaasen, F/O E.N. "Norm" 76, 80, 82, 83, 86, 88, 93-4
Rose, Sgt John 288
Ross, F/O Bill 181
Roulston, Maj John 224, 258
Roundel 267
Royal Air Force squadrons: 2 157, 164, 165; 14 23, 161; 15 159; 17 17; 43 165; 54 159-161; 67 62; 82 103; 96 124; 132 35; 139 89; 166 140; 243 27; 256 124; 329 46; 453 35; 519 51; 602 35
Royal Air Force other units:
1 Tactical Exercise Unit 49, 55
2 TAF 24, 28, 35, 42, 64
4 EFTS 48
5 FIS 48
11 Group 42
24th Airfield Construction Group 31
53 OTU 28
57 OTU 51
58 OTU 49
83 Group 23, 25, 26, 29, 39, 42
83 Group Support Unit 26, 55
125 Wing 35, 36, 42, 43
Bomber Command 42, 43, 46, 56, 64
Central Depository 62
Central Fighter Establishment 85, 86
Observer Corps 85
RAF College (Cranwell) 48
Strike Command 215
Royal Air Force stations:
Acklington 85, 90, 91
B.3 Ste-Croix-sur-Mer 31, 49, 260
B.11 Longues 35, 49
B.19 Lingèvres 36, 49
B.40 Beauvais 37, 49
B.52 Douai 37, 49
B.70 Antwerp 37, 49
B.86 Helmond 46, 56
B.90 Petit Brogel 46, 56
Bournemouth 51, 55
Brize Norton 127, 265
Brough 48
Bruggen 160, 161
Coltishall 158, 159
Digby 24, 46, 55, 56
Farnborough 296
Ford 28
Funtington 25, 26
Gütersloh 164
Hawkinge 42-44, 46, 49, 52
High Wycombe 215
Holmsley South 24, 55
Horsham St. Faith 88, 89, 117
Hunsdon 46
Hutton Cranswick 26, 27
Kenley 61
Kinloss 265
Laarbruch 159
Leuchars 123, 165
Lossiemouth 265, 266
Skaebrae 44, 46, 52, 65
Sumburgh 53
Tangmere 24
Tealing 49
Watton 90
West Raynham 82, 86, 91
Westhampnett 25, 26
Wildenrath 196

Royal Canadian Air Force/Canadian Forces squadrons:
1 13
111 23
118 13, 23, 60, 61
119 60
123 23
125 12-21, 23, 47, 229
126 17, 47
127 23, 54
400 121
401 92
402 28, 42
403 17, 26, 33, 61
404 188
405 176
409 250, 256, 275, 276
410 71, 74, 84, 88, 92, 213, 225-227, 238, 256, 260, 264, 266, 268, 285, 292, 306, 312
411 60, 95, 102, 413 71, 74, 92
414 71, 160 187, 229, 242, 252, 305
416 71, 73, 74, 99, 237, 250, 252, 255, 256, 260, 264, 268, 274, 310, 313
417 140, 157, 163, 174, 185, 187, 189, 190, 207
419 71, 187, 205, 208, 227, 237, 251, 255, 263, 268, 284, 285, 306
421 71, 65, 134, 140, 170, 174, 196, 197, 200, 207, 209, 213, 256, 258, 285
422 71, 112, 113, 170
423 71
425 29, 175, 188, 204, 238, 239, 252, 256, 274
427 71, 134, 138, 140, 142, 170
429 262
430 71, 140, 144, 170
431 (Snowbirds) 185, 250, 259, 263
433 237, 252, 256, 268, 269, 274
434 71, 112, 113, 140, 160, 189, 192
435 134, 215
437 65, 189, 229, 237, 256, 266, 267, 293
438 23, 73, 92
439 23, 71, 88, 112, 113, 140, 145, 146, 151, 170, 197, 207, 213, 256, 263, 285
440 23, 143, 215
442 23, 24, 35, 53, 71, 73, 118, 254
443 23-26, 28, 30, 31, 35, 51, 55
444 71, 112, 140
445 71
880 258

Royal Canadian Air Force/Canadian Forces other units:
1 Air Armament School 92
1 Air Division 69-170
1 Air Maintenance Squadron 266, 295
1 Canadian Air Division 292
1 Canadian Air Group 155, 160, 170-223, 258, 266
1 EFTS 60
1 FIS 187, 263
1 FTS 187, 258, 263
1 Manning Depot 47, 92
1 (F) OTU (wartime) 23, 51, 54, 54
1 (F) OTU (postwar) 95
1 Overseas Ferry Unit 90, 99
1 PGS 121
1 (F) Wing 71-169
1 (Recce) Wing 136-156, 164-165, 168-170, 215-223
1 SFTS 47, 48 60
1 "Y" Depot 23, 55
2 AFS 121, 215
2 CFFTS 227, 275, 305
2 (F) Wing 71, 100
2 FTS 188
2 SFTS 17, 54
3 AW (F) OTU 188
3 (F) Wing 71, 138
3 FTS 121
3 PPCLI 280
3 PRC 23
4 (F) Wing 97
4 FTS 95
4 Regular Support Unit 188
4 Release Centre 50
4 Software Engineering Squadron 272
5 ITS 47
6 (ST/R) OTU 140, 142, 143, 175, 181, 192, 196, 215
8 SFTS 47
12 EFTS 48
13 EFTS 54
17 EFTS 47
19 EFTS 17
42 Radar 239
126 Wing 35
137 (T) Flight 98
144 (F) Wing 23-25, 27, 30, 32, 35, 260
6402 Servicing Echelon 42, 46
6441 Servicing Echelon 24, 40
Air Defence Command 138
Air Weapons Unit (Trenton) 109, 155
Air Weapons Unit (Decimomannu) 215, 220, 221
Collège Royal Militaire 275, 305
DAOT 258
Eastern Air Command 13-23, 54
Experimental and Proving Establishment 62
FOTEF 312, 313
Home War Establishment 13-23, 61
Fighter Group 251, 261, 268
Flying Instructors School 306
ICP School 210
Institute of Aviation Medicine 86
National Defence College 206
PFS 204, 263
Royal Military College 135, 204, 205, 215, 263, 266, 269, 305
Royal Roads Military College 206, 215, 280, 305, 313
Sabre Transition Unit 140, 141, 144, 215
Staff College 163, 205, 210, 215, 238, 264, 277, 292, 313
Task Force Aviano 274-297
Winter Experimental Establishment 90
Women's Division 62
Yellow Jacket 128, 130, 216
Royal Canadian Air Force/Canadian Forces stations/bases:
Baden-Soellingen 97, 160, 161, 167, 168, 188, 190, 191, 200-223, 225, 256, 258
Bagotville 23, 51, 54, 55, 256, 275, 290
Cambridge Bay 188
Camp Borden 48, 51, 204
Centralia 92, 95
Chatham 73, 74, 95, 140, 144, 237
Chilliwack 207
Claresholm 120
Cold Lake 196, 205, 224-314
Comox 229-231, 237, 250-254, 269, 270, 275, 277, 284, 307, 313
Dartmouth 13, 14, 54, 61
Digby 24
Gander 275
Gimli 176, 187, 204
Goose Bay 99
Grostenquin 71, 97
Lachine 23, 51
Lahr 150, 155, 167-169, 199, 210
Langar 98
MacDonald 95, 121, 142
Marville 71, 96-169
Metz 71, 218
Moose Jaw 205, 207, 237, 255, 264, 305, 306
North Bay 187, 242, 243
North Luffenham 71, 78-95, 225
Penhold 95
Portage la Prairie 95, 121, 175, 187, 207, 215, 263, 266
Shearwater 258
Shilo 261
St. Hubert 73-78, 92, 93
Sydney 13, 16
Torbay 14-21
Trenton 92, 95, 215
Uplands 195, 195
Wainwright 229, 260
Zweibrucken 71, 90, 91, 97-99, 101, 138, 143
Royal Canadian Legion 266, 310
Royal College of Heralds 65, 66
Royal York Hotel 62
Rozdeba, F/L E.J. 133, 205
Rueck, West Germany 178
Ruel, Maj Pierre 285, 289
Ruggle, F/L Frank A. 27, 66
Ruggles, Sgt D.B. 19
Rung, Sgt Gary 189
Runge, Sgt Muriel 258
Runnymede Memorial 28, 264
Ryan drones 235, 239, 244, 248
Ryan, Capt Bill 227, 228, 235, 250
Ryan, Maj B.J. 246-249

Sabine, Capt Tom 237
Saladana, Capt Kurt 258, 259
Salinas, California 302, 303
SAM 279, 281, 284, 286, 292
Sanche, F/O Jacques 107, 118
Sanderson, Gary 199
Sardinia 109-111, 114, 115, 167
Saulnier, LCol Remi 139, 198, 202, 223, 227, 235
Saunders, F/O Leslie C. 24, 39
Saunders, Sandy 25
Savard, Capt M.J. 204, 209, 213, 214
Savard, Hugette 222
Savard, MCpl M. 214
Savoie, Capt Luc 227, 233, 237
Sawchuck, Capt Guy 227, 228, 237
Sawchuk, Ray 192
Saxberg, Bob 215
Schlägel, Maj 295
Schleswig, Germany 157, 158
Schmidt, Sgt Garth 282
Schoenenberger, Cpl D. 251
Schofield, Maj Chris 266
Schultz, Col R.D. 210
Schwab, S/L L.G. 54
Scott, Cpl Lorne 189
Scottish Aviation 103
sea survival 184
SEAD 279
Selby, Capt Miles 285, 302, 308, 314
Selby, Roland 302
"September 11, 2001" 309
Serbia 274-294
Sgt R. Bergeron, Sgt R. 214
Sharkey, Capt Don 204
Sheasby, F/O Bruce 72
Sheldrup, F/L Clancy 125, 173, 174, 189
Shepherd, Capt Greg 261, 267, 302
Sherwood, Capt Reah 310
Shields, MCpl Daryl 283
Ships:
Caribou 14, 17, *Carthage* 62, *Empress of Britain* 57, 59, *Empress of France* 79, *Homeric* 118, *Louis Pasteur* 23, *Graf Zepplin* 14, *Nieu Amsterdam* 62, *Ascania* 95, *Queen Mary* 51, *Stratheden* 50, *Strathmore* 62
Shockley, Les 300
Shopa, Capt Tim 302, 312
Short, MCpl Thom 307, 308
Shortt, Capt Terry 261
Sievert, Capt H.A. 151-153, 155, 170, 214
Sig Saur 9mm 308
"Silver Fox" (origin) 24
Sim, F/L Ray 35, 51
Simkins, F/L Ted 98
Simmons, F/O C.R. "Bob" 72-74, 76, 82, 84, 90, 92-94
Simmons, F/O D.B. "Don" 74, 76, 82, 84, 92, 127
Simpson, Andrea E.W. 254
Simpson, Marsh 210
Sinclair, Alex 272
Sinclair, Capt Brad 252, 257-259
Sinclair, Capt Graham 227, 230-233, 235, 269-272
Sinclair, Capts Todd 278, 284
Sinclair, Suzanne 233, 269
Sinnott, Cpl Gordon H. 16
Slessor, Sir John 70
Slimman, Don 174
Sloan, Maj W. S 165
Smiley, W/C Blake 100, 134
Smith, Capt Jason 285, 295
Smith, Cpl Shane 282
Smith, Eric G. 295
Smith, MCpl D. 194, 214
Smith, Rogers 125, 134, 295
Smith, Ron 209
Smith, Shantal 267
Snowbirds from the Beginning 262
Soellingen cemetery 223
Soesterberg, Holland 159, 179
Somerville, G/C J.D. 90, 97
Sorfleet, Capt Jim 263, 276
Soroka, Maj Kirk "Rambo" 238, 272, 278, 280-282, 288, 294,295
Sparks, Capt Brent 278, 291
Sparling, P/O 26, 27
Spencer, Capt Rob 246-249
Spencer, MCpl Craig 311
Split, Croatia 281
Sponder, Capt Chris 237
Spooner, Maj M.R. 207
sports 90, 283, 309
Spurr, Deb & Jane 119
Spurr, Larry 72-74, 111, 113, 114, 120
Spurr, Nan 119, 120
Squires, Capt D. 204, 212, 214
St-Amand, LCol J.J.P. 311-314
St-Jacques, MS 258
St. Clement Danes 198
St. John's, Newfoundland 15, 16
St. Laurent, MCpl Reg 282
St. Norbert, Manitoba 66
Stacey, F/L K.R. 124-126, 134
Stacey, F/O Jim 94
Staff cars: 41, 67, 246, 247, 295
Starfighter 138, 183
Ste. Anne, Manitoba 46, 66, 67
stealth fighter/bomber 281, 282
Stedman, F/O M.W. 126, 134
Steele, Ova 177, 178
Stef, Carl 173, 174
Stenger, Harry 57
Stevenson, Al 265
Stevenson, G/C 74
Stevenson, LCol Al 210
Stewart, Cpl I.J. 257
Stewart, F/O Dale 118
Stewart, S/L W.C. 133
Stich, Capt Ryan 278, 280
Sting of the Hornet 226
Stoney Creek, Ontario 53
Stott, Capt Bruce 161, 173
Stowe, Bill, DFC 272
Stowe, Capt Mark 251
Stoyles, Cpl W. 214
Strocel, Maj Tim 234
Struthers, LCol Ian 21, 157, 161, 183, 184, 189, 198, 199, 201, 202, 225-229, 233-235, 243, 245, 250
Stuart, Capt Jim 246-249, 258, 259
Su-27 252, 253, 272
Sullivan Jane Ann 222
Sullivan, Capt J.P. "Jim" 160, 204, 212-214
Sullivan, Cpl C.S. "Duff" 292, 311
Supermarine types:
Spitfire 22-67, 265
Swift 70, 83
Sutton, F/O Larry 111, 118, 127-129
Swallow, F/O John 113
Swyer, Phyllis 18
Sydney, NS 13, 266
Sylvester, Capt Chad 258
Syms, Don 106, 108, 110, 118, 119

TacEval 145, 162, 207, 208, 258, 263, 276, 277, 284
Tactical Leadership Program 209, 276, 278, 292
Tantarn, Bernhard 255, 265, 272, 273, 302
Tantarn, Chris 265, 272
Tarling, Turbo 182
Task Force Aviano 274-297
Taskaev, Roman 251
Taylor, Ernie 60
Taylor, F/O A.H. 134
Taylor, P/O 54
Tedder, A/C/M Sir Arthur W. 29
Ten Eyck, MCpl W.G. 257
Ten-Bruggencate, Capt Pete 225
Tessier, Capt Gino 207
Tessier, Capt Yves 280, 285, 289
test flying 193
The Courier 258
The RCAF Overseas 260
The Tumbling Sky 24
Theriault, BGen G.C.E. 201
They Shall Grow Not Old 28
Thomassin, Cpl 194
Thompson, Moira 58
Thomson, Cpl 194
Thorneycroft, Jordie 306
Thorneycroft, Kathy 306
Thorneycroft, LCol Robert 303-311
Thorneycroft, W/C Ken 181, 311
Thorneycroft, Whitney 306
Thurston, Capt Eric 172, 174, 177
Tidball, F/O Larry 127
"Tiger Meet" 263
Tinson, F/O Dave 107, 133
Todd, LCol Gordy 264
Tomcheck, Capt Ronald 151-153, 214
Tomiuk, Cpl Jason 309
Tornado 262
Toronto Island Airport 297
totem pole 170
Totti, Capt John 285
Tower, Capt Dave 264
Tracey, Sgt M 214
Transall C-160 261
Transport Canada 116
Trask, Capt Dave 180, 199
Traynor, Cpl Laurie 246
Tremblay, "Mex" 199
Trepanier, Pte R. 214
Trepenier, Luc 186
Trevena, F/L Charles W. 13
Trottier, Capt Pierre 255
Trudeau, PM P. E. 171
Trudell, Cpl Scott 282, 288
Trujillo, P/O 13
Trynchuk, Capt Dan 237
Tuck, Chris 203, 204, 212
Tuck, Susan 222
Tucker, Capts Hollis 227, 228, 230, 235, 240, 245, 246, 250, 251, 255, 270
Tupolev types:
Tu-4 69
Tu-16 69
Tu-95 Bear 235
Turkey 144, 160, 167, 190, 194, 205-6, 209, 214, 263-64
Turnbull, Capt Bill 151-153, 171, 172
Turner, F/O Jack 82, 88, 93
Twenthe, Holland 196, 263
Twenthe, Holland 260

U-boat 14-16, 20, 61
Uhldahl, Dal 156
Ukrainian Air Force 252
Umrysh, Capt Paul 305, 308
University of Toronto 50, 57
University of Western Ontario 60
Upham, Sgt Mike 282
Ursulak, John 143
US Navy bases:
Norfolk 75, 92
Oceana 165
US Navy Test Pilot School 276, 277
USAF bases:
Barksdale 235
Bergstrom 163
Bien Hoa 163
Bitburg 209, 243, 248, 249
Cannon 261
Dobbins 242, 243
Edwards 276, 277
Eglin 163, 210, 243, 248, 249
Eielson 237
Ellington 240, 243
Ellsworth 240, 246
Elmendorf 225, 229, 237, 240, 243, 251-2, 271-2
Étain 102, 129, 167
Fargo 271
Frankfurt Main 128
George 272
Great Falls 248, 249, 271
Griffiss 87
Hahn 163
Hickam 267, 288
Hill 284, 288, 308
Holloman 163, 238, 243, 272, 277, 284, 288,
Homestead 163, 262
Jacksonville 248, 249
Kadena 243, 248, 249
Kirtland 74
Klamath Falls 255, 264
Kusan 163
Langley 243, 248, 249, 264
Laughlin 163
Luke 163, 238, 267, 271, 272, 284, 288, 308, 309
Maxwell 163, 250
McCord 250
Misawa 271
Nellis 163, 242, 243, 277, 299, 308
Niagara Falls 240, 243
Offut 260
Otis 248, 249
Portland 243
Ramstein 162, 205, 210, 238
Seymour Johnson 261
Shaw 144, 162, 280
Sheppard 272
Tinker 240
Tulsa 261
Tyndall 204, 210, 234-5, 237, 239-49, 260, 271, 276, 312
U Dorn 193
Vincent 239
Westover 162, 275, 276
Williams 163, 239

USAF units:
1st TFW 243-245, 248, 249, 1st TRS 157, 3rd TFW 163, 8th TFW 163, 18th TFW 243, 248, 249, 18th TRS 157, 21st TFW 243-245, 32nd FIS 112, 32nd TFS 159, 179, 33rd TFW 243-245, 248, 249, 36th TFW 243-245, 248, 249, 43rd FS 271, 49th TFW 243-245, 50th TFW 163, 54th TFS 229, 271, 57th FIS 243-245, 95th FS 312, 102nd FW 248, 249, 107th FIG 243-245, 116th TFW 242-245, 119th 271, 120th FG 248, 249, 125th FG 248, 249, 125th FS 261, 262, 128th BS 210, 136th FIS 240, 242-245, 137th FIS 162, 142 FIG 243-245, 147th FIG 240, 243-245, 309th FS 262, 336th FS 261, 363rd FW 280, 417th 163, 422nd TES 277, 466th FS 308, 474th 242, 6512th Test Squadron 276, 7055th OS 163, Air War College 163, 250, 258, 264, 308, Interceptor Weapons School 204, Tactical Air Command 163, USAF Academy 163
Usal, Capt Siegfried 278
USMC El Toro 268, 271

Vaillant, Capt Kevin 208
Valenti, Mike 245, 248, 251
Van Lirde, Maj 83
Van Oene, Maj W.A. 151-153, 167, 216
VandenBos, Capt Michael 306
"Vanguard" 261, 303, 308, 313
Vautour, Cpl Vic 313
VE Day 46
Venman, Capt Gary 224, 238, 261, 266, 268, 284
Verdun, France 148
Vicenza, Italy 274, 278
Vickers Valiant 103
Viens, Col André 285, 290
Villeneuve, F/O Fern 76, 81, 82, 86, 88, 92, 133
Vimy Ridge 56
Vincent, 2Lt John 299
Vincent, G/C Bill 181
Vinton cameras 144, 219, 220
Virton, Belgium 169
VISTA F-16 277
VMFA-531 268
Vogan, Capt Lee 285, 289, 291
Volkel, Holland 71
Vollmer, BGen 160
Vought A-7 Corsair II 261, 262, 270
Vulcan cannon 170, 194, 205, 206, 207

Wade, R.K. 186, 202, 227-28, 240, 246, 250-52, 269
Wafer, Cpl N. 214
Walker, F/O P.C. "Slim" 72, 73, 76, 82, 84, 90
Walker, S/L R.H. "Kelly" 37-39, 46, 50, 58, 63-67
Walker, W/C James E. 24, 27
Wall, Capt Rick 157, 189, 202
Wallace, Capt Steve 268
Wallis, Capt Gord 152, 153, 156, 192, 199, 263
Walpole, G/C Nigel 164, 164
Warren, S/L Douglas "Duke" 82, 87, 91, 121
Warsaw Pact 238
Warton, UK 295
Washington, DC 267
Waters, LAC Harry J. 128
Webber, F/O Jim 91, 97, 106, 118
Weber, Sgt 266
Weeks, F/O W.R. "Willie" 72, 73
Weiche, Cpl Ron 282
Welch, Capt Ken 278
Wells, W/C Edward P. 24, 25
Wengal, Cpl Rob 283
Wenham, Capt G.B. "Judge" 157, 188-191, 194, 209
Werls, René 198, 260
West, Frank R. 47
West, P/O John E. 20, 21, 31, 32, 47, 48
West, Richard P. 47
Western Canada Aviation Museum 98
Westjet Airlines 307
Westphal, F/O Jerry 103, 108
Wheeler, Capt Dave 285
White Sands, New Mexico 98
White, Capt Reg 146
White, Cpl Allan J. 16
White, F/O K.L. "Ken" 125, 134
White, F/O Morley 94, 118
White, MCpl W. 214
Whitley, LCol Steve 135, 295
Wickham, Maj Bart 237
Wideman, WO Dave 282
Wiesman, Pte F. 214
Wightman, MGen Dave 174, 223, 263
Will, Capt Steve 261, 278, 285, 291, 295, 298-302
Willett, F/L G. "Red" 144
"William Tell" 237, 239-249, 270, 271
Williams, Capt Rick 285, 302, 303
Williams, Cpl Rob 283
Williams, G/C D.J. 108, 122, 131
Williams, Greg 300
Williams, MGen Don 261, 306
Williamson, Capt Brad 289, 312
Williamson, Capt Ken 258
Williamson, F/O Don 82-84, 88, 94
Williamson, Jim 218
Willy Messeschmitt Museum 297
Wilson, Capt D.P. 204
Wilson, LCol C.W. 201, 202, 223, 227
Wilson, Marlene 222
Wilson, P/O Frederick A.W.J. 25, 28, 30
Wilson, Rick 209, 210
Winegarden, F/O C.A. 110, 112, 113, 117, 204
Wings of Change 298
Winnipeg Free Press 233
Wise, F/O Frank 76
Wolff von Wulfing, Anne, 222
Wolff von Wulfing, Capt W.J. 204, 209
Woodfield, Capt Mike 258, 259, 307-309, 312-14
Wright, Capt Wally 173
Wright, Pte Mike 228
Wurmheller, Maj Josef 32

X-31 277

Yakachuk, F/O 101, 119, 125
Yamashita, LCol Kevin 311
Yellowjack 128, 130, 216
Yellowknife, NT 225
Young, Capt Jeff 258
Young, LCol Al 174, 182, 203, 223
Young, WO "Bud" 13, 21
Youngson, Capt Gus 157, 161, 173, 179, 189, 202

Zanner, Robert 260
Zans, LCol Gordon 184, 195, 204, 207-212
Ziegler, Cpl R. 214
Zulu Alert 98-100, 131, 134
Zyvitski, Maj Rick 258
Zylenko, Cpl Doug 282, 288